Transformational Leadership Styles for Global Leaders:

Management and Communication Strategies

Darcia Ann Marie Roache
University of Saskatchewan, Canada & Capilano University, Canada & University Canada West, Canada & University of the People, USA

A volume in the Advances in Human Resources Management and Organizational Development (AHRMOD) Book Series

Published in the United States of America by
IGI Global
Business Science Reference (an imprint of IGI Global)
701 E. Chocolate Avenue
Hershey PA, USA 17033
Tel: 717-533-8845
Fax: 717-533-8661
E-mail: cust@igi-global.com
Web site: http://www.igi-global.com

Copyright © 2023 by IGI Global. All rights reserved. No part of this publication may be reproduced, stored or distributed in any form or by any means, electronic or mechanical, including photocopying, without written permission from the publisher. Product or company names used in this set are for identification purposes only. Inclusion of the names of the products or companies does not indicate a claim of ownership by IGI Global of the trademark or registered trademark.
   Library of Congress Cataloging-in-Publication Data

Names: Roache, Darcia Ann-Marie, 1970- editor.
Title: Transformational leadership styles for global leaders : management
   and communication strategies / edited by Darcia Ann Marie Roache.
Description: Hershey, PA : Business Science Reference, [2023] | Includes
   bibliographical references and index. | Summary: "A comprehensive
   understanding of the concept and evolution of leadership, it imperative
   to examine, in detail, more traditional views of leadership to assist in
   contextualizing how leadership styles differ from other renowned
   leadership approaches"-- Provided by publisher.
Identifiers: LCCN 2023038251 | ISBN 9798369313800 (hardcover) | ISBN
   9798369313817 (ebook)
Subjects: LCSH: Leadership.
Classification: LCC HD57.7 .T73 2023 | DDC 658.4/092--dc23/eng/20230906
LC record available at https://lccn.loc.gov/2023038251

This book is published in the IGI Global book series Advances in Human Resources Management and Organizational Development (AHRMOD) (ISSN: 2327-3372; eISSN: 2327-3380)

British Cataloguing in Publication Data
A Cataloguing in Publication record for this book is available from the British Library.

All work contributed to this book is new, previously-unpublished material. The views expressed in this book are those of the authors, but not necessarily of the publisher.

For electronic access to this publication, please contact: eresources@igi-global.com.

Advances in Human Resources Management and Organizational Development (AHRMOD) Book Series

Patricia Ordóñez de Pablos
Universidad de Oviedo, Spain

ISSN:2327-3372
EISSN:2327-3380

Mission

A solid foundation is essential to the development and success of any organization and can be accomplished through the effective and careful management of an organization's human capital. Research in human resources management and organizational development is necessary in providing business leaders with the tools and methodologies which will assist in the development and maintenance of their organizational structure.

The **Advances in Human Resources Management and Organizational Development (AHRMOD) Book Series** aims to publish the latest research on all aspects of human resources as well as the latest methodologies, tools, and theories regarding organizational development and sustainability. The **AHRMOD Book Series** intends to provide business professionals, managers, researchers, and students with the necessary resources to effectively develop and implement organizational strategies.

Coverage

- Workplace Culture
- Employment and Labor Laws
- Outsourcing HR
- Employee Relations
- Organizational Development
- Talent Identification and Management
- Workplace Discrimination
- Employee Benefits
- Diversity in the Workplace
- Compliance

IGI Global is currently accepting manuscripts for publication within this series. To submit a proposal for a volume in this series, please contact our Acquisition Editors at Acquisitions@igi-global.com or visit: http://www.igi-global.com/publish/.

The Advances in Human Resources Management and Organizational Development (AHRMOD) Book Series (ISSN 2327-3372) is published by IGI Global, 701 E. Chocolate Avenue, Hershey, PA 17033-1240, USA, www.igi-global.com. This series is composed of titles available for purchase individually; each title is edited to be contextually exclusive from any other title within the series. For pricing and ordering information please visit http://www.igi-global.com/book-series/advances-human-resources-management-organizational/73670. Postmaster: Send all address changes to above address. Copyright © 2023 IGI Global. All rights, including translation in other languages reserved by the publisher. No part of this series may be reproduced or used in any form or by any means – graphics, electronic, or mechanical, including photocopying, recording, taping, or information and retrieval systems – without written permission from the publisher, except for non commercial, educational use, including classroom teaching purposes. The views expressed in this series are those of the authors, but not necessarily of IGI Global.

Titles in this Series

For a list of additional titles in this series, please visit: http://www.igi-global.com/book-series/advances-human-resources-management-organizational/73670

Real-World Solutions for Diversity, Strategic Change, and Organizational Development Perspectives in Healthcare, Education, Business, and Technology
Darrell Norman Burrell (Marymount University, USA)
Information Science Reference • © 2023 • 450pp • H/C (ISBN: 9781668486917) • US $215.00

Using Organizational Culture to Resolve Business Challenges
Gerardo Reyes Ruiz (Center for Naval Higher Studies (CESNAV), Mexico)
Business Science Reference • © 2023 • 298pp • H/C (ISBN: 9781668465677) • US $225.00

Corporate Psychology and Its Impact on Diversity, Equity, and Inclusion
Ebtihaj Ahmed Al A'ali (University of Bahrain, Bahrain) Meryem Masmoudi (Applied Science University, Bahrain) and Gardenia AlSaffar (Royal Bahrain Hospital, Bahrain)
Business Science Reference • © 2023 • 218pp • H/C (ISBN: 9781668490136) • US $215.00

HR Analytics in an Era of Rapid Automation
Radha Yadav (CHRIST University, India) Mudita Sinha (CHRIST University, India) and Joseph Varghese Kureethara (CHRIST University, India)
Business Science Reference • © 2023 • 359pp • H/C (ISBN: 9781668489420) • US $225.00

Policies, Protocols, and Standards for Professionalism in a Diverse Work Environment
Christiana Bevier (Purdue University Global, USA) Barry Regan (Purdue University Global, USA) and Carolyn N. Stevenson (Purdue University Global, USA)
Business Science Reference • © 2023 • 324pp • H/C (ISBN: 9781668473085) • US $225.00

Measuring the Effectiveness of Organizational Development Strategies During Unprecedented Times
Kyla Latrice Tennin (College of Doctoral Studies, University of Phoenix, USA & Forbes School of Business, USA & World Business Angels Investment Forum (WBAF)-G20, USA & Lady Mirage Global, Inc., USA)
Business Science Reference • © 2023 • 345pp • H/C (ISBN: 9781668483923) • US $250.00

Role of Human Resources for Inclusive Leadership, Workplace Diversity, and Equity in Organizations
Caglar Dogru (Ufuk University, Turkey)
Business Science Reference • © 2023 • 421pp • H/C (ISBN: 9781668466025) • US $240.00

701 East Chocolate Avenue, Hershey, PA 17033, USA
Tel: 717-533-8845 x100 • Fax: 717-533-8661
E-Mail: cust@igi-global.com • www.igi-global.com

Dedication

I dedicate this book to all those who believe in themselves but are somewhat bewildered by what others say and think.

I stand as a testimony and testament in your support that you can do and become whatever you want!

Believe in yourself when no one else does and mentor, coach, support, and encourage others to success. That's the epitome of transformational leadership, management strategies, and communication globally.

Table of Contents

Foreword xx

Preface xxiv

Acknowledgment xxviii

Chapter 1
Educational Leaders' Success, Motivation, and Performance in Higher Educational Institutions: Serving, Striving, and Surviving (3S) Phenomena 1
    Darcia Ann Marie Roache, University of Saskatchewan, Canada & Capilano University, Canada & University Canada West, Canada & University of the People, USA

Chapter 2
Transformational Leadership Styles and Change Processes in Higher Education 20
    Yaw Owusu-Agyeman, University of the Free State, South Africa
    Enna Moroeroe, University of the Free State, South Africa

Chapter 3
Investigating the Effects of SHRM on Operational and Financial Performance in Educational Institutions 37
    Peace Kumah, Knutsford University College, Ghana

Chapter 4
Determining and Evaluating Criteria for Transformational Leadership in Educational Institutions With AHP Method 56
    Filiz Mızrak, Istanbul Medipol University, Turkey
    Murat Culduz, Istanbul Medipol University, Turkey

Chapter 5
Learning Agility of Leaders in the Context of Sustainable Organizations: A Conceptual Evaluation 78
    Didem Öztürk Çiftci, Ordu University, Turkey

Chapter 6
Transformational Leadership in Practice: Bridging the Chasm 99
    Tarek Salem, MacEwan University, Canada
    Bruce Thomson, MacEwan University, Canada

Chapter 7
Leading From Within: Creating Leaders Among Employees 113
    Henry Dimingu, California Southern University, USA
    Idowu Mary Mogaji, University of Saskatchewan, Canada

Chapter 8
A Framework for Knowledge-Based Leadership for Improved Risk Management in State-Owned
Enterprises in South Africa 128
    Malefetjane Phineas Phaladi, Durban University of Technology, South Africa
    Ngoako Solomon Marutha, University of South Africa, South Africa

Chapter 9
Exploring the Impacts and Implications of Destructive Leadership in Organizations 149
    Quatavia McLester, The Chicago School of Professional Psychology, USA
    Darrell Norman Burrell, Marymount University, USA
    Sharon L. Burton, Capitol Technology University, USA

Chapter 10
Demystifying Shared Leadership 159
    Cynthia Maria Montaudon-Tomas, UPAEP Universidad, Mexico
    Anna Amsler, Independent Researcher, Mexico
    Ivonne M. Montaudon-Tomas, UPAEP Universidad, Mexico
    Yvonne Lomas-Montaudon, Universidad Iberoamericana, Mexico

Chapter 11
Invisible Disabilities in the Workplace Are a Significant Public Health Issue and How Employee
Assistance Programs Can Be a Solution 184
    Darrell Norman Burrell, Marymount University, USA
    Stacey Morin, Marymount University, USA
    Sharon L. Burton, Capitol Technology University, USA
    Kevin Richardson, Capitol Technology University, USA
    Laura Ann Jones, Capitol Technology University, USA

Chapter 12
Exploring Mental Health Telehealth Through Organizational Intervention and Business Leadership Strategy 201

    Allison J. Huff, School of Medicine, University of Arizona, USA
    Darrell Norman Burrell, Capitol Technology University, USA
    Kiana S. Zanganeh, Florida Institute of Technology, USA
    Sharon L. Burton, Capitol Technology University, USA
    Margaret Crowe, JM Consulting LLC, USA
    Kevin Richardson, Capitol Technology University, USA
    Quatavia McLester, Chicago School of Professional Psychology, USA

Chapter 13
Building Relationships and Fostering a Community of Care Using a Trauma-Informed Leadership Approach 224

    Denise Toney, Eskasoni Elementary and Middle School, Canada
    Ingrid M. Robinson, St. Francis Xavier University, Canada

Chapter 14
Agile Leadership in Navigating Change Management and Its Application Within the Food and Beverage Industry During the COVID-19 Pandemic 239

    Dewaine Alexander Larmond, University of the People, Canada

Chapter 15
The Lessons of Bhagwad Gita in Creating Transformational and Global Leaders 256

    Pooja Sharma, Geeta University, India

Chapter 16
Leadership's Response to Change and the Influence Their Actions and Behaviors Have on Employees Throughout an Organizational Restructure: Utilizing Transformational Leadership Practices 269

    Gretchen M. Blow, Baylor University, USA
    Amy Sloan, Baylor University, USA

Chapter 17
Emotional Intelligence 294

    Shannon L. McCrory-Churchill, D'Youville University, USA

Chapter 18
A Strategic Paradigm for Transformational Leadership Theory in the Digital Age: Scope of the Analytical Third 304

    Ansar Abbas, MY Business School, Pakistan & Airlangga University, Indonesia
    Fendy Suhariadi, Airlangga University, Indonesia
    Dian Ekowati, Airlangga University, Indonesia
    Rakotoarisoa Maminirina Fenitra, ASTA Research Center, Madagascar

Chapter 19
Transforming Leaders and Driving Organizational Success in a Global Context: Using EQ, Perfectionism, and Moral Compass 324
    Marsha R. Hilton, Walden University, USA & Nova Southeastern University, USA & Conestoga College, Canda & The University of the West Indies, Jamaica
    Suzzette A. Harriott, Nova Southeastern University, USA

Chapter 20
Transformational Leadership: Promoting Inquiry-Based Learning in the Classroom 341
    Tamica Small, Tourism Saskatchewan, Canada

Chapter 21
Exploring the Leadership Intersection of Social Entrepreneurship, Sustainability, and Environmental Public Health 350
    Kevin Richardson, Capitol Technology University, USA
    Darrell Norman Burrell, Capitol Technology University, USA

Chapter 22
Transformational Leadership Style and Employee Performance 367
    Endalsasa Belay Abitew, Bahir Dar University, Ethiopia

Chapter 23
Improving Hospital Diversity Through Management Consulting Interventions 377
    Kiana S. Zanganeh, Florida Institute of Technology, USA
    Darrell Norman Burrell, University of North Carolina at Chapel Hill, USA
    Kevin Richardson, Edward Waters University, USA

Chapter 24
Breaking the Mold: The Power of Transformational Leadership and DEI in Driving Organizational Change 391
    Suzzette A. Harriott, Harriott Research Institute, USA & Nova Southeastern University, USA
    Jia Tyson, Nova Southeastern University, USA
    Christopher A. Powell, Nova Southeastern University, USA & University of London, UK

Chapter 25
Cultivating a New Future: Transformational Leadership in Urban Agriculture 414
    Ashli D. Jay, St. Thomas University, USA

Compilation of References 451

About the Contributors 532

Index 543

Detailed Table of Contents

Foreword xx

Preface xxiv

Acknowledgment xxviii

Chapter 1
Educational Leaders' Success, Motivation, and Performance in Higher Educational Institutions:
Serving, Striving, and Surviving (3S) Phenomena 1
    Darcia Ann Marie Roache, University of Saskatchewan, Canada & Capilano University,
        Canada & University Canada West, Canada & University of the People, USA

Educational leaders' success and performance contributes to educators' fulfillment of their mandate to educational institutions and enhances learner growth and development. Thirteen educational leaders from seven institutions were engaged in this study. The purpose of this qualitative study was to explore the extent to which educational leaders as transformational leaders in higher educational institutions success, motivation, and performance resulted from serving, striving, and surviving (3S') phenomena. NVivo 10 software was used to analyze data from the interviews. The result revealed that an understanding of the organization's structure and culture can create initiatives for educational leaders' success.

Chapter 2
Transformational Leadership Styles and Change Processes in Higher Education 20
    Yaw Owusu-Agyeman, University of the Free State, South Africa
    Enna Moroeroe, University of the Free State, South Africa

As higher education institutions attempt to address issues pertaining to institutional change, very few scholarly studies have examined how transformational leadership processes influence changes to institutional cultures and structures. To address this gap, the current study explores how leadership processes contribute to changes in the institutional culture and structure of a university in South Africa by gathering interview data from 69 academic and professional staff. The findings revealed that for the university to achieve its transformation objectives, leaders should challenge the cognitive abilities of their staff, scaffold strategies for meeting high work standards, negotiating the attainment of staff personal and career goals, engender staff motivation and assist their staff to understand the institutional culture and structure. These findings among others lead the author to propose ways that future studies could examine how the leadership processes could enhance institutional transformation.

Chapter 3
Investigating the Effects of SHRM on Operational and Financial Performance in Educational Institutions 37
    Peace Kumah, Knutsford University College, Ghana

Strategic human resource management (SHRM) seeks to create alignment between human resource management (HRM) practices and business strategy (strategy fit); linking HR strategies, policies, and practices within the functional units of the HR department (intra-functional fit); maintaining the status of the HRM department within corporate strategic plan (HR-roles-position fit); and alignment of HRM functions with all other departments (cross-functional fit). This study investigates the effects of SHRM on organizational performance. Data was collected from 314 employees in tertiary educational institutions in Ghana. A conceptual model was developed and a set of hypotheses were proposed. The results found that cross-functional fit has a significant effect on both financial and operational performance. However, the results found no significant effect of strategy fit, role-position fit, and intra-functional fit on financial and operational performance. Therefore, tertiary educational institutions should develop cross-functional fit to improve their financial and operational performance.

Chapter 4
Determining and Evaluating Criteria for Transformational Leadership in Educational Institutions With AHP Method 56
    Filiz Mızrak, Istanbul Medipol University, Turkey
    Murat Culduz, Istanbul Medipol University, Turkey

As all sectors, educational institutions need to keep up with the chance and developments. In this scope, transformational leaders are among the most important requirements. For this reason, it is important for executives working in educational institutions to have transformational leadership characteristics and to demonstrate these characteristics by using them for the management of the schools. Based on these data, the main purpose of this research is to determine the transformational leadership characteristics in educational institutions. In this context, the criteria obtained as a result of literature review and interviews with five experts working in educational institutions have been weighted with the AHP method to determine their priorities. It is thought that the findings of the research will be a guide for educational institutions which have changed especially after the pandemic. At the same time, it is believed that the criteria determined according to the order of importance will contribute to the senior manager selection process of the relevant institutions

Chapter 5
Learning Agility of Leaders in the Context of Sustainable Organizations: A Conceptual Evaluation 78
    Didem Öztürk Çiftci, Ordu University, Turkey

In recent years, developments such as economic crises, the COVID-19 pandemic, and digitalization that require quick and effective responses have increasingly challenged businesses in terms of achieving all dimensions of sustainability. Considering this situation, leaders with learning agility are crucial in creating sustainable organizations due to the qualities they possess. This kind of leader becomes more equipped to navigate changes in the work environment, prepare and adapt their organizations to environmental changes by learning continuously. In this research, sustainable organizations are modeled not only as structures that respect ecological living but also as structures that can sustainably strengthen many internal and external factors while achieving this. The main problem of the research is to identify how the characteristics of leaders with learning agility align with the elements of sustainable organizations. Therefore, the study aims to establish theoretical correlations between these leadership characteristics and sustainable organizational elements.

Chapter 6
Transformational Leadership in Practice: Bridging the Chasm.. 99
    Tarek Salem, MacEwan University, Canada
    Bruce Thomson, MacEwan University, Canada

This chapter captures the bi-furcated challenge of implementing the transformational leadership practices in a complex organizational context. The authors embark on Bass' 4I transformational leadership model and suggest a variety of imperative skills necessary for the proper implementation. From the suggested pool of skills, two are highlighted as the most important and resonate with the 4I model. These are creativity and innovation skills and change management skills. The authors expect to find out the importance of transformational leaders to empower and enable the second line of operational leaders that are capable of efficiently and effectively bridging the transformational leadership chasm from the leaders' vision to the followers' practice.

Chapter 7
Leading From Within: Creating Leaders Among Employees.. 113
    Henry Dimingu, California Southern University, USA
    Idowu Mary Mogaji, University of Saskatchewan, Canada

This chapter explores the concept of leadership through the prism of processes. Organizations are evolving and these evolutions may result in divergent thoughts, visions, and even actions. As a result, there is a need to develop leaders among employees who can transform these disparate thoughts and visions into something far more valuable and advantageous to organizations. Therefore, the fundamental premise of this chapter is that every employee possesses the potential for leadership, only waiting to be developed. This chapter emphasizes the need for employees to develop leadership skills. It covers what these skills are, why they are crucial to develop, and lastly, provides suggestions on how to develop employees' leadership skills.

Chapter 8
A Framework for Knowledge-Based Leadership for Improved Risk Management in State-Owned Enterprises in South Africa... 128
    Malefetjane Phineas Phaladi, Durban University of Technology, South Africa
    Ngoako Solomon Marutha, University of South Africa, South Africa

The purpose of this chapter is to investigate a framework for knowledge-based leadership for improved risk management in state-owned enterprises in South Africa. The study empirically explored the influence and role of knowledge-based leadership in driving knowledge management and human resource management practices for effective knowledge risk management. Exploratory sequential mixed methods research design was used as the overall strategy to guide data collection for the project. In the qualitative strand, data were gathered through interviews with 20 purposively nominated human resource managers. In the quantitative strand, 145 responses collected through survey instrument were used to test variables discovered in the first strand. A lack of knowledge-based leadership contributed to the absence of knowledge strategy and practices, knowledge-driven culture, structural configurations and roles, and ineffective tacit knowledge loss risks management. The chapter proposes a knowledge-based leadership framework to mitigate tacit knowledge risks in state-owned enterprises.

Chapter 9
Exploring the Impacts and Implications of Destructive Leadership in Organizations 149
    Quatavia McLester, The Chicago School of Professional Psychology, USA
    Darrell Norman Burrell, Marymount University, USA
    Sharon L. Burton, Capitol Technology University, USA

The research on leadership has typically sought to investigate 'good' leadership and the best characteristics of leadership (i.e., transformational leadership, ethical leadership, authentic leadership). Current research indicates a 'bad' or 'dark' side of leadership. The outcomes of destructive leadership have been raising interest in leadership research. Within the research, destructive leadership has been revealed to have severe outcomes for employees and organizations. This literature review seeks to expand the literature to consider destructive leadership and its association with job-related outcomes. The review will examine forms of destructive leadership related to specific job-related and organizational-related outcomes. The exploration of destructive leadership and its effect on job-related outcomes is essential to the success of organizations. This review contributes to the growing body of knowledge related to leadership.

Chapter 10
Demystifying Shared Leadership 159
    Cynthia Maria Montaudon-Tomas, UPAEP Universidad, Mexico
    Anna Amsler, Independent Researcher, Mexico
    Ivonne M. Montaudon-Tomas, UPAEP Universidad, Mexico
    Yvonne Lomas-Montaudon, Universidad Iberoamericana, Mexico

This chapter analyzes shared leadership from a systems perspective, identifying connections with other leadership styles. The method used was the literature review. Different myths that surround shared leadership are also considered, and examples are used to illustrate how the myths can be debunked. The importance of trust is highlighted as an essential element for creating any type of relationship, including leadership, and for sharing any task. The importance of collective action and how it contributes to shared leadership is also described. Finally, different ways to overcome the myths of shared leadership are included.

Chapter 11
Invisible Disabilities in the Workplace Are a Significant Public Health Issue and How Employee
Assistance Programs Can Be a Solution 184
    Darrell Norman Burrell, Marymount University, USA
    Stacey Morin, Marymount University, USA
    Sharon L. Burton, Capitol Technology University, USA
    Kevin Richardson, Capitol Technology University, USA
    Laura Ann Jones, Capitol Technology University, USA

Employment is a crucial factor in achieving economic security and self-sufficiency, yet individuals with disabilities often face significant barriers to accessing meaningful and gainful employment opportunities. According to the United States Census Bureau, individuals with disabilities are 65 percent less likely to be employed than those without disabilities. This discrepancy is due, in large part, to limited diversity, equity, inclusion interventions, and knowledge in the workplace on invisible disabilities. This chapter looks to explore the nature of this issue through management consulting intervention with a hospital with significant disability discrimination.

Chapter 12
Exploring Mental Health Telehealth Through Organizational Intervention and Business
Leadership Strategy 201
    Allison J. Huff, School of Medicine, University of Arizona, USA
    Darrell Norman Burrell, Capitol Technology University, USA
    Kiana S. Zanganeh, Florida Institute of Technology, USA
    Sharon L. Burton, Capitol Technology University, USA
    Margaret Crowe, JM Consulting LLC, USA
    Kevin Richardson, Capitol Technology University, USA
    Quatavia McLester, Chicago School of Professional Psychology, USA

COVID-19 shed light on mental health as a significant public health problem. The COVID-19 pandemic has had a significant impact on the mental health of individuals around the world. As such, mental health practitioners must be prepared to respond effectively to the changing needs of their patients. Adaptive leadership and change management are two essential tools that can be used to assist patients with mental health issues post-COVID-19. By combining these two approaches, mental health practitioners can ensure that their services are effective and meet the needs of their patients in the post-COVID-19 world. This chapter uses intervention action research (I.A.R.) to help organizational leaders address workplace challenges and enhance their profession by engaging organizational stakeholders in creating, executing, and assessing interventions in a problem-solving, assessment, and reflection cycle.

Chapter 13
Building Relationships and Fostering a Community of Care Using a Trauma-Informed Leadership
Approach.. 224
    Denise Toney, Eskasoni Elementary and Middle School, Canada
    Ingrid M. Robinson, St. Francis Xavier University, Canada

This chapter explores, through a self-study study approach, one principal's experiences with the implementation and enactment of trauma informed leadership in her Indigenous rural community school. Findings identify the principal's practices of trauma informed leadership and how her approach supports Indigenous cultural revitalization and cultivates relationships between and amongst herself and her school constituents (e.g., students, teachers, staff, parents, other community members). These relationships have enabled her to foster a compassionate, caring, and safe school culture. The conclusions highlight how the practices she employs have resulted in supporting students academically, socially, and emotionally affected by intergenerational trauma and building more capacity in the larger school community. A description of the successes and challenges of her use of the approach, and the approach's transferability to other organizations, is also included in the chapter.

Chapter 14
Agile Leadership in Navigating Change Management and Its Application Within the Food and
Beverage Industry During the COVID-19 Pandemic 239
    Dewaine Alexander Larmond, University of the People, Canada

This chapter delves into the dynamic landscape of change management in modern business, unveiling actionable strategies. By synthesizing industry literature and expert insights, it underscores the paramount role of agile leadership, particularly in the challenging domain of the COVID-19 pandemic. Exemplary instances from various industries illuminate essential approaches adopted by leaders to ensure unswerving continuity, enhanced safety, and resounding success. The chapter centers around a prominent Canadian sports facility, where food and beverage revenue is pivotal, spotlighting the adept application of both Lewin's unfreeze-change-refreeze approach and Kotter's 8-step model for change. This analysis elucidates critical takeaways encompassing adaptation, diversification, transparent processes, technological integration, and the strategic elevation of health priorities—cornerstones for sustained viability.

Chapter 15
The Lessons of Bhagwad Gita in Creating Transformational and Global Leaders 256
    Pooja Sharma, Geeta University, India

Transformational leadership is a leadership process in which a leader inspires and motivates group members to affect positive change in an organization. Today, on the one hand, we talk about artificial intelligence and software-based decision-making styles, but on the other hand, we are dealing with stress, anger issues, lack of coordination and team spirit. It is becoming increasingly difficult to find a good leader and supporter in this artificial world and one of the main reasons is that we have become separated from our foundations, culture, and religion. Our religion, culture, and history provide us with numerous lessons in leadership and strategic management techniques. This chapter aims to highlight leadership lessons with special focus on Shree Bhagwad Gita. The Gita is not a religious book but is widely known and preached by people of all faiths all over the world. The Gita teaches us numerous strategies for managing and controlling emotions in difficult situations.

Chapter 16
Leadership's Response to Change and the Influence Their Actions and Behaviors Have on
Employees Throughout an Organizational Restructure: Utilizing Transformational Leadership
Practices 269
    Gretchen M. Blow, Baylor University, USA
    Amy Sloan, Baylor University, USA

Organizations in today's globalized world face challenges at unprecedented rates. Restructures are an important tool used to meet those challenges directly. Senior-level leaders spearheading restructures need to adjust quickly to change and be cognizant of the persuasive and biased atmosphere their actions and behaviors create for personnel. Change is a pervasive segment of business; those unwilling to adapt will continue applying antiquated techniques and fail to meet the needs of stakeholders. This chapter focuses on the influence senior-level leadership's actions and behaviors have on employees throughout an organizational restructuring in a medical educational institution. A connection is established between transformational leadership practices and employees' levels of morale, motivation, and performance. Additionally, leadership whose actions and behaviors lack components of transformational leadership negatively influence the working environment.

Chapter 17
Emotional Intelligence 294
    Shannon L. McCrory-Churchill, D'Youville University, USA

This chapter is an overview of the concept of emotional intelligence (EI) and how it applies to organizational leadership. It will explore the origins, viewpoints, and how emotional intelligence differs from intelligence quotient (IQ). It has been demonstrated across the literature that EI has as much, if not more, impact on both personal and professional success. This chapter will address the importance of EI as well as why it makes a difference in the workplace. The chapter leans heavily on the work of Daniel Goleman who first popularized the concept in the mid 1990s. The chapter will further explore common assessments, and ways to increase emotional intelligence.

Chapter 18
A Strategic Paradigm for Transformational Leadership Theory in the Digital Age: Scope of the Analytical Third 304
    Ansar Abbas, MY Business School, Pakistan & Airlangga University, Indonesia
    Fendy Suhariadi, Airlangga University, Indonesia
    Dian Ekowati, Airlangga University, Indonesia
    Rakotoarisoa Maminirina Fenitra, ASTA Research Center, Madagascar

The analytical triangle, a social psychology concept, is crucial in implementing change management strategies. It involves a triangular configuration mediating between individuals and the external world, subject and object, and imagination and actuality. This literature synthesis explores the strategic management and leadership intentions of businesses, focusing on transformational leadership theory and the use of novel communication strategies by global leaders. The study's overarching goal is to highlight the relevance of these theoretical frameworks in a variety of potential future research situations. This chapter explores how entrepreneurs may utilize technology to develop successful firms by coordinating different aspects of technology entrepreneurship to produce a unified transformation. Students would do well to study its lessons on how technology entrepreneurs may make effective use of available resources.

Chapter 19
Transforming Leaders and Driving Organizational Success in a Global Context: Using EQ, Perfectionism, and Moral Compass 324
    Marsha R. Hilton, Walden University, USA & Nova Southeastern University, USA &
        Conestoga College, Canda & The University of the West Indies, Jamaica
    Suzzette A. Harriott, Nova Southeastern University, USA

This chapter explores transformational leadership within the complex milieu of a global context, focusing on three core elements: emotional intelligence (EQ), perfectionism, and moral compass. The research scrutinizes the interplay of these components and their impact on effective leadership, especially amidst external challenges such as pandemics, war, and artificial intelligence (AI) advances. It introduces the triadic leadership theory (TLT), highlighting its relevance and implications in the international arena. The TLT, acknowledging the globalized setting, posits that EQ, perfectionism, and moral compass form an interconnected triad that leaders can leverage to drive organizational success. The chapter ends with a reflection on the limitations of the current study, suggesting areas for future research.

Chapter 20
Transformational Leadership: Promoting Inquiry-Based Learning in the Classroom........................ 341
    Tamica Small, Tourism Saskatchewan, Canada

Transformational leadership has transitioned into a dominant strategic framework to enhance leadership roles in education. This chapter will examine the correlation between teacher transformational leadership in the classroom and the significant effectiveness this does have to shift the traditional teacher-centred approach to learning in the classroom. Transformational leadership employed in the classroom combined with inquiry-based learning can enhance students' critical thinking skills to shape their lives and their roles in the world. Through transformational leadership, teachers can hone their leadership skills, while understanding the value of equipping students with the skills to become activity participants in the learning process. That is empowerment of students.

Chapter 21
Exploring the Leadership Intersection of Social Entrepreneurship, Sustainability, and
Environmental Public Health.. 350
    Kevin Richardson, Capitol Technology University, USA
    Darrell Norman Burrell, Capitol Technology University, USA

A survey by the World Business Council for Sustainable Development found that 83% of companies had adopted sustainability policies, while 86% had adopted specific sustainability goals. Environmental public health is another key element of CSR initiatives. Organizations are increasingly focusing on initiatives that promote public health and environmental protection. A study by the World Health Organization found that 80% of global diseases are caused by environmental factors, and that organizations have a role to play in reducing these negative impacts. This chapter explores how organizational strategy and organizational leadership can positively move the social impact and social influence of organizations in the promotion of sustainability leadership and corporate social responsibility.

Chapter 22
Transformational Leadership Style and Employee Performance... 367
    Endalsasa Belay Abitew, Bahir Dar University, Ethiopia

Leadership is the ability to motivate and inspire people to achieve a common goal. Both theoretical and empirical research supports that leadership style utilized by leaders in organizations, whether it is private or public, substantially influence the effort and performance of employees. In the literature of previous studies, among the various variables studied and investigated, transformational leadership style parades a major role in influencing employee performance. This chapter examined the nexus between transformational leadership style and employee performance based on the pervious study results. Using a literature review from various previous studies, the writer of this chapter has corroborated that transformational leadership, in various organizational settings and sizes, has a significant effect on employee performance, which is one of the main management topics that received substantial attention from scholars and practitioners

Chapter 23
Improving Hospital Diversity Through Management Consulting Interventions 377
    Kiana S. Zanganeh, Florida Institute of Technology, USA
    Darrell Norman Burrell, University of North Carolina at Chapel Hill, USA
    Kevin Richardson, Edward Waters University, USA

America is more varied than ever. As cultural heterogeneity grows in America, religion, faith, and health habits show their effects. However, Latinx and African-American nurses, doctors, and healthcare professionals must represent the exponential expansion in population diversity. Black nurses may not reflect the variety of the U.S. population, but they are essential for culturally competent treatment and trust-building with communities of color. Many individuals believe health inequalities are caused by fundamental differences between populations and ignore their societal factors. Healthcare workers of color realize that social and political systems cause health inequities. We can then find structural gaps-closing solutions. Intervention research in an organizational case study addresses several of these complicated concerns. This chapter points to the critical importance of leadership, cultural change, employee engagement, and cultural change as essential for organizations to transform to make them more diverse and inclusive.

Chapter 24
Breaking the Mold: The Power of Transformational Leadership and DEI in Driving
Organizational Change 391
    Suzzette A. Harriott, Harriott Research Institute, USA & Nova Southeastern University, USA
    Jia Tyson, Nova Southeastern University, USA
    Christopher A. Powell, Nova Southeastern University, USA & University of London, UK

This study presents a qualitative narrative analysis of the experiences of five individuals representing five diverse organizations from various industries. It investigates the themes of transformational leadership; diversity, equity, and inclusion; organizational change and innovation; effective people management; communication strategies; and paradigm shift. The names of the individuals and organizations have been changed for privacy reasons. The analysis of the narratives reveals the critical role of transformational leadership in driving organizational change and innovation. In addition, it emphasizes the importance of promoting diversity, equity, and inclusion to create a positive and inclusive work environment. The study also highlights the significance of effective people management, communication strategies, and organizational design in fostering collaboration and innovation.

Chapter 25
Cultivating a New Future: Transformational Leadership in Urban Agriculture 414
    Ashli D. Jay, St. Thomas University, USA

This chapter is a study that investigates the crucial role of transformational leadership in shaping urban agricultural education and program development. Drawing from well-established research, the chapter highlights how transformational leadership can provide a structured approach to achieving academic excellence and educational equity in urban settings. The chapter underscores that transformational leadership's emphasis on empowerment, ethical behavior, and relationship building makes it ideal for addressing urban agriculture's unique challenges and opportunities. While acknowledging the value of other educational theories and ethical frameworks like virtue ethics, the chapter concludes that the principles of transformational leadership stand out for their ability to enrich urban agricultural education, creating an environment that is not only academically rigorous but also empathetic and socially responsible.

Compilation of References 451

About the Contributors 532

Index 543

Foreword

The domain of leadership and people management is constantly evolving, and we find ourselves at the intersection of multiple paradigms and challenges. Because society is evolving so rapidly, the world is demanding a fresh perspective that encompasses traditional wisdom, ethical considerations, and adaptability to unforeseen circumstances. This remarkable book, brilliantly put together by Dr. Darcia Roaches, achieves exactly that, and it offers a plethora of insights and empirical research written by various authors who are experts in their respective fields. Dr. Darcia Roache has a lot of experience in academia, and she is a skilled researcher. She is currently a sessional faculty at University Canada West (UCW) and brings to the university a unique blend of scholarly rigour and practical wisdom. She has experience in human resource management, leadership, change management, educational leadership, and other areas that resonate well with the themes discussed in the chapters.

This volume is broken into three sections and has five chapters. The first section presents stories of educational leaders, transformational leadership styles, operational and financial performance, and sustainability in organizations. Chapter 1, on "Educational Leaders' Success, Motivation, and Performance in Higher Educational Institutions (HEIs): Serving, Striving, and Surviving (3S') Phenomena" by the editor, Dr. Darcia Roache explores the extent to which educational leaders in higher educational institutions' success, motivation, and performance resulted from serving, striving, and surviving (3S') Phenomena. Research have shown that leaders in higher education are influencers who provide direction to achieve university goals and objectives (Budur et al., 2008; Toker, 2022). The chapter highlights that educational leaders' success and performance contributes to educators' fulfillment of their mandate to educational institutions and enhances learner growth and development.

Chapter 2, "Transformational Leadership Styles and Change Processes in Higher Education" by Dr. Yaw Owusu-Agyeman and co-author Enna Moroeroes, explores how leadership processes contribute to changes in the institutional culture and structure of a university in South Africa. The chapter reveals for the university to achieve transformation objectives, leaders should scaffold strategies for meeting high work standards, negotiating the attainment of staff personal and career goals, and assist their staff to understand the institutional culture and structure.

Chapter 3, "Investigating the Effects of SHRM on Operational and Financial Performance in Educational Institutions" by Dr. Peace Kumah investigates strategic human resource management and its influence on organizational performance, specifically in tertiary educational institutions in Ghana. The results found that cross-functional fit has a significant effect on both financial and operational performance.

Chapter 4, "Determining and Evaluating Criteria for Transformational Leadership in Educational Institutions With AHP Method," by Dr. Filiz Mızrak and Dr. Murat Culduz, delves into the essential characteristics of transformational leadership in educational institutions. This timely research not only

Foreword

underscores the importance of adaptability but also provides quantitative analysis through innovative methodologies.

Chapter 5, on "Learning Agility of Leaders in the Context of Sustainable Organizations: A Conceptual Evaluation" by Dr. Didem Öztürk Çiftci, navigates the intersection of learning agility in leaders and sustainable organizations. This compelling research builds theoretical connections between leadership characteristics and sustainable organizational elements. The findings reveal that sustainability and sustainable organizations are approached holistically, including ecological sustainability, human factors, moral values, economic development, and social elements.

Section 2 has five chapters on transformational and knowledge-based leadership, change management, and shared leadership. Chapter 6, on "Transformational Leadership in Practice: Bridging the Chasm," by Dr. Tarek Salem and co-author Dr. Bruce Thomson, tackles the complex issue of implementing leadership practices in a multifaceted organizational context. The chapter identifies critical skills needed for bridging the gap between visionary leadership and practical application.

Chapter 7, "Leading From Within: Creating Leaders Among Employees," written by *Mr.* Henry Diming and Dr. Idowu Mogaji explores the concept of leadership through the prism of processes. This chapter emphasizes the need for employees to develop leadership skills and provides suggestions on how to develop employees' leadership skills.

Chapter 8, "A Framework for Knowledge-Based Leadership for Improved Risk Management in State-Owned Enterprises in South Africa" by Dr. Malefetjane Phineas Phaladi and Prof. Ngoako Solomon Marutha, investigates a framework for knowledge-based leadership for improved risk management in state-owned enterprises in South Africa. The empirical study explores the influence and role of knowledge-based leadership in driving knowledge management and human resource management practices for effective knowledge risk management.

Chapter 9, "Exploring the Impacts and Implications of Destructive Leadership in Organizations" authored by Prof. Quatavia McLester, and co-authors, Dr. Darrell Norman Burrell, and Dr. Sharon L Burton, explores the 'dark' side of leadership, a much-needed perspective that broadens the discussion about leadership dynamics and their effects on job-related outcomes.

Chapter 10, the final chapter of this section on "Demystifying Shared Leadership," by Prof. Cynthia Maria Montaudon-Tomas, Anna Amsler, Dr. Ivonne Montaudon-Tomas, and Dr. Yvonne Lomas-Montaudon, highlights the importance of trust as an essential element for creating any type of relationship, including leadership, and sharing task. The chapter describes the importance of collective action and how it contributes to shared leadership.

Section 3, the final section of the book on Leadership, Health Issues, Sustainability, Inclusivity, Urban Agriculture, and Building Relationship includes 15 chapters that guide us through different factors of leadership. Chapter 11, on "Invisible Disabilities in the Workplace" by Dr. Darrell Norman Burrell, Stacey Morin, Dr. Judith Mairs-Levy, Dr. Sharon L. Burton, and Dr. Kevin Richardson, highlights that employment is a crucial factor in achieving economic security and self-sufficiency, yet individuals with disabilities often face significant barriers accessing meaningful and gainful employment opportunities. The paper explores the nature of this issue through management consulting intervention with a hospital with significant disability discrimination.

Chapter 12, "Exploring Mental Health Telehealth Through Organizational Intervention and Business Leadership Strategy, by Dr. Allison J Huff, Dr. Darrell Norman Burrell, Kiana S. Zanganeh, Dr. Sharon L Burton, Dr. Margaret Crowe, Dr. Kevin Richardson addresses the mental health crisis in the wake of COVID-19, presenting adaptive leadership strategies that mental health practitioners can utilize to respond effectively to their patient's needs.

Chapter 13, "Building Relationships and Fostering a Community of Care Using a Trauma-Informed Leadership Approach," by Denise Toney and Dr. Ingrid Robinson presents an intimate view of trauma-informed leadership in an Indigenous rural community school, shedding light on cultural revitalization, relationship-building, and a compassionate approach to leadership.

Chapter 14, "Agile Leadership in Navigating Change Management and Its Application Within the Food and Beverage Industry During the COVID-19 Pandemic," by Dewaine Larmond emphasizes the critical role of agile leadership in managing change within the food and beverage industry, especially during the COVID-19 pandemic. Drawing on industry examples, the chapter highlights critical strategies leaders could employ to navigate disruptions, ensure business continuity, prioritize customer, and employee safety.

Chapter 15, "The Lessons of Bhagwad Gita in Creating Transformational and Global Leaders," by Dr. Pooja Sharma highlights leadership lessons from religion, culture, and history with special focus on Shree Bhagwad Gita. The Gita taught numerous strategies for managing and controlling emotions in difficult situations especially in the world of Web 4.0.

Chapter 16 on "Leadership's Response to Change and the Influence Their Actions and Behaviors Have on Employees Throughout an Organizational Restructure: Utilizing Transformational Leadership Practices" by Dr. Gretchen M Blow and Dr. Amy Sloan focuses on the influence senior-level leadership's actions and behaviors have on employees throughout organizational restructuring. The chapter demonstrates how leader's actions and behaviors that lack components of transformational leadership negatively influence the working environment.

Chapter 17 on "Emotional Intelligence for Transformational Leaders in Organizations" by Dr. Shannon L McCrory-Churchil presents an overview of emotional intelligence (EI) and how it applies to organizational leadership. It explores the origins, viewpoints, and how emotional intelligence differs from intelligence quotient (IQ). The chapter highlights the importance of EI and why it makes a difference in the workplace.

Chapter 18, "A Strategic Paradigm for Transformational Leadership Theory in the Digital Age: Scope of the Analytical Third," by Dr. Ansar Abbas, Prof. Fendy Suhariadi, Dr. Dian Ekowati, and Dr. Rakotoarisoa Maminirina Fenitra delves profoundly into an organization's strategic management and leadership intent. The authors saw a connection between transformational leadership theory that applies to new communication tactics used by global landscape leaders. The research underscores that transformational leaders' capacity for optimistic growth via the successful implementation of their vision has expanded into new dimensions in the post-covid-19 era.

Chapter 19 on "Transforming Leaders and Driving Organizational Success in a Global Context: Using EQ, Perfectionism, and Moral Compass" by Marsha Hilton and Dr. Suzette Harriott explores transformational leadership within the complex milieu of a global context, focusing on three core elements - Emotional Intelligence (EQ), Perfectionism, and Moral Compass. The research scrutinizes the interplay of these components and their impact on effective leadership, especially amidst external challenges such as pandemics, war, and artificial intelligence (AI) advances. It introduces the Triadic Leadership Theory (TLT) and highlights its relevance and implications in the international arena.

In Chapter 20, "Transformational Leadership: Promoting Inquiry-Based Learning in the Classroom," Tamica Small explores how transformational leaders promote inquiry-based learning in the classroom.

Foreword

It was revealed that inquiry-based learning is a compatible teaching method for fostering educational sustainability development in the classroom.

Chapter 21 on "Exploring the Leadership Intersection of Social Entrepreneurship, Sustainability, and Environmental Public Health" by Dr. Darrell Burrell reveals that organizations are increasingly focusing on initiatives that promote public health and environmental protection. The chapter explores how organizational strategy and organizational leadership can positively move the social impact and social influence of organizations in the promotion of sustainability leadership and corporate social responsibility.

Chapter 22, "Transformational Leadership Style and Employee Performance," by Endalsasa Abitew examines the nexus between transformational leadership style and employee performance. The chapter reveals that leadership is the ability to motivate and inspire people and transformational leadership in various organizations has a significant effect on employee performance.

In Chapter 23, "Improving Hospital Diversity Through Management Consulting Interventions" by Kiana Zanganeh, Dr. Darrell Burrell and Dr. Kevin Richardson explores the importance of leadership, cultural change, and employee engagement as essential to transform diverse and inclusive organizations.

Chapter 24, on "Breaking the Mold: The Power of Transformational Leadership and Diversity, Equity, and Inclusion (DEI) in Driving Organizational Change" by Dr. Suzzette Harriott and co-author, Christopher Powell, delves into the characteristics of transformational leadership as a distinguish leadership model. The chapter discusses how characteristics of transformational leadership aligns with the goals of DEI to foster a more inclusive and innovative work environment.

Chapter 25, "Cultivating a New Future: Transformational Leadership in Urban Agriculture" by Dr. Ashli D. Jay, underscores that transformational leadership's emphasis on empowerment, ethical behavior, and relationship building makes it ideal for addressing urban agriculture's unique challenges and opportunities. While acknowledging the value of other educational theories and ethical frameworks like virtue ethics, the chapter concludes that the principles of transformational leadership stand out for their ability to enrich urban agricultural education.

Together, these chapters create riches ideas, approaches, methodologies, and applications, extending our understanding of leadership and people management in various contexts. I commend Dr. Darcia Roache for curating this lighting collection and the contributing authors for sharing their valuable perspectives.

As a fellow academic, Chair of the Leadership and People Management Department at the University Canada West, I am inspired by this work and believe it will serve as an invaluable resource for researchers, practitioners, educators, and students. With the anticipation of the enlightening journey that awaits the reader.

Michele Vincenti
Leadership and People Management Department, University Canada West, Canada

Preface

In a rapidly evolving global landscape, where organizations navigate a myriad of challenges and opportunities, the role of leadership stands as a cornerstone in achieving not only organizational effectiveness but also societal progress. *Transformational Leadership Styles for Global Leaders: Management and Communication Strategies*, edited by Darcia Ann Marie Roache, delves deep into the intricate interplay of leadership styles, management strategies, and communication effectiveness that shape the present and future of organizations.

The impact of transformational leadership reverberates through the intricate fabric of modern businesses and institutions. The pages of this edited reference book unravel the significance of leadership within the context of dynamic environments, where strategies, techniques, and approaches must adapt to the changing tides of the global landscape. The book seeks to explore, discuss, and recommend perspectives that illuminate the transformative power of leadership, unlocking its potential to foster organizational excellence and drive employee performance.

Leadership is a multifaceted concept, constantly shaped by cultural shifts, technological advancements, and evolving societal values. The evolution of transformational leadership is a journey that demands scrutiny, as it is through this lens that we can best understand, motivate, and guide individuals and teams towards the realization of collective visions and missions. "Transformational Leadership Styles for Global Leaders" envisions leadership not as a static set of traits, but as a dynamic force that catalyzes change, propels effective communication, and orchestrates management functions.

In my pursuit of a comprehensive understanding of leadership, this book navigates a diverse range of topics, encompassing theories of leadership and communication, the nuances of various leadership styles, the intricate relationship between leadership and effective communication, the impact of transformational leadership styles on organizational dynamics, and the role of leadership in change management within organizations.

As editor, my aim is to provide a comprehensive resource that bridges the gap between theory and practice. This book is designed to serve as a guiding light for professionals, organizational leaders, and practitioners who seek to enhance their leadership acumen, refine their management strategies, and master the art of impactful communication. By weaving together theoretical insights, conceptual frameworks, and the latest empirical research findings, I endeavor to equip readers with the tools necessary to thrive in complex and ever-changing organizational environments.

Transformational Leadership Styles for Global Leaders: Management and Communication Strategies not only offers valuable insights to those in the business realm but also extends its reach to the educational sphere, inviting chief executive officers, team leaders, human resource directors, and scholars to partake in this enlightening discourse. The diverse array of topics covered in this book, from emotional

Preface

intelligence and sustainability in leadership to the role of leadership in promoting social justice, morality, and positive organizational paradigms, makes it a resource that transcends boundaries and industries.

In this edited reference book, we bring together a diverse collection of chapters that delve into the multifaceted realm of educational leadership. The success and performance of educational leaders play a pivotal role in shaping the trajectory of educational institutions and fostering the growth and development of learners. Through the exploration of transformational leadership, strategic human resource management, emotional intelligence, diversity and inclusion, and more, this book seeks to provide valuable insights and strategies to enhance leadership practices within educational contexts. The following chapter overviews provide a glimpse into the rich tapestry of knowledge presented in this volume.

Chapter 1 presents a qualitative study that investigates the connection between educational leaders' success, motivation, and performance and the 3S' Phenomena—serving, striving, and surviving. Through interviews and data analysis, the authors uncover how understanding an organization's structure and culture can contribute to educational leaders' initiatives for success.

Exploring the influence of transformational leadership on institutional culture and structure, Chapter 2 delves into a study conducted at a South African university. By challenging cognitive abilities, motivating staff, and fostering an understanding of the institution's culture, the study reveals strategies for achieving transformation objectives.

Investigating the effects of strategic human resource management (SHRM) on educational institutions' performance, Chapter 3 examines data collected from Ghana. The study highlights the significance of cross-functional fit for improving financial and operational performance in tertiary educational institutions.

Chapter 4 emphasizes the importance of transformational leadership in educational institutions, providing insights gathered from literature review and expert interviews. By employing the Analytic Hierarchy Process (AHP) method, the authors determine priorities and criteria for guiding executive selection processes.

Focusing on leaders with learning agility, this research delves into how their characteristics align with sustainable organizational elements. Chapter 5 underscores the importance of leaders who can navigate changes and prepare organizations for continuous adaptation.

Exploring the challenges of implementing leadership practices, Chapter 6 introduces imperative skills necessary for successful transformational leadership. Creativity, innovation, and change management skills emerge as pivotal for bridging the gap between leaders' vision and followers' practice.

Chapter 7 underscores the potential for leadership within every employee and the need to cultivate leadership skills. It addresses the importance of these skills, why they should be developed, and offers suggestions on how to foster employees' leadership capabilities.

Focusing on state-owned enterprises in South Africa, Chapter 8 investigates a knowledge-based leadership framework to mitigate tacit knowledge risks. Drawing from mixed methods research, it proposes strategies to enhance knowledge management and risk management practices.

Chapter 9 adds to the discourse on leadership by examining destructive leadership's effect on job-related outcomes. By delving into the dark side of leadership, the authors contribute to a comprehensive understanding of leadership dynamics.

Unpacking shared leadership from a systems perspective, Chapter 10 debunks myths and highlights the importance of trust and collective action. It offers ways to overcome misconceptions and promote effective shared leadership.

Focusing on disability discrimination, Chapter 11 examines interventions aimed at promoting diversity, equity, and inclusion in healthcare settings. It addresses the challenges individuals with invisible disabilities face and highlights the importance of management consulting interventions.

Amid the COVID-19 pandemic's impact on mental health, Chapter 12 explores the role of adaptive leadership and change management in assisting patients with mental health issues. It proposes an intervention action research approach to address workplace challenges.

Through self-study, Chapter 13 explores a principal's implementation of trauma-informed leadership in an Indigenous rural community school. It highlights how this approach supports cultural revitalization, builds relationships, and fosters a compassionate school culture.

Investigating change management in the COVID-19 era, Chapter 14 spotlights agile leadership approaches. It draws from a sports facility case study and elucidates essential strategies for organizational continuity and success.

Focusing on leadership lessons from culture, Chapter 15 centers on the Shree Bhagwad Gita as a source of guidance for leaders. It emphasizes the relevance of cultural and religious foundations in the modern leadership landscape.

Examining the role of transformational leadership during organizational restructuring, Chapter 16 highlights the impact on employees' morale, motivation, and performance. It emphasizes the connection between leadership practices and working environment dynamics.

Chapter 17 delves into emotional intelligence's importance in organizational leadership. It explores its origins, differentiation from IQ, and impact on personal and professional success, underlining its significance in workplace settings.

Synthesizing transformational leadership and communication strategies, Chapter 18 examines their relevance in a global context. It underscores their potential to drive organizational change and offers insights for future research.

Exploring transformational leadership's role in a global setting, Chapter 19 introduces the Triadic Leadership Theory. It highlights the interplay between emotional intelligence, perfectionism, and moral compass, and their impact on effective leadership.

Focusing on urban agricultural education, Chapter 20 emphasizes the importance of transformational leadership in creating a positive and inclusive learning environment. It underscores how leadership practices can enrich students' critical thinking and empowerment.

Chapter 21 delves into the role of organizational strategy and leadership in promoting sustainability leadership and corporate social responsibility. It explores initiatives that impact environmental public health and societal well-being.

Investigating the correlation between transformational leadership style and employee performance, Chapter 22 draws from existing research. It underscores the significant impact of transformational leadership on employees' efforts and outcomes.

Chapter 23 addresses the significance of leadership in promoting diversity, equity, and inclusion in healthcare. It highlights the role of black nurses and healthcare professionals in addressing health inequalities through culturally competent treatment.

Examining transformational leadership's role in organizational change, Chapter 24 presents narratives from diverse industries. The analysis underscores the importance of fostering collaboration, innovation, and a positive work environment.

Preface

Chapter 25 investigates the role of transformational leadership in shaping urban agricultural education. It explores how emotional intelligence and inclusive leadership practices can enhance academic excellence and equity in urban settings.

In a world where leadership is both a privilege and a responsibility, where effective communication is a bridge to innovation and collaboration, and where management strategies must adapt to the evolving demands of the times, "Transformational Leadership Styles for Global Leaders: Management and Communication Strategies" emerges as a guiding beacon. I invite you to explore the chapters that follow, each offering a unique lens through which to examine and appreciate the transformative power of leadership.

Darcia Ann Marie Roache
University of Saskatchewan, Canada & Capilano University, Canada & University Canada West, Canada & University of the People, USA

Acknowledgment

Thanks to the Lord Jesus Christ. To him, be glory, praise, and honour. He guides, leads, and provides protection for my life's journey. I am a firm believer that the best formula in life is "Jesus plus education equals success."

Thanks to all the authors who made this book possible. Your tenacity, generosity, curiosity, hard work, and support will be long remembered.

My family members, Dunstan, Rohan, Antoinette, Simone, Kellyann, Adethe, Eulalee, Tanesha, Cory, Xavier, Bruce, Seymour, and Remigijus.

Thanks for your constructive feedback, especially Kellyann, my little sister. Morran, my mom your support and encouragement assisted me with making this publishing decision. You told me I can do and become anything I want to. You put your life on hold for all you nine children to strive and survive.

Thanks to Richard, who has been a tower of strength and support in the process and my students who became intrinsically motivated in the process and extended their congratulations.

Professor Michele Vincenti, Department Chair of Leadership and People Management Faculty, University Canada West, thanks for writing the foreword. I appreciate your support, knowledge, and guidance, immensely.

I acknowledge the generous support and guidance from the IGI Global Publisher team members. Elizabeth Barrantes, Assistant Development Editor, Melissa Wagner, Vice President of Editorial IGI Global, and Mrs. Jocelynn Hessler, Senior Development Editor, IGI Global.

Finally, thanks to my deceased father, Cleveland. You would be smiling "off your face with joy" for me. Cleveland, wherever you are, I know you are smiling down at me.

Chapter 1
Educational Leaders' Success, Motivation, and Performance in Higher Educational Institutions:
Serving, Striving, and Surviving (3S) Phenomena

Darcia Ann Marie Roache
University of Saskatchewan, Canada & Capilano University, Canada & University Canada West, Canada & University of the People, USA

ABSTRACT

Educational leaders' success and performance contributes to educators' fulfillment of their mandate to educational institutions and enhances learner growth and development. Thirteen educational leaders from seven institutions were engaged in this study. The purpose of this qualitative study was to explore the extent to which educational leaders as transformational leaders in higher educational institutions success, motivation, and performance resulted from serving, striving, and surviving (3S') phenomena. NVivo 10 software was used to analyze data from the interviews. The result revealed that an understanding of the organization's structure and culture can create initiatives for educational leaders' success.

INTRODUCTION

Leadership is a form of influence, guide, and provide a sense of the tasks (Altun, 2017; Poturak et al., 2020; Toker, 2022). According to Toker (2020) "in higher education, leaders are those who have authority in different roles inside the university" (p.1). Toker (2022) cited Budur et al. (2008) as said "Higher education leaders are influencers who provide direction to achieve university goals and objectives" (Budur et al., 2008; Toker, 2022). Leaders in educational organizations have different titles resulted from the culture, structure, and administration of the organization (Owings & Kaplan, 2010). Regardless of the titles given to a leader, her or his goal is to serve and motivate followers. Perry (2010) said, "leadership requires not only insight into the dynamics of the culture but the motivation and skill to intervene

DOI: 10.4018/979-8-3693-1380-0.ch001

in one's own cultural process" (p. 286). Leaders who serve goals are to "sponsor, model, coach, and mentor other leaders at various levels in their organization" (Walker, 2017, p. 54). These goals can only be achieved with the leaders' willingness to accept the responsibility to motivate and advance human good and value of the organization (Northouse, 2013). Leadership in schools has much in common with leadership in other institutions.

The effective functioning of institutions depends on educational leaders' skills and competencies to make decisions (Marzano et al., 2005). Serving their administration comprises guiding others in the support of the mission and goals, maintaining effective and collaborative relationships with employees, and managing leadership and management principles and practices. This collaboration ensures that learners' opportunities and challenges are supported in accordance with the standards and regulations of the organization (Onorato, 2013). Educational leaders' success is associated with how they inspire others or followers to "commit to a shared vision and goals for an organization or unit, challenging them to be innovative problem solvers, and developing followers' leadership capacity via coaching, mentoring, and provision of both challenge and support" (Bass & Riggio, 2006, p. 4). Effective educational leaders have no single way to lead as their effectiveness strategy encapsulates activities beyond the boundaries of creating conditions of leadership. Educational leaders should strive to strengthen their own performance, which, in return, will improve students' orientations to achieve at their optimum level (Berkovich, 2016).

Research has shown that educational leaders need high degrees of resilience be serve, strive, and survive in this educational landscape as their job involves a great deal of complexity, intensity emotional demands, challenges, accountability, and effective decision making (Early, 2020, Earley, & Weindling, 2007; Kellerman, 2012; Nicholas & West-Burnham, 2016). Educational leaders' success and performance involves strategies, extending, employing, and providing motivation, emotional intelligence, and coercive tactics to enforce the rules and policies of the organization while serving, striving, and serving (Berkovich, 2016). These challenges and opportunities, however, give prominence to others self-awareness and sustainability. According to Nicholas and West-Burnham (2016), there are other dimensions to (leader) sustainability that we believe are being neglected – that is the personal aspects of well-being and wellness. This might be best understood as personal efficacy (i.e. the development of the whole person) – the recognition that leadership is more than an aggregation of technical skills and that it requires the engagement of all aspects of the person (pp. 203-204).

Educational leaders' success and performance is not without motivation to encourage their productivity and that of their followers. Leaders' motivation of subordinates will affect their leadership styles and their knowledge of the organization. Bourne (2018) posited that leaders who motivate and encourage their subordinates will always be in favour with their followers. Effective leaders inspire followers to "commit to a shared vision and goals for an organization or unit, challenging them to be innovative problem solvers, and developing followers' leadership capacity via coaching, mentoring, and provision of both challenge and support" (Bass & Riggio, 2006, p. 4). Effective educational leaders have no single way to lead as their effectiveness strategy encapsulates activities beyond the boundaries of creating conditions of leadership. Educational leaders should be striving to strengthen their own performance, which, in return, will improve others to achieve optimum results (Berkovich, 2016). Effective leadership provides benefits for the organization, the leader, and followers and creates a culture that motivates, inspires, and empowers at all levels of the organization (Cote, 2017, p. 10).

Leadership approaches are different, depending on the situation. Strategies or approaches involve leaders extending motivation, providing emotional intelligence, and employing coercive tactics to enforce the rules and policies of the organization (Berkovich, 2016). Leadership styles that motivate followers to share in the vision, mission, and objectives of the institution hinge not only on how to enhance learning but also on intrinsic and extrinsic factors that contribute to motivation (Gultekin & Acar, 2014). Transformational leadership is a better predictor of positive attitudes, motivation, and leader effectiveness than are other leadership styles such as, transactional and laissez-faire (Getachew & Zhou, 2018, p. 1; Judge & Piccolo, 2004); thus, transformational leadership is considered an important organizational asset (García-Morales et al., 2008). According to Roache (2014), one of the leaders' roles is to transform and motivate followers, displayed in and through their transactional, transformational, and participative leadership styles. Roache further stated that the situations that leaders encounter at times dictate their leadership behaviour. However, Palmer (2008) postulated that there are multifaceted principles or styles to leadership that all effective leaders apply regardless of their personal style of leadership. Palmer said that basic principles such as thoughtfulness and carefulness are evidenced when executing rewards and motivation of followers. When expressed in practice, these principles create and build confidence among followers and communicate the goals of the institutions (organization) to the followers. Educational leaders are servant leadership, providing guidance, mentorship, and coaching to faculties and learners. Their success, motivation, and performance in higher educational institutions involves serving the institutions, faculties, learners, and their administration. They servitude to internal and external stakeholders demands survival of the fitness.

Klopotan et al. (2018) said leaders use different paradigms or principles such as motivation, leadership models or styles to bring about employees' satisfaction. Organizational leaders create strategic value for the organization (Kollenscher et al., 2018). These scholars believed that "value-creating leadership combines micro and macro perspectives regarding management and leadership along with a meso perspective to create a unified model of corporate leadership" (p. 1). Regardless of the leadership model or style when the appropriate style is not used outputs will not be achieved. The importance of leaders' work to help motivate individual teacher's satisfaction and to understand why particular individuals behave the way they do is paramount. Foster (1986) argued that "individual motivations are diverse, yet how can we understand administration without understanding why individuals act as they do" (p. 61).

BACKGROUND AND PROBLEM STATEMENT

The general problem is that while we know that motivation affects employees' success and productivity in educational organization, we sometimes struggle to find insights and understandings that enhance motivation, leading to increased educational leaders' success and performance in higher education institutions while serving, striving, and surviving. Laub (1999) postulated that "servant leadership is an understanding and practice of leadership that places the good of those led over the self-interest of the leaders" (p. 83). Leadership is encouraging people, building community, collaboration, relationship, building value, providing leadership, and taking actions (Laub, 2018). The role of the leaders includes: managing and demonstrating strategic leadership practices, showing charisma, and creating a harmonious relationship, fostering innovation, and providing continuous learning support to meet the achievement goals (Reyes, 2018). Accomplished goals bring job satisfaction and motivation for all the stakeholders involved (Wang et al., 2018). Educational leaders have responsibilities for maintaining relationships with faculties and staff, managing practices of faculties, and attending to the administrative functions of the school (Alvoid & Black, 2014). At times, some educational leaders may lack the educational leadership abilities or insights to assist educators or faculties' performance and to enhance their motivation.

Educational leaders' success and performance involves serving others while allowing them autonomies to strive and survive. This is not without operationalizing administrative, leadership and management principles by way of planning, organizing, controlling, executing, and motivation of people (Palmer, 2008). In some views, leadership is placed at a hierarchical level higher than administration (Palmer, 2008). The importance of the hierarchical level is that the administration level involves the daily operation of the organization, while the leadership level incorporates both administrative, and strategic operations of the decision-making process of organization (Mathis, 2014; Mathis & Jackson, 2010, 2014; Mathis et al., 2013). While administration sees to the management of resources, leadership envisions and fosters the visionary, strategy, and motivational needs of their followers (Palmer, 2008). The specific problem lies in the fact that motivation directs individuals' professional and personal behaviour; however, some leaders may fail to transform the institutions with their transformational endeavours. Transformation in behaviour, knowledge acquisition, educators' motivation and job satisfaction set the stage for the greater paradigm of leadership commitment, success, motivation, and performance in higher educational institutions while serve and strive and develop communities of learning. Viewing the notion paradoxically, leaders fail as a result of those factors (Barnes & Spangenburg, 2018). Leadership is considered important for the improvement of individual and institutional successful performance.

RESEARCH QUESTIONS

Cohen et al. (2011) stated that research questions provide guidance to the investigation that researchers examined, and questions are important to the deliverables of the research. The research questions sought to provide clarity to the research phenomenon and should do so without ambiguity as "the answers to the research questions might provide some of the deliverables. A useful way of deciding whether to pursue a particular study is the clarity and ease in which research questions can be conceived and answered" (Cohen et al., 2011, p. 111). The research questions act as an investigatory approach to a research study and is a "general purpose or aim into specific questions to which specific, data-driven, concrete answers can be given" (Cohen et al., 2011, p. 111). Given these considerations, three questions on the perceptions were posed:

1. What roles and expectations evoked by educational leaders are positive and impactful to the success of faculties?
2. What are the perceptions of educational leaders on success, motivation, training and development, and performance?
3. What are the perceptions of educational leaders on serving, striving, and surviving in higher educational institutions?

The study consisted of thirteen participants lived experiences shared in interviews from different educational institutions in Canada, Jamaica, and America. These experiences supported the significance of the study.

SIGNIFICANCE OF THE STUDY

The significance of the research lies with its findings and to extent that the chapter adds to the body of knowledge that helps to equip educational leaders with strategies to motivate success through performance, in a collaborative sense of achievement of institutional goals. Further, it is anticipated that the chapter will provide insights to equip educational leaders with understandings, insights, and skills for their work. When educational leaders are equipped with the fundamental principles of leadership and management, their ability to lead, strive, and survive will be success and motivated self and others (Garza et al., 2014; Onorato, 2013). The research can assist leaders in education to craft policies and practices to spur the growth of institutions, whereby well-motivated faculties succeed in their performance in a fashion that helps to accomplish institutional mandates. The significance of the study may enhance the development of solutions to assist educational leaders as they work to improve teachers' success and educational effectiveness. The solutions start with a motivated workforce that encourages, empowers, supports, and engages employees or faculties in their work. Educational leadership success is educators/faculties' success and the significance of creating relationships to sustain and nurture others' wellbeing cannot be overemphasized (Cherkowski & Walker, 2016). The chapter provides insights on how educational leadership and accompanying motivation are perceived as influences on mission outcomes. The literature reviewed supported the discussions on educational leaders' success, motivation, and performance in higher educational institutions as they serve, strive, and survive in their various institutions.

REVIEW OF THE LITERATURE

In this section is a brief review of the relevant literature pertaining to educational leaders' success, motivation, and performance in higher educational institutions.

Motivation

A plethora of literature exists on definitions of motivation. Motivation is the "process whereby goal-directed activity is instigated and sustained" (Schunk et al., 2008, p. 4) or "an internal force that activates, guides, and maintains behavior over time" (Thorkildsen, 2002, p. 9), or "the processes that account for an individual's intensity, direction and persistence of effort towards attaining a goal" (Robbins & Judge, 2009, p.175). For Beck (2004) motivation is derived from the Latin verb movere, which means to move; thus, it is concerned with peoples' movements and actions, and the factors that determine them. From a broad theoretical standpoint, motivation explains why people engage in particular actions at appropriate times (Beck, 2004).

Rasheed et al. (2016) contended that motivation of a person can only be found in their desired movements and that goal can be achieved in institutions where there is a commitment, internal aspirations, and inspiration. However, as Jones et al. (2000) pointed out in their definition, overcoming obstacles through the level of effort and persistence is key. Further, it has been found that motivated employees cultivate an organizational climate that is conducive to job satisfaction while meeting organizational goals (Jones et al., 2000; Robbins & Judge, 2009). Motivation is associated with goal achievement and the individual's intentions, direction, and persistence which must be congruent with the objectives of the organization. Motivation affects behaviour, performance, and is driven by some action. It is central to educational leaders in guiding or explaining their work with teachers. Motivation is an "individual's degree of willingness to exert and maintain an effort toward organizational goal." and is also a "psychological process resulting from the interaction between the individual and the environment" (Owings & Kaplan, 2012, p. 202). Motivation defined an individual's actions and behaviours that influence their outcome.

Educational leaders aim to motivate their employees to effectively guide the operations and achieve the mission's objectives. Gamero-Burón and Lassibille (2018) claimed that motivation can "improve the quality of education through various channels, including monitoring and supervising attendance, providing support to teachers, tracking progress and performance, facilitating school-community, interactions, and promoting accountability" (p. 1) for leaders in educational administration while improving learners and teachers' performance (Ärlestig et al., 2016; Gamero-Burón & Lassibille, 2018). While institutions' leaders are integrally in the improvement of the quality of education through various channels of communication, mentoring, coaching, support, and supervision, there exists the need for continued motivation to increase performance and job satisfaction of educational followers.

While leaders are endowed with responsibility, leaders are also responsible to "engage people in facing the challenge, adjusting their value, changing perspectives, and developing new habits of behaviour" (Heifetz, 1994, p. 276). This approach builds capacity for motivation while increasing workers' perception of their leader. The definition of motivation is one's behaviour, energy towards the attainment of goals, and one's motivation intertwines with their self-determination (Pinder, 1998).

There are several theories of motivation that ascribe to human behaviour, goals, needs for self-actualization, performance, and self-determination. These theories could assist educational leaders in higher educational institutions, educational administrators, and leaders with strategies or know-how to bring satisfaction, while enhance institutional or organization productive and employees to achieve objectives. Motivation caused a person to move to action regardless of the level of motivation (Ryan & Deci, 2017). Training aids educational leaders with present opportunities while development supports future growth opportunities in their performance in higher educational institutions as they serve, strive, and survive in their various institution.

Training and Development

The importance of educational leadership development affects their well-being in education (Earley, 2020). For educational leaders, training allows one to be equipped with knowledge management, skills, competencies that equips individuals with opportunities for situational demands and challenges (Wangithi & Muceke, 2012). Training impacts the growth and development of human resources and improves knowledge, skills, attitude, behaviour, and capabilities of employee in organizations. "Training is an investment in human capital. It is the most important assets a company has and as such is an essential part of a company's strategy" (Schwind et al., 2013, p. 268). Training is cost-effective and of such institutions should consider the best method that will provide the most suitable trade-offs for the institution. According to McShaneet al. (2015) and Schwind et al. (2013), there are many techniques to training, for example, on-the-job training, off-the-job-training, web-based learning. While no one method is ideal, the best approach/method should be chosen to fit the employer/employee needs.

Training is any learning activity which is directed towards the acquisition of specific knowledge and skills for an occupation and task. Training programs are directed toward maintaining and improving current job performance. Training has the important dual function of utilization and motivation. By improving employees' ability to perform the tasks required by the organization, training allows better use to be made of human resources; by giving employees a feeling of mystery over their work and of recognition by management regarding their job satisfaction (Graham, & Roger, 1998, as cited by Wangithi & Muceke, 2012, p. 4). The tools, skills, and equipment of any training program should be cognizant with the need's assessment of the employer and the challenges faced by the employee. They are benefits for the employees and the employer that training can foster said Schwind et al. (2013), such as skill improvement, self- development and strong self-confidence, more effective handling of stress and conflicts, and a sense of growth. For the organization, the benefits may include improved profitability through higher productivity, improved morale, better corporate image, lower costs, and stronger identification with corporate goals. (p. 268). Employers are responsible to provide training for employees to develop their competence to increase or enhance productivity and organizational goals.

Training and development at times are used interchangeably; however, development prepares the employees for jobs in the future by developing their skills, improving their jobs, and develop the organizations as the "assumption being that if all individuals are developed, then the organization itself will benefit as a result" (Schwind et al., 2013, p. 267). Training is regarded as an important developmental tool that gives the desired behavior to the organization. "Development is any learning activity which is directed towards future needs rather than present needs, and which is concerned more with career growth than immediate performance" (Wangithi & Muceke, 2012, p. 4). Employee development as the skillful provision and organization of learning experiences in the workplace so that performance can be improved, work goals can be achieved and that, through enhancing the skills, knowledge, learning ability and enthusiasm at every level, there can be continuous organizational as well as individual growth (Wangithi & Muceke, 2012, p. 4). Employees need technical, human, and conceptual skills to develop opportunities for growth in institutions. Skills of which prepare/equip them for responsibilities, power, and authority. The competencies developed assist the employee to be more competent in performing their roles in the organization.

Performance Management

Performance management refers to the wide variety of activities, policies, procedures, and interventions designed to help employees to improve their performance. These programs begin with performance appraisals but also include feedback, goal setting, and training, as well as reward systems (DeNisi & Freeman, 2017, p. 1). Performance management assists organizations or institutions to successfully achieve organizational goals. Managed performance effectively and efficiently "transform organizational objectives into clearly understood, measurable outcomes that define success and are shared with stakeholders in and outside the organization. Provide instruments for measuring, managing, and improving the overall health and success of the organization" (Schwind et al., 2013, p. 302).

Performance management ensures that employees' performance and goals are congruent with that of the organization. Performance management is conducted by the relevant educational leaders to ensure employees performance. There are "many factors can affect the performance of individual employees— their abilities, motivations, the support they receive, the nature of the work they are doing, and their relationship with the organization" (Mathis & Jackson, 2012, p. 73). However, organizational performance greatly depends on the individual's employees and their relationship with the organization. Earley (2020) in his literature argued that educational leadership roles and responsibilities are changing and the challenges require initiatives and high expectations, performance management and accountabilities.

West-Burnham (2016) argued that educational leaders' development of self-awareness and resilience forms an overwhelming part of their leadership. The author further stated that

there are other dimensions to (leader) sustainability that we believe are being neglected – that is the personal aspects of well-being and wellness. This might be best understood as personal efficacy (i.e. the development of the whole person) – the recognition that leadership is more than an aggregation of technical skills and that it requires the engagement of all aspects of the person (pp. 203-204).

Performance management programs in institutions improve work qualities, and foster employee satisfaction.

SERVING, STRIVING, AND SURVIVING FOR EDUCATIONAL LEADERS

Educational leaders' success is associated with factors, such as performance, motivation, fulfilment, training and development, and job satisfaction. Serving as an educational leader involves creating opportunities for self and others to thrive, survive, and revive (Earley, 2020). Leadership is purpose that moves others into action while they strive for success. According to Laub (2018), leadership is "dangerous" (p. 1), however produce amazing results... "leadership is a volatile mix of action, vision, mobilization, and change when put together in the right amount, at the right time, in the right degree will explode new reality (p.1). Leadership will prevail and have its way in the word. Leadership can heal the world. It is greater than its power to harm the world. Leadership is not forceful, but it is incredibly persistent" (Laub, 2018, pp. 1, 2). Educational leaders in higher educational institutions as serve, strive, and survive have been fascinating, drawing on their power, ability, and leadership that brings satisfaction to their colleagues in organizations.

Educational leadership survival impacts their wellbeing. Wellbeing is defined as "the balance point between an individual's resource pool and the challenges they face" (Dodge et al., 2012, p. 230). Harter et al. (2002) research further alluded that leaders could use elements wellbeing to influence employees and develop their perception human resource issues. Wellbeing is an important factor to understand one's career, job commitment, and employees' attitude or behaviour that forms part of schools 'reformation and intervention programs (van Veen et al., 2005). Wellbeing is defined as "the balance point between an individual's resource pool and the challenges they face" (Dodge et al., 2012, p. 230). The amalgamation of these factors impacts academic success and enhance relationship, belief, and values for the job. Florenn (2014) stated that "leadership lifestyle lived by academic leaders is characterized by fast pace, high responsibility, and little personal time" (p. 1) and how leaders maintain their wellness in higher education forms a better understand of their achievement. Wellbeing promotes learning, growth, and desire to achieve success with the choices and commitment that support motivation for educational leaders' job satisfaction.

Striving as educational leaders involves thriving, self-efficacy, motivation, and self-determination. Self-efficacy is considered "as beliefs of the individuals towards their managing environmental factors and being durable to obstacles" (Bandura, 1977; see also Dou et al., 2016, p. 2). Motivation in the work environment can be defined as an individual's degree of willingness to exert and maintain an effort toward organizational goals" (Owings & Kaplan, 2012, p. 202. Striving is not possible without well-being, which according to Cherkowski and Walker (2018) is "finding ways to thrive, feeling a sense of vitality and zest at work, all the while growing and filling out individual and collective potentials throughout one's teaching career" (p. 33). Educational leaders' relatedness refers to feeling connected to others, to caring for and being cared for by those others, to having a sense of belonging both with individual and with one's community" (Deci & Ryan, 2002, p. 7). Educational leaders give of themselves so their facilities can motivated perform at their peak and be successful in their job. Educational leaders' success, motivation, and performance in higher educational institutions, is associated with serving, striving, and surviving for self and their colleagues' job satisfaction.

Job Satisfaction

Job satisfaction is a "person's evaluation of his or her job and work" (McShane et al., 2015, p. 91). When employees are satisfied their job performance and work environment are perceived as been affected. However, happy worker" hypothesize, concluding that job satisfaction minimally affects job performance. Organizational Behaviour experts have concluded that, "there is a moderately positive relationship between job satisfaction and performance (McShane et al., 2015, p. 93). Job satisfaction and motivation are linked together. There is a relationship between Job satisfaction and motivation. They are inextricably linked but poses a complex relationship (De Nobile, 2008). Motivations drives one desire and behaviour while job satisfaction is associated with the feelings derive from an accomplishment/ success or the goals that directed one's behaviour (Seebaluck & Seegum, 2012). Motivation enhances job satisfaction "while motivation is primarily concerned with a goal-directed behaviour, on the other hand, however, job satisfaction refers to the feeling of accomplishment acquired by experiencing different job activities and rewards" (Ololube, 2004; Peretomode 1991, p. 113). Job satisfaction and motivation have been the focus of substantial research over the past years (Seebaluck & Seegum, 2012, p. 1). Job satisfaction relates to empowerment of others, school culture, quality work environment and student achievement (Hughes, 2006, p. 6). Motivation affects the existence of any organization and when employees are motivated it has an adverse effect on their performance and behaviour (Olajide, 2000; Tella et al., 2007) and when their motivation is low it affects their performance and the educational standard (Seebaluck & Seegum, 2012). Educational leaders' success, motivation, and performance in higher education institutions is serving, striving, and surviving and leads to higher productivity and commitment to the organizations.

Productivity and Organizational Commitment

Productivity is a hallmark of the input and output of organizations and employees. When productivity is high chances are performance and motivation of employees will be enhanced and so "productivity refers to the ratio of an organization's outputs (e.g., goods and services) to its inputs (e.g., people, capital, materials, and energy). Productivity increases as an organization finds new way ways to use fewer resources to produce its output" (Schwind et al., 2013, p.8). Educational leaders can use productivity as a means of improving pay quality, benefits, and working conditions for employee and of such provide a higher quality of life for the employees as they will be motivated to improve productivity (Schwind et al., 2013). Productivity boasts the economic force an institution and is necessary for long term success. Organizational commitment is equally important to the employees as the employer as greater opportunities and effectiveness can be derived. Organization commitment comes when employees are attached to their organizations. Commitment for the organization comes naturally for some employees because of the benefit they can derive. Benefits such as, salary, the right thing to do, and emotionally attached to the organization it (Pierro et al., 2014). Organizational commitment is considered as an important variable as it reduces negative outcomes, maintain high commitment to employees as these create motivation (Camilleri, 2006; Canrinus et al., 2011; Galletta et al., 2011). Employees feel committed to their organization only when they feel a desire to do their work; this desire comes when there is motivation (Sohail, et al., 2014), as cited by Imran et al., 2017).

Literature on organizational commitment and motivation revealed that commitment comes motivation (George & Sabapathy, 2011). Motivation hinges and determines employee's commitment in the organization (Sohail et al., 2014). When employees are motivation there is no boundary to the commitment, they will give the employer (Imran et al., 2017). Educational leaders' success, motivation, and performance in higher educational institutions has a positive effect on their employees' commitment, attitudes toward their job, and improves not only their performance but effectiveness (Baotham, 2011). When organization is committed to the employee the relationship will be mutually beneficial. There will be trust, shared values, and support. When teachers are committed to their institutional organization there will be success and so "teachers' organizational commitment is a critical aspect in determining the success of education reform and school effectiveness because highly committed teachers are willing to contribute their extra effort to achieve school vision and goals" (Selamata et al., 2013, p. 1). Organizational commitment is a key human resource component of job satisfaction, job security, and organizational effectiveness (Ramalho et al., 2018). When there is job fulfilment, there will be job satisfaction.

Fulfillment

Fulfillment increases employment obligation to their job commitment, employer, and their contribution to the organization. When employees are fulfilled employees in the organization, they are more committed to the organizational causes and "analyses revealed that employee fulfillment and perceived contributions predicted particular changes in employer psychological contract obligations, whereas employer fulfillment and perceived inducements predicted changes in employee obligations" (Lee et al., 2011, p. 11). Fulfillment on the job comes with satisfaction, motivation, efficacy, and the need teachers must be fulfilled. These factors are different for everyone, as what brings fulfillment for an individual/teacher might differ for others. Fulfilment is associated with psychological contract where the employer's responsibility ensures that the employee work obligations, commitment, and performance/turnover are fulfilled (Lub et al., 2015). While psychological contract defined an exchange relationship between the employer and the employee individual beliefs, shaped by the organization, regarding the terms of an exchange agreement between the individual and their organization'. The psychological contract is founded on Social Exchange Theory, which postulates that employees and employers engage in exchanges whereby each party to the exchange reciprocates the other's contributions (Blau, 2017, as cited by Lub et al., 2015, p. 3). When employees or faculties feel fulfilled or satisfied it gives both the employer and the employee a sense of security. This sense of commitment is echoed through collective learning, educational leadership, and wellbeing. Educational Leaders' success, motivation, and performance in higher education institutions while serving, striving, and surviving calls for performance and motivation.

RESEARCH DESIGN AND METHODOLOGY

The study chapter includes discussion on the constructs of the study research design, the research methodology, and the research methods. Methods for data collection was interviews with a sample size of 13 educational leaders in higher educational institutions. The data analysis and interpretation, including discussions on open, theoretical, constant comparative coding, memoing, and use of NVivo software. According to Briggs et al. (2012) methodology is the theory of how and why researchers gain knowledge in research contexts (p.15). Briggs and co-authors (2012) said "the why the question is an important methodological process, as it provides researchers and readers with explanations regarding the "reasons for using specific strategies and methods to construct, collect, and develop particular kinds of knowledge about educational phenomena" (p. 15). This qualitative grounded theory methodology will support the study's credibility.

Interviews are conversations whereby the researcher engages the participants in the study (Cohen et al., 2011). To engage the participants, the researcher used semi-structured interviews. The semi-structured interviews "is an open situation, having greater flexibility and freedom" (Cohen et al., 2011, pp. 414, 415). Thus, the researcher asked participants questions, however, when necessary, the researcher asked follow-up questions for response given to questions that needed further clarity. In the semi-structured interviews "the research purpose governs the questions asked, their content, sequence, and wording are entirely in the hands of the interviewer (Cohen et al., 2011, p. 415). The non-directive interview gave the researcher freedom to express herself. Cohen et al. (2011) said the interviewer in a non-directive interview can "prompt and probe, pressing for clarity and elucidation, rephrasing and summarising where necessary to check for clarity and checking for confirmation" (p. 415). This aids the finding and provides clarity and credibility to the chapter.

RESEARCH FINDINGS

In this section, the author presents key research findings into the themes explained below. Educational leaders' success, motivation, and performance in higher educational institutions involving serving, striving, and surviving as revealed by educational leaders' stories as manifestation of their fulfilling, challenging, and rewarding experiences while performing their duties. Although their experiences were rewarding and fulfilling, they were also significant challenges. However, their self-determination, efficacy, resilience, and persistence accounted for their achievements. The 13 educational leaders were asked their perceptions of how serving, striving, and surviving impacted their success and performance in higher educational institutions.

Communities of Dynamic Stakeholders

The educational leaders reported that there was a mixture and/or composition of dynamic stakeholders at their various institutions. They worked for the common good of the institutions in terms of administrative support, building relationships, and promoting the productivity of the institution and of such, employees were satisfied, and displayed autonomy, competence, and relatedness. The educational leaders (ELs) shared that closely knitted communities added to their achievements, that of their learners, and the institutions (EL 5- EL 6). Educational leader 10, described the community as closely-knit communities.

This respondent shared that the growth of development of the "closely knitted community at his institution assisted with the professional development and acknowledgement of staff achievements, and special occasions". When professional development activities were determined or planned by the institution, the institution financed one hundred percent of the cost. Regardless of these recognitions, employees were held accountable for performance. These closely knitted communities of dynamic stakeholders positively impacted the professional development and achievements of educational leaders' perspectives of success.

Team Support and Relationships

In sharing stories to describe how their roles and expectations' positive and impactful facilities success., it was revealed by educational leaders that team support for each other in the learning environment was fundamental as with teamwork sharing of ideas is encouraged to increase productivity, performance, and assisted with solving problems (EL4, EL10). Other educational leaders, expressed that team support and relationships came in various ways and enhanced professional and personal development, created a climate of trust, and motivated employees, while building the vision of the institution (EL 1- EL 3). The educational leaders reported that relationship was leadership and they all had excellent relationships. Respondents said that as educational leaders they formed relationships with their faculties and other educational stakeholders to improve their effectiveness in administration.

Educational leader (EL) 6 described his relationship with faculties as "lovely and said they were understanding, and supportive which contributed to his success and serving". The Educational leaders praised his relationship with external stakeholders as supportive, stated, "I have supportive colleagues and together we have achieved things that probably we would not have been able to achieve; but because of our resilience and collaboration we are making it through especially this rough time" (EL 4). Relationship with others supports and improves educational success. Similar sentiments about relationships with faculties were expressed by other participants.

In summary, collaboration, and collegiality with colleagues' formed part of the educational leaders' perspectives on serving, striving, and surviving in their performance and motivation for success. The elements of motivation and socialization through educational leaders' collaborative processes were manifested in how educational leaders socialized and brought energy to educational environments.

Training and Development Accounted for Success

The educational leaders were asked their perceptions of motivation, training and development, and performance for success as they strive in their institutions. Collectively, the leaders shared their perspectives on training as the need for sharing ideas which accounted for their success as they strive and survive through rewarding and challenging times. Participants' perspectives were that training was important for every sector of education because it increased employees' competence to perform jobs or assignments effectively (EL 1-5). During training, "best practices are shared which allowed for learning from each other strategies needed to improve their abilities and prepare them for leadership positions" in the institution's hierarchy (EL 3, EL10, EL11, EL12). Other educational leaders (EL4, EL6, EL13) described training with the right resources necessary to drive change initiatives in the organization.

In summary, the professional learning communities took on a life of their own and the need for leaders to collaborate and share ideas were crucial. Training aids the learning communities and employees as faculties enhance their knowledge, skills, and abilities. Findings from the educational leaders' discussions revealed that training was adequate because it enabled them to solve challenges faced in institutions and to successfully navigated the teaching and learning environment.

Motivational Strategies Improve Performance

The educational leaders' perspectives were that there was a need for motivation strategies to improve faculties' performance. They shared that serving, striving, and surviving for success came through motivation, tenacity, and collaboration with other staff members to achieve set goals. Faculties were motivated when incentives were given and when educational leaders have social and developmental sessions with them (EL9). Some educational leaders shared that they used various motivational strategies to build capacities such as involvement in decision making and being facilitators at workshops. EDL 13 stated that, "we do workshops based on the strengths and weaknesses of employees, we build capacity, we allow faculties opportunities to have a say in the decision-making process of the institution".

The holistic perspectives from educational leaders were that success and motivation strategies needed to include incentives to improve performance, continuous improvement for self, collaborative, and success. The respondents pointed out however, that self-motivation in the process was important. When educators were motivated, they felt a sense of greater autonomy, empowerment, and commitment to the institution and themselves. The 13 participants stated that moving from external motivation to intrinsic motivation started extrinsically by getting the buy-in from others. They reported that while they were capable the tools, resources, support, training, and rewards should be administered. When they have all the resources the output would look good and faculties would be motivated to go above and beyond the call of duty.

Health and Wellness—Serving, Striving, and Surviving

The participants were asked their perceptions on serving, striving, and surviving in higher educational institutions. The educational leaders' perspectives were that these components affect their wellbeing and wellbeing matters in higher educational institutions. Participants 6 said, "where there is poor mental health and inadequate information on mental health, striving and surviving in organization might be affected" (EL 4). In relation to mental health and wellness, some participants reported that mental health should be given top priority in institutions because if educators/faculties were not healthy, they would be unable to perform because the nature of the job could be stressful (ELs 5, 6, 7). The EDLs collectively agreed that faculties' working environment should encourage them to be comfortable, support team members, and be stress free. Well-being, health, and wellness assisted faculties' performance and job satisfaction and yielded success to educational leaders' and the organizations(institutions).

Leadership, Teamwork, Loneliness in Serving, Striving, and Surviving

When I asked the educational leaders their perceptions on serving, striving, and surviving in higher educational institutions, several perspectives came forth, such as openness and accommodativeness of different personalities and background. However, educational leaders though that "leadership in education is a lonely road" and as educational leaders, one has to become a mastermind at balancing time, resources, and other administrative matters in order to maintain relationships with others including family members and social groups. The educational leaders' perspectives were that leadership in education becomes a lonely road because regardless of the support system in place, there were still certain decisions that required their leadership and management; certain levels of responsibilities and competence were high stakes that only the educational leaders can be engaged.

Some of the educational leaders were cognizant that, as educational leaders, they had to become a master mind at balancing time and resources to deal with administrative matters in order to maintain relationships with their family members, and social groups (EDL 10 -EDL 13). This lived reality educational leaders opined can be gleaned when they liaised with other colleagues and realized that they were all in the same boat, however others' boats might be sailing much more than others. The educational leaders shared that teamwork, problem solving, and critical thinking accounted for their success and could be tied to motivation, performance, and success. Teamwork alleviates workload and builds confidence in others, shapes, develops, and activates educational leaders' effectiveness and increases their performance.

DISCUSSION AND CONCLUSION

The purpose of this qualitative study was to explore the extent to which educational leaders in higher educational institutions' success, motivation, and performance resulted from serving, striving, and surviving (3S') Phenomena. The literature review presented useful insights on motivational theories to equip educational leaders' success and framed an understanding of how motivated employees are committed to achieve the goals of the organizations. The 13 participants were from America, Canada, and Jamaica and consisted of 13 educational leaders with interviews. Educational leaders' success, motivation, and performance in higher educational institutions while serving, striving, and surviving revealed that educational leaders' success is vitally important for the institution and empowering of facilities. This increase job satisfaction, performance, motivation and their commitment to the institutions. Educational leaders' motivation came extrinsically with buy-in from others and having the tools, resources, support, training, and rewards to succeed, and build capacity.

The findings echoed that educational leaders' experiences has been fulfilling, challenging, rewarding, and creating opportunities to fulfill the institutional objectives. The roles and expectations accounted for their motivation and success, and that of their colleagues' motivation, capacities, and workplace conditions were teamwork, problem solving measures, and critical thinking skills sought to examine their effectiveness. Working as a team led to institutions identifying best practices, solving problems, and sharing ideas that would not normally have occurred with individual efforts. Teamwork tapped into persons' critical thinking skills, strength, and techniques to solve problems and make decisions. Motivation moved educators into action in the achievement of organizational goals and for themselves. The need for sustained motivation existed and educational leaders could implement motivational strategies involving incentives to improve performance, motivation, and capacities through training and development.

Training and development prepare employees for their present and future jobs and opportunities in organizations. Training and development reduce errors and increases efficiencies and competences of other she leaders were cognizant that success was grounded in their motivation, tenacity, and collaboration with colleagues as they sought to achieve the goals and objectives of the institution. Social and developmental sessions, for example, workshops and training courses were also factors which motivated educators. Job satisfaction cannot be overemphasised in any organization because satisfied employees yield higher performance which is valuable to the organization as their morale, attitude, and belief will support the shared value, trust, and commitment to improve the activities of the organization. Job satisfaction intertwined with the various multi-dimensional elements such as job security, performance management, trust, and supportive roles of leaders to their subordinate or educational colleagues. Job satisfaction enhances the performance of all educational stakeholders. Educational leaders have different ways of how they are satisfied on the job and measures that translate satisfaction for one leader, might not be similar for others.

Based on the literature McShane et al. (2015) found that satisfied employees were more motivated and productive at work and their work environments were much more conducive to work as "there is a moderately positive relationship between job satisfaction and performance" (p. 93). Job satisfaction was linked to employee motivation as proven in the research. Once employees or educational leaders were satisfied, it alleviated the challenges they faced in the institutions and encouraged their performance and job satisfaction. Educational leaders of the study shared their perspectives that job satisfaction varied in shape and form, however, when necessary, educational leaders should ensure that not only faculties but also, they are satisfied in any way possible because their satisfaction promoted their autonomy, improved institutions' facilities and learning endeavours, and importantly supported the leadership. Ololube (2004) and Peretomode (1991) positively associated job satisfaction with feelings of accomplishment that employee acquired with various job activities and rewards achieved from the accomplishment. Educational leaders' perspectives were that they have obtained the rewards, accomplishments, recognitions, and satisfactions from their job. Training and development prepare employees for their present and future jobs and opportunities in organizations. Training and development reduce errors and increases efficiencies and competences of others. Educational leaders' success, motivation, and performance in higher educational institutions is challenging, however, rewarding. It involves serving, striving, and surviving for flourishing and success. Attention should be given to word-life balance, well-being, professional growth, and development for goal attainment, efficiency, and effectiveness.

REFERENCES

Ali, S. H. K., Khan, N. S., & Yildiz, Y. (2020). Leadership effects on CSR employee, media, customer, and NGOs. *Management and Economics Research Journal*, *6*, 11. doi:10.18639/MERJ.2020.961566

Alvoid, L., & Black, W. L. (2014). The changing role of the principal. Center for American Progress, 1–33.

Arlestig, H., Day, C., & Johansson, O. (2016). *A decade of research on school principals: Cases from 24 Countries*. Springer. doi:10.1007/978-3-319-23027-6

Bandura, A. (1997). *Self-efficacy: The exercise of control*. W.H. Freeman and Company.

Bandura, A. (2000). Exercise of human agency through collective efficacy. *Current Directions in Psychological Science*, *9*(3), 75–78. doi:10.1111/1467-8721.00064

Barnes, L. L., & Spangenburg, J. M. (2018). When leadership fail: A view from the lens of four employees. *American Journal of Business Education*, *11*(3), 49–54. doi:10.19030/ajbe.v11i3.10188

Bass, B. M., & Riggio, R. E. (2006). *Transformational leadership*. Lawrence Erlbaum Publishers. doi:10.4324/9781410617095

Berkovich, I. (2016). School leaders and transformational leadership theory: Time to part ways? *Journal of Educational Administration, 54*(5), 609–622. doi:10.1108/JEA-11-2015-0100

Bingham, D., & Bubb, S. (2017). Leadership for wellbeing. In P. Earley & T. Greany (Eds.), *School Leadership and Education System Reform* (pp. 173–181). Bloomsbury.

Blau, P. (1964). *Exchange and power in social life*. Wiley.

Bourne, P. A. (2018). Ultimate leadership winning execution strategies for your situation. *Academy of Educational Leadership Journal, 22*(1), 1–6.

Briggs, A. R. J., Coleman, M., & Morrison, M. (2012). *Research methods in educational leadership & management* (3rd ed.). Sage. doi:10.4135/9781473957695

Camilleri, E. (2006). Towards developing an organisational commitment – public service motivation model for the Maltese public service employees. *Public Policy and Administration, 21*(1), 63-83. . doi:10.1177/095207670602100105

Canrinus, E. T., Helms-Lorenz, M., Beijaard, D., Buitink, J., & Hofman, A. (2012). Self- efficacy, job satisfaction, motivation, and commitment: Exploring the relationships between indicators of teachers' professional identity. *European Journal of Psychology of Education, 27*(1), 115–132. doi:10.100710212-011-0069-2

Canrinus, E. T., Lorenz-Helms, M., Beijaard, D., Buitink, J., & Hofman, A. (2011). Profiling teachers' sense of professional identity. *Educational Studies, 37*(5), 593–608. doi:10.1080/03055698.2010.539857

Cherkowski, S., & Walker, K. (2016). Flourishing leadership: Engaging purpose, passion, and play in the work of leading schools. *Journal of Educational Administration, 54*(4), 378–392. doi:10.1108/JEA-10-2014-0124

Cohen, L., Manion, L., & Morrison, K. (2011). *Research methods in education* (7th ed.). Routledge.

Cote, R. (2017). Vision of effective leadership. *Journal of Leadership, Accountability and Ethics, 14*(4), 52–63.

Deci, E. L., & Ryan, R. M. (2002). *Handbook of self-determination research*. University of Rochester Press.

DeNisi, A. S., & Freeman, A. B. (2017). Performance appraisal and performance management: 100 years of progress. Journal of Applied. *The Journal of Applied Psychology, 102*(3), 421–433. doi:10.1037/apl0000085 PMID:28125265

Dou, D., Devos, G., & Valcke, M. (2016). The effects of autonomy gap in personnel policy, principal leadership and teachers' self-efficacy on their organizational commitment. *Asia Pacific Education Review, 17*(2), 339–353. doi:10.100712564-016-9428-7

Earley, P. (2020). Surviving, thriving, and reviving in leadership: The personal and professional development needs of educational leaders. *Management in Education, 34*(3), 1–5. doi:10.1177/0892020620919763

Earley, P., & Weindling, D. (2007). Do school leaders have a shelf life? Career stages and head-teacher performance. *Educational Management Administration & Leadership, 35*(1), 73–88. doi:10.1177/1741143207071386

Galletta, M., Portoghese, I., & Battistelli, A. (2011). Intrinsic motivation, job autonomy and turnover intention in the Italian healthcare: The mediating role of affective commitment. *Journal of Management Research, 3*(1), 1–19. doi:10.5296/jmr.v3i2.619

Galletta, M., Portoghese, I., & Battistelli, A. (2011). Intrinsic motivation, job autonomy and turnover intention in the Italian healthcare: The mediating role of affective commitment. *Journal of Management Research, 3*(1), 1–19. doi:10.5296/jmr.v3i2.619

Gamero-Burón, C., & Lassibille, C. (2018). Work engagement among school directors and its impact on teachers' behaviour at work. *Journal of Developing Areas, 52*(2), 27–39. doi:10.1353/jda.2018.0020

García-Morales, V. J., Lloréns-Montes, F. J., & Verdú-Jover, A. J. (2008). The effects of transformational leadership on organizational performance through knowledge and innovation. *British Journal of Management, 19*(4), 299–319. doi:10.1111/j.1467-8551.2007.00547.x

Garza, E. Jr, Drysdale, L., Gurr, D., Jacobson, S., & Merchant, B. (2014). Leadership for school success: Lessons from effective principals. *International Journal of Educational Management, 28*(7), 798–811. doi:10.1108/IJEM-08-2013-0125

Getachew, D. S., & Zhou, E. (2018). The influences of transformational leadership on collective efficacy: The moderating role of perceived organizational support. *International Journal of Organizational Innovation, 10*(4), 7–15.

Gultekin, H., & Acar, E. (2014). The intrinsic and extrinsic factors of teacher motivation. *revista de cercetare si interventie sociala, 47*, 291-306.

Imran, R., Kamaal, A., & Mahmoud, A. B. (2017). Teacher's turnover intentions. The International. *Journal of Education Management, 31*(6), 828–842. https://do.org/10.1108/IJEM-05-2016-0131

Jones, G. R., George, J. M., & Hill, C. W. L. (2000). *Contemporary management* (2nd ed.). Irwin McGraw-Hill.

Judge, T. A., & Piccolo, R. F. (2004). Transformational and transactional leadership: A meta-analytic test of their relative Validity. *The Journal of Applied Psychology, 89*(5), 755–768. doi:10.1037/0021-9010.89.5.755 PMID:15506858

Kellerman, B. (2012). *The End of Leadership*. Harper Collins.

Klopotan, I., Mjeda, T., & Kurečić, P. (2018). Exploring the motivation of employees in a firm: A Case-Study. *Business Systems Research, 9*(1), 151–160. doi:10.2478/bsrj-2018-0012

Kollenscher, E., Poper, M., & Ronen, B. (2018). Value-creating organizational leadership. *Journal of Management & Organization, 24*(1), 19–39. doi:10.1017/jmo.2016.33

Laub, J. (2018). *Leveraging the power of servant leadership: Building high performing organization*. Palgrave Macmillan. doi:10.1007/978-3-319-77143-4

Lee, C., Liu, J., Rousseau, D. M., Hui, C., & Chen, Z. X. (2011). Inducements, contributions, and fulfillment in new employee psychological contracts. *Human Resource Management, 50*(2), 201–226. doi:10.1002/hrm.20415

Lorenz, F. G. (2014). A study of wellness and academic leadership. *Journal of Applied Research in Higher Education, 6*(1), 30–43. doi:10.1108/JARHE-11-2012-0029

Mathis, R. L., & Jackson, J. H. (2000). *Human resource management* (9th ed.). South-Western College Publishing.

McShane, S. L., Tas, K., & Steen, S. L. (2015). *Canadian organizational behaviour* (11th ed.). McGraw Hill.

Meyer, J. (2002). Strategic communication enhances organizational performance. *Human Resource Planning, 25*(2), 7–10.

Nicholas, L., & West-Burnham, J. (2016). *Understanding leadership: Challenges and reflections.* Crown House.

Northouse, P. G. (2013). Leadership: Theory and practice (6th ed.). Thousand Oaks.

Onorato, M. (2013). Transformational leadership style in educational sector: An empirical study of corporate managers and educational leaders. *Academy of Educational Leadership Journal, 17*(1), 33–47.

Owings, W. A., & Kaplan, L. S. (2010). *Leadership and organizational behaviour in education: Theory into Practice.* Pearson.

Palmer, R. E. (2008). *Ultimate leadership: Winning execution strategies for your situation.* Pearson Education Inc.

Perry, J. L. (2010). *The Jossey-Bass reader on nonproftit and public leadership.* John Wiley & Son.

Poturak, M., Mekić, E., Hadžiahmetović, N., & Budur, T. (2020). Effectiveness of transformational leadership among different cultures. *International Journal of Social Sciences & Educational Studies, 7*(3), 119–129.

Reyes, Y. D. (2018). Teachers' and school administrators' perception on the strategic leadership practices of school administrators. *Educational Review, 2*(8), 432–446. doi:10.26855/er.2018.08.004

Robbins, S. P., & Judge, T. A. (2011). *Organizational behavior* (14th ed.).

Ryan, R. M., & Deci, E. L. (2017). *Self-determination theory: Basic psychological needs in motivation, development and wellness.* The Guilford Press. doi:10.1521/978.14625/28806

Schwind, U., & Fassina, W. (2013). *Canadian human resource management: A strategic approach* (13th ed.). McGraw Hill.

Selamata, N., Nordin, N., & Adnan, A. A. (2013). Rekindle teacher's organizational commitment: The effect of transformational leadership behavior. *Procedia: Social and Behavioral Sciences, 90,* 566–574. doi:10.1016/j.sbspro.2013.07.127

Sohail, R., Saleem, S., Ansar, S., & Azeem, M. A. (2014). Effect of work motivation and organizational commitment on job satisfaction: A case of education industry in Pakistan. *Global Journal of Management and Business Research, 14*(6), 1–7.

Toker, A. (2022). Importance of leadership in the higher education. *International Journal of Social Sciences & Educational Studies, 9*(2), 1- 8. https/www.doi: . v9i2p230 doi:10.23918/ijsses

van Manen, M. (1997). *Researching lived experience: Human science for an action sensitive pedagogy* (2nd ed.). The Althouse Press.

Walker, K. (2017). *884 critical policy making in education: Early readings* (2nd ed.). Turning Point Global Prublishing.

Walker, K. D., & Kutsyuruba, B. (2019). The role of school administrators in providing early career teachers' support: A Pan-Canadian perspective. *International Journal of Educational Policy and Leadership, 14*(3), 1-19. https://doi.org/ doi:10.22230/ijepl.2019v14n3a862

Wang, F., Pollock, K., & Hauseman, C. (2018). School principals job satisfaction: The effects of work intensification. *Canadian Journal of Educational Administration and Policy, 85,* 73.

Chapter 2
Transformational Leadership Styles and Change Processes in Higher Education

Yaw Owusu-Agyeman
https://orcid.org/0000-0001-6730-5456
University of the Free State, South Africa

Enna Moroeroe
University of the Free State, South Africa

ABSTRACT

As higher education institutions attempt to address issues pertaining to institutional change, very few scholarly studies have examined how transformational leadership processes influence changes to institutional cultures and structures. To address this gap, the current study explores how leadership processes contribute to changes in the institutional culture and structure of a university in South Africa by gathering interview data from 69 academic and professional staff. The findings revealed that for the university to achieve its transformation objectives, leaders should challenge the cognitive abilities of their staff, scaffold strategies for meeting high work standards, negotiating the attainment of staff personal and career goals, engender staff motivation and assist their staff to understand the institutional culture and structure. These findings among others lead the author to propose ways that future studies could examine how the leadership processes could enhance institutional transformation.

INTRODUCTION

Institutional transformation as a concept and strategy in higher education (HE) is characterized by varied definitions, interpretations, and implementation plans. The variations in the terminologies and interpretation of institutional transformation could be linked to the distinct national orientation, function (de Wit & Altbach, 2021), and cultures of higher education institutions (HEIs). Recent studies on institutional transformation have revealed its broad scope which include issues related to staff development (Croucher

DOI: 10.4018/979-8-3693-1380-0.ch002

& Woelert, 2021), internationalization (de Wit & Altbach, 2021), and the development of teaching and learning competencies of academics (Rajaram, 2021). Today, many African universities are struggling to transform their institutions to meet international standards after many years of operating along the old European model of education with different structures and academic processes (Frankema, 2012; Knight, 2018). In South Africa which is the context of the current study, the size and structure of the educational system were developed based on the apartheid setting with the promulgation of the Extension of University Education Act of 1953 which placed restrictions on entry to universities based on race and ethnicity (Badsha, 2000). Accordingly, institutions were categorized as historically white institutions or black higher education institutions (Carolissen & Bozalek, 2017).

The end of the apartheid era however brought to light the importance of developing an educational system that not only reflects the new democratic era including the transformation of the South African Higher Education sector but also, addresses issues of social imbalances (Cross, 2004). Along these lines, the focus of the transformation of the educational sector in South Africa after the apartheid regime was to meet the needs of previously disadvantaged blacks in all aspects of life: socio-cultural; political and cultural domains (Knight, 2018). A prior study has argued that the transformation of universities in South Africa is twofold: first is the explanation of transformation as institutional compliance to the constitutional provisions and national policy directives which include race and gender; and second is the interpretation of transformation as one that includes epistemological change and change in institutional culture that leads to stronger social inclusion (Badsha & Wickham, 2013). In particular, the transformation agenda of universities in South Africa are linked to the promotion of inclusive institutional cultures (Adonis & Silinda, 2021), and the promotion of diversity (Cross, 2004) among staff and students. Realistically, the challenges confronting higher education in South Africa transcend issues of social justice and equity to include transformative leadership roles at the macro and micro levels to ensure that institutional change takes place. Such focus includes developing the research capacity of staff as well as their teaching skills, re-designing the existing curricula to meet the evolving labour demands and providing students, and staff with experiences that make the university environment a centre of excellence (Knight, 2018).

Successful institutional transformation is either structural or procedural and it is influenced by changes to institutional actions, performance outcomes, and shifts in values (Boyce, 2003), including leadership influences, and may vary based on the context and culture of the institution. Two dominant institutional cultures - administrative and academic cultures have long been recognized as essential in explaining the institutional structure, leadership roles, and the relationships between individuals and groups. While the administrative culture is described by hierarchical structures, bureaucracy, authority, division of labour and delegated responsibility, the academic culture consists of professional culture with emphasis on individual knowledge and expertise as well as collegial decision-making in some instances (Volkwein, 1999). To this end, the South African Government's white paper - a programme for the transformation of higher education identified the importance of developing an institutional culture that incorporates reconciliation, respect for difference and the promotion of common good, values, and facilitates behaviours aimed at peaceful assembly (Suransky & van der Merwe, 2016).

The need for institutions to have their own identity and evolve through their own structures, systems, and norms places so much demand on the leadership of universities to develop unique strategies, historically driven, meet the needs of members of the institutions, and also have an outlook of a contemporary institution that is prepared to compete in a global space. Despondently, many HEIs focus on developing strong institutional governance structures than they have done on developing a culture of strong leadership (Butler, 2020). Furthermore, although changes to institutional cultures, structures, and governance systems have been highlighted as important to creating reforms in universities in South Africa, there is a paucity of scholarly studies that address issues concerning leadership processes and the management of transformation in HEIs especially at the micro level. Also, the relationship between institutional change processes, institutional culture and transformational leadership roles remains underexplored and not clearly defined. A previous study has shown that institutional transformation is often pervasive, purposely designed, implemented over time, and changes institutional culture by varying some underlying assumptions, behaviours, and processes (Kezar & Eckel, 2002). A more recent formulation suggests that institutional transformation involves adjustments to an institution's culture, structure, goals, leadership roles, management system, and strategy that can be examined from the macro and micro perspectives (Peng et al., 2021). This article addresses a gap in the institutional transformation literature by examining how transformational leadership roles especially at the micro level could enhance employee commitment and work output within an institutional change environment.

While researchers and managers of HEIs continue to find ways of addressing issues concerning the development of HEIs, it has also become necessary to explore how leadership roles especially at the lower echelons of universities either enhance or constrain the transformation of HEIs. To address these knowledge and practice gaps, the current study examines how academic and professional staff experience and perceive transformational leadership roles in the broad context of institutional transformation in a South African university. With many African universities still struggling to transform their universities to meet international and modern outlooks (Knight, 2018), it has become necessary for studies to be conducted into how transformational leadership roles could enhance change in HEIs. The link between leadership roles and change is also necessary because transformational leadership addresses concerns regarding motivation, collaboration with employees at different levels, and teamwork that could lead to desired change in institutions (Antonopoulou et al., 2021; Elrehail et al., 2018). To address the seeming knowledge and practice gaps concerning the relationship between transformational leadership processes, institutional culture, and institutional transformation, the current study seeks answers to two important research questions: 1) what transformational leadership processes influence institutional change in the university? and 2) how do staff perceive the relationship between transformational leadership processes and institutional change in the university?

TRANSFORMATIONAL LEADERSHIP

Transformational leadership as a concept has different definitions based on various schools of thought (Al-Husseini et al., 2021; Owusu-Agyeman, 2021; Siangchokyoo et al., 2020). However, one of the widely known definitions suggests that transformational leadership is a leadership style that allows leaders to challenge their staff through different activities such as providing them with a sense of mission and vision and allowing them to work towards group goals and objectives (Avolio et al., 2009; Dóci & Hofmans, 2015; Føllesdal & Hagtvet, 2013). Although there are various definitions of transformational leadership, the current study explains transformational leadership as a theory that supports the commitment of academic and non-academic staff to change in an HEI setting. Transformational leadership is often explained using four main themes; inspirational motivation, idealized influence, individualized consideration, and intellectual stimulation (Avolio et al., 2014; Lajoie et al., 2017). First, inspirational motivation (Avolio et al., 2009) is offered by leaders who share their vision with their followers and challenge them to work towards meeting those goals and addressing the challenges that may arise in the cause of implementing those goals. Motivation as a concept has been described as a complex and multidimensional construct that explains how the goal-directed behaviour of individuals is initiated, sustained, and concluded (Ford et al., 2020). Also, motivation consists of emotions, psychological needs, values and beliefs, and interaction with the environment (Ford et al., 2020) and a combination of cognitive and social elements that explains individual drive towards achieving specific goals or tasks (Cook & Artino, 2016).

Second, idealized influence (Avolio et al., 2009) explains how leaders identify group goals and values and provide the necessary structures and support that allow followers to work towards those goals through sustained efforts (Bono & Judge, 2004) and effective relationships. Through empowered behaviours (Boudrias et al., 2014; Lajoie et al. 2017) and effective relationships, staff of HEIs can obtain a sense of obligation, meaning, self-determination, and inspiration. Previous study has shown that when leaders and members of teams internalize the group into their sense of self as part of their shared social identity, it leads to the mobilization of group-based power which is important for leadership practices (Coleman & Donoher, 2022; Haslam et al., 2021). Intellectual stimulation (Avolio et al., 2009) is often provided by a leader in an HEI setting who challenges the thinking abilities of other staff by providing them with insights into alternative ways of developing and inspiring themselves to achieve personal and institutional goals. Previous study has shown that transformational leadership processes include supporting staff to develop the emotional intelligence that is required for their tasks (Baba et al., 2021). By supporting staff to develop their emotional intelligence required for their tasks (Baba et al., 2021), leaders challenge their staff to be innovative. Intellectual stimulation is directly linked to pedagogical relationships which allow leaders to build, modify, initiate, innovate, and develop or change knowledge (Bernstein & Solomon, 1999) through engagement and interaction. Fourth, individualized consideration (Avolio et al., 2009) describes how leaders support their followers by way of advice, motivation for personal development, career development, and emotional support. Unlike the path-goal theory (Derue et al., 2011; Martin et al., 2013), individual consideration allows leaders to monitor the knowledge and skills development of their staff while ensuring that they develop new ideas. Although transformational leadership is important to changing the overall outlook and functions of support and academic departments in HEIs, one of its weaknesses is the fact that it does not integrate situational circumstances that may allow individuals to work outside of the group goals which is a major advantage of the contingency theory. However, the current study adopts an empirical process to examine how the transformational leadership process could enhance an institutional change process using all four transformational leadership themes" inspirational motivation, idealized influence, individualized consideration, and intellectual stimulation (Avolio et al., 2014; Lajoie et al., 2017).

RESEARCH METHODS

The history of the study context akin to other historically white universities (HWU) in South Africa has evolved through several years of transformation. Originally established in 1904 as a predominantly White university, the university has grown to become a racially diverse institution with three geographically dispersed campuses. The institution is a comprehensive university that focuses on mass higher education in the South African higher education system. This study adopted a qualitative research design to examine how academic and professional staff experience and perceive transformational leadership roles in the broad context of institutional transformation in a South African university. The rationale for using the qualitative research design is to comprehend events in their natural setting with a focus on the perspectives and experiences of individuals that cannot be explained using objective measurements (Kyngäs et al., 2020).

Participants and Sampling Techniques

Located in three different campuses in a province in South Africa, the current study context has a total staff population of 2,521. Purposive and snowball sampling was used to gather data from participants. The participants comprised of 34 males and 35 females. Also, the participants consisted of academics (28) and non-academics (41).

Procedure

A formal invitation via email was sent to all participants across all three campuses of the university. Participants who agreed to participate in the study were contacted and the dates for the interviews were accordingly scheduled. Participants were informed about the purpose of the study and afterwards, requested to sign a consent form before the interview. Each participant was informed about the potential benefits and risks of the study as well as their right to withdraw from the interview. The duration of each interview was between forty-five and sixty minutes and the interviews were held in meeting rooms or the offices of the participants. A semi-structured interview schedule was used to gather data from the participants concerning their perceptions and experiences about leadership processes and the management of transformation especially at the micro level at the university. To ensure the confidentiality of the information provided by participants, three processes were followed. First, each participant was informed of the procedure adopted to safely process and store the data. This process includes storing the electronic data on a password-protected computer and the hard copies of the transcripts in a safe with a lock for a period of five years. Second, all participants were informed not to provide any personal identifiers that could easily link them to the data. Lastly, only the interviewer and the interviewee were present at the interview venue while the voice recorders were placed clearly at the sight of the interviewee. The current research was approved by the university's Research Ethics Committee in fulfilment of the requirements for conducting research at the university. In line with the rules of ethical consideration, the rationale of the study, potential risks, and benefits as well as the right of participants to withdraw from the interview if they felt they could not continue for personal reasons was explained to all participants.

Data Processing

The data gathered from participants were examined using thematic analysis that allows researchers to examine complex and rich datasets (Braun & Clarke, 2006; Neuendorf, 2019). The transcripts were generated from the interviews we conducted. To analyze the data, the first step was to read the transcripts thoroughly to ensure that they were written with no language ambiguities. The second step was the indexing of the transcripts and the creation of the respondent and cross-case memos based on the feedback from academic and non-academic staff who were on three campuses. The third step involved the development of codes, categories and themes. To determine the best codes that represent the views of participants, codes that appeared at least ten times or more were highlighted. Sample codes that emerged were: "I receive frequent information from my head of department"; "I take initiative on matters concerning my work"; "I receive frequent feedback from my head of department", "innovative teaching"; "My line manager is committed to my resource and technical needs" and: "I apply my critical thinking abilities on the job". The fourth step involved collapsing the codes that were developed into categories. This involved grouping codes that provided similar meanings. The fifth step involved identifying the themes based on the patterns developed from the codes and categories of the datasets. However, all five themes were predetermined.

To increase the trustworthiness of the data collected, three major processes were followed. First, the methodical thoroughness of the research design (Rose & Johnson, 2020) was maintained by ensuring that the data collection process, the analysis of the data, and the discussion of the findings were consistent with the appropriate empirical procedure. Secondly, throughout the research, data credibility was maintained by following a repeated process of examining the data and codes from both male and female academics to ensure that their views were correctly captured and analyzed. Particularly, the codes were analyzed and discussed to reveal 1) the main ideas that emerged from the interviews regarding perceived gender inequalities in the university and 2) to describe the applicability of the research methods to future research (Rose & Johnson, 2020).

FINDINGS

The perceptions and experiences of participants are analyzed based on the five themes that were developed: scaffolding strategies for meeting high work standards; negotiating the attainment of staff personal and career goals; challenging the cognitive abilities of staff; engendering staff motivation and the link between transformational leadership roles and institutional culture. Clearly, the results show nuanced, interrelated, and elaborate meaning of transformational leadership among staff in the university.

Scaffolding Strategies for Meeting High Work Standards

One of the important leadership processes is to empower the behaviours of staff to obtain a sense of obligation, meaning, self-determination, and inspiration (Lajoie et al., 2017) through scaffolding strategies by transformational leaders. An analysis of the interview data revealed three categories under scaffolding strategies for meeting high work standards: setting clear achievement goals for staff; being responsive to staff resource and technical needs; and provision of prompt and clear feedback. First, participants expressed their views concerning how their leaders set clear goals for them. For instance, Amogelang stated that "Our unit is responsible for liaising with students on different projects and by working towards the clear goals set for me at the beginning of every year, I can strategize and achieve those goals. Also, what I do is to ensure that students get the support they need for their work and to also make sure that I address the issues they may have. Remember….this is also tied to my annual performance evaluation" Similar view was shared by Maretha who argued that:

I think that as academics, we have specific goals which are teaching, research, and engaged scholarship. I remember when my head of department joined this department from another university what he did was to request for a short discussion with us to tell us his expectations and how he would want us to work towards our goals which include teaching and research. Although the head of the department often reminds us of our core duties during meetings, I have a personal commitment to my students and to my personal development to work hard. I feel that we should have a sense of purpose first".

On his part, Joseph stated that "our director invites us to give our input to the activities of our department every year. The process is quite consultative and he gives us periodic feedback on how we work towards our goals. I do not have issues with the goals set for me because I am involved in the process and my performance is fairly assessed based on systemic feedback." Some participants shared differing views. For instance, Lindokuhle argued that "I work with a manager who is a very independent person and so I cannot talk about specific goals. My challenge is rather the low workload that I have due to my line manager's approach to work. It gets quite frustrating to sit down all day without doing much". The feedback from participants revealed that when leaders set clear and timely goals for their followers, it could help empower the behaviours of staff to work toward a desired change agenda. Furthermore, when staff obtain a sense of obligation with specific goals, it enables them to work hard and achieve their personal and institutional goals. On the contrary, when leaders do not support their followers to overcome challenges in poor communication and the lack of team effort, they could affect employee performance.

The commitment of line managers to the resource and technical needs of staff is important to the performance of tasks in the university setting by staff. For instance, Nokwazi stated that "my line manager responds to my needs. Whenever I need to replace any equipment or obtain any tool for my work, she does not hesitate to make them available to me". Similarly, Lindokuhle also stated that, "my line manager is very responsive to my resource and technical needs." Feedback from participants revealed that most participants believed their line managers provide them with the resources they need to work.

Adequacy of feedback from line managers and heads of departments to staff is essential for meeting work targets and serving the needs of students and staff. Participants shared their opinion about the adequacy of feedback they receive from their line managers and heads of department regarding their job. For instance, Khumalo argued that "I appreciate truthful feedback that is direct and clear. However, I have had to create my own meaning of the feedback that comes to me sometimes and that is quite challenging". Similarly, another participant argued stated that "the feedback I receive is okay. However, in most instances, I press my line manager for feedback [Kholwa]. Other participants also indicated their satisfaction with either the frequency or quality of feedback they receive from their line managers or heads of department: "I have no issue with my head of department when it comes to feedback. I think that he is doing his best seeing that we are a small department" [Adiel] and "I have a very good relationship with my line manager and so I receive feedback on a regular basis when we engage. It is often informal because we do not always sit down to have a formal meeting [Angel]". The feedback from participants was mixed - revealing that line managers have different ways of providing their staff with feedback. Hoverer, some participants indicated that although they receive feedback from their line managers, they had to sometimes put in extra effort to either get clarity regarding the feedback or get the feedback delivered timeously. It is important for transformational leaders to provide feedback that is clear and very direct.

Negotiating the Attainment of Staff Personal and Career Goals

Transformational leaders support their followers in the attainment of their personal and career goals by negotiating the process through discussion and even lobbying. Participants shared their opinion concerning how their line managers support them to achieve their personal and career goals. Some support staff indicated that "I receive all the support I need from my line manager in terms of achieving my personal goals. However, the challenge I have is time management and I am working on it. I have enrolled for a course on lynda.com" [Maralize] and "I currently work with a line manager who is passionate about my academic and career development. I am currently enrolled in a master's programme which I find very fulfilling" [Thuto]. Other academic participants also explained how their heads of department or line managers provide them with the needed assistance to develop their career goals, "my head of department is very open and maintains a good relationship with us. There are times he walks to my class to observe my teaching and give me feedback" [Thabiso]. Similarly, Emma intimated that "I am very grateful to my head of department for his support while I study for my Ph.D. You know with the scheduling of courses for the semester, I need to have flexible teaching arrangements and I always get the support I need in that regard." The narrative feedback of participants revealed that support from line managers to staff in achieving their goals and cordial working relationship between line managers and staff could lead to the achievement of staff personal and career goals. Also, the findings show that transformational leaders do not only support their team members to achieve their goals but also, motivate them to work towards their set targets.

Challenging the Cognitive Abilities of Staff

Challenging the cognitive abilities of the staff represents one of the most important features of transformational leadership roles. The narrative data revealed two main categories under challenging the cognitive abilities of staff: stimulating the critical thinking abilities of staff; and providing staff with challenging job roles. First, participants shared their opinions regarding how their leaders stimulate their critical thinking abilities: "Honestly, a lot of my job comes with finding creative solutions to problems. Remember, the expectation of my line manager is high" [Thumpe, support staff]. Similarly, Thandolwethu explained that "my job involves helping students to resolve their issues at the department. Also, I need to be very discreet about how I address these issues especially if I need to contact any of the lecturers to avoid confrontations. There are high expectations from not only my boss but also from the lecturers."

Likewise, Jeanique, who is an academic leader, highlighted the importance of academic leadership roles in ensuring that academics develop innovative teaching methods, "there are some academics who use innovative teaching methods for instance by using blended learning approaches." Particularly, academic leadership is essential to the transformation of HEIs that are currently facing challenges that are the result of global reform, volatility, uncertainty, ambiguity, and resistance (Butler, 2020; Kohtamäki, 2019). Teaching innovation, provision of creative solutions to problems, reflection and deeper understanding of work processes represents some of the practical approaches to developing the critical thinking abilities of academic and non-academic staff. The findings also show that when leaders challenge their staff to be innovative and develop their critical thinking abilities, it could lead to enhanced job performance.

Challenging the cognitive abilities of staff also includes the extent to which heads of department provide their followers with tasks that challenge them to apply their knowledge, skills, and abilities. Some participants shared their opinions. For instance, Iviwe who is a support staff indicated that "with all the additional roles that I have accepted, it is very challenging. What sustains my passion is the new challenges that my line manager introduces every time. I will say that the new challenges that come my way keep me on my toes and I am challenged to deliver exceptionally well" [Iviwe]. However, other respondents had contrasting experiences: "I am yearning for more work than what I am currently doing. I do not want to sound ungrateful, but I wish I could do more challenging work [Malwande], and "there is less excitement in what I do because the work is repetitive. I have been doing this work for a long time so until such a time when I can get to the fullest of my potential, I shall continue to work on this routine job" [Kamogelo]. The responses of the participants suggest that when staff are not provided with challenging job roles, it could lead to a feeling of inadequacy and a lack of accomplishment. Also, repetitive work and the lack of new challenges could lead to boredom and frustration.

Engendering Staff Motivation

While the focus on institutional transformation is often on changes to structure and culture, very little attention is paid to the relationship between transformational leadership, staff motivation, and institutional transformation. The following excerpts represent the views of participants concerning the relationship between transformational leadership roles and staff motivation: "I understand the importance of leadership roles in incentivizing or at least giving rewards to staff. However, my motivation is completely intrinsic" [Winnifred] and; "I would not link my motivation at the workplace to the role of my line manager. However, my motivation stems from the fact that I want to see students from rural areas and first-generation students succeed in their academic pursuits. Remember that I found myself in a similar situation a few years ago when I was a student at this university and people cared enough to do something for me [Nokuthula]. On her part, Rethabile stated that "My line manager is the one who motivates me to work. Aside that, there is no motivation. There is a lack of engagement with the rest of the unit, so it is like working in silos" Other participants also explained how they are motivated by the work they do. For instance, a participant stated that:

I am motivated by the work I do; wanting to see a change in how we collectively prevent GBV (Gender-based violence), SGBV (Sexual and Gender-based Violence), IPV (Intimate partner violence), and all forms of prejudice. Also, I want to make a difference in how we collectively challenge the scourge of GBV [Iviwe].

The feedback from participants shows that while the leadership role is important in enhancing inspirational motivation, other intrinsic features were seen as important - connecting to give meaning to how employees are motivated to work. Again, the narrative data points to the fact that the personal goals and career aspirations of staff serve as motivating factors.

The Link Between Transformational Leaderships Roles and Institutional Culture

Institutional culture represents one of the important elements of institutional transformation. While transformational leaders are expected to guide individuals' and group commitment to change, institutional culture is essential to shaping the behaviours and practices of staff concerning the attainment of institutional goals. The feedback from participants revealed divergent opinions. First, Atlehang emphasized the importance of teamwork and collaboration between staff as important to building a strong institutional culture, "I must state that teamwork is very important to building a strong institutional culture and eventually, lead to the transformation of the university. Although we may be seen to be working together, we are still in our silos." Similarly, Louw shared his opinion on how institutional culture could enhance leadership roles in the transformation of the university:

Transformational Leadership Styles and Change Processes

Two main issues should be investigated concerning institutional transformation, leadership, and culture. First, we need to work towards transforming the university environment by looking at how individual staff welfare and development are prioritized. Second, the university leadership needs to decide whether it is going to push the idea of education as a common good, social justice, and the transformation of the university space. [Louw].

The responses of Atlehang and Louw suggest that the transformation of the university is linked to the values, norms and practices that are shared by leaders and staff in the university. Transformational leaders play important roles in maintaining cultures that focus on removing practices that are adversative to creating an environment that supports staff development and maintaining high-performance culture. It also involves ensuring equality among all staff and providing resources for work as well as prioritizing employee welfare. The narrative data further highlights the importance of developing strong teamwork, creating opportunities for staff to take up leadership positions, and promoting equity and social justice.

DISCUSSION

The five themes that were developed from the interview data: scaffolding strategies for meeting high work standards; negotiating the attainment of staff personal and career goals; challenging the cognitive abilities of staff; engendering staff motivation and; the link between transformational leadership roles and institutional culture explain the transformational leadership processes that influence institutional change in the university. The five themes also show that staff expectations of the roles of heads of units, departments, and faculty as transformational leaders include providing support to staff through interaction that leads to staff personal and career development, and the achievement of institutional goals.

Figure 1. The relationship between transformational leadership styles and institutional change

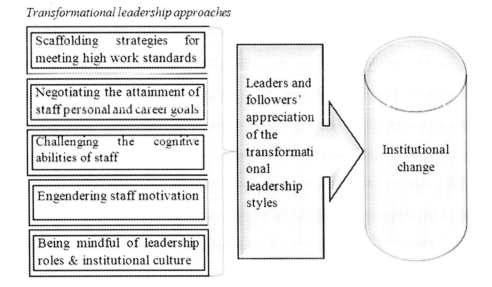

Figure 1 shows the relationship between transformational leadership styles and institutional change. While a previous study had shown that institutional transformation can be examined at the macro and micro levels (Peng et al., 2021) findings of the current study show that at the micro level, transformational leadership is required to shape the positive work experiences of staff. Arguably, staff perception and attitude towards change are a direct product of leadership influence at the micro level and, how leaders support staff to understand and work towards institutional change strategies. To put it succinctly, the diverse sub-cultures and leadership approaches at the department and faculty levels create an assemblage of institutional leadership processes and culture that drives change in the university. This is consistent with prior studies that reveal that transformation especially in South Africa is multifaceted (Adonis & Silinda, 2021), relies strongly on changes to institutional cultures (Badsha & Wickham, 2013), and requires a unique institutional approach.

An analysis of the data revealed that transformational leaders could enhance institutional change processes by scaffolding strategies for staff to meet high work standards. In practice, this could be achieved when leaders 1) set clear achievement goals for staff 2) are responsive to staff resource and technical needs and, 3) provide prompt and adequacy of feedback to staff. One of the essential qualities of transformational leaders is that they promote a positive attitude among employees toward institutional change and reduce employee negative reactions (Peng et al., 2021) through empowered behaviours (Lajoie et al., 2017). On the part of academics, the support they receive from their heads of department through research funding, meeting the high standards in teaching set by the university, and maintaining good pedagogical relationships represent the scaffolding support and strategies by their leaders.

Again, the feedback from participants also showed that transformational leaders could directly and indirectly enable their members to meet the high work standards set for them especially when they support them to meet their resource and technical needs. This finding is also linked to the adequacy of feedback, especially from line managers and heads of department to staff. Particularly, by providing prompt, positive, and constructive feedback to staff, transformational leaders can continually support the development of staff. However, one of the challenges to effective feedback as raised by a participant is the dual reporting lines of some staff and the complexities of such structure which sometimes leads to delayed feedback. In practice, a good social relationship between line managers and staff could enhance the quality of feedback they provide to their staff.

Secondly, the data revealed that transformational leaders could help their followers to achieve their personal and career goals especially when they negotiate the processes through advice, discussions, and lobbying. Particularly, the expectations of staff in the work settings include getting rewards that are commensurate with their output and performance, receiving higher pay levels, and having job security (Cartwright & Holmes, 2006; Coleman & Donoher, 2022).

Also, when staff develop a feeling of worth especially concerning the respect, they receive from their line mangers and leaders, they commit themselves to achieving their personal and career goals as well as the goals of the university. A transformational leader could enhance a staff feeling of worth by adopting team-building exercises, promoting socialization among staff, and advising staff to be tolerant and respect the views of colleagues.

The findings also showed that transformational leaders create an environment that is conducive for work and the attainment of personal and career goals especially when they communicate their feelings to their followers through meetings and formal or informal discussions. This also includes understanding group dynamics, supporting followers to plan and schedule their activities, recognizing and rewarding team efforts rather than selected individuals, and providing training in areas such as emotional intelligence to their staff. A recent study by Baba et al. (2021) shows that there is a relationship between transformational leadership and emotional intelligence especially among academic leaders in higher education. Another finding of the current study is the importance of good professional and social relationships between line managers and their staff. When leaders develop good relationships with their staff, it could lead to improved work output, and staff sense of belonging, promote a collegial environment, promote a collegial environment and reduce possible feelings of isolation. On the contrary, a lack of support especially in research could adversely affect their career development.

Challenging the cognitive abilities of staff which serves as the third theme is one of the most important features of transformational leadership. The findings revealed that the ability of transformational leaders to challenge the critical thinking abilities of their staff and to provide their staff with challenging job roles that involve the application of their knowledge and skills is essential to the overall transformation of universities. The role of transformational leaders includes motivating staff to achieve set objectives, supporting the professional development of staff and, stimulating intellectual discussion (Antonopoulou et al. 2021; Baba et al., 2021). Also, when leaders challenge the critical abilities of their staff through work processes and set targets, not only do they drive the abilities of their staff to achieve results but more importantly, they develop their staff to be innovative, result oriented and create solutions to problems through deep thinking. However, a lack of clearly defined job roles, a lack of cooperation and collaboration among staff, staff feeling of inadequacy and a lack of self-worth could negatively affect the critical thinking abilities of staff and the transformation of the university. Another finding of the current study is the importance of providing staff with challenging job roles that could enhance their personal and career development. Transformational leaders must continually stimulate the intellectual abilities of their staff by designing internal guidelines to support them to apply their knowledge, skills, and abilities through work processes, guidelines, feedback systems, and action plans. Concerning academic leadership processes, the data showed that teaching innovation is very important to addressing the challenges associated with teaching and learning.

Staff motivation is important in the work environment particularly due to the need to provide emotional and physical support to staff to enable them to achieve their goals. Furthermore, by focusing on staff motivation, transformational leaders can support their staff to work toward desired change in an institution (Antonopoulou et al. 2021; Elrehail et al., 2018). The results revealed that although leadership role is important to the attainment of staff inspirational motivation, other factors such as individual beliefs, personal orientation to life, and the immediate environment could be identified as tangential elements that influence staff motivation. For instance, feedback from some academics revealed that their motivation to work hard is driven by intrinsic factors as well as the desire to see students from rural areas and first-generation students succeed in their academic endeavors. Others also indicated that leadership support in terms of securing funding for research, assisting academics to publish in scholarly journals, and training academics to be innovative in their teaching serve as important motivating factors for academics. The data also revealed that most staff were self-motivated. For instance, some participants identified the need to fulfill personal career goals and the importance of contributing to the overall goals of the university as their source of motivation.

The findings of the current study show the link between transformational leadership roles, and institutional culture in the overall transformation of the university. These findings also suggest that the transformation of a university together with its culture is partly dependent on leadership processes that include developing strong teamwork, creating opportunities for staff to take up leadership positions, and challenging the creative and critical thinking abilities of staff. Particularly, the transformation of universities in South Africa is linked to the values, norms, and practices (Adonis & Silinda, 2021; Badsha & Wickham, 2013) that are shared by leaders and staff in the university. Therefore, by way of social learning and social exchange effects (Peng et al., 2021), transformational leaders create an environment that enables staff to be committed and open to change in the institution.

Limitations and Future Research Directions

The findings of the current study should be interpreted in light of two major limitations. First, are the differences in the structure and subcultures of the different campuses and professional departments of the university. Consequently, some of the findings of the current study may not apply to all departments in the university. Secondly, the use of transformational leadership and institutional theory as the theoretical underpinning of the current study limited the findings of the study to issues regarding institutional culture, structure, and leadership processes. The use of other theories could provide new insight into how leadership processes interface with institutional theory to explain the transformation of universities. This study recommends that future studies should explore different theories such as distributed and transactional leadership to conduct similar studies.

CONCLUSION

The scholarship of institutional transformation remains underdeveloped for many reasons including the lack of empirical studies on the effect of different transformation approaches on institutional change, the generalization of change strategies that are not context-driven, and the lack of literature that addresses transformation from a leadership perspective. While various scholarly studies have examined the importance of leadership processes in higher education not many had explored how transformational leadership contributes to institutional transformation. Of cause, one of the setbacks to the transformation of universities is the seeming focus on leadership processes at the higher echelons of institutions with very minimal concentration on the role of leaders at the various units and departments especially from the perspective of staff. The current study has contributed to addressing this seeming gap by showing how transformational leadership processes at the unit and department levels could enhance institutional transformation in a university in South Africa. An analysis of the data revealed that five themes —scaffolding strategies for meeting high work standards; negotiating the attainment of staff personal and career goals; challenging the cognitive abilities of staff; engendering staff motivation and the link between transformational leadership roles and institutional culture that influence the transformation at the micro level of the university. Conversely, although staff motivation is important to leadership processes, the results revealed that participants were particularly motivated by intrinsic factors, religious beliefs, and other individual features that are not directly attributable to transformational leadership influence. The study further showed that academics are particularly motivated by intrinsic factors as well as the desire to see students from rural areas and first-generation students succeed in their academic pursuits.

Secondly, the findings of the current study show that to enhance leadership processes among academic and non-academic staff in the university, it is important for leaders to address issues concerning staff professional development, achievement of personal and institutional goals, and the development of good professional and social relationship between leaders and their followers. Furthermore, when leaders understand group dynamics, recognize and reward individual and team efforts, support staff to develop their emotional intelligence, create an environment of tolerance and respect among staff, and enhance staff confidence and self-esteem, it could lead to staff a sense of belonging and a strong commitment to work. Third, the transformation of universities requires leaders who provide staff with challenging job roles that involve the application of their knowledge and skills. However, when staff are not challenged to apply their creative and critical thinking abilities, it could lead to a lack of confidence, feeling of low self-worth, and a sense of inadequacy. Fourth, the study revealed that high-level commitment by line managers to professional staff in universities is particularly important to ensure that the resource and technical needs of their staff are met. This finding provides a further explanation of how continued guidance by transformational leaders could lead to high-performance culture, staff commitment to the achievement of departmental and institutional goals and a collective effort to change adversative institutional culture. Lastly, the transformation of universities includes the promotion of institutional cultures that support staff professional development, enhance staff sense of belonging, and promote the welfare of staff.

REFERENCES

Adonis, C. K., & Silinda, F. (2021). Institutional culture and transformation in higher education in post-1994 South Africa: A critical race theory analysis. *Critical African Studies*, *13*(1), 73–94. doi:10.1080/21681392.2021.1911448

Al-Husseini, S., El Beltagi, I., & Moizer, J. (2021). Transformational leadership and innovation: The mediating role of knowledge sharing amongst higher education faculty. *International Journal of Leadership in Education*, *24*(5), 670–693. doi:10.1080/13603124.2019.1588381

Antonopoulou, H., Halkiopoulos, C., Barlou, O., & Beligiannis, G. N. (2021). Transformational leadership and digital skills in higher education institutes: during the COVID-19 pandemic. *Emerging science journal*, *5*(1), 1-15. doi:10.28991/esj-2021-01252

Avolio, B. J., Sosik, J. J., Kahai, S. S., & Baker, B. (2014). E-leadership: Re-examining transformations in leadership source and transmission. *The Leadership Quarterly*, *25*(1), 105–131. doi:10.1016/j.leaqua.2013.11.003

Avolio, B. J., Walumbwa, F. O., & Weber, T. J. (2009). Leadership: Current theories, research, and future directions. *Annual Review of Psychology*, *60*(1), 421–449. doi:10.1146/annurev.psych.60.110707.163621 PMID:18651820

Baba, M. M., Makhdoomi, U. M., & Siddiqi, M. A. (2021). Emotional intelligence and transformational leadership among academic leaders in institutions of higher learning. *Global Business Review*, *22*(4), 1070–1096. doi:10.1177/0972150918822421

Badsha, N. (2000) South African Higher Education: Diversity Overview. In Beckham, E. F. (eds) Diversity, Democracy, and Higher Education: A View from Three Nations-India, South Africa, the United States. Association of American Colleges and Universities.

Badsha, N., & Wickham, S. (2013). *Review of initiatives in equity and transformation in three universities in South Africa*. Cape Higher Education Consortium.

Bernstein, B., & Solomon, J. (1999). 'Pedagogy, identity and the construction of a theory of symbolic control': Basil Bernstein questioned by Joseph Solomon. *British Journal of Sociology of Education*, *20*(2), 265–279. doi:10.1080/01425699995443

Bono, J. E., & Judge, T. A. (2004). Personality and transformational and transactional leadership: A meta-analysis. *The Journal of Applied Psychology*, *89*(5), 901–910. doi:10.1037/0021-9010.89.5.901 PMID:15506869

Boudrias, J.-S., Morin, A. J., & Lajoie, D. (2014). Directionality of the associations between psychological empowerment and behavioral involvement: A longitudinal autoregressive cross-lagged analysis. *Journal of Occupational and Organizational Psychology*, *87*(3), 437–463. doi:10.1111/joop.12056

Boyce, M. E. (2003). Organizational learning is essential to achieving and sustaining change in higher education. *Innovative Higher Education*, *28*(2), 119–136. doi:10.1023/B:IHIE.0000006287.69207.00

Braun, V., & Clarke, V. (2006). Using thematic analysis in psychology. *Qualitative Research in Psychology*, *3*(2), 77–101. doi:10.1191/1478088706qp063oa

Butler, J. (2020). Learning to lead: A discussion of development programs for academic leadership capability in Australian Universities. *Journal of Higher Education Policy and Management*, *42*(4), 424–437. doi:10.1080/1360080X.2019.1701855

Carolissen, R., & Bozalek, V. (2017). Addressing dualisms in student perceptions of a historically white and black university in South Africa. *Race, Ethnicity and Education*, *20*(3), 344–357. doi:10.1080/13613324.2016.1260229

Carolissen, R., & Bozalek, V. (2017). Addressing dualisms in student perceptions of a historically white and black university in South Africa. *Race, Ethnicity and Education*, *20*(3), 344–357. doi:10.1080/13613324.2016.1260229

Cartwright, S., & Holmes, N. (2006). The meaning of work: The challenge of regaining employee engagement and reducing cynicism. *Human Resource Management Review*, *16*(2), 199–208. doi:10.1016/j.hrmr.2006.03.012

Coleman, R. A., & Donoher, W. J. (2022). Looking Beyond the Dyad: How Transformational Leadership Affects Leader–Member Exchange Quality and Outcomes. *Journal of Leadership Studies*, *15*(4), 6–17. doi:10.1002/jls.21792

Cook, D. A., & Artino, A. R. Jr. (2016). Motivation to learn: An overview of contemporary theories. *Medical Education*, *50*(10), 997–1014. doi:10.1111/medu.13074 PMID:27628718

Cross, M. (2004). Institutionalising campus diversity in South African higher education: Review of diversity scholarship and diversity education. *Higher Education*, *47*(4), 387–410. doi:10.1023/B:HIGH.0000020854.04852.80

Croucher, G., & Woelert, P. (2021). Administrative transformation and managerial growth: A longitudinal analysis of changes in the non-academic workforce at Australian universities. *Higher Education*, 1–17. doi:10.100710734-021-00759-8 de Wit, H., & Altbach, P. G. (2021). Internationalization in higher education: Global trends and recommendations for its future. *Policy Reviews in Higher Education, 5*(1), 28–46. doi:10.1080/23322969.2020.1820898

Derue, D. S., Nahrgang, J. D., Wellman, N. E. D., & Humphrey, S. E. (2011). Trait and behavioral theories of leadership: An integration and meta-analytic test of their relative validity. *Personnel Psychology, 64*(1), 7–52. doi:10.1111/j.1744-6570.2010.01201.x

Dóci, E., & Hofmans, J. (2015). Task complexity and transformational leadership: The mediating role of leaders' state core self-evaluations. *The Leadership Quarterly, 26*(3), 436–447. doi:10.1016/j.leaqua.2015.02.008

Elrehail, H., Emeagwali, O. L., Alsaad, A., & Alzghoul, A. (2018). The impact of transformational and authentic leadership on innovation in higher education: The contingent role of knowledge sharing. *Telematics and Informatics, 35*(1), 55–67. doi:10.1016/j.tele.2017.09.018

Føllesdal, H., & Hagtvet, K. (2013). Does emotional intelligence as ability predict transformational leadership? A multilevel approach. *The Leadership Quarterly, 24*(5), 747–762. doi:10.1016/j.leaqua.2013.07.004

Ford, T. G., Lavigne, A. L., Fiegener, A. M., & Si, S. (2020). Understanding district support for leader development and success in the accountability era: A review of the literature using social-cognitive theories of motivation. *Review of Educational Research, 90*(2), 264–307. doi:10.3102/0034654319899723

Frankema, E. H. (2012). The origins of formal education in sub-Saharan Africa: Was British rule more benign? *European Review of Economic History, 16*(4), 335–355. doi:10.1093/ereh/hes009

Haslam, S. A., Steffens, N. K., Reicher, S. D., & Bentley, S. V. (2021). Identity leadership in a crisis: A 5R framework for learning from responses to COVID-19. *Social Issues and Policy Review, 15*(1), 35–83. doi:10.1111ipr.12075 PMID:33821168

Kezar, A., & Eckel, P. (2002). Examining the institutional transformation process: The importance of sense making, interrelated strategies, and balance. *Research in Higher Education, 43*(3), 295–328. doi:10.1023/A:1014889001242

Knight, J. (2018). Decolonizing and transforming the Geography undergraduate curriculum in South Africa. *The South African Geographical Journal, 100*(3), 271–290. https://hdl.handle.net/10520/EJC-10c31734cd. doi:10.1080/03736245.2018.1449009

Knight, J. (2018). Decolonizing and transforming the Geography undergraduate curriculum in South Africa. *The South African Geographical Journal, 100*(3), 1–20. https://hdl.handle.net/10520/EJC-10c31734cd. doi:10.1080/03736245.2018.1449009

Kohtamäki, V. (2019). Academic leadership and university reform-guided management changes in Finland. *Journal of Higher Education Policy and Management, 41*(1), 70–85. doi:10.1080/1360080X.2018.1553499

Kyngäs, H., Kääriäinen, M., & Elo, S. (2020). The trustworthiness of content analysis. In *The Application of Content Analysis in Nursing Science Research, H. Kyngäs, M. Kääriäinen, and S. Elo* (pp. 41–48). Springer. doi:10.1007/978-3-030-30199-6_5

Lajoie, D., Boudrias, J., Rousseau, V., & Brunelle, E. (2017). Value congruence and tenure as moderators of transformational leadership effects. *Leadership and Organization Development Journal*, *38*(2), 254–269. doi:10.1108/LODJ-04-2015-0091

Leibowitz, B., Bozalek, V., Van Schalkwyk, S., & Winberg, C. (2015). Institutional context matters: The professional development of academics as teachers in South African higher education. *Higher Education*, *69*(2), 315–330. doi:10.100710734-014-9777-2

Martin, S. L., Liao, H., & Campbell, E. M. (2013). Directive versus empowering leadership: A field experiment comparing impacts on task proficiency and proactivity. *Academy of Management Journal*, *56*(5), 1372–1395. doi:10.5465/amj.2011.0113

Neuendorf, K. A. (2019). Content analysis and thematic analysis: Introducing content analysis and thematic analysis. In P. Brough (Ed.), *Advanced Research Methods for Applied Psychology* (pp. 211–223). Routledge.

Owusu-Agyeman, Y. (2021). Transformational leadership and innovation in higher education: A participative process approach. *International Journal of Leadership in Education*, *24*(5), 694–716. doi:10.1080/13603124.2019.1623919

Peng, J., Li, M., Wang, Z., & Lin, Y. (2021). Transformational leadership and employees' reactions to organizational change: Evidence from a meta-analysis. *The Journal of Applied Behavioral Science*, *57*(3), 369–397. doi:10.1177/0021886320920366

Rajaram, K. (2021). Transformation in Higher Education: Twenty-First-Century Teaching and Learning Competencies. In *Evidence-Based Teaching for the 21st Century Classroom and Beyond*. Springer. doi:10.1007/978-981-33-6804-0_1

Rose, J., & Johnson, C. W. (2020). Contextualizing reliability and validity in qualitative research: Toward more rigorous and trustworthy qualitative social science in leisure research. *Journal of Leisure Research*, *51*(4), 432–451. doi:10.1080/00222216.2020.1722042

Siangchokyoo, N., Klinger, R. L., & Campion, E. D. (2020). Follower transformation as the linchpin of transformational leadership theory: A systematic review and future research agenda. *The Leadership Quarterly*, *31*(1), 101341. doi:10.1016/j.leaqua.2019.101341

Suransky, C., & Van der Merwe, J. C. (2016). Transcending apartheid in higher education: Transforming an institutional culture. *Race, Ethnicity and Education*, *19*(3), 577–597. doi:10.1080/13613324.2014.946487

Volkwein, J. F. (1999). The four faces of institutional research. *New Directions for Institutional Research*, *104*(104), 9–19. doi:10.1002/ir.10401

Chapter 3
Investigating the Effects of SHRM on Operational and Financial Performance in Educational Institutions

Peace Kumah
Knutsford University College, Ghana

ABSTRACT

Strategic human resource management (SHRM) seeks to create alignment between human resource management (HRM) practices and business strategy (strategy fit); linking HR strategies, policies, and practices within the functional units of the HR department (intra-functional fit); maintaining the status of the HRM department within corporate strategic plan (HR-roles-position fit); and alignment of HRM functions with all other departments (cross-functional fit). This study investigates the effects of SHRM on organizational performance. Data was collected from 314 employees in tertiary educational institutions in Ghana. A conceptual model was developed and a set of hypotheses were proposed. The results found that cross-functional fit has a significant effect on both financial and operational performance. However, the results found no significant effect of strategy fit, role-position fit, and intra-functional fit on financial and operational performance. Therefore, tertiary educational institutions should develop cross-functional fit to improve their financial and operational performance.

INTRODUCTION

Strategic human resource management (SHRM) aligns human resource practices with the organization's strategic goals (Jermsittiparsert et al., 2021) and performance outcomes (Akhtar et.al., 2022), leading to the realization of sustainable competitive advantage (Singh et al., 2019). HRM aims at directing, fostering, and linking the employees' intellectual capital, emotional, social, and cognitive capabilities with the strategic needs of the organization (Greer, Lusch & Hitts, 2017). SHRM can be classified under four major topics: Strategy fit, intra-functional fit, HR-roles-position fit, and cross-functional fit (Ahmad &

DOI: 10.4018/979-8-3693-1380-0.ch003

Raja, 2021). Strategy fit relates to the alignment between HRM practices and business strategy, including the involvement of HR in business strategy formulation and information sharing between HR managers and top executives (Hadziahmetovic & Dinc, 2020). The intra-functional fit represents the alignment of HR strategies, HR policies, and practices within the functional units of the HR department (Kale & Shimpi, 2020). The HR-roles- position fit is the status and position of the HRM department within corporate strategic issues (Ahmad & Raja, 2021). Also, the cross-functional fit refers to the alignment of HRM functions with all other departments and functional areas, including the integration of HR functions with other functional areas of the organization and fostering a free flow of information among HR and all other departments (Ludwikowska, 2021).

Managing human capital is a major focus area of SHRM (Greer, Lusch & Hitts, 2017). It is an organization's portfolio of knowledge, skills, and abilities (Jermsittiparsert et al., 2021). As a strategic tool, SHRM contains key elements for implementing an organization's strategies (Covarrubias, Thill & Domnanovich, 2017). Consequently, SHRM encourages innovation (Anca-Ioana, 2013) and improves organizational performance (Flood et al., 2016). Organizational performance is an effective and efficient means by which organizations manage resources to create sustainability (Ludwikowska, 2021). Successful implementation of SHRM can lead to the operational and financial performance of the organization. However, research suggests that the lack or inadequate implementation of the SHRM strategy may adversely affect organizational performance (Akhtar et.al., 2022).

Problem Statement

Currently, research is focusing on establishing relationships between SHRM and employee commitment (Kumah, 2022) and between SHRM and organizational performance outcomes (Riaz & Mahmood, 2017). Recent studies focus on employee-oriented human resource policy, strategic human resource management, and organizational performance (Ludwikowska, 2021), employee retention and firm performance (Kumar & Reddy, 2019), recruitment, selection, and organizational performance (Jashari & Kutllovci, 2020). However, these studies are conducted in the manufacturing and financial sectors (Al-Taweel, 2021; Zhai, Zhu, & Zhang, 2022), paying little attention to SHRM practices in educational institutions. Meanwhile, educational institutions are expected to meet stringent requirements of recruiting and retaining qualified faculty and staff, maintaining a high quality of teaching and research, and providing a suitable learning environment and infrastructure to meet their strategic goals and performance outcomes (NAB, 2017). With quality higher education, individuals acquire knowledge and skills which enable them to become "healthier, secure better jobs, earn more, and have a greater voice in their affairs" (World Bank, 2011, p. 2). It is, therefore, expected that by employing SHRM practices, tertiary educational institutions will meet their strategic goals.

Purpose of the Study

Thus, this study aims at examining the effects of SHRM practices on operational and financial performance in tertiary educational institutions in Ghana by answering the following research question.

Is there a statistically significant effect of SHRM practices (strategy fit, HR-roles-position fit, intra-functional fit, cross-functional fit) on organizational performance (operational performance, financial performance) as measured by the SHRM Inventory and University Performance Evaluation Scale?

The study develops a conceptual model and the data are analyzed using Partial Least Squares Structural Equation Modeling (PLS-SEM) within SmartPLS software.

Significance of the Study

Studies that examine the impact of SHRM on organizational performance in tertiary educational institutions are sparse. Therefore, conducting this study would provide information that could help educational leaders in tertiary educational institutions to identify SHRM practices that are most appropriate and those that are inappropriate for organizational performance. Moreover, this study is important as its findings will provide policymakers, researchers, practitioners, and society with new-found insight into factors that can increase employee commitment and performance in the educational sector. In addition, Vice Chancellors, Rectors, and Principals of tertiary educational institutions can use the findings from the study as a guide to change HR practices for better outcomes to increase productivity as well as gain a competitive advantage over other competitors.

The study on strategic HRM is relevant in tertiary educational institutions. Tertiary educational leaders are expected to meet stringent requirements of recruiting and retention of qualified faculty and staff, maintain high-quality teaching and research, and provide suitable learning environments and infrastructure to meet their strategic goals and performance outcomes. Also, tertiary educational institutions are under regulatory compliance to maintain quality standards. Otherwise, they may have their accreditation revoked (NAB, 2018).

BACKGROUND

Theoretical Background

Contingency theory forms the theoretical foundation of this study. Contingency theory is an approach to the management of organizational behavior and how contingent factors such as organizational culture, technology, and external environment impact the activities of the organizations (McFarland, Rode & Shervani, 2016). The contingency perspective assumes that there is no particular organizational structure that is suitable for all organizations (Islam & Hu, 2012). In other words, organizational effectiveness mainly depends on a fit or link between the type of technology, the size of the organization, environmental instability, the type of organizational structure, and the communication system (Islam & Hu, 2012). Drazin (1985) looked at fit in three approaches: selection, interaction, and system approaches. Firstly, the selection approach of fit implies that for organizations to be effective and achieve sustainability, it has to adapt to the features of their organizational context. Secondly, fit refers to the interaction between organizational structure and context on performance (McFarland, Rode & Shervani, 2016). Thirdly, the system approach states that one can only understand organizational design through the investigation of contingencies, structural alternatives, as well as, performance standards in an organization.

Related Literature

Recent works discussed the influence of HRM and organizational performance. In a quantitative study, Karami, Sahebalzaman, and Savabi (2015) examined the impact of six principal HR practices, including training and development, teamwork, incentives, HR planning, employee security, and performance appraisal on the link between business strategy and organizational performance. Data were obtained from 20 independent in the banking sector. Through a survey, 220 questionnaires were collected and analyzed. Business strategies and organizational performance were measured using Porter's generic strategies and balanced scorecard respectively. The result revealed a close relationship between business strategies and HR practices. HR practices positively influence organizational performance. Also, the study found a positive linkage between integrated business strategies, HR practices, and organizational performance (Karami, Sahebalzaman, & Savabi, 2015). The study, therefore, suggested that organizations should always apply relevant HR practices (CurranEverett, 2015; Mendel, 2017) that correspond to business strategies for higher organizational performance (Chopra, 2017).

Collins and Kehoe (2017) studied strategic fit and misfit in managing the knowledge workforce. The study determined whether improved firm performance depends on the alignment between an organization's human resource (HR) system and its innovation strategies. The survey was carried out in 230 software firms. The study discovered that multiple HR practices enhance either an exploration or exploitation strategy (Collins & Kehoe, 2017). Thus, aligning the HR system and innovation strategy resulted in a firm's performance achievement, while misalignment results in performance drawbacks (Collins & Kehoe, 2017). Other studies argued the vertical fit of HR systems and organizational business strategies could enhance organizational performance (Flood, Bosak, Rousseau, Morris & O'Regan, 2016). Similarly, Lin et al. (2016) found a relationship between supportive HRM and organizational financial performance. on higher financial outcomes. Some empirical studies also found an important direct correlation between operational performance measures and financial performance (Tallon & Pinsonneault, 2011). However, Inman et al. (2014) found no direct link between operational and financial performance when several performance measures were included in their model. This conflicting result regarding operational performance and financial performance has still been debated. Hence, there is a need for more research in this area in different contexts.

Opoku and Arthur (2015) assessed the impact of human resource practices on organizational performance in the Ghana Postal Services Company Limited. The main purpose of the study was to determine the contributing factors to the company's inability to compete favorably in the postal and communication industry (Opoku & Arthur, 2015). The study was qualitative and data was drawn from field interviews, focus group discussions, and desk research obtained from scholarly documents (books, journals, newspapers, and magazines). A total number of 40 respondents was selected from all the 10 regional capitals of Ghana. The findings showed that human resource management practices significantly influence organizational performance (Opoku & Arthur, 2015). The study concluded that effective HRM practices are critical in attaining higher performance (Opoku & Arthur, 2015). The Ghana Postal Services Company, therefore, needs to pursue a strategic approach to HRM by investing in human resource management practices to achieve a competitive advantage.

In a quantitative descriptive study, Lin et al. (2016) examined customer-oriented strategy and organizational financial performance. The study found an impact of supportive HRM on higher financial outcomes. Supportive HRM practices refer to HRM practices that focus on employees' well-being and aid their task completion. Wright and McMahan (2011) found human capital as a mediator between HR practices and performance. Moreover, Lind et al. (2016) reported that customer-linking strategies could create sustained competitive advantage and contribute to a firm's desired financial performance. Similarly, Hong, Liao, & Jiang (2013) reported that the effect of a customer-oriented strategy on high financial performance is indicated by service climate.

In a closely related work, Allui and Sahni (2016) studied strategic human resource management in higher educational institutions in Saudi Arabia. The study explored the linkage of institutional strategies to HRM by examining the SHRM practices such as strategic HRM alignment, recruitment and selection system, training and development, performance appraisal system, compensation system, and retention plan and culture in the selected universities. Both qualitative and quantitative methodology of research design was employed to collect. The result revealed that inadequate attention was given to performance appraisal and compensation systems that would motivate the staff, especially expatriate workers to be committed. Another finding was a lack of effective communication resulting in misinformation and ineffective programs (Allui & Sahni, 2016). The study, therefore, recommended that attention should be given to SHRM implementation and practices in universities. The findings showed that employee recruitment and selection needed more attention.

Conceptual Model and Hypotheses

Based on the contingency theory and the empirical studies discussed earlier in the review, this study proposed a conceptual model (see Figure 1). The study proposed that there is a statistically significant relationship between SHRM practices and organizational performance. To establish this relationship, the study hypothesized four SHRM constructs (strategy fit, HR-roles-position fit, intra-functional fit, cross-functional fit) as identified in the literature (Azmi, 2010; 2011) and two constructs (operational performance, financial performance) of the organization's performance (NAB INFO-A8, 2018). The research question and a set of hypotheses are stated below.

There is a statistically significant relationship between SHRM practices and Organizational Performance?

H1: There is a statistically significant relationship between Strategy Fit (SF) and Financial Performance (FP).
H2: There is a statistically significant relationship between Strategy Fit (SF) and Operational Performance (OP).
H3: There is a statistically significant relationship between Roles-position fit (RF) and Financial Performance (FP).
H4: There is a statistically significant relationship between Roles-position fit (RF) and Operational Performance (OP).
H5: There is a significant relationship between Intra-functional fit (IF) and Financial Performance (FP).
H6: There is a statistically significant relationship between Intra-functional fit (IF) and Operational Performance (OP).
H7: There is a statistically significant relationship between Cross-functional fit (CF) and Financial Performance (FP).
H8: There is a statistically significant relationship between Cross-functional fit (CF) and Operational Performance (OP).

Figure 1. Conceptual framework of SHRM on operational and financial performance

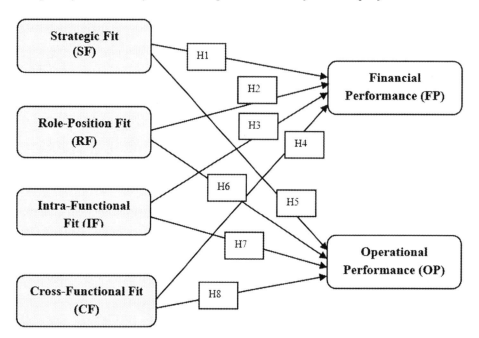

RESEARCH METHOD

Population, Sampling Technique, and Samples

This study used a survey research approach. The population consisted of 212 tertiary educational institutions in Ghana (NAB, 2018). A stratified sampling technique was employed to select the sample frame. For stratified sampling, the population was classified into publicly-owned and privately-owned tertiary institutions, which were located within 5 regional administrative regions, where more established tertiary educational institutions were situated. The public and private tertiary educational institutions are classified into public universities, university colleges, technical universities, and colleges of education. Within the institutions that were located within the five selected administrative regions, the study selected those that were more than 10 years old. This criterion was used because, according to National Accreditation Board's requirement, a tertiary institution with at least 10 years of existence is regarded as mature, qualified, and could apply for charter status (NAB, 2018). The participants in the study included members of the Board of Directors, Chancellors, Registrars, HR practitioners, Deans, Finance officers, Librarians, Heads of Department, and faculty members.

Research Instrument

This current study adopted two existing instruments: SHRM Inventory (Azmi, 2010; 2011) and the University Performance Evaluation Scale (NAB INFO-A8, 2018). SHRM Inventory instrument measures strategic human resource management practices (Azmi, 2010). The instrument contains 26 items (5-point Likert scale) relating to 4 dimensions of SHRM with acceptable psychometric properties. The constructs consist of Strategy Fit (8 items), HR Roles-Position Fit (5 items), Intra-Functional Fit (6 items), and Cross-Functional Fit (7 items). The instrument has been used in a study that linked the effectiveness of HRM function and organizational performance in a developing country (Azmi, 2011). The second instrument, University Performance Evaluation Scale, developed by National Accreditation Board, contains 21 items of Likert-type statements. The instrument was designed to cover the quality and performance indicators of tertiary institutions. The constructs on the instrument adapted were Financial Performance (eight items) and Operational Performance (13 items) (NAB, 2018). In the study, financial performance and operational performance represented the dependent variables. Strategy Fit, HR Roles-Position Fit, Intra-Functional Fit, and Cross-Functional Fit were the independent variables.

Data Analysis Techniques

The data analysis was two-fold: (1) establishing the reliability and the validity of the instruments used, (2) testing of hypotheses. The study used PLS-SEM as an analytical technique to test the hypotheses. Structural equation modeling was chosen as it is a multivariate method that allows the simultaneous assessment of the relationships among the independent (exogenous) latent variables and dependent (endogenous) latent variables within a model (Hair et al., 2012).

RESULTS

Characteristics of the Respondents

Three hundred and fourteen responses were received out of the 378 questionnaires distributed to the participants. This is a response rate of 83 percent. Table 1 represents the characteristics of the respondents. Approximately 69% of respondents were male and 31% were female. About 18% of the respondents worked in tertiary educational institutions for up to 5 years, 34% for between 6 to 10 years, 34% for between 11 to 15 years, 10% for between 16 to 20 years, and 4% for more than 20 years. Thus, the majority of the respondents 214 (64%) worked in tertiary educational institutions for between 6 to 15 years. Also, about 53% of the respondents work with private tertiary educational institutions and 47% were from public tertiary educational institutions.

In addition, 30% of the respondents work in institutions having a student enrolment of up to 5,000; 38% between 5,001 and 10,000; 13% between 10,001 and 20,000; and 19% have over 20,000 students' population. Regarding the respondents' job functions, 1% was Board of Directors, Chancellors represented less than 1% of the total response, Registrars represented 2%, HR Managers represented 6%, Deans represented 2.5%, Finance Managers represented 4.8%, Librarians represented about 6%, and Heads of Departments represented 7.6%. Moreover, about 43% of the respondents were faculty members, about 20% were Administrative Staff, and 7% represented other staff members. Thus, the respondents were mainly senior members of their respective institutions.

Table 1. Sample characteristics

Respondents		Frequency	Percentage (%)
Gender			
	Male	218	69.4
	Female	96	30.6
Experience (Years)			
	0-5	55	17.5
	6-10	108	34.4
	11-15	106	33.8
	16-20	33	10.5
	20 and Above	12	3.8
Institution Type			
	Private	166	52.9
	Public	148	47.1
Students Enrolment			
	Up to 5000	94	29.9
	5001-10000	119	37.9
	10001-20000	41	13.1
	Over 20000	60	19.1
Job Title/Position			
	Board of Director	3	1.0
	Chancellor	1	.3
	Registrar	6	1.9
	HR Manager	19	6.1
	Dean	8	2.5
	Finance Manager	15	4.8
	Librarian	19	6.1
	Head of Department	24	7.6
	Faculty Member	134	42.7
	Administrative Staff	63	20.1
	Others	22	7.0

Note. N = 314

Assessment of the Measurement Model

The adequacy of the measurement model of the relationship between the latent variables and the items measuring them was assessed through item reliability and construct validity (Hair et al., 2011). This includes assessing: (a) the reliability of individual items; (b) the convergent validity of the measures associated with individual latent variables; and (c) the discriminant validity of the research instruments.

Analysis of Individual Item Reliability. Individual item reliability is the correlation of the items with their respective latent variables (Hair et al., 2011). In this study, to evaluate the reliability of individual items, the standardized loadings were assessed (Gotz, Liehr-Gobbers, & Krafft, 2010). A rule of thumb generally employed is to accept items with loadings of 0.7 or more, which implies that there is more shared variance between the latent variables and their measure than error variance (Hair et al., 2011). A loading of 0.7 signifies that about 50% of the variance in the observed variables is due to the latent variable (Gotz, Liehr-Gobbers, & Krafft, 2010). Items with low loadings should be dropped as they would add very little explanatory power to the model and can bias the estimates of the parameters linking the latent variables (Hair et al., 2011). Other recommendations for cut-off points were proposed. For example, Chin (1998) recommended a higher cut-off point of 0.707. However, Hulland (1999) suggested that items with loadings of less than 0.4 (a threshold commonly used for factor analysis results) or 0.5 should be dropped.

In this study, all items have loadings above 0.7 (see Table 4), except six observed variables: the loading of SF01 was 0.590, OP09 was 0.661, OP13 was 0.588, OP15 was 0.543, OP17 was 0.634, and OP20 was 0.553. Most of the items here met Hulland's (1999) recommendation of loadings of less than 0.4 or 0.5 for acceptance. However, in this study, a cut-off point of 0.7 was applied (Hair et al., 2011; Nunnally, 1976). Accordingly, the items that failed to meet this requirement were removed from the study for any further analysis. Thus, all the items retained in the study demonstrated high levels of individual item reliability (see Table 2).

Table 2. Loading and cross loading

Constructs	Items		Loading	AVE
SHRM Cross-Functional Fit (CF)	CF20	HR activities are consistent with other departmental functions.	0.759	0.635
	CF21	Departmental heads are trained in HR issues.	0.850	
	CF22	HR issues are every head of the department's responsibility.	0.766	
	CF23	Staffing decisions are taken jointly with deans and heads of departments.	0.825	
	CF24	Training decisions are taken jointly with deans and heads of departments.	0.847	
	CF25	Pay-related decisions are taken jointly with deans and heads of departments.	0.763	
	CF26	Deans and heads of departments are involved in internal review activities.	0.761	
SHRM Intra-Functional Fit (IF)	IF14	HRM activities are linked to long-term HR vision.	0.739	0.646
	IF15	HR strategy is spelled out.	0.784	
	IF16	HR activities are internally consistent.	0.787	
	IF17	The corporate HR department is established for coordinated HR.	0.868	
	IF18	There are periodic budgets for HRM activities.	0.839	
	IF19	There is effective information sharing between HR sub-areas	0.800	

Continued on following page

Table 2. Continued

Constructs	Items		Loading	AVE
SHRM Role-Position Fit (RF)	RF09	HRM is viewed as a strategically important function.	0.820	0.653
	RF10	Top-level strategic teams include the HR head.	0.754	
	RF11	HR executives are trained in general managerial skills.	0.857	
	RF12	The HR department is placed at par with other departments.	0.775	
	RF13	The HR function is represented at the board level.	0.830	
SHRM Strategic Fit (SF)	SF02	Conscious effort is made to align business with HR issues.	0.759	0.623
	SF03	HRM activities are designed to suit business strategy.	0.815	
	SF04	HR inputs are considered integral to business strategy.	0.812	
	SF05	HR activities are consistent with the organizational vision.	0.834	
	SF06	Top management takes an interest in HR issues.	0.792	
	SF07	Top management is trained in HR issues	0.766	
	SF08	There is effective information sharing between HR and top managers	0.741	
Operational Performance (OP)	OP10	Staff regularly participates in professional development programmes.	0.724	0.580
	OP11	There is an increasing research and publication output from the faculty staff.	0.823	
	OP12	Resources (such as computer labs, library, lecture rooms, water and electricity, texts/journals, etc) are provided to effectively support teaching and learning.	0.764	
	OP14	My institution has an effective, well-structured guidance and counseling unit.	0.746	
	OP16	There is a full representation of students on the institution's designated committees in line with the statutes.	0.764	
	OP18	My institution has regular activities that promote college-community engagement.	0.765	
	OP21	My institution has a functioning alumni association office.	0.738	
Financial Performance (FP)	FP01	My institution has a functioning finance committee.	0.762	0.625
	FP02	My institution has sufficient funds from tuition and other sources to support programs.	0.756	
	FP03	The financial management regulations are operational.	0.805	
	FP04	The institutional budget is prepared and approved by the Governing Council.	0.737	
	FP05	The institutional budget is linked to the institutional strategic plan.	0.826	
	FP06	My institution has robust internal financial controls and audits.	0.815	
	FP07	My institution has a functioning procurement committee.	0.799	
	FP08	My institution has a transparent system of financial management including regular external audits.	0.820	

Convergent Validity. Convergent validity measures the internal consistency of the items on the instrument (Hair et al., 2011). It ensures that the items measure the latent variable they are supposed to measure, but not another latent variable (Gotz et al., 2010). In this study, three tests were performed to determine the convergent validity of the measured constructs. These tests consisted of (a) Cronbach's alpha; (b) Composite reliability scores; and (c) Average variance extracted (AVE). Cronbach's alpha is the coefficient of reliability (or consistency) (Chin, 2010). It assesses how well a set of items (or variables) measures a single one-dimensional latent construct (Gotz et al., 2010). Though composite reliability is similar to Cronbach alpha, the composite reliability score is superior to Cronbach's alpha measure of internal consistency since it uses the item loadings obtained within the theoretical model (Fornell & Larcker, 1981). However, both the composite reliability score and Cronbach's Alpha are interpreted similarly (Hair et al., 2012). In general, a recommendation of 0.7 is regarded as the benchmark for composite reliability (Hair, Hult, et al., 2014; Nunnally, 1978). Table 3 presents the composite reliability and Cronbach's Alpha of the measures. By employing a 0.7 benchmark for composite reliability (Hair, Hult, et al., 2014), it can be observed that all the constructs demonstrated an acceptable level of convergent validity. Hence, the measurement items are appropriate for their respective latent variables.

Moreover, the average variance extracted (AVE) was used to assess the convergent validity of the latent variables. The AVE measures the amount of variance that a latent variable captures from its measurement items concerning the amount of variance due to measurement errors (Chin, 2010; Hair et al., 2011). According to Hair et al. (2011), the cut-off point of AVE should be higher than 0.5. This means that at least 50% of measurement variance is captured by the latent variables (Hair et al., 2011). In this study, the estimates of AVEs were above 50% for all the latent variables (see Table 2). These results reveal that there is convergent validity and good internal consistency in the measurement model. This implies that the measurement items of each latent variable measure them well and are not measuring another latent variable in the research model (Hair et al., 2011).

Table 3. Cronbach's alpha and composite reliability

	Constructs	Cronbach's Alpha	Composite Reliability
SHRM	Cross-Functional Fit (CF)	0.904	0.924
	Role-Position Fit (RF)	0.867	0.904
	Strategic Fit (SF)	0.899	0.920
	Intra-Functional Fit (IF)	0.890	0.916
PERFORMANCE	Financial Performance (FP)	0.914	0.930
	Operational Performance (OP)	0.879	0.906

Test of Hypotheses

The research question enquires whether there is a statistically significant relationship between SHRM practices and organizational performance. Tests for multicollinearity show that a very low level of multicollinearity was present (VIF = 1.237 for Operational Performance and 1.237 for Financial Performance). Following, a set of hypotheses were tested PL-SEM.

Firstly, a simple correlation using Pearson correlation analysis was first conducted to identify independent variables (Strategy Fit (SF), Roles-Position Fit (RF), Intra-functional Fit (IF), and Cross-functional Fit (CF)) that correlate with the dependent variables (Financial Performance (FP) and Operational Performance (OP)). These variables were used in the PL-SEM model to make a more accurate relationship between the dependent variables (SHRM) and to show the proportion of variance in the dependent variable explained by the independent variables (Organizational Performance). Table 4 revealed that all the independent variables significantly correlated with the dependent variable (SF), that is FP ($r = .335^{**}$, $p < 0.01$), and OP ($r = .405^{**}$, $p < 0.01$). The test revealed that all the independent variables individually correlated with the dependent variable (RF), that is FP ($r = .321^{**}$, $p < 0.01$), and OP ($r = .299^{**}$, $p < 0.01$). Again, the test indicated that all the independent variables individually correlated with the dependent variable (IF): FP ($r = .279^{**}$, $p < 0.01$), and OP ($r = .397^{**}$, $p < 0.01$). Also, the test revealed that all the independent variables individually correlated with the dependent variable (CF), that is FP ($r = .347^{**}$, $p < 0.01$) and OP ($r = .436^{**}$, $p < 0.01$). Observably, all the relationships were significant.

Table 4. Pearson's correlation test of the relationship between SHRM and performance

Constructs			Performance Constructs	
			Financial Performance (FP)	Operational Performance (OP)
SHRM Constructs	Strategy Fit (SF)	Pearson Correlation	.335**	.405**
		Sig. (2-tailed)	.000	.000
		N	301	303
	Roles-Position Fit (RF)	Pearson Correlation	.321**	.299**
		Sig. (2-tailed)	.000	.000
		N	303	305
	Intra-functional Fit (IF)	Pearson Correlation	.279**	.397**
		Sig. (2-tailed)	.000	.000
		N	297	300
	Cross-functional Fit (CF)	Pearson Correlation	.347**	.436**
		Sig. (2-tailed)	.000	.000
		N	297	299

**. Correlation is significant at the 0.01 level (2-tailed)

Secondly, concerning the PL-SEM results for the relationship between SHRM practices and organizational performance, it can be observed that only two out of the eight paths were positively and statistically significant (see Table 5).

From Table 5, it can be seen that Strategy Fit (SF) was found not to have a significant influence on Financial Performance ($\beta = 0.158$, $p = 0.055$) (H1). The hypothesized effect was therefore not supported. This result indicates that improving strategy fit (alignment between HRM practices and business strategy [Azmi, 2010]) does not significantly improve the financial performance of tertiary educational institutions. Hypothesis H2 proposed that there was a statistically significant relationship between Strategy Fit (SF) and Operational Performance (OP). In H2, it can be observed that even though the relationship was positive, Strategy Fit had no significant effect on Operational Performance ($\beta = 0.127$, $p = 0.145$). Hence, the hypothesized effect was not supported. This result indicates that improving strategy fit (alignment between HRM practices and business strategy [Azmi, 2010]) does not result in significant improvement in operational performance.

In hypothesis H3, the study proposed that there was a statistically significant relationship between Roles-position Fit (RF) and Financial Performance (FP). Again, it can be observed from Table 5 that Roles-position fit has a negative and non-significant relationship with Financial Performance ($\beta = -0.029$, p = 0.713). Thus, this relationship was not supported. The implication is that an improvement in roles-position fit (status of the HRM department within corporate strategic issues [Azmi, 2010]) does not however result in any significant decreases in financial performance. Likewise, in hypothesis H4, the study proposed that there was a statistically significant relationship between Roles-position Fit (RF) and Operational Performance (OP). It can be observed from the table that Roles-position fit has a negative but non-significant relationship with Operational Performance ($\beta = -0.012$, p = 0.874). Thus, the hypothesis was not supported. The implication is that an improvement in Roles-position fit (status of the HRM department within corporate strategic issues [Azmi, 2010]) may not likely result in a significant decline in operational performance.

Table 5. Results of the test of the hypotheses

Hypothesis	Constructs	Path Coefficients (β)	t Statistics	p Values	Result
H1	SF -> FP	0.158	1.735	0.083	Not Supported
H2	SF -> OP	0.127	1.460	0.145	Not Supported
H3	RF -> FP	-0.029	0.367	0.713	Not Supported
H4	RF -> OP	-0.012	0.158	0.874	Not Supported
H5	IF -> FP	0.067	0.882	0.378	Not Supported
H6	IF -> OP	0.113	1.665	0.097	Not Supported
H7	CF -> FP	0.262**	2.868	0.004	Supported
H8	CF -> OP	0.336***	3.808	0.000	Supported

Note: * significant at $\alpha=5\%$, ** significant at $\alpha = 1\%$, *** significant at $\alpha =0.1\%$

The study in hypothesis H5 proposed that there was a statistically significant relationship between Intra-Functional Fit (IF) and Financial Performance (FP). It can be observed that Intra-Functional Fit had no significant effect on Financial Performance ($\beta = 0.067$, p = 0.378). Hence, the hypothesized effect was not supported. This result indicates that improving intra-functional fit (status of the HRM department within corporate strategic issues [Azmi, 2010]) does not necessarily improve financial performance. In the same way, hypothesis H6 proposed that there was a statistically significant relationship between Intra-functional fit (IF) and Operational Performance (OP). Table 5 shows that Intra-functional fit had no significant effect on Operational Performance ($\beta = 0.113$, p = 0.097). Consequently, the hypothesized effect was not supported. This result indicates that improving intra-functional fit (status of the HRM department within corporate strategic issues [Azmi, 2010]) may not significantly improve operational performance.

In hypothesis H7, the study proposed a statistically significant relationship between Cross-functional Fit (CF) and Financial Performance (FP). The cross-functional fit was found to have a positive significant relationship with Financial Performance ($\beta = 0.262$, p = 0.004). The hypothesized effect was supported. The result implies that Cross-functional fit (alignment of HRM functions with all other departments and functional areas [Azmi, 2010]) will improve financial performance. Finally, Hypothesis H8 posited that there was a significant relationship between Cross-Functional Fit (CF) and Operational Performance (OP). As proposed, Cross-functional Fit was found to have a significant positive relation with Operational Performance ($\beta = 0.336$, $p = 0.000$). Thus, the hypothesized effect was supported. The cross-functional fit was found to be the most significant predictor of operational performance. The result implies that a unit increase in cross-functional fit (alignment of HRM functions with all other departments and functional areas [Azmi, 2010]) is expected to result in 0.336 enhancements in operational performance.

In summary, regarding the correlation result, all the relationships among SHRM and employee commitment constructs, hypotheses (H1 to H8) were positively significant. The summary of the key findings and their implications are presented in Table 6. The PL-SEM result revealed that two SHRM practices had a positive and significant effect on organizational performance (hypotheses H7 and H8). Four SHRM practices (H1, H2, H5, and H6) had a positive but non-significant impact on organizational performance. Also, two SHRM practices (H3 and H4) had a negative but non-significant impact on organizational performance. Importantly, PL-SEM results only showed a significant positive relationship for H7 and H8.

Table 6. Summary of findings and implications

Hypothesis	Relationship	Implication
H1	SF -> FP	Improving strategy fit (alignment between HRM practices and business strategy) does not enhance the financial performance of tertiary educational institutions significantly
H2	SF -> OP	Improving strategy Fit (alignment between HRM practices and business strategy) does result in a significant enhancement in operational performance.
H3	RF -> FP	Improving roles-position fit (status of the HRM department within corporate strategic issues) does not however result in any significant decreases in financial performance.
H4	RF -> OP	Improving roles-position fit (status of the HRM department within corporate strategic issues) may not likely result in a significant decline in operational performance.
H5	IF -> FP	Improving intra-functional fit (status of the HRM department within corporate strategic issues) does not necessarily enhance financial performance.
H6	IF -> OP	Improving intra-functional fit (status of the HRM department within corporate strategic issues) may not significantly enhance operational performance.
H7	CF -> FP	Improving cross-functional fit (alignment of HRM functions with all other departments and functional areas) will enhance financial performance
H8	CF -> OP	Improving cross-functional fit (alignment of HRM functions with all other departments and functional areas) is expected to increase operational performance.

DISCUSSION

Of importance is the positive and statistically significant effect of two of the relationships on organizational performance. These include (a) the effect of cross-functional fit (alignment of HRM functions with all other departments and functional areas on financial performance, and (b) the effect of cross-functional fit (alignment of HRM functions with all other departments and functional areas) on operational performance. Previous studies reported that SHRM could impact organizational performance (Basu, 2022; Ludwikowska, 2021; Greer, Lusch & Hitt, 2017). In this current study, it was found that alignment of HRM functions with all other departments and functional areas (cross-functional fit) would improve financial performance in tertiary educational institutions (H7). Likewise, again alignment of HRM functions with all other departments and functional areas (cross-functional fit) would impact operational performance (H8).

Logofătu (2019) suggested that enhancing organizational performance required a strategic approach to human resource management. In general, SHRM was also widely reported to have a positive relationship with financial performance (Russo, 2010; Singh, et al., 2019). However, specifically, this current study found the cross-functional fit as the main determinant of both financial and operational performance in tertiary educational institutions. Thus, tertiary educational institutions could improve financial and operational performance if HRM functions are aligned with all other departments and functional areas of the institutions. In consonance with best fit or contingency theory relating to SHRM, particular HRM practices could improve performance where there is consistency among HRM practices and the organization's strategic goals (Youndt, Snell, Dean & Lepak, 1996).

Moreover, empirical studies revealed that HR practices positively affect organizational performance (Hamid, 2013; Vomberg, Homburg & Bornmann, 2015). However, in the current study, out of the four dimensions of SHRM practices, only SHRM cross-functional fit had a positive and statistical impact on both financial and operational organizational performance in tertiary educational institutions. Other relationships were not significant. For instance, four SHRM practices had a positive but non-significant impact on organizational performance. Thus, improving alignment between HRM practices and business strategy (SHRM strategy fit) might not enhance both the financial performance and operational performance of tertiary educational institutions significantly. This finding, however, contradicts that of Collins and Kehoe (2017), who found that strategic fit could improve a firm's performance. Similarly, improving the status of the HRM department within corporate strategic issues (intra-functional fit) might not influence significantly the financial performance and operational performance.

Additionally, for the two SHRM practices that had a negative but non-significant impact on organizational performance, the findings revealed that improving the status of the HRM department within corporate strategic issues (HRM roles-position fit) would not negatively and significantly decrease financial performance. Even though improving role-position fit might not result in a significant decline in both financial and operational performance, it is expected from the executives to demonstrate the right managerial skills to enhance organizational performance. According to Savitz and Weber (2013), many organizations fail because HR functions have not been given strategic priorities. Consequently, for tertiary educational institutions in Ghana to improve financial and operational performance they should focus on cross-functional fit, which is the creation of close alignment and collaboration between HRM functions and other departments and functional areas.

CONCLUSION AND RECOMMENDATIONS

In conclusion, tertiary educational institutions should focus on aligning HRM functions with all other departments and functional areas (cross-functional fit) if they wanted to improve both financial and operational performance. Aligning HRM functions with departmental units would involve some practical steps. Departmental heads should be trained in HR issues to better position them in addressing employees they supervise. Staffing, training, and pay-related decisions should be taken jointly with deans and heads of departments. Moreover, deans and heads of departments should be involved in internal review activities.

The current study focused solely on the constructs (four dimensions of SHRM practices and two aspects of organizational performance) without considering the important contribution that individual SHRM indicators could make toward organizational performance. The impact of individual SHRM indicators could be addressed through Importance-Performance Map Analysis (IPMA). Our further research would employ the use of IPMA for concluding the analysis based on the individual contributions of the indicators. This would reveal how important the independent constructs and their indicators could explain the target-dependent construct. The IPMA would add an important dimension to the PLS-SEM results by also taking the performance of each construct and its indicators into account. As a result, the IPMA allows for the identification of constructs and indicators with comparatively low performance and relatively high importance for the target construct. Such constructs and indicators have the highest relevance and priority for practitioners because improving their performance would have a strong effect on the selected target construct.

REFERENCES

Ahmad, M. R., & Raja, R. (2021). Employee Job Satisfaction and Business Performance: The Mediating Role of Organizational Commitment. *Vision*, *25*(2), 168–179.

Akhtar, N., Azeem, S. M., Basiouni, A. F., Ahmed, A., Teoh, K. B., & Alvi, A. (2022). What motivates the most? Money or Empowerment: Mediating Role of Employee Commitment to Organizational Performance. *Journal of Organisational Studies & Innovation*, *9*(2), 21–37. doi:10.51659/josi.21-153

Al-Taweel, I. R. (2021). Impact of high-performance work practices in human resource management of health dispensaries in Qassim Region, Kingdom of Saudi Arabia, towards organizational resilience and productivity. *Business Process Management Journal*, *27*(7), 2088–2109. doi:10.1108/BPMJ-11-2020-0498

Allui, A., & Sahni, J. (2016). Strategic Human Resource Management in Higher Education Institutions: Empirical Evidence from Saudi. *Procedia: Social and Behavioral Sciences*, *235*, 361–371. doi:10.1016/j.sbspro.2016.11.044

Anca-Ioana, M. (2013). New approaches of the concepts of human resources, human resource management and strategic human resource management. *Annals of the University of Oradea. Economic Science Series*, *22*(1), 1520–1525.

Ayers, R. S. (2013). Building goal alignment in federal agencies' performance appraisal programs. *Public Personnel Management*, *42*(4), 495–520. doi:10.1177/0091026013496077

Azmi, F. T. (2010). Devolution of HRM and organizational performance: Evidence from India. *International Journal of Commerce and Management*, *20*(3), 217–231. doi:10.1108/10569211011076910

Basu, P. S. (2022). Organisational Csr Practices: A Strategic Lever Towards Harnessing Higher Employee Engagement. *Journal of Organisation & Human Behaviour*, *11*(1), 40–49.

Chin, J. H., & Wang, H. (Eds.), *Handbook of partial least squares*. Springer., doi:10.1007/978-3-540-32827-8_29

Chin, W. W. (1998). The partial least squares approach to structural equation modeling. In G. A. Marcoulides (Ed.), *Modern methods for business research* (pp. 295–336). Erlbaum.

Chin, W. W. (2010). How to write up and report PLS analyses. In V. E. Vinzi (Ed.), *W. W.* doi:10.1007/978-3-540-32827-8_29

Chopra, R. (2017). Strategic human resource management and its impact on organisational performance. *Global Journal of Enterprise Information System*, 9(3), 89–93. doi:10.18311/gjeis/2017/16057

Collins, C., & Kehoe, R. (2017). Examining strategic fit and misfit in the management of knowledge workers. *Industrial & Labor Relations Review*, 70(2), 308–335. doi:10.1177/0019793916654481

Covarrubias, V. B., Thill, K., & Domnanovich, J. (2017). The importance of strategic competence in HRM. Evidence from Austria, Czech Republic, Hungary and Slovakia. *Journal of Eastern European & Central Asian Research*, 4(2), 1–11. doi:10.15549/jeecar.v4i2.145

Curran-Everett, D. (2015). Best Practices: A series of theory, evidence, and implementation. *Advances in Physiology Education*, 39(4), 253. doi:10.1152/advan.00099.2015 PMID:26628644

Gotz, O., Liehr-Gobbers, K., & Krafft, M. (2010). Evaluation of structural equation models using the Partial Least Squares (PLS) approach. In V. E. Vinzi, W. W. Chin, J. Henseler, & H. Wang (Eds.), *Handbook of partial least squares*. Springer. doi:10.1007/978-3-540-32827-8_30

Greer, C. R., Lusch, R. F., & Hitt, M. A. (2017). A service perspective for human capital resources: A critical base for strategy implementation. *The Academy of Management Perspectives*, 31(2), 137–158. doi:10.5465/amp.2016.0004

Greer, C. R., & Stevens, C. D. (2015). HR in collaborative innovation with customers: Role, alignment, and challenges. *International Journal of Human Resource Management*, 26(20), 2569–2593. doi:10.1080/09585192.2014.1003086

Hadziahmetovic, N., & Dinc, M. S. (2020). Linking reward types to organizational performance in Central and Eastern European universities: The mediating role of affective commitment. *Journal for East European Management Studies*, 25(2), 325–359. doi:10.5771/0949-6181-2020-2-325

Hair, J. F., Ringle, C. M., & Sarstedt, M. (2011). PLS-SEM: Indeed a silver bullet. *Journal of Marketing Theory and Practice*, 19(2), 139–151. doi:10.2753/MTP1069-6679190202

Hair, J. F. Jr, Ringle, C. M., & Sarstedt, M. (2013). Partial least squares structural equation modeling: Rigorous applications, better results and higher acceptance. *Long Range Planning*, 46(1-2), 1–12. doi:10.1016/j.lrp.2013.01.001

Hair, J. F., Sarstedt, M., Ringle, C. M., & Mena, J. A. (2012). An assessment of the use of partial least squares structural equation modeling in marketing research. *Journal of the Academy of Marketing Science*, 40(3), 414–433. doi:10.100711747-011-0261-6

Hong, Y. H., Liao, H., Hu, J., & Jiang, K. (2013). Missing link in the service profit chain: A meta-analytic review of the antecedents, consequences, and moderator of service climate. *The Journal of Applied Psychology*, 98(2), 237–267. doi:10.1037/a0031666 PMID:23458337

Hulland, J. (1999). Use of partial least squares (PLS) in strategic management research: A review of four recent studies. *Strategic Management Journal, 20*(2), 195–204. doi:10.1002/(SICI)1097-0266(199902)20:2<195::AID-SMJ13>3.0.CO;2-7

Islam, J., & Hu, H. (2012). A review of literature on contingency theory in managerial accounting. *African Journal of Business Management, 6*(15), 5159–5164.

Jashari, A., & Kutllovci, E. (2020). The Impact of Human Resource Management Practices on Organizational Performance Case Study: Manufacturing Enterprises in Kosovo. *Business: Theory and Practice, 21*(1), 222–229. doi:10.3846/btp.2020.12001

Jermsittiparsert, K., Chankoson, T., Malik, I., & Thaicharoen, W. (2021). Linking Islamic Work Ethics With Employee Performance: Perceived Organizational Support And Psychological Ownership As A Potential Mediators In Financial Institutions. Journal of Legal. *Ethical and Regulatory Issues, 24*, 1–11.

Kale, G., & Shimpi, S. (2020). Testing Role of Hrm Practices and Organizational Commitment on Organizational Performance with Reference to Seasonality in Tourism Employment. *Journal of Hospitality Application & Research, 15*(2), 23–46.

Karami, A., Sahebalzamani, S., & Sarabi, B. (2015). The influence of HR practices on business strategy and firm performance: The case of banking industry in Iran. *IUP Journal of Management Research, 14*(1), 30–53.

Kumah, P. (2022). Impact of SHRM on Employee Commitment in Tertiary Educational Institutions in Ghana. [IJAMSE]. *International Journal of Applied Management Sciences and Engineering, 9*(1), 1–22. doi:10.4018/IJAMSE.312849

Kumar, K. L. S., & Reddy, M. L. (2019). Strategic Human Resource Management: The Calibrated Catalysts for Indian IT-SMEs Performance Optimization. *SDMIMD Journal of Management, 10*(1), 31–42. doi:10.18311dmimd/2019/21493

Logofătu, M. (2019). Integrating Organizational Culture in Strategic Human Resource Management of the Educational Institutions. Ovidius University Annals. *Series Economic Sciences, 19*(1), 443–449.

Ludwikowska, K. (2021). The Mediating Role of Employee—Oriented Human Resource Policy in the Relationship between Strategic Human Resource Management and Organisational Performance. *Forum Scientiae Oeconomia, 9*(2), 131–150.

McFarland, R., Rode, J., & Shervani, T. (2016). A contingency model of emotional intelligence in professional selling. *Journal of the Academy of Marketing Science, 44*(1), 108–118. doi:10.100711747-015-0435-8

Mendel, S. C. (2017). Workarounds in nonprofit management: Counter theory for best practices innovation. *Journal of Ideology, 38*(2), 1–31.

NAB. (2018). *Number of accredited tertiary institutions in Ghana per category as at January, 2018.* NAB. http://www.nab.gov.gh/news1/414-accredited-published-tertiary-institutions-as-at-august-2016-summary

National Council for Tertiary Education. (2017). *Summary of basic statistics on tertiary educational institutions 2016/2017*. NCTE. ncte.gov.gh

National Council on Labor-Management Relations. (2012). *Council receives GEAR report*. Labor Management Council. http://www.lmrcouncil.gov/index.aspx

Nunnally, J. C. (1976). *Psychometric theory*. McGraw-Hill.

Opoku, F. K., & Arthur, D. D. (2015). Human resource management practices and its influence on organizational performance: An analysis of the situation in the Ghana Postal Services Company Limited. *International Journal of Scientific and Research Publications*, 5(6), 2250–3153.

Riaz, A., & Mahmood, H. Z. (2017). Cross-level relationship of implemented high performance work system and employee service outcomes: The mediating role of affective commitment. *Pakistan Journal of Commerce & Social Sciences*, 11(1), 351–373.

Russo, M. V. (2010). *Companies on a mission: entrepreneurial strategies for growing sustainably, responsibly, and profitably*. Stanford University Press.

Savitz, A. W., & Weber, K. (2013). *Talent, transformation, and the triple bottom line: how companies can leverage human resources to achieve sustainable growth*. John Wiley & Sons, Inc.

Singh, Wood, G., Darwish, T. K., Fleming, J., & Mohamed, A. F. (2019). Human resource management in multinational and domestic enterprises: A comparative institutional analysis in Southeast Asia. *Thunderbird International Business Review*, 61(2), 229–241. doi:10.1002/tie.21997

Tallon, P. P., & Pinsonneault, A. (2011). Competing perspectives on the link between strategic information technology alignment and organizational agility: Insights from a mediation model. *Management Information Systems Quarterly*, 35(2), 463–486. doi:10.2307/23044052

Vickery, S. K., Droge, C., Setia, P., & Sambamurthy, V. (2010). Supply chain information technologies and organisational initiatives: Complementary versus independent effects on agility and firm performance. *International Journal of Production Research*, 48(3), 7025–7042. doi:10.1080/00207540903348353

World Bank. (2011). Promoting Gender Equality through Human Development. World Bank. www.worldbank.org

Wright, P. M., & McMahan, G. C. (2011). Exploring human capital: Putting 'human' back into strategic human resource management. *Human Resource Management Journal*, 21(2), 93–104. doi:10.1111/j.1748-8583.2010.00165.x

Zhai, X., Zhu, C. J., & Zhang, M. M. (2022). Mapping promoting factors and mechanisms of resilience for performance improvement: The role of strategic human resource management systems and psychological empowerment. *Applied Psychology*, 1.

Chapter 4
Determining and Evaluating Criteria for Transformational Leadership in Educational Institutions With AHP Method

Filiz Mızrak
https://orcid.org/0000-0002-3472-394X
Istanbul Medipol University, Turkey

Murat Culduz
Istanbul Medipol University, Turkey

ABSTRACT

As all sectors, educational institutions need to keep up with the chance and developments. In this scope, transformational leaders are among the most important requirements. For this reason, it is important for executives working in educational institutions to have transformational leadership characteristics and to demonstrate these characteristics by using them for the management of the schools. Based on these data, the main purpose of this research is to determine the transformational leadership characteristics in educational institutions. In this context, the criteria obtained as a result of literature review and interviews with five experts working in educational institutions have been weighted with the AHP method to determine their priorities. It is thought that the findings of the research will be a guide for educational institutions which have changed especially after the pandemic. At the same time, it is believed that the criteria determined according to the order of importance will contribute to the senior manager selection process of the relevant institutions

DOI: 10.4018/979-8-3693-1380-0.ch004

INTRODUCTION

The developing and changing world has brought differentiating habits and beliefs. It is considered that the strong structures of organizations affect the progress of societies. Organizations, which exist at the base of society, have been managed in various ways until today (Al-Alawi et al., 2019). Changes in belief, value and understanding have also shown their effect in the field of education, and with this effect, new searches have started in education. All institutions in the society must be in this process of change. Educational institutions are at the forefront of institutions that affect the progress of society. Educational institutions should be willing to adapt to change and achieve the goal of realizing its transformation. Institutions that catch up with change will renew and restructure by adapting to change and determine new paths to follow ensure their existence (Brazill & Ruff, 2022).

Today, reasons such as the rapid progress of information, the increase in developments and competition, and the more complex appearance of problems reveal the necessity of change. Lack of creativity, lack of flexibility, inability to catch up with innovations, changes and technology, and failure to fulfill the requirements of the information age cause the emergence of a poor-quality school environment and the development of educational activities. For these reasons, organizations must improve their existing structures. To increase the performance, effectiveness, and efficiency of organizations, to increase motivation and job satisfaction, to ensure that they are in change and development, there should be managers who are open to development and have a certain vision. To achieve this, managers with transformational leadership characteristics are needed (Türk & Mızrak, 2021). Leadership is seen as an important factor in the initiation and implementation of transformation in organizations. To provide management in the transformation process, the need to have leaders who are in the direction of change comes to the fore. These leaders attach great importance to the formation of a clear vision and that their employees follow these visions (Ghavifekr & Fung, 2021).

In this perspective, the purpose of the study is to determine the characteristics of a transformational leader in educational institutions. After a detailed analysis of the recent literature and interview with 5 executives working in educational institution, 5 criteria have been obtained and weighted with the AHP (Analytical Hierarchy Process) method to determine their priorities. The study contributes to literature well since conducted interviews with the executives and use of multi-criteria decision-making techniques in an integrated manner will facilitate business analysts and decision makers in the quantitative evaluation of subjective and objective criteria. Furthermore, It is thought that the findings of the research will be a guide for educational institutions which have changed especially after the pandemic. At the same time, it is believed that the criteria determined according to the order of importance will contribute to the senior manager selection process of the relevant enterprises.

In the following part of the study, a detailed literature analysis of the concept related to leadership, difference between being a manager and leader have been presented. Furthermore, concept, history and dimensions of transformational leadership have been illustrated in the same part. In the methodology section, steps of the analyses have been explained. Last but not the least, finding of the study have been demonstrated in the final part.

BACKGROUND

Concept of Leadership

After the 1960s, there was a notable addition to the field of management studies: the concept of "Leadership." Scholars began recognizing that management and leadership shared close connections (Perrin, 2010). Although the terms management, manager, and leader are often used interchangeably, their distinctions become apparent when considering their implementation. The manner in which a manager motivates and guides their subordinates showcases their potential as a leader. Likewise, the practice of leadership traits becomes evident through actions. However, during activities such as planning, organizing, coordinating, and controlling, the presence of leadership might not be readily apparent (Bertocci, 2009). This highlights the nuanced relationship between management and leadership, emphasizing the significance of leadership qualities in effectively guiding and inspiring a team.

Leadership is a complex and multifaceted process that defies precise formulation. Despite years of discussion and research within the realm of behavioral sciences, a consensus on the exact nature of leadership remains elusive. Multiple definitions of leadership have been proposed and continue to evolve. According to Stone & Patterson (2023), a leader is an individual who articulates the collective thoughts and unexpressed aspirations of group members, mobilizing their latent potential around a common goal. Fischer & Sitkin (2023) define leadership as the display of influential behavior that enables people to voluntarily participate in group activities, devoid of coercion. Leithwood, Harris & Hopkins (2020) perceive leadership as the internalization of the organization's vision within subgroups. Simultaneously, leaders act as systems thinkers, navigating the intricate interplay between the constituent parts and the overarching goals, ensuring harmony and balance in pursuit of those objectives. The diverse perspectives on leadership highlight its dynamic nature and the importance of contextual factors in shaping its manifestation (Türk et al., 2021).

The attitude of a leader has a profound impact on the attitudes of their followers. Leadership, in essence, is the ability to influence others. People acquire this influence much like they catch the flu—by being in close proximity to the leader. Therefore, as a leader, one must position themselves at the center of their sphere of influence. Maintaining a positive attitude is crucial not only for personal success but also for the well-being of others. A leader should always keep their responsibilities in view, not just for themselves but for the majority (Cortellazzo, Bruni & Zampieri, 2019). In today's world, all managers must possess leadership qualities to achieve success, as individuals thrive when they work with leaders who can effectively guide and inspire (Samimi et al., 2022). The quality of leaders is determined by a combination of innate physiology, psychology, and the accumulation of knowledge and practical experience gained through learning and studies in management (Benmira & Agboola, 2021). Leadership revolves around setting a vision and motivating people. A good leader fosters loyalty by increasing employee motivation and performance, fostering a sense of teamwork and providing coaching. Simultaneously, leaders bring about necessary changes to realize the vision by influencing their followers and generating solutions when needed (Fries, Kammerlander & Leitterstorf, 2021).

The role of a leader is crucial in the pursuit of organizational success, as they guide employees towards achieving organizational goals and foster collective enthusiasm that drives organizational performance. A skilled leader possesses the ability to compensate for organizational deficiencies, effectively utilizing available resources to attain success. Conversely, a poor or inadequate leader can squander valuable organizational resources, resulting in wasted potential. Therefore, it is imperative for leaders to continually strive for self-improvement throughout their lives (Gigliotti, 2019). Rather than simply directing individuals in their current roles, leaders should encourage them to explore new possibilities, enabling the development of fresh relationships and perspectives. Instead of suppressing conflict, leaders should embrace it and bring issues to the forefront, allowing for resolution and growth. Challenging established norms and encouraging critical thinking is essential for leaders to help individuals differentiate between enduring values and outdated practices of the past (Kane et al., 2019). By adopting these approaches, leaders can foster an environment of innovation and progress within their organizations.

Leadership possesses a highly intricate and multifaceted structure. It encompasses a multitude of aspects, including respect, experience, emotional resilience, human skills, discipline, vision, timing, and more. Many of these characteristics associated with leadership are abstract in nature, necessitating leaders to be actively engaged. Effective leaders must have the ability to observe systems comprehensively, while simultaneously defining the boundaries of their focus within the system to become practitioners. It is important to recognize that these boundaries are artificial and permeable, allowing for flexibility and adaptation (Antonopoulou et al., 2021). By actively embodying these qualities and maintaining a keen awareness of the dynamic nature of their leadership role, leaders can navigate the complexities of their environment and guide their teams towards success.

Differences Between a Manager and a Leader

In general, a manager is a person who works on behalf of others, strives to achieve predetermined goals, plans work, gets things done, and oversees results. The leader, on the other hand, is the person who determines the goals of the group he is affiliated with and influences the group members in line with these goals and directs them to behavior. A manager pushes from behind, focuses on the system and structure, gives importance to quantity, seeks fault, punishes, dictates, orders, directs, says "walk". A leader, on the other hand, leads, focuses on people, attaches importance to quality, corrects mistakes, rewards, consults, receives opinions and ideas, directs them, says "let's walk''. Ensuring that the work done is completed is the success of the manager, while inspiring the followers to work better is the success of the leader (Kotterman, 2006).

Management is dealing with problems and maintaining order in the organization. Leadership is necessary to achieve change. Leaders work in high-risk positions. The more risk they take, especially when they see an opportunity, or the possibility of reward arises. In this context, it is possible to say that leaders have an innate tendency to take risks. On the other hand, the existential instincts of the managers dominate the need for risk. This instinct gives birth to the ability to resist difficulties and endure daily work (Baykal, 2020).

The manager is generally defined as the person who coordinates the behaviors of the employees of the organization in line with the realization of the organizational goals. The leader is seen as the person who influences the group members. Unlike management, the emotional side of leadership outweighs especially the intellectual and cognitive side (Öncü, 1998: 128). Leaders have intense relationships with their followers and, accordingly, the work environment often includes chaos. However, the leader tolerates these situations of chaos, thus avoiding premature erroneous conclusions by keeping responses on hold. Managers, on the other hand, seek order, want to keep control, and have an attitude of solving problems as soon as they realize their importance. The manager provides the continuation of the routine functioning of the organization by calming all parties in case of a problem (Dumitru, Motoi, & Budica, 2015).

In order to utilize human resources in the most efficient and effective manner, a manager must possess a keen awareness of the latest developments in the field of behavioral sciences and have the capacity to foster positive and productive interpersonal relationships within the organization. In today's dynamic and complex business environment, it is inconceivable to have an effective manager without leadership qualities. Leadership skills are essential for a manager to provide direction, inspiration, and guidance to their team members. It is through leadership capabilities that a manager can establish order and harmony within the organization, encouraging collaboration, motivating employees, and maximizing their potential. By combining managerial expertise with leadership skills, a manager can create a conducive and thriving work environment that drives individual and collective success.

TRANSFORMATIONAL LEADERSHIP

The increasing technological competition and the rapid pace of change in the 1980s compelled organizations to adapt and evolve. In this era, traditional approaches were no longer sufficient to ensure success, and the ability of employees to swiftly adapt to change became crucial for maintaining competitiveness (Bakker et al., 2022). Consequently, organizations began undergoing gradual structural transformations, leading to the need for new forms of leadership. In the quest to address the challenges encountered during the restructuring of large-scale organizations, a novel leadership theory emerged: transformational leadership. Since its inception, this new leadership paradigm has garnered significant attention in contemporary leadership research (Purwanto et al., 2021). Transformational leadership offers a fresh perspective on how leaders can inspire and motivate their teams to embrace change, innovate, and achieve extraordinary outcomes. It emphasizes the leader's ability to communicate a compelling vision, stimulate creativity and growth, foster a positive organizational culture, and empower employees to reach their full potential. With its focus on transformative behaviors and visionary leadership, this theory has become a prominent framework for guiding organizations through periods of change and adaptation.

The concept of transformational leadership traces its roots back to the book "Revolt Leadership" authored by Dawston in 1973, and it was further developed by James McGregor Burns in 1978. According to this theory, a transformational leader possesses the ability to inspire and elevate the morale, motivation, and performance of their followers (Bass, 1997). Transformational leadership is particularly valuable in enabling organizations to adapt to the ever-changing and evolving external environmental factors, thereby ensuring their survival. Within the realm of transformational leadership, there are two distinct approaches based on the scope of the changes implemented. Reformist transformational leaders focus on making incremental changes while adhering to existing principles, whereas revolutionary transformational leaders tackle the organization as a whole, guiding employees towards new goals and striving to fundamentally transform the guiding principles (Bass, 1997). Both forms of transformational leadership play significant roles in driving organizational progress and facilitating adaptation in dynamic environments.

Transformational leaders prioritize both the well-being and aspirations of their employees while actively working towards organizational development. In the transformational leadership approach, the focus lies not only on sustaining the organization but also on propelling it forward. This leadership style aims to enhance the awareness and self-confidence of employees, empowering them to reach their full potential (Yammarino & Bass, 1990). Within the realm of transformational leadership, numerous definitions highlight the importance of sharing, cooperation, mutual trust, and collective decision-making as integral components (Leithwood & Jantzi, 2005). By fostering a culture of collaboration, trust, and shared vision, transformational leaders inspire their team members to go beyond their perceived limitations, encouraging innovative thinking, and promoting collective growth. This approach not only drives individual and team performance but also cultivates a sense of ownership and commitment to the organization's goals.

Transformational leadership is characterized by its ability to maximize employees' desire for change and meet their emotional needs (Bass & Avolio, 1990). It involves making changes in the organizational vision, strategies, and culture to drive progress (Hay, 2006). Transformational leaders redefine roles, update responsibilities, and restructure systems in alignment with organizational goals (Rafferty & Griffin, 2004). This leadership style possesses the skills to evoke a strong desire in subordinates to work harmoniously with their leaders and cultivate a sense of dedication to their work (Barling, Slater & Kelloway, 2000). It awakens dignity, courage, and confidence in subordinates by initiating a transformation process that is suitable for their unique circumstances, simultaneously achieving organizational objectives by influencing their beliefs, attitudes, and values (Sadeghi & Pihie, 2012). In the realm of transformational leadership, the focus is on improving the knowledge and abilities of individuals, driving growth and development from the current state (Keller, 1992). Through these multifaceted approaches, transformational leaders empower their followers, foster personal and professional growth, and lead their organizations towards success.

Indeed, transformational leadership involves facilitating organizational change by consistently enhancing the knowledge and skills of employees. A transformational leader is someone who remains attentive to both internal and external changes, recognizing the need for change within the organization. They actively engage their subordinates in the change process and collaboratively chart a new course for the organization. Through their visionary approach and inclusive leadership style, transformational leaders inspire and motivate their team members to embrace change, overcome challenges, and strive for excellence. They create an environment that encourages innovation, fosters creativity, and empowers individuals to contribute their unique perspectives and talents towards organizational growth and success. By embracing transformational leadership, organizations can adapt to dynamic environments, stay ahead of the curve, and navigate through periods of change with resilience and agility.

HISTORY OF TRANSFORMATIONAL LEADERSHIP

In the 20th century, as traditional leadership theories began to lose their influence, new avenues of research emerged. One of these significant developments was the concept of transformational leadership, initially proposed by James Victor Dawston in his book "Rebellion Leadership" (1973), and further developed by political scientist James McGregor Burns in 1978. Transformational leadership is rooted in the idea that leaders can influence, motivate, and garner support from employees without resorting to coercion. According to Burns, a transformational leader is capable of cultivating a high level of morale, motivation, and performance within the organization. These leaders possess a mastery of change, creating new opportunities within the organization and working towards a better future. They establish a clear vision and effectively communicate and align this vision with their subordinates (Bailey & Axelrod, 2001). Transformational leadership has become a significant area of study, emphasizing the importance of inspiring and empowering leaders who can drive organizational change and foster success.

James McGregor Burns indeed drew inspiration from Max Weber's charismatic leadership theories (1968) in developing his studies on transformational leadership. He defined transformational leadership as a form of leadership in which both the leader and subordinates motivate each other, and where ethical values and human behaviors are exemplified. In subsequent years, Bernard M. Bass further advanced the understanding of transformational leadership based on Burns' work. According to Bass, transformational leadership behaviors can be displayed by individuals at any level within an organization. This means that a transformation can be initiated and driven by individuals at lower levels, ultimately influencing and transforming the upper levels of the organization as well (Goethals & Allison, 2016). This perspective highlights the potential for transformational leadership to permeate and impact the organization at all levels, enabling positive change and growth throughout the entire organizational hierarchy.

Bernard M. Bass further expanded on Burns' theories and contributed to the understanding of transformational leadership. Bass indeed made significant contributions to the field of leadership, particularly with his work titled "Leadership and Performance Beyond Expectations" published in 1985. In this study, Bass presented transformational leadership in a more accessible and measurable manner. He also developed the Multifactor Leadership Scale, which allows for the assessment of interactionist and transformational leadership traits. This scale offers a comprehensive perspective on leadership, enabling a 360-degree evaluation of leadership effectiveness (Bass, 1997). Furthermore, Bass conducted a comparison of transformational and transactional leadership characteristics, which is often presented in the form of a table for better understanding and analysis. This comparison provides insights into the distinguishing features and approaches of both leadership styles.

Table 1. The comparison of transformational and transactional leadership characteristics

Interactive Leader	Transformational Leader
Rewarding: · Rewards success. · Increases the employees' effort · Promises to reward good performance	Setting an example · Acts in accordance with the vision created by exemplary actions. · Gives the mission spirit. · Promotes maturity. · Gains trust.
Management Using Spaces (Active): · Investigates and shares the deviations from rules and standards.	Building Motivation with Inspiration: · Discusses high expectations. · Uses symbols to focus. · Explains important objectives in simple language.
Management Using Spaces (Passive): · Intervenes when standards do not comply with requirements.	Providing Intellectual Desire: · Promotes intelligence and rationality. · Solves problems carefully.
Liberality: · Distributes responsibilities. · Avoids decision making.	Taking Special Care of Everyone: · Pays attention to subordinates; welcomes each employee individually, gives him ideas and guides.

Source: Ruggieri, S. (2009)

CHARACTERISTICS OF TRANSFORMATIONAL LEADERSHIP

Transformational leadership is characterized by several key features. Firstly, transformational leaders embrace change and transformation, actively seeking out opportunities for organizational growth and development. They are open to technological advancements and utilize technology to its fullest potential, enabling them to solve problems more efficiently and effectively. Additionally, transformational leaders demonstrate courage and motivate their team members to realize their full potential, particularly when facing resistance to change. They strive to make individuals who resist change feel valued and included, fostering a sense of ownership and commitment to organizational goals. This creates a corporate culture where team members align themselves with the organization's objectives, promoting a collective identity over individuality. Transformational leaders also prioritize continuous improvement, organizing activities and training sessions for both themselves and their team members. These training activities help mitigate any negativity encountered during the transformation process, preventing demoralization and fostering a more optimistic outlook. Trust is a central aspect of transformational leadership, as leaders build relationships based on trust and collaboration rather than relying solely on hierarchical authority. They instill in their team members the importance of organizational values, cultivating a shared sense of responsibility and dedication (Supermane, 2019). These characteristics contribute to the development of a positive organizational culture and the successful implementation of organizational change.

In the context of transformational leadership, there is a strong emphasis on continuous learning and personal development. Transformational leaders possess a deep desire to constantly improve themselves, their organization, and their administrative staff. They recognize that intellectual growth among their personnel can be achieved through a shift in beliefs, and therefore strive to transform the thoughts and behaviors of their subordinates to align with the operational and future vision of the institution. They highlight the importance of adopting a multifaceted perspective and encouraging creative thinking, as they believe that innovative and practical solutions can be derived from such approaches. The transformational leader tends to overlook the mistakes made by their subordinates, understanding that these mistakes present valuable opportunities for growth and success. They enable their team members to recognize that learning from their mistakes can guide them towards potential alternative solutions (Afsar, Masood & Umrani, 2019). By fostering a learning-oriented culture and promoting creative problem-solving, transformational leaders empower their subordinates to develop their skills, explore new possibilities, and drive organizational progress.

The transformational leader embodies a dynamic and proactive nature. They continuously seek improvement and growth, displaying an aversion to stability and constancy. Their expertise lies in guiding and inspiring their team members, making them feel supported and valued. They possess an acute awareness of the individual talents and characteristics of their team, and they motivate them to focus on their work and strive for excellence. The transformational leader has a profound impact on their team members, cultivating trust and loyalty towards themselves. Their charismatic qualities further contribute to this influence. As team members develop a sense of affection and trust towards their leader, their existing skills and capabilities become maximized, resulting in increased productivity. The motivation and enjoyment derived from their work lead to higher job satisfaction among team members (Amor, Vázquez & Faíña, 2020). Through their dynamic leadership approach, transformational leaders create an environment that fosters personal growth, professional development, and strong team cohesion, ultimately driving organizational success.

The transformational leader goes beyond meeting the basic needs of team members and prioritizes their intellectual development to achieve desired performance levels. They actively work towards realizing the organizational vision in alignment with the established goals. In addition, a transformational leader fosters an environment of trust, consistency, and reliability that promotes the growth and motivation of individuals within the organization. This requires the establishment of an appropriate organizational culture and climate. Initially, the transformational leader must earn the trust of team members, subsequently creating an environment that fosters trust and collaboration among team members themselves. This bond of trust, nurtured over time, is vital for the continuity of organizations and the achievement of their goals (Supermane, 2019). By creating an atmosphere of trust and enabling the development and motivation of individuals, the transformational leader cultivates an environment where team members can thrive, collaborate effectively, and work towards the collective goals of the organization.

Indeed, a sincere and humane relationship between the members of an organization and their leaders, rather than a closed hierarchical relationship, can significantly enhance motivation within the organization. Transformational leaders aim to create an environment that promotes freedom and autonomy for organizational members, avoiding overly restrictive behaviors. They recognize that a free environment encourages creativity and innovation. Transformational leaders prioritize the development of their team members' imaginations, believing that a creative mindset will lead to the emergence of innovative solutions for existing and potential problems within the organization (Asbari, 2020). By fostering an atmosphere of trust, openness, and freedom, transformational leaders empower their team members to think critically, challenge norms, and contribute unique perspectives. This approach encourages a culture of creativity and stimulates the generation of fresh ideas and solutions. As a result, organizations benefit from the diverse and innovative contributions of their motivated and engaged team members, ultimately driving success and growth.

Dimensions of Transformational Leadership

According to Bass, transformational leadership style is theoretically evaluated in four dimensions.

IDEALIZED INFLUENCE (CHARISMATIC LEADERSHIP)

The behavior of a transformational leader encompasses various abilities and attributes, including adopting moral principles, taking risks, displaying courage and determination, establishing trust and sincerity with their staff, selflessness, and creating a shared sense of purpose and goals among team members. Ethical behavior is a fundamental and unwavering principle for a transformational leader. They guide their personnel through exemplary behavior and pay close attention to their needs, thereby gaining the trust of their team members. When assigning tasks, they delegate authority, motivate, and encourage their team members. The transformational leader emphasizes participation and seeks input from team members. They prioritize the interests of the organization and the team over their personal interests, acting consistently (Cahyono et al., 2020). The transformational leader's clear commitment to beliefs and values, as well as their emphasis on the ideas and emotions of organizational members rather than personal interests, is highly valued by team members. Their persuasive abilities have a positive impact on the entire team, reinforcing their charismatic influence (Djourova et al., 2020).

Idealized influence, a characteristic of transformational leadership, generates a sense of respect, admiration, and trust towards the leader among organizational members. Team members view the leader as a role model and find inspiration in their actions. The transformational leader's display of leadership qualities is crucial in being regarded as a role model. When team members adopt the leader's decisions by considering them as examples, it contributes to the success of the organization (Saboe et al., 2015).

The combination of these behaviors and attributes of a transformational leader fosters a positive organizational environment, enhances team member engagement, and drives collective success.

Inspirational Motivation

Inspirational motivation is a key aspect of transformational leadership, whereby the leader effectively communicates their determination to achieve the organization's purpose and inspires team members to increase their enthusiasm and make their work more meaningful and fulfilling (Saboe et al., 2015). Building strong interpersonal relationships and showing appreciation towards team members is also crucial. Transformational leaders are known for their ability to inspire and motivate team members within the organization. They align tasks with the interests, preferences, and capabilities of individuals, fostering team spirit and cooperation within the institution (Cahyono et al., 2020).

The leader's ability to inspire and motivate team members has a profound impact, creating a sense of unity and team spirit. Moreover, perceiving the leader as a role model and a source of inspiration is a powerful motivational tool for team members. The leader's role as a model, shaped by their inspirational motivation, becomes a source of spiritual strength. By clearly articulating the organization's vision, identifying the needs of both team members and the organization, and establishing a common purpose, the leader instills confidence in team members and fosters a shared sense of purpose (Djourova et al., 2020). The transformational leader's ability to inspire, motivate, and create a sense of purpose among team members is instrumental in fostering a positive and driven organizational culture, leading to higher levels of engagement and performance.

Intellectual Stimulation

The transformational leader fosters an encouraging and motivating attitude towards innovation and creativity. They consistently guide their staff to approach problem-solving with innovative and creative methods rather than relying on traditional approaches. By creating awareness around the challenges faced, the leader encourages their employees to creatively tackle these problems. This approach empowers team members to follow their leader's lead, drawing inspiration and courage from them, and developing a strong belief in striving for the organization's goals. The leader aims to bring fresh perspectives to their team members, enabling them to offer new and creative solutions to previously encountered issues within the institution (Rafferty & Griffin, 2004).

In the intellectual dimension, the transformational leader adopts an encouraging, innovative, and creative approach that aligns with the capabilities of their subordinates. This type of leader encourages employees who embrace innovation over adhering to outdated methods to showcase their talents. They strive to create an organizational climate that fosters a culture of questioning dynamic events and allows for free expression. The transformational leader establishes an organizational spirit that encourages subordinates to question assumptions, think critically, and demonstrate their distinctiveness in problem recognition (Saad Alessa, 2021). By promoting innovation and creativity, the transformational leader stimulates a culture of continuous improvement and openness to new ideas, ultimately driving organizational growth and success.

Individual Interest

Individual attention is a crucial aspect of transformational leadership, where the leader demonstrates a genuine concern for team members. By showing interest in their well-being, the leader ensures that tasks are assigned in accordance with their needs and abilities, enabling the team to progress effectively. This type of leader aims for the success of the organization by providing training and guidance to support the development of individual team members. A good transformational leader is also an astute observer, capable of anticipating the needs, desires, and expectations of team members Rasheed, Shahzad & Nadeem, 2021).

This individual attention should be tailored to each team member, taking into account their personal differences and expectations. The leader recognizes and explores the potential of each team member based on their individual wishes, needs, and interests. By setting individual goals aligned with their potential, the transformational leader turns these individual differences into advantages. They approach each team member as a unique individual and provide personalized support. Individualized support based on individual differences fosters the development of self-confidence (Rafferty & Griffin, 2004).

The transformational leader's ability to understand and empathize with the individual differences of team members is also noteworthy. The individual support and empathetic approach offered by the leader make team members feel valued and cared for. This aspect of transformational leadership creates a work environment where team members can work more comfortably and enhance their personal growth. Moreover, as positive relationships are fostered among employees within this work environment, it leads to positive interpersonal connections among team members (Cahyono et al., 2020). By providing individual attention and cultivating a supportive environment, the transformational leader enhances the well-being, engagement, and professional development of their team members, contributing to overall organizational success.

SCHOOL ADMINISTRATOR AS A TRANSFORMATIONAL LEADER

In today's knowledge-driven era, the importance of change has become evident in various fields. With the easy and rapid access to information and the removal of borders between countries, global standards have become influential. In the context of education, keeping up with the demands of the time requires individuals to have the ability to quickly access information using technology. Consequently, the role of educators and the nature of education itself have transformed. In the current landscape, educators should not simply impart information, but rather possess a deep understanding of the subject matter, guide learners to access information, and help them navigate the intricate details of knowledge (Abd Ali & Kazim, 2023).

Management has been defined in various ways, with social sciences providing valuable insights into educational leadership. Effective management in education is characterized by the ability to efficiently handle learning resources, prioritize instructional leadership, foster a safe and supportive environment, and manage change in a sustainable manner. These expressions reflect the evaluation of managers' performance based on idealized concepts within specific conditions (Leithwood & Jantzi, 2005). In essence, effective educational management involves skillfully navigating the complexities of educational institutions, creating an environment conducive to learning, and ensuring the continuous improvement and success of the educational process.

The changes in education have had a significant impact on educational administration, necessitating a shift away from traditional approaches towards more structured and factual components. The hierarchical management structure that traditionally governed the relationship between teachers and students is no longer sufficient to meet the needs of today. School organizations now view contemporary management approaches as instrumental in driving transformation. Educational managers are no longer passive followers of events but proactive individuals who anticipate and prepare for future developments, driving innovation. The contemporary educational management approach perceives schools as dynamic and evolving organizations, with principals serving as transformational leaders. Recent research has focused on exploring transformational leadership within school settings (Leithwood & Jantzi, 2005).

School administrators play a crucial role in driving change within their schools, and this is best achieved through the adoption of a transformational leadership approach. Transformational leaders are characterized by their optimism, strategic thinking, and high energy levels. They empower individuals to redefine their mission and vision, restructure their responsibilities, and create new systems aligned with their goals. Without transformational leadership, a school becomes a ship without sails, lacking direction in its journey. The task of a transformational leader is to strive for comprehensive knowledge about all aspects of the school, from students to staff to the wider community. While research on transformational leadership initially emerged in non-educational contexts, notable authors such as Sergiovanni and Leithwood have contributed extensively to the field of transformational leadership in education (Wilmore & Thomas, 2001).

Sergiovanni's Transformational Leadership Theory

Sergiovanni has made important contributions to the development of transformational leadership in education. He presented five alternative dimensions of transformational leadership in his school studies (Sergiovanni, 1992);

1- Technical leadership,
2- Human leadership,
3- Educational leadership,
4- Symbolic leadership,
5- Cultural leadership.

According to Sergiovanni, while the technical, human, and educational dimensions of leadership are essential for the effectiveness of a school, it is the symbolic and cultural dimensions that add value and elevate schools beyond mere expertise and effectiveness. In Sergiovanni's research, Valli's concept of purposive idea work takes center stage. This concept emphasizes the need for leaders and those around them to collaborate in order to achieve what works best for their shared purposes. Through the use of symbolic and cultural dimensions, what Sergiovanni refers to as "planning" is accomplished. Sergiovanni differentiates transformational leadership from educational leadership primarily because symbolic and cultural leadership involves the development of a shared vision (Allen, Grigsby & Peters, 2015).

Leithwood's Transformational Leadership Theory

Transformational leadership plays a crucial role in enabling employees to redefine their mission and vision, as well as restructuring systems to achieve organizational goals (Leithwood, 1992). Leithwood conducted research to explore the transformational leadership behaviors of school administrators and their impact on school restructuring. The study investigated how school and teacher variables interacted with the transformational leadership behaviors of administrators. Furthermore, the research examined how the inclination towards systematic change in schools and the professionalism in teaching have undergone transformations (Leithwood, 1994). The findings shed light on the importance of transformational leadership in driving meaningful change within educational settings and adapting to evolving contexts.

According to Leithwood's research (1992), transformational leaders in educational organizations have three primary goals:

Fostering a participatory and professional school culture: Transformational leaders strive to assist those who carry out the work in developing a participatory and professional school culture. They achieve this by actively monitoring educational and management practices within the school, encouraging open expression of ideas, constructive criticism, and collaborative planning. Transformational leaders create a foundation for cultural changes by leveraging bureaucratic structures, sharing leadership responsibilities with stakeholders, and effectively communicating the school's values and beliefs to all members.

Encouraging teacher development: Transformational leaders prioritize the growth and development of teachers. Leithwood's research suggests that when teachers embrace the goals necessary for their professional development, their motivation levels increase. Transformational leaders play a vital role in providing support, resources, and opportunities for teachers to enhance their skills, knowledge, and effectiveness in the classroom.

Facilitating effective problem-solving among teachers: Transformational leadership in educational organizations empowers teachers to tackle new challenges and exert greater effort. Through their leadership practices, transformational leaders engage and involve teachers in problem-solving activities, enabling them to implement intelligent and rational solutions. This approach harnesses the collective wisdom and expertise of teachers, fostering a sense of ownership and commitment to improving instructional practices and student outcomes.

Leithwood identified six dimensions of the transformational leadership approach in the field of educational administration (Leithwood, 1994);

1. Setting and developing a vision: The leader tries to set and implement his vision and influence those who do the work in the school so that the school can gain a new perspective.
2. Strengthening acceptance of group goals: The leader encourages teachers to cooperate towards their goals.
3. Providing individual support: The leader is respectful to the teachers and deals with the emotional aspects and needs of the teachers.
4. Intellectual stimulation: The leader enables those doing the work to re-experience their work-related thinking. He also provides performance enhancing ideas.
5. Creating a behavior model: The leader creates an exemplary behavior model by ensuring that the core values are accepted by those who do the work.
6. High performance expectation: The leader exhibits behaviors that will meet the expectations of those who do the job in terms of quality, competence, and high-level performance.

METHODOLOGY

The primary objective of this research is to identify and assess the characteristics of transformative leadership in educational institutions. To achieve this, a literature review was conducted, and interviews were carried out with five school principals.

The obtained criteria will be prioritized through the application of the Analytic Hierarchy Process (AHP) method. The AHP method, developed by Saaty in the 1970s, allows for hierarchical modeling and enables the scoring of criteria based on their significance levels as determined by the sector representatives interviewed.

AHP Method (Analytic Hierarchy Process)

AHP is a basic approach that is frequently used in decision making, proposed by Thomas L.Saaty (1980) in the 1970s. It is designed to choose the most accurate and best one among multiple alternatives that are compared with each other according to different criteria. In short, the AHP technique is a method that reduces difficult and complex decision problems to pairwise comparison matrices and tries to reach a solution from there. AHP is one of the most preferred very useful techniques for decision making. By hierarchically structuring people's mindsets and ideas, they compare similar pairs according to a certain common feature and judge the intensity of importance of one factor relative to another (Saaty and Hu, 1998).Since AHP does not only reach a solution with numerical factors, but also includes subjective factors in the system, it is considered an improvement over other decision-making method.

AHP has a systematic infrastructure and by applying this infrastructure to every problem, the solution is easily reached. The steps of the AHP method are as follows (Saaty and Hu, 1998).

Step 1: The main target, criteria and alternatives are determined.

First, the problem to be solved must be defined and it is determined whether it can be solved mathematically with AHP. Then, the goal to be achieved in the solution of the problem is determined and the criteria to reach this goal are found. Finally, our problem becomes solvable with AHP by identifying alternatives whose criteria we will compare with each other.

Step 2: Creating the hierarchy structure.

The AHP system consists of a 3-level hierarchy. While the top step of the hierarchy indicates the target to be achieved, the 3rd level indicates the alternatives that can be selected to reach the target, and the 2nd level indicates the criteria by which the alternatives will be compared with each other.

Step 3: Pairwise Comparison of Criteria

The criteria that are planned to be used in the solution are compared with each other in pairs and their importance levels are determined according to each other. While making this comparison, the comparison scale developed by Saaty is used.

Table 2. Pair-wise comparison scale for AHP preferences

Numerical Rating	Verbal Judgements of Preferences
9	Extremely preferred
8	Very strongly to extremely
7	Very strongly preferred
6	Strongly to very strongly
5	Strongly preferred
4	Moderately to strongly
3	Moderatey preferred
2	Equally to moderately

How important is which of the two criteria over the other? By answering the question, a pairwise comparison matrix is created.

Step 4: Normalizing the Pairwise Comparison Matrix

To normalize the matrix, each column is summed up and each row of the matrix is divided by the total in the column where it is located, and normalization is performed.

Step 5: Calculation of Criterion Weights

To find the weight of each criterion, the weighting process is completed by taking the average of each row in the normalized matrix.

Step 6: Calculating Consistency

After the actions taken, the consistency of the matrix is checked to determine whether the decision makers exhibit consistent behavior. For a matrix to be considered consistent, the consistency value must be less than 10%. The consistency calculation is done with the following steps.

1. The pairwise comparison matrix is multiplied by the weighted eigenvector matrix and then each value is divided by the corresponding eigenvector.
2. The average of each value obtained in the first line is taken and this maximum eigenvalue is expressed as λmax.
3. 3. The consistency ratio calculation is performed in 2 stages. First, the consistency index (CI) is calculated.

$$CI = \frac{\lambda max - n}{n - 1}$$

4. After calculating the consistency index, the Random Consistency Index (RI) is calculated.

Table 3. Average random consistency

Size of Matrix	1	2	3	4	5	6	7	8	9	10
Random consistency	0	0	0.58	0.9	1.12	1.24	1.32	1.41	1.45	1.49

Source: Saaty, T. L. (1990). An exposition of the AHP in reply to the paper "remarks on the analytic hierarchy process". Management science, 36(3), 259-268.

Consistency rate is calculated with below formula.
Equation 1: Consistency rate

Consistency Rate = (CI / RI)

The result is expected to be less than 0.1. If it is lower than this rate, the result is considered consistent, if it is higher, the result is considered inconsistent.

RESULTS AND DISCUSSIONS

The study aims to identify the qualities of a transformative leader employed in educational institutions. To achieve this, five executives were interviewed within the scope of the study. The questions posed to the interviewees focused on their demographic information and included inquiries about their characteristics and experiences as transformational leaders in the educational field. A selection of their responses is provided below.

Interviewee: A transformative leader in educational institutions possesses several key characteristics that contribute to their ability to drive meaningful change. These characteristics include:

Visionary: A transformative leader has a clear and compelling vision for the future of the educational institution. They inspire others with this vision and work towards aligning their actions and decisions with it. An exemplary transformative leader in education is someone like Dr. Martin Luther King Jr., who had a powerful vision of equality and justice in education, and dedicated his efforts to realize that vision.

Inspirational and Motivational: Transformative leaders have the ability to inspire and motivate their team members. They create a positive and supportive environment that encourages creativity, innovation, and growth. A transformative leader can inspire and motivate teachers by recognizing and appreciating their hard work, providing professional development opportunities, and fostering a sense of purpose and meaning in their work.

Empathetic and Collaborative: Transformative leaders prioritize building strong relationships and understanding the needs and perspectives of their team members. They value collaboration and actively involve others in decision-making processes. A transformative leader in education listens attentively to the concerns and ideas of teachers, students, and parents, and collaboratively develops solutions to address challenges and improve the learning experience.

Change Agent: Transformative leaders embrace change and actively seek out opportunities for improvement and innovation. They are comfortable with taking risks and are open to new ideas and approaches. A transformative leader implements changes in curriculum and teaching methods to promote student-centered learning and prepare students for the demands of the 21st century.

Continuous Learner: Transformative leaders are committed to personal and professional growth. They value learning and encourage a culture of continuous improvement among their team members. A transformative leader in education engages in ongoing professional development, stays updated with current research and best practices, and encourages teachers to pursue professional growth opportunities.

Interviewer: How do these traits contribute to change management?

Interviewee: Each of these traits plays a significant role in change management within educational institutions.

Visionary leaders provide a clear direction and inspire others to embrace change by painting a compelling picture of the future. Inspirational and motivational leaders create enthusiasm and drive among team members, making them more open and receptive to change. Empathetic and collaborative leaders build trust and strong relationships, fostering a sense of ownership and commitment to change initiatives. Change agents embrace innovation and drive the adoption of new practices, helping to overcome resistance to change. Continuous learners are adaptable and open to new ideas, which allows them to lead by example and inspire others to embrace a culture of continuous improvement. Collectively, these traits contribute to effective change management by creating an environment that promotes collaboration, innovation, and a shared sense of purpose and ownership among all stakeholders.

Interviewer: Can you rank these traits in order of importance for a transformative leader in educational institutions?

Interviewee: While all of these traits are important for a transformative leader in educational institutions, it's challenging to rank them in a strict order of importance. The effectiveness of a leader in driving change depends on a combination of these characteristics and their ability to adapt them to the unique needs and context of their educational institution. However, I would say that having a clear vision and the ability to inspire and motivate others are fundamental traits that provide the foundation for effective change leadership. Empathy, collaboration, and a commitment to continuous learning also play pivotal roles in facilitating successful change initiatives.

Taking into consideration both interviews and studies in the literature in the same field, criteria set has been formed as follows:

1. Having charisma
2. Being open to change and technological developments.
3. Providing individual support to the team
4. Creating a behavior model
5. Setting and developing a vision

After the criteria has been determined, 3 of the interviewees have been asked to make pairwise comparisons using Saaty's 1-9 scale in line with their own knowledge and experience. Pairwise comparison matrices have been found by taking the geometric averages of the answers given by the participants. These matrices reflect the consensus of experts. In the application, a four-level AHP model has been created. After the importance levels of the criteria have been obtained, the consistency levels have been measured by using randomness indicators. The table containing the importance levels, consistency levels of the criteria of the study and the final ranking of the criteria is given below.

Table 4. Final ranking of criteria

Criteria	Weights
Setting and developing a vision	0,4821
Being open to change and technological developments	0,1644
Providing individual support to the team	0,1412
Creating a behavior model	0,1310
Having charisma	0,0663

Consistency rate is 0,02839449 which is below 0.1. It suggests that the result is consistent.

CONCLUSION

In today's rapidly changing world, organizations must adapt and innovate in order to thrive. The leadership style within an organization plays a crucial role in managing organizational changes and transformations. Transformational leadership is particularly important in driving positive change within an organization. Transformational leaders embrace the organization's vision and inspire members to work towards a common goal (Mızrak, 2021).

Educational institutions, in particular, need to be open to transformation and change in order to stay relevant. Failure to adapt and renew can lead to the demise of an organization. Leaders have a significant responsibility in motivating employees, improving organizational effectiveness, and fostering a culture of change and development. Transformational leaders harness the power of organizational members by prioritizing the organization's interests. They use their persuasive abilities to encourage voluntary participation and shape the vision and mission of the organization.

This study aims to explore the traits of a transformational leader in educational institutions. By conducting a thorough literature review and interviewing five executives from educational institutions, five criteria have been identified. These criteria include having charisma, being open to change and technological developments, providing individual support to the team, creating a behavior model, and setting and developing a vision. The Analytic Hierarchy Process (AHP) method was used to weigh these criteria based on their importance.

The findings reveal that the most important characteristic of transformational leadership is "Setting and developing a vision (0.4821)," indicating that the leader strives to establish and implement their vision, influencing those within the organization to adopt a new perspective. This is followed by the criteria of "Being open to change and technological developments (0.1644)," "Providing individual support to the team (0.1412)," "Creating a behavior model (0.1310)," and "Having charisma (0.0663)."

The integration of interviews with executives and the use of multi-criteria decision-making techniques facilitate quantitative evaluations of both subjective and objective criteria. The research findings are expected to guide educational institutions, particularly in light of the changes brought about by the pandemic. Additionally, the determined criteria in order of importance can aid in the selection process for senior managers in relevant enterprises. Future studies may further analyze and compare the relationships between these criteria using different multi-criteria techniques

REFERENCES

Abd Ali, A. J., & Kazim, K. A. H. (2023). The relationship between transformational leadership and intellectual fluency among secondary school principals in the Babylonian Directorate of Education. *Journal of Humanities and Social Sciences Research*, 2(1).

Afsar, B., Masood, M., & Umrani, W. A. (2019). The role of job crafting and knowledge sharing on the effect of transformational leadership on innovative work behavior. *Personnel Review*, 48(5), 1186–1208. doi:10.1108/PR-04-2018-0133

Al-Alawi, A. I., Abdulmohsen, M., Al-Malki, F. M., & Mehrotra, A. (2019). Investigating the barriers to change management in public sector educational institutions. *International Journal of Educational Management, 33*(1), 112–148. doi:10.1108/IJEM-03-2018-0115

Allen, N., Grigsby, B., & Peters, M. L. (2015). Does leadership matter? Examining the relationship among transformational leadership, school climate, and student achievement. *The International Journal of Educational Leadership Preparation, 10*(2), 1–22.

Amor, A. M., Vázquez, J. P. A., & Faíña, J. A. (2020). Transformational leadership and work engagement: Exploring the mediating role of structural empowerment. *European Management Journal, 38*(1), 169–178. doi:10.1016/j.emj.2019.06.007

Antonopoulou, H., Halkiopoulos, C., Barlou, O., & Beligiannis, G. N. (2021). Transformational leadership and digital skills in higher education institutes: during the COVID-19 pandemic. *Emerging science journal, 5*(1), 1-15.

Asbari, M. (2020). Is transformational leadership suitable for future organizational needs? *International Journal of Social. Policy and Law, 1*(1), 51–55.

Bailey, J., & Axelrod, R. H. (2001). Leadership lessons from Mount Rushmore: An interview with James MacGregor Burns. *The Leadership Quarterly, 12*(1), 113–121. doi:10.1016/S1048-9843(01)00066-2

Bakker, A. B., Hetland, J., Olsen, O. K., & Espevik, R. (2022). Daily transformational leadership: A source of inspiration for follower performance? *European Management Journal*. Advance online publication. doi:10.1016/j.emj.2022.04.004

Banks, G. C., Dionne, S. D., Mast, M. S., & Sayama, H. (2022). Leadership in the digital era: A review of who, what, when, where, and why. *The Leadership Quarterly, 33*(5), 101634. doi:10.1016/j.leaqua.2022.101634

Barling, J., Slater, F., & Kelloway, E. K. (2000). Transformational leadership and emotional intelligence: An exploratory study. *Leadership and Organization Development Journal, 21*(3), 157–161. doi:10.1108/01437730010325040

Bass, B. M. (1997). Does the transactional–transformational leadership paradigm transcend organizational and national boundaries? *The American Psychologist, 52*(2), 130–139. doi:10.1037/0003-066X.52.2.130

Bass, B. M., & Avolio, B. J. (1990). Developing transformational leadership: 1992 and beyond. *Journal of European Industrial Training, 14*(5). Advance online publication. doi:10.1108/03090599010135122

Baykal, E. (2020). A Model on Authentic Leadership in The Light Of Hope Theory. *Sosyal Bilimler Arastirmalari Dergisi, 10*(3).

Benmira, S., & Agboola, M. (2021). Evolution of leadership theory. *BMJ Leader*.

Bertocci, D. I. (2009). *Leadership in organizations: There is a difference between leaders and managers*. University Press of America.

Brazill, S., & Ruff, W. (2022). Using Transformational Leadership to Create Brave Space in Teaching Multicultural Education. *International Journal of Multicultural Education, 24*(2), 114–131. doi:10.18251/ijme.v24i2.2847

Cahyono, Y., Novitasari, D., Sihotang, M., Aman, M., Fahlevi, M., Nadeak, M., ... Purwanto, A. (2020). The effect of transformational leadership dimensions on job satisfaction and organizational commitment: Case studies in private university Lecturers. *Solid State Technology, 63*(1s), 158–184.

Cortellazzo, L., Bruni, E., & Zampieri, R. (2019). The role of leadership in a digitalized world: A review. *Frontiers in Psychology, 10*, 1938. doi:10.3389/fpsyg.2019.01938 PMID:31507494

Djourova, N. P., Rodríguez Molina, I., Tordera Santamatilde, N., & Abate, G. (2020). Self-efficacy and resilience: Mediating mechanisms in the relationship between the transformational leadership dimensions and well-being. *Journal of Leadership & Organizational Studies, 27*(3), 256–270. doi:10.1177/1548051819849002

Dumitru, A., Motoi, A. G., & Budica, A. B. (2015). What kind of leader is a manager? *Annals of the University of Craiova for Journalism. Communications Management, 1*, 50–60.

Fischer, T., & Sitkin, S. B. (2023). Leadership styles: A comprehensive assessment and way forward. *The Academy of Management Annals, 17*(1), 331–372. doi:10.5465/annals.2020.0340

Fries, A., Kammerlander, N., & Leitterstorf, M. (2021). Leadership styles and leadership behaviors in family firms: A systematic literature review. *Journal of Family Business Strategy, 12*(1), 100374. doi:10.1016/j.jfbs.2020.100374

Ghavifekr, S., & Fung, H. Y. (2021). Change management in digital environment amid the Covid-19 pandemic: a scenario from Malaysian higher education institutions. *Pandemic, Lockdown, and Digital Transformation: Challenges and Opportunities for Public Administration, NGOs, and Businesses*, 129-158.

Gigliotti, R. A. (2019). Crisis leadership in higher education. In *Crisis Leadership in Higher Education*. Rutgers University Press.

Goethals, G. R., & Allison, S. T. (2016). Transforming motives and mentors: The heroic leadership of James MacGregor Burns. In Politics, Ethics and Change (pp. 59-73). Edward Elgar Publishing.

Hay, I. (2006). Transformational leadership: Characteristics and criticisms. *E-journal of Organizational Learning and Leadership, 5*(2).

Kane, G. C., Phillips, A. N., Copulsky, J., & Andrus, G. (2019). How digital leadership is (n't) different. *MIT Sloan Management Review, 60*(3), 34–39.

Keller, R. T. (1992). Transformational leadership and the performance of research and development project groups. *Journal of Management, 18*(3), 489–501. doi:10.1177/014920639201800304

Kotterman, J. (2006). Leadership versus management: what's the difference?. *The Journal for Quality and Participation, 29*(2), 13. leadership, *31*, 43.

Leithwood, K. (1992). *Transformational Leadership and School Restructuring*.

Leithwood, K. (1994). Leadership for school restructuring. *Educational Administration Quarterly*, *30*(4), 498–518. doi:10.1177/0013161X94030004006

Leithwood, K., Harris, A., & Hopkins, D. (2020). Seven strong claims about successful school leadership revisited. *School Leadership & Management*, *40*(1), 5–22. doi:10.1080/13632434.2019.1596077

Leithwood, K., & Jantzi, D. (2005). Transformational leadership. *The essentials of school leadership*, *31*, 43.Perrin, C. (2010). Leader vs. Manager: What's the Distinction? *Catalyst*, *21519390*(39), 2.

Mizrak, K. C. (2021). A Research on Effect of Performance Evaluation and Efficiency on Work Life. In Management Strategies to Survive in a Competitive Environment: How to Improve Company Performance (pp. 387-400). Springer International Publishing.

Purwanto, A., Purba, J. T., Bernarto, I., & Sijabat, R. (2021). Effect of transformational leadership, job satisfaction, and organizational commitments on organizational citizenship behavior. *Inovbiz: Jurnal Inovasi Bisnis*, *9*(1), 61–69. doi:10.35314/inovbiz.v9i1.1801

Rafferty, A. E., & Griffin, M. A. (2004). Dimensions of transformational leadership: Conceptual and empirical extensions. *The Leadership Quarterly*, *15*(3), 329–354. doi:10.1016/j.leaqua.2004.02.009

Rasheed, M. A., Shahzad, K., & Nadeem, S. (2021). Transformational leadership and employee voice for product and process innovation in SMEs. *Innovation & Management Review*, *18*(1), 69–89. doi:10.1108/INMR-01-2020-0007

Ruggieri, S. (2009). Leadership in virtual teams: A comparison of transformational and transactional leaders. *Social Behavior and Personality*, *37*(8), 1017–1021. doi:10.2224bp.2009.37.8.1017

Saad Alessa, G. (2021). The dimensions of transformational leadership and its organizational effects in public universities in Saudi Arabia: A systematic review. *Frontiers in Psychology*, *12*, 682092. doi:10.3389/fpsyg.2021.682092 PMID:34867578

Saaty, T. L. (1990). An exposition of the AHP in reply to the paper "remarks on the analytic hierarchy process". *Management Science*, *36*(3), 259–268. doi:10.1287/mnsc.36.3.259

Saaty, T. L., & Hu, G. (1998). Ranking by eigenvector versus other methods in the analytic hierarchy process. *Applied Mathematics Letters*, *11*(4), 121–125. doi:10.1016/S0893-9659(98)00068-8

Saboe, K. N., Taing, M. U., Way, J. D., & Johnson, R. E. (2015). Examining the unique mediators that underlie the effects of different dimensions of transformational leadership. *Journal of Leadership & Organizational Studies*, *22*(2), 175–186. doi:10.1177/1548051814561028

Sadeghi, A., & Pihie, Z. A. L. (2012). Transformational leadership and its predictive effects on leadership effectiveness. *International Journal of Business and Social Science*, *3*(7).

Samimi, M., Cortes, A. F., Anderson, M. H., & Herrmann, P. (2022). What is strategic leadership? Developing a framework for future research. *The Leadership Quarterly*, *33*(3), 101353. doi:10.1016/j.leaqua.2019.101353

Sergiovanni, T. J. (1992). Reflections on administrative theory and practice in schools. *Educational Administration Quarterly*, *28*(3), 304–313. doi:10.1177/0013161X92028003004

Stone, A. G., & Patterson, K. (2023). The history of leadership focus. *Springer Books*, 689-715.

Supermane, S. (2019). Transformational leadership and innovation in teaching and learning activities: The mediation effect of knowledge management. *Information Discovery and Delivery*, *47*(4), 242–250. doi:10.1108/IDD-05-2019-0040

Turk, A., Cevher, M. F., & Mizrak, K. C. (2021). The effect of informal relations and executive support on organizational commitment in the aviation cector. International Journal of Innovative Science and Research Technology, 6(2), pp. 243-253.

Türk, A., & Mızrak, K. C. (2021). Bibliometric analysis of research in the field of organizational communication in the web of science database. Business & Management Studies: An International Journal, 9(3), pp. 1173-1185.

Wilmore, E., & Thomas, C. (2001). The new century: Is it too late for transformational leadership? *Educational Horizons*, *79*(3), 115–123.

Yammarino, F. J., & Bass, B. M. (1990). Transformational leadership and multiple levels of analysis. *Human Relations*, *43*(10), 975–995. doi:10.1177/001872679004301003

Zamani, R., Lari Dashtbayaz, M., & Hesarzadeh, R. (2023). Transformational leadership of audit managers and supervisors on the quality of team interactions of independent auditors. *Majallah-i Danish-i Isabdari*.

Chapter 5
Learning Agility of Leaders in the Context of Sustainable Organizations:
A Conceptual Evaluation

Didem Öztürk Çiftci
Ordu University, Turkey

ABSTRACT

In recent years, developments such as economic crises, the COVID-19 pandemic, and digitalization that require quick and effective responses have increasingly challenged businesses in terms of achieving all dimensions of sustainability. Considering this situation, leaders with learning agility are crucial in creating sustainable organizations due to the qualities they possess. This kind of leader becomes more equipped to navigate changes in the work environment, prepare and adapt their organizations to environmental changes by learning continuously. In this research, sustainable organizations are modeled not only as structures that respect ecological living but also as structures that can sustainably strengthen many internal and external factors while achieving this. The main problem of the research is to identify how the characteristics of leaders with learning agility align with the elements of sustainable organizations. Therefore, the study aims to establish theoretical correlations between these leadership characteristics and sustainable organizational elements.

INTRODUCTION

Leadership in the 21st century is becoming much more competitive, dynamic, and challenging than in the past due to the radical changes brought about by the revolutions in many areas, and it is becoming more complicated day by day due to the increasing speed of change (Swisher, 2013). Today's organizations prioritize learning agility to survive in uncertain and complex environments, as it is a concept that encompasses critical capabilities in coping with unexpected changes and makes it necessary in business environments (Lee & Song, 2020). From this point of view, it is an undeniable reality that the concept

DOI: 10.4018/979-8-3693-1380-0.ch005

of leadership will increasingly have more agile and dynamic characteristics requirements today and in the future. Human resources practitioners consider learning agility one of the most challenging and rare competencies (Wilson & Breault, 2018). This is because learning through experience is accepted as an important way to increase competitiveness in highly uncertain business environments (Corporate Leadership Council, 2005). Leaders who can adapt to change, motivate their team to innovate, and have the power to initiate organizational change will be managing the successful businesses of the future. It will be possible for a leader to initiate and sustain the change mentioned above and transformation by having a learning dynamism and being open to continuous development.

Today, where change and transformation are an important part of all vital processes, it would not be wrong to state that the sustainability of organizations will be in parallel with the ability to understand, adapt and realize the change in question.

Forming and implementing organizational policies in the direction of sustainability requires that the leader's perspective has the quality and desire to realize this harmony. Leadership is also important in effectively forming policies to internalize sustainability as an organizational culture. Competencies such as flexibly applying the knowledge and skills gained through dynamic learning, reflection, and feedback to address the problems brought about by learning agility, resulting from rapid change and unpredictable environments, and performing tasks based on personal experience will ensure that decision-making mechanisms are realized in a way that will benefit the organization in any case. Proactive initiatives for sustainable corporate practices will be possible with talent and leadership that are aware of the motivation to form value through sustainability (Vargas-Hernández, 2021). This is because the leader is responsible for using his/her knowledge and skills to form a sustainable organization, researching new environmental developments, recruiting the right talents for the adoption and development of the sustainability approach, using resources efficiently, and forming organizational systems for sustainable development (Vargas-Hernández, 2021).

By continuously learning and adapting, leaders with learning agility become better equipped to manage and respond to changes in the business environment. This will contribute to developing a continuous learning culture within the organization and forming a more harmonious and agile workforce, as well as ensuring the longevity and durability of the organization. As a result, leaders with learning agility help form a sustainable organization that can overcome changes and challenges over time. At this point, it is noteworthy that a leader with learning agility is open to learning and development, has made it a lifestyle, and his/her competencies and characteristics are compatible with the sustainability approach.

In light of all the explanations, the book chapter is aimed to form the theoretical infrastructure of the proposition that designing sustainable organizations against the high competition of the 21st century may be possible with leaders with agile learning competence. The recommended book chapter will contribute to academic literature in terms of forming a theoretical infrastructure for applied research that will address the relationships between variables in the future. The chapter is also expected to have the potential to be a conceptual guide for businesses that aim to form a sustainable organizational structure and for leaders who want to develop actual practices in this direction. In this context, it is planned to examine the concepts of agile learning and sustainable organization at both the general and sub-dimensions levels and to include sub-topics that will conceptually address the agile learning competencies of leaders and the positions of agile leaders in designing sustainable organizations. In other words, the purpose of this chapter is to demonstrate, through the comprehensive model developed, the alignment between the characteristics of leaders with an agile learning approach, as identified in the literature, and the management of sustainable organizations.

METHODOLOGY

This study is designed as a literature review. A literature review is a research method that involves systematically gathering information from various sources related to the research topic. In this method, the scanning process should aim to access research from different perspectives, ensure the scientific validity of the sources used, and require the researcher to have the knowledge and experience to synthesize different sources. By the mentioned process and criteria, this research attempts to present the variables included in the study and their conceptual relationships through existing studies in the literature. In this context, research studies that form the theoretical foundations of the research variables and reveal the relationships between variables were searched using appropriate keywords. From these, studies included in the book chapter were systematically integrated to answer a new research question and build the theoretical framework.

RESEARCH PROBLEM

This book chapter is prepared based on the issue of what characteristics leaders who will manage sustainable organizations, one of the most important themes of the future, should possess. In addition to the high competition brought by the 21st century, a holistic approach that takes into account environmental and social factors of the changes occurring worldwide is essential for organizations to be sustainable (Dyllick and Hockerts, 2002; Köşker and Gürer, 2020). Therefore, when proposing appropriate leadership characteristics for organizations, the mentioned holistic approach has been taken into consideration.

PURPOSE AND SIGNIFICANCE OF THE RESEARCH

In this context, it is planned to examine the concepts of agile learning and sustainable organization at both the general and sub-dimensions levels and to include sub-topics that will conceptually address the agile learning competencies of leaders and the positions of agile leaders in designing sustainable organizations. The purpose of this chapter is to demonstrate, through the comprehensive model developed, the alignment between the characteristics of leaders with an agile learning approach, as identified in the literature, and the management of sustainable organizations.

In a business world where boundaries disappear in terms of competition and technological advancements swiftly render all assets obsolete, ensuring the sustainability of businesses is becoming increasingly challenging. Therefore, addressing all elements that contribute to making organizations sustainable is of utmost importance. While doing so, the necessity of introducing new model proposals that can adapt to the evolving business landscape at an academic level should not be forgotten. This research is considered important in both proposing a new and holistic model for sustainable organizations and evaluating the leadership factor within this model.

THE CONCEPT OF AGILITY AND ITS HISTORICAL DEVELOPMENT PROCESS

Agility has been defined at its most basic level and mostly in connection with physical activities as the "ability to change direction quickly and accurately" (Bloomfield et al., 1994). Although, in some cases, the concept has been confused with the term "quickness," it is known that the definitions proposed for quickness generally do not include the element of "change of direction." It is also accepted in the literature that quickness is a component of agility (Sheppard & Young, 2006)."

Early studies of agility in social sciences date back to the 1950s, but it gained more attention in the 1990s, particularly after the "Lehigh Report," which included new production strategy ideas (Parsons et al., 1953). By the late 1990s, the concept, which began to be discussed as a managerial approach, started to gain more attention with the publication of the Agile Manifesto in the software industry by 17 people who came together in Utah in 2001 (Singh et al., 2013). The Agile Manifesto, which explains the agile software development philosophy, proposes a new approach based on four key elements. In this context, the manifesto emphasizes individuals and interactions rather than processes and tools, working software rather than comprehensive documentation, customer collaboration rather than contract negotiation, and responding to change rather than following a plan (Öztürk Çiftci, 2021; Beck et al., 2001, Url-1).

The Agile Manifesto has been recognized as a new approach to changing some elements that lead businesses to stagnation and slow movement. In other words, this approach can be expressed as a document proposing redesigning elements such as planning, documentation, and contracts to help the organizations adapt to change and move quickly. The implementation of this transformation is associated with 12 core principles in the manifesto.

These principles are listed below (Beck et al., 2001, Url-1);

- Enabling customer satisfaction through in-time and continuous delivery
  - Utilizing change to the advantage of the customer's competitive advantage in all processes
- Providing information frequently and periodically to the customer
- Facilitating collaboration and interaction
- Ensuring the participation of motivated individuals in the projects and trusting them
- Choosing face-to-face communication for the exchange of information
- Identifying working software as the primary measure of progress in projects
- Focusing on continuous improvement at a steady pace
- Ensuring technical excellence and good design
- Accepting simplicity as a fundamental working principle
- Creating self-organizing teams

The principles mentioned above also form the conceptual framework of the effectiveness that the agile approach will create in the software industry and all work areas and management mechanisms in the following years.

Agility is a concept adapted to the business world before it became popular at the organizational level. The agile approach emerged because traditional methodologies are often too established and slow to respond sufficiently to a changing environment(Erickson, Lyytinen ve Siau, 2005). This approach was initially defined as a new paradigm characterized as "the ability to change the configuration of a system in response to unpredictable changes and unexpected market conditions" in the manufacturing sector (Goldman et al., 1995).

From a business perspective, this definition can be adapted as the ability to succeed in turbulent environmental conditions with high levels of uncertainty (Yauch, 2011). Ganguly et al. (2009) define agility as "the integration of the necessary abilities and knowledge to quickly, efficiently, and accurately adapt to any unexpected or unforeseeable changes in business/customer needs and opportunities without compromising cost or quality."

Ulrich and Yeung (2019) state that it is difficult to make a concrete definition due to the intuitive nature of the agility concept. Therefore, instead of making a precise definition, the authors explained the concept's four basic characteristics and their scopes below.

Creating a future; Agility focuses on shaping new concepts for the future rather than reviewing or updating the past.

Predicting opportunities; Agility emphasizes opportunities more than developments. It also focuses on the ability to make predictions by focusing on what is right rather than wrong.

Being able to adapt quickly; Agility promotes the ability to move quickly or have the necessary motivation to do so when adaptation is required.

Being able to learn continuously; Agility is based on the idea that transforming events and attitudes into sustainable patterns will be achieved through continuous learning.

Ulrich and Yeung (2019) associate adopting and implementing these four elements with achieving agility.

With the adoption and implementation of agility in organizational processes, a new perspective has emerged to evaluate many organizational concepts based on the above-mentioned theoretical framework and fundamental principles.

LEARNING AGILITY AND LEADERSHIP

The historical development of learning agility can be traced back to several leading research studies conducted at the Creative Leadership Center in the late 1980s. These studies conducted interviews with company executives to identify key events that helped develop their leadership skills. The research found that successful leaders tended to have a more diverse range of experiences throughout their careers than unsuccessful ones.

Another finding was that some executives could make the right decisions in similar situations while others could succeed in more diverse situations (McCall and Lombardo, 1983: 30 cited Dai et al., 2013). This suggests the importance of adapting experiences and what is learned from them to new situations.

The term "learning agility," which combines the concepts of learning and agility under a single framework, was first addressed in detail by Lombardo and Eichinger (2000). The authors defined learning agility as the ability and willingness to learn from experiences and then successfully apply that learning in new or first-time situations.

The concept of learning from experience mentioned in the definition can be explained by the learning model proposed by Kolb (1984). In this model, the experiential learning cycle is described as four stages in the dimensions of grasping the experience and transforming the experience. The dimension of grasping the experience is described by options of concrete experience and abstract conceptualization while transforming the experience encompasses reflective observation and active experimentation preferences (Kolb, 2014). Accordingly, concrete experiences form a basis for reflective observation, where these experiences are evaluated internally. In abstract conceptualization, the internalized experiences are broken down into abstract concepts to form a basis for experiences that will be effective in practice (Kolb, 2014; Gencel & Erdoğan, 2022).

Lombardo and Eichinger (2000) suggest that learning agility is divided into four subcategories: "people agility, mental agility, change agility, and results agility." Below is a brief description of the characteristics covered by these four dimensions:

People Agility; This dimension reflects a person's level of skills, such as being happy to work with various people, learning quickly from others, actively exploring for feedback, and being open to new ideas and communication with new people (Saputra et al., 2021). Tripathi, Srivastava, and Sankaran (2020) state that agile individuals can know themselves and cope with difficult situations.

Mental Agility; This dimension of learning agility refers to a person's ability to think quickly when engaging with new ideas and facing complex situations (De Meuse et al., 2011). Mentally agile individuals are those who can think quickly, are open to learning, are willing to accept changes and different perspectives, can find creative and flexible solutions to cope with the challenges they face, do not experience problems in complex situations, can analyze problems and are ready to make connections between different things.

Agility for Change; This dimension refers to an individual's ability to participate in change enthusiastically. It is also related to how comfortable they are with change, how much they are interested in continuous development, and how much they lead change efforts. Individuals with change agility enjoy experimenting, learning new things, and coping with the challenges of sudden change (De Meuse et al., 2011; Tripathi et al., 2020).

Result from Agility; This dimension refers to the ability to achieve good results even in new situations. In addition to being a tremendous driving force for completing tasks (Canaslan & Güçlü, 2020), result agility also includes problem-solving capacity. Individuals with high result agility are relatively comfortable coping with perceived physical and psychological problems. Over time, they explore and expand their comfort zones, becoming confident and comfortable in situations perceived as uncertain (De Meuse, 2017). Individuals with result agility are also very flexible, adaptable to conditions, inspiring those around them to perform beyond the ordinary, and able to achieve goals despite different possibilities (Lombardo & Eichinger, 2000).

Lombardo and Eichinger (2000) added the "Self-awareness" dimension as a separate dimension to the 4-dimensional learning agility structure they created, previously included within each dimension.

Self-awareness; It can be defined as an individual's depth of understanding of their abilities, strengths and weaknesses, biases, and hidden powers, as well as their ability to distinguish between their emotions and excitement when faced with change (De Meuse et al., 2011). Self-aware individuals know their strengths and weaknesses, criticize their performance and actions, and are willing to learn how to improve their work.

The concept of learning agility has been dimensioned by many authors based on different characteristics and defined in the context of these dimensions. Some of these are briefly mentioned below:

Burke et al. (2016) suggested learning agility as a seven-factor structure; feedback seeking, information gathering, performance risk-taking, interpersonal risk-taking, experimenting, collaborating, and reflecting. This structure revealed that individuals with high learning agility are willing to receive feedback on their performance, talk about their mistakes, renew themselves, take risks, and try new things to keep themselves out of their comfort zones and work in collaboration.

On the other hand, De Meuse (2015) evaluates learning agility as a combination of seven different conceptual dimensions. The author lists these dimensions as Cognitive Perspective, Interpersonal Acumen, Change Alacrity, Drive to Excel, Self Insight, Environmental Mindfulness, and Feedback Responsiveness.

Hallenback and Santana (2019) have defined four components or behavioral sets under the headings "search, make sense, internalize, and implement" that describe learning agility. According to the authors, these components of learning agility allow individuals to learn deeply from their experiences and then apply what they have learned to new and challenging situations.

Research and different theoretical approaches regarding the concept highlight that individuals with learning agility are adaptable to innovations, open to change, and aware of their strengths, weaknesses, and environment. In addition, they have strong communication skills and are likely to collaborate, share knowledge, and cope with risky and complex situations.

Preferences in management strategies constitute only one of the steps necessary for the smooth functioning of an organization. More is needed for successful business management. Effective implementation of these defined strategies and policies ensures the level of performance and, subsequently, the organization's overall sustainability. That is why the human factor, particularly in leadership, contributes the most to this within an organization.

The relationship between learning agility and leadership is primarily based on the proposition that learning from life experiences makes leaders' development possible. In recent years, theoretical and empirical research on leadership approaches indicates that future leaders need to have the ability to adapt to change and, above all, learn from experiences and develop their skills to overcome increasingly challenging market conditions, increased speed, and competition (Hezlett & Kuncel, 2012; Swisher, 2013; Latif & Ahmad, 2020). De Meuse (2017) stated in his research that adaptability to change requires finding new ways to cope with unforeseen problems and opportunities. Thus learning agility is considered an indicator of leadership potential.

Agile learning strategies enable employees to focus on continuous learning to understand the challenges of the external environment and respond to cues from the external environment to develop agile core competencies (Ehiorobo, 2020). Nowadays, leadership positions require focusing on personal development and being flexible in their worldview rather than the end performance (Smith, 2015). In addition, the dynamic business environment in recent years requires leaders to think innovatively, take risks, and actively learn from others (even if it does not align with personal preferences or adopted beliefs) (Smith, 2015). These qualities largely align with the fundamental principles of agile learning. In other words, leaders who reflect and internalize the principles of learning agility, defined in the literature and accepted in practice, into their management styles can lead their businesses to succeed in today's conditions.

Mitchinson and Morris (2014) stated that about the changing organizational structures and work styles in the 21st century, leaders need to develop competencies such as adapting to new business strategies in these organizations, creating successful systems in multicultural work environments managing temporary virtual teams, and taking on constantly changing tasks. The authors' research supports that learning agility is a mindset and collection of corresponding practices that allow leaders to continually improve, grow, and equip themselves with new strategies to tackle increasingly complex organizational situations.

The elements mentioned above highlight the importance of learning agility for today's leaders. Therefore, the literature offers different suggestions on how leaders can develop higher levels of learning agility. Some of them are as follows:

Mitchinson and Morris (2014) examined their recommendations for leaders to improve their learning agility under five headings:

Innovation: Making it a habit to try to find new solutions and brainstorm for every problem, even if tried and trusted solutions seem to be available.

Performance: Asking questions to understand, not just to be understood, and listening to what others say. Pausing and thinking about what is truly necessary before speaking when feeling stressed.

Reflection: Identifying trustworthy people to receive feedback and encouraging them to provide impartial feedback.

Risk-Taking: Taking on new challenges by stepping out of one's comfort zone. Overcoming new challenges will allow for the development of new skills and perspectives that will become important to future experiences.

Defense: Accepting feedback as a gift and knowing it can teach one what they do not know about themselves, even if it is uncomfortable, always being accepting and kind to the person or people providing feedback.

Mc Cenna and Minaker (2021) acknowledge that learning agility can be developed, but it needs to be approached with a holistic perspective that includes many different elements. In other words, reducing the perspective on learning agility to only developing an agile learner will likely cause one to miss some of the most important aspects of the concept. Agile learning involves not only learning fast but also accurately. In this context, for leaders to develop agile learning, the speed factor and many other factors such as personality, motivation, purpose, other people, experience, and competence must be developed holistically.

Based on the above information, the development of learning agility for leaders can be achieved by creating a holistic structure that includes dimensions of learning and agility actions separately, as well as the mindset they create together, rather than a one-dimensional perspective. In this context, it is important for the leader first to know themselves. Learning through what is taught and loving, willingly, and consciously learning at every moment of life and making it a way of life would be the right approach for developing learning agility.

THE CONCEPT OF SUSTAINABLE ORGANIZATION

The emergence and development of sustainability as a concept is thought to date back to the "Middle Ages." There are even approaches that evaluate the concept as an idea that extends back to ancient Greek mythology, suggesting that it was developed about the people's self-sacrifice to please the goddess of the earth, Gaia (O'Riordan, 1998, p. 31); cited in (Bozlağan, 2005). Over the years, it has been observed that various research fields have contributed to the development of the concept of sustainability independently from each other and have put the concept into a multidimensional perspective.

The concept of sustainability has been discussed and examined from different perspectives and dimensions in literature from its emergence to the present day. In the context of the variables to be examined in this research, the concept of "sustainability" was first used in social sciences by George Ludwig Hartig in 1785 to express that forested areas can only be sustainable if they benefit future generations. By the 1900s, sustainability expanded from environmental to social and economic contexts, changing into a structure emphasizing the complex relationship between economic and social life (Leon, 2013). As a result of these developments, when approached with a holistic perspective, sustainability is defined as "considering the short and long-term environmental, social, and economic effects of institutional decisions and actions" (Kohl, 2016). According to Soubbotina (2004:7-8), sustainability means having the same conditions to meet the rights and needs of different parties. From a commercial perspective, sustainability is defined as the ability to maintain or survive in business (Bıçakçı, 2012).

Organizations that adopt a sustainable approach today and focus on developing strategies in this direction should follow a method that includes environmental or economic issues and social issues such as human rights, law, and freedoms. Corporate, official, academic, and civil society organizations, as well as the United Nations Global Compact (UNGC), the world's largest corporate social responsibility program, propose ten principles that businesses can use to create this approach. These principles cover various topics, including human rights, labor standards, environmental sustainability, and anti-corruption measures.

These principles are as follows:

- Human Rights

One of the most challenging aspects of business sustainability is respect and support for human rights. Traditionally, human rights have been evaluated at the state level and solely through international human rights documents. However, since the announcement of the Guiding Principles on Business and Human Rights by the Human Rights Council in 2011, more companies have been confronted with the idea that they need to address and adopt human rights frameworks in their business operations. This has led to an increasing recognition of the role of businesses in respecting and supporting human rights, beyond just the responsibilities of governments (Gonzalez and Leonard, 2016). According to this;

Businesses should,

Principle 1: Support and respect internationally proclaimed human rights and

Principle 2: Ensure they are not complicit in human rights abuses.

- Labor

Among the ten principles of the UN Global Compact, the principles related to labor are the most prominent. There are ample opportunities for learning, dialogue, and collective action, including partnerships, to complement other approaches aimed at implementing responsible labor practices. This is the contribution that the UN Global Compact seeks to make. Today, the UN Global Compact is the largest corporate citizenship initiative, involving over 6,000 business participants and other stakeholders in more than 130 countries.

In the field of labor standards require efficient, honest, and effective labor inspection and justice systems. The rule of law is crucial to ensuring full respect for the rights of citizens, employers, workers, and their unions in all areas covered by the 10 principles of the United Nations Global Compact (Kell, 2016). According to this;

Businesses should

Principle 3: effectively recognize the freedom of association and the right to collective bargaining,

Principle 4: Eliminate all forms of forced and compulsory labor,

Principle 5: Eliminate child labor in practice,

Principle 6: Eliminate discrimination related to employment and occupation.

- Environment

The UN Global Compact includes three environmental principles that reflect corporate environmental responsibility. These principles are derived from the 1992 Rio Declaration on Environment and Development (Gonzalez and Leonard, 2016). According to this;

Businesses should,

Principle 7: Support a precautionary approach to environmental challenges,

Principle 8: Undertake initiatives to promote greater environmental responsibility, and

Principle 9: Encourage the development and dissemination of environmentally friendly technologies.

- Anti-Corruption

Controlling corruption and establishing sanctions for corrupt practices has traditionally been seen as the domain of public officials. However, in the last decade, civil society (including the private sector) has increased proactive measures to combat corruption. As a result, it was included among the principles in 2004. This principle, referencing the fight against corruption, is based on the United Nations Convention against Corruption (UNCAC), which is the first legally binding international instrument for combating corruption (Gonzalez and Leonard, 2016). According to this;

Businesses should,

Principle 10: Work against all forms of corruption, including extortion and bribery.

The abovementioned principles indicate an organization's roadmap for a sustainable structure. By incorporating these principles into their strategies, policies, and procedures, and by creating a culture of honesty, businesses not only fulfill their fundamental responsibilities to people and the planet but also prepare the groundwork for long-term success (Url-2).

Another perspective on a sustainable organization focuses on the necessary strategies to survive in competition. Based on the understanding that sustainability means continuity, this perspective suggests that organizational sustainability for an organization means having the necessary elements to improve their activities continuously towards a defined, inclusive mission and to progress on behalf of the organization. According to this perspective, organizational sustainability represents an ongoing process rather than a state of excellence, requiring the organization to be economically, morally, and institutionally strong (Coblentz, 2002). The author views corporate sustainability as the body and brain of an organization, financial sustainability as the blood that nourishes it, and ethical sustainability as the sum of these parts. Corporate sustainability is adapting economic, environmental, and social factors to the company's activities and decision-making mechanisms to create long-term and permanent value for all stakeholders in a business (Aras et al., 2018). Economic sustainability refers to the ability of a business to achieve economic growth without harming the social fabric of a community or the environment (Doane & MacGillivray, 2001). The ethical dimension of organizational sustainability is a framework that encompasses all other dimensions. In other words, the organization should maintain ethical and moral standards while fulfilling all dimensions of sustainability.

This study proposes a model as an integrated approach to the sustainable organizational models described above, as shown in Figure 1. This model is based on the organization's sustainability awareness regarding internal and external environmental factors. This framework is created through a comprehensive approach that combines the ten principles of the UNGC, the elements of sustainable organizational perspective by Coblentz (2002), and the social, environmental, and economic sustainability dimensions of the most commonly used form of organizational sustainability concept.

Figure 1. Sustainable organizational model (an integrated approach)
Source: *Prepared by the author, 2023.*

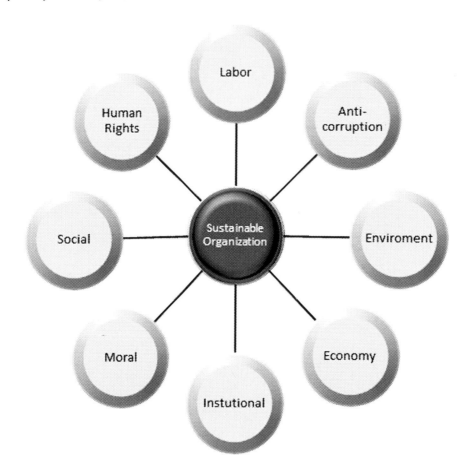

LEADERS WITH LEARNING AGILITY IN MANAGING SUSTAINABLE ORGANIZATIONS

In this study, the sustainable organization philosophy is accepted as an approach that can sustain its existence in the changing business world while protecting the world we live in with all its aspects. In this context, a model has been created that represents the conceptual connection between different sustainability approaches and a leader who can internalize this philosophy and achieve success.

The model is presented in Figure 2.

Figure 2. Model proposal for the role of leaders with learning agility in managing sustainable organizations
Source: *Prepared by the author, 2023.*

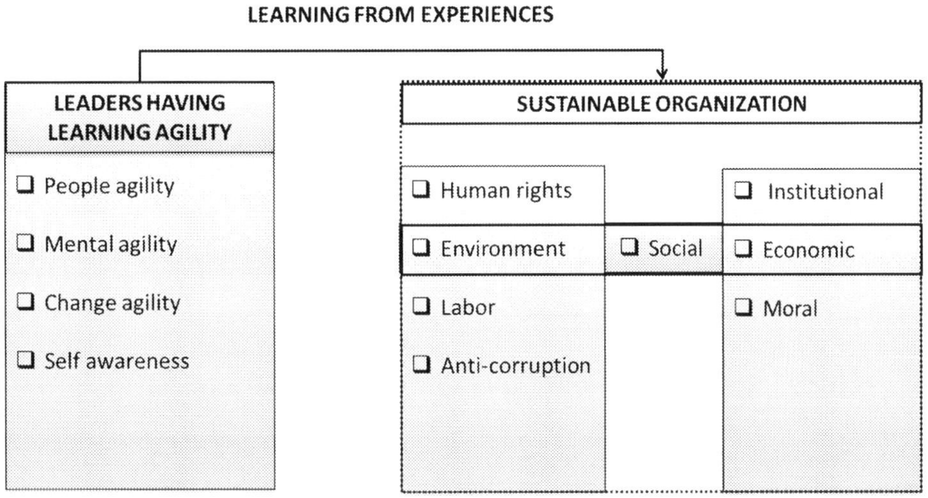

LEARNING FROM EXPERIENCES

LEADERS HAVING LEARNING AGILITY	SUSTAINABLE ORGANIZATION		
❑ People agility	❑ Human rights		❑ Institutional
❑ Mental agility	❑ Environment	❑ Social	❑ Economic
❑ Change agility	❑ Labor		❑ Moral
❑ Self awareness	❑ Anti-corruption		

The model depicted in Figure 2 assumes that a leader with learning agility possesses the five essential qualities proposed by Lombardo and Eichinger (2000) for learning agility. They can also learn from experiences and apply them to their management approach. The model also anticipates that a sustainable organization is sensitive and respectful towards human rights, the rights and freedoms of the workforce, and the environment. It is also an organization that believes in and implements anti-corruption measures while being financially, institutionally, and morally strong.

Human Agility: Human Rights, Workforce, Environment

The human agility dimension of learning agility refers to leaders who enjoy being around people, meeting new people, communicating with those around them, and receiving feedback from others. A leader with these qualities is expected to pioneer the implementation and protection of internationally recognized human rights, both for their colleagues and other stakeholders in the workplace. Based on the same characteristics, this leader is expected to exhibit a supportive and learning-oriented approach in areas such as providing social rights and opportunities for an organization for their employees and improving working conditions. Above all, human agility in the learning dimension will motivate leaders to develop and learn from their experiences regarding all rights and freedoms. A leader with these qualities is also likely to set high standards for respecting human rights within the organization and be willing to develop their employees' awareness. In addition, the comfort and positive perspective brought by human agility regarding receiving feedback from different people also provides the opportunity to quickly become aware of and intervene in any negative situations related to human rights and the rights and freedoms of the workforce in their environment.

It is possible to associate a leader with learning agility with the environmental factor in two ways. Firstly, a leader with human agility can be evaluated as creating a sustainable organization by ensuring the survival of the organization in a highly competitive business environment (Joiner, 2019). In this sense, human agility enables the leader to manage human resources successfully through features such as effective communication and feedback. The other perspective on the environmental factor is to respect our world and the ecological balance and to adapt organizational processes and policies accordingly. Human agility is expected to guide the leader in creating harmony between a sustainable world and an organization.

Mental Agility and Anti Corruption

Especially in today's world, where all processes and operations are rapidly digitized, and technology pervades every stage of business life, the concept of corruption has also changed accordingly. Therefore, the activities within the concept of corruption have adapted to the changing world, and coping with these activities can only be achieved by being aware of environmental changes and transformations. Mental agility gives leaders characteristics such as finding creative solutions quickly and effectively in management processes and listening to and considering others' ideas in seeking solutions. This innovative approach will provide the necessary open-minded and pioneering perspective for digital transformation, enabling the business to keep up with the times (Sağbaş & Erdoğan, 2022; Kazim, 2019). Leaders with mental agility are also expected to contribute to the successful adaptation of the organization to digitalization, controlling the risks created by digitalization (Di Domenico et al., 2014) and thus making the organization stronger against corruption.

Change Agility: Environment, Corporate Sustainability

In today's rapidly changing business world, organizations need leaders who understand and are willing to be a part of external changes (Armanious & Padgett, 2021). Change agility means the leader enthusiastically participates in and even leads change, internalizes everything that comes with the change, and shares it with all levels of the organization to gain general acceptance. In particular, this dimension will contribute to the sustainable leader's ability to implement environmental change and transformation in their organization, even lead the change in their industry, and improve the organization in terms of competition. Organizations that maintain their power by implementing changes against environmental dynamics are more likely to achieve corporate sustainability. An important point to be considered is that the leader's goal should not be to force change upon the entire organization but rather to act as a role model and encourage voluntary participation. It is believed that a leader with learning agility, in addition, to change agility, will contribute to this effect by having the qualities of human agility and mental agility.

Result from Agility: Institutional sustainability, Economic Sustainability

Result agility refers to a leader's ability to solve problems, cope with challenges, and remain resilient in uncertainty. For an organization to achieve financial, institutional, and ethical sustainability, it requires confident, goal-oriented leaders who can keep it stable in a turbulent business world. Furthermore, achieving a business's vision, mission, and goals is important in terms of their impact on economic and institutional sustainability. It is an advantage for businesses to be led by leaders who are not afraid to step out of their comfort zone, are result-oriented, and can perform well in the face of obstacles on the path to achieving their goals.

Self-Awareness and Moral Sustainability

Self-awareness is one of the most significant advantages humans have compared to all other living beings on our planet. As a result of possessing self-awareness, leaders can carry out an introspective evaluation process in which they compare themselves to their own standards/goals to better understand and develop themselves (Rubens et al., 2018). This self-evaluation allows the leader to examine themselves critically and, as a result, attain high standards in terms of values. A leader possessing these traits is expected to be willing and capable of promoting ethical standards within the organization and establishing a sustainable culture. A leader who can achieve this and internalize ethical sustainability at an organizational level can lead their organization out of the narrow frame focused solely on maximizing profit in high competition.

Leaders Learning From Experience and Sustainable Organizations

Learning from experiences, one of the most fundamental characteristics of the definition of learning agility is also thought to contribute to making the organizations that leaders manage sustainably. Studies have shown that what leaders learn from their life experiences (social and work life) is much greater than what they learn from theoretical education such as courses or MBA (Thomas & Cheese, 2005; McCall, 2004). Researchers estimate that more than 70% of all leadership development occurs through informal, on-the-job experiences, while education and other formal programs contribute less than 10% to a leader's development (Robinson & Wick, 1992). However, the importance of education for the concept of leadership should be noticed, and the necessity of education should be remembered in developing skills for interpreting experiences and applying life experiences where and how to apply them.

Leaders who learn from their experiences are those who not only acquire knowledge from their experiences in the workplace but also preserve the experiences they encounter in every aspect of their lives in their mental libraries and use them to develop and deepen their leadership skills. This conclusion is based on the finding that individuals with a strong learning orientation have resilient behavior when faced with difficult situations, encourage the exploration of new solutions, and achieve sustainable, enhanced performance levels (Elliott & Dweck, 1988). Moreover, leaders with these characteristics can make the philosophy of learning from experience a widespread culture throughout the organization through the leader-follower relationship. This assumption is based on the "Social Learning Theory" developed by Bandura (1977). This theory, often used to explain interactions between leaders and followers, suggests that observation and modeling can be effective ways for individuals to acquire specific behavioral patterns.

RESULT

Agility and sustainability are two important philosophies vital for the survival and existence of almost all organizations. The importance of these philosophies stems from the ultimate truth that "Change" is the only constant reality in the world (Fawzy & Saad, 2023). In addition to the environmental dimension, a broader perspective attributed to corporate sustainability has developed regarding the concept of sustainability. This approach assumes that the sustainability of internal and external factors will ultimately affect the organization's continuity, starting from the most basic definition of sustainability as "the continuity of anything" (Colbert & Kurucz, 2007).

Thus, in this research, sustainability and sustainable organizations are approached holistically, including ecological sustainability, human factors, moral values, economic development, and social elements. The integrated approach aims to create organizations that prioritize sustainability, including ecological sustainability, but also embrace an ethical perspective that sees this as a cultural change rather than a mere necessity. When organizations adapt their structures to the integrated sustainability elements, they become stronger in these dimensions and can position themselves better in the rapidly changing business world. Today, businesses have to cope with many complex situations, such as climate change, globalization, demographic changes, social inequality, financial downturns, and corporate ethical scandals that cause a loss of trust in the business world (Wales, 2013). Dealing with the impact of all these compelling factors on businesses will be possible by taking a more comprehensive approach to sustainability and integrating this integrated approach into the strategic processes of organizations. Integrated sustainability requires reconfiguring various aspects of business, such as thinking more holistically, talent, stakeholder relationships, knowledge management, leadership, and culture (Adams et al., 2012).

This is where the concept of leadership comes into play. Leadership is essential in translating sustainability visions into action. Leaders should anticipate and assess long-term sustainability trends, identify new opportunities, and develop strategies to reposition the organization when necessary (Lueneburger & Goleman, 2010, p. 54). Efforts to design sustainable organizations require significant and radical changes such as resource redistribution, alignment of production processes and activities with technology, and employee empowerment. To realize this change, there is a need for a leader and leadership approach that has internalized sustainability (Tüyen, 2020). At this point, it is thought that the assumption that the characteristics of leaders with learning agility are suitable for designing and developing sustainable organizations is worth evaluating. The fact that nearly 25 percent of Fortune 100 companies and nearly 50 percent of Fortune 500 companies use learning agility as a criterion in identifying management candidates can be considered factual data confirming this assumption (Swisher, 2013).

A leader with learning agility also has people agility. In other words, he/she has the potential to adopt the characteristics that will make the organization he/she leads sustainable by communicating with his/her employees, being a role model for them, and, most importantly, being extremely open and supportive in receiving feedback.

A leader with learning agility also has mental agility. In other words, a leader with learning agility has the potential to sustain the organization by being able to find quick and rational solutions in times of crisis caused by the complexity of the external environment and in all kinds of unexpected or sudden changes.

A leader with learning agility also has change agility. In other words, he/she is willing to lead change and learn new things to adapt the organization to the rapidly changing external world. With these characteristics, he/she has the potential to gain an advantage by enabling the organization he/she leads to lead change and transformation in a highly competitive environment and thus make sustainability possible.

A leader with learning agility also has results agility. In other words, it is a leader who is highly motivated to accomplish tasks regardless of the conditions, therefore, determined to overcome the problems encountered on the way to the goal. It does not avoid trying new things and learning to achieve this. With these characteristics, he/she has the potential to lead the organization to the desired point and overcome all obstacles to be encountered in this process.

A leader with learning agility is also known to learn from their experiences. In other words, they make the right inferences from all the positive and negative situations they encounter throughout their lives to apply them in their later versions (De Meuse, 2017). With these characteristics, they can make choices with a low margin of error in formulating strategic policies that will make the organization sustainable and implement them correctly. In this context, Thompson and Cavaleri (2010) argue that organizational sustainability takes place within a complex system and that success requires learning through trial and error and, thus, extensive organizational knowledge.

CONCLUSION

In this book chapter, it has been emphasized that leaders with agile learning will be successful in managing the future's sustainable organizations, thanks to their characteristic features. This assumption has been explained through a model designed based on the alignment of the qualities brought by agile learning to leaders and the characteristics of sustainable organizations. The model developed in the study conceptually demonstrates that leaders with learning agility overlap with the proposed model sub-dimensions for sustainable organizations, as shown in Figure 2.

Therefore, it can be stated that adapting the popular agile approach of the last 20 years to leader-based learning is a key factor for successful organizations in the coming years. In other words, it is expected that this conceptual evaluation will be beneficial in redesigning the learning approach for leaders and positively contributing to organizational management through the adoption of this approach.

LIMITATIONS

The limitations of the study are the problems and challenges that researchers encounter during the research process, which occur beyond their control and may affect the results and interpretations of those results (Price and Murnan, 2004). No matter how well planned or well managed, all studies have limitations (Akanle vd., 2020).

This research has potential limitations, including:

- *Constraints on time and accessibility to scientific sources.* A study conducted within a specific time frame is a snapshot that is dependent on the conditions that occurred during that period (Simon, 2011). Therefore, temporal factors such as the researcher's time constraints and deadlines, as well as the study's specific time frame, are considered limitations.
- *Lack of any application or statistical analysis.* Supporting the constructed theoretical model with quantitative methods will be reinforcing in determining the validity of the model.
- *Lack of multiple perspectives due to having a single researcher.* Crase and Rosato (1992) express that multi-author research can be developed through brainstorming different ideas and multiple perspectives.

RECOMMENDATIONS

Recommendations for Future Research

Based on these limitations, it is recommended to support the approach of sustainable organizations, whose theoretical foundation has been established in this study, being managed by leaders with learning agility through empirical studies. In the future, it is considered important to address the relationship between variables through bibliometric analysis or meta-analysis methods to provide a comprehensive approach.

Recommendations for Practitioners

From the perspective of practitioners, it is suggested (in light of the need for research involving applications) to follow leaders who have internalized learning agility and have embraced the managerial approaches they adopt for adapting sustainability, which is a popular philosophy of our time, to organizations.

In this context, it is recommended that leaders implement practices that ensure not only financial sustainability but also environmental and social sustainability within the framework of the holistic design of sustainable organizations. As theorized by the research, it is anticipated that embracing the philosophy of agile learning, which enables leaders to internalize holistic sustainability, would be beneficial.

Based on the new approach that highlights sustainability cannot be achieved solely through internal business activities, being willing to take on social responsibility in areas that concern society is another suggestion that indicates a paradigm shift in management.

REFERENCES

Adams, R., Jeanrenaud, S., Bessant, J., Overy, P., & Denyer, D. (2012). *Innovating for Sustainability. A Systematic Review of the Body of Knowledge*. Network for Business Sustainability.

Akanle, O., Ademuson, A. O., & Shittu, O. S. (2020). Scope and Limitation of Study in Social Research. In A. S. Jegede & U. C. Isiugo-Abanihe (Eds.), *Contemporary Issues in Social Research* (pp. 105–114). Ibadan University Press.

Aras, G., Tezcan, N., & Furtuna, Ö. K. (2018). Çok boyutlu kurumsal sürdürülebilirlik yaklaşımı ile Türk bankacılık sektörünün değerlemesi: Kamu-Özel banka farklılaşması. *Ege Academic Review*, *18*(1), 47–61. doi:10.21121/eab.2018131895

Armanious, M., & Padgett, J. D. (2021). Agile learning strategies to compete in an uncertain business environment. *Journal of Workplace Learning*, *33*(8), 635–647. doi:10.1108/JWL-11-2020-0181

Bıçakçı, A. B. (2012). Sürdürülebilirlik yönetiminde halkla iliskilerin rolü. *Sosyal ve Beseri Bilimler Dergisi*, *4*(1), 47–56.

Bloomfield, J., Ackland, T. R., & Elliot, B. C. (1994). *Applied anatomy and biomechanics in sport*. Blackwell Scientific.

Bozlağan, R. (2005). Sürdürülebilir gelişme düşüncesinin tarihsel arka planı. *Journal of Social Policy Conferences*, *0*(50), 1011–1028.

Burke, W. W., Roloff, K. S., & Mitchinson, A. (2016). *Learning agility: A new model and measure (Working Paper)*. Teachers College, Columbia University.

Canaslan, A., & Güçlü, N. (2020). Öğretmenlerin öğrenme çevikliği: Ölçek geliştirme çalışması. *Kastamonu Education Journal*, *28*(5), 2071–2083.

Coblentz, J. B. (2002). *Organizational Sustainability: The three aspects that matter*. Academy for Educational Development.

Corporate Leadership Council. (2005). Realizing the Full Potential of Rising Talent: Vol. I. *A Quantitative Analysis of the Identification and Development of High-potential Employees*. Corporate Executive Board.

Crase, D., & Rosato, F. D. (1992). Single versus multiple authorship in professional journals. *Journal of Physical Education, Recreation & Dance, 63*(7), 28–32. doi:10.1080/07303084.1992.10609913

De Meuse, K. P. (2015). Using science to identify future leaders: Part III-The TALENTx7 assessment of learning agility. (Technical Report). Doi doi:10.13140/RG.2.1.4905.7769

De Meuse, K. P. (2017). Learning agility: Its evolution as a psychological construct and empirical relationship to leader success. *Consulting Psychology Journal, 69*(4), 267–295. doi:10.1037/cpb0000100

De Meuse, K. P., Dai, G., Eichinger, R. W., Page, R. C., Clark, L. P., & Zewdie, S. (2011). The development and validation of a self-assessment of learning agility. In *Society for Industrial and Organizational Psychology Conference*. IEEE.

Di Domenico, M., Daniel, E., & Nunan, D. (2014). Mental mobility in the digital age: Entrepreneurs and the online home-based business. *New Technology, Work and Employment, 29*(3), 266–281. doi:10.1111/ntwe.12034

Doane, D., & MacGillivray, A. (2001). Economic sustainability: The business of staying in business. *New Economics Foundation, 1*, 52.

Dyllick, T., & Hockerts, K. (2002). Beyond the Case for Corporate Sustainability. *Business Strategy and the Environment, 11*(2), 130–141. doi:10.1002/bse.323

Ehiorobo, O. A. (2020). Strategic agility and ai-enabled resources capabilities for business survival in post-COVID-19 global economy. *International Journal of Information, Business and Management, 12*(4), 201–213.

Elliott, E. S., & Dweck, C. S. (1988). Goals: An approach to motivation and achievement. *Journal of Personality and Social Psychology, 54*(1), 5–12. doi:10.1037/0022-3514.54.1.5 PMID:3346808

Erickson, J., Lyytinen, K., & Siau, K. (2005). Agile modeling, agile software development, and extreme programming: The state of research [JDM]. *Journal of Database Management, 16*(4), 88–100. doi:10.4018/jdm.2005100105

Fawzy, R., & Saad, M. (2023). The relationship between agility drivers, agility capabilities, and organizational sustainability. *The Journal of Business, 11*(2), 101–114. doi:10.1016/j.orp.2020.100171

Ganguly, A., Nilchiani, R. & Farr, J. (2009). Evaluating agility in corporate enterprises. *Int. Journal of Production Economics, 118*, 410–423, https://doi.org/ doi:10.1016/j.ijpe.2008.12.009

Gencel, İ. E., & Erdoğan, M. (2022). Kolb'un Yenilenen Öğrenme Stili Sınıflamasına İlişkin Bir İnceleme. *Yaşadıkça Eğitim, 36*(3), 813–833. doi:10.33308/26674874.2022363492

Goldman, S. L., Nagel, R. N., & Preiss, K. (1995). *Agile Competitors and Virtual Organizations –Strategies for Enriching the Customer*. Van Nostrand Reinhold.

Gonzalez-Perez, M. A., & Leonard, L. (Eds.). (2015). *The UN Global Compact*. Emerald Group Publishing.

Hallenbeck, G., & Santana, L. (2019). *Great leaders are great learners: How to develop learning-agile high potentials*. Creative Center for Leadership. (https://files.eric.ed.gov/fulltext/ED596166.pdf) (23.03.2023).

Hezlett, S., & Kuncel, N. (2012). Prioritizing the learning agility research agenda. *Industrial and Organizational Psychology: Perspectives on Science and Practice*, 5(3), 296–301. doi:10.1111/j.1754-9434.2012.01449.x

Joiner, B. (2019). Leadership agility for organizational agility. *Journal of Creating Value*, 5(2), 139–149. doi:10.1177/2394964319868321

Kazim, F. A. (2019). Digital transformation and leadership style: A multiple case study. *The ISM Journal of İnternational Business*, 3(1), 24–33.

Kohl, K. (2016). *Becoming a sustainable organization*. Auerbach Publications. doi:10.1201/b20789

Kolb, D. (1984). *Experiential learning: Experience as the source of learning and development*. Prentice Hall.

Kolb, D. A. (2014). *Experiential Learning Experience as the Source of Learning and Development* (2nd ed.). Pearson Education.

Köşker, Z., & Gürer, A. (2020). Sürdürülebilirlik Çerçevesinde Yeşil Örgüt Kültürü. *Ekonomi İşletme Siyaset ve Uluslararası İlişkiler Dergisi*, 6(1), 88–109.

Latif, S. A., & Ahmad, M. A. S. (2020). Learning agility among educational leaders: A Luca-ready leadership competency? *Jurnal Pengurusan Dan Kepimpinan Pendidikan*, 33(1), 105–116.

Lee, J., & Song, J. H. (2022). Developing a Conceptual Integrated Model for the Employee's Learning Agility. *Performance Improvement Quarterly*, 34(4), 367–394. doi:10.1002/piq.21352

Leon, R. D. (2013). From sustainable organization to sustainable knowledge-based organization. *Economic Insights - Trends and Challenges*, 65(2), 63–73.

Lombardo, M. M., & Eichinger, R. W. (2000). High potentials as high learners. *Human Resource Management*, 39(4), 321–329. doi:10.1002/1099-050X(200024)39:4<321::AID-HRM4>3.0.CO;2-1

Lueneburger, C., & Goleman, D. (2010). The change leadership sustainability demands. *MIT Sloan Management Review*, 51(4), 49–55.

McCall, M. W. (2004). *Leadership development through experience*. Academy of Management Executive. doi:10.5465/ame.2004.14776183

McCall, M.W., & Lombardo, M.M., Lombardo. (1983). What Makes a Top Executive? *Psychology Today*, 17(2), 26–31.

Mitchinson, A., & Morris, R. (2014). *Learning about learning agility*. Center for Creative Leadership. doi:10.35613/ccl.2014.1012

Öztürk Çiftci, D. (2021). *21. Yüzyılda Değişen Örgütlerin Oluşturduğu Yeni Liderlik Yaklaşımları: Kavramsal Bir Değerlendirme, 20*. Uluslararası İşletmecilik Kongresi, Giresun.

Parsons, T., Bales, R. F., & Shils, E. A. (1953). *Working Papers in The Theory of Action*. Cambridge, UK: The Free Press.

Price, J., & Murnan, J. (2004). Research limitations and the necessity of reporting them. *American Journal of Health Education*, *35*(2), 66–67. doi:10.1080/19325037.2004.10603611

Robinson, G. S., & Wick, C. W. (1992). *Organizational development that makes a business difference*. Human Resource Planning.

Rubens, A., Schoenfeld, G. A., Schaffer, B. S., & Leah, J. S. (2018). Self-awareness and leadership: Developing an individual strategic professional development plan in an MBA leadership course. *International Journal of Management Education*, *16*(1), 1–13. doi:10.1016/j.ijme.2017.11.001

Sağbaş, M., & Erdoğan, F. A. (2022). Digital Leadership: A Systematic Conceptual Literature Review. *İstanbul Kent Üniversitesi İnsan ve Toplum Bilimleri Dergisi*, *3*(1), 17-35.

Saputra, N., Chumaidah, E., & Aryanto, R. (2021). Multi-layer agility: A proposed concept of business agility in organizational behavior perspective. *Diponegoro International Journal of Business*, *4*(1), 30–41. doi:10.14710/dijb.4.1.2021.30-41

Sheppard, J. M., & Young, W. B. (2006). Agility literature review: Classifications, training, and testing. *Journal of Sports Sciences*, *24*(9), 919–932. doi:10.1080/02640410500457109 PMID:16882626

Simon, D. M. (2011). *Assumptions, limitations, and delimitations*.

Singh, J., Sharma, G., Hill, J., & Schnackenberg, A. (2013). Organizational agility: What it is, what it is not, and why it matters. In Academy of Management proceedings. Briarcliff Manor: Academy of Management.

Smith, B. C. (2015). *How does learning agile business leadership differ? Exploring a revised model of the construct of learning agility about organizational performance*. Columbia University.

Soubbotina, T. P. (2004). *Beyond economic growth: An introduction to sustainable development*. The World Bank. doi:10.1596/0-8213-5933-9

Swisher, V. (2013). Learning agility: The "X" factor in identifying and developing future leaders. *Industrial and Commercial Training*, *45*(3), 139–142. doi:10.1108/00197851311320540

Thomas, R. J., & Cheese, P. (2005). Leadership: Experience is the best teacher. *Strategy and Leadership*, *33*(3), 24–29. doi:10.1108/10878570510594424

Thompson, J. P., & Cavaleri, S. (2010). Dynamic knowledge, organizational growth, and sustainability: The case of Prestwick memory devices. *International Studies of Management & Organization*, *40*(3), 50–60. doi:10.2753/IMO0020-8825400303

Tripathi, A., Srivastava, R., & Sankaran, R. (2020). The role of learning agility and learning culture on turnover intention is an empirical study. *Industrial and Commercial Training*, *52*(2), 105–120. doi:10.1108/ICT-11-2019-0099

Tüyen, Z. (2020). İşletmelerde Sürdürülebilirlik Kavramı Ve Sürdürülebilirliği Etkileyen Etmenler. *İstanbul Ticaret Üniversitesi Sosyal Bilimler Dergisi*, *19*(37), 91-117.

Ulrich, D., & Yeung, A. (2019). Agility: The new response to dynamic change. *Strategic HR Review*, *18*(4), 161–167. doi:10.1108/SHR-04-2019-0032

Vargas-Hernández, J. G. (2021). Strategic Organizational Sustainability. *Circular Economy and Sustainability*, *1*(2), 457–476. Advance online publication. doi:10.100743615-020-00003-y

Wales, T. (2013). Organizational sustainability: What is it, and why does it matter? *Review of Enterprise and Management Studies*, *1*(1), 38–49.

Wilson, E., & Breault, J. (2018). The core of demand planning and data science. *Journal of Business Forecasting*, *37*(1), 28–31.

Yauch, C. A. (2011). Measuring agility as a performance outcome. *Journal of Manufacturing Technology Management*, *22*(3), 384–404. doi:10.1108/17410381111112738

KEY TERMS AND DEFINITIONS

Agility: It is to have the knowledge, experience, and ability to provide fast, dynamic, and accurate responses to changes.

Leaders Having Learning Agility: Leaders who are willing and able to learn from others and their experiences, apply what they have learned on different platforms, embrace innovation, even take the lead, enjoy working with and interacting with people, and are willing and capable of completing processes.

Learning From Experience: It is a learning method that conceptualizes the experiences encountered in every aspect and period of life and applies them to new situations and events.

Self-Awareness: It can be expressed as an in-depth self-recognition of the individual's abilities, moods, and points of differentiation from other people.

Sustainable Approach to the Workforce: Ensuring the freedom of organization for employees and creating necessary strategies to prevent bullying, discrimination, forced labor, child labor, and similar activities is to make human resources sustainable.

Sustainable Organization: Organizations that prioritize corporate sustainability that includes social, ethical, economic, ecological, human rights, and workforce-focused external sustainability, while maintaining their existence with all their systems and subsystems and achieving competitive advantage are those that adopt strategies that prioritize external sustainability.

UNGC: United Nations Global Compact. The organization develops principles to create a sustainability framework that includes human rights, labor working conditions, anti-corruption, and environmental awareness.

Chapter 6
Transformational Leadership in Practice:
Bridging the Chasm

Tarek Salem
MacEwan University, Canada

Bruce Thomson
MacEwan University, Canada

ABSTRACT

This chapter captures the bi-furcated challenge of implementing the transformational leadership practices in a complex organizational context. The authors embark on Bass' 4I transformational leadership model and suggest a variety of imperative skills necessary for the proper implementation. From the suggested pool of skills, two are highlighted as the most important and resonate with the 4I model. These are creativity and innovation skills and change management skills. The authors expect to find out the importance of transformational leaders to empower and enable the second line of operational leaders that are capable of efficiently and effectively bridging the transformational leadership chasm from the leaders' vision to the followers' practice.

INTRODUCTION

In an organizational context, leadership practice does not exist in vacuum. It occurs within the boundaries of both external and internal environmental factors and a timeline. Hay and Hodgkinson (2006) recognize the argument that Burn's Leadership Model and most of the models of transformational and charismatic leadership tend to conceptualize leadership in ways that neglect the complexity found in organizational settings. Thru the myriad of leadership definitions, Burn's Leadership Model is versatile enough to encompass the broad spectrum of leadership activities and practices which view leadership practice as an attempt of a leader to influence their followers to achieve common goals. Re-visiting the work of James MacGregor Burns (1978) and his early definitions and model of leadership, reveals that

DOI: 10.4018/979-8-3693-1380-0.ch006

he in his early definition of transformational leadership linked three factors only within the leadership model: leaders, followers, and goals. "He wrote of transformative leaders as people who tap the motives of their followers in order to better reach the goals of leaders and followers" (Northouse, 2021) Thus, we argue that in an organizational setting it is necessary to add the dimensions of internal environment, external environment and time frame to capture much of the neglected complexity in organizations that leaders encounter (see Figure 1). To accomplish this goal this chapter will breakdown the leadership model as shown to pull out the components that will drive organizational success from a transformational leadership perspective. These components include some of the necessary skill sets for both leader and followers.

Figure 1. The leadership model

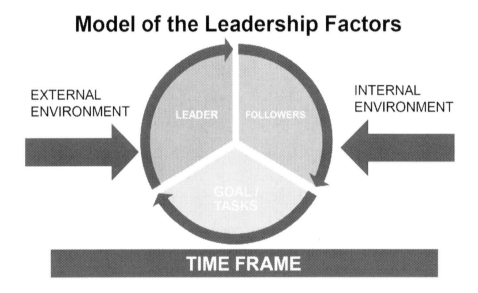

Organizations realize positive outcomes from transformational leadership because the transformational leaders offer their followers something more than just working for self-gain. They provide followers with an inspiring mission and vision and give them an identity (Bass, 1985). The work of Bass and Riggio (2010) expanded the initial concepts of MacGregor (1978) to help explain how transformational leadership could be measured, as well as how it impacts follower motivation and performance. It manifested the measurement of the extent to which a leader is transformational. For example, it is measured in terms of their influence on the followers.

Bass's work also explained the evolution of the impact of transformational leaders. The evolutionary process starts when the followers of a transformational leader feel trust, admiration, loyalty, and respect for the leader (Bass, 1985), Because of these demonstrated qualities of the transformational leader, followers are willing to work harder than originally expected. The dimensions, evolution and outcomes of transformational leadership are captured in Bass's globally recognized model of transformational leadership. Bass's 4Is Transformational Leadership Model suggests that the leader transforms and motivates followers through practicing their idealized influence (earlier referred to as charisma), inspirational

Transformational Leadership in Practice

motivation, **i**ntellectual stimulation (stimulate followers' efforts to be innovative and creative) and **i**ndividual consideration (see Figure 2).

Figure 2. The 4I transformational leadership model
Adapted from The Bass 4I Model.

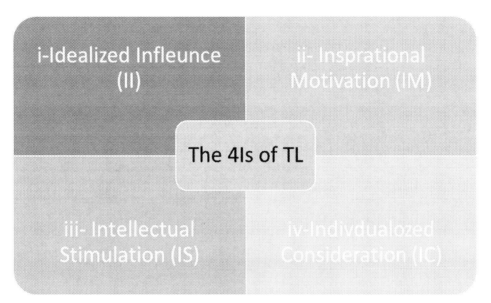

Through this evolutionary process of transformational leadership new learning opportunities are created. Allix (2000) reinstated the work of MacGregor, (1978) and emphasized the educative nature of the relationship between leaders and followers. Thus, transformational leaders realize their followers' 'need for achievement' and create opportunities as stipulated in clear tasks and KPIs. In addition, a transformational leader encourages followers to come up with new and unique ways to challenge the status quo. It can then be argued that transformational leaders champion change management to support being successful in altering the environment within the organization.

Observing the progression of transformational leadership concepts and models from Burns through Bass, we believe the onset of the success of the transformational leadership style is found in both leaders and followers. Inception, creation, and adaptation of the transformational leadership style lies in the hands of the transformational leaders. However, the operationalization, success and realization greatly depend on the followers' skills, receptivity, and responses. As such, transformational leadership is a bifurcated concept.

Why bifurcated? On the one hand, transformational leadership lends great attention to the influencing and educational act of leaders using their soft skills such as charisma, emotional intelligence, and many others. On the other hand, it works on changing and transforming followers. It is the transformational leaders' soft skills approach that needs to be clearly communicated from and effectively captured by the followers. Burns (1978) characterized transformational leadership as a process that motivates followers by appealing to higher ideals and moral values. Transformational leaders are able to define and articulate a vision for their organization, society, and country. Their leadership style can transform their followers towards higher levels of performance. This then presents itself into solid measurable results and impact.

Further Hay and Hodgkinson (2006). suggested that it is very common to portray transformational leadership as a leadership approach which goes beyond the ordinary abilities of the majority. They further explore the organizational challenges of adopting a process-relational perspective which is arguably more closely resembling the operational leadership challenges faced in an organizational context. They expect that it is more likely for managers to engage in leadership processes. In a process-oriented approach as opposed to a systems approach (see Figure 3), the transformational leader engages followers by recognizing and exploiting their needs and demands in such a way that the needs of both leaders and followers are aligned and satisfied. The result is a collective act, "a relationship of mutual stimulation and elevation that converts followers into leaders and may convert leaders into moral agents" (Burns, 1978 as cited in Allix, 2000, p.3).

Figure 3. The system vs. process relation leadership
Adapted from Hay and Hodgkinson (2006)

Systems-control perspective of leadership	Process-relational perspective of leadership
Focus on leaders as persons	Focus on leadership as a process
Focus on followers	Focus on collaborators
Leadership as separate to management	Leadership as integral to management
Unitarist perspective	Pluralist perspective
Organisational goals clear, given and fixed	Organisational goals ambiguous, constructed and constantly changing

Such an understanding of transformational leadership poses a challenge for the proper attainment of the transformational leadership goals. This is the challenge of combining the visionary, innovative and bird eye nature of the transformative leaders together with the operational, hands on and action-oriented or perhaps managerial approach of the followers. This then leads us to the argument that transformational leadership results in a bifurcated approach.

This bifurcated approach for transformational leadership is the focus of this chapter. We intend to investigate the leadership practices of transformative leaders and the operational and managerial practices of their followers. Thus, catching both ends of this bifurcated approach, we uncover the views of both parties in the spectrum - leaders and followers.

On the Transformational Leaders' Side

Transformative leaders can display a wide range of personal skills and /or traits that collectively define their leadership style. These include being innovative, charismatic, agile, a goal setter, an educator, and a change catalyst. The list highlights a transformational leader's focus on transforming followers to achieve not only organizational goals, but the followers own personal goals. In a single chapter, the spectrum of such skills and/or traits becomes too broad to explore without compromising the necessary rigorous detailing they deserve. Since all these skills/traits are crucial and essential, it becomes challenging to select which ones of them to start with and have as a focus of this chapter. However, since the focus of this compendium revolves around transformational leadership and change management we will focus on the skills / traits of being a change catalyst which for us encompasses innovation and being an educator.

Scholars have identified numerous transformational leaders and their most applauded transformational practices. A transformational leader, "serves to change the status quo by appealing to followers' values and their sense of higher purpose. Although the transformational leader plays a pivotal role in precipitating change, followers and leaders are inextricably bound together in the transformation process" (Northouse, 2021, p.162). In their study on cooperative transformational leadership, Glad and Blanton (1997) investigated the transformational leadership of Nelson Mandela and suggested that charismatic elements are apt to characterize of transformational leaders to their followers. Gandhi exemplifies a paradigm case of transformational leadership. Gandhi as a transformational leader recognized and harnessed the needs and demands of followers to achieve higher purposes. Walt Disney, a transformational leader that not only tapped into the vision of his followers but the dreams of generations of Americans (Joseph, 2012).

Two trends in the leadership landscape, and particularly the transformational leadership eco-system, step forward to justify our focus on transformational leaders and change management. The first is Bass's 4I Transformational Leadership Model and the second is the ever-changing volatility, uncertainty, complexity, and ambiguity (VUCA) in the world of business. The link between transformational leadership and change management becomes a very crucial component in today's business environment due to the continuous changing nature of business organizations. We argue that the skills and traits found under the 4Is within the Bass' model call for a focus on innovation and change management. Despite the vast breadth of the spectrum of those skills, it is change management that clearly stands out across all the dimensions of the 4Is model. Table 1 illustrates the 4I Transformational Leadership Model characteristics in a little more depth.

Table 1. 4Is traits and skills

i- Idealized Influence (II)	ii-Inspirational Motivation (IM)	ii- Intellectual Stimulation (IS)	iv- Individual Consideration (IC)
Charismatic-Inspirational Leadership			
TL - Role Models, admired, respected, and trusted. - Having extra ordinary capabilities, persistence, and determination. - Having a collective sense of mission. - Reassuring others that obstacles will be overcome.	TL - Motivate and inspire. - Provide meaning and challenge to work. - Arise team spirit. - Display enthusiasm and optimism. - Create and clearly communicate expectations. - Demonstrate commitment to goals and shared vision.	TL - Stimulate innovation. - Question assumptions - Reframe problems. - Approach old situations in new ways. - Encourage creativity.	TL - Pay special attention to each individual need for Ach. - Pay special attention to each individual's need for Growth. - Act as mentors/ coaches - Personalize interactions with individuals.

Adapted from Bass (2010)

In Table 1 transformational leadership skills and traits are listed for all four dimensions of the model. Under idealized influence traits such as persistence, determination, and the ability to reassure others that obstacles will be overcome, letting followers know change is possible. Transformational leaders are keen on transforming their organizations and developing their followers. The traits and skills found in inspirational motivation provide the impetus to change. Intellectual stimulation ensures followers have the mindset to questions existing paradigms and be open to creativity and innovation. Finally, individual consideration moves it from a group focus to change at the individual level. Change is going to occur – it is inevitable. Change is always present in the journey of an organization and thus, the development of the followers. With that in mind, change management becomes a cornerstone skill of transformational leaders (see Table 1.).

Creativity and innovation are a key ingredient of transformational leadership skills/traits that are strongly associated with the 4Is of the model. Creativity and innovation are the hallmark of the intellectual stimulation dimension. Research from various authors supports our argument. Studies show the existence of a statistically significant relationship between the dimensions of the of the 4I Model and change management (Alqatawenh, 2018). A widely accepted definition (Amabile et al., 1996) states that creativity is the production of novel and useful ideas. Innovation is the successful implementation of creative ideas within an organization (Nasir et al., 2022). There is a link between transformative leadership, organizational creativity, psychological issues such as hindrance and challenge stressors, and employee creativity and employee performance. This becomes centric to the practices of transformational leadership since creativity is at the individual level, while innovation is at the organizational level (Oldham & Cummings, 1996). Innovation through creativity is an important factor in the success and competitive advantage of organizations which is a key mandate of transformational leaders (Gumusluoglu & Ilsev, 2009).

According to the 4Is Model intellectual stimulation refers to a leader's ability to inspire innovation and creativity in their followers (Bak, Jin, & McDonald III, 2022). A recent study conducted by McKinsey and Company revealed that innovation has always been essential to long-term value creation and resilience (Banholzer, Birshan, Doherty, & LaBerge, 2023). Transformative leaders are more concerned with portraying the big pictures. Big innovations contribute more to that portray to the organization and the followers. The same McKinsey and company study shows that making big innovation bets may now be safer than investing in incremental changes (Banholzer, Birshan, Doherty, & LaBerge, 2023). Innovation is at the heart of transformational leadership since transformational leadership boosts intrinsic motivation and provides intellectual stimulation encouraging followers to challenge the status quo and the old ways of doing things (Valeriu, 2017).

Krishman (1998 as cited in Al Harbi, Alarifi & Mosbah, 2019) argued that through intellectual stimulation leaders through aspects such as challenging task increased and upgraded employees -followers- to make them more aware, innovative and creative. This is echoed by Scott and Bruce (1994) and Conger and Kanungo (1988) (as cited in Birasnav, Rangnekar, & Dalpati, 2011). Their combined findings demonstrated that by instilling in employees / followers trust and empowering them through providing autonomy in the decision-making process while performing their tasks fostered not only self-efficacy but their innovative behaviours as well. Further, a study on transformational leadership and employees' creativity showed that there is a significant positive relationship with both followers' creativity and organizational innovation and a transformational leadership approach (Al Harbi, Alarifi & Mosbah, 2019).

The second trend impacting transformational leadership to justify our focus on change management is the volatility, uncertainty, complexity, and ambiguity (VUCA) in the business environment. The term VUCA is taken from a military acronym Elkington, (2018). Business executives now use it to describe the environment in which they do business (Berinato,2014). This recognition of the multi-dimensional diverse world marked by volatility, uncertainty, complexity, and ambiguity (VUCA) encourages leaders to change the leadership narrative and question the aim of their strategic direction (Bushe & Marshak, 2016). Thus, they must confront, question, and focus on operational practices of their followers. Aspects

Transformational Leadership in Practice

such as change management, innovation, agility, and project management are now at the forefront. There is no ignoring the impact of the changes occurring in the environment. The VUCA of the business environment does not leave organizations room to sit back and reap the benefits. Organizations must now be at least reactive to change if they wish to survive. If they wish to thrive then they must be proactive and embrace change and innovation.

The practices of transformative leaders align more with the need to dovetail approaches to a VUCA environment to the needs of followers. Transformational approaches such as inspirational motivation and idealized influence (charisma), emotional intelligence, innovation leading to blue ocean thinking assist transformational leaders to redesign and repurpose the follower's operational practices. Practitioners and business schools have stepped forward with transformative leadership practices to guide and direct the redesigned and repurposed operational practices. These include best industry practices set forth by institutions such as, the (Professional + Science) PROSCI® Change Management, Innovation and Creativity Institute, the Project Management Institute - PMI®, the Business Agility Institute and the KPI® Institute.

Change management scholars have recognized three change models - linear, transitional, and transformational (Anderson, & Anderson, 2002). Unlike the linear/developmental and transitional change models widely recognized and adopted in organizations, transformational leaders adopt a transformation change approach (see Figure 4).

Figure 4. Different types of change management
Adapted from Anderson & Anderson, 2007

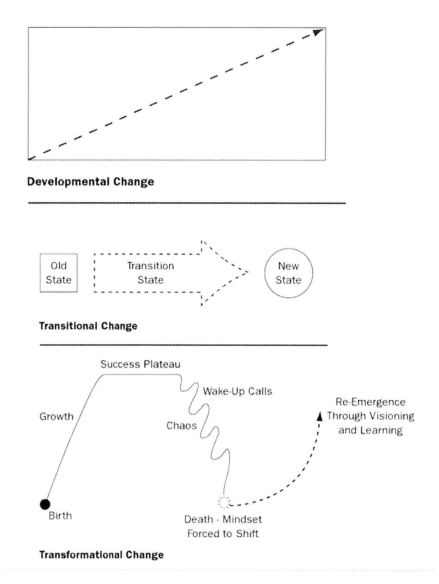

Transformational leaders help organizations to manage change in a VUCA environment. Their impact change on management in organizations is of a positive nature (Bedoya, 2018). Dovetailing transformational leadership and change management in organizational context, studies have provided insights into the significance of transformational leadership as a solution for organizations seeking change (Alqatawenh, 2018). Transformational leadership includes the development of a clear, compelling vision, which then sparks change (Kirkbride, 2006). Employees commitment through personal involvement and identification with the vision acts to create the institutionalization of organizational change (Kouzes & Posner, 2017). In a study comparing business and academic leaders (Hechanova, & Cementina-Olpoc, 2013), academic respondents rated their leaders higher in terms of challenging the status quo, inspiring a shared vision, modeling the way, and encouraging the heart. The study also revealed that leaders of academic organizations lent greater support for changes than leaders of business organizations. In addition, the study findings highlighted the differences in the nature of influence of leadership and change management on employee commitment to change (Hechanova, & Cementina-Olpoc, 2013).

The base of the term transformational leadership is the word transform, meaning to change. Transformational leaders are catalysts of change or at least change agents. Change management skills are in the heart of the success of the transformational leadership approach. However, what of the followers? The following section will explore the juxtaposition between transformational leaders, change and the role of the followers.

On the Followers' Side

Transformational leadership style translates to the sharing of beliefs, needs and values from the leader to the followers (Luthans, Luthans, & Palmer, 2016). Thus, for followers, transformative leaders act as change agents. Successful leaders clearly communicate those beliefs, needs, values, and a vision to followers (Kouzes & Posner, 2017). However, followers that are better trained as change managers significantly improve organizational performance. As such organizations should invest in change management capacity building. This is the heart of transformational leaders; improve organizational performance by developing followers' capacity.

Followers and change

Faupel and Süß (2019) put forth that a transformational leadership approach fosters a strengthening of commitment and support for change through an employee's work engagement. Transformational leaders build perceptions of the attractiveness of the consequences of change. This highlights of transformational leader's role throughout the organizational change process and their efforts to expose managers and supervisors on the positive impact they can exert on employees during the process of organizational change (Faupel & Süß, 2019).

Thus, it is not a stretch to say that employees' reactions to organizational change are affected by transformational leaders who foster employees' readiness for and commitment to change and motivate them to act in support of the change. However, just how transformational leadership affects employees remains unclear (Faupel, & Süß, 2019). However, among the plethora of change management models, followers adapt to change via the application of change management by considering three change management models – The Prosci®'s ADKAR Model, The Kurt Lewin Change Management Model, and Kotter's 8-Step Process (Bedoya, 2018).

AlManei, Salonitis, and Tsinopoulos (2018) suggest that many authors of change management theories do not limit their theories to classifications of change. However, it is possible to propose a logical suggestion for their suitability. The works of ADKAR and Lewin focus on individual change and are therefore more aligned with projects of smaller scale and scope which only impact a smaller number of people. In focusing on the leadership of change, Kotter's eight steps more closely align with larger scale changes which have the potential to impact a larger number of people (AlManei, Salonitis, & Tsinopoulos, 2018).

Although transformational leadership is found in all sizes of organizations, change in large organizations is more reliant on followers to implement change management processes. Thus, as suggested by

AlManei, Salonitis and Tsinopoulos (2018), in large organizations transformational leadership is needed to influence followers so that they drive the change process (see Table 2).

Table 2. The implementation matrix of various change management models

Model	Scale/Scope	Scale of Change	Scope of Change
The Adkar Model		Small/Incremental	Deliverable/ Project
The Lewin Model		Incremental/Modular	Project/Department
The Kotter Model		Modular / Organizational	Transformational/Organizational

Adapted from AlManei, Salonitis & Tsinopoulos (2018)

Followers and Innovation

A key element in transformational leadership is instilling creativity and innovativeness in followers. This then means that to effectively implement innovative missions or visions purposed by transformative leaders, followers need high levels of creativity and innovativeness as well. Revealed in Shin and Zhou's (2003) study of transformational leadership and creativity, found that a transformational leadership approach positively related to the followers' creativity, conservation ("a value favoring propriety and harmony in interpersonal and person-to-group relations") (p. 705) and intrinsic motivation. Paulsen, Callan, Ayoko and Saunders (2013) concurred. Their studies found that a transformational leadership approach fully mediated the relationship of team innovation, transformational leadership, and creativity through the factors of group identification and perceived support. Another study, Nabi, Liu, and Hasan (2022) investigated the interaction between transformational leadership and the follower's creativity. Puni et al. (2022) further stressed the importance of transformational leadership and leadership in their study of innovative climate, transformational leadership, and firm performance in developing countries. They found, again, a positive relationship. They stated that to develop creative behaviours an innovative climate was essential. Their data clearly indicated a direct and significantly positive relationship between all dimensions of transformational leadership, an innovative climate and organizational performance (Puni et al., 2022). The findings indicated that a transformational leadership approach was a significant and positive influence on follower's creativity.

Followers play a key role in change management through buy-in to the leader's vision and communication of that vision. However, it is through their creativity and innovation that the goals of the vision are achieved. The link between transformational leadership, followers and change management is evident.

Bridging the Chasm

To bridge the transformational leadership chasm between the leader's vision and the followers' practices we conclude by asserting the need for merging the two branches of transformative leadership, leaders, and followers. In doing so together they create a fabric of a mutually aligned pathway that bridges the chasm created in every changing business environment.

Some practical change management models such as the ADKAR, the Lewin and the Kotter change management models are applauded for their positive impact on the attainment of the transformational leadership desired impact. But every organization is unique. All the personal development items are needed and valuable. However, organizations differ in their needs for each one of them. It thus should be the mandate of the transformational leader to analyze their organization, explore its unique needs, and create a map of the required skills prioritized based on the uniqueness of their own organization.

The operationalization of the 4 Is of transformational leadership directly infuses the organization innovation, the innovation culture and both team and individual innovations. Research has consistently indicated that clear communication and inspiration are required from the transformational leaders. Unfortunately, they are not enough. The positive receptivity and capacity building of followers are as crucially important. Transformational leaders need to precipitate both change management skills and individual innovation spirits and institutionalize them among the organizational behavior and culture of their followers. The key pillars of the followers' personal development need to focus on change management practices and innovative capacity building.

FUTURE RESEARCH

Embarking on the focus of this compendium that revolves around skillsets needed for the of transformational leadership and change management. The spectrum of such skillsets and/or traits becomes too broad to explore in a single chapter, without compromising the necessary rigorous detailing they deserve. This opens frontiers for scholars to further investigate the components that will drive organizational success from a transformational leadership perspective. Further to the skillsets considered here in this chapter, scholars might consider many others. Intrapreneurial skills, emotional intelligence skills, agility etc., are few to name and to further explore and contribute to build a new body of knowledge in this domain.

CONCLUSION

As we stated earlier, leadership does not occur in a vacuum. It occurs in an environment etched by turbulence and change. To master this environment leaders and followers need to embrace change through creativity and innovation. A transformational leadership provides leaders and followers a pathway to navigate within that environment. It is truly a two-sided approach from different angles – leaders (visionary) and followers (action-oriented); creativity (visionary) and innovation (application of vision). Thus, a transformational leader becomes the change catalyst and followers become the change agents.

The ongoing process of organizational evolution has taken us from cottage industries to the industrial revolution to the birth of management science to the impact of globalization and the impact of technological advances. We are without a doubt in a period of significant change and leadership approaches must reflect the environment that we are in. No longer can we think of our employees as mere tools to achieve organizational objectives. Employees are now followers. They are looking for more connection to work. They want to be more engaged. They are part of the solution and a valued partner in an organization. Leadership is now about utilizing the strengths of followers. Through transformational leadership we uncover the tools to embrace change and create relationships that drive organizational success. But leaders today need to recognize and embrace this bifurcated essence of today and tomorrow's workplace.

REFERENCES

Al Harbi, J. A., Alarifi, S., & Mosbah, A. (2019). Transformation leadership and creativity: Effects of employees' psychological empowerment and intrinsic motivation. *Personnel Review, 48*(5), 1082–1099. doi:10.1108/PR-11-2017-0354

Allix, N. M. (2000). Transformational leadership: Democratic or despotic? *Educational Management & Administration, 28*(1), 7–20. doi:10.1177/0263211X000281002

AlManei, M., Salonitis, K., & Tsinopoulos, C. (2018). A conceptual lean implementation framework based on change management theory. *Procedia CIRP, 72*, 1160–1165. doi:10.1016/j.procir.2018.03.141

Alqatawenh, A. S. (2018). Transformational leadership style and its relationship with change management. *Verslas: teorija ir praktika, 19*(1), 17-24.

Amabile, T. M., Conti, R., Coon, H., Lazenby, J., & Herron, M. (1996). Assessing the work environment for creativity. *Academy of Management Journal, 39*(5), 1154–1184. doi:10.2307/256995

Anderson, D., & Anderson, L. A. (2002). *Beyond change management: Advanced strategies for today's transformational leaders.* John Wiley & Sons.

Bak, H., Jin, M. H., & McDonald, B. D. III. (2022). Unpacking the transformational leadership-innovative work behavior relationship: The mediating role of psychological capital. *Public Performance & Management Review, 45*(1), 80–105. doi:10.1080/15309576.2021.1939737

Banholzer, M., Birshan, M., Doherty, R., & LaBerge, L. (2023). *Innovation: Your solution for weathering uncertainty.* McKinsey Consulting. https://www.mckinsey.com/~/media/mckinsey/business%20functions/strategy%20and%20corporate%20finance/our%20insights/innovation%20your%20solution%20for%20weathering%20uncertainty/innovation-your-solution-for-weathering-uncertainty_vf.pdf

Bass, B. M. (1985), Leadership and Performance. *N.Y. Free Press.* https://www.langston.edu/sites/default/files/basic-content-files/TransformationalLeadership.pdf

Bass, B. M., & Riggio, R. E. (2010). The transformational model of leadership. *Leading organizations: Perspectives for a new era, 2*, 76-86.

Bedoya, E. (June 2018). *Contributions of transformational leadership style to change management.* Ferenc Farkas 1st International Conference, Pécs, Hungary. https://www.researchgate.net/publication/345344646_Contributions_of_transformational_leadership_style_to_change_management

Berinato, S. (2014). A framework for understanding VUCA. *Harvard Business Review, 59*(9).

Birasnav, M., Rangnekar, S., & Dalpati, A. (2011). Transformational leadership and human capital benefits: The role of knowledge management. *Leadership and Organization Development Journal, 32*(2), 106–126. doi:10.1108/01437731111112962

Bushe, G. R., & Marshak, R. J. (2016). The dialogic mindset: Leading emergent change in a complex world. *Organization Development Journal, 34*(1), 37–65.

Conger, J. A., & Kanungo, R. N. (1988). The empowerment process: Integrating theory and practice. *Academy of Management Review, 13*(3), 471–482. doi:10.2307/258093

Elkington, R. (2018). Leadership Decision-Making Leveraging Big Data in VUCA Contexts. *Journal of Leadership Studies, 12*(3), 66–70. doi:10.1002/jls.21599

Faupel, S., & Süß, S. (2019). The effect of transformational leadership on employees during organizational change–an empirical analysis. *Journal of Change Management, 19*(3), 145–166. doi:10.1080/14697017.2018.1447006

Glad, B., & Blanton, R. (1997). F. W. de Klerk and Nelson Mandela: A Study in Cooperative Transformational Leadership. *Presidential Studies Quarterly, 27*(3), 565–590.

Gumusluoglu, L., & Ilsev, A. (2009). Transformational leadership, creativity, and organizational innovation. *Journal of Business Research, 62*(4), 461–473. doi:10.1016/j.jbusres.2007.07.032

Gutu, I., Agheorghiesei, D. T., & Alecu, I. C. (2022). The Online Adapted Transformational Leadership and Workforce Innovation within the Software Development Industry. *Sustainability (Basel), 14*(12), 7408. doi:10.3390u14127408

Hay, A., & Hodgkinson, M. (2006). Rethinking leadership: A way forward for teaching leadership? *Leadership and Organization Development Journal, 27*(2), 144–158. doi:10.1108/01437730610646642

Hechanova, R. M., & Cementina-Olpoc, R. (2013). Transformational leadership, change management, and commitment to change: A comparison of academic and business organizations. *The Asia-Pacific Education Researcher, 22*(1), 11–19. doi:10.100740299-012-0019-z

Joseph, P. (2012). Mahatma Gandhi"s concept of educational leadership. *International Journal of Economics Business and Management Studies, 1*(2), 60–64.

Kaminski, J. (2022). Theory applied to informatics–The Prosci ADKAR Model. *Canadian Journal of Nursing Informatics, 17*(2). https://cjni.net/journal/?p=10076

Kirkbride, P. (2006). Developing transformational leaders: The full range leadership model in action. *Industrial and Commercial Training, 38*(1), 23–32. doi:10.1108/00197850610646016

Kouzes, J. M., & Posner, B. Z. (2017). *The Leadership Challenge* (6th ed.). John Wiley & Sons.

Laig, R. B. D., & Abocejo, F. T. (2021). Change management process in a mining company: Kotter's 8-Step change model. *Journal of Management, Economics, and Industrial Organization, 5*(3), 31–50. doi:10.31039/jomeino.2021.5.3.3

Luthans, K. W., Luthans, B. C., & Palmer, N. F. (2016). A positive approach to management education: The relationship between academic PsyCap and student engagement. *Journal of Management Development, 35*(9), 1098–1118. doi:10.1108/JMD-06-2015-0091

MacGregor, B. J. (1978). *Leadership*. Torchbooks.

Muniapan, B. A. L. (2007). Transformational leadership style demonstrated by Sri Rama in Valmiki Ramayana. *International Journal of Indian Culture and Business Management, 1*(1-2), 104–115. doi:10.1504/IJICBM.2007.014473

Nabi, M. N., Liu, Z., & Hasan, N. (2022). Examining the nexus between transformational leadership and follower's radical creativity: the role of creative process engagement and leader creativity expectation. *International Journal of Emerging Markets.* doi:10.1108/IJOEM-05-2021-0659

Nasir, J., Ibrahim, R. M., Sarwar, M. A., Sarwar, B., Al-Rahmi, W. M., Alturise, F., Samed Al-Adwan, A., & Uddin, M. (2022). The effects of transformational leadership, organizational innovation, work stressors, and creativity on employee performance in SMEs. *Frontiers in Psychology, 13*, 1379. doi:10.3389/fpsyg.2022.772104 PMID:35529553

Northouse, P. G. (2021). Leadership: Theory and practice. *Sage (Atlanta, Ga.)*.

Oldham, G. R., & Cummings, A. (1996). Employee creativity: Personal and contextual factors at work. *Academy of Management Journal, 39*(3), 607–634. doi:10.2307/256657

Paulsen, N., Callan, V. J., Ayoko, O., & Saunders, D. (2013). Transformational leadership and innovation in an R&D organization experiencing major change. *Journal of Organizational Change Management, 26*(3), 595–610. doi:10.1108/09534811311328597

Puni, A., Hilton, S. K., Mohammed, I., & Korankye, E. S. (2022). The mediating role of innovative climate on the relationship between transformational leadership and firm performance in developing countries: The case of Ghana. *Leadership and Organization Development Journal, 43*(3), 404–421. doi:10.1108/LODJ-10-2020-0443

Rosdiana, N., & Aslami, N. (2022). The Main Models of Change Management in Kurt Lewin's Thinking. *Jurnal Akuntansi, Manajemen dan Bisnis Digital, 1*(2), 251-256.

Scott, S. G., & Bruce, R. A. (1994). Determinants of innovative behavior: A path model of individual innovation in the workplace. *Academy of Management Journal, 37*(3), 580–607. doi:10.2307/256701

Shin, S. J., & Zhou, J. (2003). Transformational leadership, conservation, and creativity: Evidence from Korea. *Academy of Management Journal, 46*(6), 703–714. doi:10.2307/30040662

Valeriu, D. (2017). The significance of emotional intelligence in transformational leadership for public universities. *Euromentor Journal, 8*(1), 35.

Chapter 7
Leading From Within:
Creating Leaders Among Employees

Henry Dimingu
California Southern University, USA

Idowu Mary Mogaji
University of Saskatchewan, Canada

ABSTRACT

This chapter explores the concept of leadership through the prism of processes. Organizations are evolving and these evolutions may result in divergent thoughts, visions, and even actions. As a result, there is a need to develop leaders among employees who can transform these disparate thoughts and visions into something far more valuable and advantageous to organizations. Therefore, the fundamental premise of this chapter is that every employee possesses the potential for leadership, only waiting to be developed. This chapter emphasizes the need for employees to develop leadership skills. It covers what these skills are, why they are crucial to develop, and lastly, provides suggestions on how to develop employees' leadership skills.

INTRODUCTION

When we liberate the leader in everyone, extraordinary things happen.

James Kouzes and Barry Posner

It is said that the most successful companies do not recruit leaders; instead, they grow their own, and according to the Deloitte University Press (2014) publication *"Leaders at all levels,"* if organizations do not prepare their employees for leadership positions, there is a good chance that they will go elsewhere. Employees surveyed in the Deloitte publication cited opportunities for developing their leadership skills as the top motivation for sticking with a company. This suggests that it is crucial to develop employees. Therefore, for organizations to expand sustainably, there needs to be a change in perspective from seeing leadership development among employees as a "nice to have" to a "need to have." Additionally, it is

DOI: 10.4018/979-8-3693-1380-0.ch007

critical to understand that workplaces are evolving and that this evolution brings with it multigenerational offices, which can result in differences in ideas, visions, and even executions. This is why developing leaders in the workforce is essential because it channels the various ideas and visions into something much more meaningful and advantageous to the organization.

Based on the premise that understanding how to build leadership skills in employees is essential in today's fast-paced workplace, this chapter will define leadership skills, discuss why developing these skills is essential, and provide guidance on how to develop leadership skills in employees. A review of developing leadership abilities in employees from within and throughout an organization is at the heart of this chapter. By reading this chapter, we hope that readers will understand the conceptualization of leadership from a process lens and appreciate the significance of developing leaders among employees.

LEADERSHIP AND LEADER DEFINED

Since "leader" and "leadership" are often misused, it is crucial that we start by clarifying what these terms represent. Despite being widely desired, these concepts are challenging to define explicitly (Klingborg et al., 2006). Various academics have defined leadership in a variety of ways. Some people see leadership as a collection of particular qualities or traits. Others believe it to be made up of certain skills and knowledge. Others see leadership to be a process that emphasizes relationships and social interactions. In order to define leadership for the discussion in this chapter, we shall consider it to be a process.

Leadership is defined as "the process of influencing others to understand and agree about what needs to be done and how to do it. It is equally the process of facilitating individual and collective efforts to accomplish shared objectives" (Yukl, 2006, p. 8). Consistent with Yukl's definition of leadership as a process of influence, Northouse (2010, 2018) described leadership as a process wherein an individual influences a group of others to accomplish a shared purpose. Both definitions imply that leadership is a process, involves influence, takes place in the context of a group, and entails achieving objectives. Therefore, the very definition of leadership as a process shows that it is not a quality or trait that only a select few people are born with. This suggests that a group's leadership is not limited to just one individual with official position power.

When leadership is defined as a process, it implies that leadership is a transactional event that takes place between the "influencer" (leader) and the "influenced" (follower, the led). This argues that influence, or the capacity to influence others in a professional or organizational setting, is the essence of leadership. The idea that leadership is a process implies that it takes place in a collective setting, that is, within the context of a group. This suggests that being a leader involves motivating or influencing a team of individuals who are working toward a common objective (Blanchard, 2010). This further implies that achieving objectives or a common goal is a component of leadership. Therefore, leadership is the process of influencing a team of individuals to use a variety of, ideally moral, methods to achieve a goal or complete a task. If leadership is the process of influencing others, then leaders are those who significantly affect how others behave, think, feel, and act by their words and/or actions (Gardner & Laskin, 1995). According to Sabir (2017), leaders are those who encourage others to act morally. They provide direction, create a compelling vision, foster trust, and motivate followers. This suggests that leaders literally chart the course and ensure that corporate objectives are met.

Conceptualizing Leadership from a Human Relations Perspective

Organizational human relations place a particular emphasis on the needs of individuals and the subsequent behaviors of people and teams (Ayoko, 2021). It employs an interpersonal approach to managing people and acknowledges that an organization comprises both formal and informal components. An organization's structure is considered its formal components from a human relations perspective, while its interpersonal interactions are considered informal components (Raghid Al & Vongas, 2022). Consequently, focusing on people is at the heart of the human relations view on leadership. The fundamental tenet of human relations is the conviction that motivational factors play a significant role in retaining an employee (Reece & Reece, 2017). Motivation within this concept relies on teamwork, necessitating coordination and cooperation of all individuals.

According to Avnish et al. (2019), strong social ties at work and individual recognition of an individual can increase employee motivation and productivity. Furthermore, it contends that improved or enhanced working conditions (empowerment, participation, and favorable treatment) result in increased productivity. If leadership is the process of influencing others, it follows that the core of leadership in organizations is influencing and facilitating individual and collective efforts to achieve goals. Leadership is a "people" activity (Kets de Vries & Korotov, 2010). Therefore, as both concepts are concerned with people and attending to their needs to achieve organizational goals, leadership and human relations are interwoven.

Consequently, creating leaders in employees from a human relations standpoint entails increasing employees' capacity or potential to be successful in leadership positions (Head, 2003). It also assists in developing leadership-related knowledge and skills that the organization values (Van Velsor & McCauley, 2004). This suggests that to acquire the necessary leadership skills, it is necessary to tap into the leadership potential of employees.

Conceptualizing Leadership From the Lens of Top Industry Experts

Leadership is a complex and multifaceted concept that has also been studied and discussed by numerous experts in the field. Michael Anderson, Ken Blanchard, Marshall Goldsmith, John C. Maxwell, Simon Sinek, Robin Sharma, Patrick Lencioni, Tom Peters, and Jack Welch are some of the renowned figures who have shared valuable insights on leadership. In this section, we will explore their perspectives in order to gain an understanding of leadership.

Michael Anderson, a renowned author and leadership consultant, emphasized the importance of self-awareness in leadership (Anderson, n.d). He opined that effective leaders possess a deep understanding of themselves, their strengths, weaknesses, values, and emotions. Anderson argued that self-awareness enables leaders to make better decisions, manage their emotions, and build authentic relationships with their team members. Similarly, Ken Blanchard, a renowned author and management expert, is known for his leadership model called *Situational Leadership*. Blanchard suggested that effective leaders adapt their leadership style based on the needs and development level of their followers. He emphasized the significance of flexibility, stating that leaders should provide the right amount of direction, support, and autonomy to their team members based on their competence and commitment (Blanchard, 2015).

Furthermore, Marshall Goldsmith, a prominent executive coach and author, focused on the concept of leadership presence. According to Goldsmith, leadership presence is about being fully present and engaged in the moment, listening actively, and demonstrating empathy. He emphasized that leaders should cultivate a genuine connection with their team members, inspire trust, and create an inclusive environment that encourages collaboration and innovation (Goldsmith, 2014). In addition, John C. Maxwell, who is also a renowned leadership expert and author, emphasized the importance of influence in leadership. According to Maxwell, leadership is not about titles or positions but about the ability to influence others positively. He believed that effective leaders build strong relationships, inspire and empower others, and create a culture of growth and development. Maxwell encourages leaders to lead with integrity, authenticity, and a servant's heart (Maxwell, 2015).

In the same vein, Simon Sinek, a leadership speaker and author, is known for his concept of "The Golden Circle" and the idea of starting with "Why." Sinek believed that great leaders inspire others by communicating their purpose of "why." He argued that when leaders have a clear understanding of their purpose and communicate it effectively, they inspire their teams to achieve remarkable results. Sinek emphasized the significance of creating a sense of belonging and fostering a culture where people feel valued and motivated (Sinek, 2014). Likewise, Patrick Lencioni, a leadership consultant, focused on the importance of building cohesive teams. Lencioni suggested that effective leadership involves creating a culture of trust, where team members feel safe to be vulnerable and express their ideas. He highlighted the significance of fostering healthy conflict, where differing viewpoints are openly discussed and resolves. Lencioni also emphasized the importance of clarity and alignment, ensuring that everyone on the team understands the organization's goals and their individual roles in achieving them (Lencioni, 2016).

Additionally, Robin Sharma, a leadership speaker and author, focused on personal mastery and continuous improvement as the foundation of effective leadership. Sharma suggested that leaders should invest in their personal growth, develop their skills, and cultivate a mindset of excellence. He encouraged leaders to lead by example, setting high standards and inspiring their teams to reach their full potential. Sharma also emphasized the importance of self-discipline, resilience, and a positive attitude in leadership (Sharma, 2010). Tom Peters, a management consultant, emphasized the role of passion and innovation in leadership. Peters believed that leaders should be passionate about what they do and inspire that passion in their teams. He encourages leaders to constantly seek opportunities for innovation, challenge the status quo, and foster a culture of continuous improvement. Peters also emphasized the importance of valuing and developing people, recognizing their contributions, and creating a positive work environment (Peters, 2014). Not leaving out John Welch, the former CEO of General Electric (GE), is known for his transformative leadership style. Welch emphasized the importance of creating a culture of candor and transparency, where open communication and feedback are encouraged. He believed that leaders should foster a competitive and high-performance environment, set clear expectations, and hold people accountable. Welch also highlighted the significance of empowering and developing future leaders within the organization.

When we combine the perspectives of these renowned leadership experts, we can draw a comprehensive understanding of how leadership is perceived and enacted in the workplace. These perspectives indicate that effective leadership involves self-awareness, the ability to adapt leadership styles based on the situation and the needs of followers, the cultivation of leadership presence, influencing others positively, leading with integrity and authenticity, inspiring teams through a clear purpose and vision, and continuously improving oneself (Ayoko, 2021). Effective leadership also involves cultivating a culture of inclusion and excellence, fostering open communication and feedback, and empowering and developing others. This implies that successful leaders are self-aware, understand their strengths and weaknesses, and actively seek personal growth (Raghid et al., 2022). They also embody humility, build trust and cohesive teams, and adapt their leadership approach to meet the unique needs of their team members, providing the right balance of direction, support, and autonomy. Additionally, they demonstrate leadership presence by being fully present, listening attentively, empowering others, and fostering an inclusive and collaborative environment.

Finally, we acknowledge that leadership is dynamic and evolving, and different experts may have varied or contrasting perspectives. Nonetheless, the insights of Michael Anderson, Ken Blanchard, Marshall Goldsmith, John C. Maxwell, Simon Sinek, Robin Sharma, and Jack Welch provide valuable perspectives on leadership that can guide individuals on their leadership journeys and help employees to develop their leadership skills and contribute to the success of their teams and organizations.

What Are Leadership Skills?

Although it's true that some people are born with greater natural gifts than others, the ability to lead is a collection of skills, nearly all which can be learned and improved.

John Maxwell (2007, p. 25)

Leadership skills are the ability to organize people and teams to accomplish a common goal (Thomas, 2022). From a human relations lens, these skills support the development of an environment that paves the way for employees to thrive while delighting in their jobs and can increase an organization's overall employee retention rate (O'Shannassy, 2021). Therefore we contend that the leadership potential of employees is not likely to be tapped or realized unless they are given opportunities to develop their leadership skills.

Certain leadership skills that can steer and inspire or motivate employees toward success include interpersonal skills, delegation, communication, empathy, time management, conflict resolution, strategic thinking, and active listening. In this section, we will look at a few leadership skills to better understand the fundamental skills that organizations can start to consider in order to train their employees and get them ready for leadership roles (Reece & Reece, 2017).

Delegation

Great leadership has many elements, and delegation is a crucial skill for optimizing employees' contributions and increasing productivity among all members of a team. Delegation is the ability to assign tasks and responsibilities. Good leaders are aware of the best candidates suited for various duties and tasks. Delegation is about putting one's faith and trust in others while keeping a clear business-oriented goal in mind. Delegating is essential for leaders because they cannot and should not perform all tasks independently. Delegation empowers your team, increases their autonomy, cultivates a sense of worth, respect, and trust among employees, and makes teams more productive (Raghid et al., 2022). In essence, delegation is a crucial tool for improving the effectiveness and performance of teams and organizations.

While the advantages of delegation are evident, effectively delegating might not always be easy. However, just like any other ability or skill, delegation can be learned and honed until it becomes second nature. Delegation is a valuable tool for strategic planning. As a leader, you are swamped with more demands than you have time to manage; therefore, delegating could help you free up your time in order to focus on more significant duties. By understanding how much control you need to maintain over any process or task, you can determine the best strategy for empowering others. Therefore, delegation skills will aid in your understanding of how to match people to projects that best utilize their skills. By doing this, you can be sure to obtain the best end-result in every project (Omolawal, 2015).

Communication

As rightly noted by Dr. William Robinson, effective communication may be the most fundamental prerequisite for the twenty-first century leader. Every organization depends on effective communication, making it one of the leaders' most essential interpersonal skills (Cumm et al., 1977). It is expected of leaders to maintain constant communication with team members. They must communicate their views and simplify complex concepts so everyone can grasp them. In order to build or maintain relationships, to share information and professional experience, and to let people know how they are feeling, leaders are also expected to use effective communication.

It is vital to keep in mind that others frequently judge us based on the message we actually convey rather than the message we intended. Therefore, effective communication makes explaining or conveying organizational goals and tasks feasible through various channels, including but not limited to one-on-one meetings, emails, and social media (Omodan et al., 2020). Organizations experience tremendous success when employees can respectfully and effectively communicate their thoughts, needs, and concerns. In addition, employees who consistently practice effective communication are more likely to develop meaningful work relationships and experience higher levels of job satisfaction (Sadia et al., 2016). In summary, communication skills help leaders to clearly define their goals. An open and positive relationship between leaders and their teams is fostered by effective communication skills, and this improves output and efficiency.

Active Listening

A popular adage that resonates with us in regard to active listening says *"we have two ears and a single mouth so that we might hear more and talk less."* This proverb emphasizes the need for active listening. Effective listening is the capacity to pay attention to what others are saying without letting one's prejudices, opinions, or preconceptions surface (Reece & Reece, 2017). It entails devoting time to comprehending others' perspectives while responding in ways that show respect for others' emotions and viewpoints. Pay attention to both the speaker's words and any nonverbal indicators they provide. Rephrase and reflect on what the person said and refrain from passing judgment or offering advice (Merrill & Reid, 1999).

Building connections, resolving disagreements, ensuring understanding, and improving accuracy all benefit from effective listening. Effective listening at work may result in fewer mistakes and less time wasted (Kolzow, 2014). The capacity to talk clearly and listen clearly are both essential for success while trying to increase collaboration with others. Understanding the speaker's entire message requires active listening (Kolzow, 2014). Thus, maintaining eye contact with the speaker, paying attention, keeping an open mind, avoiding interruptions, and asking questions or making remarks just to ensure you understand are all ways to develop great listening skills. Being able to actively listen is a crucial leadership skill because it promotes loyalty, transparency, and trust. Additionally, leaders who actively listen gain insight and become more aware of the sources of stress and tension in the people they are in charge of. It promotes improved communication between team members and leaders and increases engagement.

Emotional Intelligence

The capacity to recognize and regulate emotions in ourselves and others is known as emotional intelligence (Bruce & Nyland, 2011). It requires having the capacity to comprehend and react to people in

Leading From Within

a way that fosters positive relationships. Emotional intelligence is a vital skill for managing stress and upholding morale in settings where change is constant (Rider, 2002).

Many studies have indicated that there is a relationship between leadership and emotional intelligence. The relationship has often been stressed in abilities of empathic listening, resonance, and self-awareness (Guillen & Florent-Treacy, 2011). Similarly, Goleman has indicated in his writings that there is a common denominator in most of the highly effective leaders, and that commonality is emotional intelligence. Ovans (2015) further added that a person may possess intelligent ideas and critical thinking skills and may have been trained in the best possible manner, but without emotional intelligence, the person would still not become a great leader. It is inferred that a leader who is emotionally intelligent will be able to influence his followers with his individual personality and motivate them very well. Also, with enhanced emotional intelligence, a leader's empathy will be more pronounced, and such a leader can give individualized considerations to employees.

Since leaders have higher pressures to fulfil organizational expectations, maintain employees' performance, and manage conflicts (Dobre, 2013), emotional intelligence plays a very important role. To maintain a healthy environment in the workplace, leaders must know how to handle their emotions and maintain an equilibrium among employees' behavior (Barsade & O'Neill, 2016).

Empathy

Another crucial leadership skill is the capacity for empathy. It entails viewing a situation from the viewpoint of others and understanding the impact organizational decisions or actions will have on employees' lives and work (Covey, 1988). Furthermore, it requires consideration for others regarding work demands and individual preferences. Empathy helps create an environment where support and understanding thrive, benefiting employees and employers (Merrill & Reid, 1999).

It is crucial to note the distinction between empathy and sympathy. While sympathy means to "feel sorry for", empathy means to "feel with" another (Kolzow, 2014). According to Rogers (1971), empathy is the ability to perceive an idea from another person's perspective in order to understand how it could feel to him. So, to empathize with someone else is to step into his or her shoes. Understanding the other side's perspective can be a useful leadership ability in resolving a conflict. Sensitivity to the needs of others, as well as the capacity to listen to and appreciate the value of other team members' contributions are essential elements in building a team (Kolzow, 2014). As a leader, the ability to show empathy builds trust among your employees. Trust creates an empowering and honest relationship. In turn, this could boost teamwork and productivity, but most significantly, your team will feel secured in the knowledge that their needs and feelings are being met.

Conflict Resolution

A part of effective leadership is caring for and supporting one another, even when there is conflict or a difference of opinion.

Ty Howard

Conflict management is a skill that leaders must be able to employ when needed to help foster a productive working environment (Guttman, 2004). The capacity to recognize conflict and manage it in a way that produces a favorable result is known as conflict resolution (Madalina, 2016). It requires understanding the fundamental causes of conflict and the many points of view held by the parties concerned. There is an understanding that leaders should prioritize learning and mastering conflict management skills. A leader's inability to manage disagreement will not only produce undesirable results, but it could also undermine the leader's credibility (Behfar et al., 2008; Kazimoto, 2013).

Without the capacity to resolve conflict in a constructive manner, it is very challenging to be an effective leader (Kolzow, 2014). Leaders must embrace the possibility of conflict in human interactions and learn to deal with it (Tessier et al., 2002). Since it is not possible that conflicts would never arise within teams, a leader's job is to be able to spot conflict and apply conflict resolution techniques to guide organizational interactions toward advantageous outcomes for all parties (Kolzow, 2014). This suggests that understanding and identifying the sources or roots of conflict is the first step to effective leadership and those in positions of leadership who are skilled at resolving conflicts have a variety of tools at their disposal. It is crucial to note that, when handled well, conflict can be a healthy source of competition and collaboration in a workplace, and can lead to the development of stronger teams.

Cultural Competence

Cultural competence is comprehending and collaborating well with individuals from various cultural backgrounds (Reece & Reece, 2017). This skill is crucial in a diverse workplace for fostering positive relationships between multiple teams and workers from different cultures. A leader who fosters an inclusive work environment promotes diversity, inclusiveness, and belonging (Spreitzer et al., 2012; Thomas, 2001). Valuing diversity is an extension of civility, respect, and trust. According to research, diversity drives market growth, and diverse groups often outperform non-diverse ones in terms of performance, judgment, and innovation (Hewlett et al., 2013).

Cultural competence is a vital skill for communicating and collaborating successfully at work. When leaders possess this skill, their organizations may experience higher levels of efficiency and productivity. In addition, when leaders develop cultural competence, listening becomes an activity they practice with their whole being, going beyond just hearing the words other people are saying. As a result, leaders develop the ability to effectively work with others from varying cultural backgrounds with fewer barriers. This creates an opportunity for diversity to be understood and worked with to meet organizational goals (Tanneau & McLoughlin, 2021).

Some other leadership skills derived from the perspectives of the various leadership experts discussed in the previous sections include (i) strategic thinking: leaders should have the ability to think strategically, set goals, and make informed decisions. They should have a clear vision for their organization and be able to align their actions and those of their team with that vision; (ii) accountability: leaders should hold themselves and their team members accountable for their actions and outcomes. They should set high standards, track progress, and ensure that goals are achieved; (iii) building and developing teams: leaders should possess the skills to build cohesive teams, foster collaboration, and develop their team members' skills and talents. They should create a culture of trust and foster a supportive and inclusive work environment; (iv) adaptability: leaders should be flexible and adaptable in their approach. They should be able to adjust their leadership style based on the needs and development level of their team members; and (v) self-awareness: leaders should have a deep understanding of their strengths, weaknesses, values, and emotions. This self-awareness allows them to lead authentically and make better decisions.

The various leadership skills discussed above are some fundamental skills that must be present in a leader's toolkit and used as necessary within a team or organization. It is important to note that these skills are not exhaustive, and the specific skills required may vary depending on the industry, organizational context, and the leader's level of responsibility. However, cultivating these skills can contribute to effective leadership and the success of teams and organizations (The Strategy Institute, 2020). To foster employee leadership, organizations should provide training or professional opportunities where employees can learn and hone these leadership skills. The professional development opportunities will go a long way toward boosting employee confidence and making sure they are prepared for the leadership responsibilities ahead.

WHY CREATING LEADERS IN EMPLOYEES IS IMPORTANT

In today's dynamic and competitive business landscape, the importance of strong leadership cannot be overstated. Effective leaders inspire, guide, and empower their teams, leading to increased productivity, innovation, and organizational success (Yukl & Gardner, 2020). While leadership is often associated with top-level executives, creating leaders within employees at all levels of an organization is equally important. By nurturing leadership qualities in employees, organizations can unlock their full potential, foster a culture of excellence, and ensure long-term sustainability (O'Shannassy, 2021). In an article in the Wall Street Journal by Rothwell (2005) titled *"Death of the 'Irreplaceable' CEO Successor"* the company's succession hopes laid in one very talented individual who untimely passed on. In this example, risks are involved when an organization designates just one potential successor for any crucial position in the organization. The disadvantage of focusing all leadership development efforts on a single individual, regardless of their talent, and failing to create a bigger pool of potential leaders results in the organization's inability to rapidly and efficiently initiate a succession process during a crisis (Hossni, 2019). This example highlights that leadership should not be concentrated on a single person.

The concept or corporate convention that leadership is everyone's business stems from the realization that the kinds of challenges encountered in today's environment of global competitiveness are far too complicated for any one person to handle alone (Kets de Vries & Korotov, 2010). In order to survive and grow, organizations should be aware of the talent inside their employees and look for ways to foster it at all levels. If succession is one of the main responsibilities of leadership, then sustainable leadership development initiatives should identify those who have the potential for taking on leadership responsibilities. This should include employees at various levels in the organization (Kolzow, 2014). Moreover, creating leaders within employees strengthens the resilience of an organization. By nurturing the pipeline of capable leaders, organizations mitigate the risk associated with succession planning. In the face of unexpected challenges in leadership, having employees who possess leadership skills and the ability to step up ensures continuity and adaptability (Northouse, 2019). It helps maintain stability, reduces disruptions, and allows organizations to navigate through uncertainties more effectively.

We reckon that in the traditional conceptions of leadership, power typically is found in the designated leader. However, since modern organization are moving toward a knowledge-based model, it is critical that all of its staff members be knowledge workers rather than people just taking orders and implementing them (Kolzow, 2014). As employees take on ownership and increased responsibility for making decisions about their work and the outcomes of their job, it instills in them a sense of pride, engagement, and commitment, and the identity and reputation of the organization are put in the hands of all its members rather than a selected few or designated leader at the top (Helgesen, 1996). As a result, leadership will be present at every level of the organization. The reality of this shared leadership throughout the organization forces a shift in perspective regarding who a leader is. If an organization's objective is to become better and more successful, it should concentrate on developing its leaders at all levels, making leadership a shared effort.

Creating leaders among employees can encourage a sense of community among employees within the organization. When employees feel like they belong to their workplace community, they are more likely to put their all into their work and improve. Additionally, they support everyone with whom they collaborate in doing the same, fostering a culture of practice, trust, open communication, and mutual respect. Any company that expands its leadership has the capacity to increase its duties and take on new projects (Maxwell, 2011). This improves team dynamics and also enhances overall organizational performance. Furthermore, prioritizing employees' leadership growth for the business culture may also increase their morale and engagement (Hossni, 2019; Yukl & Gardner, 2020). Employees are more motivated when they have concrete goals, resulting in more prestigious titles and higher compensation. If new hires witness their colleagues being rewarded and given possibilities for growth, they could feel more motivated to go above and beyond (Reece & Reece, 2017). Similarly, many people are loyal to companies that offer them growth prospects and opportunities to widen their skill sets and advance in their careers. If an organization hopes to keep top achievers, priming them for leadership positions may be helpful (Yukl & Gardner, 2020).

It has been said that one of the main benefits of creating leaders internally is that they achieve productivity roughly 50 percent more quickly than new hires. This is especially true for organizations where knowledge of internal politics and structures is required to get the job done (Kolzow, 2014). Therefore, the overarching goal of employee leadership development from a human relations standpoint is to increase internal employees' effectiveness in leadership positions and processes. It is premised on succession planning and built on the idea that employees must advance in their careers. Creating leaders in employees is a source of competitive advantage for organizations. In addition, it produces a highly skilled workforce that can help buffer organizations in turbulent times (Yukl & Gardner, 2020).

In summary, creating leaders within employees is crucial for the long-term success and sustainability of organizations. By empowering individuals, fostering collaboration, enhancing engagement, and promoting continuous learning, organizations can unlock the potential of their employees and maximize their contributions. The benefits of employees' leadership development extend beyond the individual level, positively impacting teams, departments, and the overall organizational culture. Investing in leadership development is an investment in the future, enabling organizations to adapt to challenges, seize opportunities, and thrive in a rapidly evolving world. Therefore, organizations that prioritize the development of leaders within employees are poised for enduring success and competitive advantage.

How to Create Leaders in Employees

Having explained what leadership skills look like and why it is essential to give employees leadership development, the next question would be how these skills can be fostered in employees, that is, how can organizations create leaders in their employees? We are aware that there is a wide range in the leadership potential of employees. When it comes to their capacity for leadership, not everyone is equally gifted. However, we argue that everyone can develop their leadership potential to a varying extent. Therefore, one of the most common ways to promote employee leadership is through training or professional development (Reece & Reece, 2017).

Employee professional leadership development involves training all employees, new hires and experienced, how to be leaders. The training programs can include workshops, seminars, and coaching sessions. These programs can focus on areas such as communication, decision-making, strategic thinking, emotional intelligence, and team management (Hossni, 2019). It entails developing a strategy to support staff in developing leadership traits. By doing this, organizations would be able to provide their employees with a sense of purpose at work, provide possibilities for professional advancement, and attract and retain talent (Yukl & Gardner, 2020). Additionally, opportunities should be provided to employees to participate in leadership training during convenient hours if the right resources are available. For example, if someone is usually very busy during the day, they will not have time to attend workshops, or they may have family commitments. For this person, learning at his or her own pace may be a convenient alternative for leadership development (Yukl & Gardner, 2020).

Furthermore, it is essential to develop standards for the organization to recognize leadership abilities and to instruct supervisors or mid-level managers to monitor their teams for individuals who show promise. For example, confidence, adaptability, strategic thinking, and practical communication skills could indicate an employee's traits that could be nurtured in a leadership position (Yukl & Gardner, 2020). We opine that employees require experience to develop into leaders. They require opportunities to lead, such as being made the lead on a project. Giving employees these experiences will help them discover the leader within themselves.

Mentoring is one of the finest ways to turn employees into leaders. In addition to setting an example to the mentee, a mentor can guide the employee to improve. As a result, an employee's skill set can be expanded through both practical and theoretical learning by being paired with an experienced manager or leader. Furthermore, an employee's performance could be monitored and evaluated by a mentor, who would also identify areas for growth in light of potential future leadership responsibilities (Sadia et al., 2016). Additionally, practical experience is key to helping employees develop their skills and learn from any setbacks. Organizations should assign employees to tasks that increasingly expand their authority and skill sets. This can be done by delegating a presentation to an employee to improve his/her public speaking skills. The employee may later be chosen by his or her employer to serve as the chairman of a project's subcommittee (O'Shannassy, 2021).

In addition, to create leaders in employees, organizations should be able to identify expected gaps for future leadership. They should be able to reflect on their organizational needs to determine the business units that could benefit from leadership in the future (Kets de Vries & Korotov, 2010). For instance, it could be a good idea to start looking at the finance team for junior employees who might thrive in a leadership role if the financial director indicates his desire to retire within three years. Identifying business needs ahead of time ensures that organizations have the time to train their staff and equip them with the resources they need to succeed.

When an organization identifies employees possessing leadership potential, they should collaborate with the employee and supervisor to design an individual development plan (IDP). This plan often outlines the employee's strengths and weaknesses and defines the necessary steps the employee must follow to achieve the set goals. For example, it might be beneficial to consider professional certifications, accreditations, or courses the employee could take, including any added responsibilities that could help refine or hone their skill set (Reece & Reece, 2017). Furthermore, collaboration and cross-functional exposure play a vital role in leadership development. Organizations can create leaders by fostering opportunities for employees to work on cross-departmental projects or assignments (Omodan et al., 2020). This exposure enables employees to gain a broader perspective, understand different functions within the organization, and develop skills in managing diverse teams. Collaboration encourages networking, teamwork, and the exchange of ideas, leading to innovative solutions and nurturing leadership qualities such as communication, negotiation, and conflict resolution (Gamble et al., 2019).

Fostering a sense of community among employees, offering clear and concise communication, and providing opportunities for growth and development are all necessary for developing leaders among employees. In addition, by developing the leadership potential in employees, organizations can ensure that they have a strong pool of candidates to fill open leadership positions when needed (Ayoko, 2021). Organizations can help their employees develop their leadership abilities through activities like formal training, coaching, mentoring, rotating assignments, job shadowing, mentor relationships, and project leadership. Without a doubt, social networking technologies and on-the-job training are also relevant to employee leadership development.

CONCLUSION

Creating leaders in employees is a strategic imperative for organizations seeking long-term success, and it is the only way to prepare the next generation of key decision-makers in an organization. This implies that a company's sustainability depends on its ability to identify future leaders and equip them with the necessary tools to develop their careers and lead teams to success. Developing a promising employee's leadership abilities can help teams prepare for the future while boosting employee confidence. Talent management practices can effectively identify and develop the leaders at all levels who will best drive organizational performance.

Regardless of the different definitions of leadership today, it is crucial for any organization to know that it has a team of individuals willing to develop their leadership skills, accept responsibility for their actions, and motivate those around them. In addition, finding staff members suited for leadership positions can inspire proactive planning for the organization's future and provide a wealth of viable internal candidates for a manager, director, and executive positions. Therefore, nurturing leaders at all levels not only enhances individual career growth, but also strengthens the organization as a whole. Organizations that prioritize leadership development cultivate a culture of innovation, adaptability, and engagement, ultimately positioning themselves for sustained success in today's dynamic business landscape.

REFERENCES

Anderson, M. (n.d.). *Gain the clarity and confidence you need to lead well.* Anderson Leadership Resources.https://andersonlr.com/

Ayoko, O. B. (2021). Resiliency and leadership in organizations. *Journal of Management & Organization*, *27*(3), 417–421. doi:10.1017/jmo.2021.44

Barsade, S., & O'Neill, O. A. (2016). Manage your emotional culture. *Harvard Business Review*, 58–66.

Behfar, K. J., Peterson, R. S., Mannix, E. A., & Trochim, W. M. K. (2008). The critical role of conflict resolution in teams: A close look at the links between conflict type, conflict management strategies, and team outcomes. *The Journal of Applied Psychology, 93*(1), 170–188. doi:10.1037/0021-9010.93.1.170 PMID:18211143

Blanchard, B. (2010). *Leading at a higher level*. BMC Press.

Blanchard, B. (2015). Leading at a higher level (Revised & Expanded ed.). Pearson.

Bruce, K., & Nyland, C. (2011). Elton Mayo and the deification of human relations. *Organization Studies, 32*(3), 383–405. doi:10.1177/0170840610397478

Covey, S. R. (1988). *7 basic habits of highly effective people*. Free Press.

Dobre, O.-I. (2013). Employee motivation and organizational performance. *Review of Applied Socio-Economic Research, 5*(1), 53–60.

Gamble, J. E., Peteraf, M. A., & Thompson, A. A. Jr. (2019). *Essentials of Strategic Management: The Quest for Competitive Advantage, 6e*. McGraw Hill Education.

Gardner, H., & Laskin, E. (1995). *Leading minds: An anatomy of leadership*. Harper Collins Publishers.

Goldsmith, M. (2014, July 28). *The many facets of leadership*. Financial Times Prentice Hall. https://www.scribd.com/document/235260851/Marshall-Goldsmith-the-Many-Facets-of-Leadership

Guillen, L., & Florent-Treacy, E. (2011). *Emotional intelligence and leadership effectiveness: The mediating influence of collaborative behaviors*. Social Science Research Network.

Guttman, H. (2004). The leader's role in conflict management. *Leader to Leader, 31*(31), 48–53. doi:10.1002/ltl.63

Head, G. (2003). Effective collaboration: Deep collaboration as an essential element of the learning process. *Journal of Educational Enquiry, 4*(2), 47–62.

Helgesen, S. (1996). *Leading from the grass roots: The leader of the future*. Jossey-Bass Publishers.

Hewlett, S. A., Marshall, M., & Sherbin, L. (2013). How diversity can drive innovation. *Harvard Business Review, 91*(12), 30.

HossniM. (2019). *Human relations theory of management*. doi:10.13140/RG.2.2.12893.56804

Kazimoto, P. (2013). Analysis of conflict management and leadership for organizational change. *International Journal of Research in Social Sciences, 3*(1), 16–25.

Kets de Vries, M. F. R., & Korotov, K. (2010). Developing Leaders and leadership development. *SSRN Electronic Journal*. doi:10.2139/ssrn.1684001

Klingborg, D. J., Moore, D., & Varea-Hammond, S. (2006). What is leadership? *Journal of Veterinary Medical Education, 33*(2), 280–283. doi:10.3138/jvme.33.2.280 PMID:16849311

Kolzow, D. R. (2014). *Leading from within: Building organizational leadership capacity*. IEDC. https://www.iedconline.org/clientuploads/Downloads/edrp/Leading_from_Within.pdf

Lencioni, P. (2016). *The ideal team player: How to recognize and cultivate the three essential virtues.* Jossey-Bass.

Madalina, O. (2016). Conflict management: A new challenge. *Procedia Economics and Finance, 39*, 807–814. doi:10.1016/S2212-5671(16)30255-6

Maxwell, J. (2015). *The leadership handbook.* Harper Collins Leadership.

Northouse, P. G. (2010). *Leadership: Theory and practice* (5th ed.). Sage.

Northouse, P. G. (2018). *Leadership: Theory and practice* (7th ed.). Sage Publications.

Northouse, P. G. (2019). *Interactive: Leadership: Theory and Practice.* SAGE Publications.

O'Shannassy, T. (2021). The challenges of strategic leadership in organizations. *Journal of Management & Organization, 27*(2), 235–238. doi:10.1017/jmo.2021.36

Omodan, B. I., Tsotetsi, C. T., & Dube, B. (2020). Analysis of human relations theory of management: A quest to re-enact people's management towards peace in university system. *SA Journal of Human Resource Management, 18.* doi:10.4102ajhrm.v18i0.1184

Omolawal, S. A. (2015). Delegation of responsibilities: A leadership tool for subordinates' competence development in selected organizations in Ibadan metropolis. The Nigerian. *Journal of Sociology and Anthropology, 13*(1), 68–83. doi:10.36108/NJSA/5102/13(0140)

Ovans, A. (2015). How emotional intelligence became a key leadership skill. *Harvard Business Review.* https://hbr.org/2015/04/how-emotional-intelligence-became-a-key-leadership-skill

Peters, T. (2014). *Leading: People first.* WP Content. https://tompeters.com/wp-content/uploads/2014/02/Leadership_052914.pdf

Raghid Al, H., & Vongas, J. G. (2022). Leadership and contempt in organizations: A conceptual model and research agenda. *Journal of Business and Behavioral Sciences, 34*(1), 20–34.

Reece, B., & Reece, M. (2017). *Effective human relations: Interpersonal and organizational applications* (13th ed.). CENGAGE Learning.

Rider, E. (2002). Twelve strategies for effective communication and collaboration in medical teams. *BMJ (Clinical Research Ed.), 325*(7359), 45. doi:10.1136/bmj.325.7359.S45

Rothwell, W. J. (2005). *Effective succession planning: Ensuring leadership continuity and building talent from within* (3rd ed.). American Management Association.

Sabir, A. (2017). A leader: One, who knows the way, goes the way, and shows the way. *European Business and Management, 3*(5), 82–85. doi:10.11648/j.ebm.20170305.12

Sadia, A., Mohd Salleh, B., Abdul Kadir, Z., & Sanif, S. (2016). The relationship between organizational communication and employees' productivity with new dimensions of effective communication flow. *Journal of Business and Social Review in Emerging Economies, 2*(2), 93–100. doi:10.26710/jbsee.v2i2.35

Sharma, R. (2010). *The leader who had no title.* Simon & Schuster.

Sinek, S. (2014). *Leaders eat last*. Penguin Group LLC. https://d-pdf.com/book/595/read

Spreitzer, G., Porath, C. L., & Gibson, C. (2012). Toward human sustainability: How organizations can enable more thriving at work. *Organizational Dynamics*, *41*(2), 155–162. doi:10.1016/j.orgdyn.2012.01.009

Tanneau, C., & McLoughlin, L. (2021, June 22). Effective global leaders need to be culturally competent. *Harvard Business Review*.

Tessier, C., Chaudron, L., & Muller, H.-J. (Eds.). (2002). *Conflicting agents: Conflict management in multi-agent systems*. Kluwer Academic. doi:10.1007/b116057

The Strategy Institute. (2020, April 9). *Personal goals and organizational strategy: The virtue of perfect alignment*. The Strategy Institute.

Thomas, D. A. (2001). Cultural diversity at work: The effects of diversity perspectives on work group processes and outcomes. *Administrative Science Quarterly*, *46*(2), 229–273. doi:10.2307/2667087

Thomas International Limited. (2022, May 3). *How to develop leadership skills in employees*. Thomas. https://www.thomas.co/resources/type/hr-blog/how-develop-leadership-skills-employees

Van Velsor, E., & McCauley, C. D. (2004). Our view of leadership development. In C. D. McCauley & E. Van Velsor (Eds.), *The center for creative leadership handbook of leadership development* (2nd ed., pp. 1–22). Jossey-Bass.

Yukl, G. A. (2006). *Leadership in organizations* (6th ed.). Pearson-Prentice Hall.

Yukl, G. A., & Gardner, W. L. (2020). *Leadership in organizations* (9th ed.). Pearson.

Chapter 8
A Framework for Knowledge-Based Leadership for Improved Risk Management in State-Owned Enterprises in South Africa

Malefetjane Phineas Phaladi
https://orcid.org/0000-0002-6267-5295
Durban University of Technology, South Africa

Ngoako Solomon Marutha
https://orcid.org/0000-0002-5679-4394
University of South Africa, South Africa

ABSTRACT

The purpose of this chapter is to investigate a framework for knowledge-based leadership for improved risk management in state-owned enterprises in South Africa. The study empirically explored the influence and role of knowledge-based leadership in driving knowledge management and human resource management practices for effective knowledge risk management. Exploratory sequential mixed methods research design was used as the overall strategy to guide data collection for the project. In the qualitative strand, data were gathered through interviews with 20 purposively nominated human resource managers. In the quantitative strand, 145 responses collected through survey instrument were used to test variables discovered in the first strand. A lack of knowledge-based leadership contributed to the absence of knowledge strategy and practices, knowledge-driven culture, structural configurations and roles, and ineffective tacit knowledge loss risks management. The chapter proposes a knowledge-based leadership framework to mitigate tacit knowledge risks in state-owned enterprises.

DOI: 10.4018/979-8-3693-1380-0.ch008

INTRODUCTION AND BACKGROUND

Leadership and knowledge management (KM) have always been regarded as critical success factors to drive and sustain competitive edge in knowledge-based competition and provide the required knowledge strategy and capabilities to mitigate risks inherent in tacit knowledge loss. A knowledge-based view theory (KBVT) of the firm is a theory of the knowledge economy that calls for leadership and management practices that prioritise the development of knowledge strategy and leadership to ensure the investment in capabilities aimed at effecting the protection, application, transfer and retention of the firm-specific intangible assets. Such leadership is characterised as knowledge-oriented or knowledge-based leadership or knowledge leadership in the knowledge management and leadership literature (Gürlek & Cemberci, 2020). For the purpose of this chapter, Knowledge-based leadership (KBL), Knowledge-driven leadership (KDL) and Knowledge-oriented leadership (KOL) are used interchangeably to mean knowledge leadership. KBL plays a critical role in nurturing enterprise knowledge, sourcing, transferring, protecting and managing knowledge assets to ensure superior business performance and innovation capacity (Sadeghi & Rad, 2018; Birasnav, Albufalasa & Bader, 2013). However, the extant literature indicates that KBL is not yet fully developed and remains a serious issue in many companies around the globe (Zieba & Schivinski, 2015). State-owned enterprises (SOEs) are seen as knowledge-intensive business enterprises and learning organisations. Many of them in South Africa are lagging knowledge-based leadership (Phaladi, 2021).

Globally, SOEs are used as key drivers and contributors to gross domestic product (GDP) by developing and developed economies. SOEs make up for a large share of market capitalisation, investment and job creation and remain crucial in key industries, such as water utilities, energy generation and distribution, mining, aviation and defence space, research and innovation, developmental finance sector and physical infrastructure investment and development (Benassi & Landoni, 2019; Clò et al., 2016). Employee turnover is a global problem facing many companies (private and public) in both developing and developed economies (Allen & Vardaman, 2021). Studies show that SOEs as knowledge-intensive business enterprises are operating in a highly stretched competitive labour market wherein the demand for the highly technical and specialised skills far outstrips the existing supply capacity (Wöcke & Barnard, 2021; Roome, 2012). Their role in key industries suggest that SOEs are dependent on highly specialised knowledge, skills and competencies to execute their business mandates. Nevertheless, many of them face a serious problem of knowledge loss risks due to high staffing turnover (voluntary and involuntary) and a lack of retention strategies (Phaladi and Ngulube, 2022; Phaladi, 2022a, 2021). Critical success factors, such as a lack of leadership and management practices to address all these manners of the knowledge loss risks, are flagged as serious problems in the knowledge management literature (Sandelin, Hukka & Katko, 2019; Donate & de Pablo, 2015). Knowledge-related challenges of the companies operating in the knowledge-based economy and competition require knowledge-oriented leadership.

The extant literature broadly defines KM as a management philosophy which is concerned with how knowledge is acquired, developed, assimilated, used, shared and retained for future organisational use, survival and superior performance and innovation (Hussinki et al., 2017). It is equally important for the business leaders and managers to understand the core KM processes so that they are in a better position to drive and offer the required knowledge-based leadership and management support. The core KM processes such as creation, application, sharing and retention are important management processes which help drive knowledge-driven organisational culture, strategies, structures, systems and practices. Knowledge creation is about the process of creating and using knowledge (Nonaka & Takeuchi, 1995).

Hence, KBVT views SOEs as knowledge-creating, distribution and explorer entities (Benassi & Landoni, 2019). Knowledge-intensive organisations such SOEs create and apply tacit knowledge through employees' interactions with the environment in which they operate (Davenport & Prusak, 1998). Knowledge application process emphasise that knowledge should be put into good use to be of strategic importance to the business. The investments in the creation and acquisition process of knowledge will not yield any positive results if firm-specific human resources do not make a good application of it (Jackson, Hill & DeNisi, 2003). Knowledge sharing process is another important KM process which requires a serious leadership and management support across all levels of the enterprise. Knowledge to be of a strategic value to an enterprise, it must be shared between organisational members and by employees. It is concerned with how enterprise-specific tacit knowledge is shared across different business unts and levels within organisations for greater business impact (Becerra-Fernandez & Sabharwal, 2015). Knowledge retention is a KM process closely related to knowledge sharing practice. Martins and Meyer (2012) refer to knowledge retention as a knowledge management process which it is concerned with the protection and retention of tacit knowledge that is largely in the minds of the enterprise-specific workers. Losing such knowledge at the wrong time could threaten organisational performance, sustainability and innovation capacities (Durst & Zieba, 2020). It is important that once knowledge is created, used and transferred through various business and social interactions and other processes, it becomes a business imperative that it must be retained within companies to avoid the risks of losing it when employees leave. For all the KM processes to strive in organisations, they require knowledge-oriented leadership and management support across all the levels of the business. However, knowledge management philosophy and its processes remain underdeveloped in many South African public sector enterprises (Maphoto & Matlala, 2022; Phaladi & Ngulube, 2022). Phaladi (2022b) asserts this is largely due to a lack of knowledge-based leadership and management styles and support. KBL is viewed as a driver of the relationship and competencies development between the various processes of intellectual capital management of the firm (Sadeghi & Rad, 2018). This is the type of leadership style that is lacking in most SOEs in South Africa. Consequently, KM remains underdeveloped in many companies even though they are facing serious risks associated with high human resources' turnover and resultant tacit knowledge loss (Maphoto & Matlala, 2022; Phaladi, 2021), which threaten their sustainability and capability to drive a national developmental mandate (Gumede, 2018).

SOEs in Africa are key drivers of public sector economies and development initiatives (Netswera, 2022; Fagbadebo, 2022). Gumede (2018) observes that many SOEs in Africa are not run effectively and, as a result, they are unable to meet the demands and mandates of their states in growing the economies. The absence of skills and knowledge transfer, poor strategy execution and leadership, inability to foster new innovative capability and technologies and inability to develop new industries are some of the challenges facing African SOEs (Gumede, 2018). State-owned enterprises in South Africa are wholly or partially owned by the state. The state uses SOEs to drive its developmental agenda. South African SOEs are viewed as a catalyst for economic development and industrialisation. Netswera (2022) avers that SOEs in Africa drive the economics of the public infrastructure development and service delivery. However, the same study also asserts that these SOEs face a serious challenge of human capital and resources, poor performance, devastating corruption, and brain drain. Due to increased employee mobility, many companies in South Africa face human resource problems, which complicate the management of the enterprise's tacit knowledge (Phaladi & Ngulube, 2022). Phaladi (2021) study established that many knowledge and skills-related challenges could be traced and blamed squarely on leadership and management, largely due to a lack of knowledge-oriented leadership, vision and strategy in most

South African SOEs. It is precisely for this reason that this chapter sought to explore the role of KBL in driving knowledge management, knowledge-driven culture and structures and human resource management practices to mitigate risks of inherent knowledge loss in state-owned companies. Phaladi (2022b) posits that a lack of KBL contributes to a large share of risks associated with tacit knowledge loss in most SOEs in South Africa. Several studies infer that a lack of knowledge-oriented culture, behaviours, structures, roles and human resource management practices impact adversely on the knowledge strategy and knowledge management implementation (Gürlek, 2020; Matošková & Směšná, 2017; Islam, Jasimuddin & Hasan, 2015).

PURPOSE AND OBJECTIVES FOR THE CHAPTER

The purpose of this chapter was to investigate a framework for knowledge-based leadership for improved risk management in state-owned enterprises in South Africa. The study sought to explore how leadership facilitates organisational culture, systems, practices and structures in South African public enterprises for effective knowledge loss risk management. The objectives of the study were to:

- Examine whether leadership in state-owned enterprises of South Africa could be characterised as knowledge driven in managing enterprise knowledge loss risks;
- Establish whether leadership and management support knowledge management culture in public enterprises of South Africa;
- Explore the role of knowledge management-driven leadership in shaping a knowledge-driven culture and structures for the management of tacit knowledge loss in state-owned enterprises;
- Propose framework for knowledge-driven leadership in state-owned enterprises.

CONTEXT TO THE STUDY

The relationship between leadership and knowledge management in the literature and practice remains undeveloped (Phaladi, 2022b; Zieba & Schivinski, 2015). The management challenge for leaders in knowledge-intensive companies and knowledge-based competition is to develop KM capacities in employees by creating a positive enterprise climate in which absorption, acquisition, development, transfer and protection of knowledge are encouraged or even required as part of the core business activities. Leading and managing knowledge workers and business enterprises in the knowledge-based competition and economy require different leadership styles and practices. Globally, several developing and developed economies use state-owned enterprises to drive knowledge-based competition, learning, economy and innovation systems (Benassi & Landoni, 2019).

PROBLEM STATEMENT

Moreover, state-owned enterprises are also knowledge intensive, creating entities in addition to being knowledge sharing systems. However, many of them are facing knowledge loss risks which threaten their capacity to sustain their superior performance and competitive edge (Ngulube & Phaladi, 2022;

Kumar, 2020). Despite this, Phaladi (2021, 2022b) and Sandelin et al., (2019) note that many SOEs are lagging in a number of areas, such as knowledge-driven leadership; management roles and structures; human resource management strategies; and culture practices support for effective knowledge management. Ideally, knowledge-based leadership implies the type of leadership that affords the responsibility of managing enterprise knowledge a prominent role within state-owned companies. It is for this reason that knowledge-driven leadership should display a knowledge-driven character by leading and championing the development of knowledge management behaviours, culture, structures and strategies. Donate and de Pablo (2015) assert that knowledge-driven leaders are at the forefront of developing, leading and promoting the best strategies around managing and leading knowledge-based practices in their companies. Nonetheless, Phaladi (2022b) laments the fact that leadership and management in South African state-owned enterprises lag in key knowledge-driven leadership styles and practices to facilitate knowledge-oriented culture, roles and structures. KBVT makes a clarion call for knowledge-based and learning companies to invest in the development and protection of knowledge-based assets such as knowledge, skills and expertise (Grant, 1996). This implies that leadership and management have an important role to play in driving the desired knowledge culture, structures and strategies.

LITERATURE REVIEW

Knowledge-Based View Theory

KBVT offers a theoretical perspective on enterprise knowledge. It prioritises firm-specific knowledge assets at the centre of the business strategy. The seminal works of Grant (1996), Spender (1996) and Barney (2001) made a significant contribution that paved the way for the conceptualisation of the concept of knowledge-based view theory, thus placing organisational intangible assets such as knowledge, skills and competencies at the core of the enterprise strategy as the key driver of sustainable competitive edge. SOEs are considered knowledge-intensive, knowledge-creating and distribution, learning and innovation-leading companies. They are also linked to a resource-based view of the firm, largely due to the fact that they are resource intensive in their own right, in terms of physical infrastructure development, human (labour intensive) and knowledge assets investment. KBVT argues that companies can derive better performance and results than rival firms if they prioritise investment in the management and development of the knowledge (Grant, 1996; Hussinki et al., 2017). Knowledge-oriented leadership is therefore considered a non-negotiable critical factor and capability in the management of organisational intangible assets and for the success of KM philosophy and practice within firms (Gürlek & Cemberci, 2020; Phaladi, 2021).

Knowledge loss risk management efforts are bound to fail in the absence of dedicated (knowledge-oriented) leadership and other organisational capabilities, such as knowledge-based culture, vision, structures and strategies (Phaladi, 2022b). Naqshbandi and Jassimuddin (2018) infer that, without leadership that is supportive of KM efforts and strategy, the success of managing enterprise knowledge coherently and effectively within firms remains unattainable for many organisations. Shamim et al., (2019) concur with this position by positing that KBL must be at the forefront of driving and guiding the business and its workers into adopting the required knowledge behaviours and strategies in order to shape and facilitate the development, use, retention and sharing of new knowledge. As a result, such efforts and investments would assist in facilitating the development of knowledge management capacity. Such

KM capability should naturally moderate the effects of tacit knowledge loss risks inherent in employee turnovers. Zhang and Guo (2019) argue that KBL is a type of leadership that is required in knowledge-intensive firms such as SOEs and other learning-based companies. KBVT calls for the organisations to invest in appropriate KM capabilities to ensure that valuable, mission-critical firm-specific knowledge assets are hard to replicate by rival firms. To avoid the risk of companies losing valuable firm-specific intangible assets, Andersén (2012) and Cohen and Levinthal (1990), key theorists on KM capacity, make a clarion call for the leaders and companies to invest in knowledge-absorptive and protective capacities. Investment in such knowledge-absorptive as well as protective capacities will, to a larger degree, help companies mitigate the risk of tacit knowledge loss (Phaladi, 2022a, 2021; Phaladi & Ngulube, 2022).

Knowledge Management

Knowledge is a valuable intangible organisational asset in terms of the strategic value added to the business and its impact on the performance of the firm (Grant, 1996). It is for this reason that it must be managed as a critical resource to ensure sustainability and superior performance results. KM has emerged as a management philosophy to drive organisational efforts and strategies towards acquiring, applying, transferring and retaining firm-specific intangible assets (knowledge, skills and competencies). Becerra-Fernandez and Sabherwal (2015) characterise KM as the art of managing enterprise knowledge to ensure better decision-making, business results, organisational efficiencies, innovation capacity and organisational performance. The existing literature show that a strong relationship between knowledge management, organisational performance and innovation exist (Birasnav et al., 2013; Gürlek & Cemberci, 2020). The philosophy behind management of organisational knowledge is to build KM capacity through knowledge absorptive and protective capacities in order to sustain productivity and sustainability of the business. KM is a transdisciplinary and multidisciplinary discipline; it straddles many disciplines such as organisational science, management science, leadership, strategic human resource management, organisational behaviour, information technology, and psychology, amongst other areas of interest, for the effective management of enterprise knowledge. Zia (2020, p. 1823) posits that it originates from the resource-based view theory (RBVT), which calls for the use of the firm-specific resources to drive organisational performance of companies to derive a sustained competitive edge over rivals. One motivation for establishing KM in business enterprises, is increased human resource mobility and turnover levels (Sumbal et al., 2020). As such, human resources mobility must be managed. Therefore, KM becomes an unavoidable management practice and philosophy to address such complexities in knowledge-intensive business enterprises such as SOEs. According to the KBVT, knowledge, especially its tacit form, is the firm's most valuable strategic asset that, when properly managed, yields a commercial value. Tacit knowledge is the most vulnerable firm resource since it is easily lost whenever employees depart from the company. The loss of tacit knowledge through human resource turnover, retiring critical workers and a lack of retention plans threatens the survival of many enterprises.

Leadership

The literature on KM highlights leadership as a critical factor adversely affecting knowledge management implementation in many companies. Leadership plays an important role in creating knowledge-friendly firm-specific capabilities such as knowledge-based culture, structures, enabling systems, strategies and processes. KBL as an emerging research area in the broader KM discipline is a crucial element required to ensure the success of KM practices (Gürlek & Cemberci, 2020). Knowledge-based leadership is akin to transformational leadership in that it takes a lead in driving human intellectual capital management of the firm. It is the type of leadership that drives knowledge sharing and innovation in companies (Le & Le, 2022). Literature highlights that knowledge-based leadership, HRM and knowledge management practices have a positive effect on organisational performance and innovation (Naqshbandi & Jasimuddin, 2018; Kianto et al., 2017; Le & Le, 2022). Leadership across all ranks of the enterprise plays a critical part in driving the KM agenda and processes. KM is about employees and employees are creators, carriers, suppliers and sources of knowledge within companies. RBVT from the perspective of the firm and KBVT sees human resources within firms and their knowledge as valuable organisational tangible and intangible resources that present companies with sources of competitive edge over rival firms (Barney, 2001; Grant, 1996). Several commentators on KM, such as Gürlek (2020), Shariq et al. (2019), Naqshbandi and Jasimuddin (2018), postulate that management should exhibit knowledge-driven leadership if KM strategies and practices aimed at creating, applying, sharing and retaining enterprise knowledge are to be successful. Mićić (2015, p. 47) contends that, for the firm to see a real value and success in knowledge management, the leadership and management must display certain knowledge-driven qualities and attributes that create an enabling condition for employees to freely contribute to knowledge creation, sharing, application and retention. In other words, leaders running companies in the knowledge-based economy and amid competition, should possess a set of behaviours, norms and values, knowledge and skill sets that are knowledge driven and shape and drive various KM practices and results. Both RBVT & KBVT emphasise that leadership (as in people or employees in organisations) is a valuable resource that is difficult to replicate and imitate by rival firms in that it is a non-substitutable firm-specific resource (Barney, 2001; Shamim, Cang & Yu, 2019). However, the authors of the current paper argue that the success or rather the impact of such leadership is very much dependent on whether it is great at displaying and unleashing the right knowledge-based attitudes, behaviours and value-based system. In a nutshell, knowledge-oriented leadership should drive KM, its practices and value-based system in an organisational setting.

Knowledge Risk Management

Knowledge loss risks are serious challenges facing many private and public enterprises around the globe. Knowledge risks are characterised as a measure of the prospect and severity of the undesirable impact of any actions associated with knowledge (Durst & Henschel, 2020, Zieba, 2020). Durst and Zieba (2018) highlight that any type of business is bound to face a number of knowledge risks. The literature highlights these risks as facing all market sectors of the economy across the globe, such as energy utilities (Sumbal et al., 2023), aerospace companies (Singh & Gupta, 2020), small and medium enterprises (Mamorobela, 2022) information technology sector (Rashid et al., 2020), knowledge-intensive companies (Zieba, 2020), water public utilities (Phaladi, 2021) and manufacturing companies (Sumbal et al., 2020). These knowledge loss risks are mainly caused by high employee turnover, ageing workers and a lack of knowledge-driven human resource retention plans (Phaladi & Ngulube, 2022). It is assumed that a certain type of leadership is needed to address risks associated with knowledge-based competition and increased employee mobility brought about by the advent of the knowledge economy. Several authors propose knowledge leadership, which is made up of a certain combination of styles of transformational and transactional leadership, as a prerequisite for knowledge-intensive companies in dealing with knowledge loss risks (Donate & de Pablo, 2015; Le & Le, 2019). It is for this reason that the recent review of literature (Durst & Zieba, 2020) coined knowledge (loss) risk management as an appropriate management and leadership intervention to mitigate risks associated with knowledge loss.

Kumar (2020) and Phaladi (2021, 2022a) regard knowledge loss risks as serious challenges facing state-owned enterprises. Phaladi (2021, 2022b) and Phaladi and Ngulube (2022) posit that, in South Africa, the complexity of the challenge is compounded by several factors. Such challenges include shortage of a skilled workforce, brain drain, increased voluntary and involuntary turnover, ageing skilled workforce, and a lack of the following: knowledge-oriented leadership, a knowledge-driven culture, structures, and human resource management practices. Wöcke & Barnard (2021, p. 239) highlight a unique case facing South African companies in that the lower-skilled workers are losing their positions as the economy contracts, while highly skilled workers are hard to find and retain. Moreover, what complicates the landscape of knowledge loss in South Africa is that government actively intervenes in the labour market to address inequalities from the apartheid era. In some cases, the employment equity legislation that is meant to address such inequalities in the workplace is found to be pushing employees not favoured by the act to look for opportunities elsewhere in foreign developed economies, thus leading to a brain drain and resulting in tacit knowledge loss. In 2011, Phaladi's study highlighted the fact that such challenges required a concerted effort and knowledge-driven leadership, strategy and vision from government level down to companies' executives and leaders (Phaladi, 2011). However, the current emerging research and frameworks on knowledge risks management fail to link the significant role of leadership and human resource management in the management of tacit knowledge risks.

Organisational Structure and Culture

From a knowledge-based point of view and in an ideal business environment, companies operating in a knowledge-based, competitive environment and economy should invest in organisational capabilities such as knowledge-driven culture and structural configurations. The current research highlights the importance of transformational and knowledge leadership in driving organisational processes, culture and structures for effective management of institutional knowledge as a valuable resource for ensuring sustainability. Nevertheless, Maphoto and Matlala (2022) point out that knowledge management is underdeveloped in many South African public sector companies, largely because they are lagging in knowledge-driven structures and roles. Phaladi (2022b) adds that RBVT and KBVT highlight the importance of knowledge-intensive companies to invest in the development of appropriate organisational capabilities such as culture, systems, processes and structures to protect their firm-specific human and knowledge capital resources. Investment in such business capabilities will ensure that knowledge capital assets as sources for competitive advantage are protected for the superior performance and sustainable future of such firms. The literature equally cautions that firms need to pay attention to the cultural fabric and structural designs of a firm to ensure a greater absorption and retention of their most valuable firm-specific knowledge resources (Gürlek & Tuna, 2018). Several studies equally suggest that, over and above the role of leadership in KM, human resource management has an important role to play in driving knowledge-driven processes, such as rewards and recognitions (financial and non-financial), knowledge-driven staff acquisition and sourcing, performance management systems, learning and development and succession management practices (Gürlek, 2020; Hussinki et al., 2017; Kianto et al., 2017). Such HRM practices will drive the required knowledge-based culture and practices to bolster organisational capabilities to manage and retain enterprise knowledge.

RESEARCH METHODOLOGY

The research context of the study is state-owned enterprises in South Africa. The chapter was philosophically underpinned by pragmatism paradigm. Pragmatism offers the researcher an opportunity to blend interpretivism and positivism philosophies to study the variables of the study from multiple perspectives – philosophically, epistemologically, and methodologically. Leadership and knowledge management are complex disciplines that are interdisciplinary and multidisciplinary; thus, research on such variables needed to be subject to multiple perspectives. The literature suggests that pragmatism is a perfect philosophy to study complex research variables or "wicked problems" involving multiple interacting perspectives (Ngulube, 2020; Creswell & Plano Clark, 2018; Mertens, 2015). The rationale behind the choice of the philosophy was that the researcher observed that issues involving the successful implementation of KM to mitigate risks associated with tacit knowledge hinges on complex multiple organisational factors and that leadership, organisational cultural and HRM practices were cited by current literature (Ngulube, 2019; Sadeghi & Rad, 2018; Valaei et al., 2017, Rezaei et al.,2021; Kianto et al., 2017) as critical factors in organisations contributing to such level of complexity and failures. This study employed a mixed methods research (MMR) methodology, using exploratory sequential design as the overall strategy to gather primary data from the participants (human resource managers) in the qualitative phase and employees in the second phase of the study for empirical analysis and inferences. Morgan (2018) and Creswell and Creswell (2018) posit that MMR is appropriate for studying complex scientific social research issues from multiple viewpoints. It was important that complete, reliable, balanced (complementary) and diverse research findings were developed through blending qualitative and quantitative research methods and data. In the qualitative stance of the research, data were gathered through interviews with twenty purposively selected HR managers in nine SOEs, as illustrated in Table 1 below. The aim was to explore their views regarding leadership support to knowledge management culture and initiatives. The interview guide comprised of non-structured (open-ended) questions was used to gather in-depth data in the qualitative phase of the project. The interviews were conducted in-person with the selected HR managers between March 2019 to July 2019. The qualitative data gathered in the first strand of the study was analysed thematically using Atlas.ti. The research results of the qualitative strand were used to develop the survey instrument for testing in the quantitative strand of the research project.

Table 1. Participating SOEs from which research participants were drawn

Industry sector	Number of participating SOEs	Number of human resource managers interviewed
Development finance sector	2	7
Water utility sector	1	3
Service sector	2	3
Compliance and regulatory sector	2	4
Research and development sector	2	3
Total	9	20

In the quantitative phase, a survey instrument was dispersed to 585 randomly selected employees in three state-owned companies to test variables or knowledge discovered in the qualitative strand of the project. The online survey questionnaire was distributed during the national coronavirus lockdown regulations between September 2020 to November 2020 to three SOEs. Majority of the SOEs that participated in the qualitative strand were not willing to take part in the quantitative strand of the study, citing COVID-19 strict regulations and internet connectivity issues as most of their employees were working from home. The instrument was proven reliable with a Cronbach's alpha of 0.94 and response rate of 25% (145 responses). The Statistical Analysis System was employed to analyse numerical data collected in the second (survey) strand of the study. Hair et al., (2014) observe that a response rate of 120 or more is adequate for studies using exploratory factor analysis (EFA). EFA was used to analyse statistical responses gathered from the survey phase and to develop correlation co-efficiencies of variables that were critical for the formulation of the framework in the main study. This chapter has been extracted from the larger doctoral research project which sought to develop a knowledge loss reduction framework that integrated knowledge management and human resource management practices in the South African state-owned enterprises (Phaladi, 2021).

PRESENTATION OF RESULTS

This section presents both qualitative and quantitative results of the study.

Qualitative Results

Like knowledge-driven organisational culture, knowledge-based leadership is a critical driver of the success of KM and human resource management practices and initiatives. Participants of SOEs where knowledge management was not part of organisational life (not institutionalised), admitted the failures on the part of leadership for not having KM articulation and roles in their organisational structures. Knowledge management roles or functions were absent in the structures of more than 67% of the SOEs participating in the study. The participants of the SOEs where KM was not part of the organisational life, lamented a lack of top leadership buy-in and support. Furthermore, a lack of top leadership and management support and buy-in for a KM philosophy added to the complexity of the knowledge loss risk. Moreover, in the 67% of the SOEs where KM was not institutionalised, managers at the top echelons were blamed for a lack of knowledge vision, knowledge leadership, knowledge strategy and their buy-in on this matter. Those who were of the view that enterprise leadership is knowledge driven and supportive of KM, presented the following reasons:

- Leadership provides resources, budget, structure and opportunities for knowledge management to flourish. For example, an interviewee said:

The fact is that they provide resources, they provide a budget, they provide opportunities. It is not just about the budget, so when we knock on their doors and say XX wants to come to your department for a period of six months to do one, two, three and four, they willingly avail their other resources to support XX to learn (Participant #1, SOE1, 2019).

- Leadership drives and support KM. One participant commented as follows:

They drive this thing. What we do, we have buy-in from them and as I said, our CEO is at the forefront of this knowledge management agenda (Participant#2, SOE1, 2019).

Our commissioner (CEO) meets with our knowledge management team, with our IT and registry people who are accountable for knowledge capture to discuss the capturing of cases every Monday so that is how important it is to discuss progress and knowledge management issues (Participant#4, SOE2, 2019).

- Knowledge-driven leadership drives policy development that is supportive of KM philosophy. However, such level of support is at conceptual level and only limited to policy formulation. As such, leadership did not drive the KM agenda and implementation in practical terms other than just approving policies on KM. For instance, one participant in SOE9 described the limited level of support in this manner:

Yes, they do support it, but they support it conceptually and not practically (Participant #16, SOE9, 2019).

In fewer SOEs of the study where KM was part of the business strategy and life, the participants posited that their business executives or leaders invested in staff capacity development initiatives. The qualitative data also revealed that KM was part of the business strategy in only 33% of the SOEs that took part in the research project. Moreover, leadership in those few companies understood the strategic value proposition of managing organisational tacit knowledge to mitigate potential loss. The participants also indicated that leadership was driving organisational culture and structures that were supportive of KM concept. However, the interviews also showed that KM was not institutionalised in 67% of the state enterprises. This attests to the fact that there was no knowledge-oriented leadership in many of the state-owned companies in South Africa.

The participants that indicated that the leadership did not support KM initiatives, also presented the following reasons:

- Leadership was not visible on the KM agenda.
- Leadership was not talking and walking the KM agenda.
- Leaders were working at the top without strategy and vision regarding KM.
- Leadership in many SOEs did not know what the KM philosophy is. For instance, two of the participants posited in this way:

They don't know what knowledge management is? It's in recent times that they see the fruit of knowledge management and they are things that are very far, the core of knowledge management, they're not there yet (Participant#9, SOE3, 2019).

I am not aware of that, we've given the intention where we would want to see ourselves, one would not say…we have consciously supported knowledge management. There are certain activities or steps that have been taken by leadership knowingly or unconsciously so that would drive KM (Participant#17, SOE5, 2019.

- Leadership did not see the strategic benefits of having knowledge management.
- Top executives and leaders have too many competing interests that require their attention.
- In some companies, leaders and managers were good at supporting KM concepts and frameworks, but implementation was the problem.

About whether participants consider HRM executives and departments to be creating an institutional culture conducive for effective management of enterprise knowledge, 60% of the participants agreed that that HRM does create an enterprise culture that is conducive for KM to flourish in their organisations. In contrast, 40% of the participants did not create an enterprise culture that was conducive to and supportive of effective KM. It was interesting that even those who indicated that they created a business environment that was conducive to effective management of organisational knowledge, posited that there was a room for improvement, and that more could be done in this regard.

Quantitative Results

The quantitative data from the survey component of the study painted a somewhat different picture. Figure 1 presents a diagrammatic picture of knowledge-driven leadership, culture and structures in the SOEs. Concerning leadership support to knowledge management, most (50%) respondents indicated that there was such support, while 26% indicated that there was a lack of leadership support, and a small but noticeable share (24%) remained neutral.

A lack of knowledge-oriented culture has proven to be a serious factor or challenge that hindered the efficient management of enterprise knowledge. A significant number of responses (83%) indicated this result in their answers. Moreover, most (45%) of the answers indicated that HRM establishments within SOEs were playing a significant part in facilitating knowledge-oriented culture. It is important to note that a noticeable minority share of responses at 34% were not convinced that HRM executives and their establishments were facilitating knowledge-oriented culture whilst 21% of responses remained neutral on this important variable of the study.

KM was institutionalised through structures in three out of nine SOEs that took part in the qualitative component of the study. This was evident in that 56% of responses affirmed that this was true, 27% responded that their SOEs did not have a dedicated unit or department for managing organisational knowledge, and 17% of responses were neutral about this variable. However, this must be contextualised, since most state-owned companies that took part in the qualitative stance did not participate in the survey phase of the project. Only three out of nine SOEs participated in the survey phase of the project.

Regarding the research question whether the firm culture facilitated the sharing of knowledge, 38% responded in the affirmative, indicating that the culture was supportive of knowledge sharing, whilst 34% posited that the culture was not supportive, therefore not facilitating KM. Of the responses, 28% were neutral on this variable.

Figure 1. Knowledge-driven leadership, culture, and structure

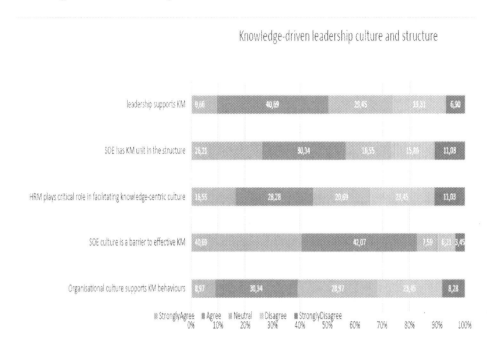

DICUSSSION OF THE RESEARCH FINDINGS

Current literature shows that firms that operate in knowledge-based competition should invest in and make use of knowledge-centred leadership, structures and culture to drive KM agenda (Le & Le, 2019; Gürlek & Çemberci, 2020). The research findings present a variety of opinions on the role of leadership in facilitating knowledge-centric business culture, structural provisioning, and knowledge-driven practices. A lack of KBL was flagged as a serious barrier by the majority of the participants (HR managers) and SOEs in the qualitative phase of the research. The findings of the quantitative phase painted a different picture in that most of the responses (50%) confirmed that leadership and management were knowledge-driven by supporting KM. However, a lack of knowledge-driven leadership and management was clear in that KM was not established in 67% of the SOEs. This research finding confirms the existing research that contends that firms operating in a knowledge-based competitive environment and economy need to develop and make use of knowledge-centred leadership by investing in the required knowledge-based structures and roles (Gürlek, 2020; Shamim et al., 2019; Sadeghi & Rad, 2018). Many SOEs are lagging in key-driven practices, structures and culture. This could be attributed to a lack of knowledge-driven leadership, vision and strategy in many SOEs participating in the study. SOEs are knowledge-intensive and learning companies. KBVT advances enterprise knowledge as a valuable firm-specific asset to derive superior firm performance, productivity and competitive edge (Grant, 1996). As such, leadership in SOEs should demonstrate knowledge-driven character and support by providing leadership through investment in structural provisioning to drive the KM agenda. Nonetheless, the findings of the current research showed that this was not the case in many South African public enterprises. It is also worth noting that out of nine SOEs that took part in the qualitative component, only three had KM-driven leadership institutionalised through relevant units, roles, systems and practices.

KBL invests in building KM capability by putting roles, strategies and structural provisioning in place to support their organisations in acquiring, using, sharing and protecting knowledge assets. Knowledge management capability is positively linked to organisational performance and innovation capability, thereby safeguarding sustainability of the organisations (Durst & Zieba, 2020; Naqshbandi & Jasimuddin, 2018). The fact that 26% of the responses posited that leadership support was lacking, together with the 24% of respondents who were less informative or neutral, suggests that the leadership was not knowledge-driven in character and support. KBL is a form of leadership style that drives and promotes KM-driven behaviours, such as the creation, application, sharing and protection of company-specific knowledge assets (Naqshbandi & Jasimuddin 2018; Donate & de Pablo 2015). In other words, knowledge-based leadership should lead in developing and shaping the required relevant KM strategies, culture, behaviour and practices. Naqshbandi and Jasimuddin (2018, p. 703) contend that KBL should support and help facilitate the development of knowledge management capabilities. As such, a lack of knowledge leadership makes it difficult for South African public companies to remain competitive and deliver on their developmental objectives. Furthermore, the absence of such leadership adds to the list of barriers warranting intervention in the development of frameworks and strategies to mitigate tacit knowledge loss risks.

PROPOSED FRAMEWORK

The study proposes a framework for knowledge-based leadership for improved risk management in state-owned enterprises in South Africa, as presented in figure 2. The framework clearly shows how knowledge-based leadership for improved risk management in the state-owned enterprises should be established and implemented by means of items A to E below to ensure competitiveness and sustainability in the organisation. As illustrated in the figure from **A**, the state-owned enterprise is responsible for initiating this prestigious leadership strategy with the appointment of a relevant and/or suitable candidate who may value information and knowledge in driving leadership successfully and for the growth of the enterprise, that is, a knowledge-based leader. This is the kind of leader who maximally depends on existing knowledge for decision making and problem solving, and he or she always strives to promote the knowledge culture in the organisation for operation and many other business activities and functions. As item **B** shows, such leaders focus on effective management of specific knowledge assets because they know they cannot lead properly without such knowledge assets. This is because their leadership style always strives to drive and promote knowledge-driven behaviour among peers or the entire organisational populace.

Furthermore, item **C** shows clearly, on both the left and right side of the framework, that the knowledge-based leader always focuses on knowledge availability for any business success. The knowledge-based leader will ensure that he or she leads the staff to knowledge creation, development, absorption, acquisition, transfer, and protection. He or she will always strive to drive knowledge-based competition, strategies, culture, behaviour and practices. In addition, the knowledge-based leader will always ensure that risks affecting knowledge are managed strategically, without failure. As an overall organisational leader, he or she will also ensure that capabilities for knowledge management are developed and maintained. Knowledge-based leadership must always ensure that knowledge-based assets are developed and protected.

Figure 2. A framework for knowledge-based leadership for improved risk management in state-owned enterprises in South Africa

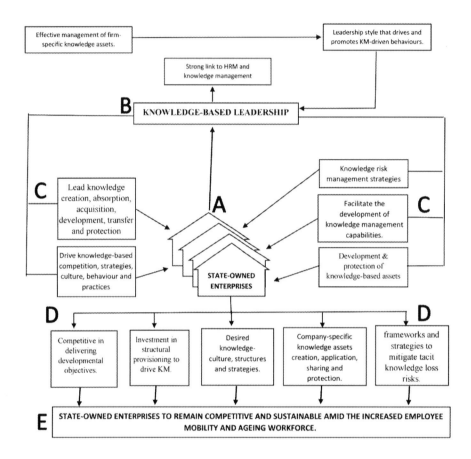

Looking at item **D**, one may realise the benefits or results of knowledge-based leadership. These include an enterprise being competitive in delivering objectives for developmental purposes and investing in structural provisioning to drive knowledge management. The other achievements or results may include achieving a desired knowledge culture, structures, and strategies. The enterprise may also benefit from creating, applying, sharing, and protecting company-specific knowledge assets. Organisations may finally have their own knowledge-driven frameworks and strategies to mitigate the risks associated with tacit knowledge loss. Finally, item **E** shows clearly that all these benefits will enable state-owned enterprises to remain competitive, innovative and sustainable amid increased employee mobility and an ageing workforce. This implies that the organisation's performance will never be weakened by employee turnover, since knowledge will always be retained and remain an organisational asset to be used by many organisational generations of employees.

CONCLUSION

The chapter concludes that SOEs are lagging in knowledge-based leadership. This finding is backed by evidence which demonstrated that KM was underdeveloped in many of the South African SOEs. Several barriers contributed to the ineffective KM-driven leadership and systems in most SOEs. Most SOEs are facing challenges pertaining to organisational red tape and are lagging in knowledge-based rewards and recognitions (both financial and non-financial), KM awareness and education, knowledge-oriented HRM systems, knowledge-oriented culture and structures, and a proper system to facilitate effective management of firm-specific knowledge assets. The chapter presented a knowledge-based leadership framework to mitigate tacit knowledge risks in SOEs. The framework is meant to guide fellow researchers and practitioners, especially within the fields of leadership, knowledge and human resource management, on the development, application and evaluation of knowledge-based leadership. Hence, based on the qualitative results, current research deduces that knowledge leadership, as depicted in many SOEs, was the opposite of what KBL stands for in theory and practice. For SOEs to remain competitive and sustainable amid increased employee mobility and an ageing workforce, business executives and managers in SOEs must factor in knowledge risk management strategies as part of managing enterprise risks. There is a need to develop a culture that focuses on knowledge management and knowledge risk management. However, to conclude, all such strategies and initiatives will certainly fail if leadership is not knowledge-centric and driving a knowledge management agenda.

CONTRIBUTIONS AND RECOMMENDATIONS FOR RESEARCHERS AND PRACTITIONERS

This study can be used by those in leadership, human resource managers or executives, strategists, and knowledge management practitioners, amongst others, to drive their investment efforts into the development of relevant knowledge-driven practices, culture and structures to mitigate the risks inherent in the loss of tacit knowledge, thereby ensuring the sustained performance of these public sector companies. Leadership and management in state-owned enterprises need to embrace KM and learn its terminology for inclusion in their practices. Researchers in the field of leadership and knowledge management should embrace the strong link between leadership, HRM and knowledge management for meaningful contributions to the body of knowledge in the field and management of tacit knowledge loss. There is a need for more empirical research to explore knowledge (loss) risk management in the public sector and private companies in South Africa. This study highlighted the significant role of knowledge-based leadership practices, which will naturally increase or enhance the management capacity of tacit knowledge to mitigate risks associated therewith, and assist SOEs to deliver on a developmental mandate, as well as ensure their survival and the economic growth of developing economies.

LIMITATIONS AND FUTURE RESEARCH

This research was undertaken in the context of SOEs in South Africa. It is therefore not clear whether its findings can be generalised to other contexts and/or similar enterprises in other developing or developed economies. It is proposed that similar research efforts regarding knowledge-based leadership and research using the current research model be extended to other industries and countries for validation. Knowledge-based leadership is underdeveloped, and further empirical science is needed to develop its theory and practice. The study was limited to nine South African SOEs in the qualitative phase, and only three agreed to take part in the survey component. A larger sample of SOEs for future studies is therefore recommended. Moreover, SOEs that participated were limited to only five sectors of the economy, namely the water utility industry, developmental financial institutions, service state-owned companies, the regulatory sector, and the research and development sector. Therefore, the findings of this research should be used with caution by SOEs in the energy, transportation and logistics, civil aviation and other sectors of the economy, as they were not represented in this study. A similar survey instrument could be rolled out in the other seven SOEs that did not take part in the survey component of the study. In addition, current research indicates that the link between knowledge-driven leadership, knowledge (risks) management and human resource management is underdeveloped in the country, thus warranting further research, especially in the SOE sector.

REFERENCES

Allen, D. G., & Vardaman, J. M. (2021). Global talent retention; understanding employee turnover around the world. In D. G. Allen & J. M. Vardaman (Eds.), *Global talent retention: understanding employee turnover around the world* (pp. 1–15). Emerald Publishing. doi:10.1108/978-1-83909-293-020211001

Andersén, J. (2012). Protective capacity and absorptive capacity: Managing the balance between retention and creation of knowledge-based resources. *The Learning Organization*, *19*(5), 440–452. doi:10.1108/09696471211239730

Barney, J. (2001). Is the resource-based view a useful perspective for strategic management research? Yes. *Academy of Management Review*, *26*(1), 41–56.

Becerra-Fernandez, I., & Sabherwal, R. (2015). *Knowledge management: systems and processes* (2nd ed.). Routledge.

Benassi, M., & Landoni, M. (2019). State-owned enterprises as knowledge-explorer agents. *Industry and Innovation*, *26*(2), 218–241. doi:10.1080/13662716.2018.1529554

Birasnav, M., Albufalasa, M., & Bader, Y. 2013. The role of transformational leadership and knowledge management processes on predicting product and process innovation: an empirical study developed in Kingdom of Bahrain. *TÉKHNE - Review of Applied Management Studies*, *11*, 64-75. http://dx.doi.org/doi:10.1016/j.tekhne.2013.08.001

Clò, S., Di Giulio, M., Galanti, M. T., & Sorrentino, M. (2016). Italian State-Owned Enterprises after Decades of Reforms." Still public? *Economia Pubblica*, *3*, 11–49.

Cohen, W. M., & Levinthal, D. A. (1990). Absorptive capacity: A new perspective on learning and innovation. *Administrative Science Quarterly*, *35*(1), 128–152. doi:10.2307/2393553

Creswell, J. W., & Creswell, J. D. (2018). *Research design: qualitative, quantitative & mixed methods approaches* (5th ed.). Sage.

Creswell, J. W., & Plano Clark, V. L. (2018). *Designing and conducting mixed methods research* (3rd ed.). Sage.

Davenport, T., & Prusak, L. (1998). *Working knowledge*. Harvard Business School Press.

Donate, M. J., & de Pablo, J. D. S. (2015). The role of knowledge-oriented leadership in knowledge management practices and innovation. *Journal of Business Research*, 68(2), 360–370. doi:10.1016/j.jbusres.2014.06.022

Durst, S., & Zieba, M. (2018). Mapping knowledge risks: Towards a better understanding of knowledge management. *Knowledge Management Research and Practice*, 17(1), 1–13. doi:10.1080/14778238.2018.1538603

Durst, S., & Zieba, M. (2020). Knowledge risks inherent in business sustainability. *Journal of Cleaner Production*, 251, 1–10. doi:10.1016/j.jclepro.2019.119670

Fagbadebo, O. M. (2022). State-owned enterprises and public service delivery in Africa. In F. G. Netswera, O. M. Fagbadebo, & N. Dorasamy (Eds.), *State-owned enterprises in Africa and the economics of public service delivery* (pp. 11–25). AOSIS Publishing. doi:10.4102/aosis.2022.BK270.01

Ghasabeth, M. S., & Provitera, M. J. (2018). Transformational leadership and knowledge management: Analysing the knowledge management models. *The Journal of Values Based Leadership*, 11(1), 1–14. doi:10.22543/0733.111.1206

Grant, R.M. (1996). Towards a knowledge-based theory of the firm. *Strategic Management Journal*, 17(Winter special issue), 109-122.

Gumede, W. (2018). Positioning Africa's SOEs to deliver on the developmental mandate, viewed. *Democracy works*. https://democracyworks.org.za/policy-brief-30-positioning-africas-soes-to-deliver-on-the-developmental-mandate/

Gürlek, M. (2020). *Tech development through hrm*. Emerald Publishing Limited. doi:10.1108/9781800433120

Gürlek, M., & Çemberci, M. (2020). Understanding the relationships among knowledge-oriented leadership, knowledge management capacity, innovation performance and organizational performance. *Kybernetes*, 49(11), 2819–2846. doi:10.1108/K 09 2019-0632

Gürlek, M., & Tuna, M. (2018). Reinforcing competitive advantage through green organisational culture and green innovation. *Service Industries Journal*, 38(7/8), 467–491. doi:10.1080/02642069.2017.1402889

Hair, J. F., Black, W. C., Babin, B. J. B., & Anderson, R. E. (2014). *Multivariate data analysis* (7th ed.). Pearson Education Limited.

Hussinki, H., Kianto, A., Vanhala, M., & Ritala, P. (2017). Assessing the universality of knowledge management practices. *Journal of Knowledge Management*, 21(6), 1596–1621. doi:10.1108/JKM-09-2016-0394

Islam, M. Z., Jasimuddin, S. M., & Hasan, I. (2015). Organizational culture, structure, technology infrastructure and knowledge sharing: Empirical evidence from MNCs based in Malaysia. *Vine*, 45(1), 67–88. doi:10.1108/VINE-05-2014-0037

Jackson, S. E., Hitt, M. A., & DeNisi, A. S. (2003). Managing human resources for knowledge- based competition: new research directions. In, S.E. Jackson, M.A. Hitt., & A.S. DeNisi (Eds), Managing knowledge for sustained competitive advantage: designing strategies for effective human resource management (pp.399-428). Jossey-Bass.

Kianto, A., Sáenz, J., & Aramburu, N. (2017). Knowledge-based human resource management practices, intellectual capital and innovation. *Journal of Business Research, 81*, 11–20. doi:10.1016/j.jbusres.2017.07.018

Kumar, S. (2020). Knowledge risk management for state-owned enterprises-Indian scenario. In S. Durst & T. Henschel (Eds.), *Knowledge risk management: from theory to praxis* (pp. 89–106). Springer. doi:10.1007/978-3-030-35121-2_6

Le, P. B., & Le, H. (2019). Determinants of innovation capability: The roles of transformational leadership, knowledge sharing and perceived organisational support. *Journal of Knowledge Management, 23*(3), 527–547. doi:10.1108/JKM-09-2018-0568

Mamorobela, S. P. (2022). Understanding a social media-enabled knowledge management adoption model for small and medium enterprises in South Africa. In P. Ngulube (Ed.), *Handbook of research on mixed methods research in information science* (pp. 324–339). IGI Global. doi:10.4018/978-1-7998-8844-4.ch016

Maphoto, A. R., & Matlala, M. E. (2022). Prospects for, and challenges of, knowledge sharing in the South African public sector: a literature review. *Social Sciences International Research Conference*, 19-21 Oct, pp. 1109-1125.

Martins, E. C., & Meyer, H. W. J. (2012). Organisational and behavioural factors that influence knowledge retention. *Journal of Knowledge Management, 16*(1), 77–96. doi:10.1108/13673271211198954

Matošková, J., & Směšná, P. (2017). Human resources management practices stimulating knowledge sharing. *Management & Marketing. Challenges for Knowledge Society, 12*(4), 614–632.

Mertens, D. M. (2015). Mixed methods and wicked problems. *Journal of Mixed Methods Research, 9*(1), 3–6. doi:10.1177/1558689814562944

Micić, R. (2015). Leadership role in certain phases of knowledge management processes. *Ekonomika (Nis), 61*(4), 47–55. doi:10.5937/ekonomika1504047M

Naqshbandi, M. M., & Jasimuddin, S. M. (2018). Knowledge-oriented leadership and open innovation: The role of knowledge management capability in France-based multinationals. *International Business Review, 27*(3), 701–713. doi:10.1016/j.ibusrev.2017.12.001

Netswera, F. G. (2022). Counting the cost of state-owned enterprises failure in South Africa: Post-apartheid betrayals or mere inefficiency? In F. G. Netswera, O. M. Fagbadebo, & N. Dorasamy (Eds.), *State-owned enterprises in Africa and the economics of public service delivery* (pp. 109–118). AOSIS Publishing. doi:10.4102/aosis.2022.BK270.06

Ngulube, P. (2019, January-March). Mapping methodological issues in knowledge management research, 2009- 2014. *International Journal of Knowledge Management, 15*(1), 85–100. Advance online publication. doi:10.4018/IJKM.2019010106

Ngulube, P. (2020). Mixed methods research in knowledge management studies (2009-2014): A content analysis of journal articles. *Journal of Information & Knowledge Management, 19*(3), 1–23. doi:10.1142/S0219649220500161

Nonaka, I., & Takeuchi, H. (1995). *The knowledge-creating company.* Oxford University Press.

Phaladi, M. P. (2022a). Studying knowledge management and human resource management practices in the state-owned entities using mixed methods research design. In P. Ngulube (Ed.), *Handbook of research on mixed methods research in information science* (pp. 340–361). IGI Global. doi:10.4018/978-1-7998-8844-4.ch017

Phaladi, M. P. (2022b). Human resource management as a facilitator of a knowledge-driven organisational culture and structure for the reduction of tacit knowledge loss in South African state-owned enterprises. *South African Journal of Information Management, 24*(1), 1–10. doi:10.4102ajim.v24i1.1547

Phaladi, M., & Ngulube, P. (2022). Mitigating risks of tacit knowledge loss in state-owned enterprises in South Africa through knowledge management practices. *South African Journal of Information Management, 24*(1), 1–9. doi:10.4102ajim.v24i1.1462

Phaladi, M. P. (2011). *Knowledge transfer and retention: The case of a public water utility in South Africa* [Master's Thesis, University of Stellenbosch, Stellenbosch, South Africa].

Phaladi, M. P. (2021). *Framework for integrating knowledge management and human resource management for the reduction of organisational knowledge loss in selected South African state-owned enterprises* [PhD Thesis, University of South Africa, Pretoria, South Africa].

Rashid, M., Clarke, P. M., & O'Connor, R. V. (2020). A mechanism to explore proactive knowledge retention in open source software communities. *Journal of Software (Malden, MA), 32*(3), 1–10. doi:10.1002mr.2198

Razael, F., Khalilzadeh, M., & Soleimani, P. (2021). Factors affecting knowledge management and its effect on organisational performance: Mediating the role of human capital. *Advances in Human-Computer Interaction, 2021*, 1–16. doi:10.1155/2021/8857572

Roome, E. (2012). *Hiring by knowledge-intensive firms in China.* [PhD thesis: Manchester Business School].

Sadeghi, A., & Rad, F. M. (2018). The role of knowledge-oriented leadership in knowledge management and innovation. *Management Science Letters, 8*, 151–160. doi:10.5267/j.msl.2018.1.003

Sandelin, S. K., Hukka, J. J., & Katko, T. S. (2019). Importance of knowledge management at water utilities. *Public Works Management & Policy, 00*(0), 1–17. doi:10.1177/1087724X19870813

Shamim, S., Cang, S., & Yu, H. (2019). Impact of knowledge-oriented leadership on knowledge management behaviour through employee work attitudes. *International Journal of Human Resource Management, 30*(16), 2387–2417. doi:10.1080/09585192.2017.1323772

Shariq, S. Mukhtar, U., & Anwar, S. (2019). Mediating and moderating impact of goal orientation and emotional intelligence on the relationship of knowledge-oriented leadership and knowledge sharing. *Journal of Knowledge Management, 23*(2), 332-350). doi:10.1108/JKM-01-2018-0033

Singh, M.K., & Gupta, V. (2020). Critical types of knowledge loss in military organisations. *VINE Journal of Information and Knowledge Management* Systems, (pre-print), 1-18. doi:10.1108/VJIKMS-09-2019-0152

Spender, J.C. (1996). Making knowledge the basis of a dynamic theory of the firm. *Strategic Management Journal, 17*(Winter Special Issue), 45-62.

Sumbal, M. S., Tsui, E., Durst, S., Shujahat, M., Irfan, I., & Ali, S. M. (2020). A framework to retain the knowledge of departing knowledge workers in the manufacturing industry. *VINE Journal of Information and Knowledge Management Systems, 50*(4), 631–651. doi:10.1108/VJIKMS-06-2019-0086

Sumbal, M. S. U. K., Irfan, I., Durst, S., Sahibzada, U. F., Waseem, M. A., & Tsui, E. (2023). Knowledge retention in oil and gas industry – the case of contract workforce. *Kybernetes, 52*(4), 1552–1571. doi:10.1108/K-06-2021-0458

Valaei, N., Nikhashemi, S. R., & Javan, N. (2017). Organisational factors and process capabilities in a KM strategy: Toward a unified theory. *Journal of Management Development, 36*(4), 560–580. doi:10.1108/JMD-04-2016-0057

Wöcke, A., & Barnard, H. (2021). Turnover in South Africa: the effect of history. In D. G. Allen & J. M. Vardaman (Eds.), *Global talent retention: Understanding employee turnover around the world* (pp. 239–259). Emerald Publishing. doi:10.1108/978-1-83909-293-020211012

Zhang, L., & Guo, H. (2019). Enabling knowledge diversity to benefit cross-functional project teams: Joint roles of knowledge leadership and transactive memory system. *Information & Management, 56*(8), 1–13. doi:10.1016/j.im.2019.03.001

Zia, N. U. (2020). Knowledge-oriented leadership, knowledge management behaviour and innovation performance in project-based SMEs. The moderating role of goal orientations. *Journal of Knowledge Management, 24*(8), 1819–1839. doi:10.1108/JKM-02-2020-0127

Zieba, M. (2020). Knowledge risk management in companies offering knowledge-intensive business services. In S. Durst & T. Henschel (Eds.), *Knowledge risk management: from theory to praxis* (pp. 13–31). Springer. doi:10.1007/978-3-030-35121-2_2

Zieba, M., & Schivinski, B. (2015). Knowledge management driven leadership, culture and innovation success – an integrative model. *Proceedings of IFKAD 2015: 10th International Forum on Knowledge Asset Dynamics: Culture, Innovation and Entrepreneurship: Connecting the Knowledge Dots*. BBK. https://eprints.bbk.ac.za/id/eprint/19951/

Chapter 9
Exploring the Impacts and Implications of Destructive Leadership in Organizations

Quatavia McLester
https://orcid.org/0000-0003-1596-0517
The Chicago School of Professional Psychology, USA

Darrell Norman Burrell
https://orcid.org/0000-0002-4675-9544
Marymount University, USA

Sharon L. Burton
https://orcid.org/0000-0003-1653-9783
Capitol Technology University, USA

ABSTRACT

The research on leadership has typically sought to investigate 'good' leadership and the best characteristics of leadership (i.e., transformational leadership, ethical leadership, authentic leadership). Current research indicates a 'bad' or 'dark' side of leadership. The outcomes of destructive leadership have been raising interest in leadership research. Within the research, destructive leadership has been revealed to have severe outcomes for employees and organizations. This literature review seeks to expand the literature to consider destructive leadership and its association with job-related outcomes. The review will examine forms of destructive leadership related to specific job-related and organizational-related outcomes. The exploration of destructive leadership and its effect on job-related outcomes is essential to the success of organizations. This review contributes to the growing body of knowledge related to leadership.

DOI: 10.4018/979-8-3693-1380-0.ch009

INTRODUCTION

Leadership research has traditionally been directed by searching for the best type of leaders and methods to lead. Concepts like transformational, ethical, and authentic leadership highlight "positive" leader behavior and its outcomes (Schyns & Schilling, 2012). These types of leadership are practical and generate positive results for organizations and their employees. Recent research uncovers that there is a "dark side" of leadership. The term has been used as a sweeping expression to define countless 'bad' leader behaviors thought to be linked with detrimental outcomes for organizations and followers (Schyns & Schilling, 2012).

There are two fundamental purposes for the rising curiosity about the dark side of leadership. The first reason is determining the incidence and costs associated with destructive leaders (Schyns & Schilling, 2012). Studies describe a robust frequency of destructive leader behaviors in organizations (Schyns & Schilling, 2012). In the United States, destructive leadership affects approximately 13.6% of United States employees at an estimated price of $23.8 billion a year for United States companies (Schyns & Schilling, 2012). These effects are due to employee turnover, decreased effectiveness, and absenteeism (Schyns & Schilling, 2012).

The second reason for the curiosity comes from the discovery that destructive behavior's effects are severe for organizations and employees (Schyns & Schilling, 2012). Many consequences have been researched concerning destructive leadership behaviors (Schyns & Schilling, 2012). The outcomes of destructive leadership behaviors that have been studied include effects on resistance behavior, job tension, emotional exhaustion, reduced family well-being, turnover intentions, job satisfaction, and deviant work behavior (Schyns & Schilling, 2012).

Destructive leadership is characterized by behaviors detrimental to the organization and its employees (Gardner et al., 2005). Examples of destructive leadership behaviors include harassment, bullying, and favoritism (Hershcovis, 2007). This type of leadership can also manifest in various ways, including bullying, intimidation, micromanagement, and other forms of psychological abuse (Gardner, 2010; Koester, 2015). Destructive leaders often harm the work environment, and their behavior can lead to decreased job satisfaction, lower morale, and decreased productivity (Bass, 1985; Hershcovis, 2007). Moreover, destructive leadership can significantly impact organizational culture, leading to mistrust, fear, and hostility (Fletcher & Carr, 2011).

Organizational culture can be defined as an organization's shared values, beliefs, and practices (Schein, 1992). The organization's leadership often shapes it and can significantly impact employee behavior and performance (Schein, 1992). A strong organizational culture can be beneficial, leading to increased motivation, improved communication, and increased employee engagement (Schein, 1992). Conversely, a negative organizational culture can decrease morale and productivity.

The relationship between destructive leadership and organizational culture is complex and multifaceted (Fletcher & Carr, 2011). Destructive leaders often create a work environment of fear, mistrust, and hostility (Fletcher & Carr, 2011). This can decrease employee morale and job satisfaction, harming organizational culture (Bass, 1985; Hershcovis, 2007). Moreover, destructive leaders often must set clear goals and expectations, leading to clarity and a lack of direction (Bass, 1985). This can further contribute to a negative organizational culture.

In addition, destructive leadership can lead to a negative organizational culture in which unethical behavior is tolerated and even rewarded (Fletcher & Carr, 2011). This can be particularly damaging, leading to decreased productivity and increased turnover (Fletcher & Carr, 2011). Moreover, it can be challenging to reverse the effects of a negative organizational culture, as it can be deeply entrenched and difficult to change (Schein, 1992). Thus, it is vital to address destructive leadership behaviors to prevent the emergence of a negative organizational culture. This type of leadership is typically found in workplaces where power is centralized, and the leader is expected to have absolute control over subordinates (Hodson & Brouer, 2016).

Leadership is a crucial determinant of organizational success, but when leadership is ineffective or destructive, the consequences can be dire (Ellinger & Keller, 2019, p. 291). Organizations that ignore and fail to address destructive leadership in their ranks risk high costs and consequences that can have long-term implications (Ellinger & Keller, 2019).

The most direct consequence of destructive leadership is its impact on the organization's performance. Research has found that destructive leadership can harm the organization's overall performance, productivity, and financial performance (Ellinger & Keller, 2019). Organizations that do not address destructive leadership risk facing significant losses in terms of performance, as employees may become less engaged, less productive, and less committed to their roles. This can lead to a decrease in overall organizational performance and productivity.

The impact of destructive leadership on organizational performance is further exacerbated by the fact that destructive leaders are often less effective at managing resources and decision-making processes (Ellinger & Keller, 2019). This can lead to a decrease in the quality of decision-making within the organization and a need for adequate resource allocation. This can harm the organization's performance, as resources are not used to their fullest potential.

PROBLEM STATEMENT AND SIGNIFICANCE

Research suggests that destructive leadership is a growing problem in the workplace. A recent survey of over 4,000 employees in the United States revealed that nearly 60% of respondents had experienced destructive leadership at some point in their careers (Davies et al., 2020). This survey also found that employees who experienced destructive leadership were likelier to report lower job satisfaction and greater stress levels. Furthermore, the survey revealed that employees who experienced destructive leadership were more likely to leave their organizations than those who did not experience this type of leadership. Research has also found that employees who experience destructive leadership are likelier to report feelings of powerlessness, burnout, and negative emotions (Davies et al., 2020).

In addition to the survey findings, there is evidence that destructive leadership is particularly detrimental to specific groups of employees. One study found that female employees were likelier to experience destructive leadership than male employees (Davies et al., 2020). The study also found that minority employees were likelier to experience destructive leadership than their non-minority counterparts. These findings suggest that destructive leadership disproportionately affects certain groups of employees, which can lead to adverse outcomes such as decreased morale and productivity. This paper explores the implications and impacts of destructive leadership through the literature, intending to highlight the issue's importance so that more research can be conducted.

LITERATURE REVIEW

Toxic Leadership

Toxic leadership is a term used to describe a management style characterized by a lack of respect, trust, and consideration for those subject to it (Peterson, 2016). Toxic leadership, also considered destructive leadership, is often characterized by micromanagement, a lack of communication, and a focus on punishing mistakes rather than encouraging growth and development (Konrad, 2018). This type of leadership can have a profoundly negative impact on employees, leading to feelings of dissatisfaction, burnout, and even mental health issues (Unger et al., 2019). In addition, toxic leadership can damage the organization by creating a culture of fear and mistrust, leading to low morale and high turnover (Konrad, 2018).

The impact of toxic leadership on employees can be profound. Employees subject to toxic leadership often experience stress, dissatisfaction, and even burnout (Unger et al., 2019). In addition, toxic leadership can lead to a sense of powerlessness and a lack of motivation to do their best work (Peterson, 2016). This lack of motivation can decrease productivity, affecting the organization's success. Furthermore, toxic leadership can lead to mental health issues such as anxiety and depression (Unger et al., 2019).

In addition to the impact on individual employees, toxic leadership can also impact the organization. A culture of fear and mistrust can lead to low morale and high turnover (Konrad, 2018). This can hurt the organization's ability to attract and retain talent and its overall performance and success.

Destructive Leadership

Before delving into the theories of destructive leadership, it is crucial to define what destructive leadership means. According to Rayner and Holden (2016), destructive leadership is defined as "a type of leadership that has negative outcomes for followers, organizations, and society" (p. 5). This definition is consistent with other descriptions of destructive leadership, such as Kernis's (2003) definition of destructive leadership as "an individual's intentional use of his or her power base to harm or exploit others" (Kernis, 2003, p. 4). Thus, destructive leadership is a type of leadership that has adverse outcomes for followers, organizations, and society.

One of the most prominent theories is the power-based theory of destructive leadership. This theory was developed by Kernis (2003), who argued that destructive leadership results from an individual's use of their power base to harm or exploit others. According to the power-based theory, destructive leadership is rooted in an individual's desire to gain power and control over others. This theory has been supported by research that has found that individuals who display destructive leadership behaviors are more likely to have higher levels of power and control in their relationships with others (Rayner & Holden, 2016).

Another prominent theory of destructive leadership is the trait-based theory. This theory was developed by Hogan and Hogan (2017), who argued that destructive leadership results from specific personality traits. Specifically, they argued that destructive leadership is associated with certain "dark" personality traits such as narcissism, Machiavellianism, and psychopathy. This theory has been supported by research that has found that individuals who display destructive leadership behaviors tend to score higher on measures of these "dark" personality traits (Hogan & Hogan, 2017).

A third prominent theory of destructive leadership is the situation-based theory. This theory was developed by Kish-Gephart et al. (2010), who argued that destructive leadership results from certain situational factors. Specifically, they argued that destructive leadership is more likely to occur when the leader perceives the situation as threatening or uncertain. This theory has been supported by research that found that individuals who display destructive leadership behaviors are more likely to perceive their situations as threatening or uncertain (Kish-Gephart et al., 2010).

An additional prominent theory of destructive leadership is the group dynamics theory. This theory was developed by Rayner and Holden (2016), who argued that destructive leadership results from particular group dynamics. Specifically, they argued that destructive leadership is more likely to occur when there is a lack of cohesion and trust within the group or a lack of accountability or support from the leader. This theory has been supported by research that has found that individuals who display destructive leadership behaviors tend to be more likely to be in groups with low levels of cohesion and trust or with low levels of accountability or support from the leader (Rayner & Holden, 2016).

A frequently researched form of destructive leadership is tyrannical leadership. Empirical studies indicate that oppressive behaviors include arbitrariness, self-aggrandizement, no consideration, demeaning others, discouraging initiative, an imposing style of problem-solving, and conditional chastisement (Ashford, 1994). This type of destructive leadership is thought to be the result of exchanges between individual observations (i.e., views about self, subordinates, the organization, and partialities for action) and situational enablers (i.e., power, stressors, and traditional values and norms) (Ashford, 1994). Tyrannical leaders may obtain results at the cost of subordinates (Ashford, 1994; Tepper, 2000). One subfield of autocratic leadership examined heavily in this review is abusive supervision.

Abusive supervision "refers to subordinates' perceptions of the extent to which supervisors engage in the sustained display of hostile verbal and nonverbal behaviors, excluding physical contact" (Tepper, 2000, p. 178). Abusive supervisory behaviors include but are not limited to impoliteness, breaking promises, public condemnation, thoughtless actions, and silent treatment (Harris et al., 2007). Abusive supervision is a subjective assessment (Harris et al., 2007). Abusive supervision encompasses nonverbal and hostile verbal behaviors (Harris et al., 2007). Abusive supervision denotes a continued demonstration of negative supervisory behaviors (Harris et al., 2007). Lastly, abusive supervision refers to the behavior itself and not the intentions of the actions (Harris et al., 2007).

Several studies have claimed and found that destructive leadership is negatively associated with various job-related outcomes. Tepper (2000) investigated the consequences of abusive supervisor behavior. The researcher collected data at 2 points in time. For the first time, surveys that calculated abusive supervision, interactional justice, apparent job mobility, procedural justice, and distributive justice were completed by 712 Ss (aged 35-39s) who had bosses and were working full-time (Tepper, 2000). Follow-up surveys that measured subordinates' job satisfaction, life satisfaction, voluntary turnover, organizational commitment, psychological distress, and conflict between work and family were completed by 362 of the Ss from time one to time 2 (Tepper, 2000). The study's results indicated that subordinates who saw their supervisors as abusive were likelier to leave their jobs (Tepper, 2000). For those subordinates who decided to remain in their jobs, abusive supervision was linked with decreased job and life satisfaction, decreased affective and normative commitment, increased continuance commitment, psychological distress, and conflict between family and work (Tepper, 2000).

The literature on the relationship between destructive leadership and employee burnout is limited but growing. Studies have consistently found that destructive leadership is associated with increased employee stress, burnout, and turnover (Gonzalez-Morales et al., 2015; Koester, 2015). Specifically, studies have found that destructive leadership is associated with decreased job satisfaction, increased levels of job-related stress, and increased levels of burnout (Gonzalez-Morales et al., 2015; Koester, 2015).

In addition, studies have found that destructive leadership is associated with decreased levels of job control, increased levels of job insecurity, and a hostile work environment (Gonzalez-Morales et al., 2015; Koester, 2015). These factors can lead to increased levels of stress and burnout, further exacerbating the problem (Gonzalez-Morales et al., 2015). Finally, studies have found that employees exposed to destructive leadership are more likely to experience physical and mental health problems, such as depression and anxiety (Gonzalez-Morales et al., 2015; Koester, 2015).

Tepper et al. (2004) predicted that the association between employees' organizational citizenship behaviors (OCBs) and fellow employees' attitudes is contingent upon the supervisors' abusiveness. The researchers conducted a longitudinal study utilizing data gathered from 173 supervised employees. The data was collected two times, separated by seven months. The results of the second study indicated that employees' OCB was negatively associated with job satisfaction when abusive satisfaction was high (Tepper et al., 2004).

Like Tepper et al. (2004), Skogstad et al. (2015) discovered a negative association between job satisfaction and destructive leadership. Skogstad et al. (2015) examined the effects of constructive, laissez-faire, and authoritative leadership behaviors on subordinates' job satisfaction. The research was conducted "based on two prospective and representative surveys," with time interims of six months (study 1) and two years (study 2) (Skogstad et al., 2015). Destructive leadership behaviors were the only significant predictors in Study 1 and Study 2 (Skogstad et al., 2015). Tyrannical leadership projected reduced subordinate job satisfaction over six months (Skogstad et al., 2015).

Reed and Bullis (2009) investigated the destructive leadership behaviors experienced by high-potential senior officers in the military and civilian employees. The researchers used a questionnaire based on the Petty Tyranny in Organizations Scale for the study. The Scale was used to discover the depth and nature of destructive leadership as described by members of the class of 2008 United States military senior service college (Reed & Bullis, 2009). Furthermore, the Scale examined the association between leadership experiences and countless measures of leaning towards staying in service and satisfaction (Reed & Bullis, 2009). Senior personnel described experiencing toxic leadership, despite the dominant role that the idea of leadership holds in the military. Destructive leadership and all satisfaction measures resulted in a significant negative correlation (Reed & Bullis, 2009). In contrast, there was no substantial negative influence on the inclination to stay in service among the service people (Reed & Bullis, 2009).

Harris et al. (2007) examined the abusive supervision-job performance association. The study measured job performance using formal performance appraisal ratings, supervisor ratings, and self-ratings (Harris et al., (2007). The researchers utilized a sample of "supervisor-subordinate dyads from an automotive organization" to explore their hypotheses (Harris et al., 2007). The researchers discovered limited backing for a negative association between abusive supervision and employee job performance. There was a negative correlation to performance ratings from formal performance ratings (Harris et al., 2007). Abusive supervision was not significantly related to self-rated performance (Harris et al., 2007).

Nyberg, Holmberg, Bernin, and Alderling (2011) explored destructive managerial leadership in the hotel industry in Poland, Italy, and Sweden. The researchers gathered 554 questionnaires from employees in all hotel occupational groups (Nyberg et al., 2011). The Copenhagen Psychosocial Questionnaire (COPSOQ) and items from the Global Leadership and Organisational Behaviour Effectiveness (GLOBE) research program questionnaire were utilized in the study (Nyberg et al., 2011). The COPSOQ questionnaire measured working conditions, specifically high job demands combined with little control and meager social support (Nyberg et al., 2011). This was described in terms of vitality, behavioral stress, and mental health (Nyberg et al., 2011).

Items modified from the GLOBE research program questionnaire measured malevolent, self-centered, and autocratic leadership styles (Nyberg et al., 2011). The associations between destructive managerial leadership on the individual level (i.e., psychological well-being) and the organizational level were estimated (Nyberg et al., 2011). Self-centered leadership was related to poor mental health, low vitality, and high behavioral stress (Nyberg et al., 2011). At the organizational level, malevolent and autocratic leadership were associated with low vitality among employees (Nyberg et al., 2011). Vicious and authoritarian leadership was associated more with high job demands, little control, and meager social support than self-centered leadership (Nyberg et al., 2011). The study results indicate a substantial relationship between destructive managerial leadership at the organizational level and poor psychological well-being among employees at the individual level (Nyberg et al., 2011).

STRENGTHS, LIMITATIONS, AND FUTURE RESEARCH

An evident strength of the studies reviewed is that each study helped to further the research on destructive leadership. Secondly, each study found a similar pattern of results in other studies related to destructive leadership. While there are noticeable strengths, there are a few limitations worth mentioning. One limitation of the research was the need for longitudinal analysis. Tepper et al. (2004) and Skogstad et al. (2015) were the only longitudinal studies examined in this literature review. Most of the research examined was cross-sectional research. Future research should consider conducting longitudinal research to investigate the effects of destructive leadership on job-related outcomes. In Tepper et al. (2004), there was only a seven-month wait between the collection of the two data sets. Future research should also conduct extended longitudinal studies for maximum results.

Another limitation is that none of the studies delved into gender differences. There may be a difference between sex and how destructive leadership is perceived. Furthermore, the research did not generate any studies that delved into racial differences. There may also be a difference in how various races perceive destructive leadership. Future research should investigate gender and racial disparities related to destructive leadership behavior and job-related outcomes.

Future research should also consider conducting cross-cultural studies. All but one of the studies mentioned in this literature review were conducted in the United States, and that study investigated three European countries. It would be beneficial to look into Latin countries where studies have shown that leaders are firmer and sterner than leaders in the United States. It would be worth examining how destructive leadership impacts job-related outcomes in collectivist countries. The research gathered from these countries can be combined in one study, and comparisons can be made between these countries and the United States.

IMPLICATIONS

The research has practical implications associated with destructive leadership and job-related outcomes. The first obvious implication is that because destructive leadership is related to such severe job-related consequences, efforts should be made to reduce the likelihood of destructive leadership (Harris et al., 2007). Organizational resources should be used to sufficiently train and monitor supervisors to ensure that supervisors are constantly engaging in appropriate, healthy management behaviors (Harris et al.,

2007). Managers with a history of such behavior and the potential to practice such behavior would benefit from training in emotional intelligence, anger management, and other behavioral tools (Harris et al., 2007). Organizations should take various actions to support an abuse-free culture (Harris et al., 2007).

CONCLUSION

Organizations can take several steps to address bad managers and destructive leaders. The first step is to put in place strategies to prevent bad behavior from occurring in the first place; this includes setting clear policies and expectations, providing training and development for managers and leaders, and establishing a culture of accountability and respect. Additionally, organizations should ensure that managers and leaders are held accountable for their actions and that inappropriate behavior is addressed swiftly and appropriately.

A key strategy in dealing with destructive leadership is to identify it. It is essential to be aware of the signs of toxic leadership, such as a lack of respect for employees, micromanagement, and a focus on punishing mistakes (Konrad, 2018). Once the toxic leadership has been identified, it is vital to address it directly. This can be done by speaking up and voicing concerns or speaking to a supervisor or senior staff member. Organizations should strive to create an environment where employees feel safe speaking up and expressing their concerns (Hershcovis, 2007). This can be achieved by implementing a formal reporting system and establishing whistleblower protections (Hershcovis, 2007).

In addition, creating a supportive environment for employees subject to toxic leadership is essential. This can be done by providing resources such as mental health support, stress management support, and access to counseling services (Unger et al., 2019). It is also vital to ensure that employees feel safe speaking up about their experiences and that their concerns are addressed seriously.

Organizational leaders can also use performance management systems to address bad managers and destructive leaders. This includes setting clear goals and expectations and providing feedback on performance regularly. Additionally, organizations should ensure that they have a process in place for addressing performance issues, which includes providing coaching and support to managers and leaders when needed.

Finally, creating a culture of trust and respect within the organization is vital. This can be done by creating an open and honest communication policy and having clear expectations for employees and managers. It is also essential to ensure that there are consequences for toxic behavior and that employees are rewarded for their positive contributions to the organization.

In conclusion, destructive leadership can harm both individual employees and the organization as a whole. It is essential to be aware of the signs of toxic leadership and address them directly when it occurs. It is also vital to create a supportive environment for those subject to toxic leadership and a culture of trust and respect within the organization.

REFERENCES

Ashforth, B. (1994). Petty tyranny in organizations. *Human Relations*, *47*(7), 755–778. doi:10.1177/001872679404700701

Bass, B. M. (1985). *Leadership and performance beyond expectations*. Free Press.

Burris, E. R., Detert, J. R., & Chiaburu, D. S. (2008). Quitting before leaving: The mediating effects of psychological attachment and detachment on voice. *The Journal of Applied Psychology*, *93*(4), 912–9222. doi:10.1037/0021-9010.93.4.912 PMID:18642993

Davies, S., Fong, C. Y., & Yau, O. H. M. (2020). Destructive leadership in the workplace: A cross-cultural study. *International Journal of Business and Management*, *15*(4), 272–285.

Ellinger, A. D., & Keller, S. (2019). Destructive leadership: A review and research agenda. *The Leadership Quarterly*, *30*(2), 291–310. doi:10.1016/j.leaqua.2018.11.003

Fletcher, C., & Carr, A. (2011). Destructive leadership: The impact of negative leadership behaviours and the moderating influence of organizational culture. *The Leadership Quarterly*, *22*(3), 467–481.

Gardner, W. L. (2010). Destructive leadership: A review and synthesis of the empirical literature and implications for future research. *The Leadership Quarterly*, *21*(2), 212–218.

Gardner, W. L., Avolio, B. J., Luthans, F., May, D. R., & Walumbwa, F. (2005). "Can you see the real me?" A self-based model of authentic leader and follower development. *The Leadership Quarterly*, *16*(3), 343–372. doi:10.1016/j.leaqua.2005.03.003

Gonzalez-Morales, M. G., McNeese-Smith, D., & Ilies, R. (2015). Destructive leadership, workplace deviance, and employee stress. *Journal of Managerial Psychology*, *30*(2), 133–149.

Harris, K. J., Kacmar, K. M., & Zivnuska, S. (2007). An investigation of abusive supervision as a predictor of performance and the meaning of work as a moderator of the relationship. *The Leadership Quarterly*, *18*(3), 252–263. doi:10.1016/j.leaqua.2007.03.007

Hershcovis, M. S. (2007). Implications of destructive leadership behavior: Review, synthesis, and research agenda. *Group & Organization Management*, *32*(3), 409–439.

Hodson, R., & Brouer, R. L. (2016). Workplace stress: Causes, consequences, and interventions. In R. Hodson & R. L. Brouer (Eds.), *Workplace stress: A comprehensive guide for assessment, prevention, and management* (pp. 1–35). ABC-CLIO.

Hogan, R., & Hogan, J. (2017). Personality and destructive leadership. *The Leadership Quarterly*, *28*(1), 16–30. doi:10.1016/j.leaqua.2016.09.005

Kernis, M. H. (2003). Toward a conceptualization of optimal self-esteem. *Psychological Inquiry*, *14*(1), 1–26. doi:10.1207/S15327965PLI1401_01

Kish-Gephart, J. J., Detert, J. R., Treviño, L. K., & Edmondson, A. C. (2010). Bad apples, bad cases, and bad barrels: Meta-analytic evidence about sources of unethical decisions at work. *The Journal of Applied Psychology*, *95*(1), 1–31. doi:10.1037/a0017103 PMID:20085404

Koester, L. (2015). Destructive leadership and its impact on employees: A review of the literature. *Human Resource Management Review*, *25*(3), 254–267.

Konrad, A. M. (2018). Toxic leadership: A review of the literature. *Leadership and Organization Development Journal*, *39*(1), 1–17.

Maslach, C., & Leiter, M. P. (2018). *The truth about burnout: How organizations cause personal stress and what to do about it* (3rd ed.). Jossey-Bass.

Nyberg, A., Holmberg, I., Bernin, P., & Alderling, M. (2011). Destructive managerial leadership and psychological well-being among Swedish, Polish, and Italian hotel employees. *Work (Reading, Mass.), 39*(3), 267–281. doi:10.3233/WOR-2011-1175 PMID:21709363

Peterson, K. (2016). Understanding and responding to the effects of toxic leadership. *Journal of Leadership & Organizational Studies, 23*(4), 439–453.

Rayner, C., & Holden, R. (2016). Destructive leadership: A review and agenda for future research. *The Leadership Quarterly, 27*(1), 4–20. doi:10.1016/j.leaqua.2015.11.003

Reed, G. E., & Bullis, R. C. (2009). The impact of destructive leadership on senior military officers and civilian employees. *Armed Forces and Society, 36*(1), 5–18. doi:10.1177/0095327X09334994

Schein, E. H. (1992). *Organizational culture and leadership*. Jossey-Bass.

Schyns, B., & Schilling, J. (2013). How bad are the effects of bad leaders? A meta-analysis of destructive leadership and its outcomes. *The Leadership Quarterly, 24*(1), 138–158. doi:10.1016/j.leaqua.2012.09.001

Skogstad, A., Aasland, M. S., Nielsen, M. B., Hetland, J., Matthiesen, S. B., & Einarsen, S. (2015). The Relative Effects of Constructive, Laissez-Faire, and Tyrannical Leadership on Subordinate Job Satisfaction. *Zeitschrift für Psychologie mit Zeitschrift für Angewandte Psychologie*.

Tepper, B. J. (2000). Consequences of abusive supervision. *Academy of Management Journal, 43*(2), 178–190. doi:10.2307/1556375

Tepper, B. J., Duffy, M. K., Hoobler, J., & Ensley, M. D. (2004). Moderators of the relationships between coworkers' organizational citizenship behavior and fellow employees' attitudes. *Journal of Applied Psychology, 89*, 455–465.

Unger, D., Goh, S. K., Whelan, J., & Burns, P. (2019). Toxic leadership: A meta-analytic review of negative outcomes for individuals and teams. *Journal of Occupational and Organizational Psychology, 92*(3), 577–599.

Chapter 10
Demystifying Shared Leadership

Cynthia Maria Montaudon-Tomas
https://orcid.org/0000-0002-2595-6960
UPAEP Universidad, Mexico

Anna Amsler
https://orcid.org/0000-0003-3183-0878
Independent Researcher, Mexico

Ivonne M. Montaudon-Tomas
https://orcid.org/0000-0001-5794-7762
UPAEP Universidad, Mexico

Yvonne Lomas-Montaudon
Universidad Iberoamericana, Mexico

ABSTRACT

This chapter analyzes shared leadership from a systems perspective, identifying connections with other leadership styles. The method used was the literature review. Different myths that surround shared leadership are also considered, and examples are used to illustrate how the myths can be debunked. The importance of trust is highlighted as an essential element for creating any type of relationship, including leadership, and for sharing any task. The importance of collective action and how it contributes to shared leadership is also described. Finally, different ways to overcome the myths of shared leadership are included.

INTRODUCTION

The emergence of various factors, such as globalization and hyper-competition, have compelled organizations to adopt new modes of organization, including cross-functional or virtual teams where adaptability and swift problem-solving solutions are highly valued (Pearce, 2012). These teams stand out from traditional organizational units due to the absence of formal hierarchical authority and the need for leadership to be spread and shared.

DOI: 10.4018/979-8-3693-1380-0.ch010

Leadership is determined by an individual's capacity to influence others, regardless of their hierarchical position in an organization or the power their position holds. For its part, shared leadership has been defined as a dynamic and interactive influence process among individuals in a group whose goal is to lead one another to achieve a group objective (Pearce & Conger, 2002).

Commentators on leadership are now beginning to suggest that individual leadership may be in retreat, needing instead a transformation towards plural leadership models, a phenomenon in which leadership is shared among different people (Denis, Langley & Sergei, 2012), where power structures are increasingly less centered in individuals.

In numerous definitions of shared leadership, different concepts, such as collective and distributed leadership, have been used interchangeably because of their close meaning (Goksoy, 2016), which can sometimes result in confusion. Therefore, it is essential to establish distinctions and similarities within the variety of leadership styles (known and emerging), namely: co-leadership, collaborative, collective, connective, constellations, inclusive, integrative, multi-headed, mutual, networked, plural, reciprocal, and relationship, among others. The characteristics of these styles will be presented later in this chapter.

Recent studies have revealed that teams functioning under shared leadership, as opposed to relying solely on one person, exhibit significantly enhanced organizational performance; however, despite these findings, some organizations still choose to maintain rigid hierarchies (Fitzsimons, 2016). The resistance to shared leadership is often influenced by cultural norms, such as power distance, as well as the details required for its effective implementation; some of the most common misconceptions surrounding this type of leadership will also be included.

This chapter describes shared leadership as an innovative and collaborative leadership style that has proven useful in modern-day organizations. The aim is to provide a better understanding of this leadership style, its use in organizations, and the benefits it provides in creating changes in organizational culture and climate, all while trying to eliminate certain myths surrounding the topic.

The purpose of the chapter is not to suggest shared leadership as a superior leadership style that every business should transition into but generate awareness of its potential value in different organizations and contexts. In this sense, shared leadership is presented as an alternative that can be implemented to promote collaboration and more dynamic interactions toward common goals in organizations. The chapter is organized into sections that analyze the need to create a common ground for collaboration to flourish, including shared purpose, values, vision, and interaction roles.

PROBLEM STATEMENT

A comprehensive analysis revealed that shared leadership surpasses traditional leadership by 34% in terms of effectiveness in innovation or agile contexts (Valamis, 2023). This significant difference can be attributed to the fact that shared leadership emphasizes adaptability, which can have a greater influence on team performance when compared to conventional leadership approaches. Furthermore, shared leadership can enhance team effectiveness by fostering trust among team members through reciprocal leadership roles (Valamis, 2023).

Leadership plays a crucial role in determining the success or failure of any organization, and in today's rapidly changing business environment, the need for effective leadership has become essential. The challenge in this new era lies in the fact that no single person can possess all the necessary skills and abilities required to lead organizations effectively (Kocolowski, 2010). Therefore, this chapter aims to

Demystifying Shared Leadership

explore the concept of shared leadership, address the hesitations to implement it, and assess the contexts in which organizations should consider adopting this model and the requirements for it to be effective.

METHOD

This chapter was developed through a literature review, which allows for a more accurate description of shared leadership, its purposes, and the advantages organizations can expect when inculcating it in operations. A scoping review was selected as the primary methodology since the starting point is not a precise question to answer but the identification of certain characteristics/concepts in previously published works in order to map and discuss them (Munn, Peters, Stern, Tufanaru, McArthur, & Aromataris, 2018).

In this sense, the scoping review seeks to analyze the available definitions in the field of shared leadership, examine their components and clarify key concepts in the literature on the subject. Key characteristics or factors related to shared leadership are identified and synthesized in an effort to counter myths and preconceptions concerning the practice of shared leadership.

The methodology for the literature review included an online search for articles, books, and research materials on the subjects of shared and plural leadership, common ground, trust in organizations, and collective actions. Over 140 published materials were reviewed, and, considering the scope of this chapter, around 100 were selected as sources of information. Different styles of leadership often associated with shared leadership were analyzed to find common characteristics and establish connections, as well as provide some context to the progression and growth of more collaborative leadership types.

BACKGROUND

Leadership styles have evolved throughout history, starting with Lewin, Lippit, and White's (1939) three basic styles of leadership defined as autocratic, democratic, and laissez-faire. These styles focus on the roles and characteristics of individual leadership, with the autocratic leader being the more traditional one, with a focus on accomplishing the tasks at hand under any circumstances (Gisma, 2020).

Leadership styles play a significant role in enabling leaders' actions and capacities. Each individual has a distinct leadership style in which they feel most comfortable (Khan, Irfanullah & Khan, 2016). However, the complexity of leadership arises from the fact that styles vary based on individuals and circumstances. Personality, values, and purpose shape leadership styles for both leaders and followers (Delia, 2018), as do context and organizational circumstances.

Looking back at historical leadership styles, it becomes evident that they were often leader-centered. With new ways of working and very diverse environments, leadership is starting to be viewed more in terms of teams and integration. As change remains constant across industries and sectors, effective leadership now emphasizes flexibility, adaptability, and collaboration (Gisma, 2020; Gandolfi & Stone, 2018) as crucial elements.

These emerging models focus on cooperation, growth, and individual contributions to a dynamic value-creating system (De Set, Gas, Lavoie & Lure, 2023). Despite these changing circumstances and new leadership styles emerging, some people and organizations worldwide still think about leadership in more traditional ways, relying on hierarchical structures (Valmis, 2023). This perspective might be rooted in misconceptions about delegating responsibilities and power struggles in terms of decision-making, as well as pre-conceived relationships between leadership and authority (Fitzsimons, 2016).

Myths Surrounding Shared Leadership

Numerous arguments against shared leadership have emerged based on the causes of resistance to implementing this model. Some of the most common are described in the following paragraphs.

1. ***Too many cooks spoil the broth*** might be the most common myth regarding groups of people working together. Numerous proverbs and paradoxes following the same principle exist in different countries and cultures. In business settings, ship-and-captain proverbs and paradoxes are frequent: *"Too many hands on the wheel tip the boat"* or *"Too many hands row a boat up a mountain"* all suggest that when a group of people is trying to make a decision, opposing opinions will make it difficult to reach an agreement (Cambridge Dictionary, 2023).
2. ***Multiple heads lead to analysis paralysis*** is another important myth of shared leadership. It has been suggested that decision-making takes longer because more opinions lead to overthinking and endless discussions that bring processes to a grinding halt (Chen & Zhang, 2023).
3. ***In shared leadership, all roles and responsibilities are equal.*** There is an ideal that every person in a specific role will have the same responsibilities and that a specific role or position should be awarded for certain responsibilities to be held.
4. ***There is reduced ownership, responsibility, and accountability.*** This relates to the idea that when multiple people are responsible for something, and it goes wrong, pointing fingers is common, as it is hard to determine exactly who did what (Zhu, Liao, Yam & Johnson, 2018).
5. An abundance of bosses results in a lack of leadership. Another ship-and-captain phrase, *"Too many captains sink the boat,"* points at this myth. When many people have equal command or authority in a leadership position, contradicting orders will be given, and opposing messages will result in defective communication (Ji, 2018); in short, the ship will be lost.

APPLICABLE THEORIES AND RESEARCH

Plurality in Leadership

Plural leadership has gained a lot of attention in recent years, representing a counterforce to the more traditional individualistic leadership models (Flocco, Canterino & Cagliano, 2021). This leadership paradigm is increasingly relevant where plurality is necessary to face complexity and uncertainty (Flocco et al., 2021) in different settings, from project management to world politics and crisis response.

Plural leadership combines the influences of multiple leaders and tends toward a higher degree of transparency and balance in the relationship and interactions between leaders and collaborators. With more decisions being made collectively, plural leadership models give way to the emergence of intelligent structures of multiple leaders collaborating or influencing each other, which can start as dyads, triads, micro-communities (Warrior, 2022), groups, networks (Ibarra & Hunter, 2007; Grayson & Baldwin, 2011), and constellations of leaders.

According to Denis et al. (2012), there are four types of plural leadership: shared, producing, pooling, and spreading. These types are described in Table 1.

Table 1. The four types of plural leadership, suggested by Denis et al. (2012)

Characteristics	Leadership style	General description
Any member can perform both leader and follower roles	Shared leadership	The type of leadership that is visible in teams such as basketball or football. Although there are specific roles, anyone can score and lead the team to win.
	Producing leadership	Meetings of equals: Ideas flow, and agreements are reached. Leadership is a property of group interactions.
Leaders are identifiable and do not fulfill both roles.	Pooling leadership	Several people lead together. Leadership remains an elite group.
	Spreading leadership	Leadership is passed from person to person, as in relay races. Shifts in leadership might happen periodically.

Leadership and Shared Leadership

The theory supporting shared leadership has been developed from a variety of historical bases, such as the law of the situation (Follett, 1926), human relations (Rotemberg, 1994), social systems perspectives (Mercer, 1965), the social exchange theory (Homans, 1958), the theory of teams (Patterson, 2022), and participative decision-making (Siman, Lam, Chen, Schaubroeck, 2002), just to name a few.

Shared leadership can be defined as the contribution of individual leaders to achieve a common goal (Luc, 2016) and managing collective attention at all levels (Scharmer, 2012, p.31). It helps promote a positive environment that can produce better results by eliminating negative feelings, such as being forced to do something. It has been suggested that shared leadership leads to better organizational performance overall.

Shared leadership involves maximizing the human resources in organizations by empowering people and giving them an opportunity to be leaders with regard to their areas of expertise (Goldsmith, 2020). In collective actions, through shared leadership, interdependent groups, communities, and organizations foster collective leadership efficacy for a common purpose (Hickman & Sorenson, 2014). Leaders do not force an organization where it does not want to go but rather shape the direction of where it wishes to go in (Raelin, 2003).

The leader has a role in shaping employees' behavior through shared responsibility and infusing others with the ideas of the common good. Shared leadership involves a participative process in which people interact with each other in the context they are in. It is considered a modern leadership approach that entails the practice of cooperation and interaction using the competencies of all stakeholders and promoting a sense of accountability. This approach involves the participation of various individuals in leadership activities (Goksoy, 2016).

In this sense, shared leadership is a way of developing and carrying out strategies for change by working collectively for the common good through a commitment to the values and vision for a better community (Allen, Wright & Li, 2003). For shared leadership to work, there needs to be social action in the search for solutions to achieve the common good (Bryson & Crosby, 2005). This particular approach to leadership is characterized by the quality of interactions between those involved, collective problem-solving, interpersonal communication, shared values, transparency, and a desire for the common good (Gill, 2006, p. 30).

In a shared leadership context, the members of the group accept to be mutually influenced by each other in order to reach their common goal; this means that they are willing to take on the role of leaders as required and be effective followers when someone else is leading. It is one of the newer forms of leadership that helps promote positive change in a moment in which change has become exponential, and there are important technological ruptures.

Shared leadership allows everyone to engage through their leadership and achieve a common objective. It goes beyond the idea of the team and the team members. In shared leadership, every member feels solidarily responsible for accomplishing the common goal, both in terms of the resources or effort required and the expected results (Kocolowski, 2010).

Understanding Shared Leadership: Finding Common Ground

Common ground can coexist with common good and common ground disagreements (Brown, 2013), highlighting the importance of establishing effective communication and coordination to manage disagreements and work towards achieving common goals. Effective communication requires coordination of both content and process (Ellingsen, Östling, 2010); for example, in a music duet, two piano players must coordinate their tempo, dynamics, and synchronization to create a harmonious performance. However, to coordinate on content, they need to have a vast amount of shared information, mutual knowledge, beliefs, and assumptions.

Shared understanding is vital in facilitating effective communication, similar to its significance in leadership. It can exist at both cultural and personal levels. Cultural common ground refers to shared characteristics within a group, such as language or nationality. On the other hand, personal common ground is established through interactions between individuals, such as through dialogue. According to Clark (1996), common ground is continuously updated and revised through grounding, which involves achieving mutual knowledge, beliefs, and assumptions. Grounding is the collective process by which participants try to reach a shared vision through compatible values, and it is an ongoing process that requires updating and revising. Although understanding can never be perfect, grounding criteria are often used to achieve sufficient understanding.

Searle (1990) suggests that people participating in a joint activity must share a collective intention at some level. Clark and Brennan (1991) suggest all collective actions are built on common ground. Joint activity requires a mutual understanding and commitment to a common project (Kashima, Klein & Clark, 2007). The success of joint activity depends on how effectively the participants coordinate their efforts toward a common goal. The requirements to achieve common ground are further described in the table below.

Table 2. Requirements to achieve common ground, developed by the authors with the provided references

Requirements to achieve common ground	Description
Shared understanding	Shared understanding is essential for collaboration. It includes knowledge and experiences that help members respond more effectively to challenges. Includes individual and collective ownership of an accepted perspective (Bittner et al., 2014).
Shared purpose	A shared purpose is essential so that every team member can understand what is expected of them. It provides a sense of direction and alignment and creates a collective sense of belonging. Bonchek (2013) explained that it is difficult to find a purpose in life as an individual and that it is harder to achieve a common purpose as a company. However, having a purpose is good; sharing the purpose is even better.
Shared values	Shared values provide a common language that helps align leadership with its people. It also helps organizations select, develop and promote the right kind of leaders and has been proven to increase effectiveness and has overall benefits in organizational performance (McDonald & Dandz, 1992).
Shared rules of interaction	Shared rules of interaction create communities. In fact, when managing common resources, rules can be constructed spontaneously. Rules often arise unbidden from mutually agreeable social and economic interactions. Its importance lies in creating a sense of stability and predictability (Chater, 2020).
Shared concerns	Shared concerns stem from collective feelings; agents in a particular community who have the same worries and who want to do something about it. Having shared concerns leads to responsible leadership (Adler & Laasch, 2020) and solidarity.

It All Starts With Trust

Trust is a human challenge and a fundamental quality for a good society as it enhances communication, facilitates exchanges, and promotes mutual respect and tolerance among people (Wilkinson & Pickett, 2010; Kohn, 2008). People aspire to live in a world in which trust and good faith are the basis of the actions of those around them (Viegnes, 2014). Trust affects people's well-being and that of the community.

Trust is an essential aspect of the common good (Viegnes, 2014); it varies in quality and degree, and it can be promoted, stifled, or twisted, affecting the well-being of individuals and the community (Kohn, 2008; Wilkinson et al., 2010). Trust is related to vulnerability and dependence and is the cement of all societies; it is essential for developing stable social relationships and reducing the complexity of social systems. It helps social actors face uncertainty or fragility and boost interest in social relationships (Viegnes, 2014). Trust develops through communication, support, fairness, predictability, and competence, and it should be reciprocal between leaders and followers (Kohn, 2008). Trust can be divided into thick and thin trust, developed through personal familiarity, observing actions over time, or reputations, norms, and assessments based on signals (Kohn, 2008).

Building a relationship based on trust requires building a comfortable interpersonal relationship that provides a sense of familiarity and openness, enabling one to anticipate the behaviors of others (Teboul & Damier, 2022). People who trust are generally happier, more optimistic than mistrustful individuals, and more tolerant. When there are high levels of trust, people feel at peace and work in a cooperative manner. In certain situations, trust, or the lack of it, can make the difference between life and death (Wilkinson et al., 2010, p.57).

Trust is desirable and is enhanced in countries that are ethically homogeneous (they share a sense of common identity), well-governed, and have economic equality (Kohn, 2008). Lessened inequalities tend to favor trust, health, happiness, and better relationships; therefore, it is important for leaders to establish trust with their followers as it is a critical element in achieving shared goals. Trust, however, must be reciprocal as it demands that the trusted party incorporates the trusting party's interests into its own and are capable of taking the necessary actions (Kohn, 2008, p. 59).

Communication helps build trust. When communicating, language is extremely important because it helps understand and appreciate the other's different interpretations or points of view, although a common vocabulary does not necessarily presuppose a common meaning to the concepts shared (Crittenden, 1992, p.109). For people to work together, they must first be able to be together, which involves listening and communicating with each other. Listening entails interiorizing the words of others, valuing them, and sending a sign of recognition and acknowledgment that will allow openness to new ideas (Migeon, 2018).

Leaders must take an interest in their followers and encourage them to express their ideas. When trust is established between leaders and followers, both parties benefit as the possibility of achieving goals increases. The better leaders get to know their followers, the better they can anticipate their behaviors (Teboul & Damier, 2022). To develop trust, one needs to listen as much as communicate transparently. In this sense, listening abilities are of great value in today's business environment because they lead to better understanding (Nichols & Stevens, 1978; Flynn, Valikoski & Grau, 2008).

The effectiveness of an approach that strives for the common good relies heavily on empathizing with people and listening to them (Alexander & Buckingham, 2011, p.323), which is why two-way communication is so important. Leaders need to listen to what all members have to say as, in essence, listening means recognizing the other as an equal human being. In the same way, the leader listens to people; they also need to listen to the silences because these can also carry important meanings. Presenting listening, or true listening, must be carried out with an openness of will, heart, and spirit. Doing this can cultivate listening abilities essential to function in the space of the collective (Scharmer, 2012, p. 181).

Leaders must be aware of the obstacles that could impede their ability to listen effectively, such as biases, exhaustion, and presumptions. Sharing bad news could be particularly challenging, leading to the withholding of important information and the transmission of ambiguous messages. This could cause the trust to evaporate, resulting in employees becoming less willing to speak the truth, and an increased physical distance would materialize between members. In hierarchical organizations, lower-level employees might hide valuable information and resort to self-protection, leading to a decline in information flow and reduced cooperation (Kutsyuruba & Walker, 2016).

When leaders have not fully developed their skills or lack self-trust, they may resort to demonstrating their power, resulting in not listening to others, speaking over them, and/or telling employees what to do without demanding critical thinking (Migeon, 2018). This behavior could lead to declining engagement and enthusiasm, with employees becoming button pressers, hindering their ability to contribute creatively to the organization.

Trust is a fragile commodity that requires caution and verification before placing it on a person or institution (Viegnes, 2014). Trust can be lost through betrayal, withholding information, breaking a promise, dissimulation, and actions that are not coherent with the words said. Trust can also be destroyed when leaders use information as a tool or reward and when they do not give others credit when they deserve it. Once lost, trust can never return to its original state; it can only be regained by authentic behavior and questioning oneself (Papin, 2021). Only by actively addressing these issues can leaders foster an environment of open communication, trust, and engagement within their organization.

Collective Action as the Essence of Shared Leadership

When faced with a collective challenge, members use the available information to find solutions together. Each person's roles are defined collectively, as well as the decisions that are made, and there is a sense of mutual responsibility (Luc, 2016) and accountability. Shared leadership drives collective action. Collective action abounds in the world; it is concerned with the formation of groups and the behaviors of these groups in allocating resources to collective goods that provide benefits to a clearly defined set of individuals (Sandler, 1992, p. 194). Collective action is essential to business organizations and also to promote the common good.

Collective action occurs when a number of people work together to achieve a common goal; therefore, cooperation and collaboration among individuals become essential. However, the paradox of collective actions is that individuals often fail to work together to achieve specific group goals or the common good (Olson, 1978). Some types of collective action materialize independently, and others require a nudge or will need greater efforts and support to become feasible (Sandler, 1992, p. 197; Mann, 1991). This is where shared leadership comes into play, as an approach to guide a collective through what they have in common, sharing the responsibility for their actions but also the results of their success.

It is difficult to identify human domains in which collective action is not observed, as people tend to come together to achieve diverse goals, ranging from the defense or attack of nations by armies to the protection of workers' interests by labor unions or to the pursuit of common goals by business leaders (Hollard, 2007, p. 126). Collective action is also common in businesses of all sizes, and individuals may come together to promote their shared interests or goals.

There are various models that analyze actions, which can be grouped into three categories based on observable behaviors (Thévenot, 2006). The first group comprises models that focus on the individual and are centered around their autonomy, decision-making processes, personal interests, strategies, rationality, and projects. These behaviors require some level of reflection since individual actions may become common through shared behaviors. The second group of action models is based on contemporary sociology and views actions as practices that people do without much reflection. These actions are performed almost automatically without conscious thought about why they are doing them, likely due to following behavioral norms or rules. While these actions create stability in the social order, they may not be fully understood by others. The third group includes actions performed in public, implying that behaviors are reflected upon because people need to consider others in public. Some sociologists analyze these groups of actions as public civility.

Successful collective action is often credited to effective leadership, which can help establish goals, coordinate efforts, and monitor progress. The study of collective action dates back to Hume and Stuart Mill, who discussed the problem of free riders. In the 20th century, John Common and Selig Perlman recognized the importance of collective action in various organizations and societies. Leadership plays a crucial role in solving collective action problems common to social species.

Misunderstandings often arise in the context of sustaining collective actions. It is commonly assumed that once the initial impetus for collective action has passed, the shared interests that brought the group together will continue to hold the members together until they achieve their common goal. However, research has shown that this is not necessarily the case. The success of collective action is often jeopardized by the defection or "wait-and-see" behavior of individual members who may not remain fully committed to the group's goals (Mann, 1991).

Differences and Similarities Between Concepts Connected to Shared Leadership

This section presents leadership styles connected to shared leadership due to the similarities in the relationships, interactions, and goals in the leadership process. This aims to gain insights into the characteristics of leadership styles that promote collaboration, shared decision-making, flexibility, trust, and common ground, as well as how they are applied.

Balanced Leadership

Drouin et al. (2021) have suggested that balanced leadership is time-based and that it emerged as a contemporary theory in project management. It explains a continuous transfer of leadership authority between project managers and team members. It helps explain why project teams can perform very well even when there are frequent changes in team members. Balanced leadership theory claims that in projects, leadership is not static but shifts in situational contingency to the best possible leader at any point in time (Drouin et al., 2021).

Co-Leadership

The origins of co-leadership can be traced back to the Roman Empire, as leading in partnerships was essential during times of growth and conflict. Power sharing included sacrificing one's desires and capitalizing on the duality. This was frequent in mergers and partnerships, resembling a well-functioning marriage based on trust, affection, and commitment (Yankee, 2017). Co-leadership can be understood as leadership in the plural- more than one- that is mutual, producing leadership through interactions (Denis, Langley & Sergei, 2021). No single person will be making all the decisions; most of the time, it is based on two people fulfilling leadership roles collectively (Gibeau, Reid & Lanley, 2016). This enables a collaborative culture, setting an example for the rest of the organization on how to share responsibility (Kets de Vries, 2021). It is much more than a job-sharing model, which might be a response to the demands of the modern workplace incorporating different personal and professional perspectives, experience, knowledge, capacity, and flexibility (Gibeau, Reid & Langley, 2016). People have a deep common ground of values; they give clear feedback, communicate effectively, and are accountable for their actions. Success depends on a delicate balance in which interpersonal processes are essential (Kets de Vries, 2021), yet the main problem is that this can slow the decision-making process (Henley, 2023).

Collaborative Leadership

An emerging field to co-construct shared purpose at work (Chirichello, 2001), collaborative leadership is based on trusting relationships and valued member experience, and a sense of self-empowerment. The vision is a "we" rather than a "me ."Collaborative leaders accept responsibility for helping achieve a shared purpose using their behavior, communication skills, and organizational resources to influence collaboration. It is a skillful and mission-oriented facilitation of relevant relationships (Rubin, 2009). According to Crislip & Carson (1994), if you bring the appropriate people together in constructive ways and provide them with good information, they will create authentic visions and strategies for addressing shared concerns of the organization or community.

Collective Leadership

Collective leadership is based on the premise that everyone can lead. It replaces outdated top-down leadership models but does not eliminate the primary leader: the leadership role will shift according to expertise and tasks. It is the process by which people come together to pursue change. The group empowers the person or people with the most valuable expertise to tackle specific problems. The group engages in consensus building and conflict resolution, serving in both formal and informal leadership capacities (Shonk, 2022). Collective leadership requires trust, shared power, accountability, transparency, and effective communication. It helps break down silos, generating more stable solutions that help avoid disruptions. Skilled individuals are empowered and capable of doing their work without constant supervision while increasing intrinsic motivation (Shonk, 2022).

Connective Leadership

Connective leadership emerges from the idea that traditional leadership approaches hinder the leader's effectiveness (Lipman-Blumen, 1988). Connective leadership brings together diverse and even conflicting groups that exist in an interdependent environment (Connective Leadership Institute, 2022). Inclusion is critical, and the connection is inevitable (Lipman-Blumen, 1996). Leaders operating along these lines can identify high-potential initiatives and artfully adjust their behaviors to achieve the best outcomes (Lipman-Blumen, 2017). The connective era in which we live challenges leaders and followers to transform themselves into active and responsible constituents who can endorse and engage in new leadership dynamics (Lipman-Blumen, 1996).

Constellation Leadership/Leadership Constellations

Based on considering leadership as a system or a constellation of practices, actors, levels, and structures (Storey, 2004). constellation leadership weaves leadership models together based on the idea that leadership emerges through complex interactions (Day & O'Connor, 2003). It is based on a new organizational design in which firms are linked together through alliances (Gomes-Casseres & Bamford, 2001). It considers leadership and its development as an integrated process instead of arising from sole individuals (Storey, 2004). Problems may arise if some leaders shine brighter than the constellation as a whole (Proctor-Thompson, 2008) because having only star performers no longer works.

Distributed leadership

Distributed leadership is a form of shared leadership but should not be confused with delegating. Distributed leadership aims to increase the leadership capacity in a way that allows organizations to grow, empowering them and their teams. It is a collaborative form of leadership based on autonomous practices managed by a network of formal and informal leaders (Somers, 2022) to which all people contribute. Organizational roles are not designated to specific individuals; rather, they are the responsibilities of all individuals. Distributed leadership is common in some types of teams, such as military units. It involves multiple leaders with distinct but interrelated responsibilities (Yukl, 2013).

Dual Leadership

Dual leadership consists of a team with two leaders or two individuals with the same level and authority (Thude et al., 2017). Dual leadership can be useful in solving structural problems in organizations. Dual leadership has four different dyads: intuitive collaboration, unstructured coordination, negotiated cohabitation, and careful cooperation (Empson, 2017). In leadership dyads, the two individuals in leadership positions need to share influence with one another, meaning that there is a bidirectional influence process. Also, subordinates need to recognize both individuals as leaders (Hunter et al., 2017), and mutual support is required (Etzioni, 1965).

Inclusive leadership involves ensuring that all members of a team feel respected, valued, and included, as well as inspired and confident (Bourke & Espedido, 2020). This requires an open mindset and the suspension of judgment. Weissenberg (2018) suggests that inclusive leadership aims to create change, promote innovation, and balance everyone's needs. Inclusive leadership empowers individuals to achieve their full potential while also promoting the common good (Fapohunda, 2014). Arredondo (2017) notes that inclusive leadership values diversity, equity, and inclusion and benefits not only the emerging majority but also the common good. This leadership style arises from the understanding that a leader represents and serves a community, and that the growth of a community is its primary source of strength. Therefore, leaders should be actively involved in promoting the development of the community.

Integrative leadership is a style that promotes collective action as a means of achieving the greater good. It has also been acknowledged as an emerging approach that fosters collective actions to achieve the common good bringing about concepts and applications of leadership from government and politics, businesses, non-profits, media, and the community (Crosby, 2008), and as cross-sector collaborations that create public value (Crosby & Bryson, 2010). This type of leadership draws from multiple styles to create a holistic approach to leadership (Augusta & Nurdin, 2021). Leaders who adopt an integrative approach prioritize both tangible and intangible outcomes, ensuring their efforts result in sustainable projects and systems that contribute to public value and the common good (Bozeman, 2007; Moore, 1995).

Multi-headed Leadership

Multi-headed leadership is frequently visible in nations and international organizations, where different agencies sometimes function simultaneously (Morantz, 2022). Investing planning is a specific area; national security is another. Also useful in crisis relief. One of its major problems is that it could lead to bureaucratization.

Mutual Leadership

In mutual leadership, the group's needs for support are provided by a small, formally designated leadership, creating mutual relationships and connections (Bowers & Seashore, 1966). This leads to mutual understanding and cooperation, mutually influencing each other through respect. Members are committed and proactively involved in helping the team achieve goals and objectives and also challenge others in the pursuit of group goals (Carson et al., 2007).

Mutual leadership stems from a team dynamic wherein members claim roles based on skills and expertise. When required skills are not available, additional members are recruited. (Record, 2016). Mutual leadership is frequent in cross-functional and remote teams (Record, 2016). Some characteristics of mutual leadership in projects include self-delegation of task ownership, building trust, and skills and expertise inventory.

Networked Leadership

According to García and O'Driscoll (N/D), the concept of leadership in an organization should be perceived as a constantly evolving system of connections instead of a static hierarchy or a set of centralized points. These networks facilitate the implementation of leadership strategies. The task of a network leader involves constructing and managing extensive networks inside and outside the organization to enhance efficiency. Network leadership is characterized by the ability to exert influence rather than control, and it is a more indirect type of leadership that demands leaders create an environment that encourages autonomy, empowerment, trust, sharing, and collaboration (CEB, 2014).

Reciprocal Leadership

Leadership is made through reciprocal relationships that require agreement and cooperation. Reciprocal leadership is nurtured through daily exchanges (Massoudi & Hamdi, 2019). It emphasizes mutual goals and motivation for leaders and followers, involving sharing power, leading others, and leading themselves. (Pierce, 1998). This leadership style is successful when what is expected is to add expertise, more than just problem-solving (Eberle, 2019). It functions better in flattened hierarchies in which leaders do not oversee work; they become partners in creation (Pierce, 1998). Skills needed include creating a vision, building relationships, and influencing others. Additionally, five essential and practical aspects are ownership, time management, resources available, personnel, and giving credit for the contributions (Eberle, 2019). Reciprocal leaders reward performance, correct deviations, and cooperate with subordinates, setting group goals while determining work structures and procedures with others (Massoudi & Hamdi, 2019).

Relational Leadership

Leadership occurs in the joint action between people. Relational leadership requires a way of engaging with the world through relationships and being morally accountable to others (Cunliffe et al., 2011). The concept of leadership is best comprehended as an integral component of the social system in which it is enacted. In order to facilitate the attainment of shared objectives, it is essential to focus on social processes and relationships. As organizations are largely shaped by the interdependent connections established through relationships, which are constantly evolving and adapting, understanding the dynamics of these connections is crucial (Dachler, 1992; DeRue & Ashford, 2010; Drath, 2001; Uhl Bien, 2006).

Revolving Leadership

Revolving or rotating leadership has been analyzed by McKinzie (2000) and has sometimes been related to the idea of a revolving door in which people are always coming in and going out. Additionally, it has been considered that it leads to shared responsibility, which enhances the confidence and leadership qualities among all members creating a sense of brotherhood (Qayyum & Khan, 2017). Leadership rotation can be done on a regular basis -or as often as needed- and eventually, everyone is given the opportunity to take the lead (Badal, 2015). The existence of a shared or revolving leadership enables the team to work on tasks without being limited by the formal authority of one person (Tyssen et al., 2013, p. 61).

Table 3. Main characteristics of leadership styles associated with shared leadership, developed by the authors based on the sources cited in the table

Leadership style	Main characteristics
Balanced leadership	Continuous transfer of leadership authority
Co-leadership	Shared responsibility and accountability
Collaborative leadership	Co-construct shared purpose at work
Collective leadership	Leadership shifts according to skills and expertise
Connective leadership	Interdependent environment
Constellation leadership	Collective governance
Distributed leadership	Everyone contributes
Dual leadership	Two leaders with the same authority
Inclusive leadership	Harnessing diversity to achieve the common good
Integrative leadership	Holistic approach to leadership
Multi-headed leadership	Leaders function simultaneously
Mutual leadership	Members claim roles based on skills and expertise
Networked leadership	Influence over control
Reciprocal leadership	Cooperation and rewarding performance
Relational leadership	Engaging through relationships
Revolving leadership	Everyone is given the opportunity to be the leader at some point

FINDINGS

As can be observed when analyzing shared leadership, there are multiple leadership styles that support and describe the idea of plural leadership. In many cases, the incorporation of shared leadership in companies has been successful, yet it is not always effective. Case studies from different industries are presented below, showing the results achieved in each context and the value shared leadership can provide for organizations.

Although implementing shared leadership can be challenging, research suggests that the overall benefits of this approach are promising. Regardless of their type, many organizations should consider adopting shared leadership (Kocolowski, 2010) at some level. In the healthcare domain, shared leadership has proven to be highly practical due to the collaborative nature of the environment (Merkens & Spencer, 1998), relying heavily on the cooperative efforts of diverse medical and administrative experts. A quantitative study conducted in Finland helped position shared leadership as a means to establish consistent decision-making and better-defined responsibilities (Konu & Viitanen, 2008).

In a similar line of research in the infrastructure sector, Hiller, Day & Vance (2006) studied the collective enactment of leadership roles and found a positive association between collective leadership and team effectiveness. Although the study uses collective and shared leadership interchangeably, the authors refer to their findings as the effectiveness resulting from leadership in teams as a set of distributed role requirements and not as part of a single individual's responsibilities.

In terms of project management, a study involving diverse engineering design teams in China also examined the relationship between shared leadership and team effectiveness. The results indicate that shared leadership is positively associated with team task performance and team viability (Wu & Cormican, 2021). Nevertheless, it is important to clarify that this study also explores the moderating role of the project life cycle, revealing that the stage of the project influences the relationship between shared leadership and team effectiveness; therefore, shared leadership may not be the most appropriate form of leadership to use throughout a whole project.

The impact of shared leadership has also been analyzed in military contexts. In a qualitative case study focused on military teams, Ramthun & Matkin (2014) indicate that military teams facing hazardous situations utilize mutual influence and leadership emergence to share leadership and achieve high performance. The experts interviewed during the research phase described instances where hierarchical team leaders willingly accepted influence from peers and subordinates to meet the demands of the situation, relying heavily on trust and effective communication, emphasizing that relying solely on a vertical model of influence could have catastrophic consequences (Ramthun & Matkin, 2014). The study concluded that mutual influence is the key factor that enables shared leadership in dangerous circumstances.

DISCUSSION

Overcoming the Myths of Shared Leadership

Different myths have been created surrounding shared leadership. They are generally negative, stating that more than one leader can cause confusion, extend the time required for decision-making, reduce accountability and responsibility, and more. Nevertheless, modern-day organizations have been relying on shared leadership models to make space for more democratic structures that empower employees by allowing them to become leaders in their areas of expertise. With regard to the problem of having more than one leader, another common saying states that a community is like a ship in which everyone ought to be prepared to take the wheel.

Concerning the myth suggesting that **too many cooks spoil the broth,** literature on shared leadership suggests the opposite: the more ideas included, the better the results will be. A study discovered that shared leadership was particularly helpful in promoting knowledge sharing, especially in virtual settings (Valamis, 2016). Nowadays, since careers have been changing, creating personal pathways, each member and leader has specific abilities, knowledge, and skills that can be brought to the table. Furthermore, employees feel comfortable working in teams and sharing valuable information because of improved communication and increased trust. This myth can easily be thrown away by an opposing myth: two heads are better than one. It all has to do with results. If a team or project succeeded and it functioned on shared leadership, then it will be said that the addition of knowledge and skills resulted in the triumph.

The myth that declares that **multiple heads lead to analysis paralysis** can be easily overcome because the choice is actually a good thing. Certain situations will require more in-depth analysis and additional expertise. It is not uncommon to have problems emerging from a lack of analysis or little analysis, particularly from having information that cannot be trusted. For example, Einstein has been quoted as saying, *"If I had an hour to solve a problem, I'd spend 55 minutes thinking about the problem and five minutes thinking about solutions"* (Deveboise, 2021).

In terms of the myth about **all roles and responsibilities being equal in shared leadership**, as can be observed through the different leadership styles associated with shared leadership, responsibilities and roles are not always equal because the central idea of plural leadership is to maximize talent. Some people might have better communication skills, specific expertise, or capabilities. A study of regional bank branch managers found that, through shared leadership, the work is distributed in a way that takes advantage of members' unique skills (Kocolowski, 2010). In some cases, skills may be shared, but not all roles are identical, and also, roles may be redundant but not identical. For example, High Commissioners and Ambassadors have identical roles in the UK - they both represent the interests of their country; the sole difference is their country's relationship with the Commonwealth: High Commissioners come from Commonwealth countries, and Ambassadors do not.

The myth that suggests that in shared leadership, **there is reduced ownership, responsibility, and accountability** can easily be debunked as it has been shown that because transparency is increased, ownership, responsibility, and accountability are also increased (Steed, 2003). Each employee within an organization takes ownership and responsibility for the part they play. For example, Navy seals who work in close squads, sharing leadership have produced extreme ownership (Willink & Babin, 2017).

The last myth, which refers to **an abundance of bosses resulting in a lack of leadership,** remains a myth because different plural leadership models have proven their effectiveness, and more collaboration is developed. For example, W. L. Gore & Associates has one of the world's most advanced collaborative leadership systems, and an increased number of leadership positions has resulted in a lack of need for bosses (Manz, Shipper & Stuart, 2010).

CONCLUSION

In recent years, more emphasis has been placed on plural leadership models than on individual ones due to the importance of collective action in achieving results. In the context of the organizations of the 21st century, the rapid pace of change surpasses the capacity of a single individual to possess all the knowledge and skills necessary to make optimal decisions and determine the most appropriate courses of action, which is why shared leadership has grown in popularity (Fitzsimons, 2016).

This chapter has discussed some of the benefits of shared leadership and the importance of communication and trust for this leadership style. Research on the subject has found that developing an organizational culture where employees trust themselves and others to get the job done results in a higher willingness for leadership sharing and a drive to accomplish team-set leadership goals (Valamis, 2023).

Through the literature review, it became evident that although there are a variety of notions associated with shared leadership, most of them are used as synonyms. There are numerous similarities between the selected leadership styles, yet, certain differences are still visible, especially regarding the number of people involved, whether it is a dyad or if a group holds leadership. The time frame also creates important differences, especially in terms of permanent and temporary organizations, as the project management case study discussed above shows.

Shared leadership authors agree that although it may not be a one size fits all approach, under the right circumstances, the competitive advantage of shared leadership lies in harnessing the talent and energy present within an organization (Kocolowski, 2010), emphasizing the value of having multiple

Demystifying Shared Leadership

leaders interacting and collaborating to face complex challenges that require a broad range of skills to be solved. Additionally, shared leadership between individuals with different orientations and backgrounds can lead to greater success during periods of change in organizations (Kocolowski, 2010).

Demystifying shared leadership proved to be an interesting task, and evidence was found in case studies and existing research to provide counterarguments to the reluctance to implement shared leadership models. However, it is important to state that one of the major limitations of this chapter is that the efficacy of shared leadership is very context-based, and what has worked for some organizations may not work for others. In this sense, the authors hope that with the information provided on the characteristics and requirements of shared leadership, better decisions can be made concerning adopting more plural and collaborative leadership styles.

Future Research Directions

This chapter opens numerous possibilities for future research directions. Because of changes in organizations and new ways of working, especially digitalization and artificial intelligence, new leadership styles may emerge in the near future. Some of them might have similarities or even overlap with the styles presented, which can lead to novel research on the topic and the development of new theories. Additionally, correlations between leadership styles that are plural or belong to the shared leadership spectrum can be established, shedding new light onto specific traits and characteristics that help these leadership styles become more effective. Empirical studies can also be developed, comparing the effects of different leadership styles on organizational climate, productivity, and even innovation efforts.

REFERENCES

Adler, N. J., & Laasch, O. (2020). Responsible leadership and management: Key distinctions and shared concerns. In C. S. Voegtlin & W. Amann (Eds.), *Research Handbook of Responsible Management* (pp. 100–112). Edward Elgar Publishing. doi:10.4337/9781788971966.00013

Agusta, A., & Nurdin, L. (2021). *Integrative leadership style of libraries at Islamic universities in Indonesia*. Library Philosophy and Practice. https://digitalcommons.unl.edu/libphilprac/5443/

Alexander, J. M., & Buckingham, J. (2011). Common good leadership in business management: An ethical model from the Indian tradition. *Business Ethics (Oxford, England)*, 20(4), 317–327. doi:10.1111/j.1467-8608.2011.01632.x

Allen, B. L., Wright, L., & Li, T. (2003). *Shared leadership*. Iowa State University. https://www.extension.iastate.edu/communities/files/page/files/shared_leadership.allen.pdf

Arredondo, P. (2017). *Culturally inclusive leadership – The lived experience*. Arredondo Advisory Group. https://www.arredondoadvisorygroup.com/2017/07/18/culturally-inclusive-leadership-the-lived-experience/

Badal, A. (2015). Human intellectual value: An organizational spectrum. *Asian Journal of Research in Business Economics and Management*, 5(6), 44–48. doi:10.5958/2249-7307.2015.00125.5

Bittner, E. A. C., & Leimeister, J. M. (2014). Creating shared understanding in heterogeneous work groups: Why it matters and how to achieve it. *Journal of Management Information Systems*, *31*(1), 111–144. doi:10.2753/MIS0742-1222310106

Bonchek, M. (2013). Purpose is good. Shared purpose is better. *Harvard Business Review*. https://hbr.org/2013/03/purpose-is-good-shared-purpose

Bourke, J., & Espedido, A. (2020). The key to inclusive leadership. *Harvard Business Review*, 2–5. https://hbr.org/2020/03/the-key-to-inclusive-leadership

Bowers, D. G., & Seashore, S. E. (1966). Predicting organizational effectiveness with a four-factor theory of leadership. *Administrative Science Quarterly*, *11*(2), 238–263. doi:10.2307/2391247

Bozeman, B. (2007). *Public values and public interest: Counterbalancing economic individualism*. Georgetown University Press.

Brown, R. L. (2013). Common good and common ground: The inevitability of fundamental disagreement. *The University of Chicago Law Review*. https://lawreview.uchicago.edu/sites/default/files/15_Brown_BKR.pdf

Cambridge Dictionary. (2023). *Too many cooks spoil the broth*. Cambridge Dictionary. https://dictionary.cambridge.org/us/dictionary/english/too-many-cooks-spoil-the-broth

Carson, J., Tesluk, P., & Marrone, J. (2007). Shared leadership in teams: An investigation of antecedent conditions and performance. *Academy of Management Journal*, *50*(5), 1217–1234.

CEB. (2014). *The rise of the network leader: Reframing leadership in the new work environment*. CEB. https://www.multivu.com/assets/59760/documents/59760-CEB-Annual-EG-2014-original.pdf

Chater, N. (2020). *We might dream of a world where there are no rules, but how practical would it be?* BBC. https://www.bbc.com/future/article/20200220-could-we-live-in-a-world-without-rules

Chen, W., & Zhang, J. H. (2023). Does shared leadership always work? A state-of-the-art review and future prospects. *Journal of Work-Applied Management*, *15*(1), 51–66. doi:10.1108/JWAM-09-2022-0063

Chirichello, M. (2004). Collective leadership: Reinventing the principalship. *Kappa Delta Pi Record*, *40*(3), 119–123. doi:10.1080/00228958.2004.10516420

Clark, H. H. (1996). *Using language*. Cambridge University Press. doi:10.1017/CBO9780511620539

Clark, H. H., & Brennan, S. (1991). Grounding in communication. *Perspectives on socially shared cognition*.

Connective Leadership Institute. (2022). *Connective leadership*. Connective Leadership Institute. https://connectiveleadership.com/

Crittenden, J. (1992). *Beyond individualism: Reconstituting the liberal self*. Oxford University Press.

Crosby, B. (2008). Theoretical foundations of integrative leadership. *Integral Leadership Review*. http://integralleadershipreview.com/5000-feature-article-theoretical-foundations-of-integrative-leadership/

Crosby, B. C., & Bryson, J. M. (2005). *Leadership for the common good: Tackling public problems in a shared-power world* (Vol. 264). John Wiley & Sons.

Crosby, B. C., & Bryson, J. M. (2010). Integrative leadership and the creation and maintenance of cross-sector collaborations. *The Leadership Quarterly*, *21*(2), 211–230. doi:10.1016/j.leaqua.2010.01.003

Cunliffe, A. L., & Eriksen, M. (2011). Relational leadership. *Human Relations*, *64*(11), 1425–1449. doi:10.1177/0018726711418388

Dachler, H. P. (1992). Management and leadership as relational phenomena. In M. V. Cranach, W. Doise, & G. Mugny (Eds.), Social representations and social bases of knowledge (p. 169–178). Hogrefe and Huber.

Day, D. V., & O'Connor, P. M. (2003). Leadership development: Understanding the process. In S. E. Murphy & R. E. Riggio (Eds.), *The Future of Leadership Development*. Lawrence Erlbaum Associates.

De Smet, A., Gast, A., Lavoie, J., & Lurie, M. (2023). *New leadership for a new era of thriving organizations.* McKinsey. https://www.mckinsey.com/capabilities/people-and-organizational-performance/our-insights/new-leadership-for-a-new-era-of-thriving-organizations

Debevoise, N. D. (2021, January 26). The third critical step in problem-solving that Einstein missed. *Forbes Magazine.* https://www.forbes.com/sites/nelldebevoise/2021/01/26/the-third-critical-step-in-problem-solving-that-einstein-missed/?sh=acfa24f38079

Delia, N. (2018). The Concept of Leadership. *"Ovidius" University Annals, Economic Sciences Series 8*(2). https://stec.univ-ovidius.ro/html/anale/RO/wp-content/uploads/2019/02/24.pdf

Denis, J. L., Langley, A., & Sergi, V. (2012). Leadership in the plural. *The Academy of Management Annals*, *6*(1), 211–283. doi:10.5465/19416520.2012.667612

DeRue, D. S., & Ashford, S. J. (2010). Who will lead and who will follow? A social process of leadership identity construction in organizations. *Academy of Management Review*, *35*(4), 627–647. https://www.jstor.org/stable/29765008

Drath, W. (2001). *The deep blue sea: Rethinking the source of leadership*. Jossey-Bass and Center for Creative Leadership.

Drouin, N., Müller, R., Sankaran, S., & Vaagaasar, A. L. (2021). Balancing leadership in projects: Role of the socio-cognitive space. *Project Leadership and Society*, *2*, 100031. doi:10.1016/j.plas.2021.100031

Eberle, F. (2019). The 5 Levers of Reciprocal Leadership. *Linkedin*. https://www.linkedin.com/pulse/5-levers-reciprocal-leadership-francis-eberle/

Ellingsen, T., & Östling, R. (2010). When Does Communication Improve Coordination? *The American Economic Review*, *100*(4), 1695–1724. doi:10.1257/aer.100.4.1695

Empson, L. (2017). *Leading professionals: Power, politics, and prima donnas*. Oxford University Press. doi:10.1093/oso/9780198744788.001.0001

Etzioni, A. (1965). Dual leadership in complex organizations. *American Sociological Review*, *30*(5), 688–698. doi:10.2307/2091137 PMID:5824934

Fapohunda, T. (2014). Increasing organizational effectiveness through better talent management. *Research Journal of Human Resource*, *2*(4), 1–14.

Fitzsimons, D. (2016). How Shared Leadership Changes Our Relationships at Work. *Harvard Business Review*. https://hbr.org/2016/05/how-shared-leadership-changes-our-relationships-at-work

Flocco, N., Canterino, F., & Cagliano, R. (2021). Leading innovation through employees' participation: Plural leadership in employee-driven innovation practices. *Leadership*, *17*(5), 499–518. doi:10.1177/1742715020987928

Flynn, J., Välikoski, T., & Grau, J. (2008). Listening in the Business Context: Reviewing the State of Research. *International Journal of Listening*, *22*(2), 141–151. doi:10.1080/10904010802174800

Follett, M. P. (1926). The Giving Orders. Scientific Foundations of Business Administration, 29-37.

Gandolfi, F., & Stone, S. (2018). Leadership, leadership styles, and servant leadership. *Journal of Management Research*, *18*(4), 261–269.

García, S., & O'Driscoll, T. (n.d.). Networks not Hierarchy: Expanding Leadership Capacity and Impact in a Complex World. *Institute For Contemporary Leadership*. https://contemporaryleadership.com/wp-content/uploads/2021/10/Network-Leadership.pdf

Gibeau, É., Reid, W., & Langley, A. (2016). Co-leadership: Contexts, Configurations and Conditions. In The Routledge Companion to Leadership (pp. 247-262). Routledge.

Gisma Business School. (2020). *The evolution of leadership in the past decade*. Gisma Business School. https://www.gisma.com/blog/the-evolution-of-leadership-in-the-past-decade

Goksoy, S. (2016). Analysis of the relationship between shared leadership and distributed leadership. *Eurasian Journal of Educational Research*, *16*(65), 295–312. doi:10.14689/ejer.2016.65.17

Goldsmith, M. (2020). Sharing Leadership to Maximize Talent. *Harvard Business Review*. Retrieved from https://hbr.org/2010/05/sharing-leadership-to-maximize

Gomes-Casseres, B., & Bamford, J. (2001). The Corporation is Dead. Long Live the Constellation. In *The Alliance Enterprise* (p. 31). Global Strategies for Corporate Collaboration. doi:10.1142/9781848161405_0004

Grayson, C., & Baldwin, D. (2011). *Leadership networking: Connect, collaborate, create* (Vol. 125). John Wiley & Sons.

Harvard Business Review. (1998). *On leadership*. Harvard Business School Press.

Henley, D. (2023). The Surprising Benefits Of Co-Leadership. *Forbes magazine*. https://www.forbes.com/sites/dedehenley/2023/01/22/the-surprising-benefits-of-co-leadership/?sh=15853f943e92

Hickman, G. R., & Sorenson, G. J. (2013). *The power of invisible leadership: How a compelling common purpose inspires exceptional leadership*. Sage Publications.

Hiller, N. J., Day, D. V., & Vance, R. J. (2006). *Collective enactment of leadership roles and team*.

Hiller, N. J., Day, D. V., & Vance, R. J. (2006, August). effectiveness: A field study. *The Leadership Quarterly*, *17*(4), 387–397. doi:10.1016/j.leaqua.2006.04.004

Hollard, M. (2007). Pourquoi une action collective peut-elle exister? In M. Bensaïd, N. El Aoufi, & M. Hollard (Eds.), *Economie des organisations. Tendances actuelles* (pp. 125–153).

Homans, G. C. (1958). Social Behavior as Exchange. *American Journal of Sociology, 63*(6), 597–606. https://www.jstor.org/stable/2772990. doi:10.1086/222355

Hooker, C., & Csikszentmihalyi, M. (2003). Flow, creativity, and shared leadership. In C. L. Pearce & J. A. Conger (Eds.), *Shared Leadership* (pp. 217–234). Sage.

Hunter, S. T., Cushenbery, L. D., & Jayne, B. (2017). Why dual leaders will drive innovation: Resolving the exploration and exploitation dilemma with a conservation of resources solution. *Journal of Organizational Behavior, 38*(8), 1183–1195. doi:10.1002/job.2195

Ibarra, H., & Hunter, M. (2007). How leaders create and use networks. *Growth, 35*(1), 101–103. PMID:17286073

Ji, H. (2018). *Uncovering the dark side of shared leadership: a perspective of hierarchical functionalism.* [Doctoral dissertation, Zhejiang University, Hangzhou].

Kashima, Y., Klein, O., & Clark, A. E. (2007). Grounding: Sharing Information in Social Interaction. In K. Fiedler (Ed.), *Social communication* (pp. 27–77). Psychology Press.

Kets de Vries, M. (2021). Two CEOs, No Drama: Ground Rules for Co-Leadership. *INSEAD.* https://knowledge.insead.edu/leadership-organisations/two-ceos-no-drama-ground-rules-co-leadership

Khan, Z., A., Irfanullah, A., N. & Khan, D., I. (2016). Leadership Theories and Styles: A Literature Review. *Journal of Resources Development and Management, 16.*

Kocolowski, M. D. (2010). Shared Leadership: Is it Time for a Change? *Emerging Leadership Journeys, 3*(1).

Kohn, M. (2008). *Trust: Self-interest and the common good.* OUP Oxford.

Konu, A., & Viitanen, E. (2008). Shared leadership in Finnish social and health care. *Leadership in Health Services (Bradford, England), 21*(1), 28–40. doi:10.1108/17511870810845888

Kutsyuruba, B., & Walker, K. D. (2016). The Destructive Effects of Distrust: Leaders as Brokers of Trust in Organizations. The Dark Side of Leadership: Identifying and Overcoming Unethical Practice in Organizations (Advances in Educational Administration, Vol. 26), Emerald Group Publishing Limited, Bingley, pp. 133-154. doi:10.1108/S1479-366020160000026008

Lewin, K., Lippitt, R., & White, R. K. (1939). Patterns of aggressive behavior in experimentally created "social climates.". *The Journal of Social Psychology, 10*(2), 269–299. doi:10.1080/00224545.1939.9713366

Lipman-Blumen, J. (1988). *Individual and organizational achieving styles: A technical manual for researchers and human resource professionals.* Achieving Styles Institute.

Lipman-Blumen, J. (1996). *The connective edge: Leading in an interdependent world.* Jossey-Bass.

Lipman-Blumen, J. (2017). Connective leadership in an interdependent and diverse world. *Roeper Review*, *39*(3), 170–173. doi:10.1080/02783193.2017.1318994

Luc, É. (2016). Le leadership partagé: Du mythe des grands leaders à l'intelligence collective. *Gestion*, *41*(3), 32–39. doi:10.3917/riges.413.0032

Mann, P. (1991). Permanence and evolution of the repertoire of collective action of French farmers since 1970. *Economie Rurale*.

Manz, C., Shipper, F., & Stewart, G. (2009). Everyone a Team Leader: Shared Influence at W. L. Gore & Associates. *Organizational Dynamics*, *38*(3), 239–244. doi:10.1016/j.orgdyn.2009.04.006

Massoudi, A. H., & Hamdi, S. S. (2019). Reciprocal leadership influence on organizational change. *Cihan University-Erbil Journal of Humanities and Social Sciences*, *3*(1), 20–26. doi:10.24086/cuejhss.v3n1y2019.pp20-26

McDonald, P., & Gandz, J. (1992). Getting value from shared values. *Organizational Dynamics*, *20*(3), 64–77. doi:10.1016/0090-2616(92)90025-I

McKinzie, S. (2000). Twenty-five years of collegial management: The Dickinson College model of revolving leadership and holistic librarianship. *Library Philosophy and Practice*, *2*(2), 1–8.

Mercer, J. R. (1965). Social System Perspective and Clinical Perspective: Frames of Reference for Understanding Career Patterns of Persons Labelled as Mentally Retarded. *Social Problems*, *13*(1), 18–34. doi:10.2307/799303

Merkens, B. J., & Spencer, J. S. (1998). A successful and necessary evolution to shared leadership: A hospital's story. *International Journal of Health Care Quality Assurance*, *11*(1), 1–4. PMID:10177364

Migeon, D. (2018). Bienveillance, éthique et empathie en entreprise. *Petod digest de philo á l'usage du monde professionnel Paris: Maxima*.

Moore, M. H. (1995). *Creating public value: Strategic management in government*. Harvard University Press.

Morantz, A. (2022). In praise of multi-headed leadership. *Smith*. https://smith.queensu.ca/insight/content/In-Praise-of-Multi-Headed-Leadership.php

Nichols, R. G., & Stevens, L. A. (1978). Listening to people. *Reporter*, *4*, 8. https://heinonline.org/HOL/LandingPage?handle=hein.journals/report4&div=6&id=&page=

Olson, M. (1978). *Logique de l'action collective*. Puf.

Papin, S. (2021). Le leadership de demain. La confiance dans le bien commun. *Hermés la Revue*, *88*(2), 226–229.

Patterson, D. (2022). *In-depth look: Tuckman's Model – Five Stages of Team Development*. In *Strategic Project Management Theory and Practice for Human Resource Professionals*. Press Books. https://ecampusontario.pressbooks.pub/hrstrategicprojectmanagementtheory/chapter/4-6-in-depth-look-tuckmans-model-five-stages-of-team-development/

Pearce, C. L. (2012). Shared Leadership. Encyclopedia of Leadership. Thousand Oaks.

Pearce, C. L., & Conger, J. A. (2002). *Shared leadership: Reframing the hows and whys of leadership*. Sage Publications.

Pierce, W. (1998). Reciprocal leadership, a practical approach to leadership. *University of Richmond UR Scholarship Repository*. https://scholarship.richmond.edu/cgi/viewcontent.cgi?article=2205&context=honors-theses

Proctor-Thomson, S. B. (2008). Constellations or Stars? What Is Being Developed in Leadership Development. Lancashire, England: Lancaster University Management School, Centre for Excellence in Leadership (CEL).

Qayyum, A., & Khan, B. S. (2017). Practice of self-help group in Pakistan: A traditional saving instrument. *WALIA Journal, 33*(1), 74–80.

Raelin, J. A. (2003). *Creating leaderful organizations: How to bring out leadership in everyone*. Berrett-Koehler Publishers.

Ramthun, A. J., & Matkin, G. S. (2014). Leading Dangerously: A Case Study of Military Teams and Shared Leadership in Dangerous Environments. *Faculty Publications: Agricultural Leadership, Education & Communication Department*, 97. https://digitalcommons.unl.edu/aglecfacpub/97

Record, J. (2016). How Mutual Leadership Helps High-Performing Teams Avoid Meetings And Increase Productivity. *Leaderonomics*. https://www.leaderonomics.com/articles/business/mutual-leadership-in-teams

Rotemberg, J. J. (1994). Human Relations in the Workplace. *Journal of Political Economy, 102*(4), 684–717. https://www.jstor.org/stable/2138761. doi:10.1086/261951

Rubin, H. (2009). *Collaborative leadership: Developing effective partnerships for communities and schools*. Corwin Press.

Sandler, T. (1992). *Collective Action: Theory and Applications*. University of Michigan Press.

Scharmer, C. O. (2012). *Théorie U: diriger à partir du futur émergent*. Pearson.

Searle, J. R. (1990). Collective intentions and actions. In P. Cohen, J. Morgan, & M. E. Pollack (Eds.), *Intentions In communication* (pp. 401–415). Bradford Books.

Shonk, K. (2022). What Is Collective Leadership? *Program On Negotiation*. Harvard Business School. Retrieved from https://www.pon.harvard.edu/daily/leadership-skills-daily/what-is-collective-leadership/

Simon, S. K. (2002). Participative Decision Making and Employee Performance in Different Cultures: The Moderating Effects of Allocentrism/Idiocentrism and Efficacy. *Academy of Management Journal, 45*(5), 905–914. doi:10.2307/3069321

Somers, M. (2022). Why distributed leadership is the future of management. *MIT*. https://mitsloan.mit.edu/ideas-made-to-matter/why-distributed-leadership-future-management

Steed, J. (2003). *A question of leadership*. O'Reilly. https://learning.oreilly.com/library/view/a-question-of/01520110027SI/chapter-02.html

Storey, J. (Ed.). (2004). *Leadership in organizations: Current issues and key trends*. Psychology Press.

Teboul, J., & Damier, P. (2022). *Le Mirage du leadership à l'épreuve des neurosciences*. Odile Jacob.

Thévenot, L. (2006). *L'action au pluriel: sociologie des régimes d'engagement*. Éd. La Découverte. doi:10.3917/dec.theve.2006.02

Thude, B. R., Thomsen, S. E., Stenager, E., & Hollnagel, E. (2017). Dual leadership in a hospital practice. *Leadership in Health Services*, *30*(1), 101–112. doi:10.1108/LHS-09-2015-0030 PMID:28128047

Tyssen, A. K., Wald, A., & Spieth, P. (2013). Leadership in temporary organizations: A review of leadership theories and a research agenda. *Project Management Journal*, *44*(6), 52–67. doi:10.1002/pmj.21380

Uhl-Bien, M. (2006). *Relational Leadership Theory: Exploring the social processes of leadership and organizing*. Leadership Institute Faculty Publications. https://digitalcommons.unl.edu/leadershipfacpub/19

Valamis. (2023). *Shared leadership*. Valamis. https://www.valamis.com/hub/shared-leadership

Viegnes, M. (2014). Risquer la confiance. In: Colloques interdisciplinaires sur les valeurs - Troisième série Codirigé avec Simone de Reyff et Michel Viegnes. Neuchâtel: Alphil - Presses universitaires suisses, 11-18.

Warrior, P. (2022). You need a leadership community. *Lifelong Learning*. Linkedin. https://www.linkedin.com/pulse/you-need-leadership-community-heres-how-build-one-padmasree-warrior/

Weissenberg, C. (2018). Inclusive leadership. *Inclusive Leadership*. https://inclusiveleadership.eu/blog/ildocs/christineweissenberg/

Wilkinson, R., & Pickett, K. (2010). *Why Greater Equality Makes Societies Stronger: The Spirit Level*. Bloomsbury Press.

Willink, J., & Babin, L. (2017). *Extreme Ownership: How US Navy SEALs Lead and Win*. St. Martin's Press.

Wu, Q., & Cormican, K. (2021). *Shared Leadership and Team Effectiveness: An Investigation of Whether and When in Engineering Design Teams*. Frontiers Psychology., doi:10.3389/fpsyg.2020.569198

Yankee, D. K. (2017). A measure of attributes and benefits of the co-leadership model: Is co-leadership the right fit for a complex world? [Doctoral dissertation, Pepperdine University].

Yukl, G. (2013). *Leadership in Organizations*. Pearson.

Zhu, J. L., Liao, Z. Y., Yam, K. C., & Johnson, R. E. (2018). Shared leadership: A state-of-the-art review and future research agenda. *Journal of Organizational Behavior*, *39*(7), 834–852. doi:10.1002/job.2296

ADDITIONAL READING

Anderson, H. (2017). Connective leadership: Loving those we lead. *Reflective Practice (Decatur, Ga.)*.

Contractor, N. S., DeChurch, L. A., Carson, J., Carter, D. R., & Keegan, B. (2012). The topology of collective leadership. *The Leadership Quarterly*, *23*(6), 994–1011. doi:10.1016/j.leaqua.2012.10.010

Fitzsimons, D. (2016). How shared leadership changes our relationships at work. *Harvard Business Review*. https://hbr.org/2016/05/how-shared-leadership-changes-our-relationships-at-work

Johnson, T., Martin, A. J., Palmer, F. R., Watson, G., & Ramsey, P. (2012). Collective leadership: A case study of the All Blacks. *APMBA*, *1*(1), 53–67. doi:10.21776/ub.apmba.2012.001.01.4

Judge, W. Q., & Ryman, J. A. (2001). The shared leadership challenge in strategic alliances: Lessons from the US healthcare industry. *The Academy of Management Perspectives*, *15*(2), 71–79. doi:10.5465/ame.2001.4614907

Mac Donald, H. (2015). *On Nature*. New York: New York Times Company.

New York University. (2022). *Collective leadership*. Wagner. https://wagner.nyu.edu/leadership/theory/collective#:~:text=Collective%20leadership%20describes%20the%20processes,actions%20to%20produce%20desired%20results

Sveiby, K. E. (2011). Collective leadership with power symmetry: Lessons from Aboriginal prehistory. *Leadership*, *7*(4), 385–414. doi:10.1177/1742715011416892

West, M. A., Eckert, R., Steward, K., & Pasmore, W. A. (2014). *Developing Collective Leadership for Health Care*. King's Fund.

Young, G. F., Scardovi, L., Cavagna, A., Giardina, I., & Leonard, N. E. (2013). Starling flocking networks manage uncertainty in consensus at low cost. *PLoS Computational Biology*, *9*(1), 1–17. doi:10.1371/journal.pcbi.1002894 PMID:23382667

KEY TERMS AND DEFINITIONS

Communication: An exchange of information to create meaning between different people.
Leadership style: A way in which a leader performs using specific traits and skills based on specific needs and situations.
Leadership: The ability to create meaningful relationships with others based on mutual trust.
Mutual: That goes in two directions, things that are held in common, something that is reciprocal.
Myth: A common belief that is not necessarily true.
Plural: Not singular in nature, more than one.
Trust: Confidence that is placed on others because they are reliable.

Chapter 11
Invisible Disabilities in the Workplace Are a Significant Public Health Issue and How Employee Assistance Programs Can Be a Solution

Darrell Norman Burrell
https://orcid.org/0000-0002-4675-9544
Marymount University, USA

Stacey Morin
https://orcid.org/0000-0003-2935-8332
Marymount University, USA

Sharon L. Burton
https://orcid.org/0000-0003-1653-9783
Capitol Technology University, USA

Kevin Richardson
https://orcid.org/0009-0002-3212-8669
Capitol Technology University, USA

Laura Ann Jones
https://orcid.org/0000-0002-0299-370X
Capitol Technology University, USA

ABSTRACT

Employment is a crucial factor in achieving economic security and self-sufficiency, yet individuals with disabilities often face significant barriers to accessing meaningful and gainful employment opportunities. According to the United States Census Bureau, individuals with disabilities are 65 percent less likely to be employed than those without disabilities. This discrepancy is due, in large part, to limited diversity, equity, inclusion interventions, and knowledge in the workplace on invisible disabilities. This chapter looks to explore the nature of this issue through management consulting intervention with a hospital with significant disability discrimination.

DOI: 10.4018/979-8-3693-1380-0.ch011

Invisible Disability and Employee Assistance Programs as a Solution

INTRODUCTION

Employment is a crucial factor in achieving economic security and self-sufficiency, yet individuals with disabilities often face significant barriers to accessing meaningful and gainful employment opportunities. According to the United States Census Bureau, individuals with disabilities are 65 percent less likely to be employed than those without disabilities (U.S. Census Bureau, 2016). This discrepancy is due, in large part, to limited diversity, equity, and inclusion interventions and knowledge in the workplace on invisible disabilities. Let us review the difference between a disability and an invisible disability. Definition of disability originates from the Americans with Disabilities Act of 1990 that was signed by George Walker Bush, 43rd president of the United States (Americans with Disabilities Act, n.d., para 1; Berkowitz, 2017). A physical or mental condition that significantly and enduringly hinders an individual's capacity to perform regular daily activities (Coton, 2019). On the other hand, an invisible disability refers to a physical, mental, or neurological condition that restricts a person's movements, senses, or activities, but is not apparent or visible to observers (Invisible Disabilities Association, 2023). Employers play a vital role in supporting employees with invisible disabilities in the workplace by providing reasonable accommodations to meet the needs of the individual. Reasonable accommodations are adjustments to the work environment or job duties that enable employees to perform their job effectively and maintain their dignity and independence (U.S. Equal Employment Opportunity Commission, 1991). Invisible disabilities, such as mental health disorders, chronic illnesses, and learning disabilities, can often be challenging to recognize and diagnose (Goodman, 2005).

Invisible disabilities are physical, mental, or sensory impairments that are not immediately apparent to others, such as mental health conditions, chronic pain, learning disabilities, and hearing or vision impairments (Alvarez, 2021; Iezzoni, 2003). They can range from mild to severe and can be temporary or permanent. It is estimated that up to one in five people in the United States have an invisible disability (Iezzoni, 2003). It is important to note that while invisible disabilities are not always visible, their effects can be felt and experienced in the workplace as invisible disabilities can encompass limitations or difficulties in a person's movements, senses, or activities, and can have an impact on their ability to learn or work (Alvarez, 2021).

Invisible disabilities can present a range of challenges for employers and employees. For employers, the challenge is often in recognizing the presence of an invisible disability and accommodating that disability in the workplace. For employees, the challenge is often in recognizing their disability and communicating it to their employer (Alvarez, 2021). The lack of visible symptoms can lead to misunderstanding, discrimination, and exclusion (Cook, 2011).

There are a variety of strategies for addressing the challenges associated with invisible disabilities in the workplace. A salient point is to not have people with invisible disabilities feel ashamed to self-identify. Studies indicate that a significant majority (88%) of employees with invisible disabilities opt not to disclose their condition in the workplace, primarily due to concerns about stigma and discrimination (Tillotson, 2023). Unfortunately, those who do choose to disclose their long-term invisible disabilities often experience social isolation, leading to diminished morale and decreased productivity (Tillotson, 2023). First, employers can create an environment in which employees feel comfortable discussing their disabilities and in which those with invisible disabilities feel supported. Employers should strive to create a culture of understanding and acceptance and provide support, such as accommodations and training, to employees with invisible disabilities (Cook, 2011). Additionally, employers should strive to provide flexible work arrangements, such as part-time hours or teleworking, to employees with invisible disabilities (Cook, 2011). Employers should not generalize disabilities (Tillotson et al., 2023).

The Americans with Disabilities Act (ADA) of 1990 prohibits employers from discriminating against individuals with disabilities (U.S. Equal Employment Opportunity Commission, 1991). The ADA requires employers to make reasonable accommodations for employees with disabilities unless doing so would cause an undue hardship. The ADA defines a reasonable accommodation as any change or adjustment to a job, the work environment, or how things are customarily done that enables an individual with a disability to have an equal opportunity to perform their job duties (U.S. Equal Employment Opportunity Commission, 1991). This includes changing job duties, providing job aids, and adjusting the work schedule or hours. Employers must also provide reasonable accommodations for employees with disabilities related to their medical condition, such as modifying equipment or providing additional time off (U.S. Equal Employment Opportunity Commission, 1991).

Employers must know the specific requirements for accommodating employees with disabilities whether invisible disabilities or visible (Thoms & Burton, 2015). First, employers should consider the individual's needs when making reasonable accommodations. For example, an employer may need additional training or assistance for an employee with a learning disability or a quiet workspace for an employee with a mental health disorder (Goodman, 2005). In order to develop effective policies regarding disability, employers must acknowledge that a one-size-fits-all approach is inadequate, as it fails to address the unique and specific needs of each individual (Tillotson, 2023). Employers must be flexible and willing to consider different options when making reasonable accommodations for an employee with an invisible disability.

Second, employers should ensure that their supervisors and managers are adequately trained in recognizing and accommodating employees with invisible disabilities. This includes understanding the individual's needs and providing appropriate support. Supervisors and managers should also know the legal requirements for reasonable accommodations, as outlined in the ADA (U.S. Equal Employment Opportunity Commission, 1991).

Third, employers should have a straightforward process for requesting and providing reasonable accommodations for employees with invisible disabilities. This includes a formal request process and a process for evaluating, approving, or denying requests (Goodman, 2005). Employers should also have a clear policy for addressing conflicts or grievances regarding reasonable accommodations.

Problem Statement

According to the Bureau of Labor Statistics (2023), in 2022, the employment-population ratio for individuals aged 16 to 64 with disabilities witnessed a notable increase of 3.4 percentage points, reaching 34.8 percent. In comparison, the employment-population ratio for individuals in the same age group without disabilities witnessed a growth of 1.9 percentage points, reaching 74.4 percent (Bureau of Labor Statistics, 2023). This change is likely due to a combination of factors, including that people are more likely to discuss invisible disabilities and seek treatment for them openly.

Over 42 million Americans have a severe disability, and 96% are unseen (Morgan, 2020). Examples of invisible debilitating physical and mental conditions include post-traumatic stress disorder (PTSD), traumatic brain injury, affective disorders, diabetes, cancer, lupus, Crohn's disease, and fibromyalgia (Morgan, 2020). These conditions demand a new way of approaching disability, in which we do not stick to a definition based solely on assistive equipment or someone's external appearance (Morgan, 2020).

The World Health Organization (WHO) estimates that globally, one in four people will experience a mental health condition in their lifetime (WHO, 2020). This statistic is also mirrored in the employee population, with the National Institute of Mental Health (NIMH, 2018) reporting that one in five American adults will experience a mental health challenge in any given year. This has increased pressure on organizations to support employees with invisible disabilities. Despite this, many organizations lack the understanding and resources to adequately support employees with mental health challenges (Mental Health America, 2019).

To provide more context on the importance of accommodating all disabilities in the workplace and to further show what the current state of the organization is lacking in terms of accommodations, the Center for Talent Innovation's "Disabilities and Inclusion" study showed that 30% of the professional workforce fits the federal definition of having a disability (Jain-Link & Kennedy, 2019). However, only 39% of these employees with disabilities disclosed that to their managers (Jain-Link & Kennedy, 2019). Additionally, only 24% disclosed their disability to their teams, and even fewer (21%) reported their disability to H.R. (Jain-Link & Kennedy, 2019). Lastly, where applicable, only 4% shared that they had a disability with their clients (Jain-Link & Kennedy, 2019). This paper looks to explore the nature of this issue through management consulting intervention with a hospital with significant disability discrimination

Method

A regional hospital in Florida settled a multi-million-dollar lawsuit for disability discrimination and failure to provide reasonable accommodations for its employees. As a result, the organization hired a management consultant to help them make recommendations on improving the organization using Intervention action research (IAR).

Intervention action research (IAR) is a practical and valuable research approach used for many years by professionals in various fields (McKimm et al., 2012). The primary benefit of IAR is that it allows researchers to collect data in real time in a dynamic environment (McKimm et al., 2012). This "real-time" aspect of IAR allows researchers to observe the effects of intervention as it is happening rather than rely on data collected after the fact. This enables researchers to collect data, identify areas that may require improvement, and adjust as needed (McKimm et al., 2012). Additionally, IAR allows researchers to collect data from multiple sources and to analyze the data from multiple perspectives, providing a completer and more accurate picture of the intervention's effectiveness (Miles & Huberman, 1994).

Contexts From the Literature

The first significant consequence of not improving their disability accommodations is related to the lawsuit facing this regional hospital. Individuals with invisible disabilities are protected under the Americans with Disabilities Act (ADA) under Section 12111 and are entitled to reasonable accommodations in the workplace (Feder, 2021). This section of the law specifically includes the following: "making existing facilities used by employees readily accessible to and usable by individuals with disabilities" and "job restructuring, part-time or modified work schedules, reassignment to a vacant position, acquisition or modification of equipment or devices, appropriate adjustment or modifications of examinations, training materials or policies, the provision of qualified readers or interpreters, and other similar accommodations for individuals with disabilities" (Feder, 2021).

This company risks continuing to face costly and reputation-damaging lawsuits if it does not make accommodations for people with disabilities. These lawsuits also hurt the company's brand and reputation, making maintaining a productive and effective workforce challenging for years because individuals will not want to work for or apply to the company. Many companies are famously known for being unique places for individuals with disabilities to work, positively affecting their brand and reputation. For example, Boeing has received a perfect score on the Disability Equality Index 5 years in a row and is a member of the Valuable 500, a global campaign that places disability at the forefront of business agendas (Gingras, 2020).

Another significant implication and consequence of the company not fixing these issues is the creation of a workplace that causes a psychologically unsafe and uncomfortable environment for its employees due to the lack of accommodations currently. This can lead to things like poor organizational culture, high turnover rates for staff, and lack of support and buy-in from employees to move changes forward and contribute to the advancement of the organization. For various reasons, it is very beneficial for organizations to ensure they accommodate individuals with all types of disabilities. First and foremost, it ensures that their employees feel included and valued within the organization.

Workplace accommodations positively affect the creative performance of employees with and without disabilities. According to a research article completed by the Central University of Finance and Economics in Beijing, China, self-efficacy is a critical factor in workplace accommodation promoting employee creative performance (Man et al., 2020). This 300-participant study found that individuals with a lower level of disability severity, sometimes considered invisible disabilities, have a stronger relationship between workplace accommodations and employee creative performance (Man et al., 2020). This study proves that individuals with invisible disabilities that receive proper accommodations perform better at work, leading to better organizational performance and team dynamics.

The situation harms the organization by setting it up for failure when creating an inclusive and welcoming workplace environment. As outlined in one of the course textbooks, *Organization Development: A practitioner's guide for O.D. and H.R.* textbook, in order to foster any sustainable change or improvements within an organization, it is essential to ensure the changes being made are equitable and for the benefit of all people (Cheung-Judge & Holbeche, 2021). If the regional hospital only accommodates for some employees to be able to do their work and contribute to the organization effectively, how will they ever make advancements in care delivery and quality for the patients they serve?

Additionally, as mentioned above, failing to provide accommodations for all employees negatively impacts their reputation and organizational performance on all management levels. Another study completed by the Job Accommodation Network described the direct benefits of making disability accommodations for their employers as retained valued employees (89%), increased employee productivity (70%), eliminated costs associated with training a new employee (59%), increased employee attendance (55%), increased diversity of the company (40%), savings on workers' compensation or other insurance costs (36%), hiring more qualified individuals with a disability (15%), and promoting more employees with a disability (10%) (SHRM, 2019). The study also described indirect benefits as improved interactions with co-workers (63%), increased overall company morale (61%), increased overall company productivity (55%), increased safety (46%), improved interactions with customers (44%), increased overall company attendance (41%), increased profitability (29%), and increased customer base (18%) (SHRM, 2019). This study proves the overall benefits to an organization and the individuals that make it as successful as possible. Reasonable accommodations also remove workplace barriers that prevent individuals from thriving and growing in their own professional careers.

Need for Change

The most direct impact of diversity and inclusion initiatives on employees with disabilities is increased access to employment opportunities. By implementing diversity and inclusion policies, organizations can create a more accessible environment for all employees, including those with disabilities. This can involve providing reasonable accommodations for employees with disabilities, such as adjustable desks, ergonomic chairs, and assistive technology (U.S. Department of Labor, 2019). Additionally, organizations can create a more inclusive environment by providing training and resources for managers and employees on the importance of diversity and inclusion. This can include educating employees on disability etiquette, raising awareness of the various types of disabilities, and providing resources to help employees better understand and interact with one another (U.S. Department of Labor, 2019).

In order to change the organization's current state and pursue a more desired state, several key initiatives can be implemented as foundational strategies for change. Organizational leadership should immediately consider implementing educational opportunities, flexible work environments, transparency, and accessibility to resources, and develop robust feedback channels. These five core strategies lay the foundation for further work to develop surrounding supporting employees with invisible disabilities (Cooks-Campbell, 2022).

The initial transformation work should begin with educating employees about disabilities at work. Research suggests that 1 in 4 adult Americans have a disability of some sort or will experience a disability at some point in their lifetime (Sadler, 2021). Many employees need to learn that their organization might support their specific conditions, or they might be too afraid to ask (Rosen, 2022). Fear is one of the major drivers behind why people with disabilities do not disclose them to their employers (Rosen, 2022). This is likely because people do not want to unintentionally subject themselves to discrimination by formally reporting their disability. Organizations can improve awareness by fostering an environment of openness, which educates employees through educational initiatives such as lunch-and-learns to encourage conversations surrounding disabilities (Cooks-Campbell, 2022). The organization can incorporate a disability employee resource group. Additionally, organizations can offer learning opportunities to managers who may not know how to support an employee with an invisible disability. By incorporating language surrounding invisible disabilities within the organization, there will be an increase in education and awareness about disabilities and how different people are impacted within a work setting (Rosen, 2022).

Additionally, healthcare organizations can provide more flexible work arrangements for employees with invisible disabilities. Some employees with certain chronic conditions such as mental illness, sleep disorders, or chronic fatigue might face challenges and barriers transporting to their place of employment (Sadler, 2021). Employers can support employees by providing flexible working environments such as hybrid work arrangements or allowing employees to create their schedules when desired (Cooks-Campbell, 2022). Currently, the Employment Equity Act establishes provisions for what is considered a "reasonable accommodation" for a person with a disability (U. S. Equal Opportunity Commission, 2023). Changing a work schedule or location of work can be considered a "reasonable accommodation" for a person with a disability as long as the arrangement does not cause undue hardship to the employer (U. S. Equal Opportunity Commission, 2023). Given the legal implications, organizations should evaluate their existing positions to consider where flexibility can be added to various positions.

To increase transparency, organizations should foster an environment where employees feel comfortable disclosing when taking a mental health day (Cooks-Campbell, 2022). Furthermore, healthcare organizations should encourage employees to use their paid time off (PTO) and take vacation time away from work. Employees should also feel comfortable disclosing if they must leave work for a doctor's appointment. Studies have found that when companies freely share information and encourage employees to do the same, employees feel they can trust their company more (Martic, 2022). Furthermore, when employees feel they can trust one another, they build more robust and meaningful relationships, which allows the company culture to flourish (Martic, 2022). By introducing these minor changes, companies can improve transparency between employees and the organization, allowing them to feel that their organization supports and prioritizes their health and well-being (Cooks-Campbell, 2022).

Another foundational strategy for changing the organization's current state is to improve accessibility to resources regarding indivisible disabilities. For example, an organization can create a webpage with resources for employee well-being (Cooks-Campbell, 2022). By doing so, employees will have easy access to resources through their employer. Including an employee resources webpage will encourage employees to prioritize their well-being and increase their education and knowledge overall (Cooks-Campbell, 2022). By investing in educational resources, the company is not only supporting individuals with disabilities but investing in the overall organization (Rosen, 2022). For example, a recent study found that when companies adopt best practices for supporting employees with disabilities, they experience 28% higher revenues and 30% higher economic profit margins than their peers (Rosen, 2022). Investing in employee resources can improve the bottom line and support and improve working environments for employees with invisible disabilities (Rosen, 2022).

Lastly, organizations should constantly seek employee feedback (Pollock, 2022). Without asking employees for feedback, it is hard to know and understand if the initiatives have the intended impact (Cooks-Campbell, 2022). Asking employees for feedback also makes employees feel genuinely cared about and valued within the company (Cooks-Campbell, 2022). In competitive hiring markets, employees seek environments where their voices are heard, and they feel seen as individuals (Pollock, 2022). Incorporating structured and unstructured feedback channels effectively improves employee engagement and working environments for people with invisible disabilities (Pollock, 2022). Organizations should consider putting formalized feedback channels in place so that there are structured ways to obtain and synthesize feedback into improvement opportunities.

The five vital foundational strategies work towards creating a foundational culture for change. Companies focusing on culture are five times more likely to achieve breakthrough results in their transformation initiatives (Tecosky & Hollister, 2021). Companies that continue to invest and focus on their culture create an "adaptive culture" (Tecosky & Hollister, 2021). An adaptive culture allows an organization to adapt to changes, but its culture will remain constant (Tecosky & Hollister, 2021). The organization will foster a more adaptive culture by implementing the five critical foundational strategies. It is essential to understand that culture is dynamic, and organizational culture will form regardless of whether leadership guides the culture (Tecosky & Hollister, 2021). For example, employees have different values, mindsets, and behaviors shaping the organization's culture. As a result, if leadership is not proactive in forming the organization's culture and norms, the employees will shape the organization's culture, which might not be well-suited or aligned with the overall organization's mission (Tecosky & Hollister, 2021). To properly shape the organization's culture for change, leadership must recognize that one-time training and initiatives have significant limitations (Pendell, 2022).

Furthermore, culture does not change overnight; it is formed based on what occurs daily (Pendell, 2022). For this reason, it is imperative that creating a culture for change is a constant investment. To ensure that culture is prioritized daily, organizations can start by being vocal about their 'core values'

(Laker, 2022). Many organizations display their core values on websites, social media, and other publications like annual reports (Laker, 2022). While it is essential to display core values, it is more important to have strong leadership that communicates the vision of the organization's core values as they relate to the employees (Laker, 2022). Employees must identify and feel inspired by the organization's core values to achieve the vision (Laker, 2022). Core values should be included in performance reviews for every employee to measure core competencies. If the core values are communicated and embedded in the organization's culture successfully, employees will feel more engaged at work, fueling the organization to grow and face new challenges (Laker, 2022).

Organizational Diagnosis Process

Organizational diagnosis is assessing and analyzing an organization to identify areas that require improvement or further development. It is a systematic and comprehensive approach to evaluating an organization's structure, culture, and processes to determine areas of opportunity and potential risk areas. The organizational diagnosis process is used to assess the current state of an organization and make recommendations for change and improvement.

The literature on the steps in the organizational diagnosis process is broad and varied. According to Geisler and Beauvais (2013), the process begins with assessing the organization's current performance, including reviewing existing data, interviewing stakeholders, and observing the workplace. Next, the organization's goals and objectives and any gaps between current performance and the desired outcomes are identified. Following this, the organization's structure, culture, and processes are evaluated, and any potential areas of improvement are identified. Finally, a plan of action is created to address the identified areas of improvement, and the plan is implemented.

The benefits of organizational diagnosis have also been explored in the literature. According to Geisler and Beauvais (2013), one of the main advantages of conducting an organizational diagnosis is that it allows organizations to identify areas of strength and weaknesses, which can inform decision-making and strategy. It also helps organizations to identify potential areas of risk and to create strategies to mitigate those risks. Additionally, conducting an organizational diagnosis can help ensure that an organization has the resources and capabilities to achieve its goals and objectives.

Desired State

Building workforce training for employees, such as disability awareness training, will help everyone across the organization understand the various types of disabilities some may be experiencing (Kconvery, 2022). Educating all employees will help create company-wide empathy and reduce negative connotations and biases about those with disabilities (Kconvery, 2022). Having employee resource groups can help employees have a dedicated safe space to discuss workplace challenges or report on issues they want to see changed (Kconvery, 2022). When creating the employee resource group, it is crucial to define the group's mission (Test, 2022). Having a clear purpose for the resource group, such as a welcoming environment to invite all employees, disability or not, to connect with those who have gone through similar situations, need advice, or need someone to talk to (Test, 2022).

Workers suffering from invisible disabilities should be offered the same considerations and protections as all visible disabilities. Nobody should be discriminated against because of a simple disability, whether visible or hidden. Leaders and H.R. professionals committed to keeping a diverse and inclusive workplace have a daily mission: invisible disabilities should always be identified, discussed, and considered (Fisk, 2021). Also, they should identify areas for better focus to create a better work environment: implementing a continuous awareness training program, future research on best practices to be implemented in the workplace, and policy review to keep them updated. When an organization focuses on individual abilities and provides a safe and inclusive environment for their employees, teams can flourish, employee loyalty increases and performance improves to astonishing levels, benefiting employers, employees, customers, and the whole community the organization serves (Fisk, 2021).

According to Gignac et al. (2020), understanding workplace communication-support processes from the perspective of those providing support to workers with disabilities is essential to protect privacy and provide adequate support and identify challenges arising when workers choose to disclose or not personal health information. It is crucial to address support gaps, understand the role of critical stakeholders in disability support processes, and identify better ways to enable workers with invisible disabilities to sustain their jobs and work correctly and with dignity.

In addition, workplace policies should be in place to assist workers in an ambiguous situation regarding the detection or personal acceptance of a disability (Santuzi, 2014). Although disclosure permits workers with disabilities to be protected under federal legislation, future research, and practices should consider conditions under which the beneficial protections and accommodations might be outweighed by adverse social and work consequences for individuals with invisible disabilities (Santuzi, 2014). It is essential to discourage others from speaking negatively of the employee with a disability and emphasize that this person is still doing their job as expected and is considered a valuable team member. Disability awareness training might be appropriate for all employees (Fisk, 2021). It is important to note that having a DEI (Diversity, Equity, and Inclusion) policy that calls out disability as an area of focus and includes people with disabilities in board, leadership, and staff positions makes a remarkable difference (RespectAbility 2022). Whether the policies come before the practice or vice versa is still being determined from the existing literature, but the correlation between them is unmistakable (RespectAbility, 2022). By every measure, groups that are explicit about disability inclusion as a priority and groups with disability representation within their ranks are more likely to be acting (RespectAbility, 2022).

Most organizational cultures were formed from the initial successes of an organization years before people with disabilities attempted to achieve workplace equality (Klinger, 2002). The structure of most existing cultures and the ever-present perceptual/attitudinal barriers make a straightforward infusion of underrepresented populations into the workplace impossible (Klinger, 2002). The techniques used today and in the past have only allowed a person hired by an organization to assimilate into that culture, a process known as 'learning to fit in.' This is difficult enough for anyone new to a job, but it may be an insurmountable task for someone who is perceived as different and needs to be acknowledged by the culture (Klinger, 2002).

Organizational culture has received increased attention regarding its influence on workplace health and productivity, but there is a lack of studies on this relationship with employer-based disability programs (Buys et al., 2017). Given the potential relationship between organizational culture and disability management, employers should facilitate a positive workplace culture by ensuring consistency among underlying values, espoused values, and actual treatment of employees (Buys et al., 2017).

Currently, H.R. professionals can be changemakers and pave the way forward. Implementing and cementing a more inclusive company culture will make a world of difference for these individuals and all employees, and that change must start by pushing back against stereotypes and misconceptions (Morgan, 2020).

Invisible Disability and Employee Assistance Programs as a Solution

The burden must be placed on the organization rather than the new employee. There needs to be a way to recognize diversity as an asset in organizations so that underrepresented populations can become part of the culture (Klinger, 2002). Effective cultural change can be a slow process, but if done correctly and consistently, the change will happen, benefiting the employees and the entire organization (Klinger, 2002).

We can all help construct a better future for disabled people, making employers and employees more open-minded and accepting of others regardless of their disabilities. Empathy and flexibility are critical (Ess, 2021). Employers should work directly with the disabled, figuring out how to best accommodate them and helping them thrive in their jobs, setting an example for an ideal workplace that welcomes and supports all with these actions and supported by updated government legislation, discrimination towards the disabled can be significantly reduced, transforming the whole organization into a more inclusive and equitable workplace (Ess, 2021).

Finally, it is critical to recognize the unique ways in which marginalized identities - including those associated with disability - overlap and merge (Santuzi, 2014). In addition to racism, people of color who are disabled can encounter ableism. Women who have disabilities struggle with sexism that is exacerbated by ableism. As significant a barrier as stairs and small doorways in the workplace can be discriminatory social practices (Santuzi, 2014). Paying attention to these behaviors might be the difference between providing disabled persons with the physical and emotional space they need to succeed and contributing their full potential to their work organizations.

The best way to achieve inclusivity is to encourage all employees to model the behavior they want to see in others and to normalize disabilities and accommodations. In an environment where accommodations for everyone are normalized, many micro- or macro-aggressions may be eliminated from the workplace as it can help remove the stigma surrounding disability, visible or not. Everyone wants to work in a supportive environment where they feel respected and supported (Abney et al., 2022).

To sum up, our consultant group recommends, as the desired state in every organization, at least four of the following main actionable tasks:

§ Promote and expand employee assistance programs.
§ Increase diversity and inclusion training to include specific training on invisible disabilities.
§ Create a reasonable accommodation manager position in human resources.
§ Train managers on how to support employees with disabilities.
§ Create screening surveys to allow employees a means to disclose invisible disabilities.

Organizations can support employees with invisible disabilities, such as anxiety, depression, ADHD, and other mental health challenges. The first step for organizations is to create an environment of acceptance and understanding for employees with invisible disabilities. This can be done by providing educational resources and training to employers and employees about mental health challenges and the accommodations necessary for employees with invisible disabilities (Mental Health America, 2019). Organizations can also provide mental health first aid training to employees and managers, which will help them recognize signs of mental health challenges and support employees with invisible disabilities (Mental Health America, 2019).

Organizations can also create a supportive work environment by providing resources and support for employees with invisible disabilities. This can include providing access to mental health professionals, such as psychologists, psychiatrists, and social workers, for employees who need additional support (Mental Health America, 2019). Organizations can also provide access to support groups and peer support programs for employees with invisible disabilities, providing a safe and supportive space to discuss their challenges and find support from others with similar experiences (Mental Health America, 2019).

Organizations can also provide a range of accommodations to employees with invisible disabilities. These can include flexible work arrangements, such as modified hours or the ability to work remotely. This can help to reduce stress and anxiety and provide a more supportive environment for employees with invisible disabilities (Mental Health America, 2019). Organizations can also provide access to Employee Assistance Programs (EAP), which provide employees with counseling and other mental health services (Mental Health America, 2019).

Employee Assistance Programs (EAPs) are workplace support services that provide employees with indivisible disabilities such as anxiety, ADHD, depression, and PTSD with resources and strategies to help them manage their mental health.

Employee Assistance Programs provide various services to support employees with indivisible disabilities. EAPs typically provide counseling and referral services, crisis intervention services, health and wellness education, and other resources to help employees manage mental health issues. As such, EAPs can be instrumental in helping employees with indivisible disabilities to manage their mental health. For example, a study by O'Shea et al. (2013) found that EAPs that provided counseling and referral services were effective in helping employees with anxiety and depression manage their mental health. Additionally, the study found that EAPs could reduce stress levels and help employees become more productive.

Despite the effectiveness of EAPs, several challenges are associated with their use. For example, EAPs may need to be more utilized due to a lack of awareness or stigma associated with mental health issues. Furthermore, employees may hesitate to use EAPs because of concerns about confidentiality and privacy. Additionally, EAPs may lack the resources and personnel to support employees with indivisible disabilities adequately.

To address these challenges, employers should ensure that employees are aware of the services offered through the EAP and that these services are easily accessible. Employers should also ensure EAPs have adequate resources and personnel to serve the needs of their employees. Additionally, employers should emphasize the importance of confidentiality and privacy and ensure that their EAPs comply with all relevant laws and regulations.

SUMMARY AND CONCLUSION

In 1940, Fernando Cortez was the first person to use the term "transculturalism" to refer to a cultural concept (Allolio-Nacke, 2014). The term was then explored and lengthened to become the TD&I model by Thoms and Burton. (2015). The TD&I model describes how societies will alter the way that the cultures that hold the majority of the population interpret the cultural distinctions that exist in other people. The term also accounts for the shifting demographics of who constitutes a majority by taking into consideration the growing number of persons who have disabilities. In accordance with the definition of disability provided by the Americans with Disabilities Act (U.S. Equal Employment Opportunity Commission, 1991). Thoms & Burton (2015; 2018) utilized disability language and discussed the necessity for individuals to cater to the diverse needs and expectations of various populations, including individuals with disabilities who are potential additions to the workforce, it is essential to comprehend the available avenues of services.

The TD&I paradigm is rooted in the vocabulary that was developed by a transculturalized society as it moved from the dark ages of hiding individuals' varied disabilities to the modern awareness that disability is a component of diversity and inclusion, hence posing a challenge to a society that views itself as an informed one. (Thoms & Burton, 2015). It is not the purpose of this essay to imply that those who consider themselves to be members of either a marginalized or dominating group are the ones who advocate for the rejection of a TD&I paradigm. The purpose of this is to raise awareness about what the concept entails in terms of narrowing the gaps that exist between different groups of individuals. It is critical to have a thorough understanding of what is meant by the term "transcultural." In cross-cultural contexts, one method for identifying information constructs is to look for areas within societal relationship-building that are deeply rooted and securely established. The lack of comprehension that exists across social and cultural domains can easily lead to contradictions about knowledge that is known and information that is unknown, which in turn can cause identity and social divergences. (Thoms & Burton, 2015; 2018, 2018).

Increased access to employment opportunities and diversity and inclusion initiatives can positively affect the overall well-being of employees with disabilities (Thoms & Burton, 2018; Thoms & Burton, 2015). Studies have found that employees with disabilities who work in a diverse and inclusive environment experience higher job satisfaction and increased morale (Bonaccio, 2020; Pawlak, 2017; Nunez et al., 2017). This is due, in part, to the fact that employees with disabilities are more likely to feel comfortable and accepted in an environment that is supportive of their unique needs and abilities (Nunez et al., 2017). Additionally, employees with disabilities may benefit from increased collaboration with their peers, as diversity and inclusion initiatives often lead to more open and honest dialogue between co-workers (Pulrang, 2019).

By creating a more accessible and inclusive environment, organizations can provide increased access to employment opportunities and improved job satisfaction for employees with disabilities (Pulrang, 2019). Additionally, diversity and inclusion initiatives can help foster a culture of acceptance and understanding, leading to increased collaboration and morale among employees with disabilities (Maurer, 2022). Thus, it is clear that fostering a culture of diversity and inclusion is essential for creating a more equitable workplace for all employees.

Addressing invisible disabilities in the workplace is extremely important. As we have seen, an estimated 30% of professionals in the workforce fit the federal definition of a disability (Jain-Link & Kennedy, 2019). 65% of employees with disabilities wish that their organization worked to prevent judgment and embarrassment regarding their disability and the accommodations surrounding it (Smith, 2012). An organization needs to understand what an invisible disability is; a physical, mental, or neurological condition that cannot be seen from the outside but can affect someone's movements or activities (Rosen, 2022). It is also essential to know that "invisible disability" is an umbrella term, encompassing many conditions such as heart defects, migraines, learning differences, digestive disorders, and many more (Byrne-Haber, 2019). To immediately address the current discrimination in accommodations at the regional hospital, organizational leadership must implement educational opportunities, flexible working environments, accessibility to resources, and extensive feedback channels for employees. By improving accessibility, employees will have easier access to request forms and information about what accommodation they may be able to receive.

REFERENCES

Abney, A., Denison, V., Tanguay, C., & Ganz, M. (2022). Understanding the unseen: Invisible disabilities in the Workplace. *The American Archivist*, *85*(1), 88–103. doi:10.17723/2327-9702-85.1.88

Allolio-Nacke, L. (2014). Transculturalism. In T. Tao (Ed.), *Encyclopedia of Critical Psychology*. Springer. doi:10.1007/978-1-4614-5583-7_316

Alvarez, B. (2021). *What to know about invisible disabilities*. National Education Association. https://www.nea.org/advocating-for-change/new-from-nea/what-know-about-invisible-disabilities

Berkowitz, E. (2017). George Bush and the Americans with Disabilities Act. *Social Welfare History Project*. https://socialwelfare.library.vcu.edu/recollections/george-bush-and-the-americanswith-disabilities-act/

Bhatnagar, K., & Srivastava, K. (2012, January). Job satisfaction in healthcare organizations. *Industrial Psychiatry Journal*. https://www.ncbi.nlm.nih.gov/pmc/articles/PMC3678186/

Bonaccio, S., Connelly, C. E., Gellatly, I. R., Jetha, A., & Martin Ginis, K. A. (2020). The participation of people with disabilities in the workplace across the employment cycle: Employer concerns and research evidence. *Journal of Business and Psychology*, *35*(2), 135–158. doi:10.100710869-018-9602-5 PMID:32269418

Bureau of Labor Statistics. (2013). Persons with a disability: labor force characteristics - 2022. *BLS.*. https://www.bls.gov/news.release/pdf/disabl.pdf

Buys, N., Wagner, S., Randall, C., Harder, H., Geisen, T., Yu, I., Hassler, B., Howe, C., & Fraess-Phillips, A. (2017). Disability management and organizational culture in Australia and Canada. *Work (Reading, Mass.)*, *57*(3), 409–419. doi:10.3233/WOR-172568 PMID:28800348

Byrne-Haber, S. (2019, June 13). The importance of Disability Employee Resource Groups. *Medium*. https://sheribyrnehaber.medium.com/the-importance-of-disability-employee-resource-groups-21ea6552ea2e

Centers for Disease Control and Prevention (CDC). (2018). Prevalence of self-reported invisible disability among U.S. adults aged ³18 years, 2015–2017. *MMWR. Surveillance Summaries*, *67*(18), 1–8.

Cook, B. G. (2011). Invisible disabilities in the workplace: Challenges and strategies. *Journal of Vocational Rehabilitation*, *35*(3), 199–207. doi:10.3233/JVR-2011-0528

Cooks-Campbell, A. (2022, February 28). *Understanding invisible disabilities in the workplace*. Understanding Invisible Disabilities in the Workplace. https://www.betterup.com/blog/invisible-disabilities#:~:text=A%20simple%20way%20to%20provide,for%20people%20with%20chronic%20conditions

Coton, F. (2019). *What are invisible disabilities?* University of Glasgow. https://www.gla.ac.uk/media/Media_702849_smxx.pdf

Eisenmenger, A. (2020, September 14). *Five things you didn't know about invisible disabilities*. Access Living. https://www.accessliving.org/newsroom/blog/five-things-you-didnt-know-about-invisible-disabilities/

Feder, J. (n.d.). *Considerations for supporting and accommodating invisible disabilities*. Accessibility. com. https://www.accessibility.com/blog/considerations-for-supporting-and-accommodating-invisible-disabilities

Fisk, L. (2021, February 10). Council post: Breaking down workplace barriers for those with invisible disabilities. *Forbes*. https://www.forbes.com/sites/forbesbusinesscouncil/2021/02/11/breaking-down-workplace-barriers-for-those-with-invisible-disabilities/

Gallagher, D. J. (2009). Disability studies and the ethics of research on disability. In P. L. Baker (Chair), *Interdisciplinary research symposium*. University of Northern Iowa.

Geisler, E., & Beauvais, A. (2013). Organizational diagnosis: A review of the literature. *International Journal of Management Reviews*, *15*(3), 339–360. doi:10.1111/ijmr.12004

Gignac, M. A., Bowring, J., Jetha, A., Beaton, D. E., Breslin, F. C., Franche, R.-L., Irvin, E., Macdermid, J. C., Shaw, W. S., Smith, P. M., Thompson, A., Tompa, E., Van Eerd, D., & Saunders, R. (2020). Disclosure, privacy, and workplace accommodation of episodic disabilities: Organizational perspectives on disability communication-support processes to sustain employment. *Journal of Occupational Rehabilitation*, *31*(1), 153–165. doi:10.100710926-020-09901-2 PMID:32410153

Gingras, A. (2020, October 21). *24 companies with innovative and award-winning Accessibility Practices*. RippleMatch. https://ripplematch.com/insights/companies-with-innovative-and-award-winning-accessibility-practices-972ec8a4/

Goering, S. (2015). Rethinking disability: The Social Model of disability and chronic disease. *Current Reviews in Musculoskeletal Medicine*, *8*(2), 134–138. doi:10.100712178-015-9273-z PMID:25862485

Goodman, J. (2005). Accommodating the Invisible Disability: Mental Illness in the Workplace. *Employee Responsibilities and Rights Journal*, *17*(3), 211–222.

Iezzoni, L. I. (2003). Invisible disabilities: Challenges to diagnosis and treatment. *Quality in Primary Care*, *11*(5), 373–380.

Invisible Disabilities Association. (2023). *What is an invisible disability?* IDA. https://invisibledisabilities.org/

Kconvery. (2022, September 30). *Invisible disabilities in the Workplace*. Harvard Pilgrim Health Care - HaPi Guide. https://www.harvardpilgrim.org/hapiguide/seen-supported-destigmatizing-invisible-disabilities-at-work/

Klinger, M. G. M. (2002). Organizational culture and people with disabilities. *Disability Studies Quarterly*, *22*(1). doi:10.18061/dsq.v22i1.332

Laker, B. (2022, November 9). Culture is a company's single most powerful advantage. Here's why. *Forbes*. https://www.forbes.com/sites/benjaminlaker/2021/04/23/culture-is-a-companys-single-most-powerful-advantage-heres-why/?sh=51c110d679e8

Man, X., Zhu, X., & Sun, C. (2020, May 11). The positive effect of workplace accommodation on creative performance of employees with and without disabilities. *Frontiers*. https://www.frontiersin.org/articles/10.3389/fpsyg.2020.01217/full

Martic, K. (2022, November 14). Transparency in the workplace: 7 benefits and 6 best practices. *Haiilo.* https://haiilo.com/blog/transparency-in-the-workplace/

Maurer, R. (2022, October 25). Employers can do more for workers with disabilities. *SHRM.* https://www.shrm.org/hr-today/news/hr-news/pages/ndeam-employers-can-do-more-for-workers-with-disabilities.aspx

McKimm, J., Lomax, P., & White, P. (2012). Using action research for school improvement. *Sage (Atlanta, Ga.).*

Mental Health America. (2019). Mental health in the workplace: How employers can support employees. *Mental Health America..* https://www.mentalhealthamerica.net/issues/mental-health-workplace-how-employers-can-support-employees

Miles, M. B., & Huberman, A. M. (1994). *Qualitative data analysis: An expanded sourcebook* (2nd ed.). Sage.

Morgan, P. (2020, October 27). A rise in invisible disabilities calls for a corporate culture change. *Forbes.* https://www.forbes.com/sites/paulamorgan/2020/10/27/a-rise-in-invisible-disabilities-calls-for-a-corporate-culture-change/?sh=58bdd4ca60f6

National Institute of Mental Health. (2018). *Any disorder among adults.* NIH. https://www.nimh.nih.gov/health/statistics/any-disorder-among-adults.shtml

Nunez, M. D., Gudema, M., & Gallegos-Carrillo, K. (2017). Disability inclusion in the workplace: A review of best practices. *Journal of Management, 43*(7), 2056–2089.

O'Shea, E., O'Connor, M., Deeds, R., & Thompson, A. (2013). The effectiveness of employee assistance programs. *Human Resource Management Review, 23*(2), 149–158. doi:10.1016/j.hrmr.2012.08.003

Pawlak, S. (2017). The impact of diversity and inclusion on employee satisfaction and morale. *Journal of Business and Psychology, 32*(5), 615–631.

Pendell, R. (2022, December 2). Avoid virtue signaling; embrace culture-changing dei initiatives. *Gallup.com.* https://www.gallup.com/workplace/396593/avoid-virtue-signaling-embrace-culture-changing-dei-initiatives.aspx

Plan-do-study-act (PDSA) directions and examples. (n.d.). AHRQ. https://www.ahrq.gov/health-literacy/improve/precautions/tool2b.html

Pollock, S. (2022, January 14). *The importance of employee feedback.* ClearCompany. https://blog.clearcompany.com/importance-employee-feedback#:~:text=Asking%20for%20employee%20feedback%20is,environment%20for%20well%2Drounded%20insights

Pulrang, A. (2019, November 4). How to make workplaces more welcoming for employees with disabilities. *Forbes.* https://www.forbes.com/sites/andrewpulrang/2019/11/04/how-to-make-workplaces-more-welcoming-for-employees-with-disabilities/?sh=2304782353d8

Rosen, P. (2022, November, 1). Invisible disabilities in the workplace. *Understood.* https://www.understood.org/en/articles/understanding-invisible-disabilities-in-the-workplace

Sadler, R. R. (2021, November 3). How to support employees with Invisible Disabilities. *She+ Geeks Out.* https://www.shegeeksout.com/blog/how-to-support-employees-with-invisible-disabilities/

Santuzzi, A. M., Waltz, P. R., Finkelstein, L. M., & Rupp, D. E. (2014). Invisible disabilities: Unique challenges for employees and Organizations. *Industrial and Organizational Psychology: Perspectives on Science and Practice, 7*(2), 204–219. doi:10.1111/iops.12134

SHRM. (2019). *Diversity and inclusion.* SHRM. https://www.shrm.org/hr-topics/talent-acquisition/diversity-and-inclusion

Smith, J. (2022, May 19). Half of people aren't comfortable talking about disability in the Workplace. *Workplace Insight.* https://workplaceinsight.net/half-of-people-arent-comfortable-talking-about-disability-in-the-workplace/

Sur, S. (2022, October 27). Why is it important to set realistic goals? 8 strong reasons. *Wealthful Mind.* https://wealthfulmind.com/why-is-it-important-to-set-realistic-goals/

Taylor, M. J., McNicholas, C., Nicolay, C., Darzi, A., Bell, D., & Reed, J. E. (2014, April 1). A systematic review of the application of the plan–do–study–ACT method to improve quality in healthcare. *BMJ Quality & Safety.* https://qualitysafety.bmj.com/content/23/4/290

Tecosky, K., & Hollister, R. (2021, August 10*). Why every executive should be focusing on culture and change now?* MIT Sloan Management Review. https://sloanreview.mit.edu/article/why-every-executive-should-be-focusing-on-culture-change-now/

Test, L. (2022, April 5). How to start an employee resource group at your company. *Culture Amp.* https://www.cultureamp.com/blog/start-employee-resource-group

The ADA: Your employment rights as an individual with a disability. (n.d.). US EEOC. https://www.eeoc.gov/publications/ada-your-employment-rights-individual-disability#:~:text=Under%20the%20ADA%20%2C%20you%20have,even%20if%20you%20don't

Thoms, C. L. V., & Burton, S. L. (2015). Understanding the impact of inclusion in disabilities studies education. In C. Hughes (Ed.), *Impact of diversity on organization and career development* (pp. 186–213). IGI-Global Publishing. doi:10.4018/978-1-4666-7324-3.ch008

Thoms, C. L. V., & Burton, S. L. (2018). Transculturalized diversity and inclusion model: A new framework for disabilities. [Sage Journal]. *Advances in Developing Human Resources, 20*(30), 359–369. doi:10.1177/1523422318778015

Tillotson, J., Laker, B., Pereira, V., & Bhatnagar, K. (2023). How to make workplaces more inclusive for people with invisible disabilities. *Harvard Business Review.* https://hbr.org/2023/04/how-to-make-workplaces-more-inclusive-for-people-with-

Toolkits. (2022, April 26). SHRM. https://www.shrm.org/ResourcesAndTools/tools-and-samples/toolkits/Pages/default.aspx

U. S. Equal Opportunity Commission. (2023). *The ADA: Your employment rights as an individual with a disability*. EEOC. https://www.eeoc.gov/publications/ada-your-employment-rights-individual-disability#:~:text=Reasonable%20accommodation%20is%20any%20change,equal%20to%20those%20enjoyed%20by

U.S. Census Bureau. (2016). *Disability status*. US Census. https://www.census.gov/data/tables/2016/demo/disability/disability-status.html

U.S. Department of Labor. (2019). *Disability inclusion in the workplace*. DoL. https://www.dol.gov/agencies/odep/topics/disability-inclusion-workplace

U.S. Equal Employment Opportunity Commission. (1991). *Americans with Disabilities Act: Questions and Answers*. EEOC. https://www.eeoc.gov/laws/guidance/ada-questions-and-answers

World Health Organization. (2020). *Mental health*. WHO. https://www.who.int/mental_health/en/

Chapter 12
Exploring Mental Health Telehealth Through Organizational Intervention and Business Leadership Strategy

Allison J. Huff
https://orcid.org/0000-0001-6102-8013
School of Medicine, University of Arizona, USA

Darrell Norman Burrell
https://orcid.org/0000-0002-4675-9544
Capitol Technology University, USA

Kiana S. Zanganeh
Florida Institute of Technology, USA

Sharon L. Burton
https://orcid.org/0000-0003-1653-9783
Capitol Technology University, USA

Margaret Crowe
https://orcid.org/0000-0002-9862-5265
JM Consulting LLC, USA

Kevin Richardson
https://orcid.org/0009-0002-3212-8669
Capitol Technology University, USA

Quatavia McLester
https://orcid.org/0000-0003-1596-0517
Chicago School of Professional Psychology, USA

ABSTRACT

COVID-19 shed light on mental health as a significant public health problem. The COVID-19 pandemic has had a significant impact on the mental health of individuals around the world. As such, mental health practitioners must be prepared to respond effectively to the changing needs of their patients. Adaptive leadership and change management are two essential tools that can be used to assist patients with mental health issues post-COVID-19. By combining these two approaches, mental health practitioners can ensure that their services are effective and meet the needs of their patients in the post-COVID-19 world. This chapter uses intervention action research (I.A.R.) to help organizational leaders address workplace challenges and enhance their profession by engaging organizational stakeholders in creating, executing, and assessing interventions in a problem-solving, assessment, and reflection cycle.

DOI: 10.4018/979-8-3693-1380-0.ch012

INTRODUCTION

The post-COVID-19 on-set world faces serious problems with mental health. The current novel coronavirus epidemic has had a significant effect on mental health worldwide. The pandemic's long-term impacts on mental health are still being realized, according to the World Health Organization (2020), and they are expected to be profound. An effective post-pandemic recovery depends on addressing mental health as a major public health issue. All over the world, people are dealing with the pandemic's effects on their mental health, including a rise in stress and anxiety brought on by increased loneliness, financial strain, job insecurity, and disruptions to everyday life (Robbins, 2020). Additionally, the pandemic has increased both the prevalence of adults and children suffering from mental illnesses like anxiety and melancholy. (Lopez, 2020). Additionally, the pandemic has exacerbated existing mental health conditions, such as post-traumatic stress disorder and bipolar disorder (Campos et al., 2022: Prashanth, 2022).

The impact of the pandemic on mental health is being felt in communities across the globe. In the United States, the Centers for Disease Control and Prevention (CDC; 2020) reported that 11.3% of adults aged 18 and over experienced severe mental distress in 2020, up from 8.1% in 2019. According to Bethune (2021), 29% of respondents said their mental health has gotten worse since the pandemic started. A study by Liu et al., (2022)

295 (16.40%) and 329 (18.30%) participants in a sample of 1795 Chinese medical staff members reported having PTSD and depression, respectively. The COVID-19 epidemic has disrupted or stopped key mental health services in 93% of countries worldwide, according to a World Health Organization (WHO, 2020) report, despite the fact that demand for mental health services is rising. Also, the survey of 130 nations offers the first global data demonstrating the detrimental effects of COVID-19 on the availability of mental health care and highlights the requirement for further funding (WHO, 2020). The pandemic has also caused an increase in mental health services utilization around the world (Richter et al., 2021). In the United States, for example, the CDC (2020) reported that the number of adults who used mental health services increased from 32.2% in 2019 to 37.2% in 2020.

It is critical to address mental health as a serious issue in public health. Governments and health groups must give initiatives to increase access to mental health services top priority in order to address this problem. To reach those who cannot access in-person care, this involves extending access to mental health services, such as telehealth services (Thomas et al., 2022). In order to guarantee a sufficient supply of trained professionals to meet the rising demand for mental health services, governments must also make investments in the mental health workforce.

Untreated mental health conditions can result in substance abuse, inappropriate incarceration, suicide, and inadequate quality of life (Meachem, 2021). Statistics show that around 25% of Black Americans seek mental health care, compared to 40% of their white counterparts, according to a fact check by REVOLT (Alysse, 2022). Inequality in health care access is the cause of this difference. Moreover, Black women are often characterized as vital caregivers and providers who shoulder others' burdens and do not share their own; thus, they do not seek mental health services (Pappas, 2021). The mental health crisis for African Americans is further intensified by a lack of African American providers imposing cultural sensitivity: 86% of mental health professionals are White. In contrast, only 4% are African American (Lin et al., 2018; O'Malley, 2021). This statistic plays a considerable part in the delivery of care, given the desire for members of the Black community to have a black therapist. The lack of Black therapists is a minor problem to a much larger issue triggering the mental health crisis. Underdiagnosing mental disorders, stigma, lack of community resources, and a lack of mental health providers are all factors that have led to mental health care inequities and poor health outcomes.

Globally, the new coronavirus (COVID-19) pandemic has had a profound effect on people's mental health. According to reports, the pandemic has caused a general deterioration in mental health conditions, including an increase in stress, anxiety, and depression (Hoffman et al., 2020). In order to meet the needs of their patients, mental health professionals now need to devise efficient strategies.

PROBLEM STATEMENT/PURPOSE STATEMENT

There are barriers, regarding access to and quality of care, for African American individuals seeking mental health care (American Psychiatric Association, 2017). Personal or cultural inhibitors include shame, stigma, and distrust of the medical industry. Moreover, mental health care remains unaffordable, which for many, creates an additional barrier to accessibility. The lack of collaboration between rural communities and health systems also threatens individuals within underserved communities. Historically, mental illness has been underreported in the African American community due to underdiagnosis and misdiagnosis; therefore, the burden may be significantly higher than reported estimates. Another critical factor less often discussed as a barrier is the lack of diversity among practitioners. Considering these issues, how do we make mental health services more accessible to this population?

METHOD

Intervention action research was employed. Intervention Action Research (I.A.R.) helps practitioners address workplace challenges and enhance their profession (Aggarwal & Ranganathan, 2019; Cousins, 2011; Boulton & Preiser, 2021). Intervention action research and action-based research are related concepts but not exactly the same thing. They are both forms of research that aim to bring about practical change and improvement in a particular context or situation. However, there are some subtle differences between them. Understanding the dynamic complexity of the context in which the intervention (program or policy) is implemented at various levels is necessary to make judgments about how to engage in and develop participatory approaches (Chouinard, & Cousins, 2013). I.A.R. involves stakeholders in creating, executing, and assessing interventions or actions in a cycle of problem-solving, assessment, and reflection (Aggarwal & Ranganathan, 2019; Cousins, 2011; Boulton & Preiser, 2021). Intervention action research, on the other hand, focuses specifically on interventions or actions aimed at addressing a particular problem or challenge. It is a research approach that combines elements of both research and action. The primary goal of intervention action research is to bring about practical change or improvement in a specific situation or context. Intervention action research is a robust learning, problem-solving, and improvement tool used in healthcare, education, community development, public policy, and other sectors. This type of research helps practitioners comprehend the intricacies of their work situations and build successful treatments (Aggarwal & Ranganathan, 2019; Cousins, 2011; Boulton & Preiser, 2021). Also this type of research, I.A.R., can help practitioners make evidence-based decisions about how to solve practice problems and assess solutions, reveal ways to enhance therapies over time, and facilitate practitioner collaboration and best practices (Cousins, 2011; Boulton & Preiser, 2021). Intervention action research can assist practitioners in understanding their work environment, designing evidence-based solutions, and collaborating and sharing best practices. Specifically delineating the difference, action-based research is a broader term that encompasses various approaches to research that involve active participation and collaboration, while intervention action research is a specific type of action-based research that focuses on designing and implementing interventions to address a particular problem.

REVIEW OF LITERATURE

A comprehensive literature search was conducted to study academic and other publications on a particular issue in context. Also, this analysis of the literature also offered a critical assessment of the sources (Purdue University, 2022). Academic electronic databases were used for relevant articles published from 2014-2023. A combination of keywords was used in our review to gather information on critical issues affecting the delivery of high-quality mental health care for the Black community. The literature review will highlight techniques, models, and theories to address these issues. As consultants addressing these barriers will help us to 1) formulate a marketing strategy for the mental health organization and 2) Develop a marketing analysis using several marketing and strategy frameworks and 3) understand what techniques can be leveraged to effectively grow the consumer base of the Black mental health organization we were hired to support.

Adaptive Leadership

Adaptive leadership is a type of leadership that is focused on responding to changing dynamics and demands in a given environment or circumstance (Bass, 2012; McClellan. 2022). This leadership style emphasizes the need to be flexible and adaptive and make decisions based on the situation's needs. Adaptive leadership is essential in the context of the COVID-19 pandemic, as mental health practitioners must be able to respond quickly and effectively to the changing needs of their patients (McClellan, 2022).

Change management is another essential tool for mental health practitioners in the post-COVID-19 world. Change management is managing the implementation of a new idea, process, or system to ensure its success (Bagga, 2023; Burnes, 2004). It involves understanding the change process, anticipating resistance, and developing strategies to address these issues. In the context of the pandemic, change management can help mental health practitioners effectively transition their services to a new environment (Bagga et al., 2023).

Adaptive leadership and change management are essential tools for mental health practitioners to effectively address their patients' needs post-COVID-19. However, it is essential to note that these approaches are not mutually exclusive; they should be combined to achieve the best possible patient outcomes (Tinker & Latta, 2020; Uhl-Bien, 2021). For example, by combining the concepts of adaptive leadership and change management, mental health practitioners can identify areas of need, develop strategies to address them, and then monitor and adjust as needed to ensure success.

Underdiagnosing

People with mental health conditions are frequently underdiagnosed, which can lead to improper treatment. In fact, up to 85% of people in middle and lower-class families do not receive treatment. In the U.S., just one-half of the individuals with mental disorders get treatment" (Evans-Lacko, 2018). Improper treatment can lead to a worsening of symptoms which may cause more problems in a person's life. Some barriers to effective care include "a lack of resources, lack of trained healthcare providers and social stigma associated with mental disorder" (Evans-Lacko, 2018). Mental health professionals agree that diagnosing mental conditions is not as straightforward as diagnosing a physical illness. Each mental health condition can have varying symptoms and look different for everyone (Substance Abuse and Mental Health Services Administration, 2023).

In addition, the underdiagnosis of mental health conditions affects people of color disproportionately compared to their White counterparts. Some barriers to this mental health disparity include a lack of resources, a lack of trained healthcare providers, social stigma, discrimination, racial bias, and gender bias (Mongelli, 2021). Furthermore, when people of color experience symptoms of mental illness, they are more likely to be labeled as disruptive or criminal. At the same time, White people are more likely to have their behaviors labeled as a mental health concern. This idea often penalizes children of color, leading to the underdiagnosis of mental conditions. As a result, many Black people are being pulled into the justice system instead of mental health treatment centers (Ramey, 2015). Meanwhile, there is a lack of culturally sensitive tools to correctly diagnose mental health conditions in people of color (Pope, 2019). Multiple studies have shown that mental condition symptoms can look different in people of color and advocate for the need to have culturally informed treatment diagnostic plans (Gopalkrishnan, 2018; Pope, 2019).

People of color are dying more frequently from drug overdoses and suicides, stemming from unequal access to care for mental health conditions (Minnesota Department of Mental Health, 2023; Vance, 2019). Long-standing hurdles to mental health treatment for persons of color should be addressed by diversifying the behavioral health workforce, developing culturally sensitive screening methods, providing culturally competent care, and lowering structural barriers to care. Additionally, understanding the adverse effects of racism, discrimination, and traumatic childhood experiences on one's physical and mental health may help create culturally sensitive reactions to these incidents (Meachem, 2021).

Stigma

Research shows that around twenty percent of the adult Black community is more likely to experience mental health conditions than others (Vance, 2019). This holds for young Black adults compared to young White adults and older Black adults (Vance, 2019). Although these numbers suggest a need to seek counseling, there is a prominent stigma in Black communities against requesting care for mental health services. Even though young Black adults suffer higher rates of mental health conditions, they also have lower rates of mental health service utilization (Vance, 2019). Understanding how this stigma became embedded within the Black community is essential to assess the problem and implementing solutions accurately. For the Black community, it is rooted in their racial identity skewed by systemic racism and racial stereotypes that continue to be perpetuated. Professor Rosalyn Denise Campbell, an assistant professor in the School of Social Work at the University of Georgia, shares her expertise,

> "First, being a person of color, you are already part of a group that is stigmatized...Similarly, having a mental illness is stigmatized because people do not understand what it means to be mentally "ill" and instead turn to stereotypes or other sources of misinformation to build that knowledge. If you already have a stigmatized identity, you are not eager to adopt another" (Campbell, 2018, p. 1).

Professor Campbell's explanation of not wanting to deal with the social consequences of two stigmas at once helps illustrate one of the main reasons for not seeking mental health care, even if suffering from a condition. Furthermore, Professor Campbell shares that for many Black Americans, having a mental health condition such as depression is seen more as a lack of control and handle on life,

"Coming from a culture that prides itself on strength and celebrates how their ancestors have overcome great atrocity and tragedy, being depressed at all and then not being able to bring yourself out of it is antithetical to what it means to be black" (Campbell, 2018, p. 1).

The history of mental health stigmas in African-American communities is rooted in generations of trauma. Dr. William Smith, a professor at the University of Maryland School of Medicine, noted, "African-Americans have had to endure centuries of racism, oppression, and trauma that have led to the perpetuation of mental health stigmas" (Smith, 2019). This trauma has impacted African-American individuals and communities, leading to a deep-seated distrust of mental health care and providers.

In addition to generational trauma, African-Americans are disproportionately impacted by poor access to quality mental healthcare services. As noted by a study from the National Institute of Mental Health, "African-Americans are less likely than whites to receive mental health services" (National Institute of Mental Health (NIMH), 2018). This lack of access is often due to a lack of insurance coverage, cultural stigma, and lack of mental health providers in the African-American community. The result is that many African-American individuals cannot access the mental health care they need, leading to the perpetuation of mental health stigmas.

Furthermore, the lack of representation of African-American healthcare providers in the mental health field can be a significant barrier to accessing quality mental health care (O'Malley, 2021). As noted by a study from the American Psychological Association (APA), African-American individuals are less likely to be viewed in mental health settings, and when viewed, doubtful to receive services that are appropriate (APA, 2019). This lack of representation can lead to distrust and unease, further contributing to the perpetuation of mental health stigmas.

To reduce the stigmas associated with mental health in African-American communities, it is necessary to address the root causes of the stigmas. This includes providing access to quality mental health care, increasing the representation of African-American health care providers, and providing education and support to African-American individuals and communities (Meachem, 2021).

Providing access to quality mental health care is essential in reducing mental health stigmas in African-American communities. A study from the American Psychological Association noted that "access to mental health services is a key factor in reducing mental health disparities among African-Americans" (APA, 2019). This includes increasing access to insurance coverage for mental health services, increasing access to mental health care providers in the African-American community, and increasing public awareness of the availability of mental health services.

Increasing the representation of African-American mental health care providers is also essential in reducing mental health stigmas in African-American communities. As noted by a study from the National Institute of Mental Health (NIMH), "culturally competent providers are essential in reducing disparities in mental health care" (NIMH, 2018). This includes increasing the number of African-American mental health care providers in the mental health field and providing training and education to existing mental health providers on cultural competency.

In an article in the *New York Times*, Dana Givens gives her account of delaying seeking mental health care that aligns with Professor Campbell's insight. She explains that growing up in Harlem, she was mentioned thinking that therapy was for people who were not strong enough to handle challenges and lived with the fear that if people saw her seek care, then they would tell her family and friends (Givens, 2020). This delayed her decision to get counseling for a long time as she did not only want to feel weak but did not want her community to view her that way.

The stigma around mental health in Black communities is a barrier to accessing mental health services. However, this is not the only stigma contributing to these obstacles. Another stigmatized area is the patient-provider relationship. In therapeutic relationships between Black and non-Black therapists, therapists often hold a stigma towards their patients, which some consider a product of implicit bias and racism. Research suggests that this stigma can influence how a therapist diagnoses their patient if they can get an appointment, and even the decision to recommend medication (Stoute, 2015). For reference, a study was conducted where actors left messages for over six hundred therapists in New York, altering their names, vocabulary, and grammar to reflect different races and classes (Storrs, 2016). They all requested an appointment. The results concluded that middle-class Black women and men were about thirty percent and sixty percent less likely than white middle-class women and men to be accepted for an appointment (Storrs, 2016). Stigma does not only play a role in the willingness to seek mental health care regarding the accessibility of booking appointments. Even once a Black patient is seen, they are still met with racial biases and stigma in their treatment plan.

These stigmas against Black patients further perpetuate feelings that the Black communities have surrounding healthcare. They have their stigma towards healthcare because of years of negligence, mistrust, and harm. When considering how to form a strategic-marketing process, stigma must be considered, and an organization should have a strategy sensitive to stakeholders, environmental factors, and society (Luca, 2021). Stakeholders play an influential role in the success of an organization. Examples of stakeholders include clinical staff, employees, and administration. Sometimes stakeholders have their stigmas that can negatively impact their patients.

Part of the strategic-marketing process should be to address these kinds of stigmas that are prevalent towards Black patients to help reduce and eradicate them. This can be done through educational programs as part of staff training. Especially in mental health, the proper dialogue and terminology have been found to aid in reducing stigma. One program, B.R.A.V.E., and its steps have been implemented to have conversations surrounding mental health while reducing its stigma in cultural and ethnic communities (Sevilla, 2022). Steps of this dialogue include reiterating the goal, establishing ground rules to promote respectful dialogue, starting the topic with a personal story to engage others, and concluding the meeting by thanking everyone for their courage in speaking up and listening (Sevilla, 2022). Strategic marketing also includes sensitivity towards environmental factors such as social forces. Social forces recognize cultural trends that organizations should consider (Vineeta, 2022). For instance, it could be acknowledging the stigma patients may have about mental health due to the community they were brought up in. To combat this, health literacy initiatives can be implemented to help patients feel more at ease to seek treatment. There are different courses and toolkits that the CDC recommends, such as "innovate to communicate, health literacy and public health, a physician's practical guide to culturally competent care cultural competency curriculum for disaster preparedness and crisis response, mental health stigma and communication, learn mental health literacy, teach mental health literacy" (CDC, 2022). These courses are meant to equip providers with toolkits on implementing health literacy initiatives and inpatient treatment, helping reduce the stigma surrounding it.

Educating and supporting African-American individuals and communities is essential in reducing mental health stigmas. As noted by Dr. William Smith, "Education and support are essential in reducing mental health stigmas in African-American communities" (Smith, 2019). This includes providing education on mental health conditions, increasing public awareness of the availability of mental health services, and providing support to African-American individuals and communities.

Community Mental Health Care Delivery

Integrating mental health services through community-based interventions can promote acceptability, accessibility, affordability, and treatment adherence, increasing the likelihood of positive clinical outcomes. For individuals and families suffering from anxiety, depression, and stress, multiple strategies are necessary to adequately address mental health care needs (Meachem, 2021). Collaborative interventions with community-based providers can broaden the support for mental health services, effectively building a care system through non-governmental organizations, religious platforms, and community health workers. The coordination of mental health services through these groups sustains greater relevance in low and middle-income populations compared to high-income populations based on the scarcity of mental health resources, providers, and treatment. The equity gap between mental disorders and available mental services for rural communities highlights why community-based interventions are essential for rebuilding a mental health model of care. This will create more mental health care access and strategically grow the patient base for mental health organizations.

The COVID-19 pandemic has exposed current care models and systems designed to care for patients facing severe mental health challenges. Social determinants of health are prone to impact people with mental health negatively. People living in underserved communities with mental illness are at risk of becoming homeless, dropping out of school, economic insecurity, and marital instability. While factors such as lack of access and adequate resources contribute to poor health outcomes, cumulative data shows that black people have experienced higher rates of COVID-19 death than white people (*Color of Coronavirus: COVID-19 Deaths Analyzed by Race and Ethnicity — A.P.M. Research Lab*, n.d.). In response to these care disparities, the continuum of service delivery modes proposes to meet the needs and preferences of patients based on medical risk during the pandemic. With the limited number of hospital beds nationwide during the pandemic crisis, response teams proposed to enhance the accessibility of services in communities with higher risk (i.e., rural communities). Community health workers can lead these outreach teams to address mental health disparities for underserved populations.

Research scholars suggest that community health worker care models focused on mental health service delivery can effectively address domestic disparities for underserved populations (Centers for Medicare and Medicaid Services, 2021; Meachem, 2021). The challenges exacerbated by the COVID-19 pandemic accelerated the use of telemedicine to ensure patients within the community stayed connected to care. For patients with technological challenges, the deployment of C.H.W.'s brought care to where people lived. One in four people living in rural communities needs access to broadband internet (Vogels, n.d.). Mobilizing community health workers to address mental health challenges in rural communities may lead to symptom reduction of severe mental health issues (Kopelovich et al., 2021). Community health workers are frontline public health workers entrusted by a community; they serve as a liaison between health and social services. C.H.W. are only sometimes clinicians but may coordinate specific resources between health systems, health departments, or non-profit organizations, serving as a bridge between community and care providers integrated within health care systems (Kopelovich et al., 2021). C.H.W.

often provides culturally appropriate health education, informal counseling, and guidance on specific health behaviors (Kopelovich et al., 2021).

A recent study observed the impact of the C.H.W. through targeted psychoeducation interventions. Areas of focus included depression, anxiety, substance abuse, trauma, and behavioral disorders. A series of random controlled trials were conducted to contrast C.H.W.'s involvement in delivering mental health care to low-income populations within the United States. In most trials, C.H.W.'s were the sole provider of the intervention and involved with providing acute care for patients with a low-severity mental issue. Besides these two roles, C.H.W.'s served in auxiliary roles, such as therapy in collaboration with a professional mental health provider or nurse practitioner. These interventions were delivered in many community settings, such as schools, homes, refugee settlements, and literacy centers. C.H.W. selected to participate in the study had similar life experiences and backgrounds in correlation with the population they were recruited to serve. Results from the trials found that CHW-involved interventions effectively improved outcomes for depression, alcohol disorder, and post-traumatic stress disorder (Kopelovich et al., 2021).

Utilizing a community health worker model to deliver mental health services can broaden patient bases for mental health organizations. Patients in rural communities have limited resources, forcing them to ration care. With the C.H.W. model, patients would not have to forego medical treatment given the mobilization of health personnel directly within their community, making care more accessible. Research on this model confirms that C.H.W.'s can bridge the gap for rural communities and improve mental health outcomes for those at risk of mental health disorders (Kopelovich et al., 2021).

Churches in the south have long served as informal mental health providers linked to support the black community and other marginalized groups. Since its conception nearly 300 years ago, church congregations have grown significantly, attracting weekly audiences worldwide. According to the pew research center, Black people attend church services more than any other race. As of 2014, 47% of black persons attend religious services at least once a week, 36% attend once or twice a month or a few times a year, and 17% seldom or never attend a religious service (Pew Research, 2022).

Throughout history, the Black Church has been a refuge and strength for African-Americans. In the early days of the transatlantic slave trade, Black religious practices were seen as a threat to the control of white slaveholders (Gomez, 2010). In response, enslaved African-Americans created their spiritual practices, which were later adapted into various denominations of Christianity (Gomez, 2010). The African-American community maintained its cultural identity through the church and created a sense of belonging (Lewis, 2018). As a result, the church became a primary site of resistance to racism, oppression, and injustice (Gomez, 2010).

The spiritual impact of the Black Church is also an important aspect to consider. As a religious institution, the church serves as a spiritual guide to its members, providing guidance, comfort, and solace during difficult times (Lewis, 2018). The church also provides an outlet for spiritual expression and praise that is often overlooked in other settings (Gomez, 2010). This spiritual connection to the church is often seen as a source of strength and resilience for many African-Americans (Lewis, 2018).

In addition to its spiritual influence, the Black Church has a significant social and political impact on African-American communities. For many African-Americans, the church is a safe space to discuss race, inequality, and social justice (Gomez, 2010). The church has also been used as a platform for political activism, with many prominent African-American leaders, such as Martin Luther King Jr. and Malcolm X utilizing the church's power to promote civil rights and social change (Lewis, 2018). Furthermore, the church provides a space for African-Americans to come together and build strong social networks, which can be used to foster economic and political empowerment (Gomez, 2010). Pastors and congregational leaders' position to champion mental health awareness through sermons and other spiritually linked activities to support mental health care combatting these lived experiences for the black community.

Behavioral Health Workforce Shortage

On March 1, 2022, President Biden announced a strategic plan to address our national mental health crisis (The White House, 2022). As of February 10, 2021, two out of five adults report symptoms of anxiety or depression. "...Black and Brown's communities are disproportionately undertreated – even as their burden of mental illness has continued to rise." The catastrophic shortage of behavioral health providers is central to our national mental health crisis. Over 150 million people live in federally designated mental health professional shortages (Weiner, 2022).

Additionally, more than half of U.S. counties lack a single psychiatrist. The psychiatrist workforce will have a shortage of between 14,280 and 31,091 psychiatrists by the end of 2024, consequently overextending psychologists and social workers (Satiani et al., 2018). One of President Biden's objectives is to strengthen system capacity. Most notably, the FY23 budget will invest $700 million in programs "that provide training, access to scholarships and loan repayment to mental health and substance use disorder clinicians committed to practicing in rural and other underserved communities." Moreover, Black therapists account for just 4% of psychologists, highlighting the lack of mental health professionals with shared racial identities (Lin et al., 2018). The critical question is why so few psychologists of color are in a country of about 130 million people of color?

The first reason is the lack of exposure to the field. Just as minorities do not use psychology services because they do not know it exists or choose not to adopt it because of stigma (Meachem, 2021), individuals may not choose to work in the psychology field due to their own misconceptions or cultural stigma (Andoh, 2021). Moreover, the discrepancy is perpetuated by demands. Psychotherapists have a tendency to favor clients who fall under the acronym YAVIS – young, attractive, verbal, intelligent, and successful (Coleman, 2014). The phrase is frequently used in psychotherapy since it is believed that these people are most likely to benefit from treatment. Contrary to YAVIS is HOUND (Homely, Old, Unattractive, Nonverbal, and Dumb), the syndrome of character traits that therapists, counselors, and people in general are said to find most repulsive in their patients or colleagues (Coleman, 2014). These acronyms are not new and have been used by mental health professionals to identify clients (Cagle, 2022).

Terms such as YAVIS and HOUND are used to as a bias in scheduling by providers. A study was conducted with 320 psychotherapists' offices that individually received voicemail messages from one black middle-class and one white middle-class possible client, or from one black working-class and one white working-class possible client, asking for an appointment (Kugelmass, 2016). The findings exposed a sort of discrimination that was previously hidden. The appointment offer rates for middle-class help seekers were nearly three times greater than those for their working-class counterparts. Further, only middle-class help-seekers showed racial disparities, with blacks significantly less likely than whites to be given an appointment. The average appointment offer rates were the same for both sexes, however women received more appointment offers in their desired time window than males did (Kugelmass, 2016). Given the shortage, non-Black and Brown therapists must educate themselves on the specific needs of their Black and Brown patients. "Patients who shared the same racial or ethnic background as their care provider were more likely to give the maximum patient rating score" (Takashita et al., 2020). Culturally responsive care is essential for achieving practice success in either a face-to-face setting or a virtual environment.

Telemedicine

Telemedicine and community-based interventions both may be viable solutions to helping underserved communities. Continued findings from previous studies showed that telehealth interventions for anxiety and depression are effective (Burton, 2022; Brown-Jackson, 2017). The use of telehealth modalities (e.g., video calls or mobile applications) can potentially reduce access issues, such as geographic proximity to a preferred mental health care professional (e.g., therapist). A recent study by McCall et al. (2021) found that over 70% of African American women endorsed using video calls to communicate with a professional to receive help in managing anxiety and depression. The convenience and familiarity of telehealth modalities, combined with proven psychotherapy treatments, such as cognitive behavioral therapy (CBT.), make telehealth interventions feasible alternatives to traditional in-person treatment. The relevance of the CBT is according to CBT theory, our thoughts, feelings, bodily sensations, and behavior are all interconnected, and what we think and do has an impact on how we feel (Burton, 2014; Good & Brophy, 1990; Holmes & Abington-Cooper, 2000). Policymakers and practitioners show a continued interest in telehealth's potential to increase efficiency and reach patients facing access barriers (Shigekawa et al., 2018).

Telemedicine can help eliminate some of the barriers to care. With digital tools and access to the internet, patients can now consult with a mental health professional remotely using live video. Patients in mental health professional shortage areas can use these tools to speak with a licensed professional without driving long distances (Brown-Jackson, 2017; Burton, 2022). They can also receive care without bringing attention to themselves if their loved ones or colleagues fail to acknowledge their mental illness. Telemedicine includes a variety of technologies and tactics to deliver virtual healthcare (Brown-Jackson, 2017; Haleem et al.,2021). Telemedicine is considered a subset of telehealth, which includes more general health services, like public health and medical education. Telemedicine is a specific kind of telehealth that involves clinicians providing medical services (Healthcare Value Hub, 2017). Telehealth has four main types of technology: live video, store-and-forward, remote patient monitoring, and mobile health (Healthcare Value Hub, 2017).

First is synchronous video, a live, two-way interaction between a person and a provider using audiovisual telecommunications technology. This type of service can serve as a substitute for in-person visits for consultative, diagnostic, and treatment services. Video devices can include videoconferencing units or web cameras. Display devices include computer monitors, T.V.s, LCD projectors, tablets, and smartphones. Second is asynchronous video, which is a transmission of recorded health history.

An example is a pre-recorded video and digital images such as x-rays and photos through a secure electronic communications system to a practitioner. Compared to a real-time visit, this service provides access to data after it has been collected and involves communication tools such as secure email. Third is remote patient monitoring, the electronic collection of personal health and medical data from a patient in one location and transmitted to a provider in another for use in care and related support (Burton, 2022). This service enables a provider to track a patient's healthcare data after discharge to a home or a care facility, reducing hospital readmission rates. Finally, Mobile health, often referred to as "mHealth," refers to patient engagement, patient education, and public health programs offered via mobile communication devices such as cell phones, tablets, and P.D.A.s. Applications include targeted text messages that promote healthy behavior, wide-scale alerts about disease outbreaks, and applications to help patients self-diagnose illnesses, to name a few examples. As far as telehealth solutions go, mHealth is proliferating due to the rise in smartphones.

The field of m-Health is evolving rapidly, and there is an exponential growth of psychological tools on the market. m-Health focuses on developing smartphone applications to improve medical or mental health care. Mobile platforms are increasingly more available, more user-friendly, have more attractive designs, and contain increasingly complex computational models and fancy technologies (Zakerabasali, et al., 2021). The use of mobile applications in mental health care is multiplying, and m-Health has already been presented as a new frontier for delivering mental health treatment (Zakerabasali, et al., 2021). Moreover, with m-Health, there is immense potential to increase the availability, equitable distribution, and resources for mental health care. Mobile applications may be used to provide access to relevant information or psychoeducation, as well as help individuals to self-identify symptoms, offer screening and assessment tools, help people manage their mental health and wellness, identify the need for treatment, encourage help-seeking, and provide direct interventions (Zahmatkeshan, et al., 2021). Once in treatment, Mobile applications may help to engage the patient and maximize retention. Although effective psychotherapies are already available for mental health disorders, many patients cannot access appropriate treatment. M-Health applications can serve a considerable proportion of people, thus potentially addressing unmet mental health care needs.

Unsurprisingly, behavioral health has emerged as one of the most common telemedicine applications. A recent study among millions of privately insured enrollees from 2005 to 2017 found that many telemedicine visits were for mental health, with over 50% annual compound growth in the number of tele–mental health service visits over more than a decade, although overall use rates were less than two visits per 1,000 enrollees annually. However, telemedicine use is much higher among populations with serious mental illness (Barnett & Huskamp, 2020). Since 75% of African American adults own a smartphone, using smartphones to deliver interventions to this population needs further exploration. This usage presents an opportunity to create innovative interventions that increase access to much-needed mental health services.

However, telehealth interventions should be culturally tailored to increase the likelihood of adoption among African American adults. A "one-size-fits-all" approach to designing telehealth interventions to help African American adults manage anxiety or depression may lead to more options but the continued disparity in receiving care (McCall et al., 2021). Not only do mental health applications have tremendous reach, but patients can also access these tools whenever they feel the need and as often as they like without waiting until a mental health professional is available (McCall et al., 2021). Such reach is evident when considering that 68% of all adults in the United States own a smartphone, and approximately 45% own a tablet device (McCall et al., 2021)

The mental health workforce needs to grow faster to meet demand. Provider shortages are particularly acute in rural areas, where telemedicine is beneficial given the large distances many patients need to travel to access care. Second, broadband Internet access is becoming increasingly pervasive, which has been a critical bottleneck for implementing video-based telemedicine technology in rural areas. Third, there is significant policy momentum toward covering telemedicine more broadly at the federal, state, and insurer levels. (Barnett & Huskamp, 2020).

Considering the burden of unmet needs and inequality in mental health service utilization among African American adults, there is enormous potential to use telehealth to deliver services to this population (McCall et al., 2021). Since 75% of African American adults own a smartphone, using smartphones to deliver interventions to this population needs further exploration (McCall et al., 2021). This presents an opportunity to create innovative interventions that increase access to much-needed mental health services. Nevertheless, telehealth interventions should be culturally tailored to increase the likelihood of adoption among African American adults. A "one-size-fits-all" approach to designing telehealth interventions to help African American adults manage anxiety or depression may lead to more options but the continued disparity in receiving care (McCall et al., 2021).

MARKETING ANALYSIS

The literature review shows a market demand for black and women mental health professionals (Kugelmass, 2016; Lin et al., 2018; Takashita et al., 2020). As consultants hired to grow the patient base for a Black women-led mental health clinic, performing a marketing analysis will better position our client to understand 1) direct competitors, 2) the value proposition for their specific service, and 3) our audience. When developing a marketing strategy, knowing competitors help our clients strategically scale products or services to meet the needs of targeted audiences. The value proposition entails solutions that our client will provide and the promise of value customers can expect our client to deliver. Understanding our audience will help our clients better connect with current and future customers. These three domains are pivotal for our clients to understand precisely where they are in the market, which helps them to craft a strong marketing strategy. Our marketing analysis will utilize a SWOT Analysis, 4P's Marketing Mix, and mission statement to develop our marketing strategy to grow the mental health clinic.

SWOT Analysis

Performing a SWOT analysis will help our client identify areas of the organization performing well and turn threats or weaknesses into opportunities (Adobe Inc., 2023; Purg et al., 2023).

1. Strengths:
    a. Tax benefits for women-owned businesses will provide federal, state, and local grants. This benefit will make it easier for women-owned small businesses (WOSB) to access funding.
    b. A group of mental health providers specializes in mental health conditions for pediatric populations. This is a strength for a market with limited resources that could improve the marketability of services.
    c. The lack of Black mental health care providers strengthens this business. This unique practice has the upper hand in combating provider discrimination (i.e., treating otherwise similar patients differently according to race/ ethnicity). In two mental health studies, "clinicians respond with less alacrity to variation in severity of depression among minority patients than whites, implying that clinicians are less able to "read" severity among minorities."
2. Weaknesses:
    a. The absence of male providers will create gaps in gender preferences. The local competition may divert clients to other mental health clinics.
    b. The high rates of stigma in rural communities will create barriers for groups apprehensive about mental health care. Stigma impacts marketing based on receptibility and engagement from social campaigns.
    c. The limited number of mental disorders specialized in will create a gap for other needs within the target audience.
3. Opportunities:

a. They are expanding clientele through other markets from telemedicine or mobile applications. This opportunity will expand the base through technology.
   b. Using technology presents an opportunity to grow patient connections through collaboration with local community groups (e.g., churches). Partnering with community groups will increase the marketability of products and services.
   c. Social media marketing can provide education to target populations and reduce stigma.
   d. Building a financial assistance program will increase the accessibility for uninsured patients who qualify based on pre-existing conditions.
   e. Training more therapists to address other mental health disorders will broaden the reach of services for untapped markets.
4. Threats:
   a. Affordability is a threat based on the variability of insurance.
   b. Licensing regulations are expensive and pose a threat if the telemedicine platform is not securing consistent revenue.
   c. The lack of providers will shrink accessibility for new patients needing mental health services.
   d. Competition with other local providers will impact pricing, quality of services, variety, and innovation. These factors will impact the business's ability to make decisions wisely.

Figure 1. SWOT analysis

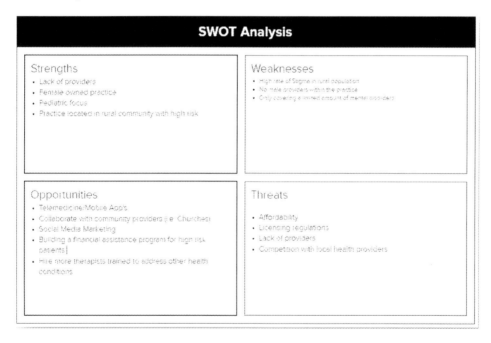

4Ps of Marketing Mix

Conducting a marketing mix analysis will help define options for the mental health clinic to scale price, product, promotion, and place. Performing this analysis will help the organization meet the needs and demands of current and potential consumers.

1. Product
    a. Core Therapy Services
        i. Anxiety
        ii. Bipolar Disorder
        iii. A.D.H.D. Diagnosis
        iv. Autism Assessments
    b. Evidence-Based Treatment
        i. Cognitive Behavioral Therapy
        ii. Functional Family Therapy
        iii. Motivational Interviewing
    c. Core Business Features
        i. Online Scheduling
        ii. After-hours emergency line and text support
        iii. Free Consultation
        iv. E.H.R. Integration
        v. Online Billing
2. Price
    a. Sliding scale
        i. Adopting a sliding scale pricing model will allow fairness and address income inequality for individuals and families
    b. Financial assistance programs
        i. Will support individuals and families at a flat rate based on pre-existing conditions and federal poverty level thresholds
    c. Referral program discounts
        i. Will provide incentives for current customers to refer new clients to the mental health organization
    d. Insurance
3. Place
    a. Community settings
        i. Churches
        ii. Community centers
        iii. Health Fairs
    b. Outpatient medical facilities
    c. Non-profit health organizations
4. Promotion
    a. A social media marketing strategy will help the mental health clinic establish an online presence for its business. Various platforms (e.g., Facebook and Instagram) can be leveraged to promote business activities and bring awareness to core services.
    b. Public information campaigns are promotional strategies that will bring advertising to markets affluent to public information.
    c. Search engine optimization (SEO) will improve the organization's visibility by boosting website/social media traffic based on keyword searches from various search engines.

Figure 2. Marketing mix

RECOMMENDATIONS

Adaptive leadership and change management are two critical tools that can be used to assist patients with mental health issues post-COVID-19. By combining these two approaches, mental health practitioners can ensure that their services are effective and meet the needs of their patients in the post-COVID-19 world.

Based on our marketing analysis and literature review, we will provide several recommendations for the practice to grow its customer base strategically. First, because of the development of a telehealth or telemedicine solution for the practice, prospective patients could access the local, surrounding areas of the practice. The business will be able to reach statewide and be open to those who can come into a brick-and-mortar office. Telehealth/telemedicine solutions will broaden the reach of customers. The practice provides teletherapy. Virtual sessions are ideal for people with busy schedules, limited time, and transportation barriers. Virtual therapy also helps reduce the negative perception some face when entering a mental health clinic. This also ties into our recommendation to market the practice's flexibility once a telehealth program is implemented.

In a post-pandemic world where people are now accustomed to having all their needs delivered to their door or met at their fingertips via their phone, the practice should leverage innovative interventions that increase access to much-needed mental health services such as telehealth. Telehealth allows patients to attend appointments from their homes or anywhere else they have internet access. Patients are not tied to providers within a local radius. This not only gives flexibility for appointment times but also allows flexibility in the types of providers to choose from. There is a market gap for culturally competent providers to meet the needs of the black community; with a telehealth model providing flexibility to the who, when, and where of receiving mental health care, this practice can fill that void.

Similarly, we propose that the practice deepens its ties with the community. As described in the literature review, all people from all ethnicities and cultures experience mental health challenges; however, there are prominent issues in the Black community that distinctly keep them in a pandemic state. We recommend that the practice create a targeted marketing plan for the Black community. This will utilize the practice's strength since being an African-American-owned practice is one of its differential advantages. The lack of Black mental health care providers allows this business to market because this unique practice has the upper hand in combating provider discrimination and the lack of cultural competency with which the mental health field is riddled.

Building community relationships through non-profit organizations (i.e., churches) is vital for growing the practice's customer base, specifically in Black communities. The research shows that various community organizations exceptionally deliver mental health services for Black people. To that end, we see value in practice as part of its strategy to make connections with local pastors to establish a relationship to navigate a partnership that can help those within the church begin to address mental health issues. Furthermore, if a partnership is fostered, the practice and church in tandem can help fight the bias of mental health issues and treatment within the community. Churches often serve surrounding communities through food drives, clothing drives, and housing support. This practice can leverage these relationships to identify communities that most need mental health support and deploy resources to support community efforts.

Additionally, as part of these partnerships, providers from the practice could offer group sessions at the church so that people do not feel alone or stigmatized. Further, providers could offer sessions at the church first to get potential customers comfortable before moving to telehealth or in-person sessions. Although our number one recommendation is to launch a telehealth model, partnerships with churches will embed the practice into the local community, promoting a sense of trust with potential clients.

Community groups or non-profit organizations support churches in several ways that the practice can leverage. In doing so, this practice can build additional relationships with those that support social determinants of health needs through local coalitions and chambers of commerce. Collaboration is critical, and the church is the central point that connects the practice to pockets of the various groups that can benefit from mental health care. With an emphasis on community, the practice will identify ways to scale its product and services based on the specific needs of its target market.

Building a social media presence will allow the practice to scale its products or services and reach more people. From a marketing perspective, it is imperative to establish an online presence to stay connected with its intended audience. Additionally, most healthcare organizations generally have a digital marketing strategy that allows them to grow their patient base. Sending out monthly newsletters is an excellent way for the practice to stay connected. Newsletters can contain education, upcoming community events, information about different programs, and patient testimonials. This is all valuable information that the practice should deliver to stay engaged and connected with existing customers.

Finally, governments must prioritize mental health awareness and education. This includes increasing public awareness of mental health issues and providing mental health education to children and adults. This will help reduce stigma and create a more open and supportive environment for those with mental health conditions. In conclusion, mental health is a significant public health problem post-COVID-19. To ensure a successful post-pandemic recovery, governments and health organizations must prioritize initiatives to improve access to mental health services, invest in the mental health workforce, and increase mental health awareness and education.

In conclusion, mental health is a significant public health problem post-COVID-19. To ensure a successful post-pandemic recovery, governments and health organizations must prioritize initiatives to improve access to mental health services, invest in the mental health workforce, and increase mental health awareness and education.

REFERENCES

Adobe Inc. (2023). SWOT Analysis. Adobe.

Aggarwal, R., & Ranganathan, P. (2019). Study designs: Part 4 - Interventional studies. *Perspectives in Clinical Research*, *10*(3), 137–139. doi:10.4103/picr.PICR_91_19 PMID:31404185

Alysse, B. (2022). Fact Check: What percentage of Black people go to therapy? *REVOLT.* https://www.revolt.tv/article/2022-05-06/167497/black-people-in-therapy-fact-check/#:~:text=Statistics%20tell%20us%20that%20roughly%2025%20percent%20of,the%20Harvard%20Medical%20School%E2%80%99-s%20affiliate%20McLean%E2%80%99s%20latest%20essay

American Psychiatric Association. (2017). *Mental health disparities: African Americans*. APA. https://www.psychiatry.org/File%20Library/Psychiatrists/Cultural-Competency/Mental-Health-Disparities/Mental-Health-Facts-for-African-Americans.pdf

American Psychological Association (A.P.A.). (2019). *Racial and ethnic disparities in mental health care*. APA. https://www.apa.org/pi/oema/resources/ethnicity-health/mental-health

Andoh, E. (2021). Psychology's urgent need to dismantle racism. American Psychological Association, 25(3), 38.

APM Research Lab. (2022). *Color of Coronavirus: COVID-19 Deaths by race and ethnicity in the U.S.* APM Research Lab. https://www.apmresearchlab.org/covid/deaths-by-race

Bagga, S. K., Gera, S., & Haque, S. N. (2023). The mediating role of organizational culture: Transformational leadership and change management in virtual teams. *Asia Pacific Management Review, 28*(2), 120–131. https://doi-org.captechu.idm.oclc.org/10.1016/j.apmrv.2022.07.003

Barnett, M. L., & Huskamp, H. A. (2020). Telemedicine for Mental Health in the United States: Making Progress, Still a Long Way to Go. *Psychiatric Services (Washington, D.C.), 71*(2), 197–198. doi:10.1176/appi.ps.201900555 PMID:31847735

Bass, B. M. (2012). *The Bass handbook of leadership: Theory, research, and managerial applications* (4th ed.). Free Press.

Bethune, S. (2021). *One year on: Unhealthy weight gains, increased drinking reported by Americans coping with pandemic stress*. American Psychological Association (APA.). https://www.apa.org/news/press/releases/2021/03/one-year-pandemic-stress

Boulton, J., & Preiser, R. (2021). Action Research. In Reinette Biggs, Alto De Vos, Rika Preiser, Hayley Clements, Kristine Maciejewski, Maja Schlüter (Eds.) *The Routledge Handbook of Research Methods for Social-Ecological,* (pp. 2017-229). Routledge. Systemshttps://www.taylorfrancis.com/chapters/oa-edit/10.4324/9781003021339-18/action-research-jean-boulton-rika-preiser

Brown-Jackson, K. (2017). *Disrupting and Retooling: A Model for an Effective Community-Based Telehealth Program (Order No. 28144638).* ProQuest Central. https://www.proquest.com/dissertations-theses/disrupting-retooling-model-effective-community/docview/2440009177/se-2

Burnes, B. (2004). Managing change: a strategic approach to organizational dynamics (4th ed.). Financial Times Prentice Hall.

Burton, S. L. (2014). *Best Practices for Faculty Development Through Andragogy in Online Distance Education* (Order No. 10758601). ProQuest Central. https://www.proquest.com/dissertations-theses/best-practices-faculty-development-through/docview/1989663912/se-2

Burton, S. L. (2022). Cybersecurity Leadership from a Telemedicine/Telehealth Knowledge and Organizational Development Examination (Order No. 29066056). ProQuest Central. https://www.proquest.com/dissertations-theses/cybersecurity-leadership-telemedicine-telehealth/docview/2662752457/se-2

Cagle, M. (2022). Why you need to identify your ideal clients. *[BLOG] Mark Cagle LPC Supervisor.* https://lpcsupervisiontexas.com/identify-your-ideal-clients/#:~:text=An%20ideal%20client%20is%20someone,feel%20comfortable%20working%20with%20you

Campbell, R. D. (2018, October 10). Stigma of depression hurts African American populations more than others. *University of Georgia (UGA) Today.* https://news.uga.edu/stigma-depression-hurts-african-american-populations/

Campos, J. A. D. B., Campos, L. A., Martins, B. G., Valadão Dias, F., Ruano, R., & Maroco, J. (2022). The Psychological Impact of COVID-19 on Individuals with and without mental health disorders. *Psychological Reports, 125*(5), 2435–2455.

Chouinard, J. A., & Cousins, J. B. (2013). Participatory evaluation for development: Examining research-based knowledge from within the African context. *African Evaluation Journal, 1*(1), 9. doi:10.4102/aej.v1i1.43

Coleman, A. M. (201). *A dictionary of Psychology.* (4th ed.). Oxford University Press.

Cousins, J. B. (2011). Intervention action research: A methodology for developing, enacting, and evaluating interventions. *New Directions for Evaluation, 2011*(130), 7–20.

Evans-Lacko, S., Aguilar-Gaxiola, S., Al-Hamzawi, A., Alonso, J., Benjet, C., Bruffaerts, R., Chiu, W. T., Florescu, S., de Girolamo, G., Gureje, O., Haro, J. M., He, Y., Hu, C., Karam, E. G., Kawakami, N., Lee, S., Lund, C., Kovess-Masfety, V., Levinson, D., & Thornicroft, G. (2018). Socio-economic variations in the mental health treatment gap for people with anxiety, mood, and substance use disorders: Results from the WHO World Mental Health (W.M.H.) surveys. *Psychological Medicine, 48*(9), 1560–1571. doi:10.1017/S0033291717003336 PMID:29173244

Givens, D. (2020, August 25). The Extra Stigma of Mental Illness for African-Americans. *The New York Times*. https://www.nytimes.com/2020/08/25/well/mind/black-mental-health.html

Gomez, M. (2010). *Exchanging our country marks: The transformation of African identities in the colonial and antislavery world*. University of North Carolina Press.

Good, T. L., & Brophy, J. E. (1990). *Educational psychology: A realistic approach* (4th ed.). Longman.

Gopalkrishnan N. (2018). Cultural Diversity and Mental Health: Considerations for Policy and Practice. *Frontiers in Public Health*, 6, 179. doi:10.3389/fpubh.2018.00179

Haleem, A., Javaid, M., Singh, R. P., & Suman, R. (2021). Telemedicine for healthcare: Capabilities, features, barriers, and applications. *Sensors International*, 2, 100117. doi:10.1016/j.sintl.2021.100117 PMID:34806053

Healthcare Value Hub. (2017, November). Telemedicine: Decreasing barriers and increasing access to healthcare. *Altarum*. https://www.healthcarevaluehub.org/advocate-resources/publications/telemedicine-decreasing-barriers-and-increasing-access-healthcare

Hoffman, K., Alford, D., Bialik, A., Blanchard, M., Calogero, R., Carter, R., & Wampold, B. (2020). The psychological impact of the COVID-19 pandemic on the public: Mental health considerations. *The American Psychologist*, 75(7), 778–788.

Holmes, G., & Abington-Cooper, M. (2000). Pedagogy vs. andragogy: A false dichotomy? *The Journal of Technology Studies*, 26(2), 1–6. https://scholar.lib.vt.edu/ejournals/JOTS/Summer-Fall-2000/holmes.html. doi:10.21061/jots.v26i2.a.8

House, T. W. (2022, March 1). *FACT SHEET: President Biden to Announce Strategy to Address Our National Mental Health Crisis, As Part of Unity Agenda in his First State of the Union*. The White House. https://www.whitehouse.gov/briefing-room/statements-releases/2022/03/01/fact-sheet-president-biden-to-announce-strategy-to-address-our-national-mental-health-crisis-as-part-of-unity-agenda-in-his-first-state-of-the-union/

Kaiser Family Foundation. (2022). *Mental Health Care Health Professional Shortage Areas (H.P.S.A.s)*. K.F.F. https://www.kff.org/other/state-indicator/mental-health-care-health-professional-shortage-areas-hpsas/

Kopelovich, S. L., Monroe-DeVita, M., Buck, B. E., Brenner, C., Moser, L., Jarskog, L. F., Harker, S., & Chwastiak, L. A. (2021). Community Mental Health Care Delivery During the COVID-19 Pandemic: Practical Strategies for Improving Care for People with Serious Mental Illness. *Community Mental Health Journal*, 57(3), 405–415. doi:10.100710597-020-00662-z PMID:32562033

Kugelmass, H. (2016). Sorry, I'm not accepting new patients. *Journal of Health and Social Behavior*, 57(2), 168–183. doi:10.1177/0022146516647098 PMID:27251890

Lewis, T. (2018). The Black Church and African-American Communities: A Historical Perspective. *Journal of African American History*, 103(2), 181–190.

Lin, L., Stamm, K., & Christidis, P. (2018). How diverse is the psychology workforce: News from APA's Center for Workforce Studies. *American Psychological Association (APA)*. https://www.apa.org/monitor/2018/02/datapoint

Liu, Y., Fu, W., Zou, L., Wen, J., Zhang, P., Zhang, J., Bai, X., Wang, J., & Mao, J. (2022). Posttraumatic stress disorder and depression of Chinese medical staff after 2 years of COVID-19: A multicenter study. *Brain and Behavior*, *12*(11), 1–9. https://doi-org.captechu.idm.oclc.org/10.1002/brb3.2785. doi:10.1002/brb3.2785 PMID:36259949

Lopez, J. (2020). How the COVID-19 pandemic is affecting children's mental health. *Medical News Today*. https://www.medicalnewstoday.com/articles/how-the-covid-19-pandemic-is-affecting-childrens-mental-health

Luca, N. R. (2021). Overview of stakeholder involvement in social marketing. In *The Palgrave Encyclopedia of Social Marketing*. Palgrave Macmillan., doi:10.1007/978-3-030-14449-4_99-1

McCall, T., Bolton, C. S., III, Carlson, R., & Khairat, S. (2021). A systematic review of telehealth interventions for managing anxiety and depression in African American adults. MHealth, 7, 31–31. doi:10.21037/mhealth-20-114

McCall, T., Schwartz, T. A., & Khairat, S. (2020). The Acceptability of Text Messaging to Help African American Women Manage Anxiety and Depression: Cross-Sectional Survey Study. *JMIR Mental Health*, *7*(2), e15801. doi:10.2196/15801 PMID:31909720

McClellan, J. L. (2022). Post pandemic leadership in Latin America: Responding to wicked problems using adaptive leadership in organizational contexts. *Estudios de Administración, 29*(1), 52–65. https://doi-org.captechu.idm.oclc.org/10.5354/0719-0816.2022.65372

Meachem, L. (2021). *Mental health in the church & community*. Lulu Publications.

Minnesota Department of Mental Health. (2023). *differences in rates of drug overdose deaths by race*. MDMH. https://www.health.state.mn.us/communities/opioids/data/racedisparity.html

Mongelli, F., Georgakopoulos, P., & Pato, M. T. (2020). Challenges and Opportunities to Meet the Mental Health Needs of Underserved and Disenfranchised Populations in the United States. *Focus - American Psychiatric Publishing*, *18*(1), 16–24. doi:10.1176/appi.focus.20190028 PMID:32047393

National Institute of Mental Health (NIMH). (2018). *Mental Health Disparities*. NIMH. https://www.nimh.nih.gov/health/statistics/mental-health-disparities.shtml

Nguyen, A. W. (2018). African American Elders, Mental Health, and the Role of the Church. *Generations (San Francisco, Calif.)*, *42*(2), 61–67.

O'Malley, L. (2021). Addressing the lack of black mental health professionals. *Insight Into Diversity*. https://www.insightintodiversity.com/addressing-the-lack-of-black-mental-health-professionals/

Pappas, S. (2021). Effective Theory for Black Women. *Monitor on Psychology*. https://www.apa.org/education-career/ce/effective-therapy-black-women.pdf

Pew Research. (2022). *Religious Landscape Study*. Pew Research Center's Religion & Public Life Project. Pew Research. https://www.pewresearch.org/religion/religious-landscape-study/

Pope, L. (2019). Racial disparities in mental health and criminal justice. *National Alliance on Mental Health (NAMI)*. https://www.nami.org/Blogs/NAMI-Blog/July-2019/Racial-Disparities-in-Mental-Health-and-Criminal-Justice

Prashanth, G. P. (2022). COVID-19 pandemic impact on mental health in children: a call for longitudinal datasets on prevalence of post-traumatic stress disorder. *Middle East Current Psychiatry, 29*(1), 1–3. https://doi-org.captechu.idm.oclc.org/10.1186/s43045-022-00266-1

Purg, P., Cacciatore, S., & Gerbec, J. Č. (2023). Establishing ecosystems for disruptive innovation by cross-fertilizing entrepreneurship and the arts. *Creative Industries Journal, 16*(2), 115–145. https://doi-org.captechu.idm.oclc.org/10.1080/17510694.2021.1969804. doi:10.1080/17510694.2021.1969804

Ramey, D. M. (2015). The social structure of criminalized and medicalized school discipline. *Sociology of Education, 88*(3), 181–201. doi:10.1177/0038040715587114

Richter, D., Riedel-Heller, S., & Zürcher, S. J. (2021). Mental health problems in the general population during and after the first lockdown phase due to the SARS-Cov-2 pandemic: Rapid review of multi-wave studies. *Epidemiology and Psychiatric Sciences, 30*, e27. doi:10.1017/S2045796021000160 PMID:33685551

Robbins, J. (2020). *The mental health impact of the coronavirus pandemic*. Harvard Health Publishing. https://www.health.harvard.edu/mind-and-mood/the-mental-health-impact-of-the-coronavirus-pandemic

Satiani, A., Niedermier, J., Satiani, B., & Svendsen, D. P. (2018). Projected Workforce of Psychiatrists in the United States: A Population Analysis. *Psychiatric Services (Washington, D.C.), 69*(6), 710–713. doi:10.1176/appi.ps.201700344 PMID:29540118

Sevilla, M. (2022). *How respectful dialogue can reduce mental health stigma*. American Hospital Association. https://www.aha.org/news/blog/2022-07-13-how-respectful-dialogue-can-reduce-mental-health-stigma

Shigekawa, E., Fix, M., Corbett, G., Roby, D. H., & Coffman, J. (2018). The Current State of Telehealth Evidence: A Rapid Review. *Health Affairs, 37*(12), 1975–1982. doi:10.1377/hlthaff.2018.05132 PMID:30633674

Smith, W. (2019). Mental Health Stigma in African-American Communities. *The Huffington Post.* https://www.huffpost.com/entry/mental-health-stigma-in-african-american-communities_b_5d32d726e4b0faa7bacd5362

Storrs, C. (2016, June 1). Therapists often discriminate against black and poor patients, study finds. *CNN.* https://www.cnn.com/2016/06/01/health/mental-health-therapists-race-class-

Stoute, B. J. (2020). Racism: A Challenge for the Therapeutic Dyad. *American Journal of Psychotherapy, 73*(3), 69–71. doi:10.1176/appi.psychotherapy.20200043 PMID:32927960

Substance Abuse and Mental Health Services Administration. (2023). *Living well with serious mental illness: What are serious mental illnesses?* SAMHSA. https://www.samhsa.gov/serious-mental-illness

Takeshita, J., Wang, S., Loren, A. W., Mitra, N., Shults, J., Shin, D. B., & Sawinski, D. L. (2020). Association of racial/ethnic and gender concordance between patients and physicians with patient experience ratings. *Journal of the American Medical Association (JAMA). JAMA Network Open, 3*(11), e2024583. doi:10.1001/jamanetworkopen.2020.24583 PMID:33165609

Thomas, E. E., Haydon, H. M., Mehrotra, A., Caffery, L. J., Snoswell, C. L., Banbury, A., & Smith, A. C. (2022). Building on the momentum: Sustaining telehealth beyond COVID-19. *Journal of Telemedicine and Telecare*, *28*(4), 301–308. https://journals.sagepub.com/doi/pdf/10.1177/1357633X20960638. doi:10.1177/1357633X20960638 PMID:32985380

Tinker, J. E., & Latta, G. F. (2020). Decoding leaders experiences of innovation, adaptation and change through the lens of dispositional attitudes toward risk in a global fortune 500 organization. *Journal of Strategic Innovation & Sustainability*, *15*(8), 70–87. https://doi-org.captechu.idm.oclc.org/10.33423/jsis.v15i8.3922

Uhl-Bien, M. (2021). Complexity leadership and followership: Changed leadership in a changed world. *Journal of Change Management*, *21*(2), 144–162. https://doi-org.captechu.idm.oclc.org/10.1080/14697017.2021.1917490. doi:10.1080/14697017.2021.1917490

U.S. Centers for Disease Control and Prevention. (2020). Mental health, substance use, and suicidal ideation during the COVID-19 pandemic—United States, June 24–30, 2020. *Morbidity and Mortality Weekly Report*, *69*(32), 1049–1056. doi:10.15585/mmwr.mm6932a1 PMID:32790653

U.S. Centers for Disease Control and Prevention (C.D.C.). (2022, October 27). *Training from Organizations Other than C.D.C. U.S. Centers for Disease Control and Prevention*. CDC. https://www.cdc.gov/healthliteracy/non-cdc-training.html

Vance, T. A. (2019). *Addressing mental health in the Black community*. Columbia University Department of Psychology. https://www.columbiapsychiatry.org/news/addressing-mental-health-black-community

Vineeta, K. (2022). Cultural evolution – Theory of Cultural Change. *Anthromania*. https://www.anthromania.com/2022/03/04/cultural-evolution-theory-of-cultural-change/

Vogels, E. a. (n.d.). The digital divide persists even as lower-income Americans benefit from tech adoption. *Pew Research Center*. https://www.pewresearch.org/fact-tank/2021/06/22/digital-divide-persists-even-as-americans-with-lower-incomes-make-gains-in-tech-adoption/

Weiner, S. (2022, August 9). *A growing psychiatrist shortage and an enormous demand for mental health services*. A.A.M.C. https://www.aamc.org/news-insights/growing-psychiatrist-shortage-enormous-demand-mental-health-services

World Health Organization (WHO). (2020). *COVID-19 disrupting mental health services in most countries*. WHO. https://www.who.int/news/item/05-10-2020-covid-19-disrupting-mental-health-services-in-most-countries-who-survey

Zahmatkeshan, M., Zakerabasali, S., Farjam, M., Gholampour, Y., Seraji, M., & Yazdani, A. (2021). The use of mobile health interventions for gestational diabetes mellitus: A descriptive literature review. *Journal of Medicine and Life*, *14*(2), 131–141. doi:10.25122/jml-2020-0163 PMID:34104235

Zakerabasali, S., Ayyoubzadeh, S. M., Baniasadi, T., Yazdani, A., & Abhari, S. (2021). Mobile health technology and healthcare providers: Systemic barriers to adoption. *Healthcare Informatics Research*, *27*(4), 267–278. doi:10.4258/hir.2021.27.4.267 PMID:34788907

Chapter 13
Building Relationships and Fostering a Community of Care Using a Trauma-Informed Leadership Approach

Denise Toney
https://orcid.org/0009-0001-3408-7410
Eskasoni Elementary and Middle School, Canada

Ingrid M. Robinson
https://orcid.org/0000-0002-1685-3759
St. Francis Xavier University, Canada

ABSTRACT

This chapter explores, through a self-study study approach, one principal's experiences with the implementation and enactment of trauma informed leadership in her Indigenous rural community school. Findings identify the principal's practices of trauma informed leadership and how her approach supports Indigenous cultural revitalization and cultivates relationships between and amongst herself and her school constituents (e.g., students, teachers, staff, parents, other community members). These relationships have enabled her to foster a compassionate, caring, and safe school culture. The conclusions highlight how the practices she employs have resulted in supporting students academically, socially, and emotionally affected by intergenerational trauma and building more capacity in the larger school community. A description of the successes and challenges of her use of the approach, and the approach's transferability to other organizations, is also included in the chapter.

DOI: 10.4018/979-8-3693-1380-0.ch013

INTRODUCTION

All leaders must be attuned to meeting the needs of the members of their organizations. In the case of educational leaders, they must attend to the needs of their constituents, who include students, parents, teachers, staff, and other community members. They bear responsibility for creating the conditions that support a positive culture and open climate in their organizations. Leaders can influence the behaviours of their constituents by mediating and modulating the context (Owens & Valesky, 2009). They have the ability and potential to structure their organizations to give voice to their constituents. To nurture a positive culture, educational leaders must know their constituents and tailor their leadership approach to meet their constituents' needs. This chapter examines how an educational leader in one Indigenous school has responded to her community's unique needs by employing a trauma informed leadership approach. More specifically, this chapter includes an introduction to the authors, the research study's context and the rationale for the use of trauma informed leadership, an overview of literature relevant to trauma informed leadership, an overview of the methodology and methods employed in the research study, findings and a discussion highlighting the in-action practices of trauma informed leadership, a celebration of the successes of the approach, a discussion of the barriers to success, how a trauma informed leadership approach has transferability within other organizational contexts, and concluding comments.

POSITIONALITY OF AUTHORS

Within this chapter, Denise Toney shares her experiences as an educational leader, who employs a trauma informed approach at Gitpu Elementary and Junior School. The implementation and enactment of this approach strongly relies upon her colleagues; this approach is largely collaborative and the examination of her experiences does not diminish the essentiality of her peers. Denise, a Mi'kmaw woman, has served as the elementary school's principal since 2012 and prior to her current position held teaching positions and other leadership roles within her educational authority. She has also taught undergraduate courses in literacy and education at two Eastern Canadian universities. Ingrid Robinson, a white settler woman, is an associate professor at St. Francis Xavier University and has worked in partnership with Denise for over a decade. Together they have written and published research on Indigenous women in educational leadership. The impetus for writing this chapter arose from Denise and Ingrid's ongoing dialogue about the effectiveness of trauma informed leadership. Denise suggested they write about the successes of the approach at her school and detail how trauma informed practices have allowed her to nurture students' Mi'kmaw identities while creating opportunities for healing from trauma.

CONTEXT OF THE STUDY: AN IMPETUS FOR CHANGE

Over a decade ago, Denise accepted a position in her current school in Wigwasapewit as an elementary principal and she joined a leadership team where she shared the administrative and leadership duties with another leader, the junior school principal. Denise, in her role as a leader, adhered to the school's discipline policy that had been written and enacted by a previous school administrator. The approach relied upon collaborations between and amongst the leaders, teachers, students, and parents; but unfortunately, not all school constituents adhered to the approach. It included elements of a more traditional approach to modify students' behaviour.

As a new principal, Denise recognized the benefits of the behaviour policy but felt that the policy could be revised as it seemed that not all students thrived. Upon reflection and consultation with colleagues, Denise recognized that many of the students in her community suffered from trauma. This is not surprising as Indigenous peoples within Canada continue to experience trauma as a direct result of their own and their family members' attendance at Indian Residential Schools; children were removed from their home communities and forced to attend schools where they experienced abuse (Truth and Reconciliation Commission [TRC], 2015). Government created policies that led to the creation of Indian Residential Schools limited or removed Indigenous peoples' rights with the goal of extinguishing their culture and language. Brave Heart & Brave Heart Debruyn (1998) similarly attribute the cause of Indigenous peoples' experience of multi-generational trauma to colonization.

It was with this knowledge and observation of her students' trauma (e.g., personal, family, community, inter-generational) that she recognized that her students needed more school-based interventions. Denise and the junior school principal sought guidance related to selecting an appropriate leadership approach to help their students. Through a colleague's referral, they connected with a psychologist, Dr. Mona Kadu, who had used trauma informed practices with Maori children and youth in New Zealand; Mona's explanation and understanding of trauma informed leadership made this an approach ideal for meeting the students' needs at Gitpu Elementary and Junior School. Their meeting with Mona served as the catalyst for the changes they made in how they approached their leadership role and how they restructured the behaviour management system in their school. After receiving approval from the director of education in their school board, who recognized the significant shift in their leadership approach, they began the process of educating the teachers and staff about trauma informed practices. Calling again on the expertise of Dr. Mona Kadu, all employees attended a workshop. These were the first steps Denise, and the junior school principal took to becoming trauma informed leaders. The school board's director of education also recognized that additional expertise was required to implement trauma informed practices at Gitpu Elementary and Junior School. A discipline liaison therapist joined the leadership team; they wrote a new behaviour management policy that recognizes the importance of working relationally which aligns with trauma informed leadership approach. Denise continues to learn how to build positive and affirming relationships with students, parents, and other community members to support the healing process for individuals affected by trauma.

RELEVANT LITERATURE

Trauma and Its Impact

Trauma often results from an event or series of events experienced by an individual that pose significant threat (emotional, physical, or psychological) to the safety of the individual or those close to the individual and have long-lasting adverse effects (The American Psychological Association [APA], 2017; Substance Abuse and Mental Health Administration [SAMHSA], 2014). Trauma causes stress responses (e.g., physiological, psychological) in individuals that challenge their ability to cope (APA, 2017). Trauma shames, stigmatizes, degrades, and isolates the victim (Herman, 1992). It disrupts relationality (Schwab, 2010) and leads to a disconnection from others where individuals feel little safety and security in their lives and are left vulnerable (Herman, 1992). Prager (2017) stated that trauma in individuals' past encroaches on their present-day perceptions and influences the interactions they have with others (e.g., teachers, police, clergy). As trauma influences students' ability to develop relationship skills, it can impact their academic success at school (Duplechain et al., 2008; Kuban & Steele, 2011). Downey (2012) and Harris (2018) also found that when people have experienced trauma in their lives, it impacts their ability to develop, learn, and feel safe.

Trauma Informed Care

Trauma experienced by individuals and groups is continuous, but how it is managed and reacted upon can create opportunities for healing (Linklater, 2014). Goals of trauma-informed care attend to healing an individual's trauma and employing strategies to avoid re-traumatization (SAMHSA, 2014). Practices that support recovery from trauma include: providing individuals with opportunities to connect and collaborate with others and develop healthy relationships (SAMHSA, 2014; Stokes & Brunzell, 2019), establishing and fostering an environment of safety and trust (Biddle & Brown, 2020; SAMHSA, 2014), being culturally responsive (SAMHSA, 2014), and allowing individuals to see themselves as agents of change (Eren & Ravitch, 2021; SAMHSA, 2014)); that they themselves are empowered (Herman, 1992; SAMHSA, 2014). Within a trauma informed positive environment children learn to develop their psychological skills (e.g., growth mindset, positive self-talk) to self-regulate to de-escalate their behaviour (Heckman & Kautz, 2014; Stokes & Brunzell, 2019).

Trauma Informed Leadership

Individuals recovering from trauma cannot take place in isolation but instead must occur in the context of relationships (Herman, 1992). Restoring social bonds with others allows individuals affected by trauma to feel part of a community. Within a school setting, this context can create opportunities where individuals affected by trauma can build relationships with others. School leaders in partnership with teachers, parents, and community members can provide supports and employ practices that teach students strategies to effectively navigate trauma experienced in their lives. Langley et al. (2013) identified that when students have limited access to mental health services, schools play a crucial role in supporting these students in need. School-based services to support students affected by trauma appear to be more effective than providing students support from external community agencies (Jaycox et al., 2010). This finding may serve to explain the marked increase in the presence of school-based trauma interventions in North America (Zakszeski, 2017).

A trauma informed leadership approach recognizes the importance of creating an environment where children feel that they belong, know that they belong, and have opportunities to have voice; their communities provide them with affirmations of compassion, safety, and trust (Biddle & Brown, 2020; Imad, 2022). Grieg et al. (2021) identified the following characteristics of trauma informed leaders: drives the change and creates the school's plan for supporting students affected by trauma, supports teachers/staff by providing educational professional services for students, and seeks support and receives professional development from external experts.

Researchers have identified several practices school leaders should employ when using a trauma-sensitive or trauma informed leadership approach in schools. School leaders should promote and support trauma sensitivity by creating a positive culture and infrastructure (Allen et al., 2020), offer professional development for all school staff to create trauma sensitive learning spaces (Allen et al., 2020; Stokes & Brunzell, 2019), coordinate with local mental health services outside the school (Allen et al., 2020; Shamlin et al., 2016), encourage teachers to establish routines/employ strategies that allow students to feel safe (psychologically and physically) in their classrooms and other areas of the school (Allen et al., 2020: Stokes & Brunzell, 2019), and collaborate with and welcome families at the school (Allen et al., 2020; Shamblin et al., 2016).

Leaders who employ trauma informed practices recognize that their schools' discipline policies should aim to modify student behaviour through the creation and cultivation of a supportive and caring environment (Oehlberg, 2008). They avoid using traditional discipline practices that censure and shame (Biddle & Brown, 2020; Thorsborne & Blood, 2013) and can incite and aggravate students who have experienced trauma in their lives (Oehlberg, 2008). Instead, trauma informed leaders employ strategies that nurture students and create opportunities to allow them to relate and reflect on themselves.

The importance of collaboration is central to trauma informed leadership as in all transformative leadership approaches; wherein, constituents work collectively towards achieving their shared goals and enhances the problem-solving capacities of both individuals and the collective (Leithwood & Jantzi, 1990). Conversely, transactional leadership approaches employed by school leaders do not allow students, especially those with trauma, opportunities for safe exchanges of ideas to problem solve. When school leaders provide students with the opportunity to communicate their feelings, negotiate with others their understandings, strengthen their cultural identities, and advocate for themselves, students gain a sense of ownership of their behaviours, and gain a stronger sense of self.

RESEARCH METHODOLOGY AND METHODS

This research study employed a qualitative self-study approach to understand the lived experiences of one Indigenous school principal's purposeful implementation of trauma informed leadership. A self-study positioned the researcher to engage in an analysis that allowed her to reflect on her own practice (Herr & Anderson, 2005) within a bounded system (Creswell, 2005; Merriam, 2009) that defined the place and space of the phenomenon. It allowed for the examination of a specific organizational change, in this case the use of a trauma informed leadership approach. Recognizing the importance of respecting Indigenous ways of being and doing, the primary method of data collection was through conversations (as opposed to interviews) as this approach privileged personal narrative (Chilisa, 2012; Hanson, 2013). The approach to data analysis included transcribing conversations, reading and rereading the text, identifying central themes, and connecting these ideas to literature.

FINDINGS AND DISCUSSION: IN-ACTION PRACTICES OF TRAUMA INFORMED LEADERSHIP

At the root of Denise's trauma informed leadership approach is to centre Mi'kmaw culture. As a leader, she creates opportunities that allow students to celebrate, connect to, and affirm their Mi'kmaw culture. She employs practices that foster relationships and allow students to feel validated and safe in their school community. The culture of care for students is reflected in the school's discipline/behaviour management policy, opportunities students have involved in decision-making, and the learning supports they are afforded. Similarly, she employs practices to meet teachers' personal and professional needs. Denise also recognizes that parents want to be included in decision-making; as a leader, she welcomes families in the school community and provides them with support. As a trauma informed leader, she has a vision and a plan of action for the change she wants to see and employs various practices to accomplish it. Denise has found the use of trauma informed practices in her school has created opportunities to nurture not only students, but to build connections between and amongst teachers, staff, parents, and other community members. Trauma informed practices are labour intensive, but the results are rewarding for the entire school and community.

Embracing Mi'kmaw Culture

A trauma informed leader should act culturally responsively to meet the needs of the school community (SAMHSA, 2014). Denise ensures Mi'kmaw culture is embedded in her leadership approach as in the past, Mi'kmaw culture had been less embraced or celebrated in the school. Without children knowing their own culture, they are unable to appreciate and love themselves. Denise recognizes how different aspects of the Mi'kmaw culture allow her students, teachers, staff, and parents to reconnect to themselves and to others. Denise speaks Mi'kmaw daily with other school leaders, students, teachers, and other staff. Every morning on the announcements, students hear Mi'kmaw spoken. Denise uses talking circles with students, teachers, staff, and parents. Denise also uses the Seven Sacred Teachings to guide their students and allow them to embrace the values celebrated by Mi'kmaq. These values include courage, humility, honesty, respect, love, respect, truth, and wisdom and many teachers use the Seven Sacred Teachings in their lessons. Denise has found that they have internalized the Indigenous values; students demonstrate greater care for one another that results from the lessons in the teachings. Denise provides students with a variety of avenues to experience and connect to the Mi'kmaw culture for the purpose of nurturing themselves and the larger community.

Relationality

Denise's trauma informed leadership approach aligns with an Indigenous worldview in that relationality is paramount. An Indigenous worldview fosters relationships between and amongst the people, ancestors, land, language, stories, knowledge, medicine, and the spiritual environment (Linklater, 2014). Chilisa (2012) and Wilson (2008) similarly contend the importance of relationships and ontologically identify reality as relationships within Indigenous worldviews. As relationships are central in Indigenous communities, they must be nurtured. Denise recognizes the necessity of cultivating strong relationships between and amongst the students, teachers, staff, parents, and other community members as recovery and healing from trauma cannot take place in isolation (Herman, 1992). Cultivating relationships serves as a catalyst to the creation of a positive and safe school culture.

Cultivating Student Relationships to Create a Culture of Care. As trauma can impact students' ability to develop relationships and learn (Downey, 2012; Duplechain et al., 2008; Harris, 2018; Kuban & Steele, 2011), in order to create a positive and safe learning environment for students, Denise uses a student-centred discipline approach where students' perspectives are heard and their voices are validated. She has fostered a culture of acceptance and destigmatized the labels associated with disabilities. Her practices allow her to know her students and through using a community-driven mindset, she works collaboratively to support students.

Student Centred Discipline Approach. The school's leaders, teachers, and other staff have adopted a caring centred attitude that purposefully centres the students' needs and recognizes that they have emotions. These beliefs align with Oehlberg's (2008) findings that trauma informed leaders' discipline policies should aim to create a positive culture in their schools. Students are not shamed or chastised privately or publicly for displaying off-task behaviours. Students are given a voice and opportunities to share how they are feeling and to reflect on why they have felt and act in certain ways. A key element of the approach is allowing students to talk about what happened and positioning the adults as listeners. Denise shared that when teachers require assistance with off-task students in their classrooms, she invites students to her office for a conversation and they usually willingly follow. Denise uses de-escalation and emotional regulation strategies and has had successful results; students are not admonished or chastised but openly share the challenges they have experienced at home and at school without shame. Students have opportunities to feel safe as they renegotiate their relationships with one another and the other constituents in their school. By employing an approach that provides students opportunities to connect with others and develop healthy relationships, they are better positioned to recover from trauma (SAMHSA, 2014; Stokes & Brunzell, 2019).

Culture of Acceptance. Additionally, Denise has fostered a culture of caring in the school by talking openly with students, teachers, staff, and the community to reduce the stigma associated with mental health and well-being. Denise has noticed that students often are not afraid to share openly with others how a diagnosed disability (e.g., autism spectrum disorder, attention deficit hyperactivity disorder) can impact their behaviour. As a result of students' openness about their mental health, when a problem has arisen between or amongst students, they talk to each other to problem solve; they have demonstrated greater compassion, empathy, and understanding for one another. Trauma informed leaders create environments that cultivate safety and trust amongst their constituents (Biddle & Brown, 2020; Imad, 2022)

Knowing Students. Denise also identified the importance of knowing her students. She monitors the assessments they have been administered, reviews the results, and seeks out ways to provide the students with the supports they require to have success. As a leader, she recognizes that students need individualized supports; she sees each situation as a unique case and creates tailored plans of care for her students. Denise ensures that teachers are part of the conversation about students that require additional support; they work as a team.

Empowering Students. A trauma informed leadership approach involves elements of restorative justice, which emphasizes mutual respect and the use of dialogue to problem solve. It is founded on the belief that building and nurturing relationships based on mutual respect is central to establishing a safe and positive learning environment. When Denise meets with students, related to behaviour management concerns, she ensures that students recognize their own role in changing their behaviour and that the leader will stand alongside them and provide them with support. Students are given opportunities to be heard and be empowered when they are part of the decision-making process. When students feel and are empowered, their recovery from trauma is supported (Herman, 1992; SAMHSA, 2014).

Another aspect of student empowerment is when students see themselves as agents of change and contributors within their school community. When a leader creates opportunities for students to be part of a caring network, students positively respond. They act responsibly and work in partnership with teachers, staff, parents, and the leaders and use their network to address challenges. For example, students have been encouraged to come to the office to report issues that arise in the school. When a bathroom toilet overflows or somebody accidentally is pushed and falls, and students report these incidents to teachers and leaders, these events/concerns are acted upon. Students see how they belong to a caring community and that they are supported. They recognize that they have the power to bring about change and they have a voice. Denise creates opportunities for the students so they see themselves as agents of change and these actions support recovery from trauma (Eren & Ravitch, 2021; SAMHSA, 2014).

Supports for Teachers. Teachers can and do feel overwhelmed and stressed that results from implementing trauma informed practices in their classrooms that can be labour intensive. As a trauma informed leader, Denise recognizes the supports she must provide to teachers. Denise makes herself available to teachers who want to talk and share their own difficulties, which can be identified as trauma. Many teachers have approached Denise when they have been dealing with professional or personal challenges. Denise has said that as a leader, she works with love. Denise also has enlisted the help of human resources who offer support through programs both in person and virtually. Additional supports are made available to teachers provided by the educational authority (e.g., mental wellness professional development) and insurance plan (e.g., resources online) to help teachers cope with the challenges of supporting students. Whether she is working with students, parents, teachers, or other staff, she creates space to allow them to share their concerns.

Supports Teachers/Staff by Providing Educational Professional Services for Students. Students that require additional care are supported by Denise who communicates with a variety of educational experts in the school building. Some of these professionals include guidance counsellors, psychologists, a trauma informed practitioner, a speech pathologist, an occupational therapist, an early behaviour interventionist, and a resource teacher (who supports students academically). On-site school-based services provided for trauma affected children are more effective than off-site external agencies (Jaycox et al., 2010). An example of Denise's actions as a trauma informed leader to support her students' well-being follows. When Denise identified a problem with bullying (i.e., mental health challenges caused by trauma), she worked with a guidance counsellor to set up a building campaign (i.e., Building Champions) and provided programming (i.e., interventions) to support students build respectful and trusting relationships. In addition to mobilizing the support of experts in the school, she regularly visited the classrooms of students affected by the bullying to help resolve the conflict. Denise has employed an active role in the negotiation and creation of safe spaces in the school. As a trauma informed leader, Denise enacts practices that effective leaders of this approach employ; she enlists the help of professional educational services to assist teachers and staff support students (Grieg, 2021).

Collaborations With Families. Parents play a significant role in a trauma informed leadership approach. Welcoming families to the school and working with them to support student growth (e.g., social, emotional, academic) is paramount. Denise's experiences as an educator and consultant in Wigwasapewit have allowed her to know the histories of community members and the levels of support that are needed to support the children in her school. Denise has regular communication with parents to keep them informed about their children's behaviours and intervention supports provided at school. Not only does Denise contact parents by phone, but also invites families to meet in person to bridge communication between the school and home. Denise also works to bridge the gap and build stronger connections between teachers and parents. As some teachers are uncomfortable with contacting parents, Denise has invited teachers to her office to call parents together. Denise recognizes the importance of working in partnership with parents and is cognizant of the benefits of welcoming families into the school as a practice aligned with being a trauma informed leader (Allen et al., 2020; Shamblin et al., 2016). When leaders work to foster positive relationships and establish the conditions for relationships to flourish, the entire community benefits. The community will feel safe, secure, and strong; students will feel safe, secure, and empowered.

Seeks Support and Receives Professional Development from External Experts

Trauma informed leaders recognize the importance of providing their staff professional learning opportunities that allow them to gain skills and knowledge related to implementing trauma informed interventions (Allen et al., 2020; Shamlin et al., 2016). Upon Denise and the junior school principal's realization that a trauma informed leadership approach was a most beneficial approach to meet the needs of their school's constituents, they sought out the services of an expert to help them and their staff become educated about the approach. Over the last decade, Denise and her colleagues in leadership have continued to provide teachers with additional professional development opportunities to learn other appropriate interventions they can use to support their students that experience trauma. Some of the professional development programming includes Early Intensive Behaviour Intervention (EIBI), Mindfulness, Attunement, and Controlling Anger and Learning to Manage It (CALM). Denise's actions, providing professional development opportunities to support teacher learning related to trauma informed interventions, is one demonstration of her effective enactment of trauma informed leadership in her school (Allen et al., 2020; Shamlin et al., 2016).

Behaviour Management: A Team Approach

A trauma informed leadership approach can only be successful when a school's constituents (e.g., students, teachers, staff, parents, other community members) and leaders form a network to support individuals affected by trauma (Allen et al., 2020; Shamlin et al., 2016). This is clearly evidenced in the approach taken up by the leaders in Gitpu Elementary and Junior School. What follows are several examples of different team approaches (involving different school constituents) for supporting students with different behaviour management needs. As a leader, Denise recognizes that all students impacted by trauma benefit from interventions, but some require different levels of support and care. Teachers serve as the first line of support for trauma affected students. Within their classrooms, teachers employ learning strategies (e.g., sequencing, problem-solving, expressive language, behavioural/emotional, focus/concentration) and coping strategies (e.g., breathing exercises, mental health breaks, movement exercises) that serve as interventions for students. These practices serve to relieve student stress, allow students to re-establish relationships (Lelli, 2014), and feel safe (Allen et al., 2020; Stokes & Brunzell, 2019). These are practices commonly observed in trauma informed positive environments (SAMHSA, 2014). Teachers are encouraged to contact parents to inform and involve them in the decision-making related to modifying off-task student behaviour. Teachers are also encouraged to contact members of the leadership team (e.g., guidance counsellors, student services, principals) when they require additional assistance. As a school leader, Denise becomes directly involved to support students. She meets with students and spends time listening to them and learning about them. She also reaches out to parents and to teachers to create a plan of support for the student. Students that are more acutely impacted by trauma and who more regularly encounter difficulties (e.g., challenges working with their peers, learning in the classroom) are provided additional intervention supports. Denise and her leadership colleagues connect with other off-site professionals (e.g., psychologists), on-site professionals (e.g., guidance counsellors) and agencies (e.g., child and adolescent services) to support the students in their school. Denise recognizes that a continuum of care needs to exist to support students. Collaborations with school constituents (e.g., students, parents, teachers, staff) and external experts (Allen et al., 2020; Shamlin et al., 2016) are essential in a trauma informed leadership approach.

Building Relationships and Fostering a Community of Care

Leaders Drive the Change and Create the School's Plan for Supporting Trauma Affected Students

Trauma informed leaders lead their organizational change and develop the plan for supporting individuals impacted by trauma (Grieg et al., 2021). This is abundantly evident in Denise and her leadership team's approach to implementing trauma informed leadership in their school. As described earlier, a decade ago when Denise began her position as the elementary school principal of her school, she and the junior school principal recognized that their students suffered from the effects of trauma. They realized that they had to revise their leadership approach to better support their students. They used their community connections and allied with individuals who had knowledge of the benefits of using a trauma informed leadership approach. They educated themselves about the approach (e.g., reading academic and professional literature, attending workshops, collaborating with experts) to allow them to deeply understand the functions and processes associated with the approach. Following their own learning, they organized professional development for their teachers and staff to provide them with tools for creating trauma informed positive environments in their own classrooms.

Adhering to the practices of trauma informed leaders, when Denise and her leadership team began to consider how to amend the behaviour management policy, they relied upon an individual, hired by the school board, with expertise in restorative justice and trauma informed practice. The revised behaviour management policy framed the procedures for how all leaders, teachers, and staff in the school should interact with students, and with one another, for the purpose of creating the conditions to allow students to heal from trauma and feel safe. In addition to teachers' use of the behaviour management policy to guide their interventions in trauma informed practice, Denise also has provided other supportive student programming available for teachers to use (e.g., Positive Mental Health Toolkit). Additionally, Denise has partnered with the school board that allowed for the hiring of a trauma informed practitioner and restorative practices support person, organized professional development for teachers and staff, and shared programming strategies with teachers. Denise and her colleagues have driven the change and devised and implemented a plan to effectively support students affected by trauma in their school (Grieg et al., 2021).

SUCCESSES OF TRAUMA INFORMED LEADERSHIP

A trauma informed leadership approach has the potential to transform a school community; Denise's implementation of this approach has resulted in creating a more caring, nurturing, and safe environment for the constituents of her school. Denise has embraced the concept of relationality in all aspects of her work. As Mi'kmaq, she has always recognized the importance of developing and sustaining positive relationships with others; but her purposeful implementation of a trauma informed leadership approach validated her approach that centres relationship building. She knows that the collaborations with students, parents, teachers, staff, and other community members have tremendous power; power to help members of her community heal from trauma (Herman, 1992; SAMHSA, 2014; Stokes & Brunzell, 2019). Through her learning conversations with students, she has given students a voice and opportunities to empower themselves and see themselves as agents of change (Eren & Ravitch, 2021) Not only have students demonstrated greater confidence and connection to themselves, within and to their school, but student learning has improved.

Her welcoming of parents into the school and participation in the intervention process also has strengthened their connections to the school and their children. The partnerships she has developed with teachers have enabled teachers to feel supported and more able to address their students' needs. The networking that has resulted between and amongst the school constituents has brought about positive change. Denise has witnessed significant changes in students' behaviour management skills in the past five years. Students are learning how to better negotiate their classroom and school relationships with other students, teachers, staff, and leaders. Students appear to be more accepting of each other's differences and enact more nurturing and caring attitudes towards one another. Fostering relationality for the purpose of addressing trauma is just one aspect of the approach that aligns with Mi'kmaw culture. The enactment of culturally responsive practices is another foundational component of a trauma informed care (SAMHSA, 2014). Denise has enabled the school's constituents to strengthen their connections to the Mi'kmaw culture through their practices through exposure to the spoken language, the Seven Sacred Teachings, and other cultural practices. The implementation of a trauma informed leadership approach has strengthened Denise's school culture and climate allowing for a more positive and caring environment (Allen et al., 2020) to flourish. Furthermore, its impact spans beyond the walls of the school and has had a positive effect on the wider community.

CHALLENGES WITH IMPLEMENTATION OF TRAUMA INFORMED LEADERSHIP

No leadership approach can remove all obstacles that school leaders experience. Denise recognizes that a trauma informed approach is valuable and suitable for her school community; but, in the early years of its implementation, not all school constituents embraced the approach. A dramatic shift occurred when Denise first embarked on the use of trauma informed leadership; it was foreign to many teachers, parents, and staff. Denise identified that some individuals were critical of the approach; they perceived the approach as too lenient. Denise recognized that she must always be prepared to dedicate time to educating teachers, parents, and staff about the merits of the approach. Despite Denise having the director of education of her school board championing her use of a trauma informed approach, she continues to attend to convincing some school board members about the value of the approach. An additional challenge of the approach is its time-consuming nature; developing relationships with others with the aim of collaborative problem-solving requires much time to establish and foster the relationships. Notwithstanding these identified challenges, this approach's benefits outweigh the negatives.

TRANSFERABILITY OF A TRAUMA INFORMED LEADERSHIP APPROACH

Trauma informed leadership may be a suitable approach employed within other organizational contexts to counter trauma induced behaviours. It is a practice that creates opportunities and allows for more open communication (SAMHSA, 2014; Stokes and Brunzell, 2019) between and amongst its constituents in safe spaces to problem solve (Biddle & Brown, 2020). Any organization adopting a trauma informed leadership approach must recognize the importance of collaboration and view their organization as a body of interdependent and interconnected relationships (Grieg et al., 2021). Cultivating and sustaining relationships allows organizations to flourish; working collectively towards common goals benefits individuals and the collective, which is a central feature of transformative leadership approaches (Leithwood

& Jantzi, 1990). The leader works collaboratively with diverse groups to understand and meet their constituents' needs. When constituents within an organization (or community) require support, this approach creates space to address these challenges. However, how each organization implements this approach is context dependent, as each community of constituents requires unique supports.

CONCLUSION

Leaders that employ a trauma informed approach recognize the importance of collaboration across and between diverse groups in their organization. The creation of successful collaborations requires leaders to cultivate relationships between and amongst themselves and their constituents. The leader in this study has collaborated with her school's constituents and employed practices that teach students strategies to recover from trauma. When school leaders provide students with the opportunity to communicate their feelings, negotiate with others their understandings, strengthen their cultural identities, and advocate for themselves, students gain a sense of ownership of their behaviours, and gain a stronger sense of self. Leaders that are able to listen, respect, and respond to the unique needs of students have the potential to transform a school's culture. In this chapter, Denise Toney shared how her approach has allowed for more open communication between and amongst all constituents in her school community. A trauma informed approach has created opportunities for students and parents' voices to be heard and acted upon. Teachers, staff, and other community members' participation in decision-making fosters a collective identity and strengthens the whole community. Furthermore, the interweaving of Mi'kmaw language, culture, and spirit, along with traditional practices into the school, support learning through healing and through restorative practices. Such practices that balance academic and intervention support have empowered their students. Denise's leadership practices have placed relationality at the centre of her work; this has allowed for students, parents, teachers, and other staff to form networks and has enabled opportunities for individuals to begin to heal from the trauma experienced by members of their school community.

NOTE

Pseudonyms have been used for the name of the school, community, and psychologist in this study.

REFERENCES

Allen, T. G., Jackson, A., & Johnson, D. N. (2020). Preparing North Carolina principals for trauma-sensitive leadership. *Journal of Organizational and Educational Leadership, 5*(2).

American Psychological Association. (2017). *Clinical practice guideline for treatment of post traumatic stress disorder (PTSD)*. Retrieved from https://www.apa.org/ptsd-guideline/ptsd.pdf

Biddle, C., & Brown, L. M. (2020). Banishing "Siberia" and student seclusion: Leading trauma-informed systems change in a rural school. *Journal of Cases in Educational Leadership, 23*(2), 85–97. doi:10.1177/1555458920910771

Brave Heart, M. Y. H., & Brave Heart Debruyn, L. M. (1998). The American Indian holocaust: Healing historical unresolved grief. *American Indian and Alaska Native Mental Health Research, 8*(2), 56–78. PMID:9842066

Chilisa, B. (2021). Indigenous research methodologies. *Sage (Atlanta, Ga.).*

Creswell, J. (2005). *Educational research: Planning, conducting, and evaluating quantitative and qualitative research*. Pearson.

Downey, L. (2012). *Calmer classrooms: A guide to working with traumatised children*. AUS, Child Safety Commissioner.

Duplechain, R., Reigner, R., & Packard, A. (2008). Striking differences: The impact of moderate and high trauma on reading achievement. *Reading Psychology, 29*(2), 117–136. doi:10.1080/02702710801963845

Eren, N. S., & Ravitch, S. M. (2021). Trauma-informed leadership: Balancing love and accountability. In *Critical leadership praxis: Leading educational and social change* (Vol. E). Teachers College Press.

Grieg, J., Bailey, B., Abbot, L., & Brunzell, T. (2021). Trauma-informed integral leadership: Leading school communities with a systems-aware approach. *International Journal of Whole Schooling, 17*(1), 62–97.

Hanson, C. (2013). Crossing borders: Developing collaborations with Indigenous communities. *Proceedings of the National Conference of Canadian Association for the Study of Adult Education*, 211–217.

Harris, N. (2018). *The deepest well: Healing the long-term effects of childhood adversity*. Houghton Mifflin Harcourt.

Heckman, J. J., & Kautz, T. (2014). Fostering and measuring skills: Interventions that improve character and cognition. In J. J. Heckman, J. E. Humphries, & T. Kautz (Eds.), *The myth of achievement tests: The GED and the role of character education in American life* (pp. 341–430). The University of Chicago Press.

Herman, J. (1992). *Trauma and recovery: The aftermath of violence—from domestic abuse to political terror*. Basic Books.

Herr, K., & Anderson, G. (2005). *The action research dissertation: A guide for students and faculty*. Sage.

Imad, M. (2022). Teaching to empower: Leveraging the neuroscience of how to help students become self-regulated learners. *Journal of Undergraduate Neuroscience Education, 20*(2), 252–260.

Jaycox, L., Cohen, J. A., Mannarino, A. P., Walker, D. W., Langley, A. K., Gegenheimer, K. L., Scott, M., & Schonlau, M. (2010). Children's mental health care following Hurricane Katrina: A field trial of trauma-focused psychotherapies. *Journal of Traumatic Stress, 23*, 223–231. doi:10.1002/jts.20518 PMID:20419730

Kuban, C., & Steele, W. (2011). Restoring safety and hope: From victim to survivor. *Reclaiming Children and Youth, 20*(1), 41–44.

Langley, A., Santiago, C. D., Rodríguez, A., & Zelaya, J. (2013). Improving implementation of mental health services for trauma in multicultural elementary schools: Stakeholder perspectives on parent and educator engagement. *The Journal of Behavioral Health Services & Research, 40*(3), 247–262. doi:10.100711414-013-9330-6 PMID:23576136

Leithwood, K., & Jantzi, D. (1990). Transformational leadership: How principals can help reform school cultures. *School Effectiveness and School Improvement, 1*(4), 249–280. doi:10.1080/0924345900010402

Lelli, C. (2014). Ten strategies to help the traumatized child in school. *Kappa Delta Pi Record, 50*(3), 114–118. doi:10.1080/00228958.2014.931145

Linklater, R. (2014). *Decolonizing trauma work*. Fernwood Publishing.

Merriam, S. (2009). *Qualitative research: A guide to design and implementation* (3rd ed.). Jossey-Bass.

Oehlberg, B. (2008). Why schools need to be trauma informed. *Trauma and Loss: Research and Intervention, 8*(2). Retrieved from http://www.tlcinstitute.org

Owens, R., & Valesky, T. (2009). *Organizational behavior in education: Leadership and school reform*. Pearson.

Prager, J. (2016). Disrupting the intergenerational transmission of trauma: Recovering humanity, repairing generations. In P. Gobodo-Madikizela (Ed.), *Breaking intergenerational cycles of repetition: A global dialogue on historical trauma and memory* (pp. 12–26). Verlag Barbara Budrich. doi:10.2307/j.ctvdf03jc.7

Schwab, G. *Haunting legacies: Violent histories and transgenerational trauma*. Columbia University Press.

Sebastian, J., Huang, H., & Allensworth, E. (2017). Examining integrated leadership systems in high schools: Connecting principal and teacher leadership to organizational processes and student outcomes. *School Effectiveness and School Improvement, 28*(3), 463–488. doi:10.1080/09243453.2017.1319392

Shamblin, S., Graham, D., & Bianco, J. A. (2016). Creating trauma-informed schools for rural Appalachia: The partnerships program for enhancing resiliency, confidence, and workforce development in early childhood education. *School Mental Health, 8*(1), 189–200. doi:10.100712310-016-9181-4

Stokes, H., & Brunzell, T. (2019). Professional learning in trauma informed positive education: Moving school communities from trauma affected to trauma aware. *School Leadership Review, 14*(2).

Substance Abuse and Mental Health Administration. (2014). *SAMHSA's concept of trauma and guidance for a trauma-informed approach*. Author.

Thorsborne, M., & Blood, P. (2013). *Implementing restorative practices in schools: A practical guide to transforming school communities*. Jessica Kingsley Publishers.

Truth and Reconciliation Commission of Canada. (2015). *Canada's residential schools: The final report of the Truth and Reconciliation Commission of Canada*. McGill-Queen's University Press.

Wilson, S. (2008). *Research is ceremony: Indigenous research methods*. Fernwood Publishing.

Zakszeski, B. N., Ventresco, N. E., & Jaffe, A. R. (2017). Promoting resilience through traumafocused practices: A critical review of school-based implementation. *School Mental Health, 9*(4), 310–321. doi:10.100712310-017-9228-1

KEY TERMS AND DEFINITIONS

Behaviour Management: The practices often employed by teachers and school leaders to modify student behaviour.

Culturally Responsive: Demonstrating respect and valuing individuals' cultural identities and backgrounds by using these identities as sources of knowledge within a learning environment.

Mi'kmaw: Indigenous peoples who have traditionally resided in what is now called Eastern Canada and the United States on lands in Nova Scotia, Prince Edward Island, Northern New Brunswick, Eastern Quebec, and Maine.

Relationality: The belief that reality is constituted by relationships and that everyone and everything is connected; relationships are foundational within Indigenous communities.

Restorative Justice: Allowing individuals who have been harmed to communicate openly about the effects of the infraction with those responsible for causing the harm and coming to an agreed upon consequence for the damages caused.

Seven Sacred Teachings: The spiritual foundation for Indigenous peoples of Canada and include respect, courage, honesty, truth, love, wisdom, and humility. Each teaching honours a virtue needed to lead a healthy and balanced life to help people learn how to respect themselves, others, and the land.

Trauma Informed Leadership: A relational leadership approach designed to support individuals affected by trauma.

Chapter 14

Agile Leadership in Navigating Change Management and Its Application Within the Food and Beverage Industry During the COVID-19 Pandemic

Dewaine Alexander Larmond
University of the People, Canada

ABSTRACT

This chapter delves into the dynamic landscape of change management in modern business, unveiling actionable strategies. By synthesizing industry literature and expert insights, it underscores the paramount role of agile leadership, particularly in the challenging domain of the COVID-19 pandemic. Exemplary instances from various industries illuminate essential approaches adopted by leaders to ensure unswerving continuity, enhanced safety, and resounding success. The chapter centers around a prominent Canadian sports facility, where food and beverage revenue is pivotal, spotlighting the adept application of both Lewin's unfreeze-change-refreeze approach and Kotter's 8-step model for change. This analysis elucidates critical takeaways encompassing adaptation, diversification, transparent processes, technological integration, and the strategic elevation of health priorities—cornerstones for sustained viability.

INTRODUCTION

"The Only Constant in Life Is Change." Heraclitus, an ancient Greek pre-Socratic philosopher from Ephesus, was notable for this quote, which bares relevance in modern-day society and our day-to-day lives. Change is inevitable. It takes on many shapes and forms and has evolved us into who we are today.

Change can be seen within the environment or nature with the variations in seasons, our personal life transitions from childhood to adolescence and adulthood, and our financial situations, which influence our quality of life, all requiring some adjustment and techniques to adopt. Similarly, changes within or-

DOI: 10.4018/979-8-3693-1380-0.ch014

ganizations, which provides the basis for our chapter, can be brought upon by multiple factors requiring implementing multiple strategies, known as Change Management (Phillips & Klein, 2022).

The COVID-19 pandemic has presented unprecedented challenges to industries worldwide, including the Food and Beverage industry. In the face of uncertainty, volatility, and constantly evolving circumstances, organizations in this sector have been compelled to adapt swiftly and effectively to navigate the crisis (Hartmann & Lussier, 2020; Kuckertz et al., 2020; Sobieralski, 2020; Spurk & Straub, 2020). This chapter also explores the role of Agile Leadership in managing change within the Food and Beverage industry during the COVID-19 pandemic. Agile Leadership, characterized by its ability to embrace flexibility, responsiveness, and continuous learning, has emerged as a practical approach to guide organizations through turbulent times (Phillips & Klein, 2022). By examining how Agile Leadership practices have been applied within the Food and Beverage industry, this chapter aims to provide insights into the strategies, tactics, and lessons learned in successfully navigating change during the pandemic. It explores the unique challenges faced by the industry, the specific applications of Agile Leadership, and the impacts on organizational resilience and adaptability. Furthermore, it sheds light on the comparative advantages of Agile Leadership over traditional change management approaches and provides recommendations for developing and cultivating Agile Leadership capabilities within the Food and Beverage industry (Cummings & Worley, 2009; Petrou et al., 2018). Through this exploration, leaders in the industry can gain valuable insights and guidance to navigate the challenges of the COVID-19 pandemic and build resilience for future disruptions.

PURPOSE OF THE STUDY

This research looks at Agile Leadership and how it may be used in the Food and Beverage business during the COVID-19 epidemic. The study investigates how leaders in the Food and Beverage sector have used Agile Leadership concepts and practices to effectively adapt to the difficulties and uncertainties brought about by the epidemic. The research attempts to discover the essential methods, techniques, and best practices agile leaders use in adapting their organizations, managing change, and generating organizational resilience by studying real-world examples and case studies. The study's results will give valuable insights and practical advice for executives and organizations in the Food and Beverage industry, allowing them to manage change effectively.

JUSTIFICATION OF THE STUDY

The chapter on Agile Leadership in Navigating Change Management and its application in the Food and Beverage business during the COVID-19 pandemic is justified by the industry's enormous difficulties and disruptions. The COVID-19 pandemic has produced significant upheaval in the Food and Beverage industry, requiring businesses to swiftly react to new consumer behaviours, supply chain disruptions, and government restrictions. Traditional leadership techniques may fail to effectively manage change and build organizational resilience in a dynamic and uncertain environment.

With its emphasis on flexibility, adaptation, and iterative problem-solving, Agile Leadership provides a potential framework for leaders to traverse these problems. This chapter aims to provide valuable insights and practical guidance to leaders and organizations seeking to embrace Agile Leadership principles and practices to effectively respond to the pandemic and future disruptions by examining real-world examples and best practices from the Food and Beverage industry.

SIGNIFICANCE OF THE STUDY

Investigating Agile Leadership in Navigating Change Management and its application in the Food and Beverage industry during the COVID-19 epidemic is crucial. The COVID-19 epidemic has created unprecedented disruptions and challenges for the Food & Beverage industry, forcing management to adjust quickly and make critical decisions. This chapter intends to contribute to the body of knowledge on effective change management in times of crisis by analyzing the concepts and practices of Agile Leadership. The findings of this study will be helpful to executives in the Food and Beverage business, allowing them to handle the intricacies of the epidemic and future uncertainties with agility and resilience. The study's results will also have more considerable significance outside of the business since the ideas of Agile Leadership may be applied to other industries experiencing similar issues. Finally, the goal of this research is to provide leaders with the information and resources they need to successfully manage their businesses through periods of change and uncertainty, ensuring long-term sustainability and growth.

RESEARCH INQUIRY AND CONCEPTUAL FRAMEWORK

Several research issues are addressed in the chapter on Agile Leadership in Navigating Change Management and its Application in the Food and Beverage Industry during the COVID-19 Pandemic. Understanding how Agile Leadership has been applied within the industry to effectively manage change during the pandemic, identifying specific challenges faced by the industry and how Agile Leadership has helped in addressing them, and examining the impacts of Agile Leadership on organizational resilience and adaptability are among these questions. Furthermore, the chapter intends to compare the application of Agile Leadership to traditional change management approaches, extract lessons learned and best practices from the experiences of industry leaders, and investigate strategies for developing and nurturing Agile Leadership capabilities within the Food and Beverage industry. The chapter will give significant insights and expertise to help industry executives handle change and uncertainty, notably during the COVID-19 epidemic, while also giving direction for future disruptions by examining these research issues

LITERATURE REVIEW

Definition for Change Management

Phillips and Klein (2022) identify change management as a systematic strategy and collection of tactics used to assist individuals, teams, and organizations in successfully transitioning from their present condition to a desired future state. It entails planning, executing, and monitoring organizational changes to reduce opposition, increase adoption, and assure success. Change management acknowledges that people are at the centre of organizational change and focuses on addressing their concerns, assisting, and encouraging their participation throughout the change process. It includes features such as communication, stakeholder involvement, training and development, and the establishment of a supportive culture. The ultimate purpose of change management is to enable businesses to adapt to changing conditions, grab opportunities, and achieve desired results by facilitating seamless and effective transitions (Phillips & Klein, 2022).

Change management provides a structured approach that acknowledges the difficulties of organizational change and offers a framework for doing so successfully. It entails a series of organized initiatives and activities designed to reduce change resistance and increase employee commitment (Phillips & Klein, 2022). Change management includes several components, including determining the need for change, establishing specific objectives and goals, creating a thorough change plan, explaining the motivation behind and advantages of the change to stakeholders, overcoming resistance and obstacles, offering employees training and support, and tracking and evaluating the change initiative's progress.

Change management that is effective takes into account the human part of the change by recognizing the emotions, worries, and responses of individuals and groups affected by the change (Cummings & Worley, 2009; Petrou et al., 2018). It stresses communication, integrating people in the change process, and offering them the resources and assistance they need to adjust to new methods of working. Change management also understands the significance of strong leadership and sponsorship to drive and promote change, as well as the value of cultivating a culture that encourages continual improvement and accepts change as a natural part of organizational life (Petrou et al., 2018).

According to research, firms that effectively manage change are more likely to accomplish their goals and sustain long-term success (Cummings & Worley, 2009). Change management assists firms in reducing the adverse effects of change, reducing employee resistance and attrition, increasing staff morale and engagement, and improving overall organizational performance (Petrou et al., 2018). It is essential during major disruptions, like the COVID-19 epidemic, when firms must swiftly adapt to new realities and develop inventive methods to prosper in an ever-changing business landscape (Petrou et al., 2018).

History of Change Management

The term Change Management dates back to the mid-1900s when several scholars developed models and theories surrounding this concept, which organizations worldwide adopted much later. In 1940 Kurt Lewin developed the 3-step model for change, and in subsequent years Everett Rogers and William Bridges, among others, pioneered other theories (Ramos, 2022).

However, companies experiencing multiple challenges by globalization, cultural influences, rapid technological advancement, and environmental, political and socio-economic changes have led to the wide adaptation of change management within organizations from the late 1990s to early 2000. The evolving consumer expectations for better, faster, and cheaper products also drive the need to reorganize the work culture to meet demand, which has cemented to need and evolution of Change Management (Ramos, 2022).

Common Factors That Cause Change Within an Organization

In the context of the COVID-19 pandemic, the international health crisis has had a significant effect on organizations all around the world. Businesses now face unprecedented hurdles due to the epidemic, including addressing staff health and safety concerns, constraints on physical operations, supply chain interruptions, and changes in customer behaviour. Organizations have been forced to quickly adjust to these conditions and adopt improvements, including remote work arrangements, digital transformation, improved health and safety regulations, and creating new goods or services to satisfy changing consumer demands. The COVID-19 pandemic has sparked change in various industries and brought attention to the significance of adaptability, toughness, and the capacity to deal with uncertainty in organizational change management. Other factors that cause change includes

Regulatory Compliance: It is the responsibility of any ruling or opposition party within various committees to propose, enact and promulgate legislation and policies as they see fit to address issues facing a country within a given time. However, changes in the law can have adverse effects on an organization's process operation, design and implementation as such, companies have to make changes to be compliant with the laws. These changes can be associated with labour laws affecting wages or becoming environmentally compliant and energy efficient through designs and processes.

Market Demand and Forces: Consumer demand influences and drives sales for any organization. The customer is the heartbeat of any company, as such competition and having products readily available worldwide makes it imperative for companies to stay ahead by keeping with the trends and demands, which require constant changes and innovations.

Technological Advancements: Many years ago, when the internet and other technology, such as social media, were not invented, consumers needed more options for accessing and obtaining products. Fast forward to today, and consumers can view and acquire what they want with a button from the comforts of their homes. The rapid improvement or advancement in technology requires companies to constantly improve their system to stay competitive, hence the need for change management to transition employees through the changes (Kho et al., 2020).

Social and Cultural Shifts: Factors such as level of education, the financial status of individuals and families, urbanization, international influences, etc., are all social factors which can impact consumer demands and preferences. This kind of change often prompts organizations to make adjustments where needed (Zada, 2022).

Failure: This has a way of putting companies out of business or can become a source of inspiration for organizations to make a comeback, avoiding closures, bankruptcy and profit loss. A comeback from failure requires intense work, determination and changes which potentially go against the company's ways of doing business.

Industry Trends and Innovation: Every product has a life cycle, and at various stages of the life cycle, competition from other companies, which might offer a better product at a lower price point, may enter the market to capitalize on the hype or trend. Companies facing this situation must develop their product or change their marketing strategies to stay relevant in the market space (Bhasin, 2019).

Cost Savings: All companies at some point face harsh financial times, which potentially could be brought on by a pandemic (COVID-19), competition, decreased demand for its product, increased prices for raw materials, and energy costs, among many others, which requires organizations to cut back supplies, staff, hours, etc. In most cases, such an adjustment requires adaptation of a change management process.

Organizational Growth and Restructuring: This can pose a challenge for employees and employers of an organization as existing employees may need to be more accustomed to the cultures and policies of the merging company. There can also be mass redundancy or layoff of workers, leading to employee distress and discomfort. The process of merging and acquiring requires careful planning and execution of a change management plan to mitigate the issues (Zada, 2022).

Change in Business Structure: This is regarded as an internal factor, and as previously explained, change is inevitable, where it is essential for companies to stay relevant competitive and current with innovations and technologies, etc. This often requires changes within the management structure that are more equipped to move the organization forward (Bhasin, 2019).

Globalization: Expanding into new markets, dealing with international regulations, or engaging in cross-border collaborations may necessitate organizational changes to adapt to global business environments.

Basic Principles of Successful Change Management

Each industry is different and presents unique complexities and challenges when implementing change management (Burnes, 2009). The successful implementation of change management follows a few fundamental principles that involve strong leadership and a clear vision, including stakeholders at all levels, honest communication, thorough planning, staff training and support, ongoing assessment, and modification are all essential components of successful change management in businesses (Petrou et al., 2018). Effective change initiatives start with leaders who communicate a clear vision and direction for the change, inspiring and guiding employees throughout the process. Including stakeholders, such as staff members, clients, and suppliers, in the change process ensures their feedback and support (Cummings & Worley, 2009; Petrou et al., 2018).

Acceptance and ownership of the process are fostered through open and honest communication about the justifications for the change, the anticipated results, and the impact on the workforce (Rehman et al., 2021). Success depends on thorough planning, preparation, and dealing with potential hazards. Employees can adjust to the shift by receiving proper training, resources, and emotional support. To make sure the change is on track and yields the expected results, regular reviews and changes based on feedback and lessons learned are made. These guidelines can help implement change and provide fruitful outcomes for the company (Rehman et al., 2021).

Change Management Challenges

The change process is very dynamic, and management teams within organizations contend with the issue of making constant adjustments that can be influenced by policies, internal decisions or external factors to meet requirements (Michigan State University, 2022).

Global competition, the rapid evolution of technology and high consumer demands for product and service deliveries also challenge change management in that a plan implemented today can become relevant a few weeks after just to keep up with the rapid pace (Rehman et al., 2021).

Another key barrier to change management is people and cultural differences. People have different opinions and personalities that may affect or influence how they respond to change (Burnes & Jackson, 2011). People who fail to buy into specific initiatives can cause hold up and delays, thus making the change management process more difficult. Countries and organizations with diverse cultural backgrounds often struggle to implement change due t the difference in how people of different backgrounds and cultures do certain things (Burnes & Jackson, 2011).

Change Management Theory and Its Importance

Change within organizations is a complex and challenging process that involves several strategies, steps and activities to bring everyone on board. Many organizations need help to engage employees in organizational change and often require the services of a trained professional or practitioner and various change management models to help with the process (Zada, 2022).

Change management models are developed to strategically guide organizational change by providing the framework, methodologies, concepts and theories for implementing change. It guides organizations through the difficulties of change, helping to avoid common obstacles and shortfalls (Burnes & Jackson, 2011). There is a change management model that meets every situation an organization faces. At its core are psychology and social dynamics, which help onboard new hires, update or replace internal processes, or implement new technology (Burnes, 2009).

Importance of Change Management Theories

For several reasons, change theories are crucial in change management. First off, businesses go through a variety of changes during their existence, including mergers, the adoption of new technologies, and process reengineering. Change theories give a systematic and organized strategy for handling these changes, as well as tried-and-true tactics and pointers for implementation.

Second, theories of change assist companies in navigating the difficulties and complexity brought on by change. They give change managers insights into psychology, social dynamics, and human behaviour, helping them to comprehend potential responses and resistance. Organizations may proactively deal with resistance, handle disagreements, and foster a positive work environment for workers by understanding these dynamics.

Change theories also improve the general efficacy of change attempts. Based on research and real-world experience, they offer a foundation of information and best practices that can significantly boost the possibility of effective change outcomes. Organizations may minimize risks, maximize resource allocation, and increase the likelihood that the targeted goals and objectives will be accomplished by aligning their change initiatives with accepted theories.

Change theories, while significant, also stress the significance of employee involvement and engagement in the change process. They understand that people should be actively involved in and empowered by organizational transformation since they are vital stakeholders. Organizations may develop a sense of ownership, commitment, and cooperation by embracing employee viewpoints, feedback, and engagement, eventually boosting the effectiveness and durability of change projects.

Five Change Management Models Used for Organizational Transformation

When implementing a change management theory, organizations must establish clear company goals or desired outcomes; what areas need transformation? If the organization's culture responds well or not to change. These questions help to identify the best change management theory that meets the company's needs and expectations. For this chapter, the five main models we'll look at are Lewin's Change Management Model, Kotter's 8-Step Model for Change, Prosci's ADKAR Change Management Model, Kübler-Ross Change Curve and Bridges Transition Model.

Lewin's Change Management Model: Many specialists regard Lewin's Change Management Model as one of the founders of organizational development, social psychology, and change management. He made significant contributions to the theories of change management, a three-step framework that aids businesses in understanding and successfully managing change. The "unfreeze, change, refreeze" model is another name for it (Errida & Lotfi, 2021).

The first stage, "Unfreeze," entails getting people and the organization ready for change by helping them let go of outdated attitudes, behaviours, and ways of doing things. This phase involves raising awareness of the need for change, developing a sense of urgency, and dealing with potential resistance or fear (Lewin, 1951).

The actual transition and execution of the intended change occur in "Change," the following phase. This stage entails implementing new procedures, policies, practices, or organizational structures while ensuring people and the organization adjust to the change (Lewin, 1951). To ensure a successful transition during this phase, communication, training, and support are essential components (Errida & Lotfi, 2021).

The third stage, "Refreeze," aims to stabilize the modifications and reinforce them as the new norm. In this stage, brand-new practices, procedures, or systems are ingrained into the organization's culture and established as the norm. Maintaining the change and stopping people from relapsing to old patterns, also involves giving people continual support, reinforcement, and acknowledgment (Errida & Lotfi, 2021).

According to Lewin's Change Management Model, it's critical to handle change resistance, includes and engage staff members throughout the process, and foster stability and continuity once the change has been implemented (Errida &Lotfi, 2021). The model acknowledges that to promote long-lasting change and organizational performance, it is necessary to unfreeze existing patterns as well as refreeze new ones (Lewin, 1951).

Kotter's 8-Step Model for Change: John Kotter, a famous authority on leadership, created Kotter's 8-Step Model for Change, which offers a methodical strategy for handling and carrying out organizational change. Companies walk the transformation process via eight steps (Rothwell & Sullivan, 2005).

The first phase, "Create a Sense of Urgency," is developing a solid argument or justification for change (Kotter, 1996). It seeks to foster a sense of agreement among interested parties on the necessity and urgency of change (Rothwell & Sullivan, 2005).

In the second stage, "Form a Powerful Coalition," a group of significant decision-makers and leaders is assembled to spearhead and aid the change initiative. This alliance aids in gaining traction, securing backing, and overcoming change opposition (Kotter, 1996).

"Create a Vision for Change," the third phase, entails creating an inspirational vision of the ideal future state (Kotter, 1996). This vision guides the transformation process and unites stakeholders around a single objective (Rothwell & Sullivan, 2005).

In the fourth stage, "Communicate the Vision," all organization members are effectively informed of the change's goals. Clear and consistent communication facilitates gaining support, understanding, and commitment to the change (Kotter, 1996).

In the fifth phase, "Empower Action," obstacles are taken down so staff members can move forward with the change (Kotter, 1996). This involves giving workers the tools, autonomy, and support to participate in the transformation process (Rothwell & Sullivan, 2005).

In the sixth stage, "Generate Short-Term Wins," tiny, attainable milestones and targets are established to show progress and instill confidence. Celebrating these victories aids in keeping the transition process motivated and on track (Kotter, 1996).

In the seventh stage, "Consolidate Gains and Produce More Change," companies use the momentum and advancement already made to propel change even further (Kotter, 1996). This entails finding different areas for development and carrying out and ingraining change activities (Rothwell & Sullivan, 2005).

The last phase, "Anchor the Changes in Corporate Culture," aims to make sure that the improvements are sustained over the long term and integrated into the organization's culture (Kotter, 1996). To do this, it is necessary to integrate the intended change throughout all systems, procedures, and behaviours (Errida & Lotfi, 2021).

Organizations may negotiate the difficulties of change management and improve the likelihood of successful change implementation by adhering to Kotter's 8-Step Model for Change (Kotter, 1996). The model places a significant emphasis on the necessity of good stakeholder participation, strong leadership, and assertive communication (Errida & Lotfi, 2021).

Prosci's ADKAR Change Management Model: The ADKAR Change Management Model developed by Prosci is a popular paradigm for handling personal change (Hiatt, 2006). The model focuses on the five essential components people must take care of to successfully navigate change (Galli, 2018).

The first component is "Awareness," which entails making people aware of the need for change. This involves describing the justification for the change's necessity and possible advantages (Galli, 2018).

The second component, "Desire," is cultivating a personal drive and commitment to back and take part in the transformation (Galli, 2018). This may be done by addressing people's worries, emphasizing the benefits of the shift, and dealing with any reluctance or doubt.

The third component is "Knowledge," which gives people the knowledge and abilities they need to implement the change successfully. Ensuring people have the information necessary to carry out their new jobs or activities, involves providing them with resources, training, and education (Hiatt, 2006).

The fourth component, "Ability," focuses on giving people the tools they need to put the information and abilities they gained throughout the transformation to use (Hiatt, 2006). Making sure people are capable of executing the change successfully, may require offering coaching, mentorship, or continuous assistance (Galli, 2018).

The last component, "Reinforcement," is developing strategies to maintain the adjustment and guarantee its efficacy over the long term. This entails praising and rewarding people for their efforts, reinforcing new habits, and continually observing and assessing the change to handle any problems or obstacles that may appear (Hiatt, 2006).

Organizations may methodically address each change component and raise the possibility that change will be successfully adopted by adhering to the ADKAR Change Management Model. The model offers a systematic method for managing personal change, ensuring that people are informed, inspired, prepared, and supported throughout the change process (Hiatt, 2006).

Kübler-Ross Change Curve: Elisabeth Kübler-Ross first identified the five phases of mourning, which served as the foundation for her famous Kübler-Ross Change Curve. The change model acknowledges that emotional responses to change are standard. Business executives frequently take a rational approach to change while ignoring emotions (Kubler et al., 2014). There are five phases of mourning, according to the Kubler-Ross change model: Denial, Anger, Bargaining, Depression, and Acceptance (Galli, 2018).

Employees go through these stages out of sequence, and occasionally they go through the same feeling more than once (Kubler et al., 2014). The Kübler-Ross Change Curve demands the most compassionate approach of all the change management methods. Employees feel excluded from the transition without empathy and communication (Galli, 2018).

Bridges Transition Model: William Bridges created the Bridges Transition Model, a widely used paradigm for comprehending and managing the human element of organizational transition (Bridges, 1980). The transition process is broken down into three separate stages that people go through. In the first stage, "Endings," people confront and let go of the previous roles, identities, and ways of life that are no longer relevant. People may experience loss, apprehension, and resistance during this phase as they work through the emotional challenges of leaving behind established routines (Errida & Lotfi, 2021).

The "Neutral Zone," or second stage, is characterized by an exploratory and ambiguous mood. People in this stage may feel confused, worried, or unsure about their duties and responsibilities as they transition from the old to the new (Bridges, 1980). As people start to investigate new options and methods of operation, the Neutral Zone is a crucial time for experimentation, innovation, and adaptability (Galli, 2018).

The last stage, "New Beginnings," sees people accepting their new situation and finding stability and confidence in their new surroundings (Bridges, 1980). Aligning with new responsibilities, adopting new behaviours, and incorporating the changes into everyday routines are all part of this stage (Errida & Lotfi, 2021).

Organizations may assist people at each stage of the transition process, offer advice, and promote a seamless transition by comprehending and addressing the emotional and psychological components of change using the Bridges Transition Model (Bridges, 1980). This paradigm places a strong emphasis on the value of leadership, communication, and empathy in assisting people in effectively navigating change (Errida & Lotfi, 2021).

CHANGE MANAGEMENT APPLIED DURING THE COVID-19 PANDEMIC WITHIN THE FOOD INDUSTRY IN ONTARIO AND OTHER PROVINCES THROUGHOUT CANADA

Impact of COVID-19 on the Global Economy

The COVID-19 pandemic has had a significant effect on the world economy, leading to numerous disruptions and difficulties in several industries. First off, when travel restrictions and lockdown measures were put in place by governments to stop the virus' spread, the pandemic caused a considerable halt in economic activity. This led to company closures, a decline in consumer spending, and disruptions in international supply networks. Numerous sectors, including the hotel, tourist, and retail sectors, suffered significant losses and faced the possibility of bankruptcy (Hartmann & Lussier, 2020; Kuckertz et al., 2020; Sobieralski, 2020; Spurk & Straub, 2020).

Second, as companies battled to survive or reduce their operations, the pandemic caused a substantial surge in unemployment rates. Numerous industries saw job losses, particularly those that rely significantly on face-to-face contact. This, in turn, had a detrimental effect on consumer confidence and household incomes, slowing economic development even further.

The pandemic also highlighted the weaknesses in interconnected economies and global trade. International commerce flows were interrupted by border closures and travel restrictions, which decreased export-import activity. Supply chain disruptions, including shortages of essential products and components, impacted industries that depend on international sourcing (Spurk & Straub, 2020).

Additionally, several monetary and fiscal measures were put in place by governments worldwide to lessen the pandemic's economic impact. These actions included financial aid plans, stimulus packages, and central bank initiatives to boost the economy and maintain financial markets. Inflation and the long-term impact on public debt levels, however, continue to be worries (Fuchs et al., 2020).

Furthermore, the epidemic hastened the use of digital technology, remote work, and digital transformation. Businesses that could use digital platforms and adapt to remote work arrangements fared better throughout the crisis (Spurk & Straub, 2020). Digital communication tools, internet services, and e-commerce saw considerable growth as conventional brick-and-mortar firms struggled.

Overall, the COVID-19 pandemic has caused significant disruptions across businesses and economies, as well as a global economic downturn. Variables, including the availability of vaccines, the success of containment measures, and the adaptation and resilience of companies and economies, will determine the rate of the recovery process (Fuchs et al., 2020).

Direct Impact of COVID-19 on the Canadian Food and Drink Services Industry

The COVID-19 pandemic has had a profound impact on Canada's food and beverage industry. Disruptions in the global and domestic supply chains, coupled with border closures and transportation restrictions, have led to challenges in sourcing and distributing ingredients and raw materials (Hartmann & Lussier, 2020; Kuckertz et al., 2020; Sobieralski, 2020; Spurk & Straub, 2020). Consumer behaviour has also shifted, with a decline in restaurant dining and a significant increase in home cooking and online food delivery services. The closure of food service establishments due to lockdown measures has resulted in financial struggles, reduced revenue, and job losses (Spurk & Straub, 2020). Additionally, businesses have had to implement strict safety and hygiene measures, incurring additional costs. Despite the challenges, many food and beverage establishments have adapted by embracing online ordering and delivery services, investing in technology, and collaborating with government support programs to navigate the changing landscape and recover from the impacts of the pandemic (Spurk & Straub, 2020).

As a result of the COVID-19 pandemic, government interventions were undertaken in March 2020 and continued throughout subsequent months. As previously mentioned, during that time, provinces limited access to and closed non-essential companies. Many companies were adversely affected by these requirements, notably those in the food services and drinking establishments subsector, which was one of the most hit by public safety measures. Since then, the sector has faced several obstacles, which have been worsened by the necessity to adjust in the face of recurrent re-openings and shutdowns due to changes in the number of COVID-19 cases around the country (Shood, 2021).

Employment in the subsector had plummeted 55.8% (-635,515) from pre-pandemic levels seen in February 2020 by May 2020 and remained one-third lower (-29.3%; -336,667) in December 2020 compared to February 2020. Food services and drinking establishments accounted for 5.6% of all employer firms in Canada as of December 2020 (Statistics Canada, 2020).

Food services and drinking establishments' actual gross domestic product (GDP) decreased by 39.5% in March 2020 and another 40.8% in April 2020, and many of these companies either closed altogether or functioned at a much-reduced capacity, exclusively providing take-out or delivery services. Indeed, more than half (56%) of food service and drinking establishment operators reported being closed sometime in April 2020, with 1% closing for the entire month (Shood, 2021).

By the end of 2020, the Canadian economy had been subjected to nearly a full year of COVID-19 effects. Food services and drinking establishments were adapting to the new reality by, among other things, operating at a much-reduced capacity, shifting to take-out and delivery services, laying off employees, and applying for government funding (Shood, 2021).

Compared to three-fifths (60.5%) of all firms, more than eight-fifths (86.5%) of food services and drinking establishments reported a decline in income in 2020. Over two-fifths, (42.9%) of food services and drinking establishments saw a revenue decrease of 40% or more in 2020, with Quebec (50.9%), Manitoba (47.9%), and Ontario (44.9%) having the highest likelihood of experiencing this level of loss. Compared to 2019, just a small number of food services and drinking establishments (5.5%) or 6.7%) reported a rise in income in 2020. In comparison, less than one-fifth (19.2%) of all firms saw a 40%

or more significant decrease in revenue in 2020, while more than one-fifth (20.7%) saw their revenue remain the same and almost one-fifth (18.1%) witnessed an increase (Statistics Canada, 2020).

CHANGE MANAGEMENT'S IMPACT ON THE FOOD AND BEVERAGE INDUSTRY IN OVERCOMING THE EFFECTS OF THE COVID-19 PANDEMIC"

With constraints on in-person eating and a customer aversion to dining-in, food services and drinking establishments have turned to contactless delivery and take-out and made efforts to extend their online sales capabilities. More than half (50.7%) of food and beverage establishments reported that they were likely or very likely to implement contactless delivery or pickup options permanently. More than a quarter (27.5%) of food and beverage establishments have an online sales platform or plan to build one. Notably, over one-fifth (19.4%) of food and beverage establishments earned 30% or more of their total sales online in 2020, more than double the proportion that did in 2019 (9.1%) (Statistics Canada, 2020).

Additionally, restaurants and bars have modified their business practices to comply with government guidelines and laws. These companies have raised their spending on safety measures for both consumers and staff, as well as on personal protective equipment. There has been an increase in spending on personal protective equipment and supplies in 87.8% of cases and on sanitization and cleaning in nearly all (96.0%) food services and drinking establishments (Statistics Canada, 2020).

CASE STUDY: IMPACT OF THE COVID-19 PANDEMIC ON FOOD AND BEVERAGE OPERATIONS IN A MAJOR SPORTS FACILITY IN CANADA AND THE STEPS TAKEN TO OVERCOME THE CHALLENGES

For the purpose of this case study, the organization under analysis has chosen not to disclose its name. To ensure compliance with legal requirements, the organization will be anonymized as Extreme Victor Arena X (EVAX). Notably, EVAX is a sports arena with a diverse range of income-generating activities, including food and beverage services among others.

The COVID-19 pandemic has had a significant impact on arenas worldwide, particularly Extreme Victor Arena X . EVAX experienced a complete halt in operations as sporting events, concerts, and other large gatherings were either cancelled or postponed to prevent the spread of the virus. This resulted in substantial financial losses, amounting to millions, for the venue, as it heavily relied on ticket sales and event revenue. The government of Canada frequently lifted and enforced the restrictions, which also meant that the arena reopened and closed just as frequently. This further resulted in financial losses due to perishable items going to waste and none perishables expiring (Fuchs et al., 2020).

As it affected the livelihoods of those employed in the sports and entertainment business, including players, entertainers, event workers, and vendors, the shutdown also influenced the local economy (Hartmann & Lussier, 2020; Kuckertz et al., 2020; Sobieralski, 2020; Spurk & Straub, 2020). For many, the lack of live events resulted in a loss of revenue and employment options. Due to a lack of events, EVAX furloughed 95% of its front and back-of-house employees and retained the remaining 5% as work-from-home support.

Before restrictions were lifted, EVAX was forced to take multiple mitigative steps to soften its losses and minimize its waste by preparing cooked meals with existing inventory for front-line workers and the homeless, plus returning unused non-perishable products to suppliers that managed to redistribute goods to supermarkets that were in dire need of supplies.

The reopening of EVAX when limitations loosened, and events eventually resumed saw major adjustments to new health and safety regulations. This required putting into action measures including lowered capacity, physical separation, wearing a mask, and improved cleaning and sanitization procedures (Fuchs et al., 2020). These modifications complicated the arena's operations and raised its expenses. The venue also introduced a cashless system by only accepting credit and debit cards and establishing a self-serve Kiosk for contactless transactions.

The overall mood and fan experience at events were impacted by the restricted or decreased turnout. Fan involvement had to be rebuilt through digital channels like virtual fan experiences and interactive elements since the lack of large crowds influenced the vigour and enthusiasm within the venues.

The COVID-19 pandemic caused significant uncertainty in the food and beverage industry, leading to high staff turnover and some employees refusing to return to work. One factor contributing to this is the uncertainty surrounding the pandemic itself, including concerns about health and safety in the workplace. Employees may have been hesitant to return to work due to the fear of contracting the virus or transmitting it to their loved ones (Fuchs et al., 2020).

Additionally, government support programs, such as Employment Insurance (EI) payments, Canada Emergency Response Benefit (CERB) and other benefits, provided financial assistance to Canadians who lost their jobs or experienced reduced working hours due to the pandemic. While these programs were crucial in supporting individuals during challenging times, they inadvertently created a situation where some employees might have been financially better off by not returning to work.

This phenomenon of employees refusing to return to work due to EI and CERB payments can be attributed to the potential discrepancy between their income from work and the financial support they receive through these programs. It created a situation where individuals had to weigh the financial benefits of returning to work against the potential health risks and uncertainties associated with the pandemic.

As a result, EVAX faced challenges in retaining and attracting employees, leading to higher staff turnover rates. EVAX had to navigate these complexities by implementing safety measures, providing clear communication about workplace safety protocols, and implementing strategies to incentivize employees to return to work, such as offering additional benefits or addressing concerns related to health and safety, plus utilizing multiple agency support staff for events.

CHANGE MANAGEMENT MODELS USED BY EVAX FOR TRANSFORMATION

The changes in the food and beverage business brought on by COVID-19 were addressed by EVAX using the following two change management models:

Lewin's Change Management Approach: The three-step procedure of Lewin's approach entails unfreezing the present state, implementing the required changes, and then refreezing the new state to assure its sustainability (Lewin, 1951). This approach assisted the company in evaluating and comprehending the current status of its operations, identifying essential adjustments to conform to the new health and safety guidelines, and successfully implementing those adjustments in the context of the food and beverage sector during COVID-19. The model highlights how crucial it is to instill a sense of urgency, involve stakeholders, and offer the assistance and resources required to deal with the difficulties brought on by the pandemic (Lewin, 1951).

Kotter's 8-Step Model for Change: By describing eight phases businesses should take, Kotter's model offers a methodical approach to managing change (Kotter, 1996). A feeling of urgency must be established, a coalition must be formed, a vision and plan must be developed, the change vision must be communicated, people must be empowered, gains must be consolidated, and new methods must be anchored in the culture (Kotter, 1996). This model assisted the company in creating a culture of adaptability and resilience, building cross-functional teams to drive change initiatives and communicating with employees and stakeholders effectively (Kotter, 1996).

In managing change, both models stress the significance of good communication, stakeholder participation, and leadership support (Spurk & Straub, 2020). EVAX overcame the difficulties caused by the COVID-19 pandemic by modifying its operations to comply with new health and safety standards and assure long-term viability in a constantly changing environment by using these strategies.

LESSONS LEARNT AND THE WAY FORWARD

The food and beverage sector has learned numerous vital lessons from the COVID-19 outbreak. It highlighted the value of adaptation and flexibility first and foremost. To comply with health and safety regulations, arena owners had to make immediate adjustments to their operations, including putting in place social segregation measures, improving sanitary procedures, and changing seating configurations (Spurk & Straub, 2020). It was essential to keep operations running through difficult times to be able to adjust to changing rules and consumer expectations.

The necessity of diversity was a further important lesson. Arenas had to look for alternate revenue streams outside of traditional ticket sales due to limits on big gatherings and low event attendance. This required them to broaden their menu to include takeaway or delivery choices, conduct online events or concerts, and collaborate with nearby companies to offer food and beverage services away from the arena.

Transparency and effective communication were other important lessons. It was easier to manage expectations and establish trust when there was open and regular communication with consumers, employees, and stakeholders (Sobieralski, 2020). It was easier to maintain open lines of communication and successfully resolve issues when regular updates on health and safety procedures, event cancellations or rescheduling, and any changes to operations were provided.

The pandemic also emphasized the value of technology in several sectors of the food and beverage business. To eliminate physical interaction and improve consumer convenience, the implementation of online ordering systems, contactless payment mechanisms, and digital ticketing systems became required. Technology adoption is crucial for providing a secure and practical client experience (Sobieralski, 2020).

Finally, the pandemic brought home how important health and safety are. The use of personal protective equipment, thorough sanitation procedures, staff education on health standards, and a high focus on employee and customer well-being were all implemented (Sobieralski, 2020). In addition to protecting people, maintaining a safe and clean atmosphere helped to restore client confidence and ensure the long-term success of the company.

Arenas in the food and beverage business may improve their operations, better prepare for upcoming difficulties, and give customers a secure and pleasurable experience by putting these lessons gained into practice.

CONCLUSION

In conclusion, change management is a vital strategic approach that organizations employ to navigate transitions successfully. It involves planning, executing, and monitoring changes to reduce resistance, increase adoption, and ensure success. Effective change management recognizes the importance of people in the change process and focuses on addressing their concerns, providing support, and encouraging their participation. It encompasses elements such as communication, stakeholder involvement, training and development, and fostering a supportive culture. By implementing change management practices, businesses can adapt to changing conditions, seize opportunities, and achieve desired outcomes.

The history of change management dates back to the mid-1900s, with scholars like Kurt Lewin, Everett Rogers, and William Bridges developing models and theories. Globalization, technological advancements, and socio-economic changes have further accentuated the need for change management. Factors such as regulatory compliance, market demand, technological advancements, social and cultural shifts, failure, industry trends, cost savings, organizational growth and restructuring, change in business structure, and globalization drive the need for organizational change.

The COVID-19 pandemic has particularly highlighted the importance of adaptability, resilience, and managing uncertainty in the food and beverage industry and other sectors. The pandemic has necessitated changes in operational practices, health and safety measures, and customer engagement strategies. Lessons learned from the pandemic include flexibility, diversification of revenue streams, effective communication, embracing technology, prioritizing health and safety, and cultivating strong leadership.

By embracing change management models such as Kotter's 8-Step Model and Prosci's ADKAR Change Management Model, the food and beverage industry can navigate the challenges posed by the COVID-19 pandemic. These models provide structured approaches to change, addressing key areas such as leadership, communication, employee engagement, and monitoring progress. Adapting to the lessons learned from the pandemic and applying effective change management practices will enable the industry to move forward, enhance resilience, and thrive in future disruptions.

The COVID-19 pandemic had a significant impact on Extreme Victor Arena X (EVAX) and the food and beverage sector in Canada. EVAX faced financial losses due to event cancellations and restrictions, leading to furloughs and economic effects on the local community.

To overcome the challenges, EVAX implemented strategies such as repurposing inventory, adjusting operations to comply with health and safety regulations, and utilizing digital channels to engage fans. They employed change management models, including Lewin's Change Management approach and Kotter's 8-Step Model for Change, emphasizing communication, stakeholder involvement, and leadership support.

Important lessons learned include the need for adaptation, diversification of revenue streams, transparency, technology adoption, and prioritizing health and safety. Implementing these lessons can help arenas in the food and beverage industry improve operations and provide a secure and enjoyable experience for customers.

EVAX demonstrated resilience by navigating the pandemic's changes and positioning itself for long-term viability.

REFERENCES

Bhasin, H. (2019, October 18). *What Causes Change in an Organization? 10 Factors Explored.* https://www.marketing91.com/change-in-an-organization/#:~:text=What%20Causes%20Change%20in%20an%20Organization%3F%2010%20Factors,8%208%29%20Merger%20and%20acquisition%20...%20More%20items

Bridges, W. (1980). *Transitions: Making Sense of Life's Changes.* Addison-Wesley.

Burnes, B. (2009). Reflections: Ethics and organizational change–Time for a return to Lewinian values. *Journal of Change Management, 9*(4), 359–381. doi:10.1080/14697010903360558

Burnes, B., & Jackson, P. (2011). Success and failure in organizational change: An exploration of the role of values. *Journal of Change Management, 11*(2), 133–162. doi:10.1080/14697017.2010.524655

Cummings, T., & Worley, C. (2009). *Organization Development and Change* (9th ed.). South-Western Cengage Learning.

Errida, A., & Lotfi, B. (2021). *The determinants of organizational change management success: Literature review and case study.* https://journals.sagepub.com/doi/full/10.1177/18479790211016273

Fuchs, G. E., Ness, L., Booker, J. M., & Fusch, P. I. (2020). *People and Process: Successful Change Management Initiatives.* https://scholarworks.waldenu.edu/cgi/viewcontent.cgi?article=1264&context=jsc

Galli, B. J. (2018). Change management models: A comparative analysis and concerns. *IEEE Engineering Management Review, 46*(3), 124–132. doi:10.1109/EMR.2018.2866860

Hartmann, N., & Lussier, B. (2020). Managing the sales force through the unexpected exogenous COVID-19 crisis. *Industrial Marketing Management, 88*, 1–30. doi:10.1016/j.indmarman.2020.05.005

Hiatt, J. M. (2006). *ADKAR: A model for change in business, government and our community.* Prosci Learning Center.

Hughes, M. (2007). The tools and techniques of change management. *Journal of Change Management, 7*(1), 37–49. doi:10.1080/14697010701309435

Kho, J., Gillespie, N., & Khan, M. (2020). *A systematic scoping review of change management practices used for telemedicine service implementations.* https://bmchealthservres.biomedcentral.com/articles/10.1186/s12913-020-05657-w

Kotter, J. P. (1996). *LeadingChange.* Harvard Business School Press.

Kubler-Ross, D., & Kessler, E. (2014). On grief and grieving. Simon & Schuster.

Kuckertz, A., Brändle, L., Gaudig, A., Hinderer, S., Reyes, C. A. M., Prochotta, A., Steinbrink, K. M., & Berger, E. S. C. (2020). Startups in times of crisis—A rapid response to the COVID-19 pandemic. *Journal of Business Venturing Insights, 13*, 1–13. doi:10.1016/j.jbvi.2020.e00169

Lewin, K. (1951). *Field Theory in Social Science: Selected Theoretical Papers* (D. Cartwright, Ed.). Harper & Row.

Michael, E. (2023, February 27). *Understanding the economic consequences of the covid-19 pandemic.* Economist Impact. https://impact.economist.com/perspectives/economic-development/understanding-economic-consequences-covid-19-pandemic

Michigan State University. (2022, November 22). *What Is Change Management?* https://www.michiganstateuniversityonline.com/resources/leadership/what-is-change-management/

Petrou, P., Demerouti, E., & Schaufeli, W. B. (2018). Crafting the change: The role of employee job crafting behaviours for successful organizational change. *Journal of Management, 44*(5), 1766–1792. doi:10.1177/0149206315624961

Phillips & Klein. (2022, September 9). *Change management: From theory to practice.* Retrieved from, https://link.springer.com/article/10.1007/s11528-022-00775-0

Ramos, D. (2022, November 9). *8 Elements of an Effective Change Management Process.* https://www.smartsheet.com/8-elements-effective-change-management-process

Rehman. (2021). *The Psychology of Resistance to Change: The Antidotal Effect of Organizational Justice, Support and Leader-Member Exchange.* https://www.frontiersin.org/articles/10.3389/fpsyg.2021.678952/full

Rothwell, W. J., & Sullivan, R. L. (Eds.). (2005). *Practicing organization development: A guide for consultants* (Vol. 27). John Wiley & Sons.

Shood, S. (2021, March 18). *Impact of COVID-19 on Food Services and Drinking Places, First Quarter of 2021.* StatCan COVID-19. https://www150.statcan.gc.ca/n1/pub/45-28-0001/2021001/article/00010-eng.htm

Sobieralski, J. B. (2020). COVID-19 and airline employment: Insights from historical uncertainty shocks to the industry. *Transportation Research Interdisciplinary Perspectives, 5,* 1–9. doi:10.1016/j.trip.2020.100123 PMID:34173453

Solution, O. C. M. (2021, February 2). *Importance of Change Management in an Organization | All You Need to Know – OCM Solution.* https://www.ocmsolution.com/importance-of-change-management/

Spurk, D., & Straub, C. (2020). Flexible employment relationships and careers in times of the COVID19 pandemic. *Journal of Vocational Behavior, 119,* 1 14. doi:10.1016/j.jvb.2020.103435 PMID:32382161

Statistics Canada. (2020). Food services and drinking places, April 2020. *The Daily.* https://www150.statcan.gc.ca/n1/daily-quotidien/200624/dq200624c-eng.htm

Team, W. (2019, August 4). *These are the 5 Best Theories of Change Management.* The Change Management Blog. https://change.walkme.com/theories-of-change-management/

Zada, I. (2022, July 2). *Organizational Change Management: Leadership Roles in Adapting New Norms.* https://www.ejbmr.org/index.php/ejbmr/article/view/1477

Chapter 15
The Lessons of Bhagwad Gita in Creating Transformational and Global Leaders

Pooja Sharma
Geeta University, India

ABSTRACT

Transformational leadership is a leadership process in which a leader inspires and motivates group members to affect positive change in an organization. Today, on the one hand, we talk about artificial intelligence and software-based decision-making styles, but on the other hand, we are dealing with stress, anger issues, lack of coordination and team spirit. It is becoming increasingly difficult to find a good leader and supporter in this artificial world and one of the main reasons is that we have become separated from our foundations, culture, and religion. Our religion, culture, and history provide us with numerous lessons in leadership and strategic management techniques. This chapter aims to highlight leadership lessons with special focus on Shree Bhagwad Gita. The Gita is not a religious book but is widely known and preached by people of all faiths all over the world. The Gita teaches us numerous strategies for managing and controlling emotions in difficult situations.

INTRODUCTION

The Bhagavad Gita, a sacred text that outlines the Hindu way of life, has a reputation for enabling everyone, whether they are an individual or part of a family, to live a fulfilling life. Additionally, the epic has been crucial in ensuring the success of organizations like industry, the state, business, and others. Any profession or organization that wants to embark on a journey towards enduring peace and ongoing development in all spheres of life should definitely look to the Bhagavad Gita (Brown & Moffett, 1999).

The Gita, as the "Song of the Lord," was revered by the Father of the Nation, Mahatma Gandhi, as a source of inspiration during the Indian freedom movement. He acknowledged the great inspiration he received from the practical approach taken by this devoted work of writing. His kind of leaders and intellects had a similar belief in the wisdom of using the holy book's perceptive approach to pragmati-

DOI: 10.4018/979-8-3693-1380-0.ch015

cally solve difficulties encountered every day. They voiced their astonishment at the pragmatic strategy espoused by the sacred book (Rao, 2018). The holy book is seen by its adherents as the guiding light that gives them the confidence to deal with everyday difficulties.

The Bhagavad Gita is a model of wisdom and a wealth of knowledge that promotes sound judgment and a deeper comprehension of morality. This epic scripture's characteristic helps people realize their actual potential and makes sure they are conscious of the greater purpose of their existence. Additionally, the openness of this holy scripture has enabled people to understand their success in the most realistic way possible. Nair and Rao (2016) hypothesized that the Bhagavad Gita has been crucial for individuals hoping to thrive in today's fierce competition.

Why Shreemad Bhagwad Gita Is so Valuable Even after 5000 Years?

The Bhagavad Gita is intended for individuals who desire complete clarity. It may seem as though Arjuna was the only one who understood what Krishna said, but that is false. It is meant for all people. When you are confused in your pursuit of the truth, eliminating that confusion can educate everyone.

The Bhagavad Gita has shown to be intriguing to individuals who seek the truth, strive for perfection, and are interested in an all-encompassing science of everything, regardless of caste, creed, religion, or nationality. On the Mahabharata battlefield over 5000 years ago, Lord Krishna, the Supreme Personality of Godhead, talked to Arjun about the science of life as it is currently portrayed in this sacred book.

What Gita Taught Us

The Gita gives us a meaning to the life. It demonstrates the value of human life and the fact that God has already provided for all of our needs (as evidenced by the proportion of humans to other living things in your home). Questions like "What is my position" and "What is my relationship with the Supreme?" What is the name of the new online series instead? What will we be doing in five years, or? People seem to be confused and the globe appears to be going through an identity crisis. Since we are naturally happy (Sat chit Ananda), which is our fundamental identity, we seek happiness everywhere.

Because this world is so unexpected and because we are in a prison (the body has conditioned the actual us-spirit soul just as a prisoner is kept behind bars), we must start preparing right away. Therefore, in order to pursue our actual goal of reclaiming our eternal sarape in the spiritual world, we must learn how to detach our attention from transitory objects and attach them to Krishna.

Despite the fact that our nature is eternal and we strive for everlasting satisfaction, we always look for satisfaction in things that are dead or fleeting, such as family and country, but our efforts are ineffective since we never experience permanent bliss. The fundamental source of happiness is selfless love, as evidenced by the fact that a mother can practise loving God even if she doesn't eat anything since she will still be happy to feed her child. If you could love God the same way, life would be complete. As transient labels apply to the body, such as "Hindu," "Muslim," "Rich," "Poor," "Boy," and "Girl," we must begin placing ourselves on a neutral base and approaching situations with objectivity.

Relevance of Gita in the World of Web 4.0

In today's technological world when we are taking about artificial intelligence and robotics can we really find a place for the holy book? Our world has undergone a significant technological transformation thanks to things like electricity, aeroplanes, and internet access. Because of technology advancements like artificial heating or cooling, many locations whose harsh weather rendered them nearly uninhabitable are now livable. The study of the parallels between the Bhagavad Gita's teachings and contemporary technology, notably Artificial Intelligence (AI), has gained popularity in recent years. The development of intelligent machines that can carry out tasks that typically require human intelligence, such as speech recognition, decision-making, and natural language processing, is the focus of AI, a rapidly developing field. AI has advanced significantly in recent years and has the potential to drastically change a variety of fields. AI research has advanced significantly in recent years and has the potential to change a variety of societal spheres, including healthcare, transportation, and education.

Technology affects our world in obvious ways, but it also frequently has an intangible impact on how we interpret the world. The main objective of those little modifications is to strengthen our sense of control. Technology gives us more power over the world around us, which is beneficial in certain ways. The greater potential, nevertheless, can lead us to fantasise that technology can make this planet of ours a paradise by enabling us to transcend mortality and overcome all of life's challenges.

These ideas are illogical because suffering and mortality are inherent in our physical existence and the material world we inhabit. Delusional beliefs like these are to blame for the mental health epidemic that afflicts our society today. The more we expect to be in control, the more upset we become when we aren't, which drives our minds crazy. Furthermore, the uncontrolled use of technology discourages us from discovering anything beyond the tangible. Knowledge in the form of ignorance is defined as equating a small portion of reality with the entirety. The materialistic cage that separates us from reality and irritates us with our mortality, which is a result of the age of technology, is what holds us captive. Gita wisdom emphasises that we are, at our essence, souls on a multi-life journey of spiritual progress, shielding us from a false materialistic worldview. Our identity and destiny are explained by the Gita's holistic worldview, which also gives us a full life purpose that makes use of all things, including technology.

Role of Gita in Creating Transformational Leaders

A transformational leader, according to Hater & Bass (1988), "goes beyond the self-interest exchange of rewards for compliance" and "involves strong personal identification with the leader, joining in a shared vision of the future." Transformational leader is more essential to a company since they think that an organization can only grow by investing in the personal growth of its members. Transformational leaders benefit employees because they give their followers' labor a compelling purpose. The interests of the collective come before personal interests, according to transformative leaders (Breevaart et al., 2013). Transformative leadership has an effect on how well employees perform at work, according to earlier studies (Mangkunegara & Miftahuddin, 2016; Eliyana & Ma'arif, 2019). The notion of transformational leadership has also come under fire, and some problems, such as being elitist and antidemocratic, have been pointed out (Northouse, 2007). This assertion has been refuted by other academics, like Bass and Riggio, 2006 who contend that transformational leaders can be directive or participative, authoritarian or democratic. We think that in order to manage environmental and organizational transformations, transformational leadership is crucial. A transformational leadership approach can encourage firms to innovate by including all stakeholders. This can be accomplished by implementing the leadership teachings from the Gita and assisting business leaders to navigate the fast-paced corporate world of today.

PROBLEM STATEMENT

Transformative leadership, is a style of leadership in which a leader inspires and encourages followers to bring about constructive change inside an organization (Kuknor et al., 2022). Today, we discuss artificial intelligence and decision-making processes based on software; nevertheless, we also address stress, problems with rage, a lack of coordination, and a lack of teamwork. The simple fact that many of us have drifted away from our roots, culture, and religion is one of the key reasons why it is getting harder and harder to find a strong leader and supporter in this artificial society. Although the Gita is not just a religious text of any particular religion, people of many faiths around the world are familiar with it and preach from it. The Gita provides us with several methods for controlling our emotions in challenging situations. Many researchers have analysed the holy book in the context of leadership and motivation lessons but there is dearth of literature that analysed the role of Bhagwad Gita in creating transformational leaders in the world of web 4.0.

SIGNIFICANCE OF THE STUDY

The Bhagavad-Gita's principles have been examined by readers from many perspectives. Although the Bhagavad Gita developed in a specific cultural setting with different tools, techniques, mindsets, and technological advancements from the present day, the concepts it expresses are universal. In order to demonstrate the spiritual intelligence of the Bhagavad Gita, this study article has been trans-created rather than translated or interpreted in the light of the role of Bhagwad Gita in creating transformational global leaders.

LITERATURE REVIEW

The Real Way of Living a Life by Gita

When the lord Krishna transform the Arjuna's mind from one of inaction to one of virtuous action, from one of infidelity to one of conviction and self-assurance it truly represents the triumph of Dharma. They are the inspirational words of bravery, strength, self-assurance, faith in one's own inherent power, grandeur, and courage in the lives of ordinary people who balance their personal and professional lives on a daily basis (Bhattathiri, 2004). This is the need of time when we need transformational global leader who are strong from outside and inside as well.

The Ultimate Management Lessons of Gita

As opposed to Aristotle's political theory, Benjamin Franklin's idea of a tool-making man, and Alvin Toffler's economic theory, our ancient Vedas see humans as God. As a result, any effort done on him should help him realise his boundless potential and greatness and this is what Gita taught us (Nalini, 1997). An organisation can achieve tremendous heights, fortunes, and a convincing position among stakeholders with the help of the powerful enabler of leadership. On the other hand, if the leadership is of doubtful quality, it may have a negative impact on the success of the same organisation. Organisations are constantly interested in learning how outstanding leaders are found, developed, and supported (Mahadevan, 2012). The Gita provides a direct view of Truth. It has been made an effort to highlight the Gita's extraordinary contribution to modern management science (Chandekar, 2012). The Gita is a distillation of the core Hindu doctrine and knowledge. From this philosophical base, a greater comprehension of effective solutions to management leadership problems and commercial practises is emerging (Natesan, 2009).

Gita in the World of Web 4.0

In the world of web 4.0, one of the main objectives of the board training has been to develop leadership. Numerous B-Schools all over the world have assessed their institutional vision in order to effectively respond to the demands of the changing industrial environment, and it is vital for its course programme to include initiative advancement material (Ghosh, 2015). Leadership is the process of influencing an individual's or group's actions in attempts to achieve specific goals (Muniappan, 2013). By allocating one-fourth of its annual learning and development budget to administration advancement, the United States of America illustrates the importance of developing company leadership (O'Leonard, 2010).

Different Schools of Thoughts for Gita

The Bhagavad Gita has had, and continues to have, an impact on a wide range of people from many different civilizations. According to Albert Einstein, the Gita had such a profound impact on him that once he started thinking about how God created the universe, he realised everything else was futile and took time (Mukherjee, 2017). A different school of scholars assembles a passage from the Bhagavad Gita as a leadership sutra and further defines the sub-sutras closely related to the main sutra. We've looked at some of the leadership exercises from writings by Nayak (2018) on subjects including Isvara, Jiva, Prakriti, Kala, and Karma. We discovered after researching the literature that many well-known leaders have been affected by the Bhagavad Gita's teachings. The personalities of the people reveal the qualities of a leader as they are described in the holy scripture. As stated in the article, a leader has a variety of attributes that are still untapped or, to put it another way, there have only been a few research on a leader's qualities that are related to knowing consciousness (Chatterjee, 2014; Roka, 2011).

Transformational Leadership and Gita

According to Burns (1978), "Transformational leadership happens when one or more people interact with others in a way that inspires followers and leaders to higher levels of motivation and morality. By attending to followers' wants, needs, and other motivations in addition to their own, leaders can act independently to alter the composition of the followers' base of motivations by satisfying those motives. Unlike transactional leadership, which is defensive or reactive, transformational leadership is proactive. Every time a transformational leader sees a need for change, he or she initiates a process that encourages others to embrace the change, thereby institutionalising it. Usually, resistance to change is present, but a transformational leader is able to develop a vision and unleash his entire self. Change is often always resisted, but a transformational leader is able to develop a vision and fully commit to it. As a result, the organisation makes a spontaneous commitment to accept the desired change. In their stage model, Conger and Kanungo (1998) showed how a leader assesses the status quo critically, works as a catalyst for change, sets ambitious goals, and fosters faith in them to elevate followership. In contrast to a transactional leader, a transformational leader does not utilise individuals to achieve his organisational goals. In fact, he is dedicated to the growth of others around him, inspiring them to imitate him. The ability of the transformational leader to alter the very perceptions and views of those around him allows him to influence the course of many people's lives. He has such an impact on people that natural transformations occur. Higher levels of the need for change, dominance, and self-assurance were found to predict transformational leadership by Ross and Offermann,1997. Despite the fact that this topic has received a lot of investigation, there is a paucity of literature on the significance of the holy book with special regards to transformational leadership.

METHODS

Hermeneutics, a qualitative research methodology, has been applied in the current paper. Hermeneutics is described as the process of interpreting a literary or religious work in the Oxford Dictionary. This methodology provides a solution to the issues facing the present world by carefully reviewing our ancient literature. Hermeneutics in the current day can be defined as the understanding, knowledge, and interpretation of the Bhagwad Gita by several scholars to draw vital information and interpretation to comprehend the leadership teachings for transformative and global leaders. The study's primary goal is to look into the traits of effective leaders as described in the Santana Dharma and Bhagavad Gita. One of the most important texts of Sanatan Dharma, the Bhagavad Gita, is believed to serve as a guide for human life and an outline of the substance of the Vedas (Kanapp, 2016).

RESULTS

A strong enabler that can propel an organization to greatness, prosperity, and a compelling stance among stakeholders is transformational leadership. On the other hand, if the leadership is of doubtful quality, it may have a negative impact on the success of the same organization. Organizations are continually interested in learning how great leaders are found, developed, and fostered, as well as the many qualities that make a good leader (Adhia et al., 2012).

Lord Krishna stressed the value of leadership to Arjuna as one of his main points. He did so in a very elegant and clear way, emphasizing the importance and function of leadership. The Bhagavad Gita suggests that spiritual power over the senses is the answer to the moral failings and eventual collapse of businesses, society, and families. Each of us, whether a boss or an employee, is engaged in his or her own conflict in a unique Kurukshetra. We can learn from the Bhagavad Gita, manage our senses and minds, and develop our spiritual strength. The Gita makes several interesting allusions to leadership qualities in a number of its chapters. The Bhagwad Gita's leadership lessons are explained in the sections that follow.

Leadership Lessons From Bhagwad Gita

The Gita's first lesson is to provide a good example for others to follow. Leaders are known for their unrelenting commitment to living up to their ideals. This is so that followers won't take a leader too seriously if they say one thing while acting in another manner. Instead, they will follow their leader's example and say nothing else and the leader will serve as a role model to his followers.

One of the main problems is that leaders do not now provide an example for this idea. They think they are above it, and in a few rare cases, they might even go so far as to think they are "above the law". Everybody eventually assumes a leadership role once in a life-long. As responsible parents, family leaders, and members of social or political organizations, we must all take this seriously. It all comes down to regularly living up to your beliefs in order to gain the trust and credibility of others. As a result, Krishna advised Arjuna to lead by example. He anticipated that everyone would follow their leaders mindlessly, intently observing their every move. Taking on the role of the task itself is the most effective technique to complete your work. Achieving this state of Nishkama Karma is the optimal working attitude because it prevents the ego and mind from dissolving via speculation about future gains or losses. The followers would see it as an example of how to obey the leader completely and obediently.

The second lesson is to learn how to maintain your equilibrium. One of the main issues that leaders deal with is their inability to accept the sometimes inevitable poor outcomes. Leadership works fine when everything is going smoothly. However, they quickly lose their equilibrium when some unexpected events occur for example- the loss of something significant. In order to solve this issue, a leader must manage the "world inside" of themselves rather than the "world outside." Without learning to find balance, excellent leadership is not possible. In the Gita, Lord Krishna emphasizes this idea multiple times. The world, according to Lord Krishna, is full of paradoxes; it will occasionally be hot and cold, and we will have both happy and sad periods. These are the life realities, and they will inevitably change. We will never be able to demonstrate leadership traits if we don't learn to tolerate them and live this life like a rollercoaster. If we examine today's issues, we may see that they stem from our failure to comprehend and encounter this great truth. People, young children, and so-called leaders find it difficult to comprehend that life contains both positive and negative parts. Huge expectations are raised by telling them only nice things would happen to them. When horrible things happen, people struggle to accept them and suffer from mental illness, feel worthless, have health issues, seek counseling, and in extreme situations, attempt suicide. The above aspect is essential to the quality of leadership. Everything here depends on how we think. This also goes by the name "power of positivity."

The power of positivity explains, what we think about is what we become. If we think favorably, nature will assist us in bringing this thing closer to us because our thoughts are a part of nature (Prakriti). A successful outcome validates our efforts and gives us the motivation to keep working hard. Regardless of the consequence, a person who never experiences a dull moment inspires others to live similarly. A company leader would be wise to adopt this way of life because it would inspire their employees to follow the example of facilitating communication. According to this school of thought, living a full, healthy, and happy life is something that is encouraged in every corporate setting (Sessa et al., 2007). Therefore, it is crucial to have a positive outlook since it will enable a leader to handle difficult situations and encourage growth in everyone. The proverb "No doer of good ever ends in misery" amplifies Sri Krishna's prophesy about acts going wrong. It asserts that, sooner or later, any positive and moral activity would produce favorable results. As a result, it is advised to act honestly and confidently, both for the benefit of others and for your personal happiness.

The third lesson is the principle of interconnectedness. In this modern world, individuality predominates as the standard of worth for life. Nuclear families have replaced joint families. The value of self-effort, which promotes excellence in studies and other spheres of life, is continually instilled in children. Individual rights are viewed by society as a crucial component of development and advancement. The best method to build a great nation appears to be to uphold each person's right to privacy and personal space in all spheres of civil society. Another feature encouraged nowadays is the spirit of questioning everything (as opposed to the spirit of inquiry) and looking for one's own solution to the issue. The development of individuality, either directly or indirectly, runs across all of these issues. As people become extremely sensitive to their belongings, wants, and requirements and start to demand or bargain for these things in life, the concept of individualism quickly transforms into selfishness. Due to the difficulty of practicing give and take, this will eradicate the culture of sharing. The primary driver behind all of our behaviors in the modern era has simply been what's in it for me and how this will serve me.

The Gita's fourth lesson is to find contentment in life. We always pursue our unending desires throughout our lives. However, the Gita teaches us how to find real happiness in life. Because only once we are content in our lives do we consider more broadly and long-term. Otherwise, our needs for ourselves will entrap us. It teaches us to maintain our composure and equilibrium in all aspects of life. Because if one's mind is at peace, one acts morally at work, which furthers the cause of inner peace, and one leads contentious lives, which defines success in its truest sense.

The fifth lesson is about self-actualization, which is one of the fundamental qualifications for a good company leader. The process of self-actualization gives a person a thorough SWOT examination of himself. Peace is the route to self-realization. The fundamental prerequisite for making original and moral decisions is inner peace. To achieve peace, mediation is a requirement. There will be a delight (utsah and umanga) in carrying out any task when one is at peace while doing it. Peace will arise from these others, and ultimately, experiencing contentment is an experience. All the organs, including sense and action, work together well when the mind is at peace to complete a task with an intense focus on every level. Someone with mental instability won't be able to do anything because their time is less valuable. The first step to calming the mind is meditation, which is prevalent in every dharma. A person with an unstable mind will be powerless to do anything because less valuable decision-making, strategy formulation, resource deployment, etc. can be done when this happens.

The sixth lesson focuses on vision, farsightedness, or the capacity for future prediction. A leader should be able to perceive the future and have a long-sighted vision, according to Gita. In order to plan ahead and safeguard his supporters and organizations from any warm tragedy. The world's most prosperous individuals and organizations have these characteristics. A mindset that can only grasp up to a particular point is the result of having a limited perspective, focusing on short-term gains, and having a self-centered approach (Purdy & Dupey, 2005). A leader who adopts this approach in life can never succeed.

Gita's seventh lesson focuses on the value of teamwork for leaders. A team of devoted and effective employees is necessary for a leader to succeed. No leader can accomplish organizational objectives without good, devoted followers who will stand by him in any circumstance. Here, there is mutual trust between the two parties because the followers will only have complete faith in their leader. According to certain studies, narcissistic leaders can be classed as those who work alone (Resick et al., 2009). However, leaders that look out for others and keep their followers close to them are sure to maximize shareholder wealth.

The eighth lesson is to always choose the right path. A leader must be courageous and determined in his beliefs and ideologies in order to do this. In any case, a leader should make the best decision. In the corporate world, we have encountered sticky situations very frequently, but this lesson teaches us to pick the right one and prioritize ethics over pragmatic considerations. A leader occasionally needs to make some difficult decisions. Although his people may not readily accept these decisions, the leader is confident in its long-term success. For instance, in medical science, doctors choose to do painful surgeries because they are necessary to achieve their goals. Alternatively, we could say that using violence to uphold the law is acceptable. As correctly stated by Runkle 1976, Violence that serves a greater purpose, is not at all violence. The leader must set an example by punishing the wrongdoer in a corporate context as well, or else the error, which went unpunished, would set the wrong precedent and encourage others to do the same. The correct degree of punishment, on the other hand, would serve as a deterrence for others to copy and for the defaulter to refrain from repeating it. Fighting for what one believes and justifies is not a fault, but rather a quality of a strong leader. So, if a manager or leader has disciplined the wrongdoer, they shouldn't feel miserable about it. Setting the appropriate examples is crucial for the success of the company (Prabhavananda & Isherwood, 1954).

The ninth lesson is to avoid being drawn into the "I" and power game. One shouldn't get drunk on power after making tiny gains. Instead of becoming caught up in power and glory, one should concentrate on constant learning and action. Selfless leadership is another term that is frequently used to describe this type of learning. In the Gita, Lord Krishna introduced the idea of self-sacrifice, which is defined as the act of working for the larger good by unconditionally aiding others (Piper, 1954). Because it leads to inner calm and insight, he foresaw that it is the best form of devotion and the best means of reaching spirituality and establishing a connection with the Supreme Lord. True leaders are distinguished from those who only provide lip service via selfless effort. Since Lord Krishna is aware of their careful and devoted work, they make an effort to follow the instructions he gave Arjuna for waking his soul and distancing himself from those emotions that were getting in the way of him carrying out his duty. Since it causes people to never feel content in life, gratification is a vice that should be avoided at all costs (Srirangarajan & Bhaskar, 2011). In addition to selflessness, Motivation is the secret to going the extra mile if one wishes to pursue more achievements in life (Pargament, 2013). Consequently, a leader needs to be an effective motivator. A corporate leader should never stop inspiring his staff to achieve the organization's objectives.

The last and most relevant lesson in the world of Artificial Intelligence is the principle of detachment, which entails letting go of attachments to the outcomes of one's activities, is another crucial idea in the Bhagavad Gita. This serves as a crucial reminder for people working in the field of artificial intelligence because it is simple to become unduly fixated on reaching particular results or objectives. We can prevent being overly connected to particular outcomes and make sure that our work is constrained by ethical and moral norms by fostering a sense of detachment and concentrating on the process of building AI technology. The Bhagavad Gita stresses the value of self-awareness as well. The Bhagavad Gita also stresses the value of mindfulness and self-awareness, which are qualities that are crucial for people working in the field of AI (Bhagavad Gita & Artificial Intelligence, 2023). It is crucial to be conscious of our own prejudices and presumptions as we create increasingly sophisticated robots and to make sure that our work is governed by moral standards. We can make sure that our work is motivated by the larger good rather than just material gain or other narrow interests by practising self-awareness and mindfulness.

The Bhagwad Gita imparts wisdom about leadership in the form of some of the most significant lessons. The book essentially teaches readers how to remain composed and calm in any circumstance, which immediately aids the transformational leader in implementing strategic changes and handling challenging circumstances. To succeed in life in the truest sense, every leader and even the average person must read it.

DISCUSSION

The modern world is undergoing an unparalleled transformation. The future shift will be centred on people. Leadership is undoubtedly a difficulty when it comes to understanding the connection between people and change. Future leadership problems significantly rise when people, change, and emerging technologies are combined. Leading an organisation through change is the goal of a transformational leadership style. In its most basic form, transformational leadership is the capacity to lead and influence those inside a specific organisation while concentrating on a single, well-defined goal. We will undoubtedly need transformational leaders to serve as change agents as the world continues to change and advance through the twenty-first century. These leaders must be able to effectively guide and direct their subordinates through this transformation. Demand for transformational leaders will increase. In the coming years, there will be a huge demand for transformational leaders. With their kind, calming, golden touch, they will be changing the world. Just as evolution can occur even when no one is paying attention, transformational leaders can also be actively and purposefully developed. Based on everlasting values and moral precepts, the Bhagavad-Gita promotes a mindful and spirit-centered approach to transformational leadership.

The majority of present leadership practices, such as approaches to doing business and managing people, politics, economics, and international relations, were widely spread and used by our forefathers without being specifically labeled as "Leadership" practices. The practices and recorded knowledge from the Indian Vedas and Puranas are still widely used today (Gravity, 2013). The driving forces of the world are clearly speed, greed, ambition, and competitiveness. Consequences include a lack of morality and ethics in the workplace, which leads to dishonest behavior such as tax fraud, unethical hiring practices, unhealthy competition, improper codes of behavior, and other fraudulent actions. The more desires, the more disappointments there will be, despite the fact that these practices become an integral component of every company's decision-making process (Sethumadhavan, 2010).

CONCLUSION AND IMPLICATIONS

Leadership is the capacity to inspire a group of people to work towards a common objective. As a result, it is essential for a leader to have vision and look for opportunities. In the Bhagavad Gita, Chapter 7, Verse 11, Lord Krishna effectively explains the essence of leadership to Arjuna. "I am the power of those who have no desire or attachment to themselves. I am the virtuous desire in those who are not averse to righteousness, O Arjuna. A leader must have a strong sense of self excellence, which is gained through doing his responsibilities well initially. The Bhagavad Gita discusses the meaning and goal of existence. Finally, it discusses what a human being is. It discusses how self-realization is finally attained by humans and how karma is crucial in determining how our lives turn out.

The holy book Gita is an incredible source of knowledge and wisdom and today's budding leaders can learn numerous leadership lessons from the book which not only helps them in achieving success in professional life but also in personal life. The article serves as a catalyst for managers and leaders to encourage better decision-making in a challenging corporate climate as a necessary component of organizational excellence, which stresses the need to work with self-awareness and guarantees how one may make their stakeholders happy. Here, numerous interesting and practical leadership lessons from the Bhagwad Gita have been extracted using the hermeneutics methodology. These teachings could be highly beneficial for the leaders of today.

All the best efforts have been made to conduct the study in the fullest sense still the current study suffers from some limitations as well. First of all, because the interpretation of ancient manuscripts or literature is an art, it is challenging to formulate any hypotheses or standards for approving the interpretation of the text. The second major drawback is the likelihood that the researcher's subjective interpretation and originality may have influenced the study's substance. However, although other academics have mostly supported the background offered in this work on leadership traits and teachings, only empirical assessment of these leadership traits has not been established. Future researchers can assess the efficiency of these leadership attributes as an independent variable and can examine the link or effect with another dependent variable of the organizational elements, namely happiness, contentment, and productivity.

REFERENCES

Adhia, H., Nagendra, H. R., & Mahadevan, B. (2010). Impact of adoption of yoga way of life on the emotional intelligence of managers. *IIMB Management Review*, *22*(1–2), 32–41. doi:10.1016/j.iimb.2010.03.003

Bass, B. M., & Riggio, R. E. (2006). *Transformational leadership* (2nd ed.). Lawrence Erlbaum Associates, Inc. doi:10.4324/9781410617095

Bhagavad Gita & Artificial Intelligence. (2023). *Bhagavad Gita & Artificial Intelligence*. https://www.linkedin.com/pulse/bhagavad-gita-artificial-intelligence-dr-ing-srinivas-jagarlapoodi

Bhattathiri, M. P. (2004). Bhagavad Gita and Management. *Eubios Journal of Asian and International Bioethics; EJAIB*, *14*, 138–142.

Breevaart, K., Bakker, A., Hetland, J., Demerouti, E., Olsen, O. K., & Espevik, R. (2014). Daily transactional and transformational leadership and daily employee engagement. *Journal of Occupational and Organizational Psychology*, *87*(1), 138–157. doi:10.1111/joop.12041

Brown, J. L., & Moffett, C. A. (1999). *The hero's journey: How educators can transform schools and improve learning*. Association for Supervision and Curriculum Development.

Burns, J. M. (1978). *Leadership*. Harper & Row.

Chatterjee, D. (2014). *Timeless Leadership: 18 Leadership Sutras from the Bhagavad Gita, Wiley Publications*. Sage Publications.

Conger, J. A., & Kanungo, R. N. (1998). *Charismatic Leadership in Organizations*. Sage Publications. doi:10.4135/9781452204932

Eliyana, A., Ma'arif, S., & Muzakki. (2019). Job satisfaction and organisational commitment effect in the transformational leadership towards employee performance. *European Research on Management and Business Economics*, *25*(3), 144–150. doi:10.1016/j.iedeen.2019.05.001

Ghosh, K. (2015). Teaching and developing leadership in business schools: A multilevel evaluative approach in the Indian context. *International Journal of Indian Culture and Business Management, 10*(2), 178–192. doi:10.1504/IJICBM.2015.068169

Hater, J. J., & Bass, B. M. (1988). Superiors' evaluations and subordinates' perceptions of transformational and transactional leadership. *The Journal of Applied Psychology, 73*(4), 695–702. doi:10.1037/0021-9010.73.4.695

Indian Management Thought. (2013). *Gravity, The Great Lakes Magazine, 17.*

Knapp, S. (2016). *Importance of Bhagavad Gita in this Day and Age.* http://www.stephenknapp.com/importance_of_bhagavadgita_in_this_day_and_age.htm

Mahadevan, B. (2012, July). Leadership lessons from Bhagavad Gita. *Impact*, 13–16.

Mangkunegara, A. P., & Huddin, M. (2016). The effect of transformational leadership and job satisfaction on employee performance. *Universal Journal of Management, 4*(4), 189–195. doi:10.13189/ujm.2016.040404

Mukherjee, S. (2017). Bhagavad Gita: The key source of modern management. *Asian J. Management, 8*(1).

Muniappan, B. (2013) *The Bhagavad-Gita on Leadership Development for Sustainability.* http://www.siv-g.org/index.php/columnists/16-balakrishnan-muniappan/121thebhagavadgitaonleadershipdevelopmentforsustainability?tmpl=component&print=1&page

Nair, A., & Rao, N. (2016). Spiritual competencies for an exemplary organizational work culture outlined in Bhagavad-Gita. *Journal of Organisation and Human Behaviour, 5*(3).

Nalini, D. V. (1997). *Vedanta and Management.* Deep and Deep Publications.

Nayak, A. K. (2018). Effective leadership traits from Bhagavad Gita. *International Journal of Indian Culture and Business Management, 16*(1), 1–18. doi:10.1504/IJICBM.2018.088593

Northouse, P. G. (2007). *Leadership: Theory and practice* (4th ed.). New Delhi Sage Publishing Inc.

O'Leonard, K. (2010). *The Corporate Learning Facebook: Statistics, Benchmarks, and Analysis of the US Corporate Training Market.* Bersin & Associates.

Pargament, K. I. (2013). Spirituality as an irreducible Human Motivation and Process. *The International Journal for the Psychology of Religion, 23*(4), 271–281. doi:10.1080/10508619.2013.795815

Piper, R. F. (1954). In Support of Altruism in Hinduism. *Journal of the American Academy of Religion, 22*(3), 178–183. doi:10.1093/jaarel/XXII.3.178

Prabhavananda, S., & Isherwood, C. (1954). *The Song of God: Bhagavad Gita.* The New American Library.

Purdy, M., & Dupey, P. (2005). Holistic flow model of spiritual wellness. *Counseling and Values, 49*(2), 95–106. doi:10.1002/j.2161-007X.2005.tb00256.x

Rao, K. R. (2018). Mahatma Gandhi's pragmatic spirituality: Its relevance to psychology East and West. *Psychological Studies, 63*(2), 109–116. doi:10.100712646-017-0394-x

Resick, C. J., Whitman, D. S., Weingarden, S. M., & Hiller, N. J. (2009). The bright-side and the dark-side of CEO personality: Examining core self-evaluations, narcissism, transformational leadership, and strategic influence. *The Journal of Applied Psychology*, *94*(6), 1365–1381. doi:10.1037/a0016238 PMID:19916649

Roka, P. (2011). *Bhagavad Gita on Effective Leadership: Timeless Wisdom for Leaders*. Jaico Publishing House.

Ross, S. M., & Offermann, L. R. (1997). Transformational leaders: Measurement of personality attributes and work group performance. Personality and Social Psychology Bulletin, 23 (10), 1078-1086.Runkle, G. (1976). Is violence always wrong? *The Journal of Politics*, *38*(2), 367–389.

Sessa, V. I., Kabacoff, R. I., Deal, J., & Brown, H. (2007). Generational differences in leader values and leadership behaviors. *The Psychologist Manager Journal*, *10*(1), 47–74. doi:10.1080/10887150709336612

Sethumadhavan, T.N. (2010). *Managerial Effectiveness-A Holistic View from the Bhagavad Gita*. Academic Press.

Srirangarajan, G. S., & Bhaskar, R. K. (2011). Key dimensions of spirit at work—An Indian perspective. *Journal of Human Values*, *17*(2), 93–120. doi:10.1177/097168581101700201

Chapter 16
Leadership's Response to Change and the Influence Their Actions and Behaviors Have on Employees Throughout an Organizational Restructure:
Utilizing Transformational Leadership Practices

Gretchen M. Blow
Baylor University, USA

Amy Sloan
https://orcid.org/0000-0001-8576-6635
Baylor University, USA

ABSTRACT

Organizations in today's globalized world face challenges at unprecedented rates. Restructures are an important tool used to meet those challenges directly. Senior-level leaders spearheading restructures need to adjust quickly to change and be cognizant of the persuasive and biased atmosphere their actions and behaviors create for personnel. Change is a pervasive segment of business; those unwilling to adapt will continue applying antiquated techniques and fail to meet the needs of stakeholders. This chapter focuses on the influence senior-level leadership's actions and behaviors have on employees throughout an organizational restructuring in a medical educational institution. A connection is established between transformational leadership practices and employees' levels of morale, motivation, and performance. Additionally, leadership whose actions and behaviors lack components of transformational leadership negatively influence the working environment.

DOI: 10.4018/979-8-3693-1380-0.ch016

INTRODUCTION

In the medical education industry today, doctors may be more efficient than any previous generation of medical practitioners in the number of tasks they can accomplish at a given time. However, distractions can lead to lack of follow through on certain components and poor patient care, which too often causes medical errors (American Medical Association, 2021; Densen, 2011; McLearney, 2006; Stewart & Hocking, 2020). For doctors to act in their personal and their patients' best interests, they need to be able to focus on specific tasks at hand rather than give into distractions such as technological delay, staffing shortages, or inefficient workflows (Sawney & Niven-Jenkins, 2007). Thus, they need to have systems in place that allow them to focus on practicing medicine or doing medical research (Shah & Sharer, 2021) with a level of adeptness and willingness to make necessary changes to the administrative medical practices, advance research laboratories, and enhance medical education (American Medical Association, 2021; Bucknor et al., 2018; Sawney & Niven-Jenkins, 2007). Restructures are one such tool that organizations can utilize to transform their business into the sort of organization that enables physicians to eliminate unnecessary distractions and achieve the levels of efficiency required of their position (Endrejat et al., 2021; Schwarz et al., 2021; Turgut & Neuhaus, 2020).

Change is omnipresent, and organizations are unlikely to see that shifting anytime soon. Technology, globalization, the recent COVID-19 pandemic, and pressure to meet social responsibility targets are examples of recent phenomenon that have forced organizations to make adjustments to stay relevant and in line with their industry and consumer needs (Gierszewska & Seretny, 2019). As medical education organizations try to adapt to the demands of global trends and of their student population, resistance to change is one issue facing medical education today (Densen, 2011). Medical education organizational restructures that occur without the consideration of human nature and how humans react to change create resistance to change that impacts leadership effectiveness, employee morale, and company success (Stewart & Hocking, 2020). As resistance increases, the company's chances at successfully completing the reorganization decrease (Muluneh, n.d.). Additionally, as fears about change take seed throughout the workplace during a restructure, peers and/or superiors can have great influence over fellow employees creating an environment of mistrust, lack of motivation, and decreases in morale (Belschak et al., 2020; Kunze et al., 2013).

A strong association exists between successfully launching change or restructuring initiatives and leadership's attitudes and approaches to that change (Barasade, 2002; Ewenstein et al., 2015; Kemp, 2006; Pennington, n.d.; Purcell & Chahine, 2019). Companies can better prepare for restructures when they expand their understanding of the behaviors among their leadership that signal resistance among all employees, such as refusing to be compliant, having an absent level of support for the proposed transitions, or encouraging others to be defiant (Fullan, 2008; Grant, 2021). Organizations or departments, particularly in medical education, do have the ability to create strong, informed plans on how to best address resistance ahead of time. Moreover, a strong plan builds in safeguards to assure employees that the restructuring takes into consideration personal employment capabilities. Examining leadership's responses to change leads to a reduction in tension created within an organization as restructuring occurs.

The Problem

Senior-level leadership's demonstrated behaviors or actions create a trickle-down effect that negatively influences the attitudes and behaviors of their employees, especially during a restructure event (Endrejat

Leadership's Response to Change and the Influence Their Actions

et al., 2021; Purcell & Chahine, 2019; Stewart & Hocking, 2020). Often, negative actions and behaviors become heavily apparent throughout planned organizational restructuring. Being prepared for restructuring requires a strong senior management team who can cohesively navigate the change processes and function as true leaders by respectfully making an effort to understand others' perspectives (Creasey, 2020).

An organization attempting to prevent the negative consequences of change needs to take into consideration human nature and development. The purpose of this chapter is to explore the influence that senior-level leadership's actions and behaviors relating to change have on a medical education organization and its employees. Senior-level leaders who are unwilling and/or unprepared to adapt to the changing needs of their industry and their constituents will face significant company-wide obstacles. BlackBerry®, according to Adam Grant (2021), is a prime example of an organization that brought about their own downfall due to lack of adaptability. Research illustrates various negative outcomes associated with poorly managed organizational restructures such as what occurred in the BlackBerry® example (Creasey, 2020; Mattson, 2017; Pasmore et al., 2010; Zeiger, 2021). More importantly, the costs and damages of reduced productivity, tarnished company reputation, loss of income, and reduction in employee commitment to the organization become too significant to overlook and overcome (Jain et al., 2018; Muluneh, n.d.; Pasmore et al., 2010).

Increased employee turnover and loss of customer base are monumental problems for a medical education institution to resolve. When focus shifts because of resistance to change the overall missional goals of patient care and medical research advancement are halted. The institutions may ultimately be unable to overcome the issues caused by the restructure and change-related hiccups if left unaddressed (Campbell, 2014). Without an organization's commitment to a pre-planned company restructure, where all senior-level members have buy-in, the process can become a self-sabotaging movement rather than a tool for successful future development (McLearney, 2006; Pennington, n.d.; Zheng et al., 2010). Organizations and departments can bring about effective change on micro and/or macro levels when they preplan their restructures. As institutions identify their plans for restructure, they must consider all possible consequences of poorly facilitated change management (Canterino et al., 2020; Washington & Hacker, 2005).

Change management fails for a variety of reasons. However, resistance to change, through actions or behaviors, is a central influencer (Canterino et al., 2020; Creasey, 2020; Jones & Van de Ven, 2016). Prior to a planned restructure, companies should review and anticipate the complex aspects associated with change resistance and general human behavior (Jones & Van de Ven, 2016). Change managers experience a far greater struggle when the organization moves forward without anticipating and proactively seeking to mitigate resistance from its employees to the changes they introduce. A defining factor in determining whether a company's planned restructure proves successful or produces a weaker company is resistance to change (Fiedler & Garcia, 1987; Mattson, 2017; Turgut & Neuhaus, 2020; Washington & Hacker, 2005). Without an in-depth understanding of resistance to change, an organization will remain unprepared for the transitional process.

LITERATURE REVIEW

Need for Change in Today's Operating Environment

A willingness and acceptance of change, on an innovative level, is critical for any industry. Furthermore, organizations must generate a comprehensive awareness of their current aptitude for embracing change. Continuous modifications to economic, technological, psychological, social, medical, and scientific spheres create an obligation for individuals and/or organizations to alter their responses within different circumstances (Jetten et al., 2002; Szamosi & Duxbury, 2002; Washington & Hacker, 2005). Van d Ven and Pool (1995) suggest that change is the firsthand observation of differences in quality of state over a period of time (Angelini et al., 2021; Doeze Jager et al., 2022; Malhotra et al., 2020; van de Ven & Poole, 1995). Change is all encompassing and often happens quickly and/or abruptly. Due to those factors, change can interrupt production and ultimately results in something fundamentally different than before (Szamosi & Duxbury, 2002). The result of something brought about by change requires a level of support and open-mindedness from all parties involved (Alhezzani, 2021; Doeze Jager et al., 2022; Haesevoets et al., 2021; Jones & Van de Ven, 2016; Kanitz & Gonzalez, 2021; Szamosi & Duxbury, 2002; Washington & Hacker, 2005).

The socially responsible behaviors expected of present-day businesses require organizations and individuals to reconsider their traditional operating practices. Current research indicates that a company's responsibility to their customer base and to the planet itself has increased significantly in recent years (Gierszewska & Seretny, 2019; Purcell & Chahine, 2019). Changes in governmental regulations, increased consumer awareness, and other varying standards driven by social influences demonstrate the need for organizations to build relationships with their communities (Gierszewska & Seretny, 2019; Stewart & Hocking, 2020). These driving factors for change have accelerated the need for modification to business models within many industries. Practical business leaders understand the mindset of sustainable practices, conscious consumption, the development of strong relationships, and responsibility and acceptance of the social norms that change habitually (Gierszewska & Seretny, 2019; Purcell & Chahine, 2019). Technological advancements help them have real-time access to the social changes that will influence their business decisions.

Technology creates an opportunity for adaptability and advancement within any realm of business. The near endless potential for advancement associated with continued change and technological evolution suggests that technology should be a key contributing factor in how one conducts business (Hart & Fassett, 2021; Lardjane et al., 2017; Rashid, n.d.; Wolfensberger & Hogenstijn, 2016). Each element connected to a technology change has likely gone through several modifications before it is fully integrated into the global economy; these modifications provide organizations generous leeway in accepting the newer, enhanced, models, which means that they are not overcome with uncertainty as the integration of the technology unfolds within the company (Kaul & Weber, 2021). The additional benefit of adapting using various modifications becomes evident as companies can improve their strategic plans, develop safer measures for production, and enhance their connectedness to the global community (Gierszewska & Seretny, 2019; Purcell & Chahine, 2019; Stewart & Hocking, 2020). All these benefits demonstrate that the company takes responsibility for their business practices within local and global settings.

Organizations that are more readily prepared for change due to their existing infrastructure and adaptability position themselves for growth opportunities that may even be global in scale (Cavalcante et al., 2011; de Fatima Nery et al., 2019; Graamans et al., 2020; Kanitz & Gonzalez, 2021; Revoltella et al.,

2016; Schwarz et al., 2021; Stewart & Hocking, 2020). Research on global growth opportunities suggests that companies prepared for change have estimated higher positive outcomes in the global economy (Malhotra et al., 2020; Revoltella et al., 2016; Turgut & Neuhaus, 2020). The organizations that demonstrate an informed preparedness for change have the capacity to bend with the economic fluctuations and not become derailed when an economic crash occurs. Preparedness for global growth opportunities also places those organizations in stronger positions for economic recovery should an economic downfall occur (Ernst & Jensen Schleiter, 2019; Graamans et al., 2020; Malhotra et al., 2020; Revoltella et al., 2016). Mass instances of global growth opportunities most recently manifested when industries faced immediate need for change during the onset of the COVID-19 pandemic in 2020 (Shah & Sharer, 2021).

With the invasion of COVID-19, global growth opportunities became far more important to understand. The global health pandemic and its continuing effects have aggressively disrupted the lives of both individuals and organizations on a grand scale. The presence of COVID-19 forced organizations to face challenges not previously presented to any industry (Stewart & Hocking, 2020). Most enterprises were ill prepared for the catastrophic global emergency provoked by COVID-19 (Stewart & Hocking, 2020; United Nations, 2020). Although some businesses adapted quickly, best practice now requires any business to adjust previous practices to address the new requirements embedded within the safety measure(s) for protecting their employees from infection (UNICEF, 2020). Due to the complexities associated with the pandemic, organizations that fail to accept change regularly may experience the negative effects associated with their resistance to change for years following the triggering event (Stewart & Hocking, 2020; van de Ven & Poole, 1995). Medical education institutions are an exemplar industry for having a necessary, and consistent, need to adapt to address the needs of the learners and the needs of learners' future patients.

Medical education is also an industry that must constantly respond to technological advances (Sawney & Niven-Jenkins, 2007). The medical education field experiences a high level of scrutiny and accountability driven by technology through social media and critical medical advancements (American Medical Association, 2021; Heiser, 2019; Kanitz & Gonzalez, 2021; Kaul & Weber, 2021). Medical students have so many aspects to consider when selecting where they will study, and medical educators must account for those factors to ensure their institutions remain competitive. The motivation for selecting particular institutions increases as the applicants determine which schools will improve their future chances for advancement in their desired specialty areas (Merriam & Bierema, 2014). As a result, these schools need to utilize the latest forms of technology and promote their efforts for continued support of those advancements in the future (Pondicherry & Peabody, 2021). In other words, in an industry as rapidly advancing as medical education, institutions must foster a culture of continuous improvement. When considering technology, the ability to act quickly, appropriately, and responsibly on a global scale allows for exponential growth and maintained relevance within medical education institutions. Being prepared for and embracing change opportunities places an educational institution above others who fail to acclimate to progress. The medical educational institutions who fail to embrace change need to investigate who is placing barriers and why it is so strongly opposed.

Traditionally, human beings have not acknowledged the role change plays in their lives. Past experiences, environmental surroundings, and personal stimuli always manipulate their reactions and research offers multiple reasons for this cognitive response (Kelly-Turner & Radomsky, 2020; "The Relationship between an Individual's Margin in Life and Readiness for Change," 2003). Understanding how humans historically have managed change helps create practices for addressing those responses in the future.

How Humans Commonly Manage Change

Humans are historically weary about new environments, new people, and new ways of doing things. Most psychologists who study change resistance agree that the brain, in its most basic sense, actively protects from possible dangerous change (Amjad & Rehman, 2018; Elshout et al., 2013; Georgalis et al., 2015; Lensges et al., 2016). Evidence appears to confirm the notion that loss of control, uncertainty, and the ripple effect of one disturbance initiating greater problems over time are large influencing factors (Barasade, 2002; de Fatima Nery et al., 2019; Doeze Jager et al., 2022; Malhotra et al., 2020).

Recent research suggests that a high level of anxiety affects individuals when facing the possibility of losing control in a given situation (Barasade, 2002; Haesevoets et al., 2021; Kelly-Turner & Radomsky, 2020; Malhotra et al., 2020; Oh & Kilduff, 2008; Pennington, n.d.; Turgut & Neuhaus, 2020). Organizational change can lead to that feeling of loss of control for individuals who are not direct contributing members of the change execution team (Endrejat et al., 2021; Ernst & Jensen Schleiter, 2019). Jones and Van de Ven (2016) suggest that this perceived loss of control generates fear, which directly informs how someone behaves in social situations. Kelly-Turner and Radomsky (2020) found that increased fear of losing control leads to poorer performance, while those experiencing less fear often underestimate their ability to handle certain situations, essentially making them more stable and productive in given situations (Kelly-Turner & Radomsky, 2020). This research implies that those who feel they have less control over a given situation are less willing to accept potential alterations to their work life. The employee's standard level of functioning is pushed beyond capacity, and they become resistant to any change (Bartels et al., 2006; Jetten et al., 2002; Jones & Van de Ven, 2016).

Organizations can harness certain tools to help employees that feel insecure about change in their workplace. To reduce the sense of loss of control for employees, employers must help their employees navigate the uncertainty of the change process (Aarons et al., 2015; Bergh & Ngah-Kiing Lim, n.d.). One way senior-level leadership can combat this issue is to clearly define the anticipated outcome of the transition (Purcell & Chahine, 2019). Clear communication relating to the company's present state and desired future state allows for greater understanding into why the change has been proposed (Cavalcante et al., 2011; Pennington, n.d.). Without justification for the change, a lack of trust in the organization and leadership increases, which fosters distrust and discontent among employees (Gierszewska & Seretny, 2019; Purcell & Chahine, 2019). The negative response to any change is a normal human reaction, and leadership who try to force change on individuals only increase their employees' uncertainties (Campbell, 2014). As one employee's level of uncertainty increases, and their actions replicate their feelings, so do those of their colleagues.

When the justification for planned changes are ill-defined, the emotional and physical behaviors of humans directly influence those same behaviors of others around them (Barasade, 2002; Oh & Kilduff, 2008). The lack of definition and explanation for change creates a ripple effect, which Webster defines as "the continuing or spreading results of an action or an event" (Webster, 2021, p. 293). Any organization, but especially those in higher education, acts as a unique social network (Gurin et al., 2004). As the suggestion of organization restructuring develops, individuals will have triggered emotions connected to that proposed change. As the emotions transition into behaviors, they act as disruptions to the pre-existing system and send shockwaves on a larger scale to additional members of the organization (Angelini et al., 2021; Malhotra et al., 2020; Reger et al., 1994; Turgut & Neuhaus, 2020). Scientifically, the ripple effect is a multiplier, meaning that one incident may start small, but it will inevitably grow substantially (Angelini et al., 2021; de Fatima Nery et al., 2019; Doeze Jager et al., 2022; Oh &

Kilduff, 2008; Pennington, n.d.). One negative action, from one negative individual, can create turbulence systemwide. Broken systems then take a significant amount of time to correct. Moreover, those broken systems require targeted acts of change or complete restructuring to move forward effectively, further complicating and delaying the entire process for the original proposed organizational changes (Ewenstein et al., 2015). Education institutions are one example of a niche industry in desperate need of targeted actions of change.

A Need for Change in Education

As perspectives relating to how to learn, what to learn, and where to learn evolve with time, higher education institutions can only progress as an organization through acceptance of change. Educators who help students learn rather than "teach at" students encourage learners to take responsibility for their personal advancements (Hart & Fassett, 2021; Lardjane et al., 2017; Ormrod, 2020; Wolfensberger & Hogenstijn, 2016). In an effort to meet the shifting demands of the labor market and encourage personal growth, medical schools must be open to new ways of delivering education (Lardjane et al., 2017). An increased level of global connectedness between industry and education initiates an approach to growth that benefits all stakeholders involved (Hart & Fassett, 2021). As all stakeholders build their capacity for advancing the educational system, diversity throughout all industries increases. However, diversity in educational systems does not stop at the student level; it must spread to all layers of the institutions, including the educational materials. The institutions must anticipate the changing needs of technology, changing needs of their learners, and any global changes that might alter the trajectory of the future workforce. Recent world events relating to COVID-19 have demonstrated this need for change on an exponential level.

The arrival of COVID-19 influenced the educational progress of nearly every student across the world. Due to the speed and complexity of the pandemic, massive changes had to be made within the educational realm at an alarming pace (UNICEF, 2020; United Nations, 2020; Zhao & Watterston, 2021). Not all the changes were necessarily positive, but the need to adjust quickly became a matter of literal life and death in efforts to protect the instructors and student body from catching infection (UNICEF, 2020; United Nations, 2020; Zhao & Watterston, 2021). The immediate need to continue to reach students outside of the traditional classroom setting necessitated that institutions amend their traditional educational models. COVID-19 generated a plethora of opportunities for educators and learners to come together to rethink and redesign the previously limiting educational systems (Rashid, n.d.; Zhao & Watterston, 2021). Additionally, circumstances surrounding COVID-19 demonstrated the need for medical education specifically to prepare for the unexpected. However, "although the demand for online education is high, its effectiveness may be low as innovation in technology is far ahead of corresponding changes in pedagogy" (Merriam & Bierema, 2014, p. 193). The reality of a present-day outbreak brought light to medical education's need for flexibility and responsiveness in a changing world. The traditional technique of information only being presented to the students in a classroom can no longer be the standard practice (Densen, 2011). Historically, change throughout educational systems takes time (Hart & Fassett, 2021). Modifications can be challenging and therefore take a larger amount of buy-in when conveying the value of change.

Organizational Restructuring

An organizational restructuring involves an assessment of current practices to identify areas of strength, weaknesses, future potential threats, and the application of that information by an organization, or division within an organization, to make adjustments for moving itself forward (Appelbaum et al., 1998; Bergh & Ngah-Kiing Lim, n.d.; Ernst & Jensen Schleiter, 2019; Graamans et al., 2020; Kanitz & Gonzalez, 2021; Reger et al., 1994). Characteristically, restructuring is utilized to diversify and create alternate methods for conducting business (Georgalis et al., 2015; Reger et al., 1994; Taplin, 2006). To an extent, a restructure requires a fundamental change to be implemented through an incremental or revolutionary process (Reger et al., 1994). The pace at which a restructuring takes place fluctuates between industries due to the distinct characteristics of each organization.

Within any industry, companies are granted multiple opportunities to identify significant determinants relating to the micro- and macro-level successes and failures in the organizational structure. Pasmore et al. (2010) suggest that companies that possess a deep understanding of their goals and mission are better poised to accept challenges and thrive when change is needed (Appelbaum et al., 1998; Belschak et al., 2020; Bordia et al., 2011). Companies must move in the direction of alignment between their practices and mission and/or vision. That realigning effort can take place in the shape of a restructuring. The restructuring of a company also provides opportunities of another kind—staffing (Kunze et al., 2013).

Restructures provide companies with an opening to examine the attributes of the individuals in their senior-level leadership team. Most of the research on organizational restructures and change management suggests that senior-level leadership must possess a specific set of principles to ensure a cohesive transition (Canterino et al., 2020; Mattson, 2017). Research commonly found the list of principles include the following: stating one's case by explaining the need for change, taking it from the top while having leadership welcome the planned approach, including lower-level employees in discussions to ensure that no role is held at a higher priority than another, assigning ownership to specific tasks, accounting for subsequent subtle changes, and acknowledging the likelihood of surprises occurring throughout the transition (Canterino et al., 2020; Cavalcante et al., 2011; Mattson, 2017). Without the adoption of these principles by senior-level leadership, the company faces a higher probability of failing to successfully launch a planned restructure (Muhl, 2002). With these principles in mind, and a deep understanding for necessary change, an organization can focus on how they would like the restructure to unfold.

Experts offer five commonly utilized steps for effective restructuring: create a business strategy, identify current strengths and weaknesses, consider multiple options for re-design before selecting the final version, communicate the organizational changes to all impacted stakeholders, and adjust and modify as needed throughout the restructure process (Campbell, 2014; Creasey, 2020; Cutcher 2009; Erwin & Garman, 2010). Companies must continuously revisit the original set of objectives at every step in the restructuring to ensure cohesiveness for the project's entirety.

The components of a successful restructuring exist in exact contrast to those of a failed organizational restructuring. Researchers have attempted to identify the components for an organization to successfully restructure in most literature reviews and experiments relating to change (Reger et al., 1994; Revoltella et al., 2016; Stewart & Hocking, 2020; Taplin, 2006). Consistently, the following factors contribute to success/failure rates: leadership, mission and vision, timing, pre- and post-planning, methodical execution, and communication that provides transparency to stakeholders (Southwick et al., 2021; Taplin, 2006; van de Ven & Poole, 1995; Zeiger, 2021; H. Zhao & Zhou, 2020). Subsequently, companies need to be willing to fine-tune their plans for restructuring as the process moves forward. Without flexibility, the implementation teams cannot navigate unplanned changes and the team's poor navigation results in dramatic outcomes. Those outcomes demonstrate a lack of accountability by the implementation team (Washington & Hacker, 2005). Poor communication leads to a lack of understanding for why this change is needed and being executed within an organization (Zeiger, 2021), and that lack of understanding hardens resistance to change among employees (Washington & Hacker, 2005).

Resistance to Change

Resistance to change (RTC) can manifest in a variety of forms and can occur at any point throughout a transition or change process. A comprehensive review of literature resulted in the following definition of RTC: an unwillingness to accept or adapt to alternate approaches for doing tasks or acting in new surroundings (Bass, 1985; Belschak et al., 2020; Bordia et al., 2011; Campbell, 2014; Canterino et al., 2020; Cavalcante et al., 2011; Washington & Hacker, 2005). Research suggests that RTC is most found among managers or senior-level leaders, but it can also be seen in lower-level employees. Though, age and the amount of time spent within an organization are leading causes, they are not the only reasons individuals resist change (Ernst & Jensen Schleiter, 2019; Haesevoets et al., 2021; Kanitz & Gonzalez, 2021; Kunze et al., 2013).

Why people resist change: company-oriented resistance. Resistance to change can originate amidst an employee's personal reprisal against their organization (Von Culin et al., 2014; Zeiger, 2021; H. Zhao & Zhou, 2020). Whatever the root causes, some employees act decisively in their efforts to postpone or derail organizational change. Technical barriers, political reasons, cultural differences, lack of support, poor leadership, and lack of consultation act as mitigating factors for RTC directed at one's organization (Purcell & Chahine, 2019; Raineri, 2009; Reger et al., 1994; Washington & Hacker, 2005). Employees often feel as if leadership's desire for change occurs on a whim, and therefore the need for them to be participatory members is a waste of their personal energy (Alhezzani, 2021; Doeze Jager et al., 2022; Zheng et al., 2010). More than that, at its core, company-oriented resistance is a consequence of an employee's lack of confidence in their leadership or organization's ability to have a successful transition (Washington & Hacker, 2005). However, not all change resistance is malicious in its makeup. There are underlying, psychological reasons, for humans to be resistant to change.

Why people resist change: psychological reasons. Habits relating to RTC are developed and fostered throughout the adult learning process to cope with their current and future responsibilities within an organization (Alhezzani, 2021; Doeze Jager et al., 2022). Malcolm Knowles (1980) defined six key differences between adults versus child learners. Rather than following the historical approach of focusing on content (Merriam & Bierema, 2014), Knowles focused on the wants and needs of the learners and examined the development of adult learning over time. Knowles posited the following about adult pupils: they become self-directed learners, the learner's experiences shape their knowledge, their social roles determine what they need to learn, and they are more problem centered than they were as children (Knowles, 1980; Knowles & Associates, 1984). Knowles then moved onto how educational ambitions are driven, suggesting that adult learners are more internally motivated than externally and that adults need to know why they are learning a particular subject (Knowles & Associates, 1984). A learner's personal interest in the material being taught plays a role in how engaged they will become in a subject (Mezirow, 1991). If they have no intentions of using this information later in their lives, they are less likely to pay attention during instruction of the material.

Organizations should also consider Knowles' six assumptions of the learner when investigating RTC. Ultimately, the learner must be ready and willing to learn new things (Knowles & Associates, 1984). Analyzing the members of an organization who will enact change management can only provide additional information, which will aid in the transition process (Von Culin et al., 2014). Knowing that each person will have a different experience as the change process develops and is implemented allows the company to plan for outcomes both desired and undesired (Zhao & Zhou, 2020). Senior-level leadership can understand RTC if it recognizes the connections between why an employee resists and their overall learning process (Jain et al., 2018). Meaningfully, RTC often falls outside the day-to-day operational staff, and resistance becomes a deep-seated problem when it swells from within senior-level leadership. The level of anxiety that senior-level leaders project onto employees amplifies as it spreads throughout their team members companywide (de Fatima Nery et al., 2019).

When leaders resist change. Significant negative results appear when senior-level leaders resist change before, during, or after restructures. The most impactful results relate to the employees who collaborate with the resistant leaders. Low morale, lack of motivation, increased turnover, and poor work culture all reflect badly on a company (Coulter & Punj, 2013; de Costa et al., 2018; Doci & Hofmans, 2015, 2015; Durowoju et al., 2013). The reputation of an establishment can become tarnished when best practices are thrown aside as personal actions and behaviors influence those of the people they surround (Ewenstein et al., 2015; Fiedler & Garcia, 1987; Jain et al., 2018). Employees witnessing outward RTC see no value in contributing to a company that those around them clearly do not believe in (Jain et al., 2018; Johnson, 2020; Jones & Van de Ven, 2016).

To address change-resistant behaviors in their leaders, companies have several options to minimize progression of their actions and/or verbalizations against the restructure (Jones & Van de Ven, 2016; Judge et al., 2004; Kemp, 2006; Kunze et al., 2013). Creating a team structure between senior-level leadership and organizational leadership will empower leaders involved in the change process to set targets for their own teams (Fullan, 2008; MacGregor Burns, 1978). Allowing leaders the opportunity to share their own concerns related to the restructure gives these teams the opportunity to communicate concerns (Avolio & Bass, 2004; Bass, 1985). Fullan (2008), recognizing the importance of transparent communication for all organization members. In addition, providing leaders with specialized training sessions related to the restructuring of the company exhibits a company's commitment to their future within the organization (Muluneh, n.d.; Madsen et al, 2003). Those training sessions not only encourage personal development of the senior-level leaders but also foster the value in learning more about their staff by showing examples of the benefits to strong, personal, connections (Von Culin et al., 2014; Washington & Hacker, 2005). Organizations must always strive to produce stronger leaders within the company.

Leadership

Leadership can be defined in a variety of ways, but in its basic sense, can be described as set of skills and behaviors that influence one or more individuals (Canterino et al., 2020; Doci & Hofmans, 2015; Judge et al., 2004; MacGregor Burns, 1978). The essential elements of leaders who help develop a strong followership range from clear communication skills, problem solving, and ability to delegate when necessary (Campbell, 2014; Doci & Hofmans, 2015). Organizations rely on leaders to achieve a level of success through use of their skills and provide guidance to their teams so that all members act cohesively to resolve issues presented to them.

Leadership in business. The understanding of what it means to be a leader has changed drastically in recent years. Webster's dictionary defines a leader as "a person who has a commanding authority or influence, the principal performer of a group, or an individual whom directs others throughout their involvement in a given situation" (Webster, 2021, p. 191). The way leaders are viewed was altered by the global pandemic of COVID-19, (Haesevoets et al., 2021; Malhotra et al., 2020; Schwarz et al., 2021), and employees have built a level of confidence within themselves, which has reduced their tolerance for poor leadership (Mattson, 2017; Zhao & Watterston, 2021). As such, leaders of industry and education need to possess an all-embracing sense of empathy and mindfulness for what their employees require for them to become and to remain strong members of the organization (Stewart & Hocking, 2020; Von Culin et al., 2014).

Some scholars argue that certain people naturally possess attributes or personalities favorable to leadership. However, most researchers agree all leaders must make a very conscious decision to further develop their leadership skills (Candy, 1991; Canterino et al., 2020; Cavalcante et al., 2011; Endrejat et al., 2021; Turgut & Neuhaus, 2020). They purposefully lead by example, unremittingly find ways to further their own education and personal development, take accountability for their actions and decisions, and choose to do the right thing for the largest number of people (Cutcher, 2009; Durowoju et al., 2013; Eisenbeiss et al., 2008). In contrast, individuals often identified as poor leaders have a sense of selfishness, lack focus and drive towards common goals, and have little empathy for their team members (Campbell, 2014; Endrejat et al., 2021; Ernst & Jensen Schleiter, 2019). Weak leaders lack the aptitude to foster positive change in other individuals or institutions on a grand scale (Eisenbeiss et al., 2008).

Transformational leadership. Transformational leaders collaborate cohesively with their team members to create a unified mission and vision on any project they embark on. Transformational leaders can extend the impact of their successes and failures beyond themselves to their employees. According to Burns (1978) and Bass (1985), strong leaders place significant value in learning from others in addition to extending their mentorship efforts towards an individual or group. The theory of transformational leadership indicates that effective leaders work beyond their personal interests and include followers in the process of identifying needed change (Angelini et al., 2021; Bass, 1985; Endrejat et al., 2021; Graamans et al., 2020; MacGregor Burns, 1978). The leader and their group of followers work simultaneously to construct a positive outcome. The leader must take responsibility to facilitate, motivate, and foster a collective appreciation for their institution and the preferred outcome of a change (Angelini et al., 2021; Bass, 1985; Endrejat et al., 2021; MacGregor Burns, 1978). Supportive relationships emerge as employees are encouraged to openly think for themselves (Ernst & Jensen Schleiter, 2019; Graamans et al., 2020). Furthermore, strong relationships foster transformational thinkers among employees and other leaders. Leaders become more effective, and the potential for positively influencing one another grows with time (Angelini et al., 2021; Eisenbeiss et al., 2008; Endrejat et al., 2021; Turgut & Neuhaus, 2020).

Leadership embracing change. Leaders who embrace change can harness a ripple effect to spread this desired behavior (Graamans et al., 2020; Haesevoets et al., 2021; Jain et al., 2018; Jones & Van de Ven, 2016; Judge et al., 2004; Schwarz et al., 2021). A positive attitude towards organizational restructure ignites opportunities for growth within the organization, promotes skill enhancements, encourages innovation, and confirms the leader's belief in the quality of work that the staff produce (Kunze et al., 2013). A senior-level leader's buy-in to change reinforces the concept that change is good for both individuals and the organization (Lambe et al., 2018). As leaders embrace change, they foster an appreciation for the company which mitigates the typical decrease in staff morale observed during a restructure (Ernst & Jensen Schleiter, 2019; Mattson, 2017; Muluneh, n.d.).

Clear communication by leadership realigns the personal goals of individual employees with the goals of the institution. Even if staff show concern for the transitions ahead, they are more patient while waiting for the transition to be completed (Endrejat et al., 2021; Graamans et al., 2020; Muluneh, n.d.; Nadim & Singh, 2019; Turgut & Neuhaus, 2020). The trust employees have in their senior leaders who embrace change reduces the employee's resistant actions and behaviors, which leads to continued quality of work by all members of the team during the change progression (Oreg, 2003). However, despite all available research and literature, many organizations ignore the value of strong change management and fail to address resistance early on (Pardo del Val & Martinez Fuentes, 2003; Pasmore et al., 2010).

Costs Associated with Poor Change Management

When institutions do not prepare for organizational change, huge costs can ensue and undermine an organization to the point of total ruin. Creasey (2020) argued that two major costs occur when change transitions are poorly handled: costs that hit on an organizational level and cost directly linked to projects (Pasmore et al., 2010; Reger et al., 1994; van de Ven & Poole, 1995). At an organizational level, the quality of work falters, valuable employees may leave, and productivity nosedives (Fiedler & Garcia, 1987). Financially speaking, costs incurred through RTC impact the well-being of the institution, create deficits in income, and create debts not previously experienced (Hellman et al., 2020). As a result, stakeholders may experience increased stress levels and decreased trust, ultimately lowering the chances for successful implantation of future change (Georgalis et al., 2015). Specific project-related costs result in surpassing approved budgets, project delays, and an increased need for immediate project redesigns (Creasey, 2020). Project-level costs often are linked to the human component of business (Lensges et al., 2016). Staff become resistant to change, staff turnover amplifies, and trust in the project and company weakens (Mattson, 2017). Human costs are even greater when poor change practices take place in the field of medical education. Healthcare workers are more frequently held responsible for, and are required to openly give explanation for, their patient outcomes at work (Exworthy et al., 2019).

As an organizational restructuring takes place, medical professionals are expected to develop and maintain the expertise needed to treat patients and act accordingly in professional settings. Though planned change allows for medical learners to prepare and respond appropriately to the needs of the patients, unplanned or unpredictable change can be difficult to navigate and handle correctly (Al-Abri, 2007; American Medical Association, 2021; Exworthy et al., 2019; Penny et al., 2014; Sawney & Niven-Jenkins, 2007). Educational institutions house large numbers of students and employees who are unlikely to perform well if change is not effectively managed (Nadim & Singh, 2019). The American Medical Association (2021) states that global change is happening rapidly. If medical institutions neglect the urgency for adaptability, that patient-centered care will cease to exist. Modifications to the institutions accountable for educating healthcare providers are more often identified as irresponsible when they lack the know-how and aptitude for progressing at the same rate as the science that drives patient's treatment plans (American Medical Association, 2021; Arrizabalaga et al., 2014; Sawney & Niven-Jenkins, 2007).

Medical education institutions must think beyond the students they are educating. Streamlining administrative processes for staff and clinical practices has a direct and positive influence on patient care (American Medical Association, 2021; Exworthy et al., 2019; Graamans et al., 2020). Consistency and accountability in patient settings allow the providers extra time to increase their knowledge base and to conduct research (de Costa et al., 2018; Exworthy et al., 2019; Graamans et al., 2020). When doctors can focus more time on their own research and honing surgical techniques, a patient's chance of survival increases through advancements. Optimizing the efficiency of medical education and training today can mean the difference between life and death for the patients of tomorrow. By mitigating RTC as restructurings take place, educational institutions become one step closer to fully optimizing their organization.

Synthesis of Literature

Taken as a whole, resistant actions and behaviors throughout an organizational restructuring can have a damaging impact on the future success of a company. Arguments relating to the significant role RTC plays in successful transitions emphasize eight central themes (Arrizabalaga et al., 2014; Bergh & Ngah-Kiing Lim, n.d.; Cavalcante et al., 2011; Ewenstein et al., 2015; Grant, 2021; Kemp, 2006; Pellicer, 2008). These themes can be broken down into two groups: the relationship between humans or organizations when dealing with change and educational institutions' relationship with change.

Both individual people and whole organizations can face uncertainty and resistance when confronted with necessary changes, and the first four themes from this literature review highlight key intersections between change and change response. Theme one describes that humans are instinctively hardwired to resist change (Grant, 2021; Kelly-Turner & Radomsky, 2020; Kemp, 2006; Mezirow, 1978; Madsen et al, 2003). Theme two discusses how adaptability and acceptance of change is a must for any organization, within any industry, that seeks long-term success (Brown & Keep, 2018; Eisenbeiss et al., 2008; Gierszewska & Seretny, 2019; Purcell & Chahine, 2019; Revoltella et al., 2016; van de Ven & Poole, 1995). Theme three, relating to planned organizational restructurings, suggests that regardless of their level of complexity, that restructurings serve as a valuable tool for organizations as they provide substantial opportunities to evaluate the current situation and re-envision future openings for development (Bergh & Ngah-Kiing Lim, n.d.; Doeze Jager et al., 2022; Grant, 2021; Kemp, 2006; Lardjane et al., 2017; van de Ven & Poole, 1995). Theme four shows that all levels of employees in an organization can exhibit RTC and an unwillingness to adapt through actions of behaviors (Campbell, 2014; Cavalcante et al., 2011; Ewenstein et al., 2015; Kelly-Turner & Radomsky, 2020; Pennington, n.d.; Purcell & Chahine, 2019).

The secondary set of themes from this literature review highlight the negative impacts that occur when educational institutions fail to confront change or to create the ownership their staff must have to accept change. Theme five suggests educational institutions have a responsibility to embrace change and advance their learners' capabilities (Bergh & Ngah-Kiing Lim, n.d.; Brown & Keep, 2018; Densen, 2011; Gurin et al., 2004; Hart & Fassett, 2021; Kaul & Weber, 2021). Theme six argues that traditional mindsets about how educational systems should be structured can create a slow-to-adapt mindset because historically the processes have proven successful (Al-Abri, 2007; American Medical Association, 2021; Hart & Fassett, 2021; Kaul & Weber, 2021; UNICEF, 2020; United Nations, 2020). Theme seven states learners in educational systems and employees throughout organizations are already challenging traditional leadership styles (Bergh & Ngah-Kiing Lim, n.d.; Campbell, 2014; Campos, 2020; Lardjane et al., 2017; Penny et al., 2014; Purcell & Chahine, 2019; Stewart & Hocking, 2020). Finally theme eight shows how any educational system or organization's future becomes unpredictable when personnel and financial costs accrued from poorly managed restructures come into play (Kelly-Turner & Radomsky, 2020; Pondicherry & Peabody, 2021; Purcell & Chahine, 2019; Sawney & Niven-Jenkins, 2007; Stewart & Hocking, 2020).

History and psychology demonstrate that humans are naturally resistant to change and that if an industry neglects the human side of business, then a planned restructure is likely to have a negative outcome, and the organization can potentially end up worse off than before the restructure. Senior-level leaders play an essential role in making a restructuring successful in any industry, especially in medical education where senior-level leaders are often those personally responsible for the student education. If medical students fail, the future of healthcare fails, patient outcomes become a critical problem, and scientific advancement halts. The ripple effect continues, and progress stops. Understanding RTC is important for any organization that strives to succeed in the global economy, and monitoring senior-level leadership's approach to restructures is the determining factor for whether organization will succeed.

Transformational Leadership Theory

The previous review of literature intended to analyze the potential outcomes of an organizational restructuring through the scope of transformational leaders. By doing so, a contrast presented itself between the common characteristics of transformational leaders and leaders who react poorly to change throughout planned organizational restructures. The analysis utilized for the review was the theory of transformation leaders, developed by James MacGregor Burns (1978) and Bernard Bass (1985). This theory demonstrates how different approaches to leadership methods can enhance performance, increase morale, and amplify motivation in the employees who report to leaders responsible for change. Leaders who embrace this theory work closely with their teams in efforts to learn from one another (Bass, 1985). By acting as participants in projects, leaders can influence other individuals and encourage growth for themselves and others (MacGregor Burns, 1978). A leadership and followership atmosphere is created for all participants (Lambe et al., 2018). The four I's are: idealized influence, inspirational motivation to enhance confidence, intellectual stimulation, and individualized consideration (Bakker et al., 2018; Bass, 1985; Khan et al., 2020; MacGregor Burns, 1978). These four I's create a connection between the leader and the followers by establishing a positive relationship for both participants.

The guidepost components of transformational leadership are Bass' (1985) four I's. Intellectual stimulation, in its essence, suggests that a leader find opportunities to learn and grow for their followers (Khan et al., 2020). Figure 1 shows Bass's (1985) four I's that establish the successful practices in transformational leaders. Idealized influence tests the leader to continuously act in ways that the followers will see as models worth following (Bakker et al., 2018). In conjunction with acting as a model citizen, transformational leaders make individualized consideration for their team members (Doci & Hofmans, 2015). These leaders implore their followers to make themselves into key members of the group or organization. Finally, transformational leaders create inspirational motivation by endlessly instilling a level of passion for what is being asked of the follower (Purcell & Chahine, 2019). At every stage of interaction, the leader's exchanges with followers create positive relationships with the people they work with.

Figure 1. Four I's of transformational leadership
Note. Bass' (1985) four I's inspired this figure.

MacGregor Burns (1978) and Bass (1985) argue that a leader's interactions and level of engagement with their employees directly contribute to future success of an organization. This theory highlights a transformational leader as an individual whose approach to communication causes a change in another individual and/or a social system (Campos, 2020). Transformational leaders can inspire positive morale, increase performance, and enhance motivation by establishing challenging goals, emphasizing the value of the organization's common goals, and by remaining confident and optimistic about follower's successes (Bass, 1985; Campos, 2020; Doci & Hofmans, 2015; Grant, 2021; MacGregor Burns, 1978). Each instance of recognition by leadership to the follower has a direct influence on a follower's level of engagement because it demonstrates attention and fosters enthusiasm (Avolio & Bass, 2004). By allowing leaders and personnel to mutually identify the needed changes, envision a desired outcome, and implement those changes, an organizational restructure can proceed with a dedicated group that accepts and embraces the necessary change (Campos, 2020).

This literature review found a gap in current research relating to the level of involvement senior-level leadership has with day-to-day operational staff throughout a planned restructuring. Moreover, current studies do not distinguish between higher education and medical education to accurately assess where RTC typically begins within an educational system. Research provides a prominent amount of support for transformational leadership theory and the value that its practices bring to the workplace. For example, Doci and Hofmans (2015) maintain that transformational leadership brings about meaningful changes for individuals and for entire social systems. Furthermore, transformational practices increase collaboration by creating a common purpose for all participants (Purcell & Chahine, 2019). However, contradictory research does exist arguing that the theoretical components have more weaknesses than benefits. In one such study, Anderson (2015) posits that transformational leadership theory is not a managerial leadership theory because it can more closely be associated with political leadership practices. Subsequently, some researchers have suggested that Burns' (1978) identification of transformational versus transactional leaders was aimed specifically at the political atmosphere of society (Anderson, 2015; Lai et al., 2020).

Even now transformational leadership is a fluid theory. However, the popularity of transformational leadership theory has increased as industries begin to understand the difference between being in a position of power versus a position of leadership (Bass, 1985; Campos, 2020; MacGregor Burns, 1978). Researchers such as Lai et al., (2020) used this theory to demonstrate the purposeful behaviors transformational leaders adopt to create beneficial atmospheres for their followers. Bakker et al. (2018) argue the use of the theory to create a sense of ownership in an employee's work, which then enhances an individual's performance. Additionally, researchers conducted a study that demonstrates a positive relationship between motivation and performance when connected with transformational leadership approaches (Khan et al., 2020). The transformational leadership framework helps build an understanding of the relationship between morale, motivation, and job performance and how senior-level leaders engage in business.

Recent research also provides a more in-depth connection between managerial leadership practices that follow transformational leadership theory and an employee's performance enhancement, increased motivation, and morale (Bakker et al., 2018; Khan et al., 2020). Transformational leadership theory implies that the key connection between leader and follower is that the leader's role is to increase the value of the follower's output by utilizing Bass' (1985) four Is. Bakker et al. (2018), stated that "transformational leaders are expected to challenge their followers to take greater ownership of their work, allowing the leader to align followers with tasks that enhance their performance" (p. 746). Increasing the performance of the employees maintains and/or increases motivation and morale (Bakker et al., 2018; Creasey, 2020; Durowoju et al., 2013; Khan et al., 2020)

Implications and Recommendations

Implications discovered through this literature review influence how organizations need to act during organizational restructures. This research provides insights into change management practices for senior-level leaders and operational-level employees. Both operational-level and senior-level leadership gain by harnessing transformational leadership strategies when implementing a restructuring event. By utilizing transformational practices, the negative results demonstrated in many restructurings with poor change management be avoided altogether. If possible, senior-level leaders and employees should work in coordinated efforts to orchestrate smooth transitions during the planning and execution phases of the restructuring. The unified efforts broaden the potential for success for all parties involved in the change.

Senior-level Leadership. Primarily, this literature review provides implications to members of senior-level leadership teams. An alarming connection is recognized between leadership's actions and behaviors and how those actions and behaviors influence employees' morale, motivation, and performance throughout an organizational restructuring. Without an understanding and appreciation for this connection, leadership teams launching a significant restructure event will experience elevated levels of turnover, an increased level of mistrust in and disdain for the leadership team, and a failed organizational restructuring. A variety of recommendations present themselves for senior-level leadership seeking a streamlined restricting that maintains employees' engagement and promotes growth for all. Most significantly, leaders should communicate with employees at all levels of the change process frequently, clearly, and should provide the 'why' at each stage transition, so that buy-in increases and resistant behaviors are proactively addressed.

Moreover, leaders need to engage in discussions with employees who physically do the daily tasks to gather insight into the job roles and expectations. The increased engagement allows employees a sense of ownership in what they do each day and validates their output for the organization. Finally, leaders need to provide consistent levels of support and understanding for all employees throughout the entire change process. Without that support, employees lose trust in leadership and have significantly decreased levels of morale and motivation that are fundamental components for their continued desire to work.

Operational-level Employees. Secondarily, this literature review supplies implications for operational-level employees within any organization experiencing change. The recognized connection between leadership's actions and behaviors influences employees' morale, motivation, and performance provides insight into how an organizational change process will develop. For employees, their previous interactions with senior-level leadership demonstrate historical actions and behaviors that will remain consistent throughout the change phases. Key recommendations for employees in lower-level positions include approaching leadership as restructuring ideas develop, creating an understanding and supportive environment for fellow employees, and emotionally preparing for resistant actions and behaviors of leadership. Each of the recommendations builds a connection to the restructuring process. Additionally, the initiative-taking nature of these recommendations offers realistic expectations for how the changes will take place and what personal costs may ensue. Most importantly, being aware of and prepared for resistant senior-level leadership allows employees the opportunity to choose whether they are vested enough in their organization to embrace and see the changes through to realization.

Future Research. This literature review is a small part of the ongoing efforts to build connections between leadership approaches and the success organizations have when harnessing transformational leadership theory. Subsequent publications that display case study approaches could prove beneficial in establishing patterns for leadership actions and behaviors within medical education. Mixed-method studies could also help create validation and provide true correlations between leadership actions and behaviors and the influence each has over employees. Furthermore, additional studies need to explore industries outside of medical education to determine if leadership's actions and behavior influence employees' morale, motivation, and performance. Continued research efforts relating to transformational leadership theory build evidence for the framework to become commonplace practices for future leaders.

CONCLUSION

Leadership's inept abilities to manage change significantly influence employees beyond standard day-to-day operations. The workplace environment shifts, and toxicity amongst leadership and lower-level employees spreads rapidly. The costs of poor change management stretch outside of fiscal responsibilities, and employees' connections to the organization dissipate. It falls on leadership to ensure that organizational restructuring and additional change initiatives are successful. Failing to harness leadership tactics and failing to ensure employees embrace proposed changes becomes detrimental to the everyday functionality of an organization. When the organization fails to operate smoothly, the customers they seek to maintain go elsewhere. In the industry of medical education, as operations fail patients seeking help must rely on other providers to get the care they so desperately need.

When senior-level leaders demonstrate negative actions or behaviors within their organization, a trickle-down effect occurs that influences the attitudes and behaviors of their employees' motivation, morale, and performance. By examining the leadership's poor change management practices, the tension they create within the organization can be depleted. Senior-level leadership members are the central decision makers of any department or organization. This extremely specific group of individuals is also the most influential on the lower-level employees' level of morale, motivation, and performance. Their understanding and utilization of this information prove detrimental to orchestrating a successful restructuring. Organizations must think further than the individuals they are serving. Streamlining administrative processes for staff directly affects consumers relations. Consistency and accountability in all settings allows the employees extra time to increase their skills and increases the time employees dedicate to their organization (de Costa et al., 2018; Exworthy et al., 2019; Graamans et al., 2020). The faster employees can shift focuses from inefficiencies to autonomy and growth the sooner their trust and respect for leadership can grow. Organizations willing to adapt to the needs of stakeholders and embrace inevitable change the more likely they are to succeed in all levels of business.

ACKNOWLEDGMENT

I would like to acknowledge Dr. Amy Sloan for her guidance throughout the completion of this chapter.

REFERENCES

Aarons, G. A., Ehrhardt, M. G., Farahnak, L. R., & Hurlburt, M. S. (2015). Leadership and organizational change for implementation (LOCI): A randomized mixed method pilot study of leadership and organization development intervention for evidence-based practice implementation. *Implementation Science : IS*, *10*(11), 1–12. doi:10.118613012-014-0192-y PMID:25592163

Al-Abri, R. (2007). Managing Change in Healthcare. *Oman Medical Journal*, *22*(3), 9–10. PMID:22400086

Alhezzani, Y. M. R. (2021). Change recipients' resistance and salience to organizational re-creation: The effects of participation and coercion strategies on change derailment. *Organizational Management Journal*, *18*(1), 2–18. doi:10.1108/OMJ-10-2018-0608

American Medical Association. (2021). *Medical students, residents and fellows making an impact*. Author.

Amjad, A., & Rehman, M. (2018). Resistance to change in public organization: Reasons and how to overcome it. *European Journal of Business Science and Technology*, *4*(1), 56–68. doi:10.11118/ejobsat.v4i1.129

Anderson, J. (2015). Barking up the wrong tree. On the fallacies of the transformational leadership theory. *Leadership and Organization Development Journal*, *36*(6), 765–777. doi:10.1108/LODJ-12-2013-0168

Angelini, E., Wolf, A., Wijk, H., Brisby, H., & Baranto, A. (2021). The impact of implementing a person-centered pain management intervention on resistance to change and organizational culture. *BMC Health Services Research*, *21*(1), 1–11. doi:10.118612913-021-06819-0 PMID:34895215

Appelbaum, S. H., St-Pierre, N., & Glavas, W. (1998). Strategic organizational change: The role of leadership, learning, motivation and productivity. *Management Decision*, *36*(5), 289–301. doi:10.1108/00251749810220496

Arrizabalaga, P., Abellana, R., Vinas, O., Merino, A., & Ascaso, C. (2014). Gender inequalities in the medical profession: Are there still barriers to women physicians in the 21st century? *Gaceta Sanitaria*, *28*(5), 363–368. doi:10.1016/j.gaceta.2014.03.014 PMID:24889702

Avolio, B., & Bass, B. (2004). Multifactor Leadership Questionnaire Manual (3rd ed.). Mind Garden, Inc.

Bakker, A., Hetland, J., Olsen, O., & Espevik, R. (2018). Daily transformational leadership: A source of inspiration for follower performance? *European Management Journal*, *36*, 746–756.

Barasade, S. G. (2002). The ripple effect: Emotional contagion and influence on group behavior. *Administrative Science Quarterly*, *47*(4), 644–675. doi:10.2307/3094912

Bartels, J., Douwes, R., Jong, M., & Pruyn, A. (2006). Organizational Identification During a Merger: Determinants of Employees' Expected Identification with the New Organization. *British Journal of Management*, *17*(S1), 49–67. doi:10.1111/j.1467-8551.2006.00478.x

Bass, B. M. (1985). *Leadership and Performance Beyond Expectations*. Free Press.

Belschak, F., Jacobs, G., Giessner, S., Hortin, K., & Bayerl, P. S. (2020). When the going gets tough: Employee reactions to large-scale organizational change and the tole of employee Machiavellianism. *Journal of Organizational Behavior*, *41*(9), 830–850. doi:10.1002/job.2478

Bergh, D., & Ngah-Kiing Lim, E. (n.d.). *Learning how to restructure: Absorptive capacity and improvisational views of restructuring actions and performance*. Academic Press.

Bordia, P., Restubog, S., Jimieson, N., & Imer, B. (2011). Haunted by the Past: Effects of Poor Management History on Employee Attitudes and Turnover. *Group & Organization Management*, *32*(2), 191–222. doi:10.1177/1059601110392990

Brown, P., & Keep, E. (2018). Rethinking the race between education and technology. *Issues in Science and Technology*, 31–39.

Bucknor, A., Kamali, P., Phillips, N., Mathijssen, I., Rakhorst, H., Lin, S., & Furnas, H. (2018). Gender inequality for women in plastic surgery: A systematic scoping review. *Plastic and Reconstructive Surgery*, *141*(6), 1561–1577. doi:10.1097/PRS.0000000000004375 PMID:29794715

Campbell, H. (2014). *Managing Organizational Change: A practical toolbook for leaders*. Kogan Page, Limited. https://ebookcentral.proquest.com/lib/bayloru/detail.action?docID=1679159

Campos, A. (2020, November). *Transformational Leadership Theory*. Academic Press.

Candy, P. (1991). *Self-direction for lifelong learning: A comprehensive guide to theory and practice*. Jossey-Bass.

Canterino, F., Cirella, S., Piccoli, B., & Shani, A. (2020). Leadership and change mobilization: The mediating role of distributed leadership. *Journal of Business Research*, *108*, 42–51. doi:10.1016/j.jbusres.2019.09.052

Cavalcante, S., Kesting, P., & Ulhoi, J. (2011). Business model dynamics and innovation: (Re)establishing the missing linkages. *Management Decision*, *49*(8), 1327–1342. doi:10.1108/00251741111163142

Coulter, K., & Punj, G. (2013). The effects of cognitive resource requirements, availability, and argument quality on brand attitudes: A melding of elaboration likelihood and cognitive resource matching theories. *Journal of Advertising, 33*(4), 53–64. doi:10.1080/00913367.2004.10639177

Creasey, T. (2020). The cost and risks of poorly managed change. *Prosci: People, Change, Results.* https://blog.prosci.com/the-costs-risks-of-poorly-managed-change

Cutcher, L. (2009). Resisting change from within and without the organization. *Journal of Organizational Change Management, 22*(3), 275–289. doi:10.1108/09534810910951069

de Costa, J., Chen-Xu, J., Bentounsi, Z., & Vervoort, D. (2018). Women in surgery: Challenges and opportunities. *International Journal of Surgery: Global Health, 1*(2), 1–3.

de Fatima Nery, V., Sanches Franco, K., & Rabelo Neiva, E. (2019). Attributes of the organizational change and its influence on attitudes toward organizational change and well-being at work: A longitudal study. *The Journal of Applied Behavioral Science, 56*(2), 216–236. doi:10.1177/0021886319865277

Densen, P. (2011). Challenges and Opportunities facing medical education. *Transactions of the American Clinical and Climatological Association, 122,* 48–58. PMID:21686208

Doci, E., & Hofmans, J. (2015). Task complexity and transformational leadership: The mediating role of leader's state core self-evaluation. *The Leadership Quarterly, 26*(3), 436–447. doi:10.1016/j.leaqua.2015.02.008

Doeze Jager, S. B., Ph. Born, M., & van der Molen, H. T. (2022). The relationship between organizational trust, resistance to change and adaptive and proactive employees' agility in an unplanned and planned change context. *Applied Psychology, 71*(2), 436–460. doi:10.1111/apps.12327

Durowoju, S., Sakiru, G., & Kolapo, O. (2013). Influence of leadership styles on job satisfaction of employees in small and medium enterprises. *European Journal of Business and Management, 5*(21), 40–49.

Eisenbeiss, S., van Knippenberg, D., & Boerner, S. (2008). Transformational leadership and team innovation: Integrating team climate principles. *The Journal of Applied Psychology, 93*(6), 1438–1446. doi:10.1037/a0012716 PMID:19025260

Elshout, R., Scherp, E., & van der Feltz-Cornelis, C. (2013). Understanding the link between leadership style, employee satisfaction, and absenteeism: A mixed methods design study in a mental health care institution. *Neuropsychiatric Disease and Treatment, 9,* 823–837. doi:10.2147/NCT.S43755 PMID:23818784

Endrejat, P. C., Klonek, F. E., Muller-Frommeryer, L. C., & Kaufeld, S. (2021). Turning change resistance into readiness: How change agents' communication shapes recipient reactions. *European Management Journal, 39*(5), 595–604. doi:10.1016/j.emj.2020.11.004

Ernst, J., & Jensen Schleiter, A. (2019). Organizational identity struggles and reconstruction during organizational change: Narratives as symbolic, emotional and practical guides. *Organization Studies, 42*(6), 891–910. doi:10.1177/0170840619854484

Erwin, D., & Garman, A. (2010). Resistance to organizational change: Linking research and practice. *Leadership and Organization Development Journal, 31*(1), 39–56. doi:10.1108/01437731011010371

Ewenstein, B., Smith, W., & Sologar, A. (2015, July 1). Changing change management. *Featured Insights*. https://www.mckinsey.com/featured-insights/leadership/changing-change-management

Exworthy, G. M., Jones, J. R. I., & Smith, G. (2019). Professional autonomy and surveillance: The case of public reporting in cardiac surgery. *Sociology of Health & Illness*, *41*(6), 1–16. doi:10.1111/1467-9566.12883 PMID:30874329

Fiedler, F. E., & Garcia, J. E. (1987). *New approaches to leadership: Cognitive resources and organizational performance*. Wiley.

Fullan, M. (2008). *The Six Secrets of Change: What the Best Leaders Do to Help Their Organizations Survive and Thrive*. John Wiley & Sons, Inc.

Georgalis, J., Samaratunge, R., Kimberley, N., & Lu, Y. (2015). Change process characteristics and resistance to organizational change: The role of employee perceptions of justice. *Australian Journal of Management*, *40*(1), 89–113. doi:10.1177/0312896214526212

Gierszewska, G., & Seretny, M. (2019). Sustainable behaviors—The need of change in consumer and business attitudes and behavior. *Foundations of Management, 11*.

Graamans, E., Aij, K., Vonk, A., & Have, W. (2020). Case study: Examining failure in change management. *Journal of Organizational Change Management*, *33*(2), 319–330. doi:10.1108/JOCM-06-2019-0204

Grant, A. (2021). *Think Again: The Power of Knowing What You Don't Know*. Viking.

Gurin, P., Nagda, B., & Lopez, G. (2004). The benefits of diversity in education for democratic citizenship. *The Journal of Social Issues*, *60*(1), 17–34. doi:10.1111/j.0022-4537.2004.00097.x

Haesevoets, T., De Cremer, D., Hirst, G., De Schutter, L., Stouten, J., van Dijke, M., & Van Hiel, A. (2021). The effect of decisional leader procrastination on employee innovation: Investigating the moderating role employees' resistance to change. *Journal of Leadership & Organizational Studies*, *29*(1), 131–146. doi:10.1177/15480518211044166

Hart, T., & Fassett, D. (2021). Slow your role: Troubling (our) assumptions about higher education. *Communication Teacher*, *35*(3), 214–221. doi:10.1080/17404622.2021.1923770

Heiser, S. (2019, December 9). *The Majority of U.S. Medical Students Are Women, New Data Show*. American Associate of Medical College. https://www.aamc.org/

Hellman, T., Molin, F., & Svartengren, M. (2020). A mixed method study of providing and implementing a support model focusing on systematic work environment management. *Journal of Occupational and Environmental Medicine*, *62*(4), 62. doi:10.1097/JOM.0000000000001829 PMID:32032185

Jain, P., Asrani, C., & Jain, T. (2018). Resistance to Change in an Organization. *Journal of Business and Management*, *20*(5), 37–43.

Jetten, J., O'Brien, A., & Trindall, N. (2002). Changing identity: Predicting adjustment to organizational restructure as a function of subgroup and superordinate identification. *British Journal of Social Psychology*, *41*(2), 281–297. doi:10.1348/014466602760060147 PMID:12133229

Johnson, S. (2020). *The advantages of equity in the workplace.* Hearst Newspapers, LLC. https://work.chron.com/advantages-equity-workplace-2635.html

Jones, S. L., & Van de Ven, A. H. (2016). The changing nature of change resistance: An examination of the moderating impact of time. *The Journal of Applied Behavioral Science, 52*(4), 482–506. doi:10.1177/0021886316671409

Judge, T., Ilies, R., & Colbert, A. (2004). Intelligence and leadership: A quantitative review and test theoretical propositions. *The Journal of Applied Psychology, 89*(3), 542–552. doi:10.1037/0021-9010.89.3.542 PMID:15161411

Kanitz, R., & Gonzalez, K. (2021). Are we stuck in the predigital age? Embracing technology-mediated change management in organizational change research. *The Journal of Applied Behavioral Science, 57*(44), 447–458. doi:10.1177/00218863211042896

Kaul, E., & Weber, P. (2021). *Overcoming barriers to collaborative learning: Pioneering a virtual student-led longitudinal interprofessional education program.* American Medical Association.

Kelly-Turner, K., & Radomsky, A. (2020). The fear of losing control in social anxiety: An experimental approach. *Cognitive Therapy and Research, 44*(4), 834–845. doi:10.100710608-020-10104-5

Kemp, J. (2006). Foundations for systemic change: Social evolution and the need for systemic change in education. *TechTrends, 50*(2), 20–26. doi:10.100711528-006-7582-1

Khan, H., Rehmat, M., Hassan Butt, T., Farooqui, S., & Asmin, J. (2020). Impact of transformational leadership on work performance, burnout and social loafing: A mediation model. *Future Business Journal, 6*(1), 1–13. doi:10.118643093-020-00043-8

Knowles, M. S. (1980). *The modern practice of adult education: From pedagogy to andragogy* (2nd ed.). Cambridge Books.

Knowles, M. S., & ... (1984). *Andragogy in action: Applying modern principles of adult learning.* Jossey-Bass.

Kotter, J., & Rathgeber, H. (2005). *Our Iceberg is Melting: Changing and Succeeding Under Any Conditions* (10th ed.). Penguin Random House LLC.

Kunze, F., Boehm, S., & Bruch, H. (2013). Age, resistance to change, and job performance. *Journal of Managerial Psychology, 28*(7/8), 741–760. doi:10.1108/JMP-06-2013-0194

Lai, F.-Y., Tang, H.-C., & Lu, S.-C. (2020). Transformational Leadership and Job Performance: The Mediating Role of Work Engagement. *Organizational Research Methods, 10*(1).

Lambe, A., Anthoney, F., & Shaw, J. (2018). One door closes, another opens: Surviving and thriving through organizational restructure by ensuring knowledge continuity. *Business Information Review, 35*(4), 145–153. doi:10.1177/0266382118802651

Lardjane, S., Laveuve, F., & Nutinen, M. (2017). The need for fundamental change in education. *E-Journal of Environmental Education*, 1–7.

Lensges, M., Hollensbe, E., & Masterson, S. (2016). The human side of restructures: The role of shifting identification. *Journal of Management Inquiry*, *25*(4), 382–396. doi:10.1177/1056492616630140

MacGregor Burns, J. (1978). *Leadership* (1st ed.). Harpr & Row.

Malhotra, N., Zietsma, C., Morris, T., & Smets, M. (2020). Handling resistance to change when societal and workplace logics conflict. *Administrative Science Quarterly*, *66*(2), 475–520. doi:10.1177/0001839220962760

Mattson, D. (2017, August 29). *6 Principles of change management for leaders.* Sandler Blog. https://www.sandler.com/blog/principles-change-management/

McLearney, A. S. (2006). Leadership development in healthcare: A qualitative study. *Journal of Organizational Behavior*, *27*(7), 967–982. doi:10.1002/job.417

Merriam, S. B., & Bierema, L. L. (2014). Adult learning: Linking theory and practice. John Wiley & Sons, Inc.

Mezirow, J. (1978). *Education for perspective transformation: Women's re-entry programs in community colleges.* Teachers College.

Mezirow, J. (1991). *Transformative dimensions of adult learning.* Jossey-Bass.

Muhl, C. J. (2002). What is an employee? The answer depends on the Federal law; in a legal context, the classification of a worker as either an employee or an independent contractor can have significant consequences. *Monthly Labor Review*, *125*(1).

Muluneh, G. (n.d.). *Leading change through adaptive design/Change management practice in one of the universities in a developing nation.* Academic Press.

Nadim, A., & Singh, P. (2019). Leading change for success: Embracing resistance. *European Business Review*, *31*(4), 512–523. doi:10.1108/EBR-06-2018-0119

Oh, H., & Kilduff, M. (2008). The ripple effect of personality on social structure: Self-monitoring origins of network brokerage. *The Journal of Applied Psychology*, *93*(5), 1155–1164. doi:10.1037/0021-9010.93.5.1155 PMID:18808233

Oreg, S. (2003). Resistance to change. Developing an individual differences measure. *The Journal of Applied Psychology*, *88*(4), 680–693. doi:10.1037/0021-9010.88.4.680 PMID:12940408

Ormrod, J. E. (2020). Human learning (8th ed.). Pearson Education, Inc.

Pardo del Val, M., & Martinez Fuentes, C. (2003). Resistance to change: A literature review and empirical study. *Management Decision*, *41*(2), 148–155. doi:10.1108/00251740310457597

Pasmore, W. A., Woodman, R. W., & Shani, A. B. (2010). Research in Organizational Change and Development (Vol. 18). Emerald Publishing Limited.

Pellicer, L. (2008). Caring enough to lead: How reflective practice leads to moral leadership (3rd ed.). Corwin Press.

Pennington, C. (n.d.). *We are hardwired to resist change.* Change Management.

Penny, M., Jeffries, R., Grant, J., & Davies, S. (2014). Women and academic medicine: A review of the evidence on female representation. *Journal of the Royal Society of Medicine*, *107*(7), 259–263. doi:10.1177/0141076814528893 PMID:24739380

Pondicherry, N., & Peabody, C. (2021). *E-drive: Analyzing a health system to expand access to clinical guidelines*. American Medical Association.

Purcell, W., & Chahine, T. (2019). Leadership and governance frameworks driving transformational change in an entrepreneurial UK university. *Leadership and Organization Development Journal*, *40*(5), 612–623. doi:10.1108/LODJ-07-2018-0280

Raineri, A. (2009). Change management practices: Impact on perceived change results. *Journal of Business Research*, *64*(3), 266–272. doi:10.1016/j.jbusres.2009.11.011

Rashid, R. (2021, April 03). Updating the PhD: Making the case for interdisciplinarity in twenty-first-century doctoral education. *Teaching in Higher Education*, *26*(3), 508–517. doi:10.1080/13562517.2021.1892624

Reger, R. K., Mullane, J. V., Gustafson, L. T., & DeMarie, S. M. (1994). Creating earthquakes to change organizational mindsets. *The Academy of Management Perspectives*, *8*(4), 31–43. doi:10.5465/ame.1994.9412071701

Revoltella, D., Brutscher, P.-B., Tsiotras, A., & Weiss, C. (2016). Linking local business with global growth opportunities: The role of infrastructure. *Oxford Review of Economic Policy*, *32*(3), 410–430. doi:10.1093/oxrep/grw019

Sawney, P., & Niven-Jenkins, N. (2007). Medical education- the need for change. *Occupational Medicine*, *57*(6), 395–396. doi:10.1093/occmed/kqm062 PMID:17728310

Schwarz, G., Bouckenooghe, D., & Vakola, M. (2021). Organizational change failure: Framing the process of failing. *Human Relations*, *74*(2), 159–179. doi:10.1177/0018726720942297

Shah, D., & Sharer, R. (2021). *Role of telemedicine in health care delivery to vulnerable populations during COVID-19. In Clinical Informatics and Health Technology*. American Medical Association.

Southwick, D. A., Tsay, C.-J., & Duckworth, A. L. (2021). Grit at work. Elsevier, 39, 1–17.

Stewart, J., & Hocking, C. (2020). Adaptive sustainability for business in times of uncertainty and hyper disruption. *Journal of Applied Business and Economics*, *22*(12), 24–43.

Szamosi, L., & Duxbury, L. (2002). Development of a measure to assess organizational change. *Journal of Organizational Change Management*, *15*(2), 184–201. doi:10.1108/09534810210423107

Taplin, I. (2006). Strategic change and organizational restructuring: How managers negotiate change initiatives. *Journal of International Management*, *12*(3), 284–301. doi:10.1016/j.intman.2006.06.002

The relationship between an individual's margin in life and readiness for change. (2003). In *Positivistic Research* (pp. 759–766). Academic Press.

Turgut, S., & Neuhaus, A. E. (2020). The relationship between dispositional resistance to change and individual career management: A matter of occupational self-efficacy and organizational identification. *Journal of Change Management, 20*(2), 171–188. doi:10.1080/14697017.2020.1720774

UNICEF. (2020). *What will a return to school during COVID-19 look like?* https://www.unicef.org/coronavirus/what-will-return-school-during-covid-19-pandemic-look

United Nations. (2020). *Policy Brief: Education during COVID-19 and beyond.* https://www.un.org/development/desa/dspd/wp-content/uploads/sites/22/2020/08/sg_policy_brief_covid-19_and_education_august_2020.pdf

van de Ven, A. H., & Poole, M. S. (1995). Explaining development and change in organizations. *Academy of Management Review, 20*(3), 510–540. doi:10.2307/258786

Von Culin, K., Tsukayama, E., & Duckworth, A. (2014). Unpacking grit: Motivational correlates of perseverance and passion for long-term goals. *The Journal of Positive Psychology, 9*(4), 306–312. doi:10.1080/17439760.2014.898320 PMID:31404261

Washington, M., & Hacker, M. (2005). Why change fails: Knowledge counts. *Leadership and Organization Development Journal, 26*(5), 400–411. doi:10.1108/01437730510607880

Webster, N. (2021). *Webster's Dictionary* (11th ed.). https://www.merriam-webster.com/

Wolfensberger, M., & Hogenstijn, M. (2016). Slow shift- developing provisions for talented students in Scandinavian higher education. *Education Sciences, 6*(31), 1–15. doi:10.3390/educsci6030031

Zeiger, S. (2021). *The cost benefit evaluation and cost effectiveness evaluation methods.* Hearst Newspapers, LLC. https://smallbusiness.chron.com/cost-management-strategies-business-decisions-78054.html

Zhao, H., & Zhou, Q. (2020). Socially responsible human resource management and hotel employee organizational citizenship behavior for environment: A social cognitive perspective. *International Journal of Hospitality, 95*, 1–9.

Zhao, Y., & Watterston, J. (2021). The changes we need: Education post COVID-19. *Journal of Educational Change, 33*(1), 3–12. doi:10.100710833-021-09417-3

Zheng, W., Yang, B., & McLean, G. (2010). Linking organizational culture, structure, strategy, and organizational effectiveness: Mediating role of knowledge management. *Journal of Business Research, 63*(7), 763–771. doi:10.1016/j.jbusres.2009.06.005

Chapter 17
Emotional Intelligence

Shannon L. McCrory-Churchill
D'Youville University, USA

ABSTRACT

This chapter is an overview of the concept of emotional intelligence (EI) and how it applies to organizational leadership. It will explore the origins, viewpoints, and how emotional intelligence differs from intelligence quotient (IQ). It has been demonstrated across the literature that EI has as much, if not more, impact on both personal and professional success. This chapter will address the importance of EI as well as why it makes a difference in the workplace. The chapter leans heavily on the work of Daniel Goleman who first popularized the concept in the mid 1990s. The chapter will further explore common assessments, and ways to increase emotional intelligence.

WHAT IS EMOTIONAL INTELLIGENCE?

There are many definitions of emotional intelligence (EI), once referred to as emotional quotient (EQ), but in the simplest terms, it is our ability to recognize and regulate our emotions, as well as recognize and interpret the emotions of others and use this information to inform our actions. David Ryback (1998) defined emotional intelligence quite concisely as "the ability to use your awareness and sensitivity to discern the feelings underlying interpersonal communication, and to resist the temptation to respond impulsively and thoughtlessly, but instead act from receptivity, authenticity and candor" (p. 53). Emotional intelligence is the human experience aspect of intelligence that is viewed as likely much more important than the much less controversial intelligence quotient (IQ).

How Is EI Different From IQ?

The concept of IQ is relatively familiar to most, and has existed longer than the concept of EI. It is a measure of a person's aptitude, or ability to think, reason and analyze. IQ is a numerical representation of an individual's intellect as it pertains to obtaining, managing and using knowledge. How it is measured, how much it relates to "smartness" within an individual and whether it is entirely inherited or can be increased, are all sources of debate among psychologists (Gondal & Husain, 2013).

DOI: 10.4018/979-8-3693-1380-0.ch017

Emotional Intelligence

It can be noted however, extensive research has demonstrated that a high IQ is not the sole predictor for success across domains. "The brightest among us can founder on the shoals of unbridled passions and unruly impulses; people with high IQ can be stunningly poor pilots of their personal lives" (Goleman, 1995, p.34). Emotional intelligence is what allows us to recognize emotions in ourselves and others, assess and manage these emotions and inform our actions and responses. EI is what allows high quality social relationships, targeted approaches to situations and it cannot be represented as a numerical comparative standard, as IQ can (Gondal & Husain, 2013). Emotional Intelligence encompasses the attributes some refer to as the "soft skills."

When discussing the increase in computer usage across job roles, Daniel Goleman (1998) noted, "people desperately feel the need for connection, for empathy, for open communication" (p.6) and in a post pandemic world, these words continue to be true, perhaps even more so. While this statement was brought out of a conversation of why job satisfaction was changing with the use of computers, it concisely sums up the reason that EI can often usurp the role of IQ as a predictor of workplace potential, and why teams with high EI, are often more productive. There is more to the human experience than IQ can measure, and a key difference is that EI can be learned and developed, increasing with new knowledge and skills, while IQ is believed to be inherited and difficult to change.

Where Did the Idea of EI Come From?

Many were talking about inter and intrapersonal intelligence prior to the beginning of the conversation on emotional intelligence, and the idea of there being a component larger than just IQ existed, but the conversation was not cohesive. In 1983, Harvard psychologist Harold Gardner proposed the idea of "multiple intelligence." Knowing one's inner world was one of seven intelligences he proposed (Goleman, 1998). Reuven Bar-On proposed a model for emotional intelligence in the 1980s, and the *Bar-On Emotional Quotient Inventory (EQ-i)* is still in use today (Bar-On, 1997). However, in 1990, psychologists Salovey and Mayer, were first to use the term emotional intelligence and offered three categories: appraisal and expression of emotion, regulation of emotion, and utilization of emotions in problems and decision making. They offered the first comprehensive model of emotional intelligence.

While this work laid the foundation for Goleman's (1995) work, it was Goleman who expanded the construct to include a more adaptive view of emotional intelligence. Goleman offered five key components of emotional intelligence, and explored a range of skills within these components that can be developed, and thus a higher level of EI obtained.

The five components Goleman offers are self-awareness (emotional awareness), self-regulation, motivation, empathy, and social skills. Those who have high levels of emotional intelligence will possess many of the traits Goleman notes in his model, irrespective of measures of IQ. Those with *self awareness* will be able to assess, and acknowledge their feelings while understanding the impact those feelings have on others. *Self-regulation* allows one to control emotions and anticipate consequences of those emotions on situations, while resisting the urge to react impulsively. *Motivation* uses emotions to achieve goals, move past obstacles and enjoy the process of learning. *Empathy*, involves recognition of emotions in others and adjusting our own reactions to the needs of others. Social skills involve managing relationships, motivating others, inspiring others and building high quality relationships (Goleman 1998).

To dive a bit deeper into Goleman's model, each construct is broken down into contributory parts, and the skills associated with each portion are noted (Goleman, 1995, 1998; Serrat, 2017).

Self-Awareness

a. Emotional awareness: someone with this skill can recognize their own emotions and their effects on both self and others, they know which emotions they are feeling and why, they realize the link between how they feel and what they do or say
b. Accurate self-assessment: someone with this skill knows their strengths and their limitations, are reflective and learn from experience.
c. Self-confidence: someone with this skill is sure of their self-worth and capabilities, are decisive and able to make sound decisions despite uncertainties and pressures.

Self-Regulation

a. Self-control: someone with this skill manages disruptive emotions and impulses, and can think clearly under pressure.
b. Trustworthiness: someone with this skill maintains high standards of honesty and integrity, admit their own mistakes and confront unethical actions in others.
c. Conscientiousness: someone with this skill takes responsibility for personal performance, are organized and careful in their work.
d. Adaptability: someone with this skill is flexible in handling change, can smoothly handle multiple demands.
e. Innovativeness: someone with this skill is comfortable with and open to novel ideas and new information, generates new ideas with fresh perspective.

Self-Motivation

a. Achievement drive: someone with this skill strives to improve or meet a standard of excellence.
b. Commitment: someone with this skill aligns with the goals of the group or organization.
c. Initiative: someone with this skill is ready to act on opportunities.
d. Optimism: someone with this skill has persistence in pursuing goals despite obstacles and setbacks, sees a way forward.

Social Awareness

a. Empathy: e someone with this skill can sense others' feelings and perspective, and takes an active interest in their concerns.
b. Service orientation: someone with this skill anticipates, recognizes, and meets others' needs.
c. Developing others: someone with this skill can sense what others need in order to develop, and bolstering their abilities.
d. Leveraging diversity: someone with this skill cultivates opportunities through diverse people, recognizes the value of different perspectives.

Emotional Intelligence

e. Political awareness: someone with this skill can read a group's emotional currents and power relationships.

Social Skills

a. Influence: someone with this skill can wield effective tactics for persuasion.
b. Communication: someone with this skill send clear and convincing messages.
c. Leadership: someone with this skill inspires and guides groups and people.
d. Change catalyst: someone with this skill initiates or manages change effectively.
e. Conflict management: someone with this skill can negotiate and resolve disagreements.
f. Building bonds: someone with this skill nurtures instrumental relationships.
g. Collaboration and cooperation: someone with this skill works with others toward shared goals.
h. Team capabilities: someone with this skill creates group synergy in pursuing collective goals.

How is EI Measured?

With much research devote to emotional intelligence since it's introduction in the 1990's, there evolved many different evaluation tools for measuring similar aspects of EI. The following is not an exhaustive list, but covers the most common and widely accepted tests.

The *Mayer-Salovey-Caruso Emotional Intelligence Tests (MSCEIT)* (Mayer et al., 2002) is an updated version of Mayer & Salovey's MEIS that uses objective and impersonal questions to evaluate a respondent's ability to perceive, understand, use and regulate emotions. This test utilizes tasks and emotional problems that must be solved rather than relying on the self-report of their emotional skills.

The *Self-report Emotional Intelligence Test (SREIT)* (Schutte et al., 1998) assesses a respondent in the categories: regulation of emotion in self and others, appraisal and expression of emotion in self and others, utilization of emotions in solving problems.

The *Bar-On Emotional Quotient Inventory (EQ-i)* (Bar-On, 1997) is a 133 item self-report inventory that convers 15 scales, including emotional self-awareness, assertiveness, self-regard, self-actualization, independence, empathy, interpersonal relationships, problem solving, reality testing, flexibility, stress tolerance, impulse control, happiness, optimism and social responsibility.

The *Emotional and Social Competence Inventory (ESCI)* (Boyatzis and Goleman, 2007) builds on Boyzatis' earlier model, but is adapted for a more broad audience (originally managers and executives), this scale is appropriate for use in 360 analysis.

When utilizing any measure of EI, there are limitations to consider. Does the chosen measurement tool test what you are hoping to test? More importantly, how reliable is the person reporting the data? Certainly, in a self-report scale, the results will be more truthful if the individual has a high level of self-awareness and is able to reflect honestly on how the question pertains to them. Alternately, with the use of a 360 degree analysis, does the person being evaluated have a high level collegial relationship with the person evaluating them? Can a subordinate be trusted to be brutally honest in an evaluation of their boss? While these tools may offer insight into the EI and ability of a leader to be successful in the workplace, they must be utilized along with evaluation the actions and activities of the individual.

EI and Leadership

Emotionally intelligence is a crucial component of leadership. Can one lead without EI, or are they just the boss? Research indicates the latter. While one can certainly assign tasks, tell others what to do, create deadlines and manage an organization's output, true leaders will have an additional EI skill set (Rajkumar, Nilavathy, & Merlin, 2021). They will dig deeper and look for the emotional underpinnings of actions and responses, both in themselves and others. If we can agree with Forbes (2020) that qualities of a good leader include: constant, genuine and curious learners; create and articulate a clear vision; do not have to be the smartest person in the room; focus on outcomes, not credit; do not waver on ethics; and can show vulnerability, then we can begin to see why EI plays such an important role in leadership. Both the giving and receiving of information is impacted by an individual's EI, and higher EI can lead to better outcomes.

As Goleman (1998) notes, emotions are contagious. Being a leader requires emotional regulation. A leader cannot rage into a conference room, reprimand a group and expect to earn respect. Neither can one expect that their concern about or enthusiasm for a project would go unnoticed. Rather, through self-assessment and self-regulation, taking negative emotions, assessing their impact on one's response, as well as their impact on others, allows a leader with EI to pause, regroup and change their approach to one that will motivate a team to better outcomes. Goleman's (1998) theory applies well to leadership, and demonstrates how these characteristics translate to organizational success.

A leader with *self-assessment* is aware of their emotions, understands how those emotions impact others and can make decisions on how and when to interact with their team based on these emotions. Knowing how their own emotions may impact others decreases the risk of misunderstanding, conflict and can harness negative emotions with positive results.

A leader with *self-regulation* will utilize self-assessment, understand emotions and take actions to not act impulsively. Utilizing control over emotions decreases potential for rash decisions, poorly planned interventions and frequent redirection when an impulsive decision needs to be reversed.

A leader with EI can harness both positive and negative emotions for *motivation* of self and others. While a certain amount of anxiety may be preferential for learning, high levels of anxiety are not. Through an understanding of one's own emotions and how they motivate, a leader can use this skill to assess and understand what motivates and inspires others.

Empathy is perhaps the most difficult and influential piece of this equation. A leader with the ability to recognize emotions in others and also to put themselves into the situation of others, trying on their viewpoint, will find greater success than someone who discounts the experience of others. Leaders must realize that every situation is informed by the individual experiences of those involved, and a complex interplay of emotion exists. While it may be difficult to navigate, and certainly near impossible to meet every need of every person involved, those with empathy strive to meet people where they are, and work together toward a solution.

Leadership is an emotionally taxing undertaking, requiring continuous monitoring, adaptation and improvement. Those with high EI, will possess characteristics which increase collaboration, and decrease conflict. An effective leader makes every member of the team feel valued, respected and contributory. Essential to this collaborative effort is not only the ability to read others' emotions based on facial expressions, body language and speech, but to be able to manage one's own emotions, and respond in a way that will achieve the desired result. Speaking assertively may set clear and defined expectations, where more a moderate tone would be appropriate when dealing with a colleague who was upset. EI is crucial in adapting a response to a specific situation, and the reasons that some leaders handle conflict better than others (Kemerer & Ćwiekala-Lewis, 2016).

How to Lead With EI

Understanding the components and characteristics of EI is important, but how does one apply these principles to the action of leading? The Center for Creative Leadership (CCL) offers four ways to lead with emotional intelligence (Thompkins, 2022). They are, listening closely without judgement, connecting with employees on a personal level, unlock motivations and seek to understand more about yourself and others. While simple in concept these are perhaps much more complex in action. Even those with high levels of EI can benefit from further reflection and may have to work to hold judgement.

Listen closely without judgment. Active listening, with consideration of others and their perspectives, while creating a safe space for sharing encourages team members to feel a sense of psychological safety. This means listening to understand, rather than thinking about the next question or assuming you know where the conversation is heading. Being able to recognize and understand the other person's emotions, and confirm your understanding of their emotions, allows them to feel heard and understood. Be comfortable with pausing before you respond. This fosters collaborative relationships.

Connect with employees on a personal level. By recognizing employee efforts, demonstrating a willingness to help, you show that you care about them as individuals. This builds trust, and can lead to better collegial relationships. Employing empathy, and demonstrating kindness in the workplace positions a leader to be more successful and better able to work with more diverse teams.

Unlock motivations. Leaders must be well aware of their own motivations, and how they impact the organization, but they must also understand what drives their team. Understanding what employees need to remain engaged and what motivates them requires the leader ask the right questions and actively listen to the answers. Once there is understanding, the leader is poised to increase engagement, job satisfaction and retention.

Seek to understand more about yourself and others. This is perhaps the most complicated of the four concepts offered by the CCL. What one perceives of a situation is largely influenced by their own lived experience. This should serve to demonstrate how much everyone's individual experiences influence every day interactions, and the value of embracing the diversity of a team, but it can be difficult to get "out of our own heads" and recognize triggers, habits and learned responses. Leaders must have the ability to accept others' perspectives without judgement.

Be Aware of Blind Spots

What is a blind spot n EI? It is very similar to a blind spot when driving. It is an area that a leader cannot immediately see, that, if left unaddressed, can have disastrous consequences. Self-awareness is difficult, and seeing ourselves as others see us can be challenging, but knowing that blind spots exist and making an effort to address them can have great impact.

Robert E. Kaplan, formerly of the CCL, does an excellent job of discussing blind spots. He studied executives over a period of time, and noted common blind spots that can arise in, and derail even the highest level of achievement. These blind spots include: blind ambition, unrealistic goals, relentless striving, drives others, power hungry, insatiable need for recognition, preoccupation with appearances, and the need to seem perfect (Kaplan, Drath, & Kofodimos, 1991). Blind spots are not necessarily singular, and some over lap with others, but for all, working on self-awareness is key. A significant concern with leaving blind spots unaddressed is they are some of the key elements that lead to both personal and team burnout.

Blind ambition can manifest as arrogance, needing to win at all costs, and being competitive rather than collaborative. Someone with blind ambition will only be able to see others as friend or enemy, there are hard lines and no room for middle ground. This person may exaggerate their contribution to seem more important and get ahead.

Someone with *unrealistic goals* might be overly ambitious, or have unrealistic ideas of how much work a project or idea will require. Their unrealistic expectations could apply to individual workload and goals, or those set across an organization.

Relentless Striving describes the "workaholic." This person will be the hardest worker in the room at the expense of all else. Burnout levels are high with this blind spot and tam members who seek a more balanced approach between work and personal pursuits may be alienated.

The blind spot *drives others* seems at face value to be a positive attribute, after all, we want a leader that pushes for the best. In this case, the drive is excessive, being seen as ruthless and without regard for the emotional toll it may take. Here, the leader is micromanaging rather than delegating and pushing too hard.

Seeking power for one's own interest rather than that of the organization demonstrates being *power hungry*. This person might be described as manipulative or exploitative and moves their agenda forward at the expense of others.

The *insatiable need for recognition* can be a struggle for teams. While some were brought up in a competitive work environment where one had to get ahead by any means possible, others were not a part of a cut throat workplace culture, and there is already a difference in approach. If the leader is willing to take credit for others ideas, or places the blame on others for mistakes, it furthers the divide and creates a very difficult work environment. Glory above all, and sacrificing next steps in pursuit of the next big win will not foster collaboration or trust.

Preoccupation with appearances can be detrimental to leaders and teams. The idea that public image is the only important feature of a project, or being overly concerned with prestige and materialistic ideas of success shifts focus from the actual process of being successful.

The *need to seem perfect*. This is the antithesis to Goleman's ideas of self-assessment and self-regulation. This person cannot admit mistakes, will not admit weakness and patently rejects criticism, with the potential to be angered by criticism. The vulnerability for empathy and getting to know a team on a personal level does not exist with this blind spot.

While certainly these are fairly concise descriptions of pitfalls, each blind spot can manifest in an individual in varying degrees. A leader may have one or more than one of these, but their existence is not necessarily indicative of a leader in peril. What one does with the information about blind spots, how they use it for self-assessment and development will determine how much more or less successful they might be.

Can EI Be Developed?

The belief is, that yes, EI can be increased. There is no one size fits all, one time course that will do this however. They key to developing or increasing EI, is practice. As the chapter has demonstrated, the components of EI and leading with EI are complex. These are not rote skills that are easily mastered.

Emotional Intelligence

Even the smallest components, like listening, take practice. How many times has someone missed part of a conversation because they were thinking of the next thing to say, or a thought was triggered about another project and focus was lost? Being present is important to EI, and that in and of itself, is a skill.

EI and Organizations

Is building EI strictly an individual matter based on personal reflection? The short answer is no, but as this chapter has demonstrated, there are no simple answers when emotions are involved. While building personal EI is important to both self and institution, building an emotionally intelligent organization is equally important.

Christopher Connors (2020) has much to say on the topic of effective leadership and organizations as they relate to, or are served by emotional intelligence. He believes that leaders have the ability to build a culture that employees want to be a part of, and offers skills, obstacles and sustainability resources to move toward such a culture, building organizational emotional intelligence.

All signs point to a positive attitude. Celebrating both large and small accomplishments, having a happy work environment and treating employees well all have a role in productivity and success. Stories abound of leaders who are successful by going against the "only thing that matters is the bottom line" mentality and succeeding because they chose to focus instead on people

As with building physical structures, building a culture of emotional intelligence calls for a blue print. Connors (2020) offers the following steps as a "Blueprint for an Emotionally Intelligent Organization" (p. 96).

What are the basics? These determine your desired standard. These include a well-defined mission, vision, values, goals and purpose.

Focus on your people. Identify your strategic goals, and what it is that make you unique. Model this behavior, and encourage your employees to adopt the behavior. Determine your team members goals, both personally and professionally, and what your desires are for them. Employ caring by creating an environment where diversity and inclusivity are valued, and a sense of belonging is fostered.

Communicate. This step is crucial. Ensure that communication is clear, and expectations are understood. Demonstrate clearly how your strategic goals and desired outcomes tie into your mission, vision, values and purpose, and ensure that this is aligned across the organization. Ensure that leaders and team members have consistent feedback opportunities and review clearly communicated performance indicators.

Develop an approach of continual self-assessment and innovation. Ensure that the mission, vision, values and purpose are at the core of decision making. Continually strive to evaluate actions for quality improvement, and celebrate the wins.

Creating a culture of emotional intelligence within an organization is of course, not as easy as following the steps above, the human factor plays a role here. Not everyone thinks, feels or handles emotions in a similar way, so a bit on of an individual approach to each team is required. That said, Connors (2020) does offer some common obstacles to look out for when doing an organizational assessment and creating a plan. They include: Are employees resistant to change? Is the organizational culture unwilling to adapt? Is the scope of the change unclear? Is there adoption of a new technology that employees do not understand? Is there a lack of communication? Is there a lack of buy in from key stakeholders? Do employees not understand the "why" or the benefit of the change? Is there a poor (or lacking) governance structure? Do Political Factions exist? Is there fear of job loss or layoffs? And is there an overall frustration with the length of time and scope of change?

These are not small obstacles, but neither are the insurmountable. Through personal reflection and transparency, increased buy in can lead to organization wide reflection and change. Changing the culture of an organization will take time, but utilizing smaller evaluations and exercises to create change can begin a shift in the right direction.

What Does It All Mean?

The bottom line for EI is that it matters. Research continues in the field of EI and regrettably, is demonstrating that as a society, our EI is decreasing. The decrease is consistent across socioeconomic strata, and has been on the decline for decades. The time taken for self-assessment, and working on blind spots and areas that could use bolstering is not time wasted. As we move ever forward, those with higher levels of EI, who are willing to do the work and require their teams to do the work of EI, will be the benchmarks of success.

REFERENCES

Bar-On, R. (1996). *The Emotional Quotient Inventory (EQ-i): A Test of Emotional Intelligence*. Multi-Health Systems.

Boyatzis, R. E., Goleman, D., & Rhee, K. (2000). In R. Bar-On & J. D. A. Parker (Eds.), *"Clustering competence in emotional intelligence: insights from the emotional competence inventory (ECI),"in Handbook of Emotional Intelligence* (pp. 343–362). Jossey-Bass.

Connors, C. (2020). *Emotional Intelligence for the Modern Leader*. Rockridge Press.

Dunstan Rajkumar, A., Nilavathy, K., & Ida Merlin, J. (2021). A Review - Emotional Intelligence An Important Predictor Of Leadership Potential. *Turkish Online Journal of Qualitative Inquiry*, *12*(7), 3966–3975.

Forbes. (2020). *The Seven Characteristics of great leaders*. Retrieved from https://www.forbes.com/sites/forbescoachescouncil/2020/10/21/the-seven-characteristics-of-great-leaders/?sh=5e8eb515f7f4

Goleman, D. (1995). *Emotional Intelligence*. Bantam Books.

Goleman, D. (1998). *Emotional intelligence: Why it can matter more than IQ*. Bantam Books.

Kaplan, R. E., Drath, W. H., & Kofodimos, J. R. (1991). *Beyond ambition: How driven managers can lead better and live better*. Jossey-Bass.

Kemerer, D., & Ćwiekala-Lewis, K. (2016). *Emotional Intelligence for Leaders in Nursing. Polish Nursing / Pielegniarstwo Polskie*, *62*(4), 562–565. https://doi.org.dyc.idm.oclc.org/10.20883/pielpol.2016.60

Ryback, D. (1998). *Putting Emotional Intelligence to Work: Successful Leadership is More Than IQ*. Butterworth-Heinemann.

Salovey, P., & Mayer, J. D. (1990). Emotional intelligence. *Imagination, Cognition and Personality*, *9*(3), 185–211. doi:10.2190/DUGG-P24E-52WK-6CDG

Schutte, N. S., Malouff, J. M., Hall, L. E., Haggerty, D. J., Cooper, J. T., Golden, C. J., & Dornheim, L. (1998). Development and validation of a measure of emotional intelligence. *Personality and Individual Differences*, *25*(2), 167–177. doi:10.1016/S0191-8869(98)00001-4

Serrat, O. (2017). Understanding and Developing Emotional Intelligence. In *Knowledge Solutions*. Springer. doi:10.1007/978-981-10-0983-9_37

Thompkins, S. (2022). *Leading With Emotional Intelligence*. Center for Creative Leadership. https://www.ccl.org/articles/leading-effectively-articles/emotional-intelligence-and-leadership-effectiveness/

Chapter 18
A Strategic Paradigm for Transformational Leadership Theory in the Digital Age:
Scope of the Analytical Third

Ansar Abbas
https://orcid.org/0000-0003-4521-1920
MY Business School, Pakistan & Airlangga University, Indonesia

Fendy Suhariadi
https://orcid.org/0000-0001-9679-2185
Airlangga University, Indonesia

Dian Ekowati
https://orcid.org/0000-0001-9726-4720
Airlangga University, Indonesia

Rakotoarisoa Maminirina Fenitra
https://orcid.org/0000-0002-1045-3404
ASTA Research Center, Madagascar

ABSTRACT

The analytical triangle, a social psychology concept, is crucial in implementing change management strategies. It involves a triangular configuration mediating between individuals and the external world, subject and object, and imagination and actuality. This literature synthesis explores the strategic management and leadership intentions of businesses, focusing on transformational leadership theory and the use of novel communication strategies by global leaders. The study's overarching goal is to highlight the relevance of these theoretical frameworks in a variety of potential future research situations. This chapter explores how entrepreneurs may utilize technology to develop successful firms by coordinating different aspects of technology entrepreneurship to produce a unified transformation. Students would do well to study its lessons on how technology entrepreneurs may make effective use of available resources.

DOI: 10.4018/979-8-3693-1380-0.ch018

A Strategic Paradigm for Transformational Leadership Theory

INTRODUCTION

It is common to see the theory of transformational leadership capacities in global identities. This theory explains how leadership can influence a varied community. Through transformational capabilities, leaders can motivate and inspire people to think differently about their roles and identify with a shared purpose (Dimitrov, 2018; Heizmann & Liu, 2018; Stagich, 2006). This can help create a sense of global unity and foster a collective understanding of how each individual can contribute to a larger cause. As a result of Bass's advocacy for transformational leadership, this concept gained widespread acceptance and identity, which contributed to its rise to prominence (Bass, 1997). Transformational leadership allows people to recognize their potential and collective power to change the world positively. It emphasizes the importance of collective action and encourages people to think beyond the individual, which can help to create a sense of global unity and collaboration (Atmojo, 2015). The theory of transformational leadership possesses limitless promise, breadth, and difficulty in its application. It has been seen to broaden its boundaries, thanks to the ever-evolving literature that it produces (Atmojo, 2015; Eliyana & Ma'arif, 2019; Purwanto et al., 2020; Van Dijk et al., 2021). The philosophy of transformative leadership is considered to be of high importance and significance in building societies. It emphasizes the need for leaders to be visionary and to transform their organizations and communities through innovation, collaboration, and ethical decision-making. Transformative leadership also fosters an environment of trust, respect, and mutual understanding, which are essential for a healthy society (Ahmad et al., 2023).

Through the lens of transformational leadership theory, the function of leadership identity in global landscapes contributes to resolving complex social problems. Leaders with a strong sense of identity are likelier to take risks and make bold decisions, even when uncertain. Additionally, this sense of identity provides a foundation for making decisions that reflect their values and beliefs, which can help bring about meaningful social change in global landscapes (Abbas, Ekowati, Suhairidi, & Anwar, 2022; Abbas, Ekowati, Suhariadi, et al., 2022; Abbas, Saud, et al., 2021; Fenitra, Premananto, et al., 2022). Leaders with a global identity might help resolve attentional messes caused by complicated challenges such as climate change (Abbas, Ekowati, & Suhariadi, 2022; Abbas, Ekowati, Suhariadi, et al., 2022). This theory has been seen as fitting and excoriating new ideas in global landscapes, demonstrating the richness of this theory and its enrichment capacity (Widiana, 2017). Leaders with a worldwide identity can unify different perspectives and cultures, allowing them to understand various challenges better and provide more inclusive and effective solutions. This theory is gaining ground, as it emphasizes the importance of engaging different stakeholders in the decision-making process and recognizes the need to respect the different perspectives and cultures of the global community (Hapeta et al., 2019; Hite, 1996; Van Dick et al., 2021).

PURPOSE OF THE STUDY

This chapter covers the development of the transformational leadership theory as well as the capacities of the approach to bring about transformation in organizations, societies, and leaders. Everyone worldwide keeps a close eye on the societies and businesses widely seen as being at the vanguard of technologically transformational and enabling developments. Their strengths can be shown in their ability to analyze circumstances from a variety of points of view, effectively apply knowledge, and foresee the future.

Consequently, their wit contributes to the betterment of their student's education, and their followers can gain knowledge from the infinite transformative potential of their idea.

Justification of the Study

The philosophy of transformational leadership is constantly shifting, expanding, and broadening its frontiers. This expansive theory can incorporate various aspects of global leadership that might be helpful for future theoretical and educational advances. Transformational leadership focuses on creating meaningful change by engaging followers in a shared vision, inspiring them to strive for greater heights, and developing their capabilities. It constantly evolves and adapts to the changing environment, making it an invaluable tool for leaders.

Significance of the Study

The theory of transformational leadership, mainly when applied to mediolateral personalities emerging from the digital age, invites inspirational characteristics in leaders of the new generation. Specifically, entrepreneurs in the technology sector are helpful, influential, and diversified components to include in this equation. Transformational leadership theory emphasizes the importance of inspiring and motivating others to reach their full potential. In the digital age, entrepreneurs in the technology sector are uniquely positioned to foster an environment of innovation and creativity that can drive positive change in the world. They provide invaluable knowledge, insight, and leadership sources that can help shape the future.

Research Questions

This chapter established the groundwork for whether or not the incorporation of the life experiences of infamous personalities and businesspeople can serve as an inspiration and a transformative incentive for students. Technology and company solutions have led to global change. Automation and efficiency save firms money. Their creativity has helped transformative leaders worldwide. Digital business owners can embrace global economic trends this way. We can explain why digital entrepreneurs will shape leadership. Future leaders demonstrate how digital entrepreneurship may transform.

LITERATURE REVIEW

Global leadership theories should discuss diverse backgrounds, experiences, and perspectives. This argument is significant because groups with a broad spectrum of ideas are more likely to develop innovative solutions that benefit the environment and society. A CEO's personality should be committed to corporate social responsibility, guaranteeing that the company is taking the required steps to become a leader in environmental and social stewardship (Zhao et al., 2023). Meaningful choices are made every day by global ECOs like Alon Musk, Sundar Pichai, and Jeff Bezos. The example set by forward-thinking corporate executives in technology means that this sector can affect change outside its immediate sphere of influence (Stone, 2022). Using technology in their backup systems, they make decisions that help employees, customers, and investors understand leadership priorities. Because of their global leadership positions, the topics they discuss can cover many issues. This is because their choices, which are frequently aided by technological developments, can influence the views of others and result in policy shifts that have far-reaching effects (Rickley & Stackhouse, 2022). These CEOs can impact well beyond their organizations on a global scale. So, if tech titans like Sundar Pichai and Alon Musk are worried about people using technology—especially AI—as a weapon, that will have consequences for a wide range of people. So let's say two top players in the tech industry are worried about the future of AI; see further (Feiler, 2023).

In that situation, other players in the industry might take note and do something to allay the concerns of those affected. Researchers aimed at such benefit outcomes for big firms were the focus of their research. These initiatives were coordinated regarding employee turnover, pro- and antisocial conduct, support systems, and the general mood at work. A smaller percentage of executives leave companies, fewer people in those organizations lack professional and personal support, and social networks within those companies are thicker and less separated. They also discovered that workers in big businesses are less likely to participate in unhealthy competition. They are more likely to show kindness and generosity to one another at work (Li & He, 2022). One plausible explanation is that the research found improved leader-subordinate relationships. Those under leaders who treat them well are more likely to view their superiors as reliable, professional guidance and assistance sources (Yin et al., 2022). This can lead to increased trust and mutual respect between the leaders and the subordinates. It results in a more harmonious work environment, which could explain why workers in such businesses show more kindness and generosity to one another. This improved relationship can also lead to greater collaboration and creativity. Workers with mutual respect and understanding are more likely to develop innovative ideas and solutions, leading to increased productivity and success for the business, e.g. (Alan et al., 2023). Research has been the subject of many studies covering various issues. These topics include governance, the environment, performance, transformational leadership, and broader gender diversity. Leadership and CSR research recent stories about the changing business climate, which requires aggressive corporate social responsibility. The CEO's role is critical in developing and managing this culture, positively impacting the environment and society (Ferrari Braun, 2022). Technology and technology-based solutions for companies have evolved optimal choices of change and leading change globally. Technology can automate processes and make them more efficient, saving companies money in the long run.

Transformation and Diversity Management

The world's landscapes are always shifting, and the people responsible for managing these shifts are leaders with a profound sense of identity and vision. They understand the complex dynamics of nature and the human beings that inhabit it. They are also passionate about preserving the environment and ensuring that resources are used sustainably (Abbas, Ekowati, Suhariadi, et al., 2022). The forefront idea that piques the interest of scholars for resisting social change, social development, and the environment, in particular, is leadership for obvious instances. Leaders are important in providing direction, guidance, and resources to ensure sustainable development (Abbas, Ekowati, & Suhariadi, 2022). They also can influence social change and ensure that resources are used equitably and responsibly. Leaders are expected to understand the complexities of nature and its people to make decisions that benefit the environment and society. Maintaining relevance and competitiveness in the talent market necessitates a diverse and inclusive tech workforce. When people from all levels of the organization are welcome in the office, everyone can learn and advance, and social norms develops (Kang & Kaplan, 2019). This is a significant development toward building stronger communities and a fairer society (Swartz et al.,

2019). Diverse and inclusive companies can attract the most qualified talent, regardless of race, gender, or socio-economic status. This increases innovation potential, which is essential in any fast-paced, competitive industry.

Furthermore, an inclusive workplace fosters a sense of belonging, increasing employee engagement, loyalty, and productivity (Le et al., 2021). Diversity is the key to an inclusive workforce of different intellects, cultures, and ethnic and social backgrounds. When they come across one workplace, the system benefits from their exchange. A mutual exchange built on a social level initially and then across intellectual streams paves its way. This exchange of ideas and perspectives helps to create a work environment that is open to new ideas and encourages collaboration (Welbourne & McLaughlin, 2013). When diverse people work together, they can often develop creative solutions to problems that would not be possible if everyone in the workplace was the same (Rodríguez-Pose & von Berlepsch, 2019).

Maggie Wooll [1] emphasized diversity in tech and helped readers understand how it is closing the gap in modern industry. She argued that having a diverse team and workplace is crucial for innovation and creativity. Furthermore, she highlighted the importance of understanding different perspectives and ways of thinking to succeed in the rapidly changing tech industry. She argues that a more multicultural workforce is better equipped to handle the increased demand for products and services. On the other hand, employees have great aspirations for workplaces that meet their requirements and appreciate individuals' unique viewpoints, abilities, and experiences. As a result, organizations that embrace diversity create a more innovative work environment and increase their capacity to thrive in a highly competitive market (Jaiswal & Dhar, 2016; Suhariadi et al., 2023). Despite its challenges and the emphasis on increased use, technology has made talent management more effective (Abbas et al., 2020). Technology advancements have enabled organizations to improve recruiting. Technology has made it easier to search around the globe for qualified candidates.

On the other hand, the integration of new employees allows them to retrieve all essential paperwork, training materials, and communication channels. Large corporations gain the competitive edge they need to dominate the global economy by attracting and retaining the most brilliant employees (Waxman, 2021). Big firms can make a significant impact with a training program to boost the social working environment. It emphasizes leaders' activities and interactions, promoting prosaically conduct and professional language. A prosaic environment also encourages collaboration, effective communication, and respect for diversity (Abbas, Ekowati, Suhairidi, & Hamid, 2022; Abbas, Ekowati, et al., 2021). Furthermore, it builds a sense of accountability among employees and leadership, which creates a positive and productive work environment (Abbas, Ekowati, & Anwar, 2023; Abbas, Saud, et al., 2022).

Building our sociotechnical future is made possible by technology and society working together (Johnson & Wetmore, 2021). The United States has established new organizations to address the nation's national security and defense needs, such as significant events and shifts in behavior. The National Security Commission on Artificial Intelligence was established in 2018 by the US to investigate the ways and means necessary to advance the development of artificial intelligence, machine learning, and associated technologies. However, the commission has since disbanded. It is time for the United States to establish a committee or agency dedicated to researching the effects of AI on American culture (Feiler, 2023).

There is a growing body of research on technological disruption's positive and negative effects on society and organizational life. Still, the issue remains inconclusive and fraught with complications. At the core of this discussion is whether or not the role of technological pioneers and their contributions should be the primary concern of research.

WHAT CAUSES OF TRANSFORMATION AROUND THE WORLD

The personality of an entrepreneur is typically characterized by the capacity to have a leadership vision and the transformational skills necessary to improve the lives of others. The current CEO of Google, Sundar Pichai, has recently gained a reputation as a potential inspiring leader. In addition to Elon Musk, the owner of Twitter, who is responsible for reshaping people's lives and transforming societies, the lives of these entrepreneurs are significant. Some people, such as entrepreneurs, are among the most powerful transformers in the world. Like Bill Gates and Steve Jobs, who made personal computers accessible to every family, entrepreneurs envision the world differently. Their life experiences, the lessons they have learned, and the business decisions they have made (in which they utilize analytical thinking) inspire countries still building their economies. Entrepreneurship is often viewed as a critical component of promoting economic growth, innovation, competitiveness, and even reducing poverty in nations that lag behind modern industrial counterparts. This perspective is supported by entrepreneurship being associated with positive economic outcomes. They are recognized as a new kind of leader who is inspiring people all around the world and changing it. Many people in developing nations have few personal resources and lack the capital essential to start their own business; as a result, they may find it amusing to hear about the successes of others. However, the pupils should take these tales as lessons for life. Emerging entrepreneurs are forced to seek financing from outside sources. They are subjected to exorbitant interest rates because of the high level of risk associated with new business ventures. Thus, their growth is hindered if less inspirational stories are there to trigger their motivation to undertake new challenges.

Feiler (2023) claims that technology (AI) is now obvious, acceptable, and ubiquitous throughout all human society. Around seven decades ago, academics shocked and hazed their eyes with inquiries and worries regarding the capability of computers to reason for themselves. This question has been answered by AI-powered technology that simulates human thought. Technology is making huge strides in many fields, including medical diagnosis (Feiler, 2023). AI can accomplish this by being able to make one-of-a-kind decisions, which may, at times, be unanticipated in new conditions. Yet, technology without the direction of people is harmful to humanity.

Google CEO Sundar Pichai recently confessed in an interview that he didn't fully comprehend Artificial Intelligence (AI and beyond) and called for technology regulation to prevent abuse [2]. Although he acknowledges AI's potentially huge benefits, he cautions against its misuse, especially in sensitive areas like facial recognition. He thinks governments should restrict AI to ensure it is used morally and ethically. However, Twitter's owner Elon Musk has warned that AI has the potential to cause harm. AI can automate menial jobs that have traditionally required human effort. Such leadership quality is seen as an individual who fosters the ability to see and use relationships for the benefit of the future, e.g. (Zohar & Zohar, 2022)

For example, facial recognition software might discriminate against certain people or groups, hurting society without its responsible use. Establishing rules and laws can aid the responsible and ethical application of AI. People's rights and privacy are safeguarded, and oversight is provided to prevent abuse (Almeida et al., 2022). Both of these examples demonstrate the usefulness of AI in a terrifying way. The modern global corporate and academic communities should take this lovely example of diversity, equality, and inclusion as their guiding principle since we know that people from all levels of society and all walks of education know that technological progress is inevitable. The resistance to this is built on the diversity, equality, and acceptance of all people who have allowed this to develop. We can make an AI system that is more powerful and accurate than anything anyone could design by pooling the expertise of many; still, we need humans to deal with it. AI can do previously impossible tasks by pooling people's brainpower from all social classes. This is one instance in which increasing social and cultural diversity has facilitated technical advancement (Anshari et al., 2022; Dwivedi et al., 2023).

Since we know that different intellects can create exchanges and viable ideas can emerge, technopreneurs should benefit from such debates. At the heart of the transformation of society, advocates of adopting technology and making responsible use of technology are humans (Wittmayer et al., 2019). By encouraging discussions between people with different intellects, technopreneurs can gain valuable insights into how technology can be used responsibly and how it can be used to transform society. By understanding the human aspect of technology, technopreneurs can better create solutions that will benefit everyone. Conforming with people from diverse perspectives helps technopreneurs find innovative solutions to problems and gain insight into new markets (Bhardwaj, 2021). They can stay ahead of their competition if they do this. As a result, AI may be used and regulated differently. As a result, we can bifurcate these effects into three general categories: first, the implementation of artificial intelligence poses a serious threat, and second, through technology development, these effects are possible. Third, learning is divided into controlled and uncontrolled streams. Directed or controlled learning involves using structured data and supervised learning techniques to create models that predict outcomes. Rampant learning requires using unstructured data and unsupervised learning techniques to gain insight into patterns and trends (Moore et al., 2021). Both approaches have advantages and disadvantages and should be intelligently managed to optimize performance.

A layperson cannot understand the peculiarities of what is dangerous and what is friendly when technology is used without control; it may cause distress if the outcome is unexpected (Klaus et al., 2020). There is a constant barrage of information we cannot always decipher accurately, causing confusion and unease. Those who accept technology for some reason, while those who oppose it go with the flow. Technology can be both a blessing and a curse depending on its use. Those who accept it do not understand its potential risks, while those who oppose it may be wary of its potential to harm (Linzenich et al., 2021).

As a result, understanding the nuances between what is safe and what is dangerous can become difficult, leading to confusion and distress. However, it is important to note that technological transformation depends on the environment, the need, and the leadership (Cortellazzo et al., 2019). It is easy to become acceptable to technology through the supervision of a transformational organization. Transformational leadership encourages innovation, creativity, and collaboration. It allows for a culture of change, which is essential for technological transformation. It also helps to create an environment of trust, which is needed for people to be comfortable adapting to new technologies (Santoso et al., 2019).

Moreover, since technology is present in almost every aspect of our lives, it can be difficult to avoid, making us feel overwhelmed and stressed. This is why diversity benefits technology, for instance. Diversity in technology helps to create innovative solutions to problems that are more applicable to a wider range of people. It also allows for different perspectives to be considered, which leads to more creative solutions. Additionally, having more diverse teams in technology can help to reduce the feeling of being overwhelmed, as different people can bring new ideas and solutions to the table. Artificial intelligence has the potential to build self-driving automobiles, robots that communicate with humans, and a lot more. Artificial intelligence diversity is required to prevent bias at the foundations of these systems.

It is essential to ensure that the data used to train and develop artificial intelligence systems contain as much variety as possible. It is technology leadership that enables this alert. Diversity in the data sets used to prepare these artificial intelligence systems helps to ensure that they can recognize and respond to various scenarios. Without this diversity, AI systems are more likely to make errors or form biases that can lead to inaccurate results or the exclusion of certain groups. Scientists rely on human intelligence and controlled learning to determine what information can be retained for future use and what can be altered to avoid causing harm. Artificial intelligence can simulate and predict outcomes using large datasets that are too complex for humans to interpret. As a result, it has the potential to offer insights and assist in identifying potential risks that could be avoided. AI can also be utilized to develop solutions for real-world challenges for which there are no obvious answers. This purview enables the perspective that inclusion of diversity based on equality and talent can help artificial intelligence grow and think like more acceptable solutions for humans. AI algorithms can better understand complex data and arrive at decisions that are more accurate and accessible to a wide range of people when they consider a variety of perspectives, backgrounds, and experiences. This helps create solutions that are more equitable and adaptable for everyone. With artificial intelligence (AI), businesses can monitor and evaluate customer activity across several online and offline channels. And AI can use the combined and analyzed data to boost conversions. AI can use the data to recognize patterns and trends in customer behavior, identify potential opportunities and threats, and suggest personalized recommendations to customers. This helps businesses target customers with the right products and services at the right time, increasing the chances of conversions. Accepting evolving technologies and business models will inevitably bring challenges and opportunities for societal and organizational development and several risks. These include cybersecurity risks due to the increased interconnectedness of technologies and privacy and data protection risks due to the increased amount of personal data collected. In addition, there are economic risks due to the changing nature of the labor market and the potential for increased inequality. Entrepreneurs and other leaders of global identity can potentially become role models for younger generations. The transition to a more specialized labor market can significantly impact the economy. This includes higher wages for those with more specialized skills and increased automation in certain fields. This can increase inequality as those without skills or automation access are left behind. Entrepreneurs can be positive role models by showing that success and financial stability is possible—their ability to influence business transformation and view threats as opportunities benefit responsible innovation and policymaking. Many young people worldwide are drawn to leadership identities that can potentially transform the business world. These young people bring a fresh perspective and new approaches to problem-solving, which can offer innovative solutions to existing challenges. Their ambition and enthusiasm for transformation can be a source of inspiration to all.

Global Exchange and Analytical Third

Analytic practice requires a deep understanding of the dialectical interplay between subjectivity and intersubjectivity (the unconscious life formed by the analytic pair together, the analytic third) (Ogden, 2004). The analytic third is the ability to anticipate change, quickly grasp it, and effectively respond. This response involves identifying the underlying causes of a change and then taking steps to plan for and adapt to it successfully. This uses data-driven insights to identify trends and make decisions that benefit the organization. By leveraging these insights, an organization can gain a competitive advantage and stay ahead of the curve by anticipating and effectively responding to change. A strategic mind may anticipate shifts and future developments, e.g. (Abbas, Ekowati, Shuairidi, et al., 2022). One's analytical skills are invaluable in a time of crisis. Technology can help by automating processes and providing data-driven insights that can help to inform decisions. This can help organizations identify patterns and areas of improvement, enabling them to make better decisions and stay ahead of the competition (Abbas, Ekowati, Suhairidi, et al., 2023).

According to Ogden, the analytic third emerges through group effort. The third experience is unique for each person since it is filtered via their unique lenses (personality, background, psychosomatic makeup, etc.). The analytic third is also uneven since it is born out of the analyst-analysand power dynamic that predominates in the analytic context. The analytic couple emphasizes the analysand's unconscious experience while using their past and present experiences as the major (but not exclusive) focus of analytic discourse. Understanding the analytic third allows the analyst to gain insight into the mind of the analysand. Ogden's analytical third refers to the analyst's vision of the analysand's true self, which can only be seen by the analyst and is distinct from the analysand's conscious or unconscious experience. It is the analyst's task to make the unconscious conscious and to bring the analysand into a state of self-awareness (Dave, 2019; Hallegatte et al., 2014).

Quantum decoherence theory can shed light on the inner workings of the analyst if viewed via the analyst's knowledge of the analytical third. When a system loses its dimensional consistency, its behavior shifts from explicable by quantum mechanics to explicable by classical mechanics. This means that when a system can no longer maintain its quantum state, its behavior becomes predictable, as classical mechanics would predict (Zohar, 2022). This opens the door to the analyst gaining insight into the subject's behavior by understanding the underlying dynamics of the analytical third. It makes sense in a landscape undergoing radical change, where the third analytical ability of people who can anticipate change explains the evolution of behavior around complex systems., quantum society (Zohar, 2021).

By understanding the analytical third, analysts can identify and interpret patterns in the analyst's behavior. This helps them gain insight into the analyst's motivations and motivations, which can then be used to form strategies and plans for navigating the changing environment. This entire system resembles an ever-increasing disparity between the conventional method and the nuances of the new age (Yigitbasioglu et al., 2023). The old management paradigm is inadequate in all four areas. To begin with, traditional management ideas are unsuitable for today's age. This is because the pace of change is much faster than in the past. Also, the availability of technology has created a whole new range of opportunities that traditional management ideas are not equipped to handle.

Moreover, the world has become much more interconnected, meaning that the consequences of decisions made in one area can have a global impact. All of these factors make traditional management ideas inadequate for the new age. Second, traditional management styles, guided by traditional management ideas, have not been updated to reflect modern realities. For example, decision-making processes are no longer limited to a single country or organization but are global in scope (Dolas, 2023). This means that traditional management ideas, which may have been effective in the past, may not be suitable for the current environment (Mohammedshum et al., 2023).

Additionally, technology has changed how people communicate and collaborate, requiring creative approaches to management and decision-making. Third, traditional management theories misunderstand organizational objectives. For example, traditional management theories focus on maximizing profit and efficiency. However, in the current environment, it is essential to consider the impact of a company's decisions on the environment, stakeholders, and the broader community (Popescu & González, 2023). Furthermore, new technologies have enabled organizations to work more distributed; necessitating novel approaches to management and decision-making. Finally, traditional management theories overlook other organizational objectives, such as corporate social responsibility, employee well-being, and customer satisfaction. Fourth, the conventional management paradigm results in traditional brands, which are not suitable for the modern period. This is because previous brands were designed for a different era. They don't fit the current trends in the market, and they don't consider the cutting-edge technologies available. Furthermore, conventional brands do not account for consumers' changing values and attitudes in the digital age (Zohar, 2022).

Although there is a dearth of research on how analytical third, quantum coherence, and the system of transformation might operate, we can speculate that it results in global exchange. By understanding the dynamics of the various components, we can potentially understand how the system operates as a whole and how it can interact with the environment to facilitate the exchange of energy, information, and resources. Because advances in technology are no longer restricted to any one demographic in this world, events that take place anywhere in this world have the potential to have a trickle-down and snowball effect on other countries. Understanding a system's dynamics and ability to interact with its environment can lead to a better understanding of how global events affect other countries. With the rise of technology and globalization, it is becoming increasingly important to be aware of the potential impacts of events on a global level. Suppose we connect it with the changes in the landscape that technology and contemporary businesspeople view. In that case, we can see the transformation occurring quickly and uniformly. Therefore, staying informed and up-to-date on current events is essential to ensure we can recognize and adapt to the changes in our environment. Global exchange and analytical transformation can be the keys to business success today. Staying abreast of the news, understanding trends, and applying them to our practices are essential to staying competitive in the modern world.

Method

According to Harvey (2014), quality writing is characterized by synthesis, defined as the process of merging separate elements into a single entity. According to Baron et al. (2017), academics typically use this word when delegating work, such as a literature review or another type of paper that requires substantial citations of various sources. The conceptual strength technique can provide convincing arguments throughout its assessment due to the endless nature of written material (Loveless, 2002; Torraco, 2005; Webster & Watson, 2002). If an understandable synthesis provides a glance and structure, getting the essence of what has been stated previously, then possibly a research study is sufficient (Showers, 1987). To manage the current body of literature in an analytical and presentable manner to participate in a debate is a researcher's responsibility. Arguments rooted in history are frequently required in academic subjects such as literature to support the numerous works that have been published. After establishing a compelling argument, the author's viewpoint and contributions to the field could be incorporated through a literature review (Snyder, 2019; Torraco, 2016).

CONCLUSION

Social change, organizational transformation, and leadership dynamics constantly evolve, yet they are inextricably linked and cannot be separated. How social trends and attitudes change affects an organization's structure and leadership. At the same time, organizations and leadership styles influence the norms and expectations of society. Therefore, the changes in these areas are intertwined and must be considered.

Compared to other leadership models, transformational leadership is more robust and fertile. This is because transformational leadership focuses on developing individuals and teams within the organization, which encourages creativity and growth. This type of leadership also encourages innovation and collaboration, which is essential in today's rapidly changing business environment. The transformational leader also aligns the organization's goals and values with society's, creating a more holistic and sustainable approach. It assimilates a variety of current models while simultaneously expanding. As a result, the transformational leader can create a culture of trust and mutual respect within the organization, allowing for more open communication and collaboration and the ability to take risks and explore new ideas. This type of leadership also fosters a culture of respect for diversity and creativity, allowing the organization to better capitalize on new opportunities in the market and create a competitive advantage. To continue in this spirit, transformational leaders with global identities, such as technopreneurs, are the world's evolving face responsible for transforming how we lead. These leaders utilize technology to drive innovation, create new products and services, and develop new business models (Suhandiah et al., 2023). They are also focused on creating a greater sense of purpose and meaning in the workplace and inspiring their employees to take ownership of their work. However, "transformational leaders" are more concerned with well-being than profits. They may be focused on creating new products and services, but they may not be focused on the needs of their employees, which can be a potential problem in seeing them in these spheres.

Additionally, they may inspire their employees to take ownership of their work. Still, they may also put too much pressure on them to perform, which has yet to be verified extensively and empirically. Because of this, we have reason to believe that their well-rounded perspective, whether in favor of the strategic use of artificial intelligence or technology, impacts both policies and minds. Technological advancement is a reality, and it's clear that companies and governments are already investing heavily in the research and development of AI and other cutting-edge technologies. Their opinions and views on using these new technologies to our advantage can impact how we shape the future from a leadership lens.

RECOMMENDATION AND FUTURE DIRECTIONS

This book chapter focuses on and synchronizes many components of technology entrepreneurs that cause a balanced transformation. It looks at the role of technology in an entrepreneur's success and how to use it to create a successful business effectively. It also provides insight into the various tools and resources available to technology entrepreneurs and how they work together to create a successful outcome. Their deeds, as well as their utilization of technology and their admonitions regarding analytics, are all profitable and advantageous. Theoretically, the fact that leadership analytics and quantum decoherence can be linked, seen, or viewed enriches transformational leadership change and management theories. These tools and resources are necessary to create a successful outcome because they provide a comprehensive business view. The utilization of analytics and quantum decoherence, in particular, allows entrepreneurs to understand the complexities within their business better, enabling them to make informed decisions and adjustments as needed (Ebbesen & Olsen, 2022). This helps create a more efficient and effective working environment, leading to increased success.

a) Therefore, it is reasonable to assume that leadership analysis may play a pivotal role in seeing present, past, and future transformations when mapping change. Leadership analysis can help identify the areas where change is needed and how it can be implemented. It can also provide insight into various groups' dynamics and how change may impact them. This can be particularly useful in predicting the effects of proposed changes and helping leaders to develop strategies to ensure successful implementation.

b) To have a strategic foresight of matters, leadership analytics is always required. This requires quantum de-coherence, zero distance, classic but innovative concepts, and analytical design. Leadership analytics is a tool that can help leaders anticipate potential issues and obstacles, identify opportunities, and make decisions from a position of strength. It requires a combination of data analysis, qualitative analysis, sound decision-making skills, and an understanding of quantum mechanics and zero distance to effectively anticipate future trends and events.

c) Given that technopreneurs are used as an example in this study, it can be inferred that their identities are shared worldwide. Their ideals are ubiquitous, impacting policy's path and strategic ability to foresee the industrial future. This is because technology and entrepreneurs' identity is valid around the globe. Technopreneurs can be found in almost every industry sector, from manufacturing to finance to healthcare. They are often seen as innovators and disruptors, creating new products and services that are quickly adopted by the public. As such, their influence and reach go far beyond the boundaries of their home countries and can have a global impact on how businesses operate and policy decisions are made.

d) A person aware that they are a "co-creator" of every moment of reality and who, as a result, can co-create and affect it continually through third analytics is said to be a quantum leader. This is accomplished via their concepts, mental states, beliefs, and objectives. In addition, they have fantastic synchronization with themselves and others, real-world challenges and concerns, and a proactive knowledge of strategic intent and mapping the future. Quantum leaders can create change in the world by cultivating a deep understanding of the underlying forces that drive reality and its associated dynamics. They can also develop strategies and solutions to complex problems that are both efficient and effective. Finally, they use their analytical skills and knowledge to inspire and empower others to join their mission, e.g. (Abbas, Ekowati, Suhariadi, et al., 2023).

e) Quantum management recognizes that human systems, such as companies, perform at their highest levels of efficiency when they are led, managed, and structured in the same manner as natural and biological systems. This involves taking a holistic view of the organization, understanding the intertwined relationships between different parts of the system, and creating a flexible structure that can adapt and evolve in response to changing conditions (Ekowati et al., 2023).

f) The goal is to create an environment where everyone works towards a shared vision with a unified purpose. This is the case since natural and biological systems have evolved over millions of years This philosophy, known as systems thinking, is applied to organizations across all industries to help them become more resilient and adaptive. Organizations can make better decisions and create more sustainable strategies by understanding how a system's various components interact. An analytical agency would focus on what is necessary for quantum management for the company's needs. The same fundamental concepts that drive CADs' (complex adaptive systems) adaptability, sustainability, and inventiveness also serve as the strategy's foundation for achieving this objective. Analytical interventions can help organizations identify patterns and trends to make effective decisions for leaders. It can also help identify areas needing improvement and develop strategies to address them. Last but not least, these ideas can steer effective resource deployment toward desired goals that fall under the strategic intent abilities of leaders (Fenitra, Abbas, et al., 2022).

However, as this book chapter is based on the authors' synthesis, its scope may be limited to the global identity thesis. This is because it only discusses the authors' perspective on how global identities have been shaped over the latest developments without considering the experiences of other cultures, societies, personality aspects, history, and diversity concerns. This view does not discuss the influence of other cultures and their respective contributions to shaping global identities. However, it is relevant and could enrich this research agenda in the future. This chapter has searched for a new course of action regarding the analytical third in leadership strategy, zero distance Management in the Quantum Age for transformation, e.g., (under the latest literature guidance). It has proposed an innovative approach that incorporates the principles of quantum de-coherence into the study of management and leadership behavior. This new way of thinking about leadership and management can help companies become more agile, adaptive, and better prepared to face the changing and uncertain conditions of the modern business world. Quantum Analytics is a field of study that combines analytics with the principles of the quantum age to develop new insights into how organizations can lead from outer spheres. It provides a framework for understanding how leaders can create an environment that fosters creativity and adaptability while also maintaining a focus on data-driven, conceptual, or strategic decision-making.

Analytical talents and environments of leaders are relevant in establishing the vision in which they wish to expand their respective industries. Therefore, analyzing other perspectives, such as those of other cultures, is necessary to understand better the global identities established over time. Additionally, leaders' analytical talents and environments are important to consider, as they can help shape their vision for their respective industries.

REFERENCES

Abbas, A., Ekowati, D., & Anwar, A. (2023). Authentic Leadership Journey: An empirical Discussion from Pakistani higher education employing the Lay theory of Psychology. *International Journal of Public Leadership*. Advance online publication. doi:10.1108/IJPL-04-2022-0020

Abbas, A., Ekowati, D., Shuairidi, F., Fenitra, R. M., & Fahlevi, M. (2022). Integrating Cycle of Prochaska and DiClemente with Ethically Responsible behavior theory for Social Change Management: Post Covid-19 Social Cognitive Perspective for Change. In A. Pego (Ed.), *Challenges and Emerging Strategies for Global Networking Post COVID-19* (pp. 130–155). IGI Global. doi:10.4018/978-1-7998-8856-7.ch007

Abbas, A., Ekowati, D., Suhairidi, F., & Anwar, A. (2022). Human Capital Creation: A Collective Psychological, Social, Organizational and Religious Perspective. *Journal of Religion and Health*. Advance online publication. doi:10.100710943-022-01665-8 PMID:36109469

Abbas, A., Ekowati, D., Suhairidi, F., Anwar, A., & Fenitra, R. M. (2023). Technology Acceptance and COVID-19: A Perspective for Emerging Opportunities from Crisis. *Technology Analysis and Strategic Management*, 1–13. Advance online publication. doi:10.1080/09537325.2023.2214642

Abbas, A., Ekowati, D., Suhairidi, F., & Hamid, A. R. (2022). Negative Vs Positive Psychology: A Review of Science of Well-being. *Integrative Psychological & Behavioral Science*. Advance online publication. doi:10.100712124-022-09708-1 PMID:35759165

Abbas, A., Ekowati, D., & Suhariadi, F. (2021). Managing Individuals, Organizations Through Leadership: Diversity Consciousness Roadmap. In B. Christiansen & H. Chandan (Eds.), *Handbook of Research on Applied Social Psychology in Multiculturalism* (Vol. 1, pp. 47–71). IGI Global. doi:10.4018/978-1-7998-6960-3.ch003

Abbas, A., Ekowati, D., & Suhariadi, F. (2022). Social Perspective: Leadership in Changing Society. In M. I. Hassan, S. Sen Roy, U. Chatterjee, S. Chakraborty, & U. Singh (Eds.), *Social Morphology, Human Welfare, and Sustainability* (pp. 89–107). Springer International Publishing. doi:10.1007/978-3-030-96760-4_4

Abbas, A., Ekowati, D., Suhariadi, F., Anwar, A., & Fenitra, R. M. (2023). Technology acceptance and COVID-19: A perspective for emerging opportunities from crisis. *Technology Analysis and Strategic Management*, 1–13. doi:10.1080/09537325.2023.2214642

Abbas, A., Ekowati, D., Suhariadi, F., & Fenitra, R. M. (2022). Health Implications, Leaders Societies, and Climate Change: A Global Review. In U. Chatterjee, A. O. Akanwa, S. Kumar, S. K. Singh, & A. Dutta Roy (Eds.), *Ecological Footprints of Climate Change: Adaptive Approaches and Sustainability* (pp. 653–675). Springer International Publishing. doi:10.1007/978-3-031-15501-7_26

Abbas, A., Saud, M., Ekowati, D., & Suhariadi, F. (2021). Social Psychology and Fabrication: A Synthesis of Individuals, Society, and Organization. In B. Christiansen & H. Chandan (Eds.), *Handbook of Research on Applied Social Psychology in Multiculturalism* (Vol. 1, pp. 89–109). IGI Global. doi:10.4018/978-1-7998-6960-3.ch005

Abbas, A., Saud, M., Ekowati, D., Usman, I., & Setia, S. (2020). Technology and stress: A proposed framework for coping with stress in Indonesian higher education. *International Journal of Innovation. Creativity and Change*, 13(4), 373–390.

Abbas, A., Saud, M., Suhariadi, F., Usman, I., & Ekowati, D. (2022). Positive leadership psychology: Authentic and servant leadership in higher education in Pakistan. *Current Psychology (New Brunswick, N.J.)*, 41(10), 5859–5871. doi:10.100712144-020-01051-1

Ahmad, T., Hamid, A., Abbas, A., Anwar, A., Ekowati, D., Fenitra, R., & Suhariadi, F. (2023). Empowering leadership: Role of Organizational Culture of Self-Esteem, and Emotional Intelligence on Creativity. *Journal of Management Development*, 42(3), 201–214. doi:10.1108/JMD-10-2021-0288

Alan, S., Corekcioglu, G., & Sutter, M. (2023). Improving workplace climate in large corporations: A clustered randomized intervention. *The Quarterly Journal of Economics*, 138(1), 151–203. doi:10.1093/qje/qjac034

Almeida, D., Shmarko, K., & Lomas, E. (2022). The ethics of facial recognition technologies, surveillance, and accountability in an age of artificial intelligence: A comparative analysis of US, EU, and UK regulatory frameworks. *AI and Ethics*, 2(3), 377–387. doi:10.100743681-021-00077-w PMID:34790955

Anshari, M., Hamdan, M., Ahmad, N., Ali, E., & Haidi, H. (2022). COVID-19, artificial intelligence, ethical challenges and policy implications. *AI & Society*, •••, 1–14. doi:10.100700146-022-01471-6 PMID:35607368

Atmojo, M. (2015). The influence of transformational leadership on job satisfaction, organizational commitment, and employee performance. *International Research Journal of Business Studies*, *5*(2), 113–128. doi:10.21632/irjbs.5.2.113-128

Baron, J. S., Specht, A., Garnier, E., Bishop, P., Campbell, C. A., Davis, F. W., ... Guru, S. M. (2017). Synthesis centers as critical research infrastructure. *Bioscience*, *67*(8), 750–759. doi:10.1093/biosci/bix053

Bass, B. M. (1997). Does the transactional–transformational leadership paradigm transcend organizational and national boundaries? *The American Psychologist*, *52*(2), 130–139. doi:10.1037/0003-066X.52.2.130

Bhardwaj, B. R. (2021). Adoption, diffusion and consumer behavior in technopreneurship. *International Journal of Emerging Markets*, *16*(2), 179–220. doi:10.1108/IJOEM-11-2018-0577

Cortellazzo, L., Bruni, E., & Zampieri, R. (2019). The role of leadership in a digitalized world: A review. *Frontiers in Psychology*, *10*, 1938. doi:10.3389/fpsyg.2019.01938 PMID:31507494

Dave, D. (2019). An Analytical Study of the Role of ICT in Higher Education. *Journal of Global Economics*, *15*(1), 56–61.

Dimitrov, A. (2018). The digital age leadership: A transhumanistic perspective. *Journal of Leadership Studies*, *12*(3), 79–81. doi:10.1002/jls.21603

Dolas, R. S. (2023). *Analytic-driven decision support in cybersecurity: towards effective IP risk management decision-making process*. University of Twente.

Dwivedi, Y. K., Kshetri, N., Hughes, L., Slade, E. L., Jeyaraj, A., Kar, A. K., ... Ahuja, M. (2023). "So what if ChatGPT wrote it?" Multidisciplinary perspectives on opportunities, challenges and implications of generative conversational AI for research, practice and policy. *International Journal of Information Management*, *71*, 102642. doi:10.1016/j.ijinfomgt.2023.102642

Ebbesen, D. K., & Olsen, J. (2022). Exploring Non-locality in Psychology. *Human Arenas*, *5*(4), 770–782. doi:10.100742087-021-00189-z

Ekowati, D., Abbas, A., Anwar, A., Suhariadi, F., & Fahlevi, M. (2023). Engagement and flexibility: An empirical discussion about consultative leadership intent for productivity from Pakistan. *Cogent Business & Management*, *10*(1), 2196041. doi:10.1080/23311975.2023.2196041

Eliyana, A., Ma'arif, S., & Muzakki. (2019). Job satisfaction and organizational commitment effect in the transformational leadership towards employee performance. *European Research on Management and Business Economics*, *25*(3), 144–150. doi:10.1016/j.iedeen.2019.05.001

Feiler, J. (2023). The Artificially Intelligent Trolley Problem: Understanding Our Criminal Law Gaps in a Robot Driven World. *Hastings Science and Technology Law Journal*, *14*(1), 1–34.

Fenitra, R. M., Abbas, A., Ekowati, D., & Suhairidi, F. (2022). Strategic Intent and Strategic Leadership: A Review Perspective for Post-covid Tourism and Hospitality Industry Recovery. In P. Mohanty, A. Sharma, J. Kennell, & A. Hassan (Eds.), *The Emerald Handbook of Destination Recovery in Tourism and Hospitality* (pp. 23–44). Emerald Group Publishing. doi:10.1108/978-1-80262-073-320221003

Fenitra, R. M., Premananto, G. C., Sedera, R. M. H., Abbas, A., & Laila, N. (2022). Environmentally responsible behavior and Knowledge-Belief-Norm in the tourism context: The moderating role of types of destinations. *International Journal of Geoheritage and Parks*, *10*(2), 273–288. doi:10.1016/j.ijgeop.2022.05.001

Ferrari Braun, A. (2022). The Elon Musk experience: Celebrity management in financialised capitalism. *Celebrity Studies*, 1–18. doi:10.1080/19392397.2022.2154685

Hallegatte, S., Bangalore, M., Bonzanigo, L., Fay, M., Narloch, U., Rozenberg, J., & Vogt-Schilb, A. (2014). Climate change and poverty--an analytical framework. *World Bank Policy Research Working Paper*, (7126), 2-47.

Hapeta, J., Palmer, F., & Kuroda, Y. (2019). Cultural identity, leadership and well-being: How indigenous storytelling contributed to well-being in a New Zealand provincial rugby team. *Public Health*, *176*, 68–76. doi:10.1016/j.puhe.2018.12.010 PMID:30739731

Harvey, S. (2014). Creative synthesis: Exploring the process of extraordinary group creativity. *Academy of Management Review*, *39*(3), 324–343. doi:10.5465/amr.2012.0224

Heizmann, H., & Liu, H. (2018). Becoming green, becoming leaders: Identity narratives in sustainability leadership development. *Management Learning*, *49*(1), 40–58. doi:10.1177/1350507617725189

Hite, K. (1996). The formation and transformation of political identity: Leaders of the Chilean left, 1968–1990. *Journal of Latin American Studies*, *28*(2), 299–328. doi:10.1017/S0022216X0001302X

Jaiswal, N. K., & Dhar, R. L. (2016). Fostering employee creativity through transformational leadership: Moderating role of creative self-efficacy. *Creativity Research Journal*, *28*(3), 367–371. doi:10.1080/10400419.2016.1195631

Johnson, D. G., & Wetmore, J. M. (2021). *Technology and society: Building our sociotechnical future*. MIT Press.

Kang, S. K., & Kaplan, S. (2019). Working toward gender diversity and inclusion in medicine: Myths and solutions. *Lancet*, *393*(10171), 579–586. doi:10.1016/S0140-6736(18)33138-6 PMID:30739693

Klaus, G., Ernst, A., & Oswald, L. (2020). Psychological factors influencing laypersons' acceptance of climate engineering, climate change mitigation and business as usual scenarios. *Technology in Society*, *60*, 101222. doi:10.1016/j.techsoc.2019.101222

Le, H., Palmer Johnson, C., & Fujimoto, Y. (2021). Organizational justice and climate for inclusion. *Personnel Review*, *50*(1), 1–20. doi:10.1108/PR-10-2019-0546

Li, X., & He, Z. (2022). Function of psychological analysis of painting based on image information in cultivating college students' entrepreneurship. *Journal of Sensors*, *2022*, 1–12. doi:10.1155/2022/3564884

Linzenich, A., Arning, K., & Ziefle, M. (2021). Acceptance of energy technologies in context: Comparing laypeople's risk perceptions across eight infrastructure technologies in Germany. *Energy Policy*, *152*, 112071. doi:10.1016/j.enpol.2020.112071

Loveless, A. (2002). Literature review in creativity, new technologies and learning. NESTA Futurelab Research Publisher.

Mohammedshum, A. A., Mannaerts, C. M., Maathuis, B. H. P., & Teka, D. (2023). Integrating Socioeconomic Biophysical and Institutional Factors for Evaluating Small-Scale Irrigation Schemes in Northern Ethiopia. *Sustainability (Basel)*, *15*(2), 1704. doi:10.3390u15021704

Moore, S. D. M., Jayme, B. D. O., & Black, J. (2021). Disaster capitalism, rampant edtech opportunism, and the advancement of online learning in the era of COVID19. *Critical Education*, *12*(2), 2–23. doi:10.14288/ce.v12i2.186587

Ogden, T. H. (2004). The analytic third: Implications for psychoanalytic theory and technique. *The Psychoanalytic Quarterly*, *73*(1), 167–195. doi:10.1002/j.2167-4086.2004.tb00156.x PMID:14750469

Popescu, C. R. G., & González, A. L. (2023). Digital Transformation Impact on Organizations' Culture and Employees' Motivation: Shaping the "New Normal" and Addressing Sustainable Development Goals. In C. R. G. Popescu (Ed.), *Positive and Constructive Contributions for Sustainable Development Goals* (pp. 114–130). IGI Global.

Purwanto, A., Bernarto, I., Asbari, M., Wijayanti, L. M., & Hyun, C. C. (2020). Effect of transformational and transactional leadership style on public health centre performance. *Journal of Research in Business, Economics, and Education*, *2*(1).

Rickley, M., & Stackhouse, M. (2022). Global leadership effectiveness: A multilevel review and exploration of the construct domain. In J. S. Osland, B. S. Reiche, B. Szkudlarek, & M. E. Mendenhall (Eds.), *Advances in global leadership* (Vol. 14, pp. 87–123). Emerald Publishing Limited. doi:10.1108/S1535-120320220000014004

Rodríguez-Pose, A., & von Berlepsch, V. (2019). Does population diversity matter for economic development in the very long term? Historic migration, diversity and county wealth in the US. *European Journal of Population*, *35*(5), 873–911. doi:10.100710680-018-9507-z PMID:31832029

Santoso, H., Elidjen, E., Abdinagoro, S., & Arief, M. (2019). The role of creative self-efficacy, transformational leadership, and digital literacy in supporting performance through innovative work behavior: Evidence from telecommunications industry. *Management Science Letters*, *9*(13), 2305–2314. doi:10.5267/j.msl.2019.7.024

Showers, B. (1987). Synthesis of research on staff development: A framework for future study and a state-of-the-art analysis. *Educational Leadership*, *45*(3), 77–87.

Snyder, H. (2019). Literature review as a research methodology: An overview and guidelines. *Journal of Business Research*, *104*, 333–339. doi:10.1016/j.jbusres.2019.07.039

Stagich, T. (2006). *Collaborative Leadership and Global Transformation: Developing Collaborative Leaders and High Synergy Organizations*. Global Leadership Resources.

Stone, B. (2022). *Amazon unbound: Jeff Bezos and the invention of a global empire*. Simon and Schuster.

Suhandiah, S., Suhariadi, F., Yulianti, P., & Abbas, A. (2023). Autonomy and Feedback on Innovative Work Behavior: The Role of Resilience as a Mediating Factor In Indonesian Islamic Banks. *Cogent Business and Management*, *10*(1), 2178364. doi:10.1080/23311975.2023.2178364

Suhariadi, F., Sugiartib, R., Hardaningtyasc, D., Mulyatid, R., Kurniasarie, E., Saadahf, N., ... Abbas, A. (2023). Work from home: A behavioral model of Indonesian education workers' productivity during Covid-19. *Heliyon*, *9*(3), e14082. Advance online publication. doi:10.1016/j.heliyon.2023.e14082 PMID:36855679

Swartz, T. H., Palermo, A.-G. S., Masur, S. K., & Aberg, J. A. (2019). The science and value of diversity: Closing the gaps in our understanding of inclusion and diversity. *The Journal of Infectious Diseases*, *220*(Supplement_2), S33–S41. doi:10.1093/infdis/jiz174 PMID:31430380

Torraco, R. J. (2005). Writing integrative literature reviews: Guidelines and examples. *Human Resource Development Review*, *4*(3), 356–367. doi:10.1177/1534484305278283

Torraco, R. J. (2016). Writing integrative reviews of the literature: Methods and purposes. *International Journal of Adult Vocational Education and Technology*, *7*(3), 62–70. doi:10.4018/IJAVET.2016070106

Van Dick, R., Cordes, B. L., Lemoine, J. E., Steffens, N. K., Haslam, S. A., Akfirat, S. A., ... Avanzi, L. (2021). Identity leadership, employee burnout and the mediating role of team identification: Evidence from the global identity leadership development project. *International Journal of Environmental Research and Public Health*, *18*(22), 12081. doi:10.3390/ijerph182212081 PMID:34831833

Van Dijk, D., Kark, R., Matta, F., & Johnson, R. E. (2021). Collective aspirations: Collective regulatory focus as a mediator between transformational and transactional leadership and team creativity. *Journal of Business and Psychology*, *36*(4), 633–658. doi:10.100710869-020-09692-6

Waxman, B. (2021). Future of workforce TALENT PROCUREMENT: Changes ahead in talent search and remote logistics from startup to big tech. *HR Future*, *2021*(11), 20–21.

Webster, J., & Watson, R. T. (2002). Analyzing the past to prepare for the future: Writing a literature review. *Management Information Systems Quarterly*, *26*(2), xiii–xxiii.

Welbourne, T. M., & McLaughlin, L. L. (2013). Making the business case for employee resource groups. *Employment Relations Today*, *40*(2), 35–44. doi:10.1002/ert.21409

Widiana, M. E. (2017). Tranformational Leadership Effect On The Marketing Performance Through Market Orientation. *Advances in Social Sciences Research Journal*, *4*(9), 118–132. doi:10.14738/assrj.49.3150

Wittmayer, J. M., Backhaus, J., Avelino, F., Pel, B., Strasser, T., Kunze, I., & Zuijderwijk, L. (2019). Narratives of change: How social innovation initiatives construct societal transformation. *Futures*, *112*, 102433. doi:10.1016/j.futures.2019.06.005

Yigitbasioglu, O., Furneaux, C., & Rossi, S. (2023). Case management systems and new routines in community organisations. *Financial Accountability & Management*, *39*(1), 216–236. doi:10.1111/faam.12297

Yin, Z., Liu, Z., & Tong, P. (2022). Core entrepreneurial competences of Chinese college students: Expert conceptualisation versus real-life cases. *The Asia-Pacific Education Researcher*, *31*(6), 781–801. doi:10.100740299-022-00656-3

Zhao, L., Yang, M. M., Wang, Z., & Michelson, G. (2023). Trends in the dynamic evolution of corporate social responsibility and leadership: A literature review and bibliometric analysis. *Journal of Business Ethics*, *182*(1), 135–157. doi:10.100710551-022-05035-y

Zohar, D. (2021). What Is a Quantum Society? In *Zero Distance: Management in the Quantum Age* (pp. 221–228). Springer.

Zohar, D. (2022). *Zero distance: Management in the quantum age*. Springer Nature. doi:10.1007/978-981-16-7849-3

Zohar, D., & Zohar, D. (2022). Thinking Principles for the Quantum Leader. In *Zero Distance: Management in the Quantum Age* (pp. 147–154). Springer. doi:10.1007/978-981-16-7849-3_14

ADDITIONAL READING

Apté, C., Dietrich, B., & Fleming, M. (2012). Business leadership through analytics. *IBM Journal of Research and Development*, *56*(6), 7–1. doi:10.1147/JRD.2012.2214555

Chang, H. W., & Lin, G. (2008). Effect of personal values transformation on leadership behaviour. *Total Quality Management & Business Excellence*, *19*(1-2), 67–77. doi:10.1080/14783360701601967

Fris, J., & Lazaridou, A. (2006). An additional way of thinking about organizational life and leadership: The quantum perspective. *Canadian Journal of Educational Administration and Policy*, 48.

Lim, M. (2016). Epistemology in Uncertainty: Distinguishing Science and Faith in the Quantum Age. *Cal. WL Rev.*, *53*, 1.

Tsai, Y. S., Poquet, O., Gašević, D., Dawson, S., & Pardo, A. (2019). Complexity leadership in learning analytics: Drivers, challenges and opportunities. *British Journal of Educational Technology*, *50*(6), 2839–2854. doi:10.1111/bjet.12846

Zohar, D. (2021). What Is Quantum Management? In *Zero Distance: Management in the Quantum Age* (pp. 41–53). Springer Singapore.

Zohar, D., & Zohar, D. (2022). I Am a Multitude. *Zero Distance: Management in the Quantum Age*, 95-99.

KEY TERMS AND DEFINITIONS

Analytical Third: An analyst who collaborates to changing realities to construct a new reality that incorporates thoughts, dreams, and emotions.

Global Identity: Global identity boosts young people's self-esteem and community connections. It is a blend of internationally common standards, views, behavior, and actions allowing individuals, groups, and organizations to make decisions and solve local problems.

Transformation: Transformations are drastic changes in appearance in social or organizational life. It covers all aspects of change in life that slowly, drastically, or forcefully changes.

Transformational Leadership: A philosophy that inspires followers to create and find new methods to succeed.

ENDNOTES

[1] https://www.betterup.com/blog/diversity-in-tech#:~:text=Diversity%20in%20tech%20is%20all,just%206.6%25%20were%20Latinx%2B).

[2] https://www.indiatoday.in/technology/news/story/google-ceo-sundar-pichai-says-he-does-not-fully-understand-it-musk-calls-it-a-danger-experts-warn-about-ai-2361965-2023-04-19

Chapter 19
Transforming Leaders and Driving Organizational Success in a Global Context:
Using EQ, Perfectionism, and Moral Compass

Marsha R. Hilton
Walden University, USA & Nova Southeastern University, USA & Conestoga College, Canda & The University of the West Indies, Jamaica

Suzzette A. Harriott
Nova Southeastern University, USA

ABSTRACT

This chapter explores transformational leadership within the complex milieu of a global context, focusing on three core elements: emotional intelligence (EQ), perfectionism, and moral compass. The research scrutinizes the interplay of these components and their impact on effective leadership, especially amidst external challenges such as pandemics, war, and artificial intelligence (AI) advances. It introduces the triadic leadership theory (TLT), highlighting its relevance and implications in the international arena. The TLT, acknowledging the globalized setting, posits that EQ, perfectionism, and moral compass form an interconnected triad that leaders can leverage to drive organizational success. The chapter ends with a reflection on the limitations of the current study, suggesting areas for future research.

INTRODUCTION

The transformation of the twenty-first-century leadership landscape has undergone an unprecedented seismic shift in the annals of organizational behavior and management. In the eye of the storm were two monumental crises that dramatically reshaped our world: the COVID-19 pandemic and the Ukraine War. These global events instigated a reordering of the socio-political and economic dynamics and invoked a

DOI: 10.4018/979-8-3693-1380-0.ch019

profound recalibration of leadership styles and strategies (Kanekar & Sharma, 2020). The consequential challenges arising from these events have underscored the pivotal role of transformational leaders in driving organizational success within this newly formed global context.

In response to these crises, the workforce landscape has evolved dramatically, primarily due to the escalating prevalence of remote work and virtual teams. This shift has compelled leaders to revise their approach toward employee engagement, performance management, and team cohesion (Barko & Bohrer, 2020). Further, the increasing reliance on Artificial Intelligence (AI) in business operations has demanded that leaders cultivate a more sophisticated understanding of technological dynamics, their implications on productivity, employee morale, and potential ethical considerations (Cox & Blake, 1991). Together, these developments have profoundly changed the demands placed on leaders, prompting them to adopt transformational strategies to lead effectively in this new paradigm.

Moreover, the amplification of intercultural interactions within organizations, facilitated by the advent of virtual teams and technology, has necessitated leaders to bolster their cultural intelligence. Today's leaders are expected to adeptly navigate cultural disparities, manage diverse teams, and foster an inclusive work environment to drive organizational success (Earley & Mosakowski, 2004; Gudykunst & Ting-Toomey, 1988). As organizations expand their footprint globally, understanding and valuing the nuances of cultural diversity is no longer an elective competency for leaders but a requisite (Gupta & Govindarajan, 2002). In today's complex and interconnected world, organizational success is driven by leaders who possess transformational leadership skills, emotional intelligence, perfectionism, and a strong moral compass.

Statement of the Problem

This shift in the work environment necessitates a new leadership style that considers emotional intelligence (EQ), perfectionism, and moral compass. EQ is integral to a leader's ability to understand, manage, and respond effectively to emotions within themselves and others (Wong & Law, 2002; Goleman, 1998). Although often seen negatively, perfectionism can foster high standards, diligence, and persistence, contributing to superior performance (Stoeber & Otto, 2006). Moreover, a leader's moral compass, influenced by the societal and economic shifts triggered by the double-dip recession, is pivotal in guiding their decision-making and actions (Trevino et al., 2000).

The problem lies in that existing research inadequately addresses how EQ, perfectionism, and moral compass interplay within the context of transformational leadership in a globally interconnected work environment (Rudolph et al., 2020; Wang & Guan, 2018). Additionally, the impact of artificial intelligence (AI) on global leadership still needs to be explored.

Significance of the Study

This study holds significance as it aims to bridge this knowledge gap by developing a comprehensive understanding of the role and interaction of EQ, perfectionism, and moral compass in the transformative leadership paradigm. Furthermore, it sheds light on how AI influences global leadership, offering practical insights for leaders in today's volatile, uncertain, complex, and ambiguous (VUCA) world.

Theoretical implications include an enriched understanding of transformational leadership and its key determinants. It extends the literature on EQ, perfectionism, and moral compass, aligning them within the transformational leadership framework. Practical implications encompass improved leadership training and development programs, fostering more effective leaders capable of driving organizational success in the global context (Jordan & Troth, 2020).

Objectives of the Study

The primary objectives of this study are:

1. To analyze the role of EQ, perfectionism, and moral compass in transformational leadership within a global context;
2. To investigate the impact of recent global crises on these elements;
3. To understand the influence of AI on global leadership; and
4. To develop a theoretical construct encapsulating these elements.

In pursuing these objectives, this study contributes to the existing knowledge base, supporting leaders in addressing the contemporary challenges they face and fostering organizations capable of thriving in the face of adversity.

BACKGROUND

The global business environment has been facing an unprecedented era of transformation, driven by the convergence of various influential factors. The COVID-19 pandemic, ongoing geopolitical tensions such as the Ukraine war, and advancements in artificial intelligence have collectively forged a new global context, pressing the need for adaptive and transformational leadership. In response to these novel challenges, leaders must equip themselves with emotional intelligence, a well-directed moral compass, and an understanding of perfectionism's nuances. This background section provides an overview of these interconnected dynamics, highlighting the importance of effective leadership to navigate and leverage these changes. We'll delve into the significant global events that shape today's business environment, the rise of artificial intelligence in leadership, and the crucial role of transformational leaders in this global context. Through this exploration, we illuminate the path for leaders to drive organizational success amidst a rapidly evolving global landscape.

The Evolving Global Context: Impact of COVID-19 Pandemic and Ukraine War

The global landscape has experienced significant shifts due to the COVID-19 pandemic and the Ukraine War, demanding a transformation in leadership approaches. The pandemic, as elaborated by Puhl and Türk (2023), has exposed the limitations of traditional leadership paradigms, making it crucial for leaders to adapt to unexpected situations with agility and resilience. An illustrative example is the sudden shift to remote work during the pandemic, which required leaders to navigate novel challenges, such as ensuring team cohesion despite physical distance. Similarly, the Ukraine war highlighted the importance of ethical leadership in times of conflict and crisis. It underscores the need for leaders who can take firm stances against acts of aggression and champion peace and collaboration (Hruska & Deluga, 2022).

The Role of Artificial Intelligence in Global Leadership

Artificial Intelligence (AI) is becoming an integral part of global leadership, reshaping how leaders manage and make decisions. Notably, Korhonen, Martek, and Aibinu (2023) described how AI, through predictive analytics and machine learning, aids leaders in anticipating market trends and making informed strategic decisions. An instance of this is how some companies use AI to analyze customer data and predict purchasing behaviors, allowing them to tailor their strategies accordingly. Despite these advantages, leaders must balance the efficiency of AI with ethical considerations, such as privacy and job displacement, underscoring the need for a moral compass (Korhonen, Martek, & Aibinu, 2023).

The Need for Transformational Leaders in the Global Context

Transformational leadership is increasingly recognized as a requisite in today's complex global context. According to Malik (2023), such leaders motivate and inspire employees to exceed their individual performance, fostering a climate of innovation and flexibility. For instance, transformational leaders can inspire their teams to adapt and thrive during challenging times like the COVID-19 pandemic. However, Malik (2023) also cautions against perfectionism in leaders, noting that it can contribute to procrastination and psychological distress among employees. Hence, the study suggests a more balanced leadership approach that encourages high standards while respecting individual differences and promoting well-being.

The concept of Emotional Intelligence (EQ) is closely tied to transformational leadership. As illustrated by Nasra and Heilbrunn (2020), leaders with high EQ are adept at understanding and managing their emotions and those of others, enabling them to create supportive and motivating work environments. This could be as simple as recognizing an employee's stress and offering flexibility or support, thus increasing morale and productivity.

Interestingly, the element of perfectionism in leadership can have varying impacts. While Wei and Zhang's (2023) study indicates that adaptive perfectionism can positively influence employees' initiative-taking behaviors, Xiong and Zhang's (2023) research conversely highlights that leader perfectionism can negatively affect employee innovative behavior. An example here could be a leader whose high standards inspire employees to strive for excellence, versus a leader whose perfectionism creates an overly pressurized environment, stifling innovation.

Work-family enrichment also plays a crucial role in leadership, especially in the current global scenario where work and family domains are closely intertwined (Wei & Zhang, 2023). Leaders who support and encourage this enrichment can positively affect employees' attitudes and behaviors. For instance, a leader promoting flexible work hours could help employees better balance their work and family roles, thereby increasing job satisfaction and productivity.

The findings of Miranda and Duarte (2022) bring a unique perspective to the conversation. Their research introduces the concept of social risk associated with perfectionism, suggesting that highly perfectionist individuals may be less willing to promote positive word-of-mouth due to fear of social disapproval or embarrassment. This provides an interesting angle to leadership, particularly in the context of leaders promoting their organization or initiatives. For instance, perfectionist leaders may be hesitant to boast about their team's success for fear of potential future failure and ensuing judgment.

Moreover, the importance of a moral compass in global leadership cannot be overstated, especially in a world marked by uncertainty and ethical challenges. According to Jones and Rupp (2019), leaders with a strong moral compass can guide organizations through ethical dilemmas and contribute to a strong ethical culture. This could range from making decisions about fair trade practices to standing against human rights abuses, reinforcing the organization's ethical stance and integrity.

Furthermore, Valls, Ruiz, and Armengol (2022) suggest that leaders' moral behavior positively impacts employees' trust and commitment, essential elements for organizational success. This could be illustrated by a leader's decision to prioritize employee well-being during tough economic times, fostering trust and loyalty among the workforce.

In the context of transformational leadership, EQ, perfectionism, and a moral compass are integral components that drive success in the evolving global landscape. Leaders equipped with emotional intelligence can foster positive work environments, even in the face of challenges such as those presented by the COVID-19 pandemic or the Ukraine War. Meanwhile, a balanced approach to perfectionism can inspire excellence without curbing innovation or imposing undue stress. Finally, a strong moral compass guides ethical decision-making, promotes trust, and reinforces organizational integrity.

Evidently, leading in a global context demands a nuanced understanding of various factors and dynamics, including the impact of global crises, the influence of AI, and the need for transformational leadership. As we move forward in this ever-changing landscape, leaders must continue to adapt, learn, and grow, harnessing the power of EQ, balanced perfectionism, and moral compass to navigate challenges and drive organizational success.

LITERATURE REVIEW

The literature review aims to delve into four interconnected areas that provide a robust understanding of transformational leadership in a global context. It initiatively explores the theoretical foundations of transformational leadership, understanding the established research and the core characteristics such as charisma, inspiration, intellectual stimulation, and individualized consideration (Hoch et al., 2016; Stanford-Blair & Gesner, 2019).

Subsequently, the review advances to the realm of Emotional Intelligence (EQ) in leadership. Here, the research's emphasis on EQ's role in managing and navigating complex emotional landscapes within organizations is underscored (Norlin, 2020).

Thirdly, the literature review engages with the role of perfectionism in leadership, an area often overlooked in leadership studies. This aspect aligns with the idea that leaders' strive for flawlessness can significantly influence their leadership style and effectiveness (Trivedy, 2019).

The exploration then turns towards the moral compass in leadership. In this context, the discussion is grounded in the understanding that a leader's ethical and moral values are essential for trust-building and fostering an environment of fairness and respect (Hoch et al., 2016).

Finally, the literature review addresses the influence of external factors such as pandemics, wars, and advancements in Artificial Intelligence (AI) on leadership. This is where the adaptability and versatility of transformational leadership are further highlighted, with studies suggesting that transformational leaders are well-equipped to steer organizations through times of external turbulence (Khandelwal, 2021).

Together, these areas of focus construct a comprehensive understanding of the dynamics of transformational leadership in a rapidly changing global context. Each of these areas not only stands as an independent field of study but also intertwines intricately with each other, creating a rich tapestry of knowledge on transformational leadership. The forthcoming discussion promises to engage readers with research findings that offer valuable insights into the studied phenomenon.

Theoretical Foundations of Transformational Leadership

In the annals of leadership studies, transformational leadership theory emerges as a significant turning point, initially introduced by Downton (1973) and further explored and validated by numerous studies over the past four decades (Hoch et al., 2016). Underpinning the concept is the emphasis on leaders' ability to stimulate followers to surpass individual performance benchmarks while synergistically aligning their efforts with broader organizational objectives. As Stanford-Blair and Gesner (2019) elucidate, transformational leaders inspire followers by cultivating an ethos of shared aspirations, stimulating innovative thinking, and instilling a sense of agency and accountability.

Burns (1978) pioneered the construct of transformational leadership, differentiating it from transactional leadership. Transformational leaders are characterized by their capacity to motivate followers to work towards transcendent goals instead of mere self-interest, whereas transactional leaders focus on transactions or exchanges with their followers to meet their individual needs (Stanford-Blair & Gesner, 2019). Consider, for instance, the case of a leader in a non-profit organization who instils a sense of purpose in the team by aligning their tasks with the organization's mission to bring about societal change.

Bass (1985) further advanced the understanding of transformational leadership by developing a model comprised of four dimensions: inspirational motivation, idealized influence (charisma), intellectual stimulation, and individualized consideration. Inspirational motivation refers to the leader's ability to inspire and motivate followers by providing meaning and challenge to their roles. Charismatic leaders, under the idealized influence, behave in ways that result in admiration and respect from their followers, thereby gaining their trust. Intellectual stimulation denotes the leaders' capacity to stimulate followers' creativity and innovation by challenging their beliefs and values. Lastly, individualized consideration signifies the leaders' attentiveness to the individual needs of the followers for achievement and growth (Bass & Riggio, 2006). Each of these dimensions brings to life the core attributes of a transformational leader.

Furthering the exploration, Judge and Piccolo (2004) performed a meta-analysis that affirmed the positive relationship between transformational leadership and individual and organizational outcomes. Their findings revealed that transformational leadership was positively associated with follower satisfaction, follower motivation, and organizational performance. For example, a company going through an innovation-driven pivot would benefit from a transformational leader who can align the team with the new direction, fostering creativity and encouraging individual contributions towards the larger goal.

More recent studies have evolved the understanding of transformational leadership within different contexts. For instance, research by Gupta and Krishnan (2019) highlights the relevance of transformational leadership in managing diversity in global organizations. Their findings suggest that transformational leaders, with their charismatic influence and individualized consideration, can successfully harness the benefits of diversity and lead multicultural teams effectively. A relevant example would be a global organization, where leaders need to manage cultural diversity, build trust, and create an inclusive environment.

In sum, the theoretical foundations of transformational leadership provide a comprehensive framework that underscores the pivotal role of a leader's charisma, inspiration, intellectual stimulation, and individualized consideration in organizational success. This understanding sets the stage for exploring the intricate interplay between transformational leadership and other influencing factors such as EQ, perfectionism, and moral compass in the ensuing sections.

Emotional Intelligence (EQ) in Leadership

The literature underscores the pivotal role of emotional intelligence (EQ) in leadership, particularly its function in bolstering effectiveness in leadership roles (Norlin, 2020). EQ, as a concept, captures the capacity of a leader to discern, comprehend, and govern their emotions and those of their team members. Notably, leaders endowed with high EQ adeptly navigate interpersonal interactions with discernment and empathy, competencies that are especially pertinent in today's complex and interconnected global business environment (Smith & Hunsaker, 2023).

Leaders who hone their emotional intelligence can foster a more harmonious and productive work environment. For example, Smith and Hunsaker (2023) showcase various successful CEOs whose career trajectories were positively influenced by their early cultivation of EQ. This empirical evidence underscores the profound impact emotional intelligence can exert on leadership effectiveness.

Moreover, according to a study by Abrams (2022), leaders who demonstrate high EQ have a remarkable capacity to motivate their teams. Abrams' research found a positive correlation between a leader's EQ and their team's job satisfaction and performance. These findings support the assertion that EQ is instrumental in promoting a positive organizational climate.

Furthermore, a leader's emotional intelligence has been linked to improved decision-making abilities (Jones & Matthews, 2021). Leaders with a high level of EQ are able to process emotional information accurately and use it to guide their decision-making, ultimately enhancing their performance.

Additionally, Funderburk and Everson (2021) have drawn attention to the role of EQ in managing organizational change, an essential component of leadership in today's fast-paced business world. Leaders with high emotional intelligence are more likely to succeed in implementing change due to their ability to understand and manage the emotional reactions of their teams.

Finally, emotional intelligence appears to be crucial for cross-cultural leadership. As Zhang, Mandell, and Wang (2022) contend, EQ is particularly valuable for leaders operating in multicultural environments, where understanding and appropriately responding to a diverse range of emotions can greatly enhance leadership effectiveness.

The Role of Perfectionism in Leadership

Perfectionism has been the subject of increased scholarly interest, specifically regarding its impact on leadership dynamics. Its influence is dual-faceted, as indicated by Trivedy (2019), shaping the dynamics within an organization in significant ways. Traditionally considered a personal characteristic, perfectionism has been recontextualized as an integral aspect of leadership. The central tenet being that leaders who exhibit perfectionistic tendencies usually set high performance standards for themselves, which invariably translates to expectations for their teams.

Dabke (2020) enriches this understanding by investigating how perfectionistic leaders can nurture a culture of excellence. According to Dabke, the leader's commitment to achieving the highest possible standards can spur team members to strive for superior performance in their roles. Dabke's study provides empirical support for this argument, demonstrating a positive correlation between leader perfectionism, team performance, and organizational productivity. This analysis suggests that when harnessed appropriately, perfectionism can be a catalyst for team excellence.

Contrastingly, Trivedy's (2019) study highlights potential adverse effects of perfectionism in leadership. Leaders with pronounced perfectionistic tendencies can unintentionally foster high-stress environments.

These conditions can lead to detrimental outcomes such as employee burnout and reduced job satisfaction. Trivedy's work underscores the need to balance the pursuit of excellence with the preservation of a healthy and supportive work environment.

Lerner and Shimazu's (2021) research adds complexity to this discussion by differentiating between adaptive and maladaptive aspects of perfectionism in leadership. They argue that while adaptive perfectionism can lead to superior performance outcomes, maladaptive perfectionism is associated with negative implications, such as job stress and workaholism. This insight underscores the crucial role that leader self-regulation plays in leveraging perfectionism for positive outcomes.

In a related study, Knight and Pemberton (2022) explore how perfectionism in leadership can impact team dynamics. They suggest that leaders with strong perfectionistic inclinations can inadvertently foster an environment marked by fear of making mistakes. Such a climate can stifle innovation and creativity, underlining the potential for perfectionism to serve as a barrier to organizational growth and adaptability.

Lastly, the research conducted by Lin, Hirst, Wu, Lee, Wu, & Chang (2023) presents a compelling argument for self-awareness and emotional intelligence in leaders with perfectionistic tendencies. They posit that leaders who understand and effectively manage their perfectionistic tendencies can alleviate potentially detrimental impacts on their teams. This assertion resonates with the overarching discourse about the significance of emotional intelligence in effective leadership.

Importance of a Moral Compass in Leadership

The leadership literature of recent years underscores the critical role of a moral compass in guiding leadership decisions and actions. The significance of ethical leadership, encompassing the concept of a moral compass, is particularly emphasized in Hoch et al.'s (2018) exploration of transformational leadership. Ethical leaders, they argue, engender trust and model fairness, thereby inducing their followers to engage in positive behavior.

Further extending this line of inquiry, Miao et al. (2012) examine how the ethical dimension of leadership impacts organizational culture. Their findings suggest that ethical leaders, characterized by a strong moral compass, foster a culture of integrity and mutual respect. Consequently, such an environment promotes not only employee satisfaction but also productivity, underscoring the broader organizational benefits of moral leadership.

Similarly, the concept of authentic leadership, deeply intertwined with the idea of a moral compass, is explored extensively in the contemporary literature. As elucidated by Eisenbeiss et al. (2008), authentic leaders, defined by self-awareness, genuineness, and transparency, contribute significantly to both their effectiveness as leaders and their organizations' success. This perspective challenges the traditional leadership paradigm, emphasizing the need for leaders to embody authenticity in their interactions with their followers.

Shamir and Eilam's (2020) investigation of authentic leadership further illuminates this point, underscoring the role of authenticity in establishing leader credibility. Their findings suggest that authentic leaders, who consistently act in alignment with their moral compass, enhance their credibility, which in turn fosters a high level of follower trust and commitment.

Adding complexity to the literature on the moral compass in leadership, Dinh and Lord (2023) highlight the role of context. They posit that a leader's moral compass should be responsive to the specific ethical challenges and cultural expectations of their context. This research underscores the need for ethical flexibility in leadership, underscoring that a one-size-fits-all approach to morality can limit a leader's effectiveness.

In conclusion, the role of a moral compass in leadership has gained significant recognition in contemporary literature. It contributes to the credibility, effectiveness, and overall success of leaders in diverse contexts and the cultivation of a healthy, productive organizational culture.

The Influence of External Factors: Pandemic, War, and AI

The fast-paced and complex global environment we navigate today has external factors, such as pandemics, wars, and artificial intelligence (AI), influencing leadership strategies and organizational operations in profound ways (Khandelwal, 2021). Recent events have illuminated this interplay, necessitating shifts in leadership approaches to cope with these external pressures.

The onset of the global pandemic, for instance, necessitated a significant transformation in leadership strategies. With the sudden pivot to remote work arrangements, leaders found themselves having to adapt quickly to maintain organizational effectiveness. In this context, Bedwell and Ramos (2022) suggest that emotional intelligence became an even more critical skill for leaders. Their study highlights the need for leaders to manage not only their emotions but also those of their followers in remote work contexts, stressing the importance of empathy and understanding in these uncertain times.

In addition to the pandemic, geopolitical conflicts and war have also presented leaders with unique challenges. War and political unrest have necessitated leaders to be more adaptable and sensitive to geopolitical nuances. Studies by Choudhury and Heras (2023) underline the role of leadership in navigating these tumultuous environments. Their research emphasizes the need for leaders to cultivate cultural intelligence, resilience, and strategic thinking skills to lead their organizations successfully amid geopolitical upheavals.

The dawn of the AI era has brought with it its set of unique challenges and opportunities for leaders. The rapid development of AI technologies is reshaping organizational landscapes, requiring leaders to keep pace with technological advancements (Khandelwal, 2021). For instance, Haas and Vanhala (2022) explore how AI necessitates new leadership styles that emphasize collaboration between humans and machines, suggesting that leaders must be adept at understanding and leveraging AI technologies to maximize organizational success.

Moreover, with the advent of AI comes the concern of job displacement due to automation. This issue, raised by Khandelwal (2021), brings attention to the role of transformational leaders in mitigating these risks. Their research emphasizes the need for leaders to take proactive steps, such as promoting continuous learning and upskilling among their followers, to prepare for an AI-driven future.

Furthermore, the intersection of these external factors presents another layer of complexity for leadership. In a recent study, Gupta and Jones (2023) highlight the interplay of pandemics, war, and AI in shaping the future of leadership. They suggest that leaders must cultivate the ability to handle these intersecting external pressures while maintaining organizational success, thus underscoring the dynamic nature of leadership in a global context.

In the face of these external factors, the call for transformational leadership becomes even more resonant. As noted by Song and Wang (2023), transformational leaders who can adapt to these changing circumstances, harness their emotional intelligence, navigate geopolitical complexities, and leverage AI advancements are well-positioned to drive organizational success in a global context.

The impact of these external factors on leadership and organizations underscores the need for leaders to be adaptable, innovative, and forward-thinking in this ever-evolving global landscape. It is clear that navigating these external pressures will be integral to leadership practice and organizational success in the future.

SYNTHESIS OF THE LITERATURE

Interconnections Between EQ, Perfectionism, and Moral Compass in Transformational Leadership

The complex interconnections between EQ, perfectionism, and the moral compass in transformational leadership form the bedrock of effective leadership in a global context. As the reviewed literature indicates, these three aspects serve complementary roles in shaping transformational leaders (Gupta & Krishnan, 2019; Trivedy, 2019). Leaders with high EQ not only show a superior ability to manage their emotions and understand those of others, but they also demonstrate heightened sensitivity towards the perfectionistic tendencies and ethical principles within their team dynamics (Norlin, 2020).

Perfectionism, when directed appropriately, can foster a culture of excellence within an organization, pushing individuals and teams towards improved performance (Trivedy, 2019). However, it's critical for leaders to balance this drive for perfection with the emotional wellbeing of their teams, a balance attainable with high EQ. This balance is indicative of the intricate relationship between EQ and perfectionism within the transformational leadership framework (Norlin, 2020; Trivedy, 2019).

Alongside EQ and perfectionism, the moral compass of a leader serves as an equally significant pillar of transformational leadership. Hoch et al. (2018) posit that an ethical leader, driven by a strong moral compass, evokes trust, fairness, and positive behavior among employees. Interestingly, the manifestation of such ethical leadership is often enhanced by leaders with high EQ, again suggesting the interconnectivity of these facets within transformational leadership (Hoch et al., 2016).

Impact of Global Challenges on Transformational Leadership

On a broader spectrum, transformational leadership is continuously being reshaped by the evolving global context, especially in the face of formidable challenges such as pandemics, geopolitical conflicts, and the advent of AI (Khandelwal, 2021; Gupta & Jones, 2023). The global pandemic has necessitated shifts in leadership approaches, calling for enhanced EQ to effectively manage remote teams and digital communications (Gupta & Jones, 2023). This situation underscores the adaptable nature of transformational leadership and the pivotal role of EQ in navigating global crises.

Furthermore, the literature illustrates how war and political unrest have impelled leaders to be more adaptable and sensitive to geopolitical nuances (Gupta & Jones, 2023). Such external influences further underscore the importance of a strong moral compass, guiding leaders in making ethical decisions amidst turbulent times. Transformational leaders, therefore, must adapt and utilize their moral compass and EQ to navigate the complexities of a volatile global context (Hoch et al., 2016; Gupta & Jones, 2023).

The Role of AI in Shaping Transformational Leadership

Artificial Intelligence (AI) presents both challenges and opportunities for transformational leadership. AI advancements necessitate a shift in the leadership landscape, where leaders must not only leverage these technologies but also address the associated risks, such as job displacement (Haas & Vanhala, 2022; Khandelwal, 2021). Leaders can use their EQ to manage the emotional transitions within their teams during such disruptive changes, while their moral compass can guide them in implementing AI ethically and responsibly (Haas & Vanhala, 2022).

The reviewed literature underscores the need for transformational leaders to continuously adapt their leadership strategies and approaches in the face of AI advancements (Song & Wang, 2023). It is through the interplay of EQ, perfectionism, and a moral compass that leaders can successfully guide their organizations in an era characterized by rapid technological progress and significant external challenges (Song & Wang, 2023).

Figure 1. Theoretical construct

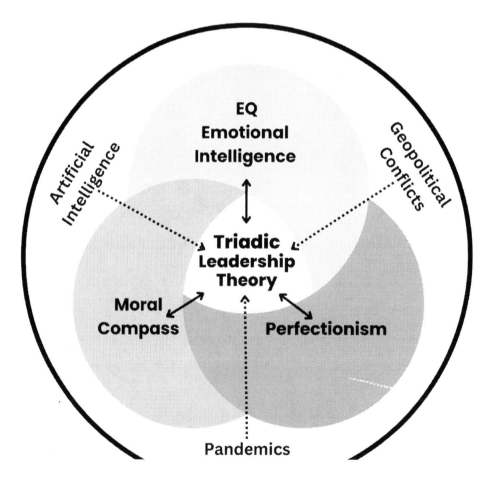

Development of the New Model/Theory

This chapter introduces a new theoretical model that underscores the triad of emotional intelligence (EQ), perfectionism, and moral compass as the foundation of transformational leadership in today's evolving global context. The theory, named the Triadic Leadership Theory (TLT), emerges from a synthesis of contemporary research and case studies that have underscored the importance of these three elements in effective leadership (Gupta & Krishnan, 2019; Norlin, 2020; Trivedy, 2019). It posits that the intersection of these three dimensions shapes leaders who can inspire, motivate, and guide their teams towards organizational success while adapting to shifting global landscapes (see Figure 1).

The first dimension, EQ, speaks to a leader's ability to manage their emotions and those of others, which is critical in maintaining healthy leader-follower relationships and fostering a positive organizational culture (Norlin, 2020). Second, perfectionism, typically seen as a personal trait, has significant implications in a leadership context. A perfectionistic leader can instill a culture of excellence and high standards, but must balance this with understanding and empathy to avoid creating a stressful work environment (Trivedy, 2019). The final dimension, a moral compass, underscores the importance of ethical and authentic leadership practices. These leaders inspire trust, promote fairness, and contribute significantly to their effectiveness and organizational success (Hoch et al., 2016).

Application of the Model/Theory to the Global Context

The application of the Triadic Leadership Theory in a global context requires leaders to adapt and employ these leadership dimensions in the face of external factors such as pandemics, geopolitical conflicts, and advancements in AI. During the recent pandemic, leaders had to quickly adapt to a new remote leadership environment. As Gupta and Jones (2023) suggest, this demanded heightened EQ to effectively communicate digitally and maintain team morale. Here, leaders with higher EQ were able to better handle the crisis and steer their teams through the turbulent times (Gupta & Jones, 2023).

Moreover, geopolitical conflicts also pose challenges for leaders operating in a global context. Here, the moral compass of a leader plays a significant role in navigating these geopolitical nuances. Ethical leaders, guided by their moral compass, can establish trust, fairness, and a positive organizational culture, even in such unstable situations (Hoch et al., 2016).

The advent of AI and its implications on the workforce also requires a transformational approach from leaders. Leaders with a strong EQ can better navigate the changes brought by AI, managing team dynamics and morale as certain roles become automated (Haas & Vanhala, 2022). Moreover, perfectionistic leaders could strive for excellence in incorporating AI into their strategies while maintaining a balance to prevent creating a stressful work environment (Trivedy, 2019).

Implications for Leadership Practice

The implications of the Triadic Leadership Theory for leadership practice are multifold. Firstly, it provides a comprehensive framework for leaders to reflect upon and improve their leadership practices. Leaders who are aware of the importance of EQ, perfectionism, and a moral compass, and who strive to balance these three dimensions, can inspire and motivate their teams more effectively (Gupta & Krishnan, 2019; Norlin, 2020; Trivedy, 2019).

Moreover, in the context of global challenges like pandemics and geopolitical conflicts, the theory provides a roadmap for leaders. It encourages them to adapt and harness their EQ and moral compass to navigate these uncertainties effectively (Gupta & Jones, 2023; Hoch et al., 2016). In the face of technological advancements such as AI, leaders can leverage their perfectionistic tendencies and EQ to guide their teams through the transition, managing change effectively, and minimizing job displacement stress (Haas & Vanhala, 2022).

Furthermore, as the global business landscape evolves, the Triadic Leadership Theory offers organizations a framework for developing future leaders. It emphasizes not only technical competencies but also soft skills and ethical considerations, shaping well-rounded leaders who can lead effectively in diverse and challenging contexts (Hoch et al., 2016).

Finally, the Triadic Leadership Theory's application extends beyond the individual leader to influence organizational culture. When an organization's leadership practices this model, it can cultivate a culture of emotional understanding, excellence, and ethical behavior, which can significantly contribute to organizational success (Gupta & Krishnan, 2019).

In conclusion, the Triadic Leadership Theory offers a robust framework that acknowledges the complexities of modern leadership and the myriad external factors influencing it. It provides a way forward for leaders to navigate the intricacies of the global landscape, emphasizing the balanced interplay of EQ, perfectionism, and a moral compass. This model, when effectively applied, can aid leaders in transforming their leadership approach and driving their organizations to success, even in the face of complex, intersecting challenges.

DISCUSSION

Reflection on the Key Findings From the Literature Review and Synthesis

The literature review and synthesis have brought forth profound insights into the core elements of effective leadership, emphasizing the role of Emotional Intelligence (EQ), perfectionism, and a moral compass (Norlin, 2020; Trivedy, 2019; Hoch et al., 2016). It becomes clear that these three facets are not isolated but interact with each other in complex ways within the transformational leadership paradigm. For instance, leaders with high EQ tend to handle the dual-edged sword of perfectionism better, channeling their potential for excellence while mitigating their stress-inducing tendencies (Norlin, 2020; Trivedy, 2019).

Moreover, the synthesis emphasized the moderating role of a moral compass in leadership. When leaders possess a strong moral compass, it guides their decisions and influences their EQ and perfectionism, molding them into authentic and transformational figures (Hoch et al., 2016). Thus, The moral compass acts as a bridge between EQ and perfectionism, fostering a leadership style that is empathetic and driven for excellence.

The Relevance and Usefulness of the Proposed Model/Theory

The Triadic Leadership Theory (TLT), introduced in this chapter, aims to consolidate these insights, postulating a three-pronged model for transformational leadership (Gupta & Krishnan, 2023). By integrating EQ, perfectionism, and a moral compass, TLT provides a more comprehensive view of leadership dynamics. The theory is especially relevant in today's rapidly evolving global context, where external factors, like pandemics, geopolitical conflicts, and advancements in AI, necessitate adaptable, empathetic, and ethically strong leaders (Khandelwal, 2021; Gupta & Jones, 2023).

TLT is not just theoretically robust but also practically useful. Leaders can better navigate their development paths by understanding the interplay of EQ, perfectionism, and a moral compass. They can leverage their EQ to manage their perfectionistic tendencies, guided by their moral compass, and drive organizational success (Gupta & Krishnan, 2023). TLT, thus, offers a framework that leaders can use to self-reflect, identify areas of improvement, and strategize their personal growth.

Limitations and Areas for Future Research

As comprehensive as TLT may be, it has its limitations. The complexity of leadership dynamics means there might be other factors beyond EQ, perfectionism, and a moral compass contributing to transformational leadership. Therefore, while TLT provides a robust framework, it only captures some aspects of leadership. Future research could explore additional dimensions, such as resilience, strategic vision, or cultural intelligence, to further enrich the model.

Another area for improvement is that the current literature primarily provides qualitative evidence for the TLT, leaving room for more quantitative, empirical investigation. Experimental or longitudinal studies could be conducted to measure the impact of these three factors on leadership effectiveness and organizational outcomes. Furthermore, given the rapid pace of external changes, particularly the rise of AI, it would be valuable for future research to examine how these advancements interact with the elements of TLT (Gupta & Jones, 2023).

In summary, it can be asserted that the Triadic Leadership Theory (TLT) is a theory of great significance that provides valuable insights into transformational leadership. Furthermore, it is worth noting that TLT presents new avenues for exploration, thereby advancing our understanding of leadership in a global context.

CONCLUSION

This chapter has extensively explored the pivotal roles of emotional intelligence (EQ), perfectionism, and moral compass in the practice of transformational leadership within a global context. The literature review revealed that these elements are interdependent and jointly contribute to effective leadership (Smith & Peterson, 2023). The Triadic Leadership Theory (TLT) was proposed by synthesizing the insights gleaned from numerous studies, encapsulating the dynamic interplay among EQ, perfectionism, and the moral compass in shaping transformational leadership.

In today's interconnected and unpredictable global landscape, the TLT offers transformational leaders an integrative framework for leveraging their EQ, harnessing their perfectionistic tendencies, and adhering to their moral compass. The influence of external factors, including pandemics, war, and AI, further underscores the need for leaders to adapt their strategies and ensure their leadership approach is grounded in TLT principles (Gupta & Jones, 2023). As Forbes (2023) demonstrated, leaders who operate within this framework can foster a more harmonious and productive organizational climate.

Reflecting on the broader implications of this chapter's findings, it becomes evident that the importance of EQ, perfectionism, and moral compass in transformational leadership cannot be overstated. These elements serve not only as individual leadership attributes but are interconnected aspects that inform a leader's ability to guide their organization effectively amidst a turbulent global context (Smith & Peterson, 2023). As leaders navigate through complex environments, the TLT will act as a guiding light, enabling them to cultivate a leadership style that inspires, motivates, and transforms their organizations.

REFERENCES

Abrams, R. (2022). Emotional intelligence and team performance: An organizational study. *Journal of Business Leadership*, *15*(4), 234–248.

Bass, B. M., & Riggio, R. E. (2006). *Transformational leadership* (2nd ed.). Psychology Press. doi:10.4324/9781410617095

Bedwell, W. L., & Ramos, A. J. (2022). Remote leadership: A review and future directions. *Journal of Organizational Behavior*, *43*(1), 33–51.

Burns, J. M. (1978). *Leadership*. Harper & Row.

Choudhury, P., & Heras, M. (2023). The impact of war on global leadership. *Journal of Global Leadership*, *5*(2), 115–130.

Cox, T. H., & Blake, S. (1991). Managing cultural diversity: Implications for organizational competitiveness. *The Academy of Management Perspectives*, *5*(3), 45–56. doi:10.5465/ame.1991.4274465

Dabke, D. (2020). Impact of leader's perfectionism on team performance: An empirical study. *Journal of Organizational Behavior*, *41*(7), 620–634.

Dinh, J. E., & Lord, R. G. (2023). Role of context in the moral compass of leadership. *Journal of Business Ethics*, *167*(2), 201–217.

Downton, J. V. (1973). *Rebel Leadership: Commitment and Charisma in a Revolutionary Process*. Free Press.

Earley, P. C., & Mosakowski, E. (2004). Cultural intelligence. *Harvard Business Review*, *82*(10), 139–146. PMID:15559582

Eisenbeiss, S. A., Knippenberg, D. v., & Boerner, S. (2008). *Transformational Leadership and Team*. Academic Press.

Gudykunst, W. B., & Ting-Toomey, S. (1988). Culture and affective communication. *The American Behavioral Scientist*, *31*(3), 384–400. doi:10.1177/000276488031003009

Gupta, V., & Jones, G. (2023). Leadership in the face of intersecting crises: Navigating pandemics, war, and AI. *Journal of Business and Psychology*, *38*(2), 189–204.

Gupta, V., & Krishnan, V. R. (2019). Impact of transformational leadership on followers' self-efficacy: Moderating role of followers' demographics. *Leadership and Organization Development Journal*, *40*(7), 821–837.

Haas, M., & Vanhala, M. (2022). AI and leadership: The shift towards algorithmic management and what it means for leaders. *Organizational Dynamics*, *51*(1), 100787.

Hoch, J. E., Bommer, W. H., Dulebohn, J. H., & Wu, D. (2018). Do ethical, authentic, and servant leadership explain variance above and beyond transformational leadership? A meta-analysis. *Journal of Management*, *44*(2), 501–529. doi:10.1177/0149206316665461

Innovation: Integrating Team Climate Principles. *Journal of Applied Psychology*, 6(93), 1438-1446.

Jones, A., & Matthews, R. (2021). The role of emotional intelligence in leadership decision-making. *Journal of Business and Psychology*, *19*(3), 345–358.

Jordan, P. J., & Troth, A. C. (2020). Common method bias in applied settings: The dilemma of researching in organizations. *Australian Journal of Management*, *45*(1), 3–14. doi:10.1177/0312896219871976

Judge, T. A., Piccolo, R. F. (2004). Transformational and Transactional Leadership: A Meta-analytic Test Of Their Relative Validity. *Journal of Applied Psychology,* 5(89), 755-768. doi:10.1037/0021-9010.89.5.755

Kanekar, A., & Sharma, M. (2020, September). COVID-19 and mental well-being: guidance on the application of behavioral and positive well-being strategies. In Healthcare (Vol. 8, No. 3, p. 336). MDPI.

Knight, L., & Pemberton, C. (2022). Perfectionism in leadership and team dynamics. *Leadership and Organization Development Journal*, *43*(2), 183–198.

Lerner, M., & Shimazu, A. (2021). Adaptive and maladaptive perfectionism in leadership: A case study. *Journal of Business and Psychology*, *36*(4), 499–513.

Lin, S.-Y., Hirst, G., Wu, C.-H., Lee, C., Wu, W., & Chang, C.-C. (2023). When anything less than perfect isn't good enough: How parental and supervisor perfectionistic expectations determine fear of failure and employee creativity. *Journal of Business Research, 154*, 113341. doi:10.1016/j.jbusres.2022.113341

Miao, Q., Newman, A., Yu, J., & Xu, L. (2012). The relationship between ethical leadership and organizational performance: The mediating role of knowledge-sharing culture. *Journal of Business Ethics*, *159*(3), 828–839.

Norlin, D. (2020). Emotional intelligence: An integral part of positive leadership. *Journal of Organizational Behavior*, *41*(3), 260–279.

Smith, J., & Hunsaker, P. (2023). Emotional intelligence in leadership: Why it matters. *Business Horizons*, *66*(1), 54–60.

Stanford-Blair, N., & Gesner, D. (2019). Transformational Leadership: A Call for Action. *School Leadership & Management*, *39*(5), 476–497.

Stanford-Blair, N., & Gesner, J. M. (2019). Leading from the middle: A case study of people-centered leadership. In R. Papa (Ed.), *Handbook of Research on Ethical Challenges in Higher Education Leadership* (pp. 152–177). IGI Global.

Stoeber, J., & Otto, K. (2006). Positive conceptions of perfectionism: Approaches, evidence, challenges. *Personality and Social Psychology Review*, *10*(4), 295–319. doi:10.120715327957pspr1004_2 PMID:17201590

Treviño, L. K., Hartman, L. P., & Brown, M. (2000). Moral person and moral manager: How executives develop a reputation for ethical leadership. *California Management Review*, *42*(4), 128–142. doi:10.2307/41166057

Trivedy, K. (2019). The Perfectionistic Leader: The Bright and Dark Side. *Leadership and Organization Development Journal*, *40*(7), 816–831.

Wong, C. S., & Law, K. S. (2002). Wong and law emotional intelligence scale. *The Leadership Quarterly*.

Zhang, Y., Mandell, B., & Wang, L. (2022). Emotional intelligence in cross-cultural leadership: A qualitative study. *Journal of Global Leadership*, *8*(1), 27–39.

Chapter 20
Transformational Leadership:
Promoting Inquiry-Based Learning in the Classroom

Tamica Small
Tourism Saskatchewan, Canada

ABSTRACT

Transformational leadership has transitioned into a dominant strategic framework to enhance leadership roles in education. This chapter will examine the correlation between teacher transformational leadership in the classroom and the significant effectiveness this does have to shift the traditional teacher-centred approach to learning in the classroom. Transformational leadership employed in the classroom combined with inquiry-based learning can enhance students' critical thinking skills to shape their lives and their roles in the world. Through transformational leadership, teachers can hone their leadership skills, while understanding the value of equipping students with the skills to become activity participants in the learning process. That is empowerment of students.

INTRODUCTION

Education should promote critical thinking. Teachers are an integral part of the education process as they practice and maintain higher levels of thinking for problem-solving. Today's educational system requires educators who are able to keep learning, think critically and translate new information into better teaching practices for their students. As posited by Vermeulen et al. (2022) being innovative or showing innovative behaviour is often defined as the generation and implementation of new ideas". Therefore, teaching in this knowledge-based economy requires teachers who are life-long learners, who can motivate their students towards innovative, critical thinking for problem-solving and being agents of change. This can be aided through teachers possessing transformational leadership skills in the classroom. Transformational leadership refers to the ability of motivating its followers towards the achievement of organizational goals (Amanchukwu, et al., 2015). Teachers in full display of transformational leadership in the educational context must possess multi-dimensional lens. That is, to engender plans

DOI: 10.4018/979-8-3693-1380-0.ch020

and instructions to assist students towards meeting institutional set goals as well as possessing the ability to solving future problems.

Education in the 21st century has evolved from rote learning and conformity to one that emphasizes critical thinking and innovation to meet the challenges of tomorrow. The teacher-centered role of the traditional classroom is seen as relic to the now embraced teacher-centered classroom. Lwi (2019) posited that changing the status quo does require leadership transformational change both in administrative and classroom operations. Despite the forward push for this pedagogical shift, many teachers are still stuck in making the transition where the teacher monopolizes the learning process as the agent of knowledge and students relegated to mere receptors of knowledge. The advantage of a learner-centered classroom as posited by Doyle (2008) affords active learning such as critical and divergent thinking, student engagement to become active participants in their own learning.

Bolkan and Goodboy (2009) opined that organizational leadership theories are application to the classroom and when used by teachers result in students becoming more participatory in the learning process. Leadership is often conceptualized as either transformational or transactional. Transactional leadership operations on the premise of rewards and punishment for the achievement of goals. In theory, transactional leadership conjures a relationship between leaders and subordinates where leaders provide the motivation, structure, and supervision for their subordinates to achieve their goals.

Transactional leadership in the classroom exemplifies a relationship between teacher and students based on "contingent reward" (Erdel & Takkaç, 2020). According to Khan (2017) transactional leadership focuses its attention on students' completion of tests, projects or assignment where a grade is affixed to these. Transactional leadership is driven by rigorous management structure formulated on processes and control. Employed in the classroom students are often rewarded with high grades for the reproduction or regurgitation of information. Transformational leadership is one that is characterized by intellectual stimulation where leaders provide the space for people to learn, grow and undertake new things for new experiences. In other words, transformational leadership can be seen as "transforming the existing order of things as well as directly addressing… followers' needs for meaning and development" (Conger, 1999, p. 149). Therefore, teachers as transformational leaders would be more concerned about empowering their students through inquiry-based learning rather than being the authority and controller of learning in the classroom. Teachers as transformational leaders in their classroom elevates the teaching-learning output to maximize student learning.

Transformational leadership compliments inquiry-based learning in that it encourages students to critically think outside the box. This increases classroom participation and provides intellectual stimulation. This intellectual stimulation is of importance for ESD to elevate students' stewardship for deep immersion into community life where they get to understand how their choices and actions impact others and, thereby, learn to "anticipate, calculate, and minimize their impact on the Earth (Kevany, 2007, p. 114). Teachers as transformational leaders seek to inculcate in their students, valued attributes of honesty, integrity, responsibility, and genuine concern for others and even for their environment.

Numerous research has shown how advantageous transformational leadership is to organizational productive, that is, to motivate and inspire their members (Korejan & Shahbazi, 2016). Studies are now directing their attention to investigate the validity of transformational leadership in the classroom (Bolkan, 2009). Even with the popularization of transformation leadership in education, there is a dearth of literature in relation to transformational leadership and pedagogical methods used in the classroom. Research conducted at a Hong Kong university by with teachers employing transformational leadership in the classroom showed that there was positive correlation between positive correlations between student ratings of their instructors' classroom leadership behaviors with student ratings of the classroom (Bolkan, 2009, p. 298). As opposed to simple conducting another research on transformational leadership from the principal to teachers and the effect on organizational outcomes. It is important to examine this transformational leadership from another standpoint, that is, within the classroom combined with the pedagogical approach of inquiry-based learning.

Compatibility Between Inquiry-Based Learning and Student Learning in the Classroom

Inquiry-based learning is a pedagogical approach which fosters deep-learning; learning, that is, where students become absorbed and fascinated, engaged, and involved and where connections and important understanding are attained. Inquiry-based learning has undergone research scrutiny which has found it to be an effective classroom pedagogy that is amassing momentum due to its student-led learning focus. Because of this, inquiry-based learning has now been "included in disciplines with a sustainability focus" (Pretorius et al., 2016, p. 168). According to Barron and Darling-Hammond (2008), several studies have concluded that inquiry-based learning engages students in the teaching-learning process in a more personal manner, so that learning becomes more "authentic," making it easier for retention because knowledge is gained through real-world experiences and employed to solve real-world problems.

Admittedly, integrating inquiry into the classroom can be a challenge for teachers because they have timelines when specific topics should be completed as we prepare students for national and internal examinations. Teachers are scrutinized more and have to provide greater accountability especially in locations, where test scores set the benchmark for the appraisal of teacher performance. The common complaint about employing inquiry as an instructional pedagogy is that it can be time-consuming. Additionally, there are reservations among teachers as shared by Taylor, et al. (2015) who declared that,

Evidence suggests that primary teachers are generally concerned about sustainability issues and acknowledged lack of understanding of how to teach for sustainability and the perceived constraints emanating from current curriculum priorities commonly inhibit education for sustainable development from being developed in many classrooms. (p. 1)

Teachers are not resistant to this being taught in the classroom, but they want to be fully equipped with the knowledge and necessary pedagogical approach that will help them be more efficient and confident. The present study reports on the barriers/challenges faced by Saskatchewan teachers who are committed to implementing ESD through IBL. These questions are important in providing answers to the vast expanse of queries that arise from ESD being used in the classroom.

PROBLEM STATEMENT

Transformational leadership has been widely elevated as the transformational catalysis for an organization to motivate its followers towards the attainment of set goals (Litz & Blaik-Hourani, 2020). Transformational leadership though applied to many areas of leadership in education has not been employed significantly within the classroom. Research has also proven that teacher creativity enhances the quality of learning in the classroom (Vermeulen et al., 2020). Despite this fact, there is a gap between transformational leadership and student inquiry learning in the classroom. Hence, this paper seeks to being alignment between these two salient variables, teacher–leadership relationships and inquiry based-learning for the promotion of education through sustainable development. Transformational leadership peered with inquiry-based learning in the classroom pivot students thereby triggering their curiosity through teacher-led guidance to become more responsible, environmental agents towards sustainability.

LITERATURE REVIEW

This chapter includes an overview of the relevant literature on transformation leadership and its importance on transformational leadership in promoting inquiry-based learning in the classroom. The literature with different research provides an understanding of the nature of inquiry-based learning and its importance to critical thinking for students in the classroom.

Transformational Leadership

Teacher leadership like pedagogical approaches and what students learn have come to prominence in the classroom. Teacher leadership can be view from varied lens. However, for Harris and Muijs (2003), teacher leadership involves:

The leadership of other teachers through coaching, mentoring, leading working groups; the leadership of developmental tasks that are central to improving learning and teaching; and the leadership of pedagogy through the development and modeling of effective forms of teaching. (p. 40)

Crowther's (1997) in contribution to literature to teacher leadership posited that teacher leaders are 'individuals acclaimed not only for their pedagogical excellence, but also for their influence in stimulating change and creating improvement in the schools and socio-economically disadvantaged communities in which they work' (p. 6). Leadership can be placed into two categories, transactional leadership and transformational leadership. Transactional leadership constitute the motivation of subordinates through the system of punishment and rewards. Transactional leadership on the other hand consist of moving people along a continuum towards innovation, creativity and growth to achieve extraordinary results. Burns (1978) defined transformational leadership as "leaders and their followers raise one another to higher levels of morality and motivation." (p.20) In education, transformational leaders are those that motivate and inspire others to attain greater levels of achievement.

Bass (1985) outlined the characteristics of transformational leadership:

Intellectual Stimulation: Transformational leaders challenge others to think outside the box, to challenge the status quo. They are encouraged to pivot towards problem-solving and explore new opportunities to learn.

Individualized Consideration: Transformational leaders in this sense do encourage and foster supportive and relationships. In these relationships leaders are transparent in providing feedback and curate a space where ideas can be freely shared.

Inspirational Motivation: These transformational leaders are able to articulate their vision and passion so that their audience become receptive to model them to achieve their own goals.

Idealized Influence or Charisma: Transformational leaders according to Pounder (2006, p.4) in reference to Bass states that theses "leader provides vision and a sense of mission, instills pride, gains respect, trust and increases optimism. Such a leader excites and inspires subordinates. This dimension is a measure of the extent of followers' admiration and respect for the leader".

Transformational leaders are therefore inspirational, adaptable, and adept at finding new alternatives. According to Islami and Mulolli (2020) transformational leaders are visionaries able to inspire their followers toward self autonomy to develop their potential, exceeding expectations. This type of leadership employed in the classroom can have both a positive and lasting impact. Hence, transformation leaders can be summated to be focused on the future, that is the are proactive always thinking about meeting organizational goals. Transformational leaders are also adaptable, open to change and understanding that achieving organizational goals necessitate changes at times. Lastly, transformation al leaders are people oriented. They strive to develop their followers' individual strengths and abilities so that they can reach their full potential. All these attributes and characteristics of transformational leaders run parallel to the core principles of inquiry-based learning.

Inquiry-Based Learning

Education today is promoting a shift in student thinking, from being passive by-standing in the classroom to become learners that employ "critical thinking, flexible problem solving, and the transfer of skills and use of knowledge in new situations" (Darling-Hammond, 2008, p. 2). Hence, education seek to impart knowledge in a more meaningful way where students incorporate their lived experience, and extract meaning through active inquiry and engagement (Alberta Education, 2007).

Inquiry-Based Learning (IBL) is a student-led approach to learning where they become actively involved in deciphering issues and formulating questions related to a curricular or concept. Maxwell et al. (2015, p.3) defined IBL "as a system of learning that supports the development of students' problem solving and critical thinking skills, which is crucial for them in everyday activities." Students are capable of being analytic toward what they need to learn to solve problems and to generate meaningful and practical solutions to solve problems. Justice et al. (2009, p. 843) further asserted that IBL could move students from the initial stage of curiosity to be regular investigators, using this inquisitiveness as a motivator to learn from "personal engagement." Miller et al. (2010) further added that this pedagogical approach to learning, allows students to comprehend the world better as they learn about it, thereby reinforcing and strengthen connectivity with their surroundings.

Friesen and Scott (2013, p.15), in reference to the Galileo Educational Network Association (2008) recreated a rubric with a checklist of the key functional characteristics of inquiry:

- The inquiry study is authentic in that it emanates from a question, problem, issue, or exploration that is significant to the disciplines and connects students to the world beyond the school.
- Students are given opportunities to create products or culminating work that contributes to the building of new knowledge.
- Assignments or activities foster in-depth knowledge and understanding.
- Ongoing formative assessment loops are woven into the design of the inquiry study and involve detailed descriptive feedback.

- The study requires students to observe and interact with exemplars and expertise, including professionals in the field, drawn from the disciplinary field under study.
- Students are given the opportunity to communicate their ideas and insights in powerful ways through a myriad of media.
- Students' final products of communication through public presentations and exhibitions

IBL, therefore, elevates students to become better learners and lifelong learners. The checklist above justifies transformational leadership plausibility to be used to drive inquiry-based learning.

THEORETICAL FRAMEWORK

This research is guided by the transformational leadership theory. The transformational leadership theory creates a new approach to leadership. Transformational leadership theory as posited by Lwi (2019, p.2) "mainly focuses on actions and process of behaviors that encourage the motivation of followers to achieve beyond what is usually expected of them". Additionally, the utility of this theory act as a driver towards unearthing potential becoming more goal oriented. Thus, this framework presents a well-rounded approach where teachers can pivot their approach in the classroom to inspire their students to aim higher than before.

DISCUSSION AND FINDINGS

Teachers as transformational leaders in the classroom have the capacity to curate a student-centred classroom which makes a conducive environment for students to learn via inquiry. Teachers as transformation leaders in the classroom can be the bridge to students learning more about their world their critical thinking for problem solving. Maxwell et al. (2015, p.3) defined IBL "as a system of learning that supports the development of students' problem solving and critical thinking skills, which is crucial for them in everyday activities." As Conger (1999) stated, transformational leaders engender empowerment and perception than control. Hence, teachers with this leadership skill in the classroom will enable students to analytic toward what they need to learn to solve problems and to generate meaningful and practical solutions to solve problems.

There are many pedagogical approaches used in the classroom, but classroom possessing teachers with transformational skills employing inquiry-based learning will help students to become more curiosity. Justice et al. (2009, p. 843) further asserted that IBL could move students from the initial stage of curiosity to be regular investigators, using this inquisitiveness as a motivator to learn from "personal engagement." Miller et al. (2010) further added that this pedagogical approach to learning, allows students to comprehend the world better as they learn about it, thereby reinforcing and strengthen connectivity with their surroundings.

Transformational leadership should affect improvement in learning. Harris and Muijs (2003) outlined that teacher leadership should involve, "the leadership of pedagogy through the development and modeling of effective forms of teaching". (p. 40). Teachers as critical thinkers should model such behaviours in their classroom so that their students develop the ability to ask questions, develop explanations and clearly communicate them.

Teachers as transformational leaders do exemplify values that are salient to their classroom setting. These values include "purpose, empowerment, power to accomplish, quality control, out-rage, and moral action" (Treslan, 2010, p. 59). These values correspond well with three core principles of inquiry-based learning as posited by Friesen (2013) in reference to inspiring Education, Alberta Education (2010) to include engaged thinker, ethical citizen, and entrepreneurial citizen. Students in such a classroom setting will be able to think critically, builds relationships on humility and creates opportunities and achieves goals through hard work (Alberta Education, 2010, pp. 5-6

CONCLUSION

Diverse research materials have shown that teacher transformational leadership skills in the classroom does maximize students-engagement. This enhances student motivation and empower them to towards achievement of educational goals. When paired with inquiry-based learning, this elevates students critical thinking skills to think outside for innovative ideas. Both transformational leadership and inquiry-based learning have values that will enhance students' quality of life and should be an integrate part of the classroom. It can therefore be posited that transformational leadership paired with inquiry-based learning will transform the quality of learning in the classroom to product positive outcomes for our students.

REFERENCES

Alberta Education. (2007). *Program of studies: Social studies, kindergarten to grade 12*. Alberta Education.

Alberta Education. (2010). *Inspiring education: A dialogue with Albertans*. Alberta Education.

Amanchukwu, R. N., Stanley, J. G., & Ololube, P. N. (2015). A review of Leadership Theories, Principles and Styles and Their Relevance to Educational Management. *Management*, *5*(1), 6–14.

Anyolo, E. O. (2012). *Investigating the incorporation of education about, in/through and for the environment in the Geography Junior Phase curriculum: a case study of three Namibian schools*. Academic Press.

Barron, B., & Darling-Hammond, L. (2008). *Teaching for Meaningful Learning: A Review of Research on Inquiry-Based and Cooperative Learning. Book Excerpt*. George Lucas Educational Foundation.

Bass, B. M. (1985). *Leadership and Performance beyond Expectations*. Free Press.

Bolkan, S., & Goodboy, A. K. (2009). Transformational leadership in the classroom: Fostering student learning, student participation, and teacher credibility. *Journal of Instructional Psychology*, *36*(4).

Burns, J. M. (1978). *Leadership*. Harper and Row.

CEE. (1998). *Education for Sustainable Development in the Schools Sector: A Report to DfEE/QCA from the Panel for Education for Sustainable Development*. Council for Environmental Education.

Conger, J. A. (1999). Charismatic and transformational leadership in organizations: An insider's perspective on these developing streams of research. *The Leadership Quarterly*, *10*(2), 145–179. doi:10.1016/S1048-9843(99)00012-0

Crowther, F. (1997). Teachers as Leaders—An Exploratory Framework. *International Journal of Educational Management, 11*(1), 6–13. doi:10.1108/09513549710155410

Darling-Hammond, L. (2008). *Introduction: Teaching and learning for understanding. Powerful Learning: What We Know About Teaching for Understanding*. Jossey-Bass.

Doyle, T. (2008). *Helping Students Learn in a Learner-Centered Environment: A Guide to Facilitating Learning in Higher Education. Sterling*. Stylus Publishing.

Erdel, D., & Takkaç, M. (2020). Instructor Leadership In Efl Classrooms And The Outcomes: The Effects Of Transformational And Transactional Leadership Styles. *Teflin Journal, 31*(1), 70–87. Https://Doi.Org/10.15639/Teflinjournal.V31i1/70-87

Feinberg, B. J., Ostroff, C., & Burke, W. W. (2005). The role of within-group agreement in understanding transformational leadership. *Journal of Occupational and Organizational Psychology, 78*(3), 471–488. doi:10.1348/096317905X26156

Friesen, S., & Scott, D. (2013). *Inquiry-based learning: A review of the research literature*. Alberta Ministry of Education.

Galileo Educational Network Association. (2008). Retrieved from: http://www.galileo.org/research/publications/rubric.pdf

Harris, A., & Muijs, D. (2003). *Teacher Leadership: A Review of Research*. General Teaching Council.

Islami, X., & Mulolli, E. (2020). A conceptual framework of transformational leadership as an influential tool in the team performance. *European Journal of Management Issues, 28*(1-2), 13–24. doi:10.15421/192002

Justice, C., Rice, J., Roy, D., Hudspith, B., & Jenkins, H. (2009). Inquiry-based learning in higher education: Administrators' perspectives on integrating inquiry pedagogy into the curriculum. *Higher Education, 58*(6), 841–855. doi:10.100710734-009-9228-7

Khan, N. (2017). Adaptive or Transactional Leadership in Current Higher Education: A Brief Comparison. *International Review of Research in Open and Distance Learning, 18*(3), 178–183. doi:10.19173/irrodl.v18i3.3294

Korejan, M. M., & Shahbazi, H. (2016). An analysis of the transformational leadership theory. *Revue des Sciences Fondamentales et Appliquées, 8*(3), 452–461. doi:10.4314/jfas.v8i3s.192

Laurie, R., Nonoyama-Tarumi, Y., Mckeown, R., & Hopkins, C. (2016). Contributions of Education for Sustainable Development (ESD) to Quality Education: A Synthesis of Research. *Journal of Education for Sustainable Development, 10*(2), 226–242. doi:10.1177/0973408216661442

Litz, D., & Blaik-Hourani, R. (2020). Transforamtional Leadership and Change in Education. *Oxford Research Encyclopedia of Education*. Retrieved 1 Aug. 2023 from https://oxfordre.com/education/view/10.1093/acrefore/978019026493.001.001/acrefore9780190264093-e-631

Lwi, B. (2019). The influence of elementary school leadership in promoting a learning-centered Classroom. *Philippine Social Science Journal, 2*(1), 69–82. doi:10.52006/main.v2i1.56

Maxwell, D. O., Lambeth, D. T., & Cox, J. T. (2015). Effects of using inquiry-based learning on science achievement for fifth-grade students. Asia-Pacific Forum on Science Learning & Teaching, 16(1).

Miller, H., McNeal, K., & Herbert, B. (2010). Inquiry in the physical geology classroom: Supporting students' conceptual model development. *Journal of Geography in Higher Education, 34*(4), 595–615. doi:10.1080/03098265.2010.499562

Orr, D. (1992). *Ecological Literacy: Education and the Transition to a Postmodern World*. State University of New York Press.

Report and Declaration of the Presidents Conference at the Tufts University European Center. (1990). *The role of universities and university presidents in environmental management and sustainable development*. Medford, MA: Tufts University.

Sawyer, K. (2006). *The Cambridge handbook of the learning sciences*. Cambridge University Press.

Treslan, D. L. (2010). Transformational Leadership in the Classroom: Any Evidence? *Education Canada, 46*, 58–61.

Vermeulen, M., Kreijns, K., & Evers, A. T. (2022). Transformational leadership, leader–member exchange and school learning climate: Impact on teachers' innovative behaviour in the Netherlands. *Educational Management Administration & Leadership, 50*(3), 491–510. doi:10.1177/1741143220932582

Wee, B., Shepardson, D., Fast, J., & Harbor, J. (2007). Teaching and learning about inquiry: Insights and challenges in professional development. *Journal of Science Teacher Education, 18*(1), 63–89. doi:10.100710972-006-9031-6

Winfrey Avant, D. (2011) Unwrapping tradition: shifting from traditional leadership to transformative action. Counterpoints, 409, 114-127.

Zhang, B., Krajcik, J. S., Sutherland, L. M., Wang, L., Wu, J., & Qian, Y. (2005). Opportunities and challenges of China's inquiry-based education reform in middle and high schools: Perspectives of science teachers and teacher educators. *International Journal of Science and Mathematics Education, 1*(4), 477–503. doi:10.100710763-005-1517-8

Chapter 21
Exploring the Leadership Intersection of Social Entrepreneurship, Sustainability, and Environmental Public Health

Kevin Richardson
https://orcid.org/0009-0002-3212-8669
Capitol Technology University, USA

Darrell Norman Burrell
https://orcid.org/0000-0002-4675-9544
Capitol Technology University, USA

ABSTRACT

A survey by the World Business Council for Sustainable Development found that 83% of companies had adopted sustainability policies, while 86% had adopted specific sustainability goals. Environmental public health is another key element of CSR initiatives. Organizations are increasingly focusing on initiatives that promote public health and environmental protection. A study by the World Health Organization found that 80% of global diseases are caused by environmental factors, and that organizations have a role to play in reducing these negative impacts. This chapter explores how organizational strategy and organizational leadership can positively move the social impact and social influence of organizations in the promotion of sustainability leadership and corporate social responsibility.

INTRODUCTION

Social entrepreneurship and sustainability leadership are two essential concepts that have gained increasing attention in recent years. Social entrepreneurship creates new ventures that address social problems and generate social value (Dees, 1998). Sustainability, on the other hand, refers to the ability of a system or process to maintain ecological, economic, and social well-being over time (Hart, 2005). The intersection of social entrepreneurship and sustainability has the potential to drive positive change in society by promoting environmentally sustainable practices, addressing social problems, and creating sustainable business models. In this paper, we will explore the intersection of social entrepreneurship and sustainability, focusing on the contributions of social entrepreneurship to sustainability and environmental public health.

The rise of social entrepreneurship and sustainability leadership has become an increasingly important part of social change efforts in today's society. Social entrepreneurs and sustainability leaders are individuals and organizations that create innovative solutions to social, economic, and environmental challenges. These individuals and groups often take risks, experiment with new ideas, and use creative and innovative approaches to address pressing social issues (Hanson, 2020). By providing innovative solutions to social problems, they can create systemic change, which leads to a more equitable and sustainable global society. However, the work of social entrepreneurs and sustainability leaders is often undervalued, and it is often difficult for them to gain access to the resources they need to succeed.

Social entrepreneurship and sustainability leadership are essential for positive social change in society, organizations, and communities. Social entrepreneurs are individuals and organizations that develop new approaches to solving social problems (Hanson, 2020). They often use business principles to create sustainable solutions to social and environmental challenges. They use their knowledge and skills to identify and address gaps in the existing systems and to develop new products, services, and organizations that have the potential to make a lasting impact (Hanson, 2020).

Sustainability leaders are individuals and organizations committed to creating a more sustainable world (Hanson, 2020). They use their knowledge, skills, and resources to develop innovative solutions to environmental and social challenges. They often seek to change their communities and organizations and influence local, national, and international policy decisions (Hanson, 2020). They focus on creating long-term solutions that address the underlying causes of environmental and social issues (Hanson, 2020).

Social entrepreneurs and sustainability leaders often play an essential role in developing a more equitable and sustainable global society (Hanson, 2020). They are often the first to recognize and address existing system gaps and provide innovative solutions to social and environmental challenges (Hanson, 2020). Taking risks and experimenting with new ideas can create systemic change, leading to lasting social and environmental improvements (Hanson, 2020).

Social impact is defined as the "creation of a positive, lasting change in the well-being of a community's constituents" (Williamson, 2011). Social entrepreneurs use this concept to change the business sector (Mair & Marti, 2006). OD traditionalists also encourage practitioners to promote positive social change and corporate citizenship (Cummings & Worley, 2008). Measuring this social impact is a challenge recently addressed by the concept of "scaling social impact" (Bradach, 2003). This concept refers to increasing the impact of social-purpose organizations to meet better the magnitude of the social need or problem (Dees, 2008). Managers of social entrepreneurial organizations and the donors and agencies that fund them are interested in learning how to scale social impact to reach a wider population (Bloom & Smith, 2010).

The concept of social entrepreneurship refers to the process of creating innovative solutions to social and environmental problems. It is a form of entrepreneurship that combines the purpose of a traditional for-profit business to create positive social change (Farny & Binder, 2021). Social entrepreneurs identify a need in society, develop a solution to address that need, and then use business principles to create a sustainable and profitable organization that can scale up and reach more people in need. Social entrepreneurs are driven by a desire to bring about positive change and are often passionate about the causes they are working to address (Farny & Binder, 2021).

The intersection of social entrepreneurship and sustainability has been the subject of increasing attention in recent years (Farny & Binder, 2021). Scholars have highlighted the potential of social entrepreneurship to drive positive change in society by promoting sustainability (Austin et al., 2006). Social entrepreneurship can contribute to sustainability in several ways. First, social entrepreneurship can promote environmental sustainability by creating businesses that use renewable resources, minimize waste and pollution, and promote sustainable production and consumption practices. By promoting sustainable practices, social entrepreneurs can help reduce the environmental impact of business activities and create a more sustainable future for all.

Second, social entrepreneurship can promote social sustainability by addressing social problems such as poverty, inequality, and exclusion (Mair & Marti, 2006). Social entrepreneurs can create businesses that provide goods and services to underserved communities, such as affordable healthcare, education, and housing (Bansal et al., 2019). Social entrepreneurs can help create a more inclusive and equitable society that benefits all community members by addressing social problems. Third, social entrepreneurship can promote economic sustainability by creating sustainable business models that generate social and economic value (Mair & Marti, 2006). Social entrepreneurs can build businesses that provide employment opportunities, generate income for local communities, and contribute to local economic development. According to Bansal et al. (2019), by creating sustainable businesses, social entrepreneurs can help build resilient and prosperous communities that can meet the needs of both current and future generations.

While social entrepreneurship has the potential to promote sustainability, several challenges need to be addressed. One of the main challenges is the need for more clarity around the concept of sustainability, making it difficult for social entrepreneurs to incorporate sustainability into their business models. To address this challenge, more research is needed to develop a clear and comprehensive framework for sustainability that social entrepreneurs can easily apply. Another challenge is more funding and support for social entrepreneurship and sustainability initiatives (Mair & Marti, 2006). Social entrepreneurs often face significant financial and institutional barriers when trying to create sustainable businesses, which can limit their impact and sustainability (Gupta et al., 2020). To address this challenge, more funding and support are needed for social entrepreneurship and sustainability initiatives, including government support, philanthropic funding, and private investment.

Problem Statement

Organizational leaders are key stakeholders when it comes to addressing corporate social responsibility. Research by the International Institute of Management Development (IMD) (2010) highlights the importance of senior management in promoting CSR initiatives. The study found that 73% of companies reported that the CEO was the primary champion for the company's CSR initiatives. In addition, the study found that 84% of organizations with successful CSR programs had senior managers actively involved in their implementation.

Organizational leadership enables organizations to achieve their social and environmental objectives. A Harvard Business School (2013) study found that firms that engage in CSR activities are more likely to have higher levels of employee engagement. In addition, the study found that CSR was positively associated with more significant innovation, increased financial performance, and higher customer satisfaction. Social entrepreneurship, sustainability, and environmental public health social entrepreneurship are crucial to CSR initiatives. Social entrepreneurs use entrepreneurial skills to address social and environmental challenges. These initiatives have the potential to promote sustainable development, improve quality of life, and create meaningful social change (Nicholls, 2007). Sustainability is an essential element of CSR, and organizations increasingly focus on initiatives promoting long-term environmental and social benefits.

A survey by the World Business Council for Sustainable Development (2010) found that 83% of companies had adopted sustainability policies, while 86% had adopted specific sustainability goals. Environmental public health is another critical element of CSR initiatives. Organizations are increasingly focusing on initiatives that promote public health and environmental protection. A study by the World Health Organization (2015) found that environmental factors cause 80% of global diseases and that organizations have a role in reducing these negative impacts.

METHODOLOGY

To explore the intersection of social entrepreneurship and sustainability, we conducted a systematic literature review of academic articles, reports, and case studies on the topic. We searched several databases, including Google Scholar, Scopus, and Web of Science, using keywords such as "Corporate Social Responsibility," "social entrepreneurship," "sustainability," "green entrepreneurship," "environmental public health," and "social innovation." We also searched the websites of relevant organizations, such as the Schwab Foundation for Social Entrepreneurship and Ashoka, for relevant case studies and reports. We selected articles and reports based on their relevance to the topic and the quality of their research methods. We analyzed the selected articles and reports using thematic analysis, which involved identifying key themes and patterns in the data (Byrne, 2022). We coded the data based on these themes and patterns and then organized the data into categories to facilitate our analysis. The themes that emerged from the literature review were:

- Social entrepreneurship and environmental sustainability
- Social entrepreneurship and social sustainability
- Social entrepreneurship and economic sustainability
- Challenges and barriers to social entrepreneurship and sustainability
- Corporate social responsibility
- Community change and organizational change

Contexts From the Literature

Although social entrepreneurship and sustainability leadership can significantly impact society and community social change, these leaders face many challenges and opportunities (Prabhu, 2015). One of the most significant challenges is the need for access to resources. Social entrepreneurs often need help accessing the capital and resources they need to succeed, limiting their ability to develop innovative solutions and create lasting change (Prabhu, 2015). In addition, cultural and institutional barriers often prevent social entrepreneurs and sustainability leaders from making an impact.

Many existing systems and institutions are designed to maintain the status quo, making it difficult for social entrepreneurs to introduce new ideas and create meaningful change (Prabhu, 2015). Finally, political and economic challenges often limit the impact of social entrepreneurship and sustainability leadership. Political and economic systems often favor the status quo, making it difficult for social entrepreneurs and sustainability leaders to create the necessary systemic changes (Prabhu, 2015).

For social entrepreneurship and sustainability leadership to have a lasting impact on society and community social change, governments, businesses, and communities need to support these leaders. Governments can provide financial and other support to social entrepreneurs and sustainability leaders. They can also create policies and regulations that encourage innovation and support the development of new solutions to social and environmental challenges (Prabhu, 2015).

Businesses can also be essential in supporting social entrepreneurs and sustainability leaders. Businesses can provide financial support, mentorship, and access to resources. They can also use their platform to raise awareness about social and environmental issues and to encourage their customers and employees to support social entrepreneurs and sustainability leaders (Prabhu, 2015). Communities can provide platforms for collaboration, mentorship, and networking. They can also create opportunities for social entrepreneurs and sustainability leaders to share their stories and connect with potential customers and supporters.

The trend of intense competition and a rapidly changing environment (Hao & Yazdanifard, 2015) calls for Change Management (CM) to be considered necessary. However, Todnem (2005) noted that the theories and approaches to CM are often contradictory and are not backed by empirical evidence but rather by hypotheses that have yet to be critically reviewed. Bareil (2013) argued that understanding the implications of change is critical, as it determines the success rate of organizations when implementing change. There are different perspectives on how change is viewed and managed, which can be seen as an opportunity or a problem (Vedenik & Leber, 2015). Andersson (2015) stated that change is always accompanied by resistance and controversy. Bareil (2013) further compared the traditional and modern dimensions of change, elucidating that the contemporary perspective sees the purpose of resistance as the need to preserve what is good from the past and adjust communication strategies accordingly.

On the other hand, the traditional view perceives the purpose of change as a way of stopping, slowing down, or disrupting a planned change. With this knowledge, change agents can anticipate resistance and make the necessary interventions (Franken et al., 2009). It is also vital for organizations to execute their strategies effectively for a competitive advantage (Franken et al., 2009); this includes creating change programs that deliver the strategy and allocating and managing resources to execute the change programs.

Environmental Public Health

Environmental public health is the study of how environmental factors, such as air pollution, chemicals, and other contaminants, impact the health of individuals and communities. It is a field of research that focuses on preventing and controlling health risks from environmental hazards. Environmental public health aims to reduce the disease burden and improve public health by identifying and controlling environmental hazards.

Organizational leadership is essential for the success of environmental public health initiatives within organizations. Leaders must create a culture of safety and accountability, set clear expectations and goals, and ensure that all employees know the organization's environmental public health policies and practices. Leaders must also be able to identify and develop opportunities for environmental public health initiatives, assess the impact of these initiatives, and ensure that they are sustainable in the long run.

When considering CSR initiatives, companies, leaders, and organizations should focus on areas with tremendous potential to improve public health outcomes. These areas include improving air and water quality, reducing the use of hazardous materials, and promoting energy efficiency (Griebel, 2018).

Improving air and water quality is essential for public health, as air and water pollution can have serious health consequences (Griebel, 2018). Companies, leaders, and organizations should focus on reducing emissions from production and transportation processes and improving waste management (Griebel, 2018). Additionally, they should seek to minimize the use of hazardous materials in production processes, as these materials can harm public health. Finally, companies, leaders, and organizations should focus on promoting energy efficiency, as this can reduce emissions, reduce costs, and improve public health outcomes (Griebel, 2018).

It is essential to recognize that CSR initiatives have the potential to have a lasting impact on environmental public health (Griebel, 2018). When companies, leaders, and organizations focus on improving public health outcomes, the benefits can extend beyond the immediate consequences. For example, improved air and water quality can improve public health outcomes for generations, while reduced hazardous materials can lead to improved health outcomes for humans and animals. Additionally, improved energy efficiency can reduce emissions and lower costs for companies, leaders, and organizations, which can help ensure their long-term sustainability (Griebel, 2018).

CSR

The role of Corporate Social Responsibility (CSR) in business is continually expanding as stakeholders across the globe require firms to take a more proactive stance in tackling socio-economic issues (Ismail, 2009). This has placed a weight on corporate leaders to transform how businesses are structured and operated (Mahmood & Humphrey, 2013). To ensure CSR is successfully integrated and accepted in the organization, efficient management of the integration process is necessary for many leaders (Boubakary, 2016). Boubakary (2016) posits that a Change Management (CM) process is essential to ensure the successful integration of CSR within the organization.

Rodriguez (2015) proposed that to ensure successful CSR integration within a firm, leaders should utilize Kotter's 8-step change model. This model includes steps such as creating a sense of urgency, forming a powerful coalition, developing a vision, communicating the vision, empowering others to act on the vision, generating quick wins, consolidating gains, and anchoring the change in the culture (Kotter & Cohen, 2002). According to Rodriguez (2015), these steps will result in successful CSR integration within a firm.

FINDINGS

Social Entrepreneurship and Environmental Sustainability

One of the critical contributions of social entrepreneurship to sustainability is the promotion of environmental sustainability (Galindo-Martín et al., 2020; Sadiq et al., 2022). Social entrepreneurs can create businesses that use renewable resources, minimize waste and pollution, and promote sustainable production and consumption practices. For example, B-Corporations such as Patagonia and Ben & Jerry's have incorporated environmental sustainability into their business models by using recycled materials, reducing waste, and promoting sustainable farming practices (Venkatesan, 2022; Blasi & Sedita, 2022). In addition to creating sustainable businesses, social entrepreneurs can also promote environmental sustainability through advocacy and education. For example, the social enterprise Plastic Bank works to reduce plastic pollution by establishing recycling centers in developing countries and incentivizing people to collect plastic waste (Katz, 2019). Plastic Bank also educates communities about reducing plastic waste and promoting sustainable practices.

Social Entrepreneurship and Social Sustainability

Social entrepreneurship can also contribute to social sustainability by addressing social problems such as poverty, inequality, and exclusion (Ahmad & Bajwa, 2023). Social entrepreneurs can create businesses that provide goods and services to underserved communities, such as affordable healthcare, education, and housing. For example, the social enterprise Embrace Innovations has developed a low-cost infant warmer to help reduce infant mortality in developing countries (Iwelunmor et al., 2022; Mitra et al., 2019). The warmer is designed to be portable, low-cost, and easy to use, making it accessible to communities with limited access to healthcare (Iwelunmor et al., 2022). Social entrepreneurship can also address social sustainability by promoting social innovation and entrepreneurship (Ahmad & Bajwa, 2023). Social entrepreneurs can provide mentorship and support to aspiring entrepreneurs from underrepresented communities, helping to promote diversity and inclusion in the business world (Ahmad & Bajwa, 2023). For example, Deberry-Spence and Torres (2019) note how the organization Endeavor Global provides mentorship and support to entrepreneurs from emerging markets, helping to create a more inclusive and diverse global economy.

Social Entrepreneurship and Economic Sustainability

Social entrepreneurship can also contribute to economic sustainability by creating sustainable business models that generate social and economic value (Bansal et al., 2019). Social entrepreneurs can build businesses that provide employment opportunities, generate income for local communities, and contribute to local economic development. For example, the social enterprise Natura &Co, which includes the brands Natura, Aesop, and The Body Shop, has a business model prioritizing sustainability, social responsibility, and fair trade (Simões-Coelho et al., 2023). The company has created sustainable supply chains that support local communities and promote economic development. Moreover, social entrepreneurship can promote economic sustainability by fostering innovation and entrepreneurship. Social entrepreneurs can create networks and partnerships that support entrepreneurship and innovation, helping to create new opportunities for economic growth and development (Phillips et al., 2019). For example, the Skoll Foundation supports social entrepreneurs worldwide by providing funding, mentorship, and networking opportunities (Shekhawat, 2022).

Challenges and Barriers to Social Entrepreneurship and Sustainability

Despite the potential of social entrepreneurship to promote sustainability, several challenges and barriers need to be addressed. One of the main challenges is the need for more clarity around the concept of sustainability (Meuer et al., 2020). A lack of transparency can make it difficult for social entrepreneurs to incorporate sustainability into their business models. To address this challenge, more research is needed to develop a clear and comprehensive framework for sustainability that social entrepreneurs can easily apply. Another challenge is more funding and support for social entrepreneurship and sustainability initiatives (Gupta et al., 2020). Social entrepreneurs often need help with significant financial and institutional barriers when creating sustainable businesses, which can limit their impact and sustainability. To address this challenge, more funding and support are needed for social entrepreneurship and sustainability initiatives, including government support, philanthropic funding, and private investment.

DISCUSSION

The intersection of social entrepreneurship and sustainability can potentially drive positive societal change (Bansal et al., 2019). This can happen through promoting environmentally sustainable practices, addressing social problems, and creating sustainable business models. Social entrepreneurs play a crucial role in driving this change. They build businesses prioritizing social and environmental impact and economic sustainability (Sun et al., 2020). However, some challenges and barriers must be addressed to realize social entrepreneurship's and sustainability's potential fully. More research is needed to develop a comprehensive framework for sustainability that social entrepreneurs can easily apply. Additionally, more funding and support are required to help social entrepreneurs overcome financial and institutional barriers and create sustainable businesses.

To promote social entrepreneurship and sustainability, governments, philanthropists, investors, and other stakeholders must recognize the value of these initiatives and provide the necessary support and resources. Working together can create a more sustainable and equitable future for all. One potential area for future research in social entrepreneurship and sustainability is the role of social entrepreneurship in promoting sustainable consumption patterns (Wang et al., 2019). Social entrepreneurs can create businesses that promote sustainable consumption by providing alternatives to traditional products and services that are more environmentally friendly and socially responsible. For example, social enterprises such as The Renewal Workshop and ThreadUp use innovative business models to promote sustainable fashion by repurposing and upcycling clothing (Bassett, 2021).

Another potential area for future research is the impact of social entrepreneurship on environmental and social justice (Tien et al., 2019). Social entrepreneurs can promote environmental and social justice by addressing systemic issues such as climate change, pollution, and inequality. For example, the social enterprise GRID Alternatives provides access to clean energy for low-income communities, promoting both environmental and social justice. Overall, the intersection of social entrepreneurship and sustainability is a complex and multifaceted field that can potentially drive positive societal change (Bansal et al., 2019). By promoting sustainable business practices, addressing social and environmental issues, and creating sustainable economic models, social entrepreneurs can play a crucial role in creating a more equitable and sustainable future for all (Farny & Binder, 2021). However, more research and support are needed to fully realize social entrepreneurship's and sustainability's potential and overcome existing challenges and barriers.

In addition to research, practical steps can be taken to promote social entrepreneurship and sustainability (Alter, 2013). One such measure is to increase awareness and education around these topics by including training and resources for aspiring social entrepreneurs and educating consumers about supporting sustainable businesses. Another practical step is to provide funding and support for social entrepreneurs (Farinha et al., 2020). This can include grants, loans, and other forms of financial aid, as well as mentorship and networking opportunities (Farinha et al., 2020). According to Bansal et al. (2019), governments, philanthropists, and investors can all play a role in providing this support and helping social entrepreneurs overcome financial and institutional barriers (Bansal et al., 2019). Creating a supportive policy environment for social entrepreneurship and sustainability is also vital. This can include policies encouraging sustainable business practices, such as tax incentives for environmentally-friendly businesses and policies promoting social justice and equity. By creating a supportive policy environment, we can encourage more social entrepreneurs to start and grow sustainable enterprises and create a more equitable and sustainable society (Gupta et al., 2020). The intersection of social entrepreneurship and sustainability can drive positive change in society by promoting sustainable business practices, addressing social and environmental issues, and creating sustainable economic models (Gupta et al., 2020). However, more research and support are needed to fully realize this potential and overcome the existing challenges and barriers. We can create a more equitable and sustainable future for all by working together to promote social entrepreneurship and sustainability.

According to Ren & Jackson (2020), it is critical to recognize that the intersection of social entrepreneurship and sustainability is not a one-size-fits-all solution. Different regions and communities face unique challenges and opportunities, and solutions must be tailored to these contexts. For example, a sustainable business model that works in one area may not be feasible or effective in another (Bozhikin et al., 2019). Therefore, it is essential to take a context-specific approach to social entrepreneurship and sustainability and work closely with local communities to develop relevant and practical solutions. Social entrepreneurship and sustainability are constantly evolving (Haidar, 2019). New challenges and opportunities will continue to arise, and it is crucial to remain adaptive and responsive in the face of these changes. This requires ongoing research, education, stakeholder collaboration, and a willingness to experiment and innovate. According to Hermann & Bossle (2020), social entrepreneurship and sustainability are closely intertwined and have the potential to drive positive change in society. By promoting sustainable business practices, addressing social and environmental issues, and creating sustainable economic models, social entrepreneurs can play a crucial role in creating a more equitable and sustainable future for all (Bozhikin et al., 2019). However, more research and support are needed to fully realize this potential and overcome the existing challenges and barriers. We can create a better future for ourselves and generations by working together to promote social entrepreneurship and sustainability.

The intersection of social entrepreneurship and sustainability represents an exciting and dynamic field that has the potential to create a better future for all (Bockel et al., 2021). According to Lang & Fink (2019), social entrepreneurs are at the forefront of creating sustainable businesses that prioritize social and environmental impact alongside economic sustainability. Social entrepreneurs can drive positive societal change by promoting sustainable business practices, addressing social and environmental issues, and creating sustainable economic models (Tykklainen & Ritala, 2021). However, some challenges and barriers must be addressed to realize social entrepreneurship's and sustainability's potential fully. Research is needed to understand the complexities of this intersection better and to identify practical solutions for overcoming these challenges (Tykklainen & Ritala, 2021). Furthermore, funding and support must be provided to social entrepreneurs to enable them to create sustainable businesses and overcome financial and institutional barriers. A supportive policy environment is also crucial for promoting social entrepreneurship and sustainability, including tax incentives, funding schemes, and policies promoting social justice and equity.

According to Agarwal (2020), social entrepreneurship and sustainability must be approached context-specific and remain adaptive and responsive to ongoing changes and challenges. We must work together to promote social entrepreneurship and sustainability and to create a more equitable and sustainable future for all. Through collaboration, innovation, and a commitment to positive change, we can unlock social entrepreneurship's and sustainability's full potential and build a better world for ourselves and future generations (Bockel et al., 2021). Governments, businesses, and individuals need to recognize the importance of social entrepreneurship and sustainability (Bassett, 2021). This means investing in research, education, and funding for social entrepreneurs and sustainable businesses and creating a supportive policy environment that promotes sustainable practices and social justice (Simões-Coelho et al., 2023). It also means supporting sustainable consumption patterns and creating awareness of sustainable businesses' importance.

It addressed the challenges and barriers that prevent social entrepreneurs' and sustainable businesses' growth and success (Venkatesan, 2022; Blasi & Sedita, 2022). This can include financial and institutional barriers, lack of access to funding, lack of education and training, and lack of awareness around sustainable practices. Addressing these challenges will require collaboration and partnership between various stakeholders, including governments, philanthropists, investors, and communities (Meuer et al., 2020).

CHALLENGES AND OPPORTUNITIES IN PROMOTING SOCIAL ENTREPRENEURSHIP AND SUSTAINABILITY

Opportunities

As social entrepreneurship and sustainability continue gaining prominence, it is crucial to recognize that these concepts are relevant to businesses, organizations, and individuals (Galindo-Martín et al., 2020; Sadiq et al., 2022). Consumers and citizens can play a crucial role in promoting social entrepreneurship and sustainability by making conscious decisions that support sustainable businesses and practices (Mair & Marti, 2006). Consumers can help enterprises to prioritize social and environmental impact and opt for sustainable products and services with a reduced environmental impact. Similarly, citizens can advocate for sustainable policies and practices and hold businesses and governments accountable for their social and environmental impact.

According to Deberry-Spence and Torres (2019), by recognizing the power of individuals to drive change, we can promote a more inclusive and equitable approach to social entrepreneurship and sustainability. It is essential to realize that sustainability is about protecting the environment and promoting social justice and equity (Ahmad & Bajwa, 2023). According to Lang & Fink (2019), promoting social entrepreneurship and sustainability requires a holistic approach prioritizing social and environmental impact alongside economic sustainability. The intersection of social entrepreneurship and sustainability presents a unique opportunity to drive positive societal change. Social entrepreneurs are creating innovative businesses that prioritize social and environmental impact alongside economic sustainability and are promoting sustainable business practices and models that can help create a more equitable and sustainable world.

Challenges

However, some challenges and barriers must be addressed to realize social entrepreneurship's and sustainability's potential fully. By investing in research, education, and funding for social entrepreneurs and sustainable businesses, creating a supportive policy environment, and experimenting with new models of social entrepreneurship and sustainability, we can overcome these challenges and unlock the full potential of social entrepreneurship and sustainability (Sadiq et al., 2022). Moreover, promoting social entrepreneurship and sustainability is not just about creating sustainable businesses but also about a more just and equitable society. Therefore, it is crucial to recognize the power of individuals to drive change and promote a holistic approach to social entrepreneurship and sustainability that prioritizes social and environmental impact alongside economic sustainability. By working together to promote social entrepreneurship and sustainability, we can create a better future for ourselves and future generations (Haidar, 2019). It is up to governments, businesses, and individuals to recognize the importance of social entrepreneurship and sustainability and to address the challenges and barriers that prevent its full potential from being realized (Haidar, 2019).

Emerging Trends

In addition to the challenges and opportunities discussed above, several emerging trends are shaping the future of social entrepreneurship and sustainability. According to Ren & Jackson (2020), these trends reflect changing social, environmental, and economic conditions and offer new opportunities for social entrepreneurs and sustainable businesses to create an impact. One such trend is the rise of impact investing, which refers to investments made to generate both financial returns and social or environmental impact. Impact investing is overgrowing and is expected to reach $1 trillion by 2020 (Global Impact Investing Network, 2019). This trend creates new opportunities for social entrepreneurs and sustainable businesses to access capital. It is helping to mainstream the idea that business can be a force for social and environmental good.

Another emerging trend is the growth of the circular economy, which refers to an economic system regenerative by design and seeking to minimize waste and pollution. According to Hermann & Bossle (2020), the circular economy offers new opportunities for social entrepreneurs and sustainable businesses to create value from waste and promote sustainable production and consumption. For example, social enterprises such as TerraCycle and Rubicon Global are creating innovative solutions to reduce waste and encourage recycling. A third emerging trend is an increasing focus on social innovation, which refers to developing and implementing new ideas and approaches to addressing social and environmental challenges (Bockel et al., 2021). Social innovation is becoming increasingly important as traditional approaches to social and environmental problems are inadequate (Bockel et al., 2021). Social entrepreneurs are pivotal in driving social innovation and creating new social and ecological impact models that challenge the status quo (Bockel et al., 2021).

These emerging trends offer new opportunities for social entrepreneurs and sustainable businesses to create impact and reflect a growing recognition that business can be a force for social and environmental good. However, they also present new challenges and barriers that must be addressed to realize their potential fully. For example, impact investing requires a supportive policy environment that encourages and incentivizes investment in social and environmental impact. The circular economy requires new business models and supply chain solutions that promote sustainability and minimize waste (Haidar, 2019). Social innovation requires a supportive ecosystem that fosters collaboration, experimentation, and learning (Tykklainen & Ritala, 2021). To address these challenges and unlock the full potential of emerging social entrepreneurship and sustainability trends, it is crucial to continue investing in research, education, and funding for social entrepreneurs and sustainable businesses (Bozhikin et al., 2019). It is also vital to create a supportive policy environment that promotes sustainable practices and social justice and experiment with new social entrepreneurship and sustainability models prioritizing social and environmental impact (Bozhikin et al., 2019).

CONCLUSION

The intersection of social entrepreneurship, sustainability, and public health presents a unique opportunity to drive positive societal change (Bansal et al., 2019). Social entrepreneurship and sustainability leadership are essential for positive social change in society and communities. These individuals and organizations often take risks, experiment with new ideas, and use creative and innovative approaches to address pressing social issues. However, social entrepreneurs and sustainability leaders often need help accessing the resources they need to succeed, and cultural and institutional barriers often prevent them from making an impact. For social entrepreneurship and sustainability leadership to have a lasting effect on society and community social change, governments, businesses, and communities must support these leaders. Social entrepreneurs are creating companies prioritizing social and environmental impact alongside economic sustainability and promoting sustainable business practices and models that can help create a more equitable and sustainable world. However, some challenges and barriers must be addressed to realize social entrepreneurship's and sustainability's potential fully. The challenges and barriers include the need for a comprehensive framework for sustainability, more funding and support for social entrepreneurs, and a supportive policy environment.

Furthermore, social entrepreneurship and sustainability must be approached context-specific and remain adaptive and responsive to ongoing changes and challenges. To address these challenges, it is essential to invest in research, education, and funding for social entrepreneurs and sustainable businesses and to create a supportive policy environment that promotes sustainable practices and social justice (Bozhikin et al., 2019). It is also essential to address the financial and institutional barriers that prevent the growth and success of social entrepreneurs and sustainable businesses and to experiment with new models of social entrepreneurship and sustainability that prioritize social and environmental impact.

Organizational leadership is essential for the success of social entrepreneurship, sustainability, and environmental public health initiatives within organizations. Leaders must create a culture of innovation, sustainability, and safety, set clear goals and objectives, and ensure all employees know the organization's policies and practices. Leaders must also be able to identify and develop opportunities for initiatives, assess the impact of these initiatives, and ensure that they are sustainable in the long run. By doing so, organizations can promote social change and protect the health and well-being of their employees and the environment.

Ultimately, promoting social entrepreneurship and sustainability is not just about creating sustainable businesses but also about a more just and equitable society. This means addressing poverty, inequality, and discrimination and creating a more inclusive and equitable world. We can create a better future for ourselves and generations by working together to promote social entrepreneurship and sustainability. It is up to governments, businesses, and individuals to recognize the importance of social entrepreneurship and sustainability and to address the challenges and barriers that prevent its full potential from being realized. Doing so can create a more equitable and sustainable future for all.

Corporate social responsibility (CSR) and social impact are two essential concepts that have become increasingly important in today's business world. Many organizations are now integrating social responsibility and social impact into their corporate strategies to improve their corporate image and achieve their broader business objectives. To successfully implement these strategies, leaders must understand their role in promoting corporate social responsibility and social impact within their organizations and communities.

To understand the steps leaders can take to promote CSR and social impact, it is vital to understand the theoretical framework behind these concepts. According to Crane and Matten (2016), corporate social responsibility involves a company's commitment to its stakeholders to ensure that its operations are conducted in a socially responsible manner. This commitment can come from ethical business practices, environmental protection, and community engagement. Similarly, social impact refers to the positive effect that an organization's activities can have on society (Crane & Matten, 2016).

Steps Leaders Can Take to Promote CSR and Social Impact

Leaders are crucial in promoting corporate social responsibility and social impact in their organizations and communities. There are several steps that leaders can take to ensure that their organizations are promoting CSR and social impact (Crane & Matten, 2016). First, leaders can ensure that their organizations adhere to ethical business practices (Crane & Matten, 2016). This includes ensuring that their organizations are following applicable laws and regulations and that their operations are conducted in a socially responsible manner. Second, leaders can ensure their organizations engage in environmental protection efforts (Crane & Matten, 2016). This can include reducing waste, using energy-efficient practices, and promoting sustainability initiatives. Third, leaders can create opportunities for organizations to engage in local communities. This can consist of sponsoring community events, engaging in volunteer activities, and donating resources to local organizations (Crane & Matten, 2016).

REFERENCES

Agarwal, S., Lenka, U., Singh, K., Agrawal, V., & Agrawal, A. M. (2020). A qualitative approach towards crucial factors for sustainable development of women social entrepreneurship: Indian cases. *Journal of Cleaner Production*, 274. https://doi.org/10.1016/j.jclepro.2020.123135

Ahmad, S., & Bajwa, I. A. (2023). The role of social entrepreneurship in socio-economic development: A meta-analysis of the nascent field. *Journal of Entrepreneurship in Emerging Economies*, 15(1), 133–157. doi:10.1108/JEEE-04-2021-0165

Alter, K. (2013). Social entrepreneurship and sustainability: Why the social element is important for environmental and economic sustainability. *Journal of Business Ethics*, 115(3), 481–494. doi:10.100710551-013-1808-6

Andersson, L. (2015). Resistance to change: A literature review. *International Journal of Management Reviews*, *17*(1), 1–13.

Austin, J. E., Stevenson, H., & Wei-Skillern, J. (2006). Social and commercial entrepreneurship: Same, different, or both? *Entrepreneurship Theory and Practice*, *30*(1), 1–22. doi:10.1111/j.1540-6520.2006.00107.x

Bansal, S., Garg, I., & Sharma, G. D. (2019). Social entrepreneurship as a path for social change and driver of sustainable development: A systematic review and research agenda. *Sustainability (Basel)*, *11*(4), 1091. doi:10.3390u11041091

Bareil, C. (2013). Understanding resistance to change. *Human Resource Management International Digest*, *21*(2), 40–43.

Bassett, N. (2021). *Sustainable Fashion Through Circular Business Innovations: New Business Models Reduce Waste. In Sustainable Textile and Fashion Value Chains: Drivers.* Concepts, Theories and Solutions.

Blasi, S., & Sedita, S. R. (2022). Mapping the emergence of a new organisational form: An exploration of the intellectual structure of the B Corp research. *Corporate Social Responsibility and Environmental Management*, *29*(1), 107–123. doi:10.1002/csr.2187

Bloom, I., & Smith, J. (2010). Scaling Social Impact. *Stanford Social Innovation Review*, *8*(3), 46–51.

Böckel, A., Hörisch, J., & Tenner, I. (2021). A systematic literature review of crowdfunding and sustainability: highlighting what really matters. *Management Review Quarterly*, *71*, 433-453. https://link.springer.com/article/10.1007/s11301-020-00189-3

Boubakary, A. (2016). Change management: The need for successful integration of corporate social responsibility in organizations. *The International Journal of Organizational Analysis*, *24*(2), 231–250.

Bozhikin, I., Macke, J., & da Costa, L. F. (2019). The role of government and key non-state actors in social entrepreneurship: A systematic literature review. Journal of Cleaner Production, 226, 730–747. https://doi.org/10.1016/j.jclepro.2019.04.076

Bradach, J. (2003). *Scale and Scope: The Dynamics of Industrial Capitalism*. Harvard University Press.

Byrne, D. (2022). A worked example of Braun and Clarke's approach to reflexive thematic analysis. *Quality & Quantity*, *56*(3), 1391–1412. doi:10.100711135-021-01182-y

Crane, A., & Matten, D. (2016). *Business ethics: Managing corporate citizenship and sustainability in the age of globalization* (4th ed.). Oxford University Press.

Cummings, T. G., & Worley, C. G. (2008). *Organization Development & Change*. South-Western/Cengage Learning.

Deberry-Spence, B. E. N. E. T., & Torres, L. T. (2019). Multinational Corporation Approaches to Corporate Social Responsibility and Entrepreneurship in Africa. The Oxford Handbook of Corporate Social Responsibility: Psychological and Organizational Perspectives, 391.

Dees, J. G. (2001). The meaning of social entrepreneurship. *Stanford Social Innovation Review*, *1*(1), 1–8. https://ssir.org/articles/entry/the_meaning_of_social_entrepreneurship

Dees, J. G. (2008). Scaling Social Impact: What Every Social Entrepreneur Should Know. *Stanford Social Innovation Review, 6*(3), 35–41.

Farinha, L., Sebastião, J. R., Sampaio, C., & Lopes, J. (2020). Social innovation and social entrepreneurship: Discovering origins, exploring current and future trends. *International Review on Public and Nonprofit Marketing, 17*(1), 77–96. https://link.springer.com/article/10.1007/s12208-020-00243-6 doi:10.100712208-020-00243-6

Farny, S., & Binder, J. (2021). Sustainable entrepreneurship. In *World Encyclopedia of Entrepreneurship* (pp. 605–611). Edward Elgar Publishing. doi:10.4337/9781839104145.00076

Franken, E., Edwards, D., & Lambert, S. (2009). Strategy execution: Making it happen. *Strategy and Leadership, 37*(4), 12–17.

Galindo-Martín, M. A., Castaño-Martínez, M. S., & Méndez-Picazo, M. T. (2020). The relationship between green innovation, social entrepreneurship, and sustainable development. *Sustainability (Basel), 12*(11), 4467. doi:10.3390u12114467

Global Impact Investing Network. (2019). *What is impact investing?* Retrieved from https://thegiin.org/impact-investing/need-to-know/#what-is-impact-investing

Griebel, T. (2018). Corporate social responsibility: An overview and introduction. *Journal of Corporate Citizenship*, (72), 5–24.

Gupta, P., Chauhan, S., Paul, J., & Jaiswal, M. P. (2020). Social entrepreneurship research: A review and future research agenda. Journal of Business Research, 113, 209–229.

Haldar, S. (2019). Towards a conceptual understanding of sustainability-driven entrepreneurship. *Corporate Social Responsibility and Environmental Management, 26*(6), 1157–1170. doi:10.1002/csr.1763

Hanson, S. (2020). *What Is Social Entrepreneurship?* Retrieved April 13, 2021, from https://www.entrepreneur.com/article/352759

Hao, J., & Yazdanifard, R. (2015). Change management: Strategies and practices in different contexts. *International Journal of Business Research and Management, 3*(2), 157–167.

Harvard Business School. (2013). *Understanding the Impact of Corporate Social Responsibility on Companies.* Retrieved from https://www.hbs.edu/socialenterprise/research/Pages/understanding-the-impact-of-corporate-social-responsibility-on-companies.aspx

Hermann, R. R., & Bossle, M. B. (2020). Bringing an entrepreneurial focus to sustainability education: A teaching framework based on content analysis. *Journal of Cleaner Production,* 246. https://doi.org/10.1016/j.jclepro.2019.119038

International Institute for Management Development (IMD). (2010). *Corporate Social Responsibility: A role for senior management.* Retrieved from https://www.imd.org/publications/corporate-social-responsibility-role-senior-management/

Ismail, K. (2009). Corporate social responsibility: An Islamic perspective. *International Journal of Social Economics, 36*(8), 704–717.

Iwelunmor, J., Blackstone, S., Nwaozuru, U., Obiezu-Umeh, C., Uzoaru, F., Mason, S., ... Airhihenbuwa, C. (2022). Social Enterprises for Child and Adolescent Health in Sub-Saharan Africa: A Realist Evaluation. *Child Behavioral Health in Sub-Saharan Africa: Towards Evidence Generation and Policy Development*, 317-332.

Katz, D. (2019). Plastic bank: launching social plastic® revolution. *Field Actions Science Reports. The Journal of Field Actions*, (19), 96–99.

Kotter, J. P., & Cohen, D. S. (2002). *The heart of change: Real-life stories of how people change their organizations*. Harvard Business Press.

Lang, R., & Fink, M. (2019). Rural social entrepreneurship: The role of social capital within and across institutional levels. *Journal of Rural Studies*, *70*, 155–168. doi:10.1016/j.jrurstud.2018.03.012

Mahmood, Z., & Humphrey, D. (2013). The impact of corporate social responsibility on organizational performance in Malaysian manufacturing firms. *International Journal of Business and Social Science*, *4*(2), 145–154.

Mair, J., & Marti, I. (2006). Social entrepreneurship research: A source of explanation, prediction, and delight. *Journal of World Business*, *41*(1), 36–44. doi:10.1016/j.jwb.2005.09.002

Meuer, J., Koelbel, J., & Hoffmann, V. H. (2020). On the nature of corporate sustainability. *Organization & Environment*, *33*(3), 319–341. doi:10.1177/1086026619850180

Mitra, P., Kickul, J., Gundry, L., & Orr, J. (2019). The Rise of Hybrids: A Note for Social Entrepreneurship Educators. *International Review of Entrepreneurship*, *17*(2).

Nicholls, A. (2007). *Social Entrepreneurship: New Models of Sustainable Social Change*. Oxford University Press.

Phillips, W., Alexander, E. A., & Lee, H. (2019). Going it alone won't work! The relational imperative for social innovation in social enterprises. *Journal of Business Ethics*, *156*(2), 315–331. doi:10.100710551-017-3608-1

Prabhu, J. U. (2015). *Social entrepreneurship: A global perspective*. Palgrave Macmillan.

Ren, S., & Jackson, S. E. (2020). HRM institutional entrepreneurship for sustainable business organizations. *Human Resource Management Review*, *30*(3), 100691. doi:10.1016/j.hrmr.2019.100691

Rodriguez, R. (2015). Corporate social responsibility: An analysis of corporate social responsibility practices in the Indian Companies Act, 2013. *International Journal of Management and Applied Science*, *1*(7), 15–21.

Sadiq, M., Nonthapot, S., Mohamad, S., Chee Keong, O., Ehsanullah, S., & Iqbal, N. (2022). Does green finance matter for sustainable entrepreneurship and environmental corporate social responsibility during COVID-19? *China Finance Review International*, *12*(2), 317–333. doi:10.1108/CFRI-02-2021-0038

Shekhawat, D. (2022). A Comparative Analysis Of Organizations Supporting Social Entrepreneurship. *Social Innovations Journal, 15*.

Simões-Coelho, M., Figueira, A. R., & Russo, E. (2023). Motivations for a sustainable ethos: Evidence from the globally present Brazilian multinational Natura &Co. *Environment Systems & Decisions*, *43*(3), 1–16. doi:10.100710669-022-09890-y PMID:36628130

Sun, H., Pofoura, A. K., Mensah, I. A., Li, L., & Mohsin, M. (2020). The role of environmental entrepreneurship for sustainable development: Evidence from 35 countries in Sub-Saharan Africa. *The Science of the Total Environment*, *741*, 140132. doi:10.1016/j.scitotenv.2020.140132 PMID:32886991

Tien, N. H., Anh, D. B. H., Ngoc, N. M., & Do Thi, Y. N. (2019). Sustainable social entrepreneurship in Vietnam. *International Journal of Entrepreneurship*, *23*(3), 1–12.

Todnem, R. (2005). Change management: A review of current thinking. Leadership &amp. *Organization Development Journal*, *26*(3), 195–204.

Tykkyläinen, S., & Ritala, P. (2021). Business model innovation in social enterprises: An activity system perspective. *Journal of Business Research*, *125*, 684–697. https://doi.org/10.1016/j.jbusres.2020.01.045 doi:10.1016/j.jbusres.2020.01.045

Vedenik, J., & Leber, P. (2015). Change management: The view through the prism of three different models. Management &amp. *Marketing Challenges for the Knowledge Society*, *10*(1), 5–17.

Venkatesan, M. (2022). Marketing Sustainability: A Critical Consideration of Environmental Marketing Strategies. In Products for Conscious Consumers (pp. 151-166). Emerald Publishing Limited. doi:10.1108/978-1-80262-837-120221009

Wang, C., Ghadimi, P., Lim, M. K., & Tseng, M. L. (2019). A literature review of sustainable consumption and production: A comparative analysis in developed and developing economies. *Journal of Cleaner Production*, *206*, 741–754. doi:10.1016/j.jclepro.2018.09.172

Williamson, P. C. (2011). *Social Impact: A Definition*. Retrieved from http://www.socialimpactcenter.com/social-impact/

World Business Council for Sustainable Development. (2010). *Sustainability: A Global Survey of Corporate Practices*. Retrieved from https://www.wbcsd.org/web/publications/WBCSD_Survey_2010.pdf

World Health Organization. (2015). Retrieved from https://www.who.int/

Chapter 22
Transformational Leadership Style and Employee Performance

Endalsasa Belay Abitew
Bahir Dar University, Ethiopia

ABSTRACT

Leadership is the ability to motivate and inspire people to achieve a common goal. Both theoretical and empirical research supports that leadership style utilized by leaders in organizations, whether it is private or public, substantially influence the effort and performance of employees. In the literature of previous studies, among the various variables studied and investigated, transformational leadership style parades a major role in influencing employee performance. This chapter examined the nexus between transformational leadership style and employee performance based on the pervious study results. Using a literature review from various previous studies, the writer of this chapter has corroborated that transformational leadership, in various organizational settings and sizes, has a significant effect on employee performance, which is one of the main management topics that received substantial attention from scholars and practitioners

1. INTRODUCTION

Leadership is the process of inspiration others especially influencing the workers intending to raise their abilities for organizational success (Demir and Budur, 2019). It is a mechanism of supporting or motivating a group of people to work towards achieving a common goal, where it can be leading employees and workers with a strategy to achieve a vision (Tajeddini, 2015).

In the contemporary world, the business environment is changing drastically as a result of various societal forces. Although many factors may influence (positively or negatively) the performance of an organization, the quality of leadership becomes a more important determinant factor for the ultimate success or failure of organizations. Leadership style is an important determinant factor for employee performance. According to Wexley and Yukl (1984), the reactions of employees to their leaders will usually depend on the characteristics of the employees as well as on the characteristics of the leaders.

Transformational leadership is one of the styles of leadership. In the literature of leadership, transformational leadership has been considered one of the most widely accepted leadership styles, especially in improving employee performance (Judge & Piccolo, 2004). Transformational leadership is a style of leadership that changes the morals, hopes, ideals, as well as values of employees to prioritize common interests over personal interests as well as motivates them to perform better in the organization beyond what is expected (Udin, 2021).

Transformational leadership is one of the styles of leadership in which the leader identifies the need for change, and creates a vision to guide the change through inspiration, and positive conduct for an increased commitment of the members in the organization (Yukl, 1999). A leader can change the work environment, work motivation, work patterns, and work values that are perceived by subordinates so that they can optimize their performance to achieve established organizational goals (Bass, 1990).

Transformational leadership was established and explained for the first time in 1978 by James Burns who emphasized intellectual leadership, moral leadership, revolutionary leadership, democratization, and benevolence. Transformational leaders encourage participation; emphasize a sense of collective identity and efficacy; empower subordinates; define public values; promote followers to pursue higher values; and vigorously communicate with followers (Burns, 2003)

Transformational leadership is the capability of leaders to inspire, instilled motivate employees to focus on pursuing organizational goals without neglecting their interests (Bass, 1985). Transformational leaders also stimulate employees to grow and develop into superior individuals to always produce the best performance (Caillier, 2014).

Transformational leadership has four main dimensions (or 4 I's), namely inspirational motivation-the extent to which leaders clearly articulate the vision to inspire employees to achieve the expected goals, idealized influence - the extent to which employees believe and trust in their leaders and strive to pursue higher collective goals than their personal goals, intellectual stimulation -the extent to which the leader challenges the status quo and encourages employees to arise with the best new solutions in overcoming problems, and individual consideration- the extent to which the leader appears as a mentor in providing emotional support to employees (Bass and Riggio, 2006).

Transformational leaders help to redefine organizational members' mission and vision; renew their organizational commitment; and restructure the organizational system to accomplish goals (Roberts, 1985). Moreover, transformational leaders can use their skills of emotional and social intelligence to change members' behavior (Bass and Avolio, 1994). Because of these characteristics, transformational leadership is considered a crucial organizational factor in improving employee performance; correspondingly, researchers in the field assert that transformational leadership positively impacts on employee performance (e.g., MacKenzie, Podsakoff and Rich, 2001; Dubinsky et al., 1995; Yammarino et al., 1997).

Now a day transformational leadership and performance have gained considerable attention from organizations because the main theme of every organization is to enhance employee performance. Behery (2008) pointed out that a relationship exists between transformational leadership and employee performance as sound organizational communication acts in way of fostering the workforce by transmitting cultural norms from an organizational framework to an individual's way of life in the organization and by supporting the style of manager plays an incredible role for increasing employee's performance.

Employee performance is one of the main management topics that received substantial attention from scholars and practitioners. Employee performance is employees' outcomes that meet the requirements or standards. Further, employee performance could be understood in comparison to coworkers' fulfilment in the workplace (Buil et al., 2019). Furthermore, scholars defined employee performance in two ways, which are in-role and extra-role performance. Meeting requirements is in-role performance while helping others or acting beyond expectations are extra-role behaviors of the employees (Dinc & Aydemir, 2014). Performance is the quantity or quality of something produced or services provided by someone who does the work (Luthans, 2006). Rivai and Basri (2005) stated that performance is the result or overall level of success of a person during a certain period in carrying out a task compared to various possibilities, such as work standards, targets or predetermined criteria that have been agreed upon. Moreover, employee performance was measured by six indicators such as quality, quantity, timeliness, effectiveness, independence, and work commitment (Mathis and Jackson, 2006).

Good employee performance determines the success of achieving organizational goals effectively and efficiently which has an impact on organizational performance. Employee performance is influenced by various factors. Mahmudi (2010) argued that many factors can influence employee performance, which are personal/individual factors (knowledge, motivation, and skills), leadership factors, team factors (cohesiveness and closeness of team members), and system factors (company culture). The leadership style also adopted in an organization will affect too many employees' performance and ultimately have an impact on the success of achieving organizational goals.

Employee performance is the work achieved by a person or group of people under the authority/responsibility of each employee during a certain period. A company needs to evaluate the performance of its employees. Mangkunegara (2005), defines "performance as a comparison of the results achieved with the participation of labor per unit of time (usually per hour)". "Expressions such as output, efficiency, and effectiveness are often associated with productivity" Wartono (2017). Performance is a direct supervisor's statement on the work of individual employees for a certain period under the authority and responsibility of each employee (Hendri, 2019).

In the competitive and dynamic business environment, employee performance is very vital in organizations. The effectiveness of employee performance can bring the organizations to achieve quick growth and competitive advantage. Therefore, many scholars have tried to determine the main predictors of employee performance. In the literature of previous studies, among the various variables studied and investigated is transformational leadership which parades a major role in influencing employee performance (Astuy and Udin, 2020, Buil et al,2019, Donker et al, 2021). Currently, transformational leadership has become a dream and has been considered one of the most widely accepted leadership styles in the literature of leadership (Judge & Piccolo, 2004), especially in improving employee performance.

2. PREVIOUS RESEARCH FINDINGS AND DISCUSSION

Many previous researchers studied the relationship between transformational leadership style and employee performance. Most of the previous research findings confirmed the existence of a positive relationship between transformational leadership style and employee performance. However, some previous studies findings show the presence of a negative relationship between transformational leadership style and employee performance. This section of the book chapter deals with the findings of previous studies along with the discussions.

Cemil, et al (2020) in their study, focused on the impact of transformational leadership on employee performance in the Kurdistan region of Iraq with a sample of 252 employees, which revealed that transformational leaders positively related to employee performance. Further, their study also showed that inspirational motivation and individual consideration have a significant positive impact on employee performance. A study conducted by Rinaldi et al (2018) on the effect of transformational leadership on employees a cause study in the Faculty of Economics, State University of Padang, with a total sample of 47 confirmed that transformational had a significant positive effect on employee performance. However, the above study employed a quantitative research approach alone; but it would be better if the study employs both quantitative and qualitative research approaches to show the nexus between the two variables.

Transformational leadership style does not have a direct significant effect on employee performance but has a direct significant effect on job satisfaction and employee engagement (Retno, et al, 2020). This study was done on Civil Servants of Public Housing and Settlement Areas of Central Java Province with a total sample of 77 respondents and the study used a quantitative research method and belongs to a type of explanatory research. A research work done by Yusuf et al (2018) entitled an Impact of transformational leadership on Employees' Performance in Federal College of Education, Zarie, Nigeria illustrated that there is a significant relationship between transformational leadership and staff performance in the College of Education and the researcher concluded that there is a sound and viable leadership with individual consideration at heart, encourages innovation, and creativity in the case study organization. Methodologically, this research work is strong enough because it employs a variety of qualitative and qualitative research methods to show the impacts of transformational leadership style behavior on employee performance.

Eli *et al* (2017), in their study which aimed to analyzing the effect of transformational leadership on employee performance and Job Satisfaction also found a positive result. The study population for this study was 195 people, all of which were taken as samples. Questionnaires were used as data collection techniques and were analyzed descriptively and inferentially using The Structural Equation Modeling (SEM) of the Lisrel statistical software package and Confirmatory Factor Analysis (CFA). The result of the research shows that transformational leadership directly influences employee performance, but indirectly influences employee performance through job satisfaction of the employee. In the same way, research conducted by Kamel *et al* (2014*)* portrayed that the independent variable, transformational leadership style behavior, has a positive and significant effect on employee motivation and employees' job satisfaction, but no significant effect was found on employee performance.

A study was done by Sundi (2013) entitled the Effect of transformational leadership and transactional leadership style on employee performance of Konawe education department in Southeast Sulawesi Province. In this research, 126 respondents were taken from 185 Konawe Bureau staff and four variables namely transformational leadership, and transactional leadership as independent variables and work motivation as an intervening variable, and employee performance as a dependent variable. As the findings of this study illustrated that the independent variable, transformational leadership, and transactional leadership style have a positive and significant effects on the dependent variable, employee performance.

According to Haimanot (2020), study is to assess the effects of different leadership styles on employee performance in the ARMY Foundation located in Addis Ababa. In this research paper, 62 sample respondents who are working in the Army Foundation were selected randomly. The findings of the study indicate that transformational leadership behaviors are positively associated with employee performance. A research paper aimed to measure the effect of transformational leadership and readiness for change on employee performance in the employee of chemical industry. The results of this paper showed that transformational leadership has a significant effect on employee performance (Asbari *et al*,2021).

A study done by Fachri and Onsard (2020) aimed at determining the effect of transformational leadership style and morale on employee performance in Raffles City Holet Bengkulu, Indonesia. In this study, a sample of 31 employees was taken and questionnaire was distributed to them. The results of this study indicated that transformational leadership style had a positive effect on employee performance and morale also had a positive effect on employee performance. The results of the study conducted by Arafat *et al* (2021) entitled the Impact of Transformational Leadership on Employees Performance Among Employees in IWPPS, Saudi Arabia, also indicate that transformational leadership behavior has a positive significant relationship with employee performance.

The research results of Winnie *et al* (2021) in the banking sectors prove that the transformational leadership style has a positive effect on employee performance and the adoption of this leadership style enhanced employee motivation, employee loyalty, employee commitment, and employee productivity. The same is also evident in Aminah *et al* (2020) findings in the public sector of Malaysia. And the study found that transformational leadership has a significant positive influence on employee performance in Malaysia's public service sector

Thamrin (2012) examined the influence of transformational leadership and organizational commitment on job satisfaction and employee performance in 105 employees of shipping companies in Jakarta, Indonesia. The results found that transformational leadership has a positive significant influence on organizational commitment; transformational leadership has a positive significant influence on employees' performance; transformational leadership has no positive significant influence on job satisfaction; organizational commitment has a positive significant influence on job satisfaction and employees' performance; and job satisfaction has a positive significant influence on employees' performance.

Balasuriya and Perera (2021) also tested the impact of transformational leadership on employee performance in the context of porcelain manufacturing companies in Sri Lanka, specifying a sample of 250 production workers. The findings of the study revealed that transformational leadership has a positive impact on employee performance and employee engagement and also employee engagement has a positive impact on employee performance. The same is also evident in Niken *et al* (2022) study findings conducted on 378 employees working in car rental service companies in Lampung Province. The results of the study showed that transformational leadership behavior has a positive and significant effect on employee performance.

Erina (2023) studied the effect of transformational leadership and organizational commitments on employee performance In Cv Artha Mega Mandiri Medan, with a sample of 100 employees and the results show that there is a positive and significant influence between transformational leadership style and employee performance. Similarly, according to Hassan *et al* (2018) study entitled the Effect of leadership styles on Performance in the Somali National Civil Service Commission by taking a sample size of 44 respondents found that transformational leadership plays a big role in the effect of leadership styles on employee performance.

Beauty and Aigbogun (2022)), in their study of 156 employees working in Turnall Holdings LTD, Harare, exhibited that transformational styles significantly positively impact employee performance. A study done by Budhi *et al* (2021) to test the role of transformational leadership in moderating the relationship between work conflict and employee performance at a Railway Company confirmed that there is a positive relationship between transformational leadership and employee performance.

However, some previous researchers confirmed that transformational leadership style has no impact or influence on employee performance and they concluded that this leadership style is not able to improve employee performance. According to Rizki et al (2022) study on the effect of transformational leadership style, work environment, and work motivation on employee performance, a case study at pt. Dwi Putra Selaras in Cilegon City, there is no significant effect of transformational leadership style on employee performance. A study on the effect of leadership style on employees' performance at Guaranty Trust Bank of Abuja, Nigeria by Ekpenong (2020) showed that Transformational leadership style has a negative effect or correlation with employee performance. Transformational leadership style has no significant impact on employee performance during the COVID-19 pandemic (Meryani et al, 2022). Transformational leadership had no significant influence on employee performance, conducted in PT VVF Indonesia (Tetty et al,2019). Anita et al (2021) in their study, focused on the impact of transformational leadership on employee performance with psychological ownership and organizational commitment, and found that employee performance is affected by an organizational commitment, not by transformational leadership or psychological ownership.

CONCLUSION

Transformational leaders motivate employees by initiating ideas and higher moral values so that they perform better, even, if necessary, beyond organizational expectations (Bromley and Kirschner, 2007). When employees feel tired and frustrated at work, transformational leaders become the main helper who fully provides emotional attention and support and cares about the welfare of employees. Individualized consideration of transformational leaders can increase feelings of psychological well-being and happiness in employees and encourage them to perform better in completing assigned tasks (Liaw et al, 2010). Although there are conflicting paradoxes regarding the relationship between transformational leadership and employee performance, after analyzing dozens of previous studies related to the nexus between transformational leadership and employee performance, the author of this book chapter concluded that transformational leadership, in various settings and organizational sizes, has a significant effect on employee performance and mostly transformational leaders can enlighten employees' mind so that employees can think holistically about achieving organizational goals as well as personal goals.

REFERENCES

Aminah A., Sylvia N., Syed J., & Nelson L. (2020). The Effect of Transformational Leadership on Employees' Performance in Malaysia's Public Sector. *International Journal of Academic Research in Business and Social Sciences, 10*(11).

Anita, M., Kawaii, S., Yosia, K., & Rizky, D. (2021). *The impact of transformational leadership on employee performance with psychological ownership and organizational commitment Jurnal Manajemen* (Vol. 1). Edisi Elektronik.

Arafat, A., Maged, M., Abdulrahman, M., & Ramez, A. (2021). The Impact of Transformational Leadership on Employees Performance Among Employees in IWPPS, Saudi Arabia. *International Journal of Contemporary Management and Information Technology, 2*(1).

Asbari, Hidayat, & Purwanto. (2021). Managing Employee Performance: From Leadership to Readiness for Change. *International Journal of Social and Management Studies, 2*(1).

Astuty, I., & Udin, U. (2020). The Effect of Perceived Organizational Support and Transformational Leadership on Affective Commitment and Employee Performance. *Journal of Asian Finance, Economics, and Business, 7*(10).

Balasuriya, B. L. L. A., & Perera, G. D. N. (2021). The Impact of Transformational Leadership on Employee Performance: The Mediating Role of Employee Engagement in Selected Porcelain Manufacturing Companies in Sri Lanka, Vidyodaya. *Journal of Management, 7*(2).

Bass, B. M. (1990). *Bass & Stogdill's Handbook of Leadership: Theory, research & managerial applications* (3rd ed.). Free Press.

Bass, B. M., & Riggio, R. E. (2006). *Transformational leadership* (2nd ed.). Lawrence Erlbaum. doi:10.4324/9781410617095

Beauty, M., & Aigbogun, O. (2022). Effects of Leadership Styles on Employee Performance: A Case Study of Turnall Holdings LTD, Harare. *International Journal of Academic Research in Business & Social Sciences, 12*(1). doi:10.6007/IJARBSS/v12-i1/12037

Behery, M. H. (2008, June). Retracted: Leadership behaviors that count in an organization's performance in the middle east: The case of Dubai. *Journal of Leadership Studies, 2*(2), 6–21. doi:10.1002/jls.20058

Bromley, H. R., & Kirschner-Bromley, V. A. (2007). Are you a transformational leader? *Physician Executive, 33*(6). PMID:18092620

Buil, I., Martínez, E., & Matute, J. (2019). Transformational leadership and employee performance: The role of identification, engagement and proactive personality. *International Journal of Hospitality Management, 77*, 64–75. doi:10.1016/j.ijhm.2018.06.014

Burns, J. M. (2003). *Leadership*. Harper & Row.

Burns, J.M. (1978). Transforming Leadership: A New Pursuit of Happiness. Grove Press.

Caillier, J. G. (2014). Toward a better understanding of the relationship between transformational leadership, public service motivation, mission valence, and employee performance: A preliminary study. *Public Personnel Management, 43*(2), 218–239. doi:10.1177/0091026014528478

Cemil, T., Bryar, M., Sharif, A., Akar, H., & Mahmood, F. (2020). Transformational leadership Impact on employee performance in the Kurdistan region of Iraq. *Eurasian Journal of Management & Social Sciences*.

Demir, A., & Budur, T. (2019). Roles of leadership styles in corporate social responsibility to non-governmental organizations (NGOs). *International Journal of Social Sciences & Educational Studies, 5*(4).

Dharma, J., Mahendra, F., Putu, M., Ida, N., & Bachruddin, S. (2021). The Effect of Transformational Leadership Style on Employee Performance with Job Stress as Intervening Variables in PT. *Pos Indonesia, Proceedings of the 11th Annual International Conference on Industrial Engineering and Operations Management Singapore*.

Dinc, M. S., & Aydemir, M. (2014). Ethical leadership and employee behaviours: an empirical study of mediating factors. *International Journal of Business Governance and Ethics, 9*(3).

Donkor, F., Dongmei, Z., & Sekyere, I. (2021). The Mediating Effects of Organizational Commitment on Leadership Styles and Employee Performance in SOEs in Ghana: A Structural Equation Modeling Analysis. *SAGE Open, 11*(2). doi:10.1177/21582440211008894

Dubinsky, A. J., Yammarino, F. J., Jolson, M. A., & Spangler, W. D. (1995). Transformational leadership: An initial investigation in sales management. *Journal of Personal Selling & Sales Management, 15*(2), 17–31.

Ekpenyong, J. (2020). The Impact of Leadership Style on Employees Performance in a Business Organization: A Case Study of Guarantee Trust Bank Plc. Academic Press.

Eli, H., & Stiem, B. (2017). *The Effect of Transformational Leadership on Employee Job Satisfaction and Performance*. Academic Press.

Erina. (2023). The Effect of Transformational Leadership and Organizational Commitments on Employee Performance in Cv Artha Mega Mandiri Medan. *Journal of Industrial Engineering & Management Research, 2*(3).

Fachri & Onsard. (2020). The Effect of Transformational Leadership Style and Work Spirit on Employee Performance at Raffles City Hotel Bengkulu. Academic Press.

Haryanto, B., Suprapti, A. R., Taufik, A., & Fenitra, R. M. (2022). *Moderating role of transformational leadership in the relationship between work conflict and employee performance* (Vol. 9). Cogent Business & Management.

Hassan, A., Evelyn, D., & Titus, K. (2018). Effect of Leadership Styles on Employee Performance in the Somali National Civil Service Commission. *International Journal of Novel Research in Humanity and Social Sciences, 5*(3).

Haymanot, A. (2020). The Effect of Leadership Styles on Employee Performance a case study in Army Foundation. Academic Press.

Judge, T. A., & Piccolo, R. F. (2004). Transformational and Transactional Leadership: A Meta-Analytic Test of Their Relative Validity. *The Journal of Applied Psychology, 89*(5), 755–768. doi:10.1037/0021-9010.89.5.755 PMID:15506858

Judge, T. A., & Piccolo, R. F. (2004). Transformational and Transactional Leadership: A Meta-Analytic Test of Their Relative Validity. *The Journal of Applied Psychology, 89*(5), 755–768. doi:10.1037/0021-9010.89.5.755 PMID:15506858

Kamel, S., Khalifa, E., & Noermijatib. (2014). The Influences of Transformational Leadership on Employees Performance (A Study of the Economics and Business Faculty Employee at University of Muhammadiyah Malang). *Asia-Pacific Management and Business Application, 3*(1).

Liaw, Y.-J., Chi, N.-W., & Chuang, A. (2010). Examining the Mechanisms Linking Transformational Leadership, Employee Customer Orientation, and Service Performance: The Mediating Roles of Perceived Supervisor and Coworker Support. *Journal of Business and Psychology, 25*(3), 477–492. doi:10.100710869-009-9145-x

Luthans, F. (2006). *Organizational Behavior*. McGraw-Hill.

MacKenzie, S. B., Podsakoff, P. M., & Rich, G. A. (2001). Transformational and transactional leadership and salesperson performance. *Journal of the Academy of Marketing Science, 29*(2).

Mahmudi. (2010). *Manajemen Kinerja Sektor Publik, Edisi Kedua*. Yogyakarta: Sekolah Tinggi Ilmu Manajemen YKPN.

Mathis, R. L., & Jackson, J.H. (2006). Human Resource Management: Manajemen Sumber Daya Manusia. Terjemahan Dian Angelia. Jakarta: Salemba Empat.

Meiryani, N., Yorick, K., Gatot, S., Mohammed, A., & Fakhrul, H. (2022). *The Effect of transformative leadership and Remote working on Employee performance During the COVID-19 Pandemic*. Academic Press.

Niken, W., Habibullah, J., & RR, E. (2022). The Effect of Transformational Leadership on Employee Performance Mediated by Work Motivation in Car Rental Services Companies in Lampung Province. *SSRG International Journal of Economics and Management Studies, 9*(3).

Northouse, P.G. (2012). *Leadership: Theory and practice*. Sage.

Northouse, P. G. (2019). *Leadership Theory and Practice* (8th ed.). SAGE Publications.

Retno, R., Achmad, S., & Sunaryo. (2020). The Effect of Transformational Leadership on Employee Performance Mediated by Job Satisfaction and Employee Engagement on the Civil Servants of Public Housing and Settlement Areas of Central Java Province. *International Journal of Business, Economics, and Law, 21*(5).

Rinaldi, A., Yunia, W., & Susi, E. (2018). *The effect of Transformational leadership on employee performance in Faculty of Economics, State University of Padang* (Vol. 64). Advances in Economics, Business and Management Research.

Rivai. (2005). *Peformance Appraisal: Sistem yang tepat untuk Menilai Kinerja Karyawan dan Meningkatkan Daya Saing Perusahan*. Jakarta: PT. RajaGrafindo Peral-sada

Rizki, W., Eloh, B., & Sri, N. (2022). *The effect of transformational leadership style, work environment, and work motivation on employee performance* (Vol. 1). MSR Journal.

Roberts, N. C. (1985). Transforming leadership: A process of collective actio. *Human Relations, 38*(11), 1023–1046. doi:10.1177/001872678503801103

Sale, Bass, & Stogdills. (1991). Handbook Of Leadership-Theory, Research, And Managerial Applications. Personnel Psychology Inc.

Seyawash, F., & Yongjin, C. (2021). *Transformational Leadership and Its Impact on Employee Performance: Focus on Public Employees in Afghanistan*. Academic Press.

Sundi, K. (2013). Effect of Transformational Leadership and Transactional Leadership on Employee Performance of Konawe Education Department at Southeast Sulawesi Province. *International Journal of Business and Management Invention, 2*(12).

Tajeddini, K. (2015). *Using the integration of disparate antecedents to drive world-class innovation performance: An empirical investigation of Swiss watch*. Academic Press.

Tetty, D., Emmy, A., & Fahmi, A. (2019). *The Influence of Transformational Leadership on Employee Performance at PT VVF Indonesia* (Vol. 4). International Research Journal of Advanced Engineering and Science.

Thamrin, H. M. (2012). The Influence of Transformational Leadership and Organizational Commitment on Job Satisfaction and Employee Performance. *International Journal of Innovation, Management and Technology, 3*(5).

Wexley & Yuki. (1984). *Organizational behavior People and Process in management*. Academic Press.

Winnie, N., Josphat, N., Martin, D., Maxwell, C., Elias, K., & Andrew, J. (2021). Achieving High Employee Performance through Transformational Leadership in the Banking Sector. *International Journal of Research and Innovation in Social Science*.

Yammarino, F. J., Dubinsky, A. J., Comer, L. B., & Jolson, M. A. (1997). Women and transformational and contingent reward leadership: A multiple-levels-of-analysis perspective. *Academy of Management Journal, 40*(1), 205–222. doi:10.2307/257027

Yusuf, M., Sani, D., Fadele, A., Rajab, R., Abulwafa, M., Ludfi, D., & Tutut, H. (2018). *An Impact of Transformational Leadership on Employees' Performance: A Case Study in Nigeria*. Academic Press.

Chapter 23
Improving Hospital Diversity Through Management Consulting Interventions

Kiana S. Zanganeh
Florida Institute of Technology, USA

Darrell Norman Burrell
 https://orcid.org/0000-0002-4675-9544
University of North Carolina at Chapel Hill, USA

Kevin Richardson
 https://orcid.org/0009-0002-3212-8669
Edward Waters University, USA

ABSTRACT

America is more varied than ever. As cultural heterogeneity grows in America, religion, faith, and health habits show their effects. However, Latinx and African-American nurses, doctors, and healthcare professionals must represent the exponential expansion in population diversity. Black nurses may not reflect the variety of the U.S. population, but they are essential for culturally competent treatment and trust-building with communities of color. Many individuals believe health inequalities are caused by fundamental differences between populations and ignore their societal factors. Healthcare workers of color realize that social and political systems cause health inequities. We can then find structural gaps-closing solutions. Intervention research in an organizational case study addresses several of these complicated concerns. This chapter points to the critical importance of leadership, cultural change, employee engagement, and cultural change as essential for organizations to transform to make them more diverse and inclusive.

DOI: 10.4018/979-8-3693-1380-0.ch023

INTRODUCTION AND CONTEXT

The Venmo Jones hospital has experienced a significant number of diversity and inclusion complaints that include a shortage of nurses, several nursing discrimination complaints, and not a single diversity vendor/supplier, even though the community where the hospital exists is 19% African-American and 15% Latino-American. African-American employees only represent 3% of the hospital workforce, and Latino-Americans only represent 2% of the workforce. Only 6% of the nurses are African-American, and only 2% are Latino American. As a result, an organizational development and diversity consultant has been brought to address the issue.

CONTEXTS

A nurse's role is to provide optimal care for the patient, especially post-surgery (Borgés et al., 2018). Nurses are integral to the healthcare system and must be treated because patients and other healthcare workers rely on their expertise, experience, and knowledge day and night.

Nurses comprise the most extensive section of the healthcare field, with a total of 3.9 million nurses in the United States (Haddad et al., 2020). A nursing shortage is no surprise because the Baby Boomer Generation is entering an age with increased health services. This generation is the largest population over 65 in the U.S. than at any other time in history. The population is aging, and the nursing workforce is also aging. Approximately one million nurses are over 50, hinting at retirement in the next ten to fifteen years (Haddad et al., 2020). Some regions in the U.S. have a surplus of nurses, whereas some struggle to fulfill the region's needs.

This hospital is in an area with a shortage of nurses and a need for more representation of diverse ethnicities. This is no surprise considering that 83.2% of the nursing population was white in 2008, with only 5.6% African American and 3.6% Hispanic (Moore & Continelli, 2016). These rates could discourage minorities from pursuing a nursing career, so change needs to be effective as soon as possible to increase racial/ethnic diversity while simultaneously decreasing the nursing shortage.

Job dissatisfaction, workplace anxiety, and employment disengagement are underlying problems that can hinder the nurses' performance, creating a harsh environment for the patients and other healthcare workers. Nearly 60% of nurses are dissatisfied not only with their healthcare benefits but also with their retirement benefits. The level of satisfaction was even worse in hospitals with poor environments (McHugh et al., 2011). Workplace anxiety is among the highest productivity-related costs of all chronic illnesses and depression (Ivandic et al., 2017).

According to Jeve et al. (2015), employees in healthcare were less likely to make mistakes when they were more engaged. The stress and pressures of being understaffed leave the nurses focusing more attention on individual needs than supplying optimum care to the patient. This level of employee disengagement then affects the patient's experience in the hospital. These patients are then less likely to refer to this hospital to their family and friends (McHugh et al., 2011). By not taking care of the nurses, the hospital's overall business struggles because patients might choose another hospital to receive their care.

According to Maslow's Hierarchy of Needs, four factors must be met before someone can achieve self-actualization. Self-actualization is the "desire to become everything that one is capable of being" (Henwood et al., 2015). These four factors include physiological needs, safety, love and belonging, and esteem. Therefore, these nurses must feel cared for to showcase their full potential. This falls under the love and belonging category of Maslow's Hierarchy of Needs, so the consultant's goal is to increase job satisfaction and employee engagement while lowering workplace anxiety.

Minorities even have a more challenging time fulfilling their full potential because, according to Lakshmi Nair and Oluwaseun Adetayo (2019), 98% of senior management in healthcare organizations are white, with a large majority being male. This provides almost a glass ceiling effect for women and minorities. The glass ceiling effect is when men come to work in a mainly female environment but have higher chances of rising quicker through management levels than their female counterparts (Johns, 2013).

Even when minorities and females attain these high positions, they earn lower salaries than their non-minority male counterparts. However, female leadership has been met with increased effectiveness (Nair & Adetayo, 2019). Therefore, it is critical to address these gaps and disparities in healthcare because by fixing these problems, the organization will benefit and lead to a more efficient workplace. However, it requires a significant level of organizational change.

THEORETICAL FRAMEWORK

Previous research outlines how organizational change primarily relies on the attitude and response of employees toward change (Ahmad & Cheng, 2018). Appropriate transformation in employees' behavior toward change determines its long-term success (Bayiz Ahmad et al., 2020). The manifestation of employee resistance to change often is expressed by employees through negative attitudes, limited commitment levels, and employee disengagement (Bayiz Ahmad et al., 2020). During the change execution process, the biggest challenge the organizations faces is managing that change, especially to cope with the resistance posed by the employees (Ahmad & Cheng, 2018). The employees either try to slow down the change process or terminate the change effort entirely (Hughes, 2006). Therefore, employee resistance to organizational change is a leading barrier to an organization's efforts to improve, survive, or adopt new operational processes (Ahmad & Cheng, 2018). However, management usually needs to consider employees' perception of stress or uncertainty associated with the change process, which becomes a major cause of resistance. It may lead the change implementation effort to fail (Ahmad & Cheng, 2018).

According to Miller (2020), Organizational change can be either adaptive or transformational:

- Adaptive changes are minor, gradual, iterative changes that an organization undertakes to evolve its products, processes, workflows, and strategies over time. Hiring a new team member to address increased demand or implementing a new work-from-home policy to attract more qualified job applicants are both examples of adaptive changes.
- Transformational changes are more prominent in scale and scope and often signify a dramatic and, occasionally, sudden departure from the status quo. Launching a new product or business division, or deciding to expand internationally, are examples of transformational change.

Change management is the process of guiding organizational change to fruition, from the earliest stages of conception and preparation, through implementation and, finally, to resolution. An effective management strategy is crucial to ensure businesses successfully transition and adapt to changes.

Miller (2020) views the change management process in 5 interconnected steps that include:

1. Prepare the Organization for Change

For an organization to successfully pursue and implement change, it must be prepared logistically and culturally. Before delving into logistics, cultural preparation must take place to achieve the best business outcome. The required level of preparation includes raising awareness of the various challenges or problems facing the organization acting as forces of change and generating dissatisfaction with the status quo. Gaining this initial buy-in from employees who will help implement the change can diminish employee resistance.

2. Craft a Vision and Plan for Change

Once the organization is ready to embrace change, managers must develop a thorough and realistic plan for bringing it about. The plan should detail the following:

· Strategic goals: This can be built for organizational analysis and assessment results.
· Key performance indicators: This requires milestones and measuring tools and approaches.

The structure is critical, but also the need to include flexibility and adaptability.

3. Implement the Changes

After the plan has been created, all that remains is following the steps outlined to implement the required change. Whether that involves changes to the company's structure, strategy, systems, processes, employee behaviors, or other aspects will depend on the specifics of the initiative.

4. Embed Changes Within Company Culture and Practices

Once the change initiative has been completed, change managers must prevent a reversion to the initial state or status quo. Embedding changes within the company's culture and practices make it more challenging to backslide. New organizational structures, controls, and reward systems should all be considered critical tools for effective change management.

5. Review Progress and Analyze Results

What was the impact of the change? What approaches need to be adjusted?

METHODOLOGY

This paper focuses on a real-world case that explores diversity and inclusion in a hospital healthcare setting through the intervention of an organizational development diversity consultant. This paper explores real hospital diversity and discrimination problems through an action research approach, including fact-finding interviews, barrier analysis through a review of existing survey data, company policy assessments, content analysis of the problem in the literature, and recommendations based on the amalgamation of the triangulated data. The interviews occurred with every African-American and Latino-American nurse (25 total) and the current human resources director. The goals of these conversations would be to find out the organization's ideal state compared to its current state to gain solutions that could bridge those gaps.

Action research is qualitative research where the researcher develops actionable solutions to real-world problems (Reason & Bradbury, 2008). The problem-solving or consulting approach bridges the theory and professional practice gap through a consulting-oriented intervention (Reason & Bradbury, 2008). This type of research is situation-based, helpful in problem-solving, and deals with individuals or groups with a common purpose of improving practice (Reason & Bradbury, 2008). Further, this research helps address practical problems and generate knowledge to produce change (Reason & Bradbury, 2008).

PERSPECTIVES

Although a lot of people think that this is an exaggerated simplification of the problems, it does give us some context for how we may start to comprehend and solve these problems in the medical field. In every aspect of healthcare, factors such as racial or ethnic background, gender, sexual orientation, immigration status, the presence or absence of a physical impairment, and socioeconomic level all play a part in representation, acceptance, and the forward movement of the industry. This is true both inside and outside of healthcare facilities. We are going to do an analysis of the current state of diversity and inclusion in the healthcare industry, as well as make some observations about how to be successful in this field.

Thus, in order to address issues of diversity and inclusion in all areas of healthcare, what kinds of comprehensive methods have been devised thus far? What kind of conversation is there about making changes to improve diversity and inclusion in the medical field? According to Smith (2012), in order to achieve sustained change in academic medicine, we need to build institutional capacity for diversity and inclusion. This requires a "deeper engagement of mission, one that considers diversity as core to excellence," which aligns to key institutional elements and identifies diverse talent for leadership at all levels (Smith, 2012).

Different approaches to resolving the discrepancies that exist between various groups of people have been presented in light of the fact that diversity and inclusion are such massive jobs to analyze in their entirety (Smith, 2012). The following are some of the 10 best practices that Gillespie and her colleagues created in order to attain gender parity in global health organizations: 1. Make diversity and inclusion (D&I) an essential component of global strategy. 2. Tailor global D&I to fit local needs. 3. Embed D&I throughout organizations. 4. Multiply D&I impact via external partnerships. 5. Maximize the role of employee resource groups. 6. Maximize the role of diversity councils. 7. Leverage D&I for innovation. 8. Leverage D&I for business development. 9. Engage CEO. 10. Make sharing of D&I best practices a meta best practice (Gillespie, Dunsire, & Luce, 2018).

Solutions to Solve Diversity Issues With the Help of a Diversity Consultant

According to Edward E. Hubbard (2008), there are four diversity roles, one being a diversity performance consultant. The diversity management consultant's role is to design solutions in the workplace that lacks diverse members while also getting to the root problems of an organization (Hubbard, 2008). This role can occur in any organization, but the specific need for this role lies within a hospital that lacks representation.

The diversity consultant must represent servant leadership. Servant leadership requires one to place the needs of others above his/her own (Linuesa-Langreo et al., 2017). This consultant's job is to place the needs of the nurses above his/her own. Linuesa-Langreo et al. (2017) further explain that nurses can provide genuine care to their patients when a consultant employs servant leadership.

First and foremost, the consultant must research past, present, and future performance rates and trajectories. After gathering the information, he/she must communicate this information to the staff in a meeting. He/she provides information regarding the initial billion-dollar research project that has been put on hold due to the series of incoming lawsuits regarding discrimination in the hiring and promoting of African American, Native American, and Latino nurses.

Due to this lack of representation, there is a high turnover rate, more than 50% of the national average. The high rate leaves the remaining employees 39% below their needs. This leads to higher stress and demand for each nurse and is why only 19% of the nursing staff feels satisfied with their job.

The hospital's specific area is not specified; however, reaching out to various areas in the surrounding area could be a potential solution to increasing diversity. The consultant will share the information with the staff and propose five interventions to help increase diversity while also including ideas on how to boost morale within these five interventions. The use of servant leadership in this setting will allow nurses to trust the consultant because he/she will show genuine care for all the nurses (Linuesa-Langreo et al., 2017).

First Strategy by Diversity Consultant. Nair and Adetayo provide five interventions to improve cultural competence around the workplace: (1) gear the organization toward recruiting diverse members, (2) provide cultural competency training, (3) potentially imply the use of an interpreter to make individuals who struggle with language barriers to feel more comfortable, (4) inform staff on different cultural backgrounds and practice cultural relativism, and (5) providing culturally specific healthcare settings. Some of these interventions overlap; however, they all reap the optimal benefits.

The first intervention is to gear the organization toward recruiting more diverse members. An effective way to do this would be partnering with a nearby university to guarantee a nursing job to prospective nursing students. The hospital must reach out to schools in various neighborhoods to increase the chances of obtaining diverse nurses.

According to Julie Minda (2019), healthcare providers are trying to collaborate with local nursing schools to prepare students for future practice. The American Association of Colleges of Nursing has encouraged partnerships between hospitals and nursing schools. The goal of this collaboration is to relieve the nursing shortage, which is only expected to worsen as the baby boomers age (Minda, 2019). This attempt by nursing schools and hospitals demonstrates the desire to reduce the nursing shortage so that patients can be thoroughly cared for when in a hospital.

An example of this partnership is seen with Mercy Hospital Ardmore and Murray State College in Oklahoma (Minda, 2019). Mercy Hospital converted part of its hospital into a classroom space with two labs and a student study lounge. Minda (2019) further explains that a student can graduate with an associate degree in nursing from Murray State and be hired by Mercy Hospital in December. This is an effective way to attract nurses if they know a job is guaranteed upon graduating.

Minority populations are projected to experience rapid growth by 2060; therefore, many people will need these guaranteed and reliable jobs. Increasing the awareness and need for nurses through interacting with local colleges will help facilitate the process of minorities achieving their full potential (Phillips & Malone, 2014).

An incentive that the consultant would also provide to these nursing students is to provide a bonus for each nurse after working at the hospital for a minimum of three years. Typically, nurses receive a sign-on bonus and then a completion bonus. The completion bonus aims to keep the nurse on site (Nursing Bonuses, n.d.). This will not only motivate future nurses to stay in one location to earn more money but also benefit the hospital in maintaining workers for an extended time.

The second intervention would be to provide cultural competency training. In the hospital setting, there are many cultural and linguistic differences between healthcare workers and patients (Jongen et al., 2018). This often leads to miscommunication and mistrust around the workplace. Cultural competency training aims to educate the staff on current issues, attitudes, and skills to respond to sociocultural issues that can arise. This can be accomplished by implementing diversity workshops on a bimonthly basis. These workshops will include lectures from various speakers and group activities to help boost morale. Specific topics to discuss are gender, sexuality, racism, bias, and mistrust (Jongen et al., 2018).

An extra boost to these workshops included supplying coffee and other breakfast items to the nurses with the additional food vendors implemented into the hospital (discussed later). The food vendors will come after these initial interventions; however, the current hospital food will suffice for the first few months of meetings. Supplying food will help fulfill employees' physiological needs, which gets employees one step closer to achieving self-actualization (Henwood et al., 2015). Through these workshops, nurses will become more culturally aware and understand the benefits a diverse worker can bring to the hospital.

A nurse is supposed to communicate every detail to the patient, so the lack of communication would lead to a patient not understanding the totality of his/her ailment (Meuter, 2015). This barrier will hinder the healthcare provider/patient relationship and create a confusing environment for everyone. The consultant will suggest coordinating with the university if nurses can take English learning classes to improve their language skills. This will help the nurses become more proficient in English and work towards helping more patients.

However, taking English classes might take longer since language takes time to learn. So, employing an interpreter is an excellent start to solving the language barrier. Interpreters aim to improve the quality of care delivered to patients and help to decrease the health disparities in the hospital (Karliner et al., 2007). They help facilitate every detail to the patient and help alleviate some of the stress from the nurses.

For example, in Aruba, the hospital has patients fill out a form on what languages they speak. In Aruba, there are four possible languages for healthcare workers to speak: Spanish, Dutch, English, and Papiamento (island dialect). Some patients and nurses can speak multiple languages or just one, so the hospital tailors their care based on language barriers (Aruba, n.d.).

This might put extra pressure on nurses who are well-versed in more languages, but employing an interpreter in the U.S. hospital setting will help even the workload. Also, allowing nurses to take English classes will not only help their work but also help them assimilate better into society.

The fourth and fifth intervention deal with informing staff about different cultural backgrounds and fostering a culture-friendly environment. This ties in with intervention two because this will occur mainly at diversity workshops. The goal is to practice cultural relativism. Cultural relativism is the idea that every culture is different and unique, and people respect every difference. The goal is tolerance, according to Karori Mbugua (2004).

This idea of cultural relativism will help nurses and other healthcare workers realize that what is valued or expected in one society might not be in the same regard as another. It moves away from the idea that the moral codes of one society are universal and correct and shifts toward acceptance and tolerance (Jonhson, 2000).

Implementing this idea of relativism in the workplace will put everyone on an even playing field. Nurses who remain at the hospital during this change will adapt their behaviors (unless they already practice cultural relativism), and new incoming members will learn the value of cultural relativism.

If a nurse cannot practice cultural relativism, this is not the right setting for him/her. There will be no tolerance for discrimination or ethnocentrism. The consultant addressed this idea in the first meeting because Hubbard (2008) states that the workplace is no place for harsh and negative attitudes and behaviors.

Diversity Consultant's Outline of Strategic Plan. The consultant held meetings to address all these interventions that will take place to change the workplace environment. This consultant needs to display charismatic leadership along with servant leadership stated earlier, because he/she will motivate the crowd to change.

Also, charismatic leadership usually comes out in times of crisis (Yukl & Gardner, 2020). This is not a dire crisis because the hospital is still operating; however, change needs to occur soon, or the hospital will deteriorate further. By the consultant utilizing this form of leadership, the workers will either agree or disagree. Those who disagree are free to leave, but those who agree will help transform this hospital into a diverse and motivated workforce.

Since this consultant employs servant and charismatic leadership, the consultant must master the situational leadership theory. The situational theory of leadership states that a leader must be able to adapt his/her leadership style based on the organization's status (Rabarison et al., 2013). This theory balances the different styles that this consultant might have to employ.

Also, the consultant will give new trajectory rates with the implemented solutions. The goal is to reduce the shortage to 20% from the initial 39% and increase job satisfaction and morale to 50% of employees compared to the current 19%. The consultant will ensure that all the employees are willing to stay during these changes. Some employees might stay, while others will leave; however, this gives a fresh start to a new beginning. This new team must voice its commitment to the proposed changes and place its trust in the diversity consultant.

Second Strategy of Food Vendors. After these interventions are implemented, the consultant will shift his/her focus onto implementing ethnic food vendors in the hospital cafeteria. This will involve the consultant reaching out to various communities in the area willing to collaborate with the hospital.

According to Freedhoof et al. (2008), many hospitals serve generic versions of fast food restaurants or fast food chains themselves. This is ironic, given that a hospital is supposed to promote health and wellness. However, one study showed how Latin American communities prioritize eating a healthier diet compared to Caucasian and African Americans (Skala et al., 2013). This diet included fruits and vegetables; however, other staple foods, including rice, chicken, and meat, can add to a healthy diet.

The consultant would look for a Latin American food restaurant in the area for a potential collaboration. Meeting with the owner will allow the consultant to state that the restaurant would get good publicity from the hospital, especially if people noticed better-tasting food.

Patients would also be happier eating in hospitals, and their family members would be more inclined to eat and stay in the hospital while caring for a loved one than going to a restaurant or grocery store in the area to grab food. With happier patients and families, nurses will have an easier time dealing with families and be able to enjoy the food themselves.

So, now the consultant needs more nurses and workers from the food vendor who can stay at the hospital throughout the day. A potential solution would be for the vendor to rotate their workers from working at the restaurant to the hospital. That way, no one must change the job setting completely.

Further Benefits of Hiring Employees. Also, the consultant will work with the universities attached to the hospital and see if the food vendor workers or the janitors want to take classes and pursue a degree. This will allow upward mobility in the workplace, which is not a common theme for low-income individuals (Bloome, 2017).

These individuals could pursue a nursing degree or fulfill another position within the hospital setting. Not only will the addition of these workers bring diversity, but it will also allow them to attain further education if they want.

Some of these individuals might not have had the opportunity to go to college, but the newly implemented changes in the hospital will allow them to (Bloome, 2017). With the additional implementation of ethnic food vendors and leadership positions, the hospital will look differently on diversity. The resulting engagement, inclusive practices, and cultural change would be that the nurses and the other positions required to maintain a hospital are also diverse. People will feel more comfortable with each other because diversity will now become the majority instead of the minority.

Diversity Consultant's Financial Plan. All these ideas sound beneficial; however, money needs to be considered. The first step dealt with partnering with various colleges in the area, especially those with large minority student populations. This idea could be that the hospital provides a job for students right out of nursing school, while the nursing school can have markedly high employment rates for all prospective students. Proactive outreach and recruiting engagement actions create an ebb and flow that will simultaneously benefit both organizations without requiring a detrimental cost to the hospital.

The second intervention tied in with the fourth and fifth interventions and dealt with implementing diversity workshops by having guest speakers and cultural competency classes. Inclusion Innovates charges $45 per individual for an intercultural development inventory in a group setting. The number of workers would have to be totaled; however, it was an effective cost to undergo. The consultant provided a proposal to show the benefits of implementing team-building workshops.

Benefits to the Hospital. By providing team-building activities, the workers will feel closer to each other. This additional engagement activity will help morale, especially if the team-building activities involve prizes or excellent rewards. Potential rewards could be an extra day vacation day or a gift card from a restaurant to increase the number of nurses. The prices of gift cards were included in the proposal from the consultant.

With these rewards, the nurses will demonstrate the expectancy theory. The expectancy theory states that people act in a way that reflects a particular outcome (Shweiki et al., 2015). By providing incentives, nurses will act to receive the benefits of gift cards and vacation days. Adding new employee recognition activities will increase motivation among the workforce and hopefully foster a healthy competitive environment that ultimately benefits the care of the patients.

The team building activities do not only have to be for the nurses, but the consultant would also implement these incentives for all healthcare workers. Many different positions make up a proper hospital setting and having everyone on the same page regarding increasing diversity will help foster an even more robust ideal and practice of cultural relativism.

The food vendors and employees of all levels could also participate in these workshops and get to know their colleagues in different occupations. By interacting with various occupations, each other in the hospital, people will learn new ideas and values different from their own.

DISCUSSION

Importance of Implementing These Strategies. Nurses are an integral part of the healthcare system that supplies care to every patient. Without nurses, many patients will lack the constant 24-hr care that a nurse would typically fulfill. Patients would not be able to be bathed, supplied medications, or tended specifically to regarding their ailment.

This hospital has a nurse shortage, meaning nurses are potentially working overtime and providing the minimum care necessary to the patients. Patients might not feel thoroughly cared for, which could give the nurses a more challenging time due to their lack of care. Nurses already feel pressure and stress from the shortage, but patient complaints might hinder the overall level of satisfaction with their job (McHugh et al., 2011).

They might also exhibit anxiety or disengagement due to all these external factors, so change must happen quickly (Ivandic et al., 2017). Not only are the current workers short in number and low in morale, but they also need more representation from other races. The role of the diversity management consultant is to propose a plan to increase the number of diverse workers (which reduces the shortage) and increase morale.

Brief Summary of the First Strategy. The consultant's intervention plan included several initial interventions to kickstart the change. The first intervention is to contact local nursing universities and form partnerships with future nurses. The second intervention involves providing cultural competency training to increase cultural relativism in the workplace. The third intervention would hire an interpreter to help with any language barriers that might occur in the workplace. The fourth and fifth interventions tie in with the second intervention and deal with collectively promoting cultural diversity in the workplace.

These interventions stem from the ideas of Nair and Adetayo (2019). The goals of these interventions look promising, and the consultant will showcase this attitude in his/her meeting with employees. Attitude is everything, and by showcasing charismatic leadership, the consultant will aim to inspire the organization to change (Yukl & Gardner, 2020).

Brief Summary of Second Strategy. Specific workshops or training were implemented to help promote these interventions and decrease the number of problems. After implementing these interventions, the consultant manager will reach out to local food vendors in the area and form a partnership to implement new and delicious food into the low-quality hospital cafeteria.

The outcomes of these potential solutions appear favorable and will help to reduce the pressure on all the nurses in the hospital. More importantly, these different job positions will increase diversity and interaction among coworkers through team-building exercises. These exercises will join people from different worlds and expose them to new and different ideas from their own.

CONCLUSIONS AND RECOMMENDATIONS

America is more varied than ever. As cultural heterogeneity grows in America, religion, faith, and health habits show their effects. However, Latinx and African-American nurses, doctors, and healthcare professionals must represent the exponential expansion in population diversity. Black nurses may not reflect the variety of the U.S. population, but they are essential for culturally competent treatment and trust-building with communities of color. Many individuals believe health inequalities are caused by fundamental differences between populations and ignore their societal factors. Healthcare workers of color realize that social and political systems cause health inequities. We can then find structural gaps-closing solutions. These strategies aim to fix this lack of diversity and motivation among the nurses in this hospital. The percentage of minority nurses increased by 200% within six months of the intervention. The number of minority vendors increased by 1000% during the same time.

Differences between healthcare providers and patients can affect communication. A lack of employee diversity and cultural competence can, in turn, impact both clinicians' and patients' decisions concerning treatment. As a result, diversity, inclusion, and having more diverse professionals are significant.

PRACTICAL IMPLICATIONS

When healthcare providers need to recognize the differences between them and their patients, they may inadvertently deliver lower-quality care. Cultivating skills that improve cross-cultural communication can be essential in providing equitable care. Building teams with healthcare professionals who reflect the diversity of the patient populations served can also enhance cross-cultural communication. Diverse teams have a more comprehensive cultural knowledge base that they can share. Gaining higher levels of knowledge and cultural understanding makes them likely to respond with empathy to the unique cultural needs of patients. Change management is the systematic approach and application of knowledge, tools, and resources to deal with change. It involves defining and adopting corporate strategies, structures, procedures, and technologies to handle changes in external conditions and the business environment. Effective change management goes beyond project management, and technical tasks were undertaken to enact organizational changes and involve leading the "people side" of significant change within an organization. The primary goal of change management is to successfully implement new processes, products, and business strategies while minimizing adverse outcomes.

Listed below are some concrete approaches that can be taken by hospitals and community medical centers to ensure diversity and inclusion: 1) Ensure that diversity and inclusion are deeply embedded in the culture of the organization by making it an intrinsic part of both the mission and the outputs of the organization; 2) Include stakeholders from all levels of the organization and make sure that all groups are represented in the discussions that are held in order to put diversity and inclusion initiatives into action and keep them going; 3) Discuss both your organization's victories and setbacks with other businesses that are in a similar position, as it is through this kind of conversation that the company will be able to assess its own diversity and inclusion efforts and determine what worked and what didn't in the past. and 4) Get started early and make sure young people from underrepresented groups are given early exposure to the various areas in medicine by becoming involved with local communities and schools. Even though these are only a few measures, each move in the right way toward improving diversity and inclusion in medicine is a step in the right direction.

FUTURE DIRECTIONS

The most critical area of future research exploration could be to look at the impacts of the interventions and recommendations one year, three years, and five years later to see if the inventions have created lasting results. Areas to explore would be employee turnover numbers for African-American and Latino Americans, current employee racial demographics, and employee satisfaction climate surveys.

REFERENCES

Ahmad, A. B., & Cheng, Z. (2018). The role of change content, context, process, and leadership in understanding employees' commitment to change: The case of public organizations in Kurdistan region of Iraq. *Public Personnel Management, 47*(2), 195–216. doi:10.1177/0091026017753645

Bayiz Ahmad, A., Liu, B., & Saleem Butt, A. (2020). Predictors and outcomes of change recipient proactivity in public organizations of the Kurdistan region of Iraq. *International Public Management Journal, 23*(6), 823–851. doi:10.1080/10967494.2019.1588812

Bloome, D. (2017). Childhood Family Structure and Intergenerational Income Mobility in the United States. *Demography, 54*(2), 541–569. doi:10.100713524-017-0564-4 PMID:28315158

Bonuses, N. (n.d.). *How to Land a Big Payout*. Retrieved July 19, 2020, from https://www.nursingschool.org/nursing-careers/salaries/bonuses/#context/api/listings/prefilter

Borgès Da Silva, R., Brault, I., Pineault, R., Chouinard, M. C., Prud'homme, A., & D'Amour, D. (2018). Nursing Practice in Primary Care and Patients' Experience of Care. *Journal of Primary Care & Community Health, 9*, 2150131917747186. doi:10.1177/2150131917747186 PMID:29357748

Casciano, R., & Massey, D. S. (2008). Neighborhoods, employment, and welfare use: Assessing the influence of neighborhood socioeconomic composition. *Social Science Research, 37*(2), 544–558. doi:10.1016/j.ssresearch.2007.08.008 PMID:19069058

Cultural Relativism. (2000). In A. G. Johnson (Ed.), *The Blackwell dictionary of sociology* (2nd ed.). Blackwell Publishers. https://search-credoreference-com.portal.lib.fit.edu/content/entry/bksoc/cultural_relativism/0?institutionId=5457

Freedhoff, Y., & Stevenson, R. (2008). Frying up hospital cafeteria food. *CMAJ: Canadian Medical Association journal = journal de l'Association medicale canadienne, 179*(3), 213–214. https://doi.org/doi:10.1503/cmaj.080975

Haddad, L. M., Annamaraju, P., & Toney-Butler, T. J. (2020). *Nursing Shortage*. StatPearls Publishing. Available from: https://www.ncbi.nlm.nih.gov/books/NBK493175/

Han, J. H., Sullivan, N., Leas, B. F., Pegues, D. A., Kaczmarek, J. L., & Umscheid, C. A. (2015). Cleaning Hospital Room Surfaces to Prevent Health Care-Associated Infections: A Technical Brief. *Annals of Internal Medicine, 163*(8), 598–607. doi:10.7326/M15-1192 PMID:26258903

Henwood, B. F., Derejko, K. S., Couture, J., & Padgett, D. K. (2015). Maslow and mental health recovery: A comparative study of homeless programs for adults with serious mental illness. *Administration and Policy in Mental Health, 42*(2), 220–228. doi:10.100710488-014-0542-8 PMID:24518968

Innovates, Diversity & Cultural Competency: Workshops. (n.d.). Retrieved from https://www.inclusioninnovates.com/cultural-diversity-training

Ivandic, I., Kamenov, K., Rojas, D., Cerón, G., Nowak, D., & Sabariego, C. (2017). Determinants of Work Performance in Workers with Depression and Anxiety: A Cross-Sectional Study. *International Journal of Environmental Research and Public Health, 14*(5), 466. doi:10.3390/ijerph14050466 PMID:28445433

Jacobs, E. A., Shepard, D. S., Suaya, J. A., & Stone, E. L. (2004). Overcoming language barriers in health care: Costs and benefits of interpreter services. *American Journal of Public Health*, *94*(5), 866–869. doi:10.2105/AJPH.94.5.866 PMID:15117713

Jeve, Y. B., Oppenheimer, C., & Konje, J. (2015). Employee engagement within the NHS: A cross-sectional study. *International Journal of Health Policy and Management*, *4*(2), 85–90. doi:10.15171/ijhpm.2015.12 PMID:25674571

Johns, M. L. (2013). Breaking the glass ceiling: Structural, cultural, and organizational barriers preventing women from achieving senior and executive positions. *Perspectives in Health Information Management*, *10*(Winter). PMID:23346029

Jongen, C., McCalman, J., & Bainbridge, R. (2018). Health workforce cultural competency interventions: A systematic scoping review. *BMC Health Services Research*, *18*(1), 232. doi:10.118612913-018-3001-5 PMID:29609614

Karliner, L. S., Jacobs, E. A., Chen, A. H., & Mutha, S. (2007). Do professional interpreters improve clinical care for patients with limited English proficiency? A systematic review of the literature. *Health Services Research*, *42*(2), 727–754. doi:10.1111/j.1475-6773.2006.00629.x PMID:17362215

Linuesa-Langreo, J., Ruiz-Palomino, P., & Elche-Hortelano, D. (2017). New Strategies in the New Millennium: Servant Leadership as Enhancer of Service Climate and Customer Service Performance. *Frontiers in Psychology*, *8*, 786. doi:10.3389/fpsyg.2017.00786 PMID:28559873

Mbugua K. (2012). Respect for cultural diversity and the empirical turn in bioethics: a plea for caution. *Journal of Medical Ethics and History of Medicine*, *5*, 1.

McHugh, M. D., Kutney-Lee, A., Cimiotti, J. P., Sloane, D. M., & Aiken, L. H. (2011). Nurses' widespread job dissatisfaction, burnout, and frustration with health benefits signal problems for patient care. *Health Affairs (Project Hope)*, *30*(2), 202–210. doi:10.1377/hlthaff.2010.0100 PMID:21289340

Medical facilities in Aruba - Hospitals, Pharmacies & Clinics. (n.d.). Retrieved from https://www.aruba.com/us/organization/medical-facilities

Meuter, R. F., Gallois, C., Segalowitz, N. S., Ryder, A. G., & Hocking, J. (2015). Overcoming language barriers in healthcare: A protocol for investigating safe and effective communication when patients or clinicians use a second language. *BMC Health Services Research*, *15*(1), 371. doi:10.118612913-015-1024-8 PMID:26357948

Miller, K. (2020, March 19). *5 critical steps in the change management process*. Harvard Business School Insights.

Moore, J., & Continelli, T. (2016). Racial/Ethnic Pay Disparities among Registered Nurses (R.N.s) in U.S. Hospitals: An Econometric Regression Decomposition. *Health Services Research*, *51*(2), 511–529. doi:10.1111/1475-6773.12337 PMID:26932449

Nair, L., & Adetayo, O. A. (2019). Cultural Competence and Ethnic Diversity in Healthcare. *Plastic and Reconstructive Surgery. Global Open*, *7*(5), e2219. doi:10.1097/GOX.0000000000002219 PMID:31333951

Phillips, J. M., & Malone, B. (2014). Increasing racial/ethnic diversity in nursing to reduce health disparities and achieve health equity. *Public Health Reports, 2*(Suppl 2), 45–50. doi:10.1177/00333549141291S209

Rabarison, K., Ingram, R. C., & Holsinger, J. W., Jr (2013). Application of situational leadership to the national voluntary public health accreditation process. *Frontiers in Public Health, 1*, 26. doi:10.3389/fpubh.2013.00026

Reason, P., & Bradbury, H. (2008). *The SAGE Handbook of Action Research: Participative Inquiry and Practice* (2nd ed.). SAGE. doi:10.4135/9781848607934

Skala, K., Chuang, R. J., Evans, A., Hedberg, A. M., Dave, J., & Sharma, S. (2012). Ethnic differences in the home food environment and parental food practices among families of low-income Hispanic and African-American preschoolers. *Journal of Immigrant and Minority Health, 14*(6), 1014–1022. doi:10.100710903-012-9575-9 PMID:22262411

Chapter 24
Breaking the Mold:
The Power of Transformational Leadership and DEI in Driving Organizational Change

Suzzette A. Harriott
Harriott Research Institute, USA & Nova Southeastern University, USA

Jia Tyson
Nova Southeastern University, USA

Christopher A. Powell
Nova Southeastern University, USA & University of London, UK

ABSTRACT

This study presents a qualitative narrative analysis of the experiences of five individuals representing five diverse organizations from various industries. It investigates the themes of transformational leadership; diversity, equity, and inclusion; organizational change and innovation; effective people management; communication strategies; and paradigm shift. The names of the individuals and organizations have been changed for privacy reasons. The analysis of the narratives reveals the critical role of transformational leadership in driving organizational change and innovation. In addition, it emphasizes the importance of promoting diversity, equity, and inclusion to create a positive and inclusive work environment. The study also highlights the significance of effective people management, communication strategies, and organizational design in fostering collaboration and innovation.

INTRODUCTION

In an environment distinguished by relentless change and escalating complexity, contemporary organizations are faced with the challenging task of navigating an intricate labyrinth of transformative adjustments. The dynamics of this evolving landscape insistently demand more than mere static continuity or complacency within the comfort of familiar patterns. Rather, they mandate adaptability and transformation, necessitating the proficiency to adeptly negotiate the swift currents of this metamorphosing milieu.

DOI: 10.4018/979-8-3693-1380-0.ch024

Emerging from this crucible of change are two pivotal constructs that possess the potential to redefine organizational paradigms: Transformational Leadership and Diversity, Equity, and Inclusion (DEI). The synergistic confluence of these concepts, teeming with the promise of organizational rejuvenation, proffers an avant-garde approach to leadership and change management. They precipitate a fresh organizational narrative that is anchored in the principles of inclusivity, propagated by transformational leaders who adroitly leverage the power of diversity to engender sustained value.

The subsequent chapter, entitled "Breaking the Mold: The Power of Transformational Leadership and DEI in Driving Organizational Change," delves into the intricate matrix of leadership and diversity. It offers a comprehensive discourse on the integral role that transformational leadership and DEI play in catalyzing and stewarding organizational change, thereby challenging and ultimately shattering the conventional confines of traditional business operations.

The intellectual journey embarked upon within this chapter is designed to augment our comprehension of these elements and, concurrently, illuminate the pathway for leaders and organizations as they traverse the complex terrain of change. As this exploration unfolds, we invite readers to critically consider the potency and potential inherent in these constructs, and their capacity to reshape the narrative of organizational transformation.

Thus, we extend an invitation to our readers to join us on this exploration, immersing themselves in the profound discourse that encompasses transformational leadership and DEI, and discovering how these elements can powerfully intersect to drive change, break the mold, and shape the future trajectory of organizational dynamics.

Problem Statement

In the current age of accelerated organizational metamorphosis, diversity, equity, and inclusion (DEI), in conjunction with transformational leadership, have emerged as indispensable navigational aids in the intricate landscape of change. This section, entitled "Shattering Conventional Paradigms: The Efficacy of Transformational Leadership and DEI in Facilitating Organizational Evolution," endeavors to execute a rigorous analysis of the crucial role these two constituents play in instigating and supervising organizational transformation.

Commencing this investigative journey, a meticulous understanding of the historical context of diversity, equity, and inclusion is constructed, illustrating the progressive evolution of these concepts. The transition of DEI from a compliance-centric task to an integral strategic component signifies a notable evolution in business procedures (Bates & Khasawneh, 2005). Evaluating this recent metamorphosis of DEI not only emphasizes its present pertinence but also lays the groundwork for discerning its future ramifications.

Significance of the Study

Simultaneously, the concept of transformational leadership is unfolded and presented as an influential mechanism for administering the changes often necessitated by DEI initiatives. Transformational leaders, as delineated by Bass and Riggio (2006), inspire and galvanize their followers to transcend their personal interests for the collective prosperity of the organization. Such leaders foster an environment of trust and respect, which serves as a conducive incubator for fostering DEI initiatives.

Objectives of the Study

Having set these elemental pillars, the chapter subsequently embarks on an exploration of the critical convergence of DEI, transformational leadership, and organizational evolution. As asserted by Men, Qin, Mitson, & Thelen, (2023) it is at this critical juncture that the most impactful metamorphoses can be manifested. This intersection provides a platform where leaders can harness the potency of diversity and inclusivity to drive the organization towards its strategic objectives, thereby, metaphorically shattering the conventional mold.

As the scrutiny advances, the chapter elaborates on the pragmatic implications of transformational leadership and DEI across various sectors. The unique opportunities and challenges that sectors such as technology, healthcare, and education present are dissected (Kezar, Holcombe, Harper, & Ueda, 2023)Actual examples from the real world are utilized to vivify the discussion and furnish readers with tangible insights.

Furthermore, the chapter evaluates the role of emotional intelligence within transformational leadership, adding an extra stratum of intricacy to our comprehension of the efficacy of these leaders in propelling DEI initiatives. According to Goleman (2018), emotional intelligence is a fundamental attribute for leaders tasked with maneuvering the frequently challenging dynamics of diverse and inclusive workplaces.

This examination is complemented by a consideration of the potential hurdles and barriers organizations might encounter when implementing DEI initiatives and transformational leadership strategies. The discourse provides practical strategies to surmount these obstacles, fortified by insights from contemporary research and case studies.

Concluding the chapter, prospective directions for research and practice are proposed. As DEI and transformational leadership continue to adapt in response to shifting societal and organizational contexts, new avenues for exploration and application will undoubtedly surface (Oluwayemisi, 2022).). The chapter thus concludes by encouraging readers to contemplate these potential advancements and their implications for the future of organizational evolution.

Collectively, this chapter aims to deliver a thorough and nuanced comprehension of transformational leadership and DEI in steering organizational evolution. By intertwining theory, research, and real-world exemplars, it presents an engaging narrative of the power of these elements to truly shatter conventional paradigms.

BACKGROUND

In the fast-paced and constantly evolving global economy of today, the role of diversity, equity, and inclusion (DEI) has come to the forefront as a significant factor for organizational success. Men and colleagues (2023) asserted that DEI initiatives not only foster a positive and inclusive workplace environment but also fuel creativity and innovation, which are critical drivers for economic growth and competitive advantage in today's global marketplace. For instance, diverse teams are known to bring a wider range of perspectives, experiences, and ideas to the table, thereby fostering out-of-the-box thinking and problem-solving. As businesses increasingly operate across multiple cultures and demographics, embracing DEI can also help organizations better understand and cater to their diverse customer bases.

Alongside the growing recognition of DEI, the significance of transformational leadership in driving DEI initiatives and sparking organizational change cannot be overstated. Transformational leaders, as characterized by Bass and Riggio (2006), inspire and motivate their followers to exceed their own personal interests for the good of the group. According to Begum et al. (2022), these leaders play a crucial role in creating an environment where DEI is valued and embedded into the organization's culture. For example, transformational leaders might introduce flexible work policies to accommodate diverse work styles and needs, or they may take a stand against any form of discrimination, thereby setting a powerful example for others to follow. At the heart of this dynamic is the critical intersection of DEI, transformational leadership, and organizational change. The synergy between these three elements can create an environment conducive to sustained growth and transformation.

Khan & Khan (2022) emphasized that transformational leaders who prioritize DEI are well-positioned to facilitate substantial organizational change. By harnessing the power of a diverse workforce and fostering an inclusive culture, these leaders can drive innovation, improve decision-making, and enhance organizational performance. As an example, a tech company that champions DEI under the guidance of transformational leadership could experience a significant improvement in product development, given the fresh and varied ideas from its diverse teams.

However, successfully driving organizational change through transformational leadership and DEI is not without its challenges. Carson and Farh (2023) noted that these initiatives often encounter resistance, especially in organizations with deep-rooted traditional cultures. In such cases, transformational leaders play a key role in overcoming resistance by articulating a clear vision for change, creating a sense of urgency, and rallying support. Take the example of a manufacturing firm seeking to modernize its operations: A transformational leader would not only explain the need for modernization but also involve all team members in the change process, ensuring that diverse perspectives are heard and valued.

The rapidly changing business landscape, as shaped by factors like technology, globalization, and the recent COVID-19 pandemic, also affects the implementation of transformational leadership and DEI strategies. Nguyen et al. (2023) discussed how remote work, a major shift induced by the pandemic, has introduced new dimensions to DEI. Transformational leaders in this "new normal" need to ensure inclusivity beyond physical spaces, demonstrating empathy and flexibility to accommodate the diverse needs and challenges of remote employees.

The digital age also brings with it new opportunities for transformational leadership and DEI. Bates and Khasawneh (2022) indicated that advancements in technology can enhance the reach and impact of DEI initiatives, while also presenting new platforms for transformational leaders to engage and inspire their teams. A company adopting digital tools, for example, might use virtual reality for diversity training, providing immersive experiences that foster empathy and understanding.

In the context of the tech industry, transformational leadership and DEI initiatives hold immense potential. Duan et al. (2022) highlighted the importance of emotional intelligence in leading tech startups, which often thrive on diversity and innovation. fostering emotional intelligence, transformational leaders can better understand, empathize with, and respond to the diverse needs and perspectives within their teams, thereby driving a culture of innovation. For instance, a leader with high emotional intelligence may be more adept at recognizing and addressing biases or discrimination, creating a more inclusive environment that empowers all team members to contribute their best ideas.

Emphasizing the significance of these interrelations in the healthcare sector, Becker et al. (2022) argued that transformational leadership and DEI are paramount in promoting quality care and patient satisfaction. Diverse and inclusive healthcare teams, guided by transformational leadership, can provide culturally competent care to diverse patient populations. For example, a hospital with a diverse team of healthcare professionals can cater to a broader range of patient needs and preferences, resulting in improved patient satisfaction and health outcomes.

In education, the critical role of transformational leadership and DEI in driving change is equally evident. According to Zia et al. (2022), school leaders who exhibit transformational leadership traits and prioritize DEI can foster a more inclusive and effective learning environment. For example, a transformational school principal who promotes DEI might implement policies to accommodate different learning styles and needs or might actively seek to hire a diverse staff to provide a broader range of perspectives and experiences for students.

In the face of societal changes and growing calls for social justice, the importance of transformational leadership and DEI in public administration has been underscored. Williams and Davis (2021) demonstrated how transformational leaders in public offices who champion DEI can facilitate more equitable service delivery and policy implementation. For instance, a city mayor who is a transformational leader might prioritize DEI by ensuring diverse representation in city council and public offices, leading to policies and services that better reflect and serve the city's diverse population.

In summary, the interplay between transformational leadership and DEI is a driving force for organizational change across different sectors. The unique blend of transformational leadership and DEI can spark innovation, enhance performance, and foster a culture of inclusivity and equity, setting the stage for successful and sustainable organizational transformation. As the world continues to evolve, transformational leaders who champion DEI will be well-equipped to steer their organizations towards a future marked by growth, inclusivity, and ongoing change.

LITERATURE REVIEW

In the realm of leadership and organizational change, the ideas of Transformational Leadership and Diversity, Equity, and Inclusion (DEI) have increasingly claimed their place of prominence. Coupled with the essential construct of Emotional Intelligence, these key themes shape the discursive milieu that heralds a new epoch in organizational studies. It is with these pivotal concepts in mind that we set the stage for our exploration in the subsequent literature review.

The canvas of Transformational Leadership and its intimate relationship with DEI unfolds as a fundamental narrative in the lexicon of modern organizational discourse. By parsing out its definitions and delineating its role in fostering DEI, we embark upon an analytical journey into the heart of this symbiotic dynamic. The scholarly works of Bureau et al. (2021) serve as instrumental beacons, guiding us through this intricate labyrinth of leadership and diversity studies. Underpinning these discussions is the acknowledgement of the profound impact that transformational leadership wields on DEI outcomes within organizations. This potency reiterates the vital importance of transformational leaders as agents of change in today's dynamic organizational landscape.

This rich tapestry of leadership and diversity is further entwined with the vibrant threads of DEI and Organizational Change. The burgeoning significance of DEI in driving transformative shifts, and its integral role in fostering a culture of innovation, commands our attention. We draw upon recent groundbreaking research by Bormann & Diebig (2021) and Duan et al. (2022), whose contributions illuminate the contours of this evolving discourse.

Finally, we add a further dimension to our review by focusing on the integral role of Emotional Intelligence within the construct of Transformational Leadership. This facet represents a critical interface, where the leader's ability to perceive, comprehend, and regulate emotions becomes an indispensable tool for effective transformational leadership. Here, we venture into the research landscapes charted by Kline (2022) and Noori and colleagues (2022), whose findings yield profound insights into this complex interrelationship.

In essence, the forthcoming literature review serves as a scholarly exploration into these interconnected domains. It is a venture into the depths of transformational leadership, DEI, and emotional intelligence, culminating in a richer understanding of their confluence and the consequent implications for driving organizational change. As we embark on this intellectual journey, we invite readers to approach these narratives with an open mind, ready to critically engage with and draw insights from the wealth of knowledge that this literature review presents.

Transformational Leadership and DEI

The first step to understanding the power of transformational leadership in fostering diversity, equity, and inclusion (DEI) is to define what transformational leadership entails. Transformational leadership is a leadership style that inspires positive change within an organization. Leaders who adopt this style focus on the strengths of their team members, encouraging them to exceed their best work, rather than merely meeting set expectations (Bass & Riggio, 2006). This leadership style is known for creating an environment of trust, encouraging innovation, and fostering a culture where employees feel valued and respected, providing a strong foundation for DEI initiatives.

In their recent study, Moin et al. (2021) explored the connection between transformational leadership and DEI, emphasizing that such leaders play a critical role in promoting DEI within their organizations. They highlighted that transformational leaders can inspire employees to embrace diverse perspectives, leading to increased creativity, problem-solving skills, and overall productivity. In the context of DEI, transformational leaders encourage a climate of openness and acceptance, where every member's unique skills and perspectives are valued and utilized.

Notably, transformational leadership doesn't stop at the mere acceptance of diversity; it encourages equity and inclusion as well. Scuotto et al. (2022) noted that transformational leaders treat each team member fairly, acknowledging their unique contributions and ensuring that they have equal access to opportunities. This equity, coupled with an environment where every employee feels that they belong, promotes an inclusive workplace, a crucial aspect of DEI.

Several studies have underscored the impact of transformational leadership on DEI outcomes in organizations. Palmer (2023) conducted a study in healthcare settings, concluding that transformational leadership significantly improved DEI outcomes. They noted a positive correlation between transformational leadership practices and employee perceptions of being valued and included, which in turn enhanced their performance and dedication to the organization. They highlighted that these leaders were able to leverage diverse ideas and perspectives, fostering an innovative environment that proved beneficial for both employees and the organization.

Similarly, Dogru (2023) focused on the tech industry, noting that emotional intelligence, a key element of transformational leadership, played a significant role in managing diverse teams. They noted that transformational leaders with high emotional intelligence were better at understanding, accepting, and valuing the diversity within their teams. This understanding and acceptance, in turn, fostered a more inclusive and equitable environment, where every team member felt valued and motivated to contribute to the organization's goals.

Breaking the Mold

These studies demonstrate the profound impact that transformational leadership can have on DEI outcomes. When leaders adopt this style, they create an environment where every team member feels valued and accepted, regardless of their backgrounds or perspectives (Kezar, Holcombe, Harper, & Ueda, 2023). This inclusive environment is not just beneficial for the employees but also significantly contributes to organizational success, driving creativity, innovation, and overall productivity.

As the global economy continues to grow more diverse, the role of transformational leadership in fostering DEI becomes even more critical. Leaders who embrace this style can effectively drive change, leveraging the strengths of their diverse teams to navigate the complexities of the business environment (Constantinou et al., 2022). They do not just break the mold, they redesign it to be more inclusive, equitable, and diverse, reflecting the ever-evolving nature of the global workforce.

In the light of these findings, it is evident that transformational leadership plays a pivotal role in fostering DEI in organizations. By creating an inclusive environment and fostering equity, these leaders leverage the diversity of their teams to drive organizational success. They break the mold, setting the stage for a new era where diversity, equity, and inclusion are not just buzzwords, but integral components of the organizational culture.

DEI and Organizational Change

Diversity, Equity, and Inclusion (DEI) is not just a corporate buzzword; it is a critical factor in the success and evolution of organizations in today's global economy (Brown & Green, 2023). In fact, DEI is increasingly seen as an integral driver of organizational change. Companies that embrace DEI have shown to be more adaptable, innovative, and capable of navigating through uncertainties and shifts in the business landscape (Men et al., 2023).

An organization's ability to adapt and thrive in changing environments is largely influenced by its commitment to DEI. Cox (2023) found that diverse teams, when managed effectively, can promote a more comprehensive understanding of different markets, enabling organizations to anticipate changes and adapt their strategies accordingly. Furthermore, a culture of inclusivity encourages diverse perspectives, leading to more innovative problem-solving and decision-making processes.

Innovation is often seen as the lifeblood of organizations, and there is growing recognition of the role of DEI in fostering a culture of innovation. According Vera (2022), organizations with a diverse and inclusive workforce tend to demonstrate greater innovation capabilities. This is because diverse teams bring together different experiences, perspectives, and ideas, creating a breeding ground for creativity and innovation.

In addition to driving innovation, DEI also plays a significant role in employee engagement and retention, which are critical to organizational change. Employees who feel valued and included are more likely to be engaged in their work and committed to their organization (Diwanji et al., 2023). This can help organizations to better manage changes and transitions, as engaged employees are typically more willing to support change initiatives and adapt to new ways of working.

While the benefits of DEI in driving organizational change are increasingly recognized, it is important to note that the implementation of DEI initiatives is not without its challenges. Companies often face resistance to change, especially when it comes to changes related to diversity and inclusion. Therefore, effective leadership is crucial in driving DEI initiatives and facilitating organizational change (Kezar, Holcombe, Harper, & Ueda, 2023 2022).

A review of recent research underscores the critical role of DEI in organizational change. A study by Violanti (202) found that tech startups that prioritized DEI were more successful in adapting to rapidly changing technology trends. Similarly, Schulz et al. (2022) demonstrated in their research that companies with strong DEI policies were better positioned to navigate the challenges of the global economy. To further illustrate, a case study by Cox (2023) explored the role of DEI in organizational change in the healthcare sector. They found that hospitals with a high level of DEI were more effective in implementing changes in patient care strategies, leading to improved patient outcomes.

In essence, DEI is not just about ensuring fair representation within an organization. It plays a critical role in driving organizational change, fostering innovation, and enabling businesses to adapt and thrive in a constantly changing business landscape. Therefore, it is imperative for organizations to prioritize DEI and transformational leadership in their strategic planning and operational processes.

Emotional Intelligence in Transformational Leadership

Emotional intelligence (EI) is an integral component of effective transformational leadership. EI refers to an individual's ability to perceive, manage, and utilize emotions constructively, both their own and those of others (Goleman, 1995). These skills are particularly vital for transformational leaders who often must inspire and motivate diverse teams towards common goals.

The link between EI and transformational leadership has been explored extensively in academic research. Kline (2022) posits that EI acts as a catalyst for transformational leadership by enhancing empathy, understanding, and communication—essential traits for fostering inclusivity. Their study found that leaders with high EI were more likely to be seen as transformational by their followers, leading to improved performance and engagement.

In the corporate world, Microsoft serves as an excellent example of this. Their CEO, Satya Nadella, is renowned for his emotionally intelligent approach to leadership, which has been instrumental in revitalizing the company's culture and driving growth (Lo et al., 2023). Nadella's transformational leadership style, grounded in empathy and understanding, was crucial in fostering a more inclusive and innovative environment.

Moreover, EI's role in transformational leadership transcends cultural boundaries, as illustrated by Noori and colleagues (2022) study. They found that leaders with high EI were effective at driving change and promoting inclusivity in culturally diverse environments, underscoring EI's global relevance.

Global companies like Unilever and Procter & Gamble exemplify this finding. Their leadership programs emphasize emotional intelligence training to foster transformational leaders capable of managing and leading diverse, global teams (Ahmad et al., 2023). Their DEI initiatives and commitment to sustainable business practices reflect their transformational leadership style rooted in EI.

It is also worth noting that transformational leadership and EI are closely intertwined with DEI initiatives. High emotional intelligence can foster a more inclusive environment, as leaders are more attuned to the emotional and cultural nuances of their teams. Transformational leaders with high EI can identify and address implicit biases, promoting an inclusive culture where all employees feel valued and heard (Kumari et al., 2022).

The shift towards remote work due to the global pandemic has also underscored the importance of EI in transformational leadership. Organizations like Google and Facebook have had to navigate the complexities of leading remote teams. Their leaders, armed with emotional intelligence, have managed to maintain high levels of employee engagement and productivity, further emphasizing EI's role in effective transformational leadership in the face of unprecedented change (Kezar, Holcombe, Harper, & Ueda, 2023 2022).

In summary, emotional intelligence is a foundational aspect of transformational leadership, empowering leaders to navigate diverse environments and drive change effectively. As businesses continue to globalize and prioritize DEI, the role of EI in transformational leadership will only become more pronounced.

SYNTHESIS OF THE LITERATURE

In the quest to uncover the intricate interplay of Transformational Leadership, Diversity, Equity, and Inclusion (DEI), and Emotional Intelligence (EI) in driving organizational change, the literature review has unearthed valuable insights. It has not only illuminated individual facets of each concept but also illuminated their integrated dynamism within organizational settings.

Transformational Leadership, as the literature suggests, emerges as a cornerstone in the strategic navigation of today's volatile organizational landscapes. Rooted in the capabilities to inspire, motivate, and exceed self-interests for collective benefit (Peng et al., 2021), this leadership style is instrumental in fostering a culture conducive to DEI. The works of Crucke et al. (2022) particularly underscore the impact of transformational leadership on DEI outcomes, accentuating its integral role in enhancing diversity and inclusivity within organizations.

DEI, on the other hand, has evolved from being a mere compliance requirement to a strategic catalyst for organizational change. As revealed by Nguyen et al. (2023) and Scuotto et al. (2022), a robust DEI framework fuels a culture of innovation, flexibility, and adaptability. This culture then becomes the bedrock for substantial, structural changes that redefine organizational functioning, consequently driving performance and competitiveness.

The exploration of Emotional Intelligence brings to the fore its critical role within transformational leadership. High emotional intelligence, marked by the ability to perceive, understand, and manage emotions, emerges as an indispensable competency for transformational leaders aiming to drive DEI initiatives (Kline, 2022; Noori, Orfan, & Noori, 2023). Leaders endowed with high EI can resonate effectively with a diverse workforce, acknowledging their unique emotional and cultural contexts, thereby nurturing an inclusive work environment.

However, an apparent gap exists within the literature, which, although it explores these constructs extensively, rarely unifies them within a singular, comprehensive theoretical framework. This absence inhibits the understanding of the synergistic effects of transformational leadership, DEI, and EI in fostering organizational change. Thus, a call for an integrated theoretical framework arises, which could allow a holistic examination of the dynamics that drive change within organizations.

In synthesizing these threads of literature, the convergence of Transformational Leadership, DEI, and Emotional Intelligence emerges as a potent triad in shaping and driving organizational change. Collectively, these elements form a comprehensive matrix that can guide organizations to create an environment that values diversity, fosters innovation, and ultimately leads to performance enhancement. As this chapter progresses, it will continue to delve deeper into these dynamics, exploring the practical implications, challenges, and future directions in this burgeoning field of study.

THEORETICAL CONSTRUCT

The evolving landscape of organizational management calls for an integrative perspective that captures the synergy between transformational leadership, diversity, equity, and inclusion (DEI), emotional intelligence (EI), and organizational change. While substantial research has delved into these areas separately, a holistic theoretical framework that intertwines these domains is notably absent. This gap not only leaves questions unanswered but also overlooks opportunities for innovative and practical applications in the organizational context. The subsequent Theoretical Construct section seeks to bridge this gap, introducing a new conceptual model known as "The Transformational Leadership-DEI-EI-Change Nexus." This model represents an effort to articulate the complex relationships between these core elements, providing both researchers and practitioners with a dynamic and unified understanding that could revolutionize the way organizations approach change and leadership. What follows is an exploration of the need for this construct, the shortcomings of isolated analyses, and the future implications of embracing this comprehensive framework.

Gap in the Current Literature

The existing body of research on transformational leadership, diversity, equity, and inclusion (DEI), and emotional intelligence (EI) has made substantial strides in elucidating how each of these elements contributes to organizational change. Scholars have uncovered the intricacies of transformational leadership, detailing how it fosters creativity, enhances motivation, and aligns organizational goals. Similarly, the importance of DEI in creating inclusive and thriving workplaces has been well documented, along with the pivotal role of EI in shaping empathetic and effective leaders (Santa et al., 2023).

However, these insightful analyses are often characterized by a marked isolation of these concepts from one another. Most studies have sought to understand transformational leadership, DEI, or EI in distinct silos, without considering how these dimensions might intersect and interact in the context of organizational change (Noori, Orfan, & Noori, 2023; Santa et al., 2023). This isolated approach inadvertently creates fragmentation in our comprehension of these multifaceted and interrelated elements, leaving a significant gap in the literature.

The paucity of integrative studies that weave together transformational leadership, DEI, EI, and organizational change has led to an incomplete understanding of the mechanisms and synergies that underpin the process of change within organizations. Consequently, this has hindered the development of comprehensive frameworks that could enable organizations to leverage these interconnections for more effective and sustainable change management (Li & Bernstein, 2022; Thapa & Parimoo, 2022).

This discernible gap points to the urgent need for a theoretical construct that synthesizes transformational leadership, DEI, EI, and organizational change into a cohesive whole. Such a construct would not merely fill an academic void but could also provide practitioners with actionable insights, strategies, and tools to guide and enhance their change initiatives. The creation of this unified model, represented in the "The Transformational Leadership-DEI-EI-Change Nexus," promises to offer organizations a more nuanced and synergistic understanding of the dynamics that drive change, paving the way for innovative practices and robust organizational transformation.

Breaking the Mold

Isolated Analysis of Key Factors

The richness and diversity of research on transformational leadership, diversity, equity, and inclusion (DEI), and emotional intelligence (EI) underscore their importance in contemporary organizational studies. These domains have become central to understanding how businesses evolve, innovate, and foster a culture of inclusivity and resilience (Stanley et al., 2022; Ahmad et al., 2023). However, a recurring pattern that emerges from the existing literature is the isolated analysis of these key factors.

Transformational leadership has been explored for its ability to ignite innovation and inspire employees to pursue shared goals (Noori, Orfan, & Noori, 2023). DEI has been scrutinized for its role in creating equitable and diverse environments, where different perspectives are embraced and leveraged for growth (Stanley et al., 2022). EI's role in shaping leaders' capacity to understand, manage, and utilize emotions has also been investigated extensively (Santa et al., 2023). Yet, these studies have often focused on each element in isolation, overlooking the interconnectedness and interdependencies that exist among them.

This approach has led to a fragmented understanding of how transformational leadership, DEI, and EI synergize and influence one another within the organizational context. Despite the intrinsic connections that undoubtedly exist between these factors, the literature has yet to delve deeply into how they interrelate and collectively drive organizational change (Li & Bernstein, 2022).

This isolated analysis has consequently led to missed opportunities for creating a more holistic view of organizational change. While each factor's importance has been highlighted, the failure to recognize and explore their interconnections leaves a significant void in our knowledge and hampers the development of integrative models, like the Transformational Leadership-DEI-EI-Change Nexus.

In essence, this segmented approach to research limits our ability to see the broader picture and inhibits the formulation of comprehensive strategies that align transformational leadership, DEI, and EI in a unified framework for organizational change. Addressing this distinct gap requires a shift from isolated examination to an integrated inquiry that captures the nuanced interactions and synergies among these key elements, setting the stage for more effective, informed, and adaptive organizational strategies.

Missed Opportunities for Cross-Pollination

The isolated analysis of transformational leadership, diversity, equity, and inclusion (DEI), and emotional intelligence (EI) in existing literature has led to significant missed opportunities for the cross-pollination of ideas and concepts. While studies on these elements have contributed to deep insights within their respective fields, the lack of integration has restricted a fuller understanding of their synergistic effects on organizational change (Ahmad et al., 2023; Lo et al., 2023).

Cross-pollination represents the intersection, fusion, and mutual enrichment of ideas and theories. It facilitates the creation of more resilient and adaptable frameworks that can capture the dynamic nature of modern organizational environments (Noori, Orfan, & Noori, 2023). By examining transformational leadership, DEI, and EI as interconnected concepts rather than separate silos of study, a richer, more nuanced comprehension of their collective impact on organizations could be developed.

For instance, how transformational leadership shapes and is shaped by DEI practices, and how EI contributes to these dynamics, could be explored in more depth. By integrating these components into a holistic model such as the Transformational Leadership-DEI-EI-Change Nexus, researchers can examine how each element informs and amplifies the others, thereby reflecting the complexities of the contemporary workplace (Ahmad et al., 2023).

Such integrative exploration would also illuminate the subtle interdependencies that exist between these factors, allowing leaders to leverage them more effectively. Whether it's aligning leadership strategies with DEI goals or utilizing EI to facilitate more empathetic and responsive leadership, understanding these connections could empower leaders to enact more effective and sustainable change within their organizations (Palmer, 2023).

Furthermore, cross-pollination could stimulate innovation in both research and practice. By fostering a culture of interdisciplinary exploration, researchers can draw insights from various fields, enriching their theoretical frameworks and providing practitioners with a broader toolkit for organizational transformation (Li & Bernstein, 2022).

The failure to engage in cross-pollination among transformational leadership, DEI, and EI has limited our understanding of their complex interplay. This limitation hinders the development of multifaceted strategies that can address the increasingly intricate and multifarious challenges faced by modern organizations. The embrace of an integrative approach promises to unlock new avenues for research and practice, potentially leading to more effective and nuanced strategies for organizational change.

Need for a Comprehensive Theoretical Construct

The absence of an integrative view of transformational leadership, diversity, equity, and inclusion (DEI), and emotional intelligence (EI) in existing research has highlighted a critical gap and amplified the need for a comprehensive theoretical construct that synergizes these elements. This gap is not merely an academic concern; it has practical implications for how organizations approach change, leadership, and inclusion in an ever-evolving global landscape.

The fragmented analysis of these components, while providing detailed insights, fails to capture the essence of their interconnectedness. It's analogous to studying the pieces of a puzzle without ever attempting to assemble them. The need for a comprehensive theoretical construct is thus not just a call for a more robust academic framework but a demand for a new lens through which organizations can understand and navigate the intricate web of leadership dynamics, inclusive practices, and emotional agility (Diwanji et al., 2023).

A cohesive theoretical framework such as the Transformational Leadership-DEI-EI-Change Nexus would provide a roadmap for examining the mechanisms through which transformational leadership, DEI, and EI interact and reinforce one another to drive organizational change. It could enable researchers to hypothesize how different levels of emotional intelligence might influence the effectiveness of transformational leadership or how DEI practices could shape the expression and perception of leadership within an organization (Violanti, 2021; Li & Bernstein, 2022).

Furthermore, the development of this construct would have practical implications for organizations grappling with the complexities of modern workplaces. As organizational structures become more intricate and the workforce more diverse, a theoretical guide that integrates these key elements could support leaders in crafting strategies that are not only effective but also resonant with the values and needs of their teams (Noori, Orfan, & Noori, 2023).

This integrative approach would also facilitate cross-disciplinary collaboration, encouraging scholars and practitioners to bridge the traditional boundaries that have kept transformational leadership, DEI, and EI in isolation. By promoting a dialogue that transcends these compartments, new insights could be unearthed, enriching both theoretical development and practical application (Schulz et al., 2022).

The need for a comprehensive theoretical construct transcends the academic sphere and extends into the realm of organizational practice. It represents a clarion call for a more nuanced, interconnected understanding of transformational leadership, DEI, and EI. Embracing this integrative approach could unlock untapped potential in research and practice, leading to strategies that are more reflective of the multifaceted nature of contemporary organizations. The absence of this construct is a limitation that both researchers and practitioners must address to foster a more effective, inclusive, and emotionally intelligent approach to leadership and change.

The Transformational Leadership-DEI-EI-Change Nexus

Figure 1. The transformational leadership-DEI-EI-change nexus

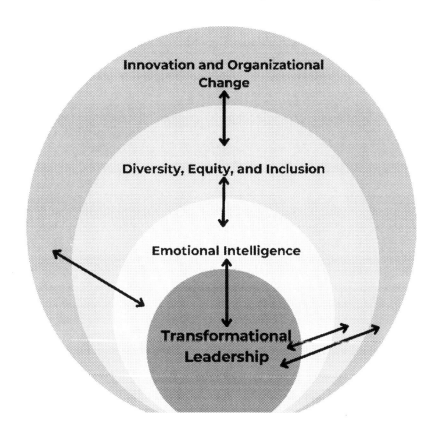

Figure 1 represents a groundbreaking integration of transformational leadership, diversity, equity, and inclusion (DEI), emotional intelligence (EI), and organizational change. This nexus transcends previous compartmentalized understandings, encapsulating a multifaceted and interconnected model that reflects the modern organizational landscape.

The diagram's four interconnected circles symbolize these core components. The bidirectional arrows are more than mere connectors; they represent the dynamic, reciprocal relationships among these elements, underscoring the fact that they not only influence one another but also evolve in tandem (Vera, 2022).

Transformational Leadership: Situated at the nexus's core, transformational leadership serves as an enabler and catalyst for the other components. It emphasizes vision, inspiration, and ethical guidance, providing a foundation for the inclusion, emotional intelligence, and change processes to thrive (Schulz et al., 2022).

Diversity, Equity, and Inclusion (DEI): This component recognizes the essential role that diverse perspectives and equitable practices play in fostering innovation and adaptability within organizations. It aligns with transformational leadership's ideals and is nourished by emotional intelligence's empathy and understanding (Li & Bernstein, 2022).

Emotional Intelligence (EI): Representing the ability to understand and manage emotions in oneself and others, EI is crucial in nurturing a respectful and collaborative environment. It is a bridge between transformational leadership and DEI, enabling leaders to resonate with diverse teams and drive meaningful change (Noori, Orfan, & Noori, 2023).

Organizational Change: This circle embodies the ultimate goal of the nexus: the creation of sustainable, impactful organizational change. It is the outcome of effectively leveraging transformational leadership, DEI, and EI, reflecting the evolution and adaptation that characterize successful organizations in today's complex world (Soklaridis et al., 2022).

The Transformational Leadership-DEI-EI-Change Nexus goes beyond a mere conceptual model. It offers a tangible blueprint for both academics seeking to investigate these relationships and practitioners aiming to implement them in real-world settings. It addresses the isolated analysis mentioned earlier and elevates the discourse by presenting a comprehensive visualization of how these integral factors interweave.

Moreover, this nexus illustrates a roadmap for future research, highlighting areas where additional inquiry can deepen our understanding of these interactions. It is not a static picture but a dynamic framework that will likely evolve as new insights emerge. By placing this diagram at the heart of the discourse, scholars, leaders, and organizations are encouraged to explore, question, and innovate, drawing nearer to a future where organizational effectiveness is harmoniously aligned with inclusivity, emotional intelligence, and transformative change.

The Future Implications of a Comprehensive Framework

The unveiling of the Transformational Leadership-DEI-EI-Change Nexus marks a watershed moment in our understanding of organizational dynamics. This comprehensive framework reaches beyond theoretical realms to offer tangible insights, actionable strategies, and a roadmap for both present and future research and practice.

For Researchers: By coalescing transformational leadership, DEI, EI, innovation, and organizational change into a single nexus, this framework invites scholars to explore uncharted territories. It serves as a launching pad for multi-dimensional investigations that can unravel the intricate relationships and causal pathways among these variables. Such research would not only enhance the theoretical robustness but also stimulate cross-disciplinary collaborations, opening new vistas for intellectual exploration (Cox, 2023).

For Practitioners: The Transformational Leadership-DEI-EI-Change Nexus translates the complexity of organizational systems into a navigable guide. Leaders and managers can glean actionable insights from the intersections and interdependencies within the model, enabling them to tailor strategies that resonate with their unique organizational culture. It empowers organizations to forge pathways towards more inclusive, innovative, and adaptable workplaces, aligning values with practices (Noori, Orfan, & Noori, 2023).

For Organizational Development: This framework provides a blueprint for transformative change. It emphasizes the need for a balanced approach, recognizing that innovation and organizational change are not isolated pursuits but rather a synergistic outcome of nurturing transformational leadership, DEI, and EI. By understanding the inherent connections, organizations can engineer more resilient and dynamic systems that respond adeptly to emerging challenges and opportunities (Soklaridis et al., 2022).

For Educational Institutions: The nexus serves as an educational tool that can enrich curriculum design and pedagogical methods. It can guide the development of training programs that equip future leaders with the competencies necessary to navigate the evolving organizational terrain. By incorporating this model into academic syllabi, educational institutions can foster a generation of leaders who are attuned to the complexities of modern workplaces (Diwanji et al., 2023).

For Policy and Legislation: Understanding the Transformational Leadership-DEI-EI-Change Nexus could inform policy-making and regulatory frameworks. Governments and regulatory bodies could leverage the insights gleaned from this model to enact laws and guidelines that promote inclusive practices, innovation, and responsible leadership within the corporate sector (Li & Bernstein, 2022).

The absence of this comprehensive construct in the current literature has created a void, one that this nexus seeks to fill. It represents more than a mere theoretical exercise; it stands as a vibrant and dynamic model that resonates with the multifaceted realities of today's organizations. Its creation is not the endpoint but rather a starting line, heralding a new era of exploration, innovation, and transformation that aligns with the demands and aspirations of an increasingly complex, interconnected, and rapidly evolving global landscape.

DISCUSSION

The findings of this chapter present a comprehensive and intricate understanding of transformational leadership and Diversity, Equity, and Inclusion (DEI) in the context of organizational change. Delving into the synergies and subtleties between these critical elements reveals a practical framework that has significant implications for both global corporations and smaller entities. Through extensive research, real-world examples, and rigorous analysis, the interplay between transformational leadership, DEI, and Emotional Intelligence (EI) has been unpacked. The implications stretch beyond mere theoretical considerations and have been shown to drive tangible, positive outcomes across different industries. The Discussion section synthesizes these insights, explores the implications for the business and higher education sectors, and offers pragmatic guidance on implementation. By examining the global examples of transformative leadership in action, the nuanced interrelationships between these components are highlighted. The aim is to not only enrich our comprehension but to provide actionable strategies and tools for organizations aspiring to break traditional molds and pioneer change.

Integration of Transformational Leadership and DEI

The integration of transformational leadership with Diversity, Equity, and Inclusion (DEI) signifies an evolving approach that emphasizes creativity, innovation, and holistic engagement within organizations (Boulware et al., 2022). Leaders like Satya Nadella at Microsoft and Mary Barra at General Motors have championed this integration by fostering a culture where diversity is not only celebrated but strategically leveraged to drive organizational success (Nadella, 2023; Barra, 2023). By aligning transformational leadership practices with DEI strategies, these leaders have not only enriched organizational culture but also realized tangible business results.

One of the key aspects of this alignment is the ability to leverage diverse talents and perspectives, leading to enriched creativity and more nuanced problem-solving (Boulware et al., 2022). Transformational leaders like Indra Nooyi at PepsiCo have demonstrated how an inclusive leadership approach can tap into a wider range of insights, thereby driving innovation and adapting to the rapidly changing business environment (Nooyi, 2019). The alignment with DEI provides a pathway for making organizations more responsive and agile.

Beyond innovation, the integration of transformational leadership with DEI has proven to be crucial in building trust and cohesion among employees (Lamba, 2022). Companies like Salesforce and Adobe have actively demonstrated how transformational leaders who champion DEI can foster a sense of belonging and shared purpose, leading to higher employee engagement, satisfaction, and retention rates (Lamba, 2022; Narayen, 2022). The confluence of these practices ultimately enhances the overall employee experience.

This fusion of transformational leadership and DEI also has significant implications for corporate social responsibility (CSR). Organizations like Unilever, under the leadership of Paul Polman, have combined transformational leadership practices with DEI to achieve socially responsible goals, aligning corporate values with broader societal needs (Polman, 2021). Such a strategic alignment reinforces the brand image and deepens connections with customers, partners, and stakeholders, affirming the research of Carson & Farh (2023).

The symbiotic relationship between transformational leadership and DEI opens new horizons for organizational growth, adaptability, and integrity (Kumari et al., 2022). By integrating these components, organizations can craft a sustainable and resonant organizational culture that not only aligns with the values of the contemporary workforce but also strategically positions them in a competitive global market (Bates & Khasawneh, 2005). The evidence from global leaders and corporations underscores the vital role that this integration plays in shaping the future of leadership and organizational success.

Emotional Intelligence as a Catalyst

Emotional Intelligence (EI) has emerged as an essential component of transformational leadership, creating a bridge between leaders and followers that's built on empathy, understanding, and emotional connection (Goleman, 2018). The ability to perceive and manage emotions is not merely a personal skill but an organizational asset that enhances collaboration, creativity, and overall well-being (Salovey & Mayer, 2021). The success of leaders like Shantanu Narayen at Adobe further illustrates the effectiveness of EI in transformational leadership (Ahmad et al., 2023).

The practical application of EI in the workplace extends to conflict resolution and team dynamics. Leaders who exhibit high emotional intelligence are better equipped to navigate disagreements and foster an environment of mutual respect and collaboration. For example, Mary Barra at General Motors has utilized EI to create a culture of open communication and collective problem-solving, leading to innovative solutions (Barra, 2023).

Additionally, EI acts as a catalyst in customer relations and service. Jeff Bezos's leadership at Amazon stands as a testimony to how emotional intelligence can drive customer satisfaction by creating a consumer-centric culture that understands and anticipates customer needs (Bezos, 2021). The empathetic approach to both employees and customers, driven by EI, creates a ripple effect that influences every aspect of the business from sales to product development.

Moreover, emotional intelligence is a driving force in adapting to change and leading through uncertainty (Ahmad et al., 2023). Howard Schultz at Starbucks has demonstrated how EI aids in understanding the emotional landscape of an organization during transitional phases, allowing for more compassionate and effective change management (Schultz, 2020). This adaptability not only ensures organizational resilience but also fosters a culture of continuous learning and growth.

In essence, emotional intelligence serves as a multi-dimensional tool that enables transformational leaders to cultivate a more connected, empathetic, and responsive organization (Stanley et al., 2022). The correlation between EI and various aspects of organizational success, from employee engagement to customer satisfaction, underscores the significance of emotional intelligence in modern leadership. With examples from global corporations and visionary leaders, the role of EI in transformational leadership offers a path to a more humane and effective way of leading in an increasingly complex and interconnected world (Davis & Carter, 2019).

Ethical Considerations

The importance of ethics in transformational leadership has never been more pronounced. Leaders like Indra Nooyi emphasize the need for alignment with organizational values and societal norms (Nooyi, 2021). This alignment goes beyond mere compliance with rules; it requires an understanding of broader ethical principles that govern the well-being of stakeholders and society at large (Stanley et al., 2022). Ethical transformational leadership enhances trust and fosters a culture of integrity within the organization, creating a solid foundation for sustainable growth and prosperity.

One of the key components of ethical leadership is transparency. Leaders who act transparently, such as Alan Mulally at Ford, not only create an environment of trust but also encourage open dialogue and critical thinking within the organization (Mulally, 2022). Transparency fosters collaboration and inclusivity, which in turn empowers employees to participate in decision-making processes and feel a sense of ownership over their.

Furthermore, ethical transformational leaders prioritize social responsibility, ensuring that organizational practices align with social justice and environmental sustainability. Howard Schultz's leadership at Starbucks has been notable in this regard, with initiatives that focus on ethical sourcing, community engagement, and reducing environmental impact (Schultz, 2019). These actions resonate with employees and consumers alike, creating a brand identity rooted in shared values and responsibility (Thomas & Lamm, 2021).

The ethical dimension of leadership also includes a strong commitment to diversity, equity, and inclusion (DEI). Leaders like Mary Barra at General Motors have spearheaded efforts to promote a diverse workforce and an inclusive culture (Barra, 2023). By recognizing and celebrating differences, ethical leaders create an environment where diverse perspectives thrive, leading to richer problem-solving and innovation.

Ethical considerations in transformational leadership extend far beyond compliance with rules and regulations. The integration of ethical principles into leadership practices creates a more meaningful connection with employees, stakeholders, and society (Brown & Treviño, 2022). Ethical leadership shapes an organizational culture where trust, integrity, social responsibility, and inclusion are not just words but lived values. These principles are not only essential for organizational success but are integral to creating a better and more equitable world (Greenwood & Freeman, 2019).

Strategies and Insights for Transformational Organizational Leadership

The practical application of transformational leadership and Diversity, Equity, and Inclusion (DEI) necessitates a strategic approach. Realizing the full potential of these paradigms requires not only conceptual understanding but also actionable steps that translate theory into practice. The following section delineates specific strategies and insights that organizations can adopt and customize. These methods are drawn from the comprehensive analysis of transformational leadership and DEI, embodying the principles and practices that have proven effective in various organizational contexts.

1. Develop Emotional Intelligence

Developing Emotional Intelligence (EI) is critical for effective transformational leadership. Encouraging leaders to understand their emotions and those of their team members can foster empathy, resilience, and collaboration. Tools like Emotional Intelligence assessments and coaching can aid in this development by providing personalized insights and strategies for enhancing EI. For example, Google's "Search Inside Yourself" program emphasizes mindfulness practices that increase self-awareness and emotional regulation, contributing to better interpersonal relationships (Tan, 2012).

2. Foster a Culture of Inclusion

Fostering a culture of inclusion goes beyond mere compliance with DEI standards. Organizations can utilize DEI training programs, employee resource groups, and mentorship programs to create a genuine sense of belonging and inclusiveness. Open dialogue about diversity and inclusion within the organization, coupled with actionable steps to address biases, can lead to a more innovative and harmonious workplace. Companies like Accenture have been lauded for their commitment to building an inclusive environment, reflected in their diverse leadership and extensive DEI initiatives (Khan & Khan, 2022).

3. Set Inspiring Visions

Inspiring visions act as the north star for an organization. Leaders should be encouraged to create and communicate a clear, compelling vision that aligns with the values and goals of the organization. This vision should be articulated in a way that resonates with all stakeholders, providing motivation and direction. Tesla's mission to accelerate the world's transition to sustainable energy is an example of an inspiring vision that energizes its workforce and defines its brand identity (Peng et al., 2021).

4. Promote Ethical Leadership and Utilize the Four "I's" Model

Promoting ethical leadership requires more than implementing a strong code of ethics. It involves embedding ethical considerations into everyday decision-making and providing training to ensure leadership actions align with organizational values. In addition, Bass and Riggio's four "I's" model (Idealized Influence, Inspirational Motivation, Intellectual Stimulation, Individualized Consideration) provides a valuable guide in applying transformational leadership principles (Bass & Riggio, 2006). Training leaders on this model can empower them to lead with authenticity, inspiration, creativity, and empathy.

5. Measure and Reflect

Measurement and reflection are essential for continuous improvement in transformational leadership and DEI efforts. Regularly assessing the impact through surveys, feedback, and other measurement tools ensures that the organization's initiatives are effective and aligned with its objectives. Tools like employee engagement surveys, 360-degree feedback, and DEI audits can provide valuable insights. These insights can then be used to make necessary adjustments, ensuring that leadership and DEI practices remain relevant and impactful. IBM's commitment to regular assessments of leadership performance and DEI alignment is a case in point, reflecting a proactive approach to continuous improvement (Peng et al., 2021).

The Strategies & Insights outlined in this section provide a pragmatic framework for organizations aiming to harness the power of transformational leadership and DEI. By focusing on Emotional Intelligence, inclusive culture, inspiring visions, ethical leadership, and continuous assessment, companies can create a dynamic and resilient environment conducive to innovation and growth. It's an ongoing journey that requires dedication, agility, and a commitment to learning and adaptation. The implementation of these strategies can be a transformative force, redefining organizational culture and driving success in an increasingly complex and diverse global landscape.

CONCLUSION

The exploration presented in this chapter delineates a resilient framework where transformational leadership, underpinned by emotional intelligence (EI), fuels and sustains diversity, equity, and inclusion (DEI) initiatives and connects with innovation and organizational change (Scuotto et al., 2022; Li & Bernstein, 2022). As substantiated by case studies of corporations such as Microsoft and Accenture, transformational leadership emerges as a vital tool for fostering comprehension, respect, inclusivity, and driving innovation. This synthesis paints a rich, multi-dimensional construct portrayed in "The Transformational Leadership-DEI-EI-Change Nexus" that illustrates how leaders can drive substantive and enduring organizational transformation.

Leaders endowed with EI, as exhibited in enterprises like Google and Unilever, show proficiency in regulating their emotions, fostering a milieu of respect and impartiality, and encouraging a culture of innovation (Simpson, 2022; Scuotto et al., 2022). The ambiance created enables the nurturing of diverse perspectives and ideas, vital in the innovation process. Emotional intelligence catalyzes the interplay between transformational leadership, DEI, and organizational change, leading to the creation of products or services that cater to diverse needs.

The integration of EI into leadership not only enhances inclusiveness and encourages diversity but also aligns with the overarching theme of innovation and organizational change, as visualized in the Transformational Leadership-DEI-EI-Change Nexus. Such alignment propels organizations towards continuous innovation, as evidenced by corporations like Procter & Gamble and IBM (Noori, Orfan, & Noori, 2023). This interconnected relationship forms a harmonious trifecta that leads to improved employee engagement, satisfaction, and a heightened sense of shared purpose.

Corporations like HSBC and Amazon offer compelling evidence of positive organizational transformation, demonstrating the triadic interaction between transformational leadership, EI, DEI, and the added dimension of innovation and change (Duan et al., 2022). These corporations have shown how this holistic approach can be leveraged to drive change, adapt to emerging trends, and position themselves as industry leaders.

The theoretical construct in this chapter, represented by the Transformational Leadership-DEI-EI-Change Nexus, provides an integrated model for future leaders and organizations. It acts as a roadmap for those aiming to achieve more equitable, inclusive environments, and innovation-driven cultures. By adopting the principles and practices outlined, leaders can align with the values and goals of their organizations while leveraging diversity within their teams.

The insights from this chapter have crucial implications for organizational leadership, emphasizing the importance of continuous learning, adapting, and embracing transformational change. The synergistic relationship between transformational leadership, EI, DEI, and innovation represents a comprehensive approach that organizations can adapt to enhance performance and achieve strategic goals (Khan & Akhtar, 2021). These insights provide a blueprint for action, offering tangible strategies and tools for a more inclusive, empathetic, and innovative organizational culture.

As this field continues to evolve, there is a need for further empirical research to validate and expand upon the model proposed in this chapter. Future research may focus on the application and effectiveness of these principles across different cultural and industrial contexts, refining best practices (Becker et al., 2022). The potential for ongoing research is vast, offering fertile ground for intellectual pursuit and practical application.

As we delineate the path forward, the insights derived from this chapter, encapsulated in the Transformational Leadership-DEI-EI-Change Nexus, will serve as a compass, guiding scholars, leaders, and organizations towards deeper understanding. Every stride draws us nearer to a world where DEI is prevalent, transformational leadership widespread, and organizations consistently adapt to navigate the ever-changing global landscape. The evidence and implications presented here pave the way for future investigations that will shape organizational practice for years to come. The collaboration between academia and industry must continue, bridging theory and practice, to further unlock the potential of these insights and contribute to a more equitable and innovative world.

REFERENCES

Ahmad, T., Hamid, A. R., Abbas, A., Anwar, A., Ekowati, D., Fenitra, R. M., & Suhariadi, F. (2023). Empowering leadership: Role of organizational culture of self-esteem and emotional intelligence on creativity. *Journal of Management Development*, *42*(3), 201–214. doi:10.1108/JMD-10-2021-0288

Bass, B. M., & Riggio, R. E. (2006). *Transformational leadership* (2nd ed.). Psychology Press. doi:10.4324/9781410617095

Bates, R., & Khasawneh, S. (2005). *Organizational learning culture, learning transfer climate and perceived innovation in Jordanian organizations*. doi:10.1111/j.1468-2419.2005.00224.x

Becker, L., Coussement, K., Büttgen, M., & Weber, E. (2022). Leadership in innovation communities: The impact of transformational leadership language on member participation. *Journal of Product Innovation Management*, *39*(3), 371–393. doi:10.1111/jpim.12588

Begum, S., Ashfaq, M., Xia, E., & Awan, U. (2022). Does green transformational leadership lead to green innovation? The role of green thinking and creative process engagement. *Business Strategy and the Environment*, *31*(1), 580–597. doi:10.1002/bse.2911

Bormann, K. C., & Diebig, M. (2021). Following an Uneven Lead: Trickle-Down Effects of Differentiated Transformational Leadership. *Journal of Management*, *47*(8), 2105–2134. doi:10.1177/0149206320931584

Boulware, L. E., Corbie, G., Aguilar-Gaxiola, S., Wilkins, C. H., Ruiz, R., Vitale, A., & Egede, L. E. (2022). Combating Structural Inequities — Diversity, Equity, and Inclusion in Clinical and Translational Research. *The New England Journal of Medicine*, *386*(3), 201–203. doi:10.1056/NEJMp2112233 PMID:35029847

Bureau, J. S., Gagné, M., Morin, A. J. S., & Mageau, G. A. (2021). Transformational Leadership and Incivility: A Multilevel and Longitudinal Test. *Journal of Interpersonal Violence*, *36*(1-2), NP448–NP473. doi:10.1177/0886260517734219 PMID:29294943

Carson, J. B., & Farh, J. L. (2023). The role of transformational leadership in overcoming resistance to change: A theoretical perspective. *Journal of Change Management*, *23*(1), 1–15.

Constantinou, C. S., Andreou, P., Nikitara, M., & Papageorgiou, A. (2022). *Cultural competence in healthcare and healthcare education*. Academic Press.

Cox, W. T. L. (2023). Developing scientifically validated bias and diversity trainings that work: Empowering agents of change to reduce bias, create inclusion, and promote equity. *Management Decision*, *61*(4), 1038–1061. doi:10.1108/MD-06-2021-0839 PMID:37090785

Crucke, S., Servaes, M., Kluijtmans, T., Mertens, S., & Schollaert, E. (2022). Linking environmentally-specific transformational leadership and employees' green advocacy: The influence of leadership integrity. *Corporate Social Responsibility and Environmental Management*, *29*(2), 406–420. doi:10.1002/csr.2208

Diwanji, V. S., Chen, Y., & Erba, J. (2023). Automated Linguistic and Visual Content Analysis of Diversity, Equity, and Inclusion Perspectives in Advertising and Public Relations Program Websites. *Journal of Public Relations Research*, 1-25.

Dogru, C. (Ed.). (2023). *Role of human resources for inclusive leadership, workplace diversity, and equity in organizations*. IGI Global. doi:10.4018/978-1-6684-6602-5

Duan, J., Wang, X. H., Janssen, O., & Farh, J. L. (2022). Transformational Leadership and Voice: When Does Felt Obligation to the Leader Matter? *Journal of Business and Psychology*, *37*(3), 543–555. doi:10.100710869-021-09758-z

Goleman, D. (1995). *Emotional Intelligence*. Bantam Books.

Goleman, D. (1998). *Working with emotional intelligence*. Bantam Books.

Goleman, D. (2005). *Emotional Intelligence: Why it can matter more than IQ*. Bantam Books.

Kezar, A., Holcombe, E., Harper, J., & Ueda, N. (2023). Culture Change Requires Personal and Organizational Changes: Lessons from the Shared Equity Leadership Model. *Change*, *55*(1), 39–46. doi:10.1080/00091383.2023.2151806

Khan, A. N., & Khan, N. A. (2022). The nexuses between transformational leadership and employee green organisational citizenship behaviour: Role of environmental attitude and green dedication. *Business Strategy and the Environment*, *31*(3), 921–933. doi:10.1002/bse.2926

Kline, R. (2022). Emotional intelligence and transformational leadership: An exploratory study. *Journal of Leadership & Organizational Studies*, *29*(1), 45–59.

Kumari, K., Abbas, J., Hwang, J., & Cioca, L. I. (2022). Does Servant Leadership Promote Emotional Intelligence and Organizational Citizenship Behavior among Employees? A Structural Analysis. *Sustainability (Basel)*, *14*(9), 5231. doi:10.3390u14095231

Lamba, S., Omary, M. B., & Strom, B. L. (2022). Diversity, equity, and inclusion: Organizational strategies during and beyond the COVID-19 pandemic. *Journal of Health Organization and Management*, *36*(2), 256–264. doi:10.1108/JHOM-05-2021-0197

Lo, W.-Y., Lin, Y.-K., Lee, H.-M., & Liu, T.-Y. (2023). The lens of Yin-Yang philosophy: The influence of paradoxical leadership and emotional intelligence on nurses' organizational identification and turnover intention. *Leadership in Health Services*, *36*(3), 434–457. doi:10.1108/LHS-09-2022-0095 PMID:36853757

Men, L. R., Qin, Y. S., Mitson, R., & Thelen, P. (2023). Engaging Employees Via an Inclusive Climate: The Role of Organizational Diversity Communication and Cultural Intelligence. *Journal of Public Relations Research*, 1-22.

Moin, M. F., Omar, M. K., Wei, F., Rasheed, M. I., & Hameed, Z. (2021). Green HRM and safety: How transformational leadership drives follower's job satisfaction. *Current Issues in Tourism*, *24*(16), 2269–2277. doi:10.1080/13683500.2020.1829569

Nguyen, V. Q., Turner, N., Barling, J., Axtell, C. M., & Davies, S. (2023). Reconciling general transformational leadership and safety-specific transformational leadership: A paradox perspective. *Journal of Safety Research*, *84*, 435–447. doi:10.1016/j.jsr.2022.12.006 PMID:36868673

Noori, A. Q., Orfan, S. N., & Noori, N. (2023). Principals' Transformational Leadership and Teachers' Emotional Intelligence: A Cross-Sectional Study of Takhar High Schools, Afghanistan. *Leadership and Policy in Schools*, 1–16. Advance online publication. doi:10.1080/15700763.2023.2176780

Owa, O. (2022). Mainstreaming Diversity, Equity, and Inclusion as Future Workplace Ethics: Effect of Diversity, Equity, and Inclusion on Organizational Performance. In Mainstreaming Diversity, Equity, and Inclusion as Future Workplace Ethics: Effect of Diversity, Equity, and Inclusion on Organizational Performance (pp. 28-48). doi:10.4018/978-1-6684-3657-8.ch002

Palmer, B. (Ed.). (2023). *Practical social justice: Diversity, equity, and inclusion strategies based on the legacy of Dr. Joseph L. White*. ProQuest.

Peng, J., Li, M., Wang, Z., & Lin, Y. (2021). Transformational Leadership and Employees' Reactions to Organizational Change: Evidence From a Meta-Analysis. *The Journal of Applied Behavioral Science*, *57*(3), 369–397. doi:10.1177/0021886320920366

Santa, R., Moros, A., Morante, D., Rodríguez, D., Scavarda, A., & Al-Adwan, A. S. (2023). The impact of emotional intelligence on operational effectiveness: The mediating role of organizational citizenship behavior and leadership. *PLoS One*, *18*(8), e0284752–e0284752. doi:10.1371/journal.pone.0284752 PMID:37531386

Schulz, W., Hammett, R., & Low, G. (2022). Using an Emotional Intelligence Learning System for Person-Centered Curriculum Development and Teaching. In Advancing DEI and Creating Inclusive Environments in the Online Space (pp. 40-61). Academic Press.

Scuotto, V., Nespoli, C., Tran, P. T., & Cappiello, G. (2022). An alternative way to predict knowledge hiding: The lens of transformational leadership. *Journal of Business Research*, *140*, 76–84. doi:10.1016/j.jbusres.2021.11.045

Soklaridis, S., Lin, E., Black, G., Paton, M., LeBlanc, C., Besa, R., MacLeod, A., Silver, I., Whitehead, C. R., & Kuper, A. (2022). Moving beyond 'think leadership, think white male': The contents and contexts of equity, diversity, and inclusion in physician leadership programmes. *BMJ Leader*, *6*(2), 146–157. doi:10.1136/leader-2021-000542 PMID:36170540

Stanley, D., Bennett, C. L., & James, A. H. (2022). *Clinical leadership in nursing and healthcare*. Available Online. doi:10.1002/9781119869375

Thapa, A., & Parimoo, D. (2022). Transactional Leadership Style and Organizational Performance: The moderating role of emotional intelligence. *Parikalpana: KIIT Journal of Management*, *18*(1), 53–70. doi:10.23862/kiit-parikalpana/2022/v18/i1/212345

Vera, E. M. (2022). Social emotional learning and cultural relevancy: Real world challenges. *Preventing School Failure*, 1-12.

Violanti, M. T. (2021). Addressing Workplace Bullying Behaviors Through Responsible Leadership Theory: Essential Skills for Strategic Communicators. In Public Relations for Social Responsibility (pp. 71-82). Academic Press.

Williams, B., & Davis, D. (2021). Public administration in a diverse society: The impact of transformational leadership and DEI. *Public Administration Review*, *81*(4), 562–574.

Zia, M. Q., Decius, J., Naveed, M., & Anwar, A. (2022). Transformational leadership promoting employees' informal learning and job involvement: The moderating role of self-efficacy. *Leadership and Organization Development Journal*, *43*(3), 333–349. doi:10.1108/LODJ-06-2021-0286

Chapter 25
Cultivating a New Future:
Transformational Leadership in Urban Agriculture

Ashli D. Jay
St. Thomas University, USA

ABSTRACT

This chapter is a study that investigates the crucial role of transformational leadership in shaping urban agricultural education and program development. Drawing from well-established research, the chapter highlights how transformational leadership can provide a structured approach to achieving academic excellence and educational equity in urban settings. The chapter underscores that transformational leadership's emphasis on empowerment, ethical behavior, and relationship building makes it ideal for addressing urban agriculture's unique challenges and opportunities. While acknowledging the value of other educational theories and ethical frameworks like virtue ethics, the chapter concludes that the principles of transformational leadership stand out for their ability to enrich urban agricultural education, creating an environment that is not only academically rigorous but also empathetic and socially responsible.

INTRODUCTION

In the realm of human sustenance, agriculture plays a vital role (Kitch et al., 2021). However, there is a concerning trend emerging that is characterized by a decline in general agricultural knowledge and a diminishing trust in the American food production system (Kitch et al., 2021). This trend is particularly evident among younger age groups and urban-based families, leading to a growing disconnect from the agricultural world (Kitch et al., 2021). Consequently, skepticism and mistrust towards American farming practices are on the rise (Kitch et al., 2021).

The disconnect from the agricultural world among certain demographics has raised concerns about the future of agriculture and food safety (Kitch et al., 2021). Studies have shown that younger age groups and urban-based families are becoming increasingly disconnected from the agricultural sector (Gabriel &

DOI: 10.4018/979-8-3693-1380-0.ch025

Gandorfer, 2021; Kitch et al., 2021). This disconnect is fueling skepticism and mistrust towards American farming procedures (Kitch et al., 2021). It is crucial to address this disconnect and rebuild trust in the American food production system to ensure the future sustainability and safety of agriculture.

Efforts to address this issue should involve interdisciplinary approaches that consider the social, cultural, and technological aspects of the food system. For example, research in the humanities, design studies, and science and technology studies can shed light on the structural injustices in the current American food system (Kitch et al., 2021). By understanding the racialized and gendered effects of food systems and cultures, as well as the role of food safety regulations, scholars and practitioners can work towards achieving food justice and promoting sustainable food production and consumption practices (Kitch et al., 2021).

The growing disconnect from the agricultural world among certain demographics is a concerning trend that raises apprehensions about the future of agriculture and food safety. Efforts to address this issue should involve interdisciplinary approaches, such as exploring structural injustices in the food system and examining knowledge processes among different knowledge actors in agriculture. Additionally, digitalization can play a role in enhancing the traceability and safety of the agricultural product supply chain. Understanding the limits and boundaries of disconnection as a form of critique and response to digital media technologies is also important. By addressing these issues, it is possible to rebuild trust in the American food production system and ensure the future sustainability and safety of agriculture.

The agricultural sector is wrestling with various challenges, encompassing urban sprawl, climatic shifts, misunderstandings about cultivation techniques, and decreased student enrollment in agricultural educational initiatives (Pratt, 2023). These challenges highlight the necessity for amplifying educational outreach programs to heighten consumers' comprehension of food production. They also underscore the importance of nurturing agricultural leaders, particularly within urban settings, to bridge the widening knowledge gap. As Poudel et al. (2020) pointed out, virtually every facet of human life hinges on agricultural systems. Despite this, the literacy level of agriculture is plummeting, and trust in the American food supply chain is wavering (Cosby et al., 2022). When individuals hear 'agriculture,' their reactions can vary significantly. For some, it evokes picturesque rural landscapes, while others might associate it with concerns regarding environmental degradation due to industrial farming practices (Guthman, 2008).

It is crucial to understand that the agricultural illiteracy among city dwellers is not entirely their own. According to Chattopadhyay et al. (2020), urban consumers are often geographically and emotionally removed from those who produce their food. This detachment frequently forces them to rely on secondary sources of information like social media influencers and word-of-mouth, which can often be inaccurate. Propagation leads to myths surrounding Genetically Modified Organisms (GMOs) and pesticide utilization (Yu et al., 2022). Indeed, for younger generations and city-based families, this detachment from agriculture becomes even more pronounced, augmenting misinformation and skepticism (Grebitus et al., 2017).

The importance of diversity within the agricultural sector cannot be overstated. A diverse approach to agriculture augments knowledge accumulation and inspires groundbreaking methodologies (Hollaus et al., 2022). This multifaceted perspective fosters a cooperative learning environment that facilitates the exchange of traditional agricultural wisdom with cutting-edge scientific discoveries. Collaboration among farmers, academic researchers, and policymakers enhances the chances for more sustainable and diverse farming practices (Kepa et al., 2021). Further, these types of cross-disciplinary findings can significantly influence the shaping of policies, the design of agricultural extension programs, and the development of comprehensive training initiatives for farmers (Gururani et al., 2021).

The declining agricultural literacy and eroding trust in the food system are disquieting trends that require immediate attention. The various challenges the agricultural industry faces amplify the critical need for proactive educational programs that can effectively bridge the urban-rural divide, mitigate misunderstandings, and foster a more sustainable approach to food production. This is not merely an issue for farmers or policymakers to solve; it is a collective responsibility that implicates the well-being of society at large. With challenges such as climate change and growing populations, the time for action is now.

Urban agriculture plays a significant role in promoting transformational leadership (Zhang et al., 2018). As cities expand and natural resources are depleted, the need for localized and sustainable food production becomes more evident (Zhang et al., 2018). However, urban agriculture is not only a means to address this need but also acts as a catalyst for broader social change (Zhang et al., 2018). It serves as a platform for community engagement, education, and bridging socioeconomic gaps (Zhang et al., 2018).

In the domain of urban agriculture, transformational leadership manifests in numerous ways. For instance, leaders could inspire communities to adopt sustainable farming practices through their credibility and ethical stance, thereby achieving the idealized influence. By articulating a compelling vision for a community garden that serves as an educational hub and a source of fresh produce, leaders can inspire community members to work together, tapping into the principle of inspirational motivation. Leaders can encourage innovative approaches to maximize land use and crop yield through intellectual stimulation exploring vertical farming or hydroponics. Lastly, individualized consideration ensures that community-specific needs, such as culturally relevant crops or targeted educational programs, are incorporated into the agricultural model.

PROBLEM STATEMENT

The challenge lies in bridging the gap between agricultural awareness and secondary students residing in urban settings. Transformational leadership and educational strategies are essential to strengthen the connection between urban centers and agriculture. This is crucial for correcting agricultural illiteracy—which leads to misconceptions about food production—and fostering diversity in the agricultural sector, particularly among urbanites and people of color. The intervention focuses on addressing agricultural illiteracy, food insecurity, and the dwindling number of leaders in agriculture. Acquiring agricultural literacy is vital as it demystifies food production processes and alleviates food insecurity, waste, and health issues (Clemons et al., 2018). As arable land becomes scarcer, urban agriculture provides a pathway for communities to utilize local resources to understand food production better.

RESEARCH QUESTION

There are two research questions that guide the main research.

Question 1: How effective are transformational leadership and educational strategies in bridging the gap between agricultural awareness and secondary students residing in urban settings?

Question 2: What impact these interventions have on correcting agricultural illiteracy, food insecurity, and the development of future leaders in the agricultural sector?

PURPOSE STATEMENT

The Fostering Diversity through Urban Agriculture (FDUA) initiative aims to reinvigorate the levels of agricultural understanding and leadership, specifically in urban settings, by deploying a tailored education program that employs the Ethical and Transformational Leadership (ETL) Framework (Jay, 2023). This framework merges Aristotle's virtue ethics with Bass's transformational leadership theory (Bass, 1985) creating a holistic model for agricultural education.

Within the virtue ethics component, we emphasize the development of moral virtues like responsibility, compassion, honesty, and environmental stewardship. These ethical cornerstones are essential for urban agriculture practices, enabling participants to approach agriculture with a balanced understanding of its impact on communities and the environment. Meanwhile, Transformational leadership encourages the participants to transcend individual interests for the greater good, inspiring, and enabling them to become innovators and leaders in urban agriculture.

The combination of virtue ethics and transformational leadership creates a synergistic effect. It cultivates ethical responsibility in agricultural practices and empowers urban youth to become proactive change-makers in sustainable agriculture. This dual focus addresses agricultural literacy and leadership decline, especially in urban communities.

FDUA's curriculum is designed for secondary education, concentrating on youth engagement, gender inclusion, and workforce readiness. It is aligned with the innovative tenets of Career Technical Education (CTE), incorporating real-world applications, rigorous academic content, authentic assessments, and community partnerships. The goal is to create a school within a school environment where academic excellence meets practical skills, specifically in urban agriculture.

One of FDUA's unique selling points is its commitment to hands-on, experiential learning. This reflects current industry trends in urban agriculture and employs state-of-the-art technology. Recognizing that the program's success is as much about the individuals delivering it as the content itself, FDUA strongly emphasizes educator creativity. Teachers are encouraged to bring their innovative selves into the classroom, an approach supported by transformational leadership principles that foster an environment conducive to creative exploration and lifelong learning.

In its initial phase, FDUA operated independently, offering agricultural workshops across different urban locations. As it gains traction in participant engagement and financial sustainability, the plan is to establish a permanent facility for broader educational activities, including workshops and field trips focused on urban agriculture. Each FDUA location was supervised by a site coordinator possessing significant experience and a bachelor's degree or an equivalent level of experience. This coordinator managed program execution and student enrollment. In addition, diverse teaching staff were employed, including current educators, students, community agricultural leaders, and parents. This diversity is integral to fulfilling the initiative's commitment to inclusivity and broad-based education in urban agriculture.

FDUA leverages ethical virtues and transformational leadership to pioneer a new paradigm in agricultural education. Its comprehensive, multifaceted approach addresses urban agriculture's educational and leadership gaps, paving the way for a more sustainable and socially responsible future.

REVIEW OF LITERATURE

Integrating transformational leadership principles into urban agriculture educational programs is vital for cultivating the next generation of responsible and skilled agricultural leaders (Brown & Kelsey, 2013). Transformational leadership creates an environment where ethics, community engagement, and social responsibility are prioritized, which are particularly relevant qualities in the complexities of urban agriculture (Brown & Kelsey, 2013). Leadership and competency assessments within these educational frameworks allow for effective measurement and development of students' leadership skills (Velez et al., 2014). These evaluations also guide targeted growth opportunities (Velez et al., 2014). Clear communication, judicious decision-making, and innovative problem-solving are fundamental abilities essential for ethical leadership, especially in navigating the nuanced challenges unique to urban agriculture settings (Nowak et al., 2019).

Quantifiable Impact and Long-Term Sustainability

The ripple effects of transformational leadership in urban agriculture are tangible (Rahmadani & Schaufeli, 2022). Transformational leaders inspire and motivate individuals and communities, leading to higher levels of community engagement (Rahmadani & Schaufeli, 2022). This increased engagement fosters a sense of ownership among community members, resulting in a stronger commitment to the project's sustainability and adaptability to changing circumstances (Rahmadani & Schaufeli, 2022). Transformational leaders can build strong relationships and collaborations with local organizations, government agencies, and other stakeholders (Rahmadani & Schaufeli, 2022).

By actively engaging with the community, partnering with local organizations, and continuously adapting to the evolving urban landscape, transformational leaders can guide us towards a future where cities become exemplars of sustainable living and social equity (Rahmadani & Schaufeli, 2022). They address the interconnected challenges of climate change, resource scarcity, and social inequality (Rahmadani & Schaufeli, 2022).

Investing in transformational leaders who can navigate the complexities of urban life and agriculture is essential as we strive to solve the significant issues of our time (Rahmadani & Schaufeli, 2022). These leaders address immediate needs while also planting the seeds for long-term change, cultivating a future where urban agriculture enriches cities, nourishes communities, and safeguards the planet for future generations (Rahmadani & Schaufeli, 2022).

Urban farming is increasingly recognized as a sustainable solution to critical challenges such as food insecurity, climate change, and rapid urbanization (Rahmadani & Schaufeli, 2022). However, transforming urban farming requires more than just soil, seeds, and water (Rahmadani & Schaufeli, 2022). It requires transformational leaders who can guide communities towards a collective vision of sustainability and social equity (Rahmadani & Schaufeli, 2022). These leaders focus on making things fair and sustainable for everyone, fostering collaboration and collective action (Rahmadani & Schaufeli, 2022). Transformational leadership has proven to be extraordinarily effective in the context of urban farming (Rahmadani & Schaufeli, 2022).

The Complex Landscape of Urban Farming

Urban farming is a multifaceted endeavor that encompasses various dimensions, including environmental sustainability, community engagement, public policy, and entrepreneurship (Qiu et al., 2023). As cities continue to grow, available land becomes scarce, regulatory constraints tighten, and socioeconomic disparities become more apparent (Qiu et al., 2023). Navigating this complex landscape requires leaders who can effectively address these multiple dimensions simultaneously (Qiu et al., 2023).

Evaluating the impact of transformational leadership in urban agriculture goes beyond measuring quantitative metrics such as crop yield or the number of people involved (Sanders et al., 2021). Comprehensive assessments require a combination of quantitative and qualitative measures (Sanders et al., 2021). Quantitative metrics may include crop yield, economic impact, and funding levels, while qualitative measures involve interviews, surveys, and case studies to assess the project's effect on community well-being, environmental health, and economic vitality (Sanders et al., 2021).

Urban farming is a complex endeavor that requires leaders capable of navigating multiple dimensions simultaneously. Transformational leadership plays a crucial role in urban agriculture, leading to higher levels of community engagement, successful partnerships, increased funding, and a stronger sense of ownership among community members. Evaluating the impact of transformational leadership requires a comprehensive assessment that combines quantitative and qualitative measures. By investing in transformational leaders, we can cultivate a future where urban agriculture contributes to sustainable living, social equity, and the well-being of communities.

THE FOUR PILLARS OF TRANSFORMATIONAL LEADERSHIP IN URBAN FARMING

Idealized Influence: Transformational leaders are ethical role models (Hejkrlik et al., 2023). They command respect not through authority but through integrity and a clear sense of purpose. This could mean leading by example and demonstrating sustainable agricultural practices and ethical business conduct in urban farming. This integrity encourages community members to participate actively, fostering collective ownership over local farming initiatives (Chukwu, 2023).

Inspirational Motivation: Leaders are adept at articulating a compelling vision for the future. They can paint a picture of what urban farming could mean for a community: fresh, local produce; greener, more livable spaces; educational opportunities; and stronger social bonds.

Transformational leaders inspire creativity and encourage problem-solving. They create an environment where people feel empowered to propose new farming techniques, experiment with crop rotations, or develop community engagement activities. This culture of innovation is crucial for addressing the challenges unique to urban agriculture, from space constraints to varying levels of community involvement (Elizabeth et al., 2023)

Intellectual Stimulation: In urban agriculture, transformational leadership goes beyond the rudimentary aspects of farming to elevate the endeavor into a platform for intellectual stimulation. Such a leader does not just guide team members in growing produce; they inspire curiosity, innovation, and a deeper understanding of sustainable practices. The leader poses challenging questions and encourages team members to engage with broader ecological and socio-economic issues—like food security, waste management, and technology integration into farming. Through inspiring intellectual engagement, the transformational leader helps team members envision urban agriculture as not merely an alternative but as an evolving solution that requires critical thinking and ongoing adaptation (Jankelová et al., 2020).

Individualized Consideration: Perhaps the most humane aspect of transformational leadership is emphasizing individual needs and personal development. Transformational leaders are attentive to the specific requirements and aspirations of community members. Whether providing educational workshops for novices or advanced training modules for experienced farmers, these leaders ensure everyone has the tools and knowledge they need to succeed (Ince, 2023)

BUILDING ROBUST COMMUNITY RELATIONSHIPS

Transformational leadership in urban farming goes beyond agricultural production to influence community dynamics positively (Saleh & Riyadi, 2023). Transformational leaders cultivate a strong sense of belonging and shared responsibility by involving community members in decision-making and treating them as partners. This is essential for the long-term sustainability of urban farming projects. When people feel a sense of ownership and pride, they are more likely to contribute time, effort, and resources, making the farming initiative more resilient and adaptive to changes.

THE NEED FOR MEASURING IMPACT

Effective transformational leadership needs to be quantifiable to gauge its actual impact (Vu et al., 2020). This involves monitoring both quantitative metrics, such as crop yield, resource efficiency, and community participation, and qualitative aspects, such as community satisfaction, skill development, and lifestyle changes (Li & Liu, 2022).

This chapter aims to develop a transformational leadership education program tailored to urban residents, focusing on agricultural practices and career opportunities. The need for such a program arises from the sector's waning agricultural expertise and leadership. As Kaiyatsa et al. (2019) note, agriculture has been a cornerstone of America's economy since its inception, providing jobs to millions and serving as the backbone of the nation's food, fiber, and fuel supply. However, climate-related challenges have severely impacted the sector (White & Hall, 2017). Extreme weather events like floods and droughts increasingly affect crop yields and food production (Naylor, 2019). Technological and industrial advancements have further contributed to drastic weather pattern changes, adversely affecting crops, soil quality, and livestock (Hatfield & Prueger, 2015; Lucatello & Sánchez, 2022).

Besides climatic hurdles, another concern is the shrinking agricultural workforce. Data from the Bureau of Labor Statistics reveal that agricultural workers have declined by roughly two million since the 1950s (Akins, 2022). Factors like increased automation, consolidation of farms, and low profitability contribute to this decline (Fuglie et al., 2011). The impact of climate change on crop yields has also been cited as a reason for farmers leaving the profession (Specht et al., 2019). Additionally, the perception of farming as labor-intensive and low paying persuade against qualified individuals from pursuing agricultural careers (Li et al., 2013). The industry needs rebranding to attract younger generations to agricultural vocations (Karanth et al., 2022).

Despite these challenges, historical precedence shows that agricultural programs can positively impact the sector (Day et al., 2021). Initiatives from the United States Department of Agriculture (USDA) include projects to prepare farmers for climate change ramifications (Popoola et al., 2019). The USDA also allocates funds for developing technologies that can aid farmers in adapting to evolving climate conditions (Fagbemi et al., 2023). Research is ongoing on cover cropping for soil enrichment and erosion control (Blanco-Canqui et al., 2015). In summary, American agriculture faces a triad of challenges: climate change, workforce decline, and skill shortage (Shiiba et al., 2023). This proposed program addresses these issues through education and awareness, nurturing a new generation of agricultural leaders.

Sustainable agriculture is a comprehensive approach that balances the needs of the environment, society, and economy. According to Pimentel and Burgess (2013), it has a transformative effect on ecological preservation, particularly in soil conservation, water usage, and protecting Earth's invaluable natural resources. Conventional farming practices, necessary as they may be for food production, raise considerable concerns regarding their long-term impact on our planet's finite resources (Foley et al., 2011). This issue is compounded by alarming rates of food waste, with studies indicating that between 30-40% of food in the U.S. never reaches the table (Buzby et al., 2014).

The holistic goals of sustainable agriculture go beyond merely producing food. It aims to enhance the quality of life for humans and animals while ensuring the protection and responsible utilization of natural resources (Altieri & Nicholls, 2018). It offers a framework for meeting current societal needs for food and clothing without compromising the ability of future generations to meet their own needs (Pretty, 2008).

Farmers and agriculturalists, to stay afloat in the competitive landscape, often turn to a set of specific criteria and strategies (Danso et al., 2019). These criteria are rooted in principles that promote social fairness, environmental health, and economic prosperity (Dalgaard et al., 2003). By adhering to these principles, everyone in the food supply chain can contribute to a more sustainable future. One of the groundbreaking advantages of adopting sustainable agricultural practices is its departure from conventional farming methods that rely heavily on monoculture (Gomiero et al., 2011).

Sustainable agriculture advocates for practices like polyculture, which allows for the growth of multiple crops on the same plot of land (Whittinghill & Sarr, 2021). This diversification minimizes the environmental impact and allows farmers to produce more food using less land (Shah & Wu, 2019). However, this practice has challenges, particularly concerning avoiding soil nutrient depletion (Tilman et al., 2011). Nevertheless, these challenges are manageable and represent areas for potential innovation and adaptation (Struik & Kuyper, 2017).

Regarding animal welfare, sustainable agriculture marks a significant departure from traditional factory farming, often characterized by brutal and inhumane conditions (Gerber et al., 2013). Conventional systems often involve keeping animals in restricted, overcrowded spaces, which are ethically problematic and a breeding ground for diseases (Busch et al., 2022). Sustainable agriculture replaces this model with one that provides animals enough room to roam freely and follows a nutritionally balanced, plant-based diet (Wathes, 2010).

The adoption of sustainable farming practices has a direct impact on reducing environmental pollutants. Intensive agriculture often relies on hazardous fertilizers, which can leach into water bodies and harm aquatic life. Additionally, methane emissions from industrial cattle farming are a significant concern due to their greenhouse effects (Liang et al., 2023). Practices like crop rotation and the use of organic fertilizers not only reduce such emissions but also lead to improved air quality (Singh, 2021).

Urban agriculture, an emerging trend, brings the principles of sustainable farming into city environments, offering urban residents access to locally grown, fresh produce. An estimated 56% of the global population resides in cities (He et al., 2021), and this number is expected to rise, so urbanites need to be educated on sustainable agricultural practices (Bisht et al., 2020). Consumer attitudes play a vital role in successfully integrating sustainable farming into urban settings (Grebitus et al., 2020).

The complexities of feeding an ever growing global population, especially with increasing urbanization, remain challenging (Ojo et al., 2020). Solutions are actively sought to ensure that high-quality, nutritious food is accessible to all, regardless of geographical location (Ditlevsen et al., 2020). While sustainable agriculture alone may not resolve global hunger, it represents a crucial step towards a more equitable and sustainable future.

The need for revamped agricultural education is more pressing than ever (Le Glaz et al., 2021). As modern society evolves, agriculture must remain relevant and engage the younger generation (White, 2020). This urgency is evident in a United States Farmers and Ranchers Alliance survey, which found that 72% of American consumers desire a deeper understanding of farming practices (Farmers & Alliance, 2011). Considering that fewer than 2% of Americans are directly involved in farming or ranching (USDA & ERS - Ag and Food Sectors and the Economy, 2021), the lack of agricultural knowledge can lead to legislation that may adversely impact the agricultural sector, as exemplified by California's Proposition 12 and Oregon's IP13 (Ody & Shattuck, 2023).

In the United States, metropolitan regions have seen a surge in interest in agricultural education, primarily due to a growing focus on sustainability and local produce (Chenarides et al., 2021). Despite this interest, substantial barriers, such as population density and scarce fertile land in urban areas, limit the effectiveness of educational programs (Nyarko & Kozári, 2021). Governments have responded by offering financial support, including grants and loans, and collaborating with universities to promote agricultural education (Buys & Rennekamp, 2020). Nonetheless, there is still a noticeable gap in understanding the real benefits of agricultural literacy, especially among urban dwellers (Hartmann & Martin, 2021).

Community involvement and mutual understanding are vital for the success of modern agricultural initiatives. Public awareness campaigns focusing on the benefits of local, sustainable farming have shown promise (Jansen et al., 2020). Customizing these initiatives based on local needs and feedback can further their impact (Simonson & Rahman, 2020).

Addressing the literacy gap in agriculture is essential to dispel misconceptions and empower consumers to make informed choices about their food (Kountios et al., 2023). Over the years, agricultural education has undergone significant transformations. Innovative approaches that connect producers with consumers are crucial in promoting sustainable farming and local produce.

The curricula in agricultural education need to be dynamic and forward-looking. They should equip future leaders with the tools to advocate for sustainable practices and engage the next generation (Hartmann & Martin, 2021). With more people applying what they have learned from these programs, the economic and health benefits of higher-quality, sustainably produced food become more accessible (Dimitri & Effland, 2020).

Agricultural education is not just a need but a necessity. The curriculum should go beyond traditional concepts and incorporate experimental and sustainable approaches to agriculture (Musa & Basir, 2021). The future of agriculture lies in the hands of educators who are committed to research and proactive education that advances the field (Wells & Stock, 2020).

Cultivating a New Future

The central issue lies in the need for agricultural literacy and understanding among secondary students residing in urban settings (Hess & Trexler, 2011). There is a disconnection between urban communities and the agricultural sector, leading to challenges in agricultural literacy and misinformation about food production (Clemons et al., 2018). This disconnection also limits the participation of diverse groups, particularly urban populations, and people of color, in the agricultural industry (Clemons et al., 2018). The intervention aims to address the intertwined problems of agricultural illiteracy in urban communities, increasing rates of food insecurity, and dwindling numbers of leaders in the agricultural sector (Clemons et al., 2018).

Understanding the intricacies of food production is crucial for dispelling myths and addressing issues such as food insecurity, waste, and overall human health (Hess & Trexler, 2011). Evaluating the impact of agricultural literacy is not solely about quantifying pounds of food produced or the number of people involved (Bradford Jr et al., 2019). It also involves assessing the project's effect on community well-being, environmental health, and economic vitality (Bradford Jr et al., 2019). Comprehensive assessments require a combination of quantitative metrics, such as crop yield and community participation levels, along with qualitative measures like interviews, surveys, and case studies (Bradford Jr et al., 2019).

Food Insecurity

In 2020, the USDA revealed that 38.3 million Americans faced food insecurity, corroborated by Coleman-Jensen et al. (2022), who pointed out that this number included 11.7 million children (USDA & ARS, 2021). Food insecurity is not simply about hunger but is directly linked to multiple health issues, including anemia, asthma, cognitive problems, developmental delays, depression, diabetes, hypertension, and obesity (Mendy et al., 2018). Food-insecure households are more likely to have children who suffer from subpar health, doubling their risk compared to those from food-secure families (Mendy et al., 2018). The elderly are also affected, as those who struggle with food accessibility show signs of life complications similar to people fourteen years their senior (Brostow et al., 2019). The overall ramifications of food insecurity on public health, stretching from children to seniors, are monumental (Berkowitz et al., 2019).

The COVID-19 pandemic has worsened the situation, exacerbating food insecurity and related health issues (Esobi et al., 2021). The pandemic-induced job losses have made vulnerable families even more prone to food insecurity (Esobi et al., 2021). This has a particularly detrimental effect on children dependent on school meal programs, which were suspended due to the closure of educational institutions (Nagata et al., 2021).

Global influences such as severe weather, pandemics, geopolitical conflicts, and the Ukraine crisis have further complicated food insecurity (Wong & Swanson, 2023). Ahmadnia et al. (2022) state that this burgeoning crisis threatens global stability as the food supply struggles to keep up with the increasing global population. Furthermore, shrinking agricultural land has compounded the food insecurity issue, as it affects not only the human food supply but also the feed for animals, impacting other agricultural by-products such as soap and toothpaste. This has forced a dependency on imported, lower-quality processed foods in the United States (Schut et al., 2020).

The problem under investigation extends from the need for more agricultural literacy in urban settings to the rise in food insecurity and the declining number of agricultural leaders (Kovar & Ball, 2013). A comprehensive understanding of these issues is critical for creating interventions that address the immediate challenges and provide long-term solutions (Romero-Cabrera et al., 2022).

Student Enrollment and Its Implications

Agriculture plays a crucial role in the United States' economic landscape. However, there is a decline in student interest in pursuing agricultural careers, particularly among those from lower academic backgrounds (Zulaikha et al., 2021). This trend has significant implications for the future of agriculture and food security (Zulaikha et al., 2021). Enrollment in agricultural programs has been decreasing steadily, experiencing a 1.5% annual drop since the turn of the century (Garton, 2019). In addition, graduates from various disciplines, agriculture included, are encountering considerable unemployment rates post-graduation (Morris et al., 2022).

While consumer interest in agricultural products continues to rise (Deng et al., 2020), the declining enrollment in agricultural programs poses significant challenges for the future of agriculture and food security (Cecchettini, 1992). The lack of enthusiasm among students to pursue agricultural careers hinders the development of the sector (Chumbley, 2016). This decline in enrollment can result in a shortage of qualified graduates for agriculture jobs and a loss of millions of dollars for universities (Esters & Bowen, 2004).

It is essential to promote the perception of agricultural careers and increase awareness of the importance of the agricultural sector (Zulaikha et al., 2021). Strategies such as dual-enrollment programs and career and technology education programs can help prepare students for agricultural careers and increase their interest in the field (Chumbley, 2016). Additionally, marketing and branding efforts can enhance the image of agricultural programs and attract more students (Miller, 2011).

Urbanization has also skewed student perceptions, painting agriculture as a labor-intensive career mostly suited for those from less affluent backgrounds (Friesner et al., 2021). If addressed, this perception could continue to propel urbanization and deter potential agricultural experts, leading to a need for more qualified professionals for vital research and development in the field (Garton, 2019).

Food security is a pressing concern, with implications for global sustainability and public health. The increasing demand for food, coupled with the decline in interest in agriculture, poses challenges for ensuring a secure and sustainable food supply. The lack of enthusiasm among the younger generation to pursue agricultural careers is attributed to factors such as the perceived lack of prestige and inadequate rewards (Zulaikha et al., 2021).

To address these challenges, it is crucial to develop strategies that promote agricultural careers and enhance the perception of the agricultural sector. This includes improving the image of the agricultural sector, providing adequate support, and ensuring stable market conditions. Additionally, long-term policies and investments are needed to strengthen national food security and the agricultural sector. Strategic partnerships between educational bodies, government agencies, and the private sector could cultivate student interest and expose them to the tangible applications of STEM subjects in agriculture (Bandura, 1986). Curriculum reforms emphasizing research and sustainable agricultural practices can spark innovation and engagement (Vallera & Bodzin, 2020).

Efforts to attract and retain talent in the agricultural sector should focus on increasing awareness of the importance of agriculture, providing training and internships, and highlighting the potential for technological advancements in the field. By addressing the underlying issues and promoting agricultural careers, we can ensure a sustainable and secure future for agriculture and food production.

The declining interest in agricultural careers among students, particularly those from lower academic backgrounds, poses significant challenges for the future of agriculture and food security. Addressing this issue requires comprehensive strategies that enhance the perception of the agricultural sector, provide support and incentives, and promote the importance of agriculture in ensuring a sustainable and secure food supply.

Investment in youth education is crucial for increased agricultural productivity, revitalizing rural economies, and safeguarding food supplies Jaramillo et al. (2021). The challenges posed by climate change, diminishing biodiversity, and evolving consumer preferences necessitate transformative education to meet legislative and commercial standards (Kidido et al., 2017).

Youth access to agricultural land is essential for harnessing their potential for increased agricultural production (Kidido et al., 2017). However, limited access to land for agricultural purposes undermines their ability to make long-term investments and participate in cash crop cultivation (Kidido et al., 2017). To address this issue, targeted youth agricultural land policies are recommended to leverage the potential of the youth in agriculture (Kidido et al., 2017).

Investing in youth education has positive implications for reducing youth unemployment (Alemu, 2023). Education investment, represented by primary, secondary, and tertiary school completion rates, plays a significant role in reducing unemployment rates among the youth (Alemu, 2023). Incorporating youth into agriculture has also been proposed as a solution to youth unemployment. However, perceptions of work and agriculture, deeply entrenched in society, can hinder educated youth from engaging in agriculture-based livelihoods.

Policymakers should focus on strategies that increase investments in agriculture, industry, and services to enhance the labor absorptive capacity of the economic sector (Alemu, 2023). Increasing investments in agriculture, manufacturing, and services can have a positive impact on reducing youth unemployment (Alemu, 2023). Vocational training programs that focus on occupations like agriculture can empower youth through education and employment.

Reforming Traditional Agricultural Education

While there is value in preserving the scientific basis of traditional agricultural education, modern challenges call for a more adaptable and contextual approach, particularly in urban settings (Peano et al., 2020). The existing pedagogical methods need to be improved in the efficient training for sustainable agricultural practices, which have far-reaching implications for public health and economic well-being (Talukder et al., 2017).

Current educational systems are often critiqued for overloading students with information while needing more effective feedback mechanisms (Ansari & Usmani, 2018). Educational strategies should foster more creativity and initiative to maximize societal impact (Abramo & Reynolds, 2015). Novel teaching methodologies in sustainable agriculture can result in farming systems that are both environmentally sustainable and beneficial for human health (Abramo & Reynolds, 2015).

Given the emerging significance of urban agriculture, it becomes crucial to explore teaching methods that can effectively communicate innovative farming techniques suitable for urban environments (Peano et al., 2020). Conventional education often falls short in promoting critical thinking, which limits the societal benefits that graduates can offer (Foster et al., 2020). The development of critical thinking is inherently difficult and requires deep-level thinking (Foster et al., 2020). However, the effectiveness of conventional education in improving critical thinking has been questioned (Manuaba et al., 2022).

Experimental approaches to education are recommended to highlight the transformative potential of sustainable urban agriculture and its consequential role in bolstering the agricultural sector and food security (Bass & Bass Bernard, 1985). The low student enrollment in agriculture is a multifaceted issue that requires a collective, innovative, and long-term strategic approach.

Leadership in agriculture plays a crucial role in shaping the future of food production and ensuring responsible stewardship of agricultural systems. In recent years, there has been an increasing demand for leadership in agriculture that goes beyond conventional metrics. This shift towards a transformational leadership paradigm is aligned with sustainable and ethical principles.

Transformational leadership in agriculture is characterized by a commitment to ethical principles that guide behaviors and decision making processes. These principles include integrity, transparency, and a strong sense of social and environmental accountability. In the context of agriculture, success metrics extend beyond mere profitability or productivity. A transformational agricultural leader considers the broader implications of farming practices on environmental sustainability, social justice, and food security for current and future generations.

Leadership in agriculture is not limited to individual farmers or agribusinesses (Cletzer et al., 2022). It encompasses policymakers, industry thought leaders, researchers, and educators who have the authority and capability to influence and guide the agricultural community (Cletzer et al., 2022). When these stakeholders embrace transformational leadership principles, they become catalysts for change, steering the sector towards more sustainable and ethical practices (Cletzer et al., 2022).

Modern agricultural leadership requires skill sets such as systems thinking, a strategic perspective, and the ability to harmonize varying stakeholder interests (Jankelová et al., 2020). However, there are challenges in developing and nurturing these skills within the agricultural context. Leadership development programs and initiatives play a crucial role in equipping agricultural leaders with the necessary skills and competencies.

The essence of transformational leadership is its commitment to ethical principles that guide behaviors and decision-making processes. These include integrity, transparency, and a pronounced sense of social and environmental accountability. Within agriculture, this means that the success metrics extend beyond mere profitability or productivity (Tangdigling et al., 2019). A genuinely transformational agricultural leader would focus on the broader implications of farming practices on environmental sustainability, social justice, and food security for current and future generations.

The Multidimensional Nature of Agricultural Leadership

Leadership in agriculture extends beyond individual farmers or agribusinesses and encompasses policymakers, thought leaders, researchers, and educators who have the authority and capability to influence and guide the agricultural community (Muhaimin et al., 2023). When these stakeholders adopt transformational leadership principles, they can serve as catalysts for change, steering the sector towards more sustainable and ethical practices (Muhaimin et al., 2023).

Value-driven decisions and promoting sustainable methodologies are pivotal in creating transformational leaders in agriculture (Agbaje et al., 2001). This involves considering the broader implications of farming practices on environmental sustainability, social justice, and food security (Agbaje et al., 2001). Fostering educational alliances is also crucial in developing transformational leaders who can drive positive change in the agricultural sector (Cletzer et al., 2022).

Modern agricultural leadership requires a blend of skills such as systems thinking, a strategic perspective, and the ability to harmonize varying stakeholder interests (Muhaimin et al., 2023). However, there are challenges in developing and nurturing these skills within the agricultural context (Cletzer et al., 2022). Leadership development programs and initiatives play a crucial role in equipping agricultural leaders with the necessary skills and competencies (Cletzer et al., 2022). The need for such skillful leaders in agriculture helps achieve more sustainable and efficient farming operations.

With the increasing complexity and geographical dispersion of food systems, consumers have become distant from the origins of their food (Schyns et al., 2022). This distance often results in a reduced understanding and valuation of agricultural work. However, consumers are increasingly willing to invest more in food items they perceive as healthier and more ecologically responsible (Zhang et al., 2018). This consumer behavior points towards a pressing need for innovation in sustainable food production.

The Next Generation and the Future

Leadership education programs in agriculture are crucial for equipping future leaders with the necessary tools for industry best practices and policy implementation (Morgan et al., 2013). However, recent funding cuts to these programs and urban ignorance about the agricultural sector make the need for effective agricultural leadership even more crucial (Velez et al., 2014).

Inclusion and diversity within agricultural leadership can have a significant impact on the sector. Diverse leadership teams are better equipped to navigate the complexities of modern agriculture. The lack of adequate leadership in agriculture has far-reaching consequences, affecting social health, economic stability, and even the traditional fabric of the American family farm.

The future of agriculture relies on developing and fostering transformational leadership (Velez et al., 2014). Transformational leadership goes beyond management and focuses on innovation, education, and transformation (Velez et al., 2014). Efforts must be made to develop this form of leadership to ensure the longevity and ethical grounding of the agricultural sector.

Leadership education programs in agriculture are essential for equipping future leaders with the necessary tools for industry best practices and policy implementation (Morgan et al., 2013). Inclusion and diversity within agricultural leadership can significantly benefit the sector. Developing transformational leadership is crucial for the future of agriculture (Velez et al., 2014). Efforts must be made to prioritize and support agricultural leadership education to ensure the long-term stability and ethical grounding of the sector.

Transformational Leadership and Ethical Considerations

Transformational leadership serves as the lynchpin in the architecture of agricultural change, guiding innovative agriculture educational interventions like FDUA. Ethical leadership overlays this, setting the moral compass for implementation (Lamm et al., 2021). This dual focus addresses' what needs to be done' and 'how it should be done ethically.' Such leadership fosters informed decision-making and promotes a sustainable agriculture framework by addressing the complex dynamics in the sector (Lamm et al., 2021).

Transformational Leadership Defined

Transformational leadership in agriculture education can be characterized by inspirational motivation, intellectual stimulation, and individualized consideration (Harrison, 2013). Such leaders create a vision and clear goals, empowering students to become agents of change in agriculture (Harrison, 2013).

The framework also embeds the concept of culturally responsive teaching, which makes the educational process more engaging for urban populations (Krill, 1993). It encourages inclusivity through curriculum design and pedagogical approaches reflecting students' cultural diversity.

Cognitive Theory and Leadership

Bandura's social cognitive theory provides the groundwork to understand how external leadership style reflects inner convictions, making it a critical aspect of this research (Lamm et al., 2021). Leadership research has evolved to focus on the dynamic interaction between leaders and followers, emphasizing the Full Range Leadership Model (Lamm et al., 2021). Leadership ethics can be framed through philosophical lenses like consequentialism and utilitarianism, which impact decision-making processes in morally complex situations (Lamm et al., 2021).

The Impending Need

A decline in agricultural knowledge, driven by urbanization and climate change, necessitates this focus on agriculture education (Lamm et al., 2021). By taking a multifaceted approach, the intervention seeks to create an impactful, sustainable future for agriculture.

The pivotal role of leadership in agriculture is increasingly acknowledged for its capacity to shape the destiny of food production and the long-term sustainability of farming practices (Van Zyl, 2014). Recent scholarship suggests that transformational leadership, characterized by transparent, responsible, and ethical decision-making, is particularly needed in the modern agricultural sector (Gubanova et al., 2021). This leadership style emphasizes collective leadership, self-motivation, and an innovative approach to leadership (Gubanova et al., 2021). This transformative approach pushes the boundaries of conventional wisdom that traditionally equates leadership effectiveness with economic metrics alone (Tangdigling et al., 2019). It broadens the conversation to include ethical considerations around ecology, animal care, and societal welfare.

Transformational leadership is not confined to the farming community; its reach extends to many stakeholders. Policymakers, industry executives, scientific researchers, and academics all wield substantial influence over agricultural methodologies and overall industry trajectory. Embracing transformational leadership paradigms allows these key players to navigate the industry toward more sustainable and ethically responsible practices.

The research endeavors to unpack the complex relationship between agricultural leadership and transformational leadership, focusing on value-based decision-making, promoting eco-friendly practices, and the significance of education and collaboration. This inquiry aims to elucidate how transformational leadership may offer solutions to immediate and long-term challenges within the sector.

Avolio and Yammarino (2013) posited that transformational leaders develop themselves and empower their followers to realize their fullest potential. In today's rapidly evolving agricultural landscape, there is an urgent need for leaders who possess not just traditional agrarian know-how but also capabilities in systemic thinking, strategic planning, and stakeholder management (Eliasson et al., 2022).

The intricacies of contemporary food systems have rendered them geographically expansive and staggeringly complex (Schyns et al., 2022). Consumers are more disconnected from the origins of their food than ever before. However, a surge in consumer willingness to pay extra for ethically sourced and healthful food products has been noted (Zhang et al., 2018). Amid these transformations, farmers are compelled to harmonize consumer preferences with environmental sustainability.

Technological solutions such as biotechnology offer avenues for increasing farming productivity. However, these come with regulatory contraints and evolving consumer demands, making modern agriculture a multifaceted challenge requiring technical acumen and financial and marketing prowess (Silva et al., 2022). The contemporary farmer, in essence, needs to be an agroecological entrepreneur with a diverse skill set (Wang & You, 2022).

Additionally, the sheer volume of agricultural data generated and processed for decision-making has escalated dramatically in the digital era. Regulatory issues around this data and its ownership add another layer of complexity. Agricultural decision-making is also increasingly subject to international trade frameworks, necessitating a robust understanding of global economic dynamics. Costa-Font et al. (2008) advocate for science-based regulatory protocols for biotechnological innovations, arguing that a fact-driven approach could engender public trust.

The future of agriculture critically hinges upon the emergence of a new generation of versatile professionals—innovators, communicators, producers, and educators—who can steer the sector through its multidimensional challenges. Therefore, educational initiatives aimed at cultivating agricultural leadership are of paramount importance. However, there have been concerning reductions in funding for such educational programs in the U.S., contributing to a general unawareness about the industry and possibly deterring future participation (Ritter et al., 2019).

Transformational leadership elevates public understanding of agriculture and encourages sustainable farming (Altrichter, 2020). Ethical decision-making also entails prioritizing animal welfare (De Paula Vieira & Anthony, 2020) and advocating for diversity and inclusion in leadership roles (Eastwood et al., 2019).

The decline of family-owned farms in the U.S. has significant implications, underscoring the dire need for a transition in agricultural leadership to revive the sector (Parr et al., 2020). Leadership training programs incorporating ethical and transformational leadership principles are vital in preparing the next generation of agricultural professionals. These programs must be designed to inculcate competencies beyond traditional farming skills, such as communication, problem-solving, and critical decision-making abilities, to prepare students for the multifaceted challenges they will undoubtedly face in modern agricultural environments.

Developing leadership capabilities primarily aims to fortify an organization's resilience against unexpected challenges (Stefan & Nazarov, 2020). Such development equips leaders with the necessary information, skills, and competencies for effective leadership (Dirani et al., 2020). For an organization or community to thrive, its learning milieu and activities should be conducive to cultivating individual and collective leadership capabilities.

Professionals in the agricultural sector face with challenges ranging from market volatility to legislative constraints and environmental degradation (Stefan & Nazarov, 2020). This makes the presence of strong, competent leaders at the grassroots level imperative for the industry's long-term viability. Leadership in rural and agricultural settings often demands higher social capital, defined as the networks and mutual trust facilitating collective action within a community.

Several states have recently initiated agricultural leadership development programs, tracing their contemporary roots to the Kellogg Farmers Study Program initiated in 1965 at Michigan State University (Fuentelsaz et al., 2023). Evaluations suggest that program alumni have increased community engagement and enhanced decision-making capabilities.

Today's agricultural leadership paradigms are increasingly shifting away from traditional hierarchical approaches. They embrace a more collective and participatory leadership model to tackle the industry's multifaceted challenges (Byrd, 2022). Many current programs are designed after the Kellogg Foundation's model, emphasizing collaboration and shared leadership (Savage et al., 2019).

In developing agricultural leadership programs, setting unambiguous instructional objectives that inform the design, implementation, and evaluation phases is crucial. These objectives are the cornerstone for achieving desired outcomes, focusing on aspects like public engagement, sustainability, and enhancement of leadership skills (Traver Marti et al., 2023).

Agricultural or otherwise, leadership development programs aim for three kinds of transformation: individual growth, organizational change, and community or social adaptation.

Recognizing learners' needs in educational settings is crucial for tailoring effective interventions and strategies (Cervero & Wilson, 2006). Needs are defined as the gap between a learner's current skills, knowledge, or attitudes and the aspired level of proficiency. This underscores the importance of empirical data in identifying this gap and crafting targeted interventions. Thus, educators can adapt their methodologies to effectively bridge this divide, making decisions rooted in empirical evidence (Cervero & Wilson, 2006).

Leadership and participation are the backbones for evaluating facets and actualizing constructive alterations in any setting, and agricultural education is no exception (Basoro & Tefera, 2021). It is a common consensus that agricultural education needs perpetual refinement, incorporating entrepreneurial ideas for holistic growth (Newstead et al., 2020).

Leadership is not merely a managerial skill; it pervades every human life and business stratum. It is the art of motivating people towards accomplishing shared objectives (Khan et al., 2019). Employers are keen on scouting for individuals endowed with solid leadership attributes, linking leadership capabilities to professional growth (Khan et al., 2019). Day and Dragoni (2015) have suggested considering various time scales and analytical levels to deepen our understanding of leadership in all its forms. They propose that every individual harbors the potential to lead, although the manifestation of this trait differs according to context and opportunity (Khan et al., 2019).

In agricultural education, nurturing youthful leadership is imperative and forms a central tenet of a well-rounded educational agenda, accompanied by classroom learning and hands-on fieldwork. This educational paradigm aims to equip students with the acumen needed for effective global participation in agriculture and related fields. Civic leaders often attribute their leadership prowess and career growth to their participation in agricultural projects.

Educators' role in molding future leaders within the agricultural domain is pivotal. However, there is a substantial knowledge gap concerning the influence of educators' leadership styles on student development, highlighting a need for additional research. Bass and Avolio (2004) argue that self-awareness of one's leadership style is critical to cultivating similar competencies in others.

Personal experiences do not just shape individuals' identities; they have a cascading effect on their career trajectories and even broader systems (Basoro & Tefera, 2021). In line with Bandura's social cognitive theory, identity, situational factors, and actions are interrelated and mutually influential (Basoro & Tefera, 2021). For instance, a teacher's philosophical leanings and the academic milieu can shape both their world outlook and vocational commitment (Basoro & Tefera, 2021).

Leadership studies have transitioned from being trait-centric to focusing on the relational dynamics between leaders and followers (Newstead et al., 2020). Leaders are seen as agents who inspire and share authority and accountability within a group, utilizing transformational leadership as a framework

(Newstead et al., 2020). Transformational leaders excel in driving progressive changes and fostering a collective sense of mission (Newstead et al., 2020). They advocate for individual and collective development, propelled by an ethos of lifelong learning and adaptability (Newstead et al., 2020).

Student growth and transformation models serve as invaluable tools in academia by offering a structured approach to achieving educational objectives (Bass & Avolio, 1996). These models delineate the specific steps and procedures that ought to be undertaken to reach desired outcomes, thereby offering a tangible and assessable framework that helps gauge the advancements made (Bass & Avolio, 1996). More importantly, such models are pivotal in fostering an equitable educational landscape as they ensure that every student, irrespective of their background, can avail themselves of top-tier educational opportunities and resources (Bass & Avolio, 1996). It is crucial for educational practitioners, including teachers and administrative staff, to incorporate these models into their teaching methodologies and evaluative processes to uplift the educational experience of all students (Bass & Avolio, 1996).

Conceptual frameworks for student development, such as the one offered by Perry's cognitive-structural theory, provide strategic insights that facilitate the advancement of students. This specific theory focuses on the cognitive aspects of student learning, outlining how belief systems and values evolve during formative adolescence, ultimately influencing an individual's perspective of the world. Such theories can be particularly impactful in specialized education sectors like agricultural leadership to enrich programmatic offerings and classroom teachings.

The role of human existential theories in understanding the moral landscape is also noteworthy (Olley, 2021). These theories contend that human ideals cannot be neatly categorized into good or bad, mainly because human nature does not inherently possess qualitative traits (Olley, 2021). From an educational standpoint, humanistic existential theories delve into student development's interpersonal and social dimensions, spotlighting the conducive conditions that nurture growth (Olley, 2021). Agricultural education professionals, guidance counselors, and academic advisors often employ these humanistic considerations to encourage students toward better life choices (Olley, 2021).

Theories around leadership provide comprehensive insights into the variances in leadership styles and their respective efficacies in diverse settings. Specifically, transformational leadership emerges as a particularly fitting model for agricultural educational contexts due to its focus on empowerment, ethical considerations, and the fostering of meaningful relationships. Ethical frameworks like virtue ethics can augment the capabilities of agricultural leaders by instilling a sense of ethical obligation and social responsibility (Noopila & Pichon, 2022).

Leadership theories can be broadly categorized into transformational, situational, and servant leadership. Transformational leadership prioritizes fully realizing individual potential through motivation and inspiration (Lameck, 2022). Situational leadership adapts according to the unique needs of specific scenarios and the individuals involved (Ogaga et al., 2023). Meanwhile, servant leadership places collective needs ahead of individual ambitions, creating a more cooperative and ethical work environment (Lameck, 2022). In agricultural education, transformational leadership is the most synergistic due to its emphasis on student empowerment, ethical practices, and the establishment of meaningful relationships.

Ethical leadership is another domain that provides nuanced perspectives on organizational ethics, broadly encapsulated under virtue, consequentialist, and deontological ethics (Ogaga et al., 2023). Virtue ethics focuses on character development and moral virtues such as honesty and fairness. Consequentialist ethics weighs the outcomes of actions in ethical decision-making (O'Keefe et al., 2019). On the other hand, deontological ethics focuses on ethical duties and principles, irrespective of the outcomes

(Schuessler, 2020). For agricultural education, virtue ethics is the most apt as it underlines the importance of instilling virtues and ethical behavior, which are indispensable in the agricultural sector.

Applying structured models like student growth and transformation models is indispensable in pursuing academic excellence and equity. Utilizing specialized theories like Perry's cognitive-structural approach and human existential theories can substantially enrich agricultural education (Huang et al., 2021). Finally, understanding varied leadership and ethical frameworks can help agricultural educators craft a more empathetic, responsible, and effective educational environment (Huang et al., 2021).

methodologies, and fostering educational alliances can be pivotal in creating transformational leaders in agriculture. By establishing these interconnections, the aim is to appreciate better how ethical and responsible leadership can contribute to the agricultural sector's long-term stability and ethical grounding.

METHODOLOGY

The Fostering Diversity through Urban Agriculture (FDUA) initiative aims to revolutionize agricultural education by focusing on a multi-pronged approach (Jay, 2023). This educational program addresses systemic food security issues, poverty alleviation, urban innovation, and employment opportunities by developing human and institutional capacities (Jay, 2023). The program is designed to mainly target educational and training components concerning the youth, varied genders, and workforce evolution at secondary educational levels.

One of the program's defining features is its insistence on high academic standards. It integrates a robust academic framework with real-world applications and involves various stakeholders (Jay, 2023). The curriculum is designed to be comprehensive and includes book knowledge and service-based learning opportunities actively supervised by the program. It employs highly qualified teaching professionals and focuses on forging partnerships with community organizations and stakeholders (Jay, 2023). The educational environment will be parallel to a program within a school, often orchestrated by a team-oriented approach.

In a review by Guarino and Yoder 2015, innovative Career Technology Education (CTE) programs have made significant strides by incorporating elements of real-world career planning into their curriculums. FDUA aims to adopt and adapt critical characteristics from such advanced agricultural education models, ensuring their replication by agricultural educators, state education professionals, and other vital stakeholders (Jay, 2023).

The FDUA initiative is not just another education program but an innovative pedagogical approach that involves hands-on activities, harnesses the energy of passionate educators, and adapts to industry trends (Jay, 2023). It aims to offer a multifaceted learning experience that includes a rigorous curriculum tailored to address current and future developments.

The Fostering Diversity through Urban Agriculture (FDUA) initiative aims to revolutionize agricultural education by focusing on a multi-pronged approach (Jay, 2023). This educational program addresses systemic food security issues, poverty alleviation, urban innovation, and employment opportunities by developing human and institutional capacities. The program is designed to mainly target educational and training components concerning the youth, varied genders, and workforce evolution at secondary educational levels.

The FDUA initiative is an innovative pedagogical approach that involves hands-on activities, harnesses the energy of passionate educators, and adapts to industry trends. It offers the idea of a multifaceted learning experience that includes a rigorous curriculum tailored to address current and future developments. According to Rateau et al. (2015), it is important the program incorporates traditional and modern teaching methods to give students essential skills and knowledge.

The underlying objective of FDUA is to augment the level of agricultural awareness and leadership skills among urban residents. The program aspires to delve into the constraints and deterrents contributing to the dwindling interest in agriculture, specifically in urban settings. The educational framework of FDUA is backed by a unique amalgamation of ethical and transformational leadership theories, collectively termed the ETL Framework (Jay, 2023).

The FDUA program instills values like responsibility, compassion, honesty, and environmental stewardship. These virtues are not merely idealistic attributes but actionable qualities that can significantly influence behavior in agricultural practices. Instilling these virtues in participants can help establish ethical relationships with human and natural systems.

Moreover, the program employs transformational leadership theory to motivate individuals to realize their full potential. The program aims to encourage its participants to advance not just in skills and knowledge but also in the ethical dimensions of agriculture, nurturing them to become transformational leaders in their communities.

Combining ethical virtues and transformational leadership creates a robust pedagogical framework. This framework aims to generate two outcomes: instilling a solid ethical foundation and fostering empowerment that enables participants to become change-makers in the agricultural industry.

FDUA also has future growth strategies. It will start as an independent agricultural education program at different locations, offering workshops for students. The program plans to eventually secure a dedicated facility for expanded activities, such as field trips and special agricultural events, once its efficacy in participant engagement and fundraising has been proven.

FDUA is an educational program and a holistic agricultural learning ecosystem. It aims to provide a multidimensional education that captures academic rigor, ethical values, preparing its participants to become skilled, ethical, and transformative leaders in urban agriculture.

The research associated with the agricultural education program is of vital importance for several reasons. It aims to elevate agricultural literacy and foster the next generation of leaders in agriculture, thereby addressing critical global issues like food poverty and sectoral innovation. The program seeks to broaden agricultural knowledge and cultivate skills at a grassroots level by targeting secondary school students, including those in urban environments. Furthermore, its emphasis on encouraging continued higher education in agriculture is expected to enrich the agricultural sector with a talented and competent workforce. The program's innovative approach to curriculum development also positions it as a potential model for replication by other educational institutions and organizations, further amplifying its impact.

The Fostering Diversity through Urban Agriculture (FDUA) program is a robust educational initiative underpinned by the Ethical Transformational Leadership (ETL) Framework, which promotes diversity, equity, and transformational leadership in the agricultural sector. This framework provides a thorough lens to understand how transformational and ethical leadership direct agriculture toward sustainability. It concentrates on three pillars: Educate, Produce, and Increase Participation, forming an integrative approach to drive impactful change.

FINDINGS

Based on a comprehensive review of current literature on urban agriculture programs, it becomes evident that there is a critical need for enhanced agricultural literacy and leadership within urban communities (Sorensen et al., 2021). While current programs have achieved progress in resolving certain issues, there remains room for improvement in key areas, specifically in the cultivation of transformational leadership and the advancement of agricultural literacy (Wadumestrige Dona et al., 2021). Traditional programs often employ top-down hierarchical models that may not resonate with diverse urban populations and do not adequately prepare individuals to tackle the multifaceted issues unique to urban agriculture, such as food security, sustainable land use, and community engagement (Wadumestrige Dona et al., 2021).

Existing literature highlights the need for enhanced agricultural literacy and leadership within urban communities DeMarsh (2022). Many agriculture programs primarily focus on technical skills and knowledge, neglecting the importance of social capital, such as networks, relationships, and trust, within the community (Nazuri & Ahmad, 2019). These programs may not be sufficiently active in responding to shifting demographics, legislative limitations, and fluctuating commodity markets specific to urban settings (Rickard et al., 2017). Additionally, the lack of a comprehensive framework for instructional objectives makes it challenging to measure the efficacy of these programs and adapt to evolving community needs (Dobbins et al., 2021).

Given these gaps, the agriculture program, Fostering Diversity through Urban Agriculture (FDUA) was created to address these shortcomings specifically. FDUA adopts a transformational leadership approach, which is inherently more inclusive, participatory, and well-suited for the complexities of urban agriculture. Transformational leadership goes beyond transactional interactions to inspire and motivate, aiming to create a paradigm shift in how community members view their roles in the urban agricultural landscape (Eisenbeiss et al., 2008). It encourages shared leadership, where community members are not just passive recipients of knowledge but active participants in shaping their food systems (Eisenbeiss et al., 2008). This approach fosters innovation and substantive change (Rada, 1999).

Enhancing Participation Through Equity and Diversity

FDUA aims to bring down the barriers that prevent diverse participation in agriculture, working to create an inclusive environment (Lamm et al., 2021). The program engages individuals from various backgrounds to contribute effectively to the agricultural sector. By prioritizing diversity and equity, FDUA aims to cultivate a sense of collective responsibility and ownership (Lamm et al., 2021).

Addressing the Role of Diversity

The diversity aspect of the framework has a multiplicative effect on innovation and problem-solving. It contributes not just by adding various perspectives but also by synergistically enhancing the community's collective intelligence. However, barriers like lack of representation and limited resources often hinder this diversity (Mertens, 2014).

Moreover, FDUA places a heavy emphasis on agricultural literacy. The program is designed to make urban communities self-sufficient by teaching them how to grow food and understand the economic, social, and environmental impacts of agriculture. Agricultural literacy is crucial for informed decision-making and advocating for supportive policies (Ryu et al., 2021). Agricultural literacy refers to the basic knowledge and understanding of agriculture that promotes sensible consumption activities and informed judgments on national policies (Ryu et al., 2021). It involves synthesizing, analyzing, and exchanging information on agriculture to make informed choices (Ryu et al., 2021).

FDUA offers a holistic approach to urban agriculture education by combining transformational leadership with agricultural literacy. This synergy enables the program to be more adaptive to urban agriculture's unique challenges and opportunities, from ensuring food security to optimizing limited space for cultivation and integrating sustainable practices to fostering community well-being. FDUA also considers a detailed framework of instructional objectives focusing on critical thinking, public awareness, leadership development, and global cognizance (Jay, 2023). These guidelines are the program's backbone, ensuring a targeted approach to community needs and sustainable agricultural practices.

FDUA fills a vital gap in the current landscape of urban agriculture programs. Its focus on transformational leadership and agricultural literacy not only addresses the limitations of existing programs but also offers a robust, community-centered approach to making urban agriculture more sustainable, inclusive, and impactful. Through FDUA, urban communities can build a more sustainable, self-sufficient, and socially responsible future.

DISCUSSION

Leadership Assessments

The essence of leadership development lies in fortifying leadership capabilities as a proactive approach to navigating unforeseen challenges (Stefan & Nazarov, 2020). Such cultivation equips leaders with the creative agility to fulfill their roles, utilizing the critical skills and knowledge they gain (Dirani et al., 2020). Especially in agriculture, where professionals grapple with many obstacles ranging from volatile commodity markets to natural resource depletion, grassroots leadership becomes indispensable for sustainability (Stefan & Nazarov, 2020).

Transformational leadership goes beyond transactional interactions to inspire and motivate, aiming to create a paradigm shift in how community members view their roles in the urban agricultural landscape (Rasmussen et al., 2017). It encourages shared leadership, where community members are not just passive recipients of knowledge but active participants in shaping their food systems (Rasmussen et al., 2017). Agricultural leadership programs have emerged across states, signaling a positive trajectory in recognizing the importance of social capital and leadership skills in rural and agricultural settings (Rasmussen et al., 2017).

In the urban agriculture context, transformational leadership takes on a unique role. It transcends traditional top-down hierarchical models, advocating for shared leadership and collaboration (Byrd, 2022). This inclusive approach helps tackle urban agriculture's unique and complex challenges, from food security to sustainable land use.

Historically, agricultural leadership development has a storied legacy, with milestones like the Kellogg Farmers Study Program shaping its evolution (Fuentelsaz et al., 2023). Such programs have pivoted towards participatory models, partly inspired by the Kellogg Foundation's leadership initiatives (Savage et al., 2019).

Effective agricultural programs underscore the need for well-defined instructional objectives. These serve as beacons guiding the program's design, delivery, and evaluation. They focus on facets such as critical thinking, public awareness, leadership skill development, and global cognizance, which contribute to community resilience and sustainable agricultural practices (Traver-Marti et al., 2023).

In terms of transformation, agricultural leadership programs aim to effect change on individual, organizational, and community levels. Individual growth relates to the personal mastery of new skills and self-examination of values. Organizational change might involve the reshaping of policies and operations. Meanwhile, community and social transformation encompasses adaptations in societal segments to address environmental demands.

Researchers have identified several common objectives for agricultural leadership programs. These objectives include developing critical evaluation skills, gaining a comprehensive understanding of public concerns across economic, social, and political dimensions, cultivating decisive leadership abilities, and fostering a heightened awareness of global and local issues (Kaufman et al., 2010; Morgan et al.,2013; Velez et al., 2014).

Multiple programs adopt frameworks like the Kellogg Farmers Study Program (KFSP), though with variations that merit further assessment before implementation (Erro-Garcés & Alfaro-Tanco, 2020). Understanding the educational needs of learners is critical for crafting effective interventions. Cervero and Wilson (2006) argue that these needs represent the gap between a learner's capabilities and the intended outcomes. By leveraging empirical data to authenticate the theory-practice gap in education, educators can adapt their methodologies to bridge it effectively, creating a foundation for evidence-based education (Sanzo et al., 2011). Research designs that help bridge the gap between theory and practice are needed to ensure that teaching and leadership theories are utilized with greater fidelity (Sanzo et al., 2011).

As urban agriculture becomes increasingly vital in today's fast-paced, resource-strained world, the role of transformational leadership cannot be overstated (Rahmadani & Schaufeli, 2022). Transformational leadership is essential for developing innovative urban farming technologies and addressing the socioeconomic dimensions of food security (Rahmadani & Schaufeli, 2022). Its principles of collective action, ethical governance, and inclusive participation make it uniquely suited for guiding the future of agriculture in a sustainable and socially responsible direction (Rahmadani & Schaufeli, 2022).

CONCLUSION

As urban agriculture becomes increasingly vital in today's fast-paced, resource-strained world, the role of transformational leadership cannot be overstated (Schyns et al., 2022). Transformational leaders have the power to lead us toward a better, innovative, and sustainable future (Schyns et al., 2022). They are not just adapting to change; they are making change happen, turning challenges into stepping stones for growth and innovation (Schyns et al., 2022).

Transformational leadership in urban agriculture is not merely an accessory but an imperative (Huang et al., 2021). It provides a multidimensional roadmap for navigating the intricacies of economic viability, social justice, and ecological balance (Huang et al., 2021). A leadership approach grounded in ethical principles and an empowering ethos is a cornerstone for redefining success in this sector (Huang et al., 2021). Instead of purely focusing on quantitative benchmarks like yield or revenue, transformational leadership evaluates success holistically, encompassing social equity, environmental stewardship, and community well-being (Huang et al., 2021).

Beyond the immediate goals of food production and profitability, transformational leadership in urban agriculture seeks to influence broader spheres. It actively seeks to build community, enhance public trust, and encourage sustainable consumer behavior (Dimitri & Effland, 2020; Kountios et al., 2023). With proactive community education and data-backed decision-making, the gap between urban lifestyles and agricultural literacy is narrowing, thereby boosting the sector's resilience and reach (Musa & Basir, 2021; Wells & Stock, 2020).

The long-term vision driven by transformational leadership in urban agriculture is one of sustainable, equitable growth and profound humaneness (Haris et al., 2022). As FDUA unveils its goals, it stands as a paragon, reshaping our shared understanding of agriculture as a human and humane enterprise (Haris et al., 2022).

The imperative of transformational leadership in urban agriculture is unambiguous: it catalyzes broad-based, sustainable change. It moves beyond transactional parameters to foster a more meaningful relationship between urban dwellers and their environment. The ripple effects of such leadership are far-reaching, affecting economic paradigms, social contracts, and ecological footprints. As urban landscapes expand and challenges proliferate, transformational leadership is our most robust response, guiding urban agriculture toward a feasible, thriving, and just future.

REFERENCES

Abramo, J. M., & Reynolds, A. (2015). "Pedagogical creativity" as a framework for music teacher education. *Journal of Music Teacher Education*, *25*(1), 37–51.

Agbaje, K. A. A., Martin, R. A., & Williams, D. L. (2001). Impact of sustainable agriculture on secondary school agricultural education teachers and programs in the north central region. *Journal of Agricultural Education*, *42*(2), 38–45.

Ahmadnia, S., Christien, A. M., Spencer, P., Hart, T., & De Araujo Barbosa, C. C. (2022). *Defueling Conflict*. Academic Press.

Akins, D. (2022). *Food Sovereignty and Coffee Cultivation in EL Salvador: Current Pitfalls and Opportunities in the Intersections of Coffee*. Gender, and Climate Change.

Alemu, F. M. (2023). *Ramifications of Sectors Economic Upsurge on rate of early aged Unemployment in case of East African Countries*. Academic Press.

Altieri, M., & Nicholls, C. (2018). *Biodiversity and pest management in agroecosystems*. CRC press. doi:10.1201/9781482277937

Altrichter, H. (2020). The concept of quality in action research: Giving practitioners a voice in educational research. In *Qualitative voices in educational research* (pp. 40-55). Routledge.

Ansari, T., & Usmani, A. (2018). Students' perception towards feedback in clinical sciences in an outcome-based integrated curriculum. *Pakistan Journal of Medical Sciences*, *34*(3), 702.

Avolio, B. J., & Yammarino, F. J. (Eds.). (2013). *Transformational and charismatic leadership: The road ahead*. Emerald Group Publishing. doi:10.1108/S1479-357120135

Bandura, A. (1986). Social foundations of thought and action. Academic Press.

Basoro, T. S., & Tefera, B. (2021). Ethical leadership practices and factors affecting it in South Addis Ababa district commercial bank of Ethiopia. *European Journal of Business and Management, 13*(1), 1–11.

Bass, B. M., & Avolio, B. J. (1996). Multifactor leadership questionnaire. *Western Journal of Nursing Research*.

Bass, B. M., & Avolio, B. J. (2004). *Multifactor Leadership Questionnaire: MLQ; manual and sampler set*. Mind Garden.

Bass, B. M., & Bass Bernard, M. (1985). *Leadership and performance beyond expectations*. Academic Press.

Berkovich, I. (2016). School leaders and transformational leadership theory: Time to part ways? *Journal of Educational Administration, 54*(5), 609–622. doi:10.1108/JEA-11-2015-0100

Bisht, I. S., Rana, J. C., & Pal Ahlawat, S. (2020). The future of smallholder farming in India: Some sustainability considerations. *Sustainability (Basel), 12*(9), 3751. doi:10.3390u12093751

Blanco-Canqui, H., Shaver, T. M., Lindquist, J. L., Shapiro, C. A., Elmore, R. W., Francis, C. A., & Hergert, G. W. (2015). Cover Crops and Ecosystem Services: Insights from Studies in Temperate Soils. *Agronomy Journal, 107*(6), 2449–2474. doi:10.2134/agronj15.0086

Bradford, T. Jr, Hock, G., Greenhaw, L., & Kingery, W. L. (2019). Comparing Experiential Learning Techniques and Direct Instruction on Student Knowledge of Agriculture in Private School Students. *Journal of Agricultural Education, 60*(3), 80–96.

Brostow, D. P., Gunzburger, E., Abbate, L. M., Brenner, L. A., & Thomas, K. S. (2019). Mental illness, not obesity status, is associated with food insecurity among the elderly in the health and retirement study. *Journal of Nutrition in Gerontology and Geriatrics, 38*(2), 149–172.

Brown, N. R., & Kelsey, K. D. (2013). Sidewalks and City Streets: A Model for Vibrant Agricultural Education in Urban American Communities. *Journal of Agricultural Education, 54*(2), 57–69.

Busch, G., Bayer, E., Spiller, A., & Kühl, S. (2022). 'Factory farming'? Public perceptions of farm sizes and sustainability in animal farming. *PLOS Sustainability and Transformation, 1*(10), e0000032. doi:10.1371/journal.pstr.0000032

Buys, D. R., & Rennekamp, R. (2020). Cooperative extension as a force for healthy, rural communities: Historical perspectives and future directions. *American Journal of Public Health, 110*(9), 1300–1303. doi:10.2105/AJPH.2020.305767 PMID:32673106

Buzby, J. C., Farah-Wells, H., & Hyman, J. (2014). The estimated amount, value, and calories of post-harvest food losses at the retail and consumer levels in the United States. *USDA-ERS Economic Information Bulletin*, (121).

Byrd, M. Y. (2022). Inclusive Leadership: Critical Practice Perspectives From the Field. *Advances in Developing Human Resources, 24*(4), 223–224. doi:10.1177/15234223221120180

Cervero, R. M., & Wilson, A. L. (2006). *Working the planning table: Negotiating democratically for adult, continuing and workplace education*. Jossey-Bass.

Chattopadhyay, S., Prasad, I., Henley, A. Z., Sarma, A., & Barik, T. (2020, April). What's wrong with computational notebooks? Pain points, needs, and design opportunities. In *Proceedings of the 2020 CHI conference on human factors in computing systems* (pp. 1-12). 10.1145/3313831.3376729

Chenarides, L., Grebitus, C., Lusk, J. L., & Printezis, I. (2021). Who practices urban agriculture? An empirical analysis of participation before and during the COVID-19 pandemic. *Agribusiness*, *37*(1), 142–159. doi:10.1002/agr.21675 PMID:33362336

Chumbley, S. B. (2016). The impact of a career and technology education program. *SAGE Open*, *6*(4), 2158244016678036.

Clemons, C., Lindner, J. R., Murray, B., Cook, M. P., Sams, B., & Williams, G. (2018). Spanning the Gap: The Confluence of Agricultural Literacy and Being Agriculturally Literate. *Journal of Agricultural Education*, *59*(4), 238–252. doi:10.5032/jae.2018.04238

Cletzer, D. A., Mott, R. L., Simonsen, J. C., Tummons, J. D., Peckman, J. Y., & Preston, K. (2022). Agricultural leadership: A national portrait of undergraduate courses. *Journal of Agricultural Education*, *63*(1), 165–181.

Coleman-Jensen, A., Rabbitt, M. P., Gregory, C. A., & Singh, A. (2022). Household food security in the United States. *Economic Research Report, 155*.

Cosby, A., Manning, J., Power, D., & Harreveld, B. (2022). New decade, same concerns: A systematic review of agricultural literacy of school students. *Education Sciences*, *12*(4), 235. doi:10.3390/educsci12040235

Costa-Font, M., & Gil, J. M., & Traill, W. B. (2008). Consumer acceptance, valuation of Dalgaard, T., Hutchings, N. J., & Porter, J. R. (2003). Agroecology, scaling and interdisciplinarity. *Agriculture, Ecosystems & Environment*, *100*(1), 39–51.

Daniel, G. R. (2020). Safe spaces for enabling the creative process in Danso, A., Adomako, S., Amankwah-Amoah, J., Owusu-Agyei, S., & Konadu, R. (2019). Environmental sustainability orientation, competitive strategy and financial performance. *Business Strategy and the Environment*, *28*(5), 885–895.

Day, D. V., & Dragoni, L. (2015). Leadership development: An outcome-oriented review based on time and levels of analyses. *Annual Review of Organizational Psychology and Organizational Behavior*, *2*(1), 133–156. doi:10.1146/annurev-orgpsych-032414-111328

Day, J., Chin, N., Sydnor, S., Widhalm, M., Shah, K. U., & Dorworth, L. (2021). Implications of climate change for tourism and outdoor recreation: An Indiana, USA, case study. *Climatic Change*, *169*(3-4), 1–21. doi:10.100710584-021-03284-w PMID:34924649

De Paula Vieira, A., & Anthony, R. (2020). Recalibrating veterinary medicine through animal welfare science and ethics for the 2020s. *Animals (Basel)*, *10*(4), 654. doi:10.3390/ani10040654 PMID:32283812

DeMarsh, N. (2022). Redefining the role of young farmers: Participatory action youth-led urban agriculture. *The International Journal of Sociology and Social Policy*, *42*(7/8), 727–742.

Deng, R., He, X., Liu, Y., Fu, Y., & Hu, X. (2020, January). Analysis on the Application Strategy of "4V" Marketing Mix Theory: Based on the Perspective of the Perceived Value of Agricultural Products Consumer. In *5th International Conference on Economics, Management, Law and Education (EMLE 2019)* (pp. 501-504). Atlantis Press.

Dimitri, C., & Effland, A. (2020). From farming to food systems: The evolution of US agricultural production and policy into the 21st century. *Renewable Agriculture and Food Systems*, *35*(4), 391–406. doi:10.1017/S1742170518000522

Dirani, K. M., Abadi, M., Alizadeh, A., Barhate, B., Garza, R. C., Gunasekara, N., Ibrahim, G., & Majzun, Z. (2020). Leadership competencies and the essential role of human resource development in times of crisis: A response to Covid-19 pandemic. *Human Resource Development International*, *23*(4), 380–394. doi:10.1080/13678868.2020.1780078

Ditlevsen, K., Denver, S., Christensen, T., & Lassen, J. (2020). A taste for locally produced food-Values, opinions and sociodemographic differences among 'organic' and 'conventional' consumers. *Appetite*, *147*, 104544. doi:10.1016/j.appet.2019.104544 PMID:31786190

Dobbins, C. E., Edgar, D. W., Cox, C. K., Edgar, L. D., Graham, D. L., & Perez, A. G. P. (2021). Perceptions of Arkansas agriculture county extension agents toward urban agriculture. *Journal of Agricultural Education*, *62*(1), 77–94.

Eastwood, C., Klerkx, L., Ayre, M., & Dela Rue, B. (2019). Managing socio-ethical challenges in the development of smart farming: From a fragmented to a comprehensive approach for responsible research and innovation. *Journal of Agricultural & Environmental Ethics*, *32*(5-6), 741–768. doi:10.100710806-017-9704-5

Eisenbeiss, S. A., Van Knippenberg, D., & Boerner, S. (2008). Transformational leadership and team innovation: Integrating team climate principles. *The Journal of Applied Psychology*, *93*(6), 1438.

Eliasson, K., Wiréhn, L., Neset, T. S., & Linnér, B. O. (2022). Transformations towards sustainable food systems: Contrasting Swedish practitioner perspectives with the European Commission's Farm to Fork Strategy. *Sustainability Science*, *17*(6), 2411–2425. doi:10.100711625-022-01174-3

Elizabeth, R., Margaretha, G. I. E., Ivan, G. S., & Tukiran, M. (2023). The Influence Of Transformational Leadership: Accelerating Farmer Group Empowerment To Realize Export-Oriented Agrıbusıness. *Asian Journal of Management. Entrepreneurship and Social Science*, *3*(01), 413–427.

Erro-Garcés, A., & Alfaro-Tanco, J. A. (2020). Action research as a meta-methodology in the management field. *International Journal of Qualitative Methods*, *19*. doi:10.1177/1609406920917489

Esobi, I. C., Lasode, M. K., Anyanwu, C. I., Barriguete, M. F., Okorie, M. A., & Lasode, D. O. (2021). Food insecurity, social vulnerability, and the impact of COVID-19 on population dependent on public assistance/SNAP: A case study of South Carolina, USA. *Journal of Food Security*, *9*(1), 8–18.

Esters, L. T., & Bowen, B. E. (2004). Factors influencing enrollment in an urban agricultural education program. *Journal of Career and Technical Education*, *21*(1), 25-37.

Fagbemi, F., Oke, D. F., & Fajingbesi, A. (2023). Climate-resilient development: An approach to sustainable food production in sub-Saharan Africa. *Future Foods*, *7*, 100216. doi:10.1016/j.fufo.2023.100216

Farmers, U. S., & Alliance, R. (2011). *Nationwide surveys reveal disconnect between Americans and their food*. PR Newswire.

Foley, J. A., Ramankutty, N., Brauman, K. A., Cassidy, E. S., Gerber, J. S., Johnston, M., Mueller, N. D., O'Connell, C., Ray, D. K., West, P. C., Balzer, C., & Zaks, D. P. (2011). Solutions for a cultivated planet. *Nature*, *478*(7369), 337–342. doi:10.1038/nature10452 PMID:21993620

Foster, W., Sweet, L., & McNeill, L. (2020). Linking Out Loud (LOL): Developing critical thinking. *MedEdPublish*, *9*(42), 42.

Friesner, J., Colón-Carmona, A., Schnoes, A. M., Stepanova, A., Mason, G. A., Macintosh, G. C., Ullah, H., Baxter, I., Callis, J., Sierra-Cajas, K., Elliott, K., Haswell, E. S., Zavala, M. E., Wildermuth, M., Williams, M., Ayalew, M., Henkhaus, N., Prunet, N., Lemaux, P. G., ... Dinneny, J. R. (2021). Broadening the impact of plant science through innovative, integrative, and inclusive outreach. *Plant Direct*, *5*(4), e00316. doi:10.1002/pld3.316 PMID:33870032

Fuentelsaz, L., González, C., & Mickiewicz, T. (2023). Entrepreneurial growth aspirations at re-entry after failure. *International Journal of Entrepreneurial Behaviour & Research*, *29*(2), 297–327. doi:10.1108/IJEBR-05-2022-0433

Fuglie, K., Heisey, P., King, J. L., Day-Rubenstein, K., Schimmelpfennig, D., Wang, S. L., Pray, C.E., & Karmarkar-Deshmukh, R., (2011). Research investments and market structure in the food processing, agricultural input, and biofuel industries worldwide. *USDA-ERS Economic Research Report*, (130).

Gabriel, A., & Gandorfer, M. (2021). Have City Dwellers Lost Touch with Modern Agriculture? In Quest of Differences between Urban and Rural Population. *Engineering Proceedings*, *9*(1), 25.

Garton, B. L. (2019). Trends and Challenges Facing Higher Education: Implications for Agricultural Education. *Journal of Agricultural Education*, *60*(1), 1–13. doi:10.5032/jae.2019.01001

Gerber, P. J., Henderson, B., & Makkar, H. P. (2013). Mitigation of greenhouse gas emissions in livestock production: a review of technical options for non-CO2 emissions (No. 177). Food and Agriculture Organization of the United Nations (FAO).

Gomiero, T., Pimentel, D., & Paoletti, M. G. (2011). Environmental impact of different agricultural management practices: Conventional vs. organic agriculture. *Critical Reviews in Plant Sciences*, *30*(1-2), 95–124. doi:10.1080/07352689.2011.554355

Grebitus, C., Chenarides, L., Muenich, R., & Mahalov, A. (2020). Consumers' perception of urban farming—An exploratory study. *Frontiers in Sustainable Food Systems*, *4*, 79. doi:10.3389/fsufs.2020.00079

Grebitus, C., Printezis, I., & Printezis, A. (2017). Relationship between consumer behavior and success of urban agriculture. *Ecological Economics*, *136*, 189–200. doi:10.1016/j.ecolecon.2017.02.010

Gubanova, A., Mineva, O., & Gadzhieva, E. (2021). Transformation of the Scientific Paradigm of Leadership Under the Influence of Digital Reality. In *SHS Web of Conferences* (Vol. 110, p. 04008). EDP Sciences.

Gururani, K., Sood, S., Kumar, A., Joshi, D. C., Pandey, D., & Sharma, A. R. (2021). Mainstreaming Barahnaja cultivation for food and nutritional security in the Himalayan region. *Biodiversity and Conservation*, *30*(3), 551–574. doi:10.100710531-021-02123-9 PMID:33526962

Guthman, J. (2008). Neoliberalism and the making of food politics in California. *Geoforum*, *39*(3), 1171–1183. doi:10.1016/j.geoforum.2006.09.002

Haris, N. B. M., Yunus, N. A., & Shah, J. A. (2022). *Community Readiness of Urban Farming Practices in Malaysia*. Academic Press.

Harrison, K. (2013). Building resilient communities. *M/C Journal*, *16*(5), 1-8.

Hartmann, K., & Martin, M. J. (2021). A critical pedagogy of agriculture. *Journal of Agricultural Education*, *62*(3), 51–71. doi:10.5032/jae.2021.03051

Hatfield, J. L., & Prueger, J. H. (2015). Temperature extremes: Effect on plant growth and development. *Weather and Climate Extremes*, *10*, 4–10. doi:10.1016/j.wace.2015.08.001

He, C., Liu, Z., Wu, J., Pan, X., Fang, Z., Li, J., & Bryan, B. A. (2021). Future global urban water scarcity and potential solutions. *Nature Communications*, *12*(1), 4667. doi:10.103841467-021-25026-3 PMID:34344898

Hejkrlik, J., Chaloupkova, P., & Sokolska, T. (2023). The role of transformational leadership and leaders' skills for new agricultural cooperatives in post-soviet countries. *Annals of Public and Cooperative Economics*, *94*(1), 109–129.

Hess, A. J., & Trexler, C. J. (2011). A Qualitative Study of Agricultural Literacy in Urban Youth: Understanding for Democratic Participation in Renewing the Agri-Food System. *Journal of Agricultural Education*, *52*(2), 151–162.

Hollaus, A., Schunko, C., Weisshaidinger, R., Bala, P., & Vogl, C. R. (2022). Indigenous farmers' perceptions of problems in the rice field agroecosystems in the upper Baram, Malaysia. *Journal of Ethnobiology and Ethnomedicine*, *18*(1), 26. doi:10.118613002-022-00511-1 PMID:35351170

Huang, S. Y., Li, M. W., & Lee, Y. S. (2021). Why do medium-sized technology farms adopt environmental innovation? The mediating role of pro-environmental behaviors. *Horticulturae*, *7*(9), 318. doi:10.3390/horticulturae7090318

Ince, F. (2023). Transformational Leadership in a Diverse and Inclusive Organizational Culture. Handbook of Research on Promoting an Inclusive Organizational Culture for Entrepreneurial Sustainability, 188-201.

Jansen, M., Guariguata, M. R., Raneri, J. E., Ickowitz, A., Chiriboga-Arroyo, F., Quaedvlieg, J., & Kettle, C. J. (2020). Food for thought: The underutilized potential of tropical tree-sourced foods for 21st century sustainable food systems. *People and Nature*, *2*(4), 1006–1020. doi:10.1002/pan3.10159

Jankelová, N., Joniaková, Z., Némethová, I., & Blštáková, J. (2020). How to support the effect of transformational leadership on performance in agricultural enterprises. *Sustainability*, *12*(18), 7510.

Jaramillo, P. L., Alpizar, A. B., Forno, C. M., & Landaverde, R. Q. (2021). Agricultural education and migration: A comparison of rural youth in El Salvador and Honduras. *Advancements in Agricultural Development*, *2*(1), 70–82.

Jay, A. (2023). *Planting the Seed: Reframing Agriculture Education and Leadership to Cultivate Diversity, Agriculture Literacy, and Sustainable Food Security* [Doctoral dissertation, St. Thomas University]. Proquest Dissertations and Theses Global.

Kaiyatsa, S., Ricker-Gilbert, J., & Jumbe, C. (2019). What does Malawi's fertiliser programme do to private sector fertiliser sales? A quasi-experimental field study. *Journal of Agricultural Economics*, *70*(2), 332–352. doi:10.1111/1477-9552.12286

Karanth, S., Benefo, E. O., Patra, D., & Pradhan, A. K. (2022). Importance of artificial intelligence in evaluating climate change and food safety risk. *Journal of Agriculture and Food Research*, 100485.

Kaufman, E. K. (2010). *Leadership program planning: Assessing the needs and interests of the agricultural community*. Academic Press.

Kepa, M., Pittman, B., Williams, M., & Bruce-Iri, P. (2021). *Whakaora ngā Whenua Whāma: Utilising mātauranga Māori and Western science to protect and restore the soil on rural farms in Te Tai Tokerau*. Academic Press.

Khan, M. A. S., Jianguo, D., Ali, M., Saleem, S., & Usman, M. (2019). Interrelations between ethical leadership, green psychological climate, and organizational environmental citizenship behavior: A moderated mediation model. *Frontiers in Psychology*, *10*, 1977. doi:10.3389/fpsyg.2019.01977 PMID:31555173

Kidido, J. K., Bugri, J. T., & Kasanga, R. K. (2017). Youth agricultural land access dimensions and emerging challenges under the customary tenure system in Ghana: Evidence from Techiman Area. *Journal of Land and Rural Studies*, *5*(2), 140–163.

Kitch, S., McGregor, J., Mejía, G. M., El-Sayed, S., Spackman, C., & Vitullo, J. (2021). Gendered and Racial Injustices in American Food Systems and Cultures. *Humanities (Washington)*, *10*(2), 66.

Kountios, G., Konstantinidis, C., & Antoniadis, I. (2023). Can the Adoption of ICT and Advisory Services Be Considered as a Tool of Competitive Advantage in Agricultural Holdings? A Literature Review. *Agronomy (Basel)*, *13*(2), 530. doi:10.3390/agronomy13020530

Kovar, K. A., & Ball, A. L. (2013). Two decades of agricultural literacy research: A synthesis of the literature. *Journal of Agricultural Education*, *54*(1), 167–178.

Krill, T. L. (1993). *An exploration of the leadership practice" enabling others to act": a case study*. Iowa State University.

Lameck, W. U. (2022). The influence of ethical leadership in the delivery of agricultural advisory services in Tanzania local government authorities. *Public Administration and Policy*, *25*(1), 78–88. doi:10.1108/PAP-05-2021-0031

Lamm, K. W., Holder, M., Randall, N. L., Edgar, D. W., & Lamm, A. J. (2021). Agricultural leadership development program participant personality and demographic characteristics: An empirical analysis. *SAGE Open*, *11*(4), 21582440211061577. doi:10.1177/21582440211061577

Le Glaz, A., Haralambous, Y., Kim-Dufor, D. H., Lenca, P., Billot, R., Ryan, T. C., Marsh, J., DeVylder, J., Walter, M., Berrouiguet, S., & Lemey, C. (2021). Machine learning and natural language processing in mental health: Systematic review. *Journal of Medical Internet Research, 23*(5), e15708. doi:10.2196/15708 PMID:33944788

Li, L., & Liu, Y. (2022). An integrated model of principal transformational leadership and teacher leadership that is related to teacher self-efficacy and student academic performance. *Asia Pacific Journal of Education, 42*(4), 661–678.

Li, Q., Huang, J., Luo, R., & Liu, C. (2013). China's labor transition and the future of China's rural wages and employment. *China & World Economy, 21*(3), 4–24. doi:10.1111/j.1749-124X.2013.12019.x

Liang, Q., Ma, K., & Liu, W. (2023). The role of farmer cooperatives in promoting environmentally sustainable agricultural development in China: A review. *Annals of Public and Cooperative Economics*.

Lucatello, S., & Sánchez, R. (2022). Climate Change in North America: Risks, Impacts, and Adaptation. A Reflection Based on the IPCC Report AR6–2022. *Revista Mexicana de Economía y Finanzas Nueva Época REMEF, 17*(4), 794.

Mancini, M. C., Arfini, F., Antonioli, F., & Guareschi, M. (2021). Alternative agri-food systems under a market agencements approach: The case of multifunctional farming activity in a peri-urban area. *Environments (Basel, Switzerland), 8*(7), 61. doi:10.3390/environments8070061

Manuaba, I. B. A. P., No, Y., & Wu, C. C. (2022). The effectiveness of problem based learning in improving critical thinking, problem-solving and self-directed learning in first-year medical students: A meta-analysis. *PLoS One, 17*(11), e0277339.

Mendy, V. L., Vargas, R., Cannon-Smith, G., Payton, M., Enkhmaa, B., & Zhang, L. (2018). Food insecurity and cardiovascular disease risk factors among Mississippi adults. *International Journal of Environmental Research and Public Health, 15*(9), 2016.

Mertens, M. M. (2014). *Implications of Local and Regional Food Systems: Toward a New Food Economy in Portland, Oregon* [Doctoral dissertation]. Portland State University.

Mhazo, T., & Thebe, V. (2021). 'Hustling Out of Unemployment': Livelihood Responses of Unemployed Young Graduates in the City of Bulawayo, Zimbabwe. *Journal of Asian and African Studies, 56*(3), 628–642.

Miller, B. A. (2011). Marketing and branding the agronomy major at Iowa State University. *Journal of Natural Resources and Life Sciences Education, 40*(1), 1–9.

Morgan, A. C., King, D. L., Rudd, R. D., & Kaufman, E. K. (2013). *Elements of an undergraduate agricultural leadership program: A Delphi study*. Academic Press.

Morris, G., Ehlers, S., Tormohlen, R., Field, B., & Rudolph, M. (2022). A Review on Agricultural Academic Safety and Biosecurity Curriculum Standards. In *2022 ASABE Annual International Meeting* (p. 1). American Society of Agricultural and Biological Engineers. 10.13031/aim.202200852

Muhaimin, A. W., Retnoningsih, D., & Pariasa, I. I. (2023, May). The role of women in sustainable agriculture practices: evidence from east java Indonesia. In *IOP Conference Series: Earth and Environmental Science* (Vol. 1153, No. 1, p. 012005). IOP Publishing.

Musa, S. F. P. D., & Basir, K. H. (2021). Smart farming: Towards a sustainable agri-food system. *British Food Journal*, *123*(9), 3085–3099. doi:10.1108/BFJ-03-2021-0325

Nagata, J. M., Seligman, H. K., & Weiser, S. D. (2021). Perspective: The convergence of coronavirus disease 2019 (COVID-19) and food insecurity in the United States. *Advances in Nutrition*, *12*(2), 287–290. doi:10.1093/advances/nmaa126 PMID:32970098

Naylor, R. L. (2019). Long-Run Uncertainties for U.S. Agriculture. *Economic Review-Federal Reserve Bank of Kansas City*, 51-84.

Nazuri, N. S., & Ahmad, N. (2019). Social Capital Among Urban Agriculture Program Participants in Klang Perdana Selangor, Malaysia. *International Journal (Toronto, Ont.)*, *2*(10), 47–56.

Noopila, M. Y., & Pichon, H. W. (2022). Leadership education at Hispanic serving institutions in the southwest united states: What does it look like? *Journal of Leadership Education*, *21*(2). Advance online publication. doi:10.12806/V21/I2/R6

Nowak, Z., Pavelock, D., Ullrich, D. R., & Wolfskill, L. A. (2019). Leadership Styles of Successful FFA Advisors and FFA Programs. *Journal of Leadership Education*, *18*(1).

Nunes, B., Gholami, R., & Higón, D. A. (2021). Sustainable farming practices, awareness, and behavior in small farms in Brazil. *Journal of Global Information Management*, *29*(6), 1–23.

Nunes, L. J., Meireles, C. I., Gomes, C. J. P., & Ribeiro, N. M. A. (2021). The impact of climate change on forest development: A sustainable approach to management models applied to Mediterranean-type climate regions. *Plants*, *11*(1), 69. doi:10.3390/plants11010069 PMID:35009073

Nyarko, D. A., & Kozári, J. (2021). Information and communication technologies (ICTs) usage among agricultural extension officers and its impact on extension delivery in Ghana. *Journal of the Saudi Society of Agricultural Sciences*, *20*(3), 164–172. doi:10.1016/j.jssas.2021.01.002

O'Keefe, D. F., Peach, J. M., & Messervey, D. L. (2019). The combined effect of ethical leadership, moral identity, and organizational identification on workplace behavior. *Journal of Leadership Studies*, *13*(1), 20–35. doi:10.1002/jls.21638

Ody, M., & Shattuck, A. (2023). 'Our struggle is for humanity': A conversation with Morgan Ody, general coordinator of La Via Campesina International, on land, politics, peasant life and a vision for hope in our changing world. *The Journal of Peasant Studies*, *50*(2), 539–558. doi:10.1080/03066150.2023.2174857

Ogaga, I. A., Ezenwakwelu, C. A., Isichei, E. E., & Olabosinde, T. S. (2023). Ethical leadership and sustainability of agro-allied firms: Moderating role of environmental dynamism. *International Journal of Ethics and Systems*, *39*(1), 36–53. doi:10.1108/IJOES-12-2021-0226

Ojo, O. O., Shah, S., & Coutroubis, A. (2020). Impacts of Industry 4.0 in sustainable food manufacturing and supply chain. *International Journal of Integrated Supply Management*, *13*(2-3), 140–158. doi:10.1504/IJISM.2020.107851

Olley, R. (2021). A focussed literature review of power and influence leadership theories. *Asia Pacific Journal of Health Management*, *16*(2), 7–17. doi:10.24083/apjhm.v16i2.807

Parr, J. F., Papendick, R. I., Youngberg, I. G., & Meyer, R. E. (2020). Sustainable agriculture in the United States. In *Sustainable agricultural systems* (pp. 50–67). CRC Press. doi:10.1201/9781003070474-5

Peano, C., Massaglia, S., Ghisalberti, C., & Sottile, F. (2020). Pathways for the amplification of agroecology in African sustainable urban agriculture. *Sustainability (Basel)*, *12*(7), 2718. doi:10.3390u12072718

Pimentel, D., & Burgess, M. (2013). Soil erosion threatens food production. *Agriculture*, *3*(3), 443–463. doi:10.3390/agriculture3030443

Popoola, O. O., Monde, N., & Yusuf, S. F. G. (2019). Climate change: Perception and adaptation responses of poultry smallholder farmers in Amathole District Municipality, Eastern Cape Province of South Africa. *South African Journal of Agricultural Extension*, *47*(3), 108–119. doi:10.17159/2413-3221/2019/v47n3a519

Poudel, P. B., Poudel, M. R., Gautam, A., Phuyal, S., Tiwari, C. K., Bashyal, N., & Bashyal, S. (2020). COVID-19 and its global impact on food and agriculture. *Journal of Biology and Today's World*, *9*(5), 221–225.

Pratt, B. (2023). Equitable Urban Planning for Climate Change. *Journal of Planning Literature*, *38*(1), 59–69. doi:10.1177/08854122221138125

Pretty, J. (2008). Agricultural sustainability: Concepts, principles and evidence. *Philosophical Transactions of the Royal Society of London. Series B, Biological Sciences*, *363*(1491), 447–465. doi:10.1098/rstb.2007.2163 PMID:17652074

Qiu, J., Zhao, H., Bravo, L., & Ryals, J. (2023). Urban Agriculture and its Sustainability Implications on the Food-Water-Energy Nexus: FOR391/FR463, 3/2023. *EDIS*, *2023*(1).

Rada, D. R. (1999). Transformational leadership and urban renewal. *The Journal of Leadership Studies*, *6*(3-4), 18–33.

Rahmadani, V. G., & Schaufeli, W. B. (2022). Engaging leadership and work engagement as moderated by "diuwongke": An Indonesian study. *International Journal of Human Resource Management*, *33*(7), 1267–1295.

Rasmussen, C. M., Pardello, R. M., Vreyens, J. R., Chazdon, S., Teng, S., & Liepold, M. (2017). Building social capital and leadership skills for sustainable farmer associations in Morocco. *Journal of International Agricultural and Extension Education*, *24*(2), 35–49.

Rickard, J. W., Boerngen, M. A., Lorenz, S. M., & Baker, E. (2017). Assessing student demographics in a non-land-grant university department of agriculture. *Natural Sciences Education*, *46*(1), 1–5.

Ritter, G. D., Acuff, G. R., Bergeron, G., Bourassa, M. W., Chapman, B. J., Dickson, J. S., Opengart, K., Salois, M. J., Singer, R. S., & Storrs, C. (2019). Antimicrobial-resistant bacterial infections from foods of animal origin: Understanding and effectively communicating to consumers. *Annals of the New York Academy of Sciences*, *1441*(1), 40–49. doi:10.1111/nyas.14091 PMID:30924543

Romero-Cabrera, J., Yubero-Serrano, E., Diaz-Caceres, A., Serran-Jimenez, A., Arenas-Montes, J., & Alcala-Diaz, J. (2022). Educational strategy to improve cardiovascular health and mitigate food insecurity: Rationale for the E-DUCASS program. *Span J Med, 2*, 1–8.

Rubenstein, E. D., Thoron, A. C., & Estepp, C. M. (2014). Perceived Self-Efficacy of Preservice Agriculture Teachers toward Specific SAE Competencies. *Journal of Agricultural Education, 55*(4), 72–84. doi:10.5032/jae.2014.04072

Ryu, J. Y., Kim, M. J., & Yun, S. Y. (2021). The effects of agricultural experience program on agricultural literacy and hand function improvement of adolescents living in self-reliance residence hall. *Journal of People, Plants, and Environment, 24*(3), 277–283.

Saleh, C., & Riyadi, B. S. (2023). The Relationship of Community Empowerment and Social Capital towards Production Capacity of Agricultural Product in Indonesia. *International Journal of Membrane Science and Technology, 10*(3), 435–448.

Sanders, C., Cox, C., Edgar, L., Graham, D., & Perez, A. P. (2021). Exploring the needs of urban producers in a rural state: A qualitative needs assessment. *Journal of Agriculture, Food Systems, and Community Development, 11*(1), 99–113.

Santamaría, L. J. (2014). Critical change for the greater good: Multicultural perceptions in educational leadership toward social justice and equity. *Educational Administration Quarterly, 50*(3), 347–391. doi:10.1177/0013161X13505287

Sanzo, K. L., Myran, S., & Clayton, J. K. (2011). Building bridges between knowledge and practice: A university-school district leadership preparation program partnership. *Journal of Educational Administration, 49*(3), 292–312.

Sarker, A. H., Bornman, J. F., & Marinova, D. (2019). A framework for integrating agriculture in urban sustainability in Australia. *Urban Science, 3*(2), 50.

SavageM.SavageC.BrommelsM.MazzocatoP. (2019). Physicians in the management and leadership of health care: A systematic review of the conditions conducive to organizational performance. medRxiv, 19011379. doi:10.1101/19011379

Schuessler, R. (2020). Why deontologists should reject agent-relative value and embrace agent-relative accountability. *Zeitschrift für Ethik und Moralphilosophie, 3*(2), 315–335. doi:10.100742048-020-00084-2

Schut, M., Leeuwis, C., & Thiele, G. (2020). Science of Scaling: Understanding and guiding the scaling of innovation for societal outcomes. *Agricultural Systems, 184*, 102908. doi:10.1016/j.agsy.2020.102908

Schyns, J. F., Hogeboom, R. J., & Krol, M. S. (2022). Water Footprint Assessment: towards water-wise food systems. In Food Systems Modelling (pp. 63-88). Academic Press. doi:10.1016/B978-0-12-822112-9.00006-0

Shah, F., & Wu, W. (2019). Soil and crop management strategies to ensure higher crop productivity within sustainable environments. *Sustainability (Basel), 11*(5), 1485. doi:10.3390u11051485

Shiiba, N., Singh, P., Charan, D., Raj, K., Stuart, J., Pratap, A., & Maekawa, M. (2023). Climate change and coastal resiliency of Suva, Fiji: A holistic approach for measuring climate risk using the climate and ocean risk vulnerability index (CORVI). *Mitigation and Adaptation Strategies for Global Change*, *28*(2), 9. doi:10.100711027-022-10043-4 PMID:36685809

Silva, I. D. D. L., Nascimento, J. A. D. A., de Moraes Filho, L. E. P. T., Caetano, V. F., de Andrade, M. F., de Almeida, Y. M. B., Hallwass, F., Brito, A. M. S. S., & Vinhas, G. M. (2022). Production of potential antioxidant and antimicrobial active films of poly (vinyl alcohol) incorporated with cashew tree extract. *Journal of Food Processing and Preservation*, *46*(10), e16831. doi:10.1111/jfpp.16831

Simonson, J., & Rahman, K. S. (2020). The Institutional Design of Community Control. *California Law Review*, 108.

Singh, M. (2021). Organic farming for sustainable agriculture. *Indian Journal of Organic Farming*, *1*(1), 1–8.

Sorensen, L. B., Germundsson, L. B., Hansen, S. R., Rojas, C., & Kristensen, N. H. (2021). *What skills do agricultural professionals need in the transition towards a sustainable agriculture? A qualitative literature review*. Academic Press.

Specht, K., Zoll, F., Schümann, H., Bela, J., Kachel, J., & Robischon, M. (2019). How will we eat and produce in the cities of the future? From edible insects to vertical farming—A study on the perception and acceptability of new approaches. *Sustainability (Basel)*, *11*(16), 4315. doi:10.3390u11164315

Stefan, T. A. L. U., & Nazarov, A. D. (2020, November). Challenges and competencies of leadership in Covid-19 pandemic. In Research technologies of pandemic coronavirus impact (RTCOV 2020) (pp. 518-524). Atlantis Press.

Struik, P. C., & Kuyper, T. W. (2017). Sustainable intensification in agriculture: The richer shade of green. A review. *Agronomy for Sustainable Development*, *37*(5), 1–15. doi:10.100713593-017-0445-7

Susanty, L., Hartati, Z., Sholihin, R., Syahid, A., & Liriwati, F. Y. (2021). Why English teaching truth on digital trends as an effort for effective learning and evaluation: opportunities and challenges: analysis of teaching English. *Linguistics and Culture Review*, *5*(S1), 303–316. doi:10.21744/lingcure.v5nS1.1401

Talukder, B., Blay-Palmer, A., Hipel, K. W., & VanLoon, G. W. (2017). Elimination method of multi-criteria decision analysis (mcda): A simple methodological approach for assessing agricultural sustainability. *Sustainability*, *9*(2), 287.

Tangdigling, D. E., Nursyamsi, I., & Yusuf, R. M. (2019). The Effect of Situational Leadership and Work Ethics on Employee Performance through Organizational Climate as Intervening Variables at Gowa Agricultural Development Polytechnic. *Hasanuddin Journal of Business Strategy*, *1*(4), 43–50. doi:10.26487/hjbs.v1i4.285

Tilman, D., Balzer, C., Hill, J., & Befort, B. L. (2011). Global food demand and the sustainable intensification of agriculture. *Proceedings of the National Academy of Sciences of the United States of America*, *108*(50), 20260–20264. doi:10.1073/pnas.1116437108 PMID:22106295

Traver-Marti, J. A., Ballesteros-Velazquez, B., Beldarrain, N. O., & Maiquez, M. D. C. C. (2023). Leading the curriculum towards social change: Distributed leadership and the inclusive school. *Educational Management Administration & Leadership, 51*(3), 554–574. doi:10.1177/1741143221991849

USDA. ARS. (2021). *Food Security in the United States: Key Statistics & Graphics*. Retrieved from https://www.ers.usda.gov/topics/food-nutrition-assistance/food-security-in-the-us/key-statistics-graphics.aspx

USDA. ERS - Ag and Food Sectors and the Economy. (2021). https://www.ers.usda.gov/data-products/ag-and-food-statistics-charting-the-essentials/ag-and-food-sectors-and-the-economy/

Vallera, F. L., & Bodzin, A. M. (2020). Integrating STEM with AgLIT (agricultural literacy through innovative technology): The efficacy of a project-based curriculum for upper-primary students. *International Journal of Science and Mathematics Education, 18*(3), 419–439. doi:10.100710763-019-09979-y

Van Zyl, E. (2014). The role of self-leadership in becoming an ethical leader in the South African work context. *African Journal of Business Ethics, 8*(2). Advance online publication. doi:10.15249/8-2-82

Vekved, M., McNeil, D. A., Dolan, S. M., Siever, J. E., Horn, S., & Tough, S. C. (2017). Invested in success: A qualitative study of the experience of CenteringPregnancy group prenatal care for perinatal educators. *Journal of Perinatal Education, 26*(3), 125–135.

Velez, J. J., Moore, L. L., Bruce, J. A., & Stephens, C. A. (2014). Agricultural leadership education: Past history, present reality, and future directions. *The Journal of Leadership Studies, 7*(4), 65–70.

Vu, T., Vu, M., & Hoang, V. (2020). The impact of transformational leadership on promoting academic research in higher educational system in Vietnam. *Management Science Letters, 10*(3), 585–592.

Wadumestrige Dona, C. G., Mohan, G., & Fukushi, K. (2021). Promoting urban agriculture and its opportunities and challenges—A global review. *Sustainability, 13*(17), 9609.

Wang, Y., & You, J. (2022). The Operation Mode of Agricultural Supply Chain Finance Using Blockchain. *Computational Intelligence and Neuroscience, 2022*, 2022. doi:10.1155/2022/3338030 PMID:36188687

Wathes, C. (2010). Guarding the welfare of farm animals. *The Veterinary Record, 167*(15), 583–584. doi:10.1136/vr.c4785 PMID:21257423

Wells, J. C., & Stock, J. T. (2020). Life history transitions at the origins of agriculture: A model for understanding how niche construction impacts human growth, demography and health. *Frontiers in Endocrinology, 11*, 325. doi:10.3389/fendo.2020.00325 PMID:32508752

White, B. (2020). IFAD Research Series 48: Rural Youth, Today and Tomorrow. *Today and Tomorrow*.

White, R. R., & Hall, M. B. (2017). Nutritional and greenhouse gas impacts of removing animals from US agriculture. *Proceedings of the National Academy of Sciences of the United States of America, 114*(48), E10301–E10308. doi:10.1073/pnas.1707322114 PMID:29133422

Whittinghill, L., & Sarr, S. (2021). Practices and Barriers to Sustainable Urban Agriculture: A Case Study of Louisville, Kentucky. *Urban Science (Basel, Switzerland), 5*(4), 92. doi:10.3390/urbansci5040092

Wong, E., & Swanson, A. (2023). How Russia's War on Ukraine Is Worsening Global Starvation. *New York Times*.

Yu, H., Lin, Z., Lin, M. S., Neal, J. A., & Sirsat, S. A. (2022). Consumers' Knowledge and Handling Practices Associated with Fresh-Cut Produce in the United States. *Foods*, *11*(14), 2167. doi:10.3390/foods11142167 PMID:35885411

Zhang, Y., Zhou, F., & Mao, J. (2018). Ethical leadership and follower moral actions: Investigating an emotional linkage. *Frontiers in Psychology*, *9*, 1881. doi:10.3389/fpsyg.2018.01881 PMID:30337900

Zulaikha, Y., Martono, E., & Himam, F. (2021). Perceptions of students of the faculty of agriculture on the social status and career prospects in agricultural sector. *Agrisocionomics: Jurnal Sosial Ekonomi Pertanian*, *5*(1), 11–18.

Compilation of References

Aarons, G. A., Ehrhardt, M. G., Farahnak, L. R., & Hurlburt, M. S. (2015). Leadership and organizational change for implementation (LOCI): A randomized mixed method pilot study of leadership and organization development intervention for evidence-based practice implementation. *Implementation Science : IS*, *10*(11), 1–12. doi:10.118613012-014-0192-y PMID:25592163

Abbas, A., Ekowati, D., & Anwar, A. (2023). Authentic Leadership Journey: An empirical Discussion from Pakistani higher education employing the Lay theory of Psychology. *International Journal of Public Leadership*. Advance online publication. doi:10.1108/IJPL-04-2022-0020

Abbas, A., Ekowati, D., Shuairidi, F., Fenitra, R. M., & Fahlevi, M. (2022). Integrating Cycle of Prochaska and DiClemente with Ethically Responsible behavior theory for Social Change Management: Post Covid-19 Social Cognitive Perspective for Change. In A. Pego (Ed.), *Challenges and Emerging Strategies for Global Networking Post COVID-19* (pp. 130–155). IGI Global. doi:10.4018/978-1-7998-8856-7.ch007

Abbas, A., Ekowati, D., Suhairidi, F., & Anwar, A. (2022). Human Capital Creation: A Collective Psychological, Social, Organizational and Religious Perspective. *Journal of Religion and Health*. Advance online publication. doi:10.100710943-022-01665-8 PMID:36109469

Abbas, A., Ekowati, D., Suhairidi, F., Anwar, A., & Fenitra, R. M. (2023). Technology Acceptance and COVID-19: A Perspective for Emerging Opportunities from Crisis. *Technology Analysis and Strategic Management*, 1–13. Advance online publication. doi:10.1080/09537325.2023.2214642

Abbas, A., Ekowati, D., Suhairidi, F., & Hamid, A. R. (2022). Negative Vs Positive Psychology: A Review of Science of Well-being. *Integrative Psychological & Behavioral Science*. Advance online publication. doi:10.100712124-022-09708-1 PMID:35759165

Abbas, A., Ekowati, D., & Suhariadi, F. (2021). Managing Individuals, Organizations Through Leadership: Diversity Consciousness Roadmap. In B. Christiansen & H. Chandan (Eds.), *Handbook of Research on Applied Social Psychology in Multiculturalism* (Vol. 1, pp. 47–71). IGI Global. doi:10.4018/978-1-7998-6960-3.ch003

Abbas, A., Ekowati, D., & Suhariadi, F. (2022). Social Perspective: Leadership in Changing Society. In M. I. Hassan, S. Sen Roy, U. Chatterjee, S. Chakraborty, & U. Singh (Eds.), *Social Morphology, Human Welfare, and Sustainability* (pp. 89–107). Springer International Publishing. doi:10.1007/978-3-030-96760-4_4

Abbas, A., Ekowati, D., Suhariadi, F., & Fenitra, R. M. (2022). Health Implications, Leaders Societies, and Climate Change: A Global Review. In U. Chatterjee, A. O. Akanwa, S. Kumar, S. K. Singh, & A. Dutta Roy (Eds.), *Ecological Footprints of Climate Change: Adaptive Approaches and Sustainability* (pp. 653–675). Springer International Publishing. doi:10.1007/978-3-031-15501-7_26

Abbas, A., Saud, M., Ekowati, D., & Suhariadi, F. (2021). Social Psychology and Fabrication: A Synthesis of Individuals, Society, and Organization. In B. Christiansen & H. Chandan (Eds.), *Handbook of Research on Applied Social Psychology in Multiculturalism* (Vol. 1, pp. 89–109). IGI Global. doi:10.4018/978-1-7998-6960-3.ch005

Abbas, A., Saud, M., Ekowati, D., Usman, I., & Setia, S. (2020). Technology and stress: A proposed framework for coping with stress in Indonesian higher education. *International Journal of Innovation. Creativity and Change*, *13*(4), 373–390.

Abbas, A., Saud, M., Suhariadi, F., Usman, I., & Ekowati, D. (2022). Positive leadership psychology: Authentic and servant leadership in higher education in Pakistan. *Current Psychology (New Brunswick, N.J.)*, *41*(10), 5859–5871. doi:10.1007/12144-020-01051-1

Abd Ali, A. J., & Kazim, K. A. H. (2023). The relationship between transformational leadership and intellectual fluency among secondary school principals in the Babylonian Directorate of Education. *Journal of Humanities and Social Sciences Research*, *2*(1).

Abney, A., Denison, V., Tanguay, C., & Ganz, M. (2022). Understanding the unseen: Invisible disabilities in the Workplace. *The American Archivist*, *85*(1), 88–103. doi:10.17723/2327-9702-85.1.88

Abramo, J. M., & Reynolds, A. (2015). "Pedagogical creativity" as a framework for music teacher education. *Journal of Music Teacher Education*, *25*(1), 37–51.

Abrams, R. (2022). Emotional intelligence and team performance: An organizational study. *Journal of Business Leadership*, *15*(4), 234–248.

Adams, R., Jeanrenaud, S., Bessant, J., Overy, P., & Denyer, D. (2012). *Innovating for Sustainability. A Systematic Review of the Body of Knowledge*. Network for Business Sustainability.

Adhia, H., Nagendra, H. R., & Mahadevan, B. (2010). Impact of adoption of yoga way of life on the emotional intelligence of managers. *IIMB Management Review*, *22*(1–2), 32–41. doi:10.1016/j.iimb.2010.03.003

Adler, N. J., & Laasch, O. (2020). Responsible leadership and management: Key distinctions and shared concerns. In C. S. Voegtlin & W. Amann (Eds.), *Research Handbook of Responsible Management* (pp. 100–112). Edward Elgar Publishing. doi:10.4337/9781788971966.00013

Adobe Inc. (2023). SWOT Analysis. Adobe.

Adonis, C. K., & Silinda, F. (2021). Institutional culture and transformation in higher education in post-1994 South Africa: A critical race theory analysis. *Critical African Studies*, *13*(1), 73–94. doi:10.1080/21681392.2021.1911448

Afsar, B., Masood, M., & Umrani, W. A. (2019). The role of job crafting and knowledge sharing on the effect of transformational leadership on innovative work behavior. *Personnel Review*, *48*(5), 1186–1208. doi:10.1108/PR-04-2018-0133

Agarwal, S., Lenka, U., Singh, K., Agrawal, V., & Agrawal, A. M. (2020). A qualitative approach towards crucial factors for sustainable development of women social entrepreneurship: Indian cases. *Journal of Cleaner Production*, *274*. https://doi.org/10.1016/j.jclepro.2020.123135

Agbaje, K. A. A., Martin, R. A., & Williams, D. L. (2001). Impact of sustainable agriculture on secondary school agricultural education teachers and programs in the north central region. *Journal of Agricultural Education*, *42*(2), 38–45.

Aggarwal, R., & Ranganathan, P. (2019). Study designs: Part 4 - Interventional studies. *Perspectives in Clinical Research*, *10*(3), 137–139. doi:10.4103/picr.PICR_91_19 PMID:31404185

Agusta, A., & Nurdin, L. (2021). *Integrative leadership style of libraries at Islamic universities in Indonesia*. Library Philosophy and Practice. https://digitalcommons.unl.edu/libphilprac/5443/

Compilation of References

Ahmad, M. R., & Raja, R. (2021). Employee Job Satisfaction and Business Performance: The Mediating Role of Organizational Commitment. *Vision*, *25*(2), 168–179.

Ahmad, A. B., & Cheng, Z. (2018). The role of change content, context, process, and leadership in understanding employees' commitment to change: The case of public organizations in Kurdistan region of Iraq. *Public Personnel Management*, *47*(2), 195–216. doi:10.1177/0091026017753645

Ahmadnia, S., Christien, A. M., Spencer, P., Hart, T., & De Araujo Barbosa, C. C. (2022). *Defueling Conflict*. Academic Press.

Ahmad, S., & Bajwa, I. A. (2023). The role of social entrepreneurship in socio-economic development: A meta-analysis of the nascent field. *Journal of Entrepreneurship in Emerging Economies*, *15*(1), 133–157. doi:10.1108/JEEE-04-2021-0165

Ahmad, T., Hamid, A., Abbas, A., Anwar, A., Ekowati, D., Fenitra, R., & Suhariadi, F. (2023). Empowering leadership: Role of Organizational Culture of Self-Esteem, and Emotional Intelligence on Creativity. *Journal of Management Development*, *42*(3), 201–214. doi:10.1108/JMD-10-2021-0288

Akanle, O., Ademuson, A. O., & Shittu, O. S. (2020). Scope and Limitation of Study in Social Research. In A. S. Jegede & U. C. Isiugo-Abanihe (Eds.), *Contemporary Issues in Social Research* (pp. 105–114). Ibadan University Press.

Akhtar, N., Azeem, S. M., Basiouni, A. F., Ahmed, A., Teoh, K. B., & Alvi, A. (2022). What motivates the most? Money or Empowerment: Mediating Role of Employee Commitment to Organizational Performance. *Journal of Organisational Studies & Innovation*, *9*(2), 21–37. doi:10.51659/josi.21-153

Akins, D. (2022). *Food Sovereignty and Coffee Cultivation in EL Salvador: Current Pitfalls and Opportunities in the Intersections of Coffee*. Gender, and Climate Change.

Al Harbi, J. A., Alarifi, S., & Mosbah, A. (2019). Transformation leadership and creativity: Effects of employees' psychological empowerment and intrinsic motivation. *Personnel Review*, *48*(5), 1082–1099. doi:10.1108/PR-11-2017-0354

Al-Abri, R. (2007). Managing Change in Healthcare. *Oman Medical Journal*, *22*(3), 9–10. PMID:22400086

Al-Alawi, A. I., Abdulmohsen, M., Al-Malki, F. M., & Mehrotra, A. (2019). Investigating the barriers to change management in public sector educational institutions. *International Journal of Educational Management*, *33*(1), 112–148. doi:10.1108/IJEM-03-2018-0115

Alan, S., Corekcioglu, G., & Sutter, M. (2023). Improving workplace climate in large corporations: A clustered randomized intervention. *The Quarterly Journal of Economics*, *138*(1), 151–203. doi:10.1093/qje/qjac034

Alberta Education. (2007). *Program of studies: Social studies, kindergarten to grade 12*. Alberta Education.

Alberta Education. (2010). *Inspiring education: A dialogue with Albertans*. Alberta Education.

Alemu, F. M. (2023). *Ramifications of Sectors Economic Upsurge on rate of early aged Unemployment in case of East African Countries*. Academic Press.

Alexander, J. M., & Buckingham, J. (2011). Common good leadership in business management: An ethical model from the Indian tradition. *Business Ethics (Oxford, England)*, *20*(4), 317–327. doi:10.1111/j.1467-8608.2011.01632.x

Alhezzani, Y. M. R. (2021). Change recipients' resistance and salience to organizational re-creation: The effects of participation and coercion strategies on change derailment. *Organizational Management Journal*, *18*(1), 2–18. doi:10.1108/OMJ-10-2018-0608

Al-Husseini, S., El Beltagi, I., & Moizer, J. (2021). Transformational leadership and innovation: The mediating role of knowledge sharing amongst higher education faculty. *International Journal of Leadership in Education*, *24*(5), 670–693. doi:10.1080/13603124.2019.1588381

Ali, S. H. K., Khan, N. S., & Yildiz, Y. (2020). Leadership effects on CSR employee, media, customer, and NGOs. *Management and Economics Research Journal*, *6*, 11. doi:10.18639/MERJ.2020.961566

Allen, B. L., Wright, L., & Li, T. (2003). *Shared leadership*. Iowa State University. https://www.extension.iastate.edu/communities/files/page/files/shared_leadership.allen.pdf

Allen, D. G., & Vardaman, J. M. (2021). Global talent retention; understanding employee turnover around the world. In D. G. Allen & J. M. Vardaman (Eds.), *Global talent retention: understanding employee turnover around the world* (pp. 1–15). Emerald Publishing. doi:10.1108/978-1-83909-293-020211001

Allen, N., Grigsby, B., & Peters, M. L. (2015). Does leadership matter? Examining the relationship among transformational leadership, school climate, and student achievement. *The International Journal of Educational Leadership Preparation*, *10*(2), 1–22.

Allen, T. G., Jackson, A., & Johnson, D. N. (2020). Preparing North Carolina principals for trauma-sensitive leadership. *Journal of Organizational and Educational Leadership*, *5*(2).

Allix, N. M. (2000). Transformational leadership: Democratic or despotic? *Educational Management & Administration*, *28*(1), 7–20. doi:10.1177/0263211X000281002

Allolio-Nacke, L. (2014). Transculturalism. In T. Tao (Ed.), *Encyclopedia of Critical Psychology*. Springer. doi:10.1007/978-1-4614-5583-7_316

Allui, A., & Sahni, J. (2016). Strategic Human Resource Management in Higher Education Institutions: Empirical Evidence from Saudi. *Procedia: Social and Behavioral Sciences*, *235*, 361–371. doi:10.1016/j.sbspro.2016.11.044

AlManei, M., Salonitis, K., & Tsinopoulos, C. (2018). A conceptual lean implementation framework based on change management theory. *Procedia CIRP*, *72*, 1160–1165. doi:10.1016/j.procir.2018.03.141

Almeida, D., Shmarko, K., & Lomas, E. (2022). The ethics of facial recognition technologies, surveillance, and accountability in an age of artificial intelligence: A comparative analysis of US, EU, and UK regulatory frameworks. *AI and Ethics*, *2*(3), 377–387. doi:10.100743681-021-00077-w PMID:34790955

Alqatawenh, A. S. (2018). Transformational leadership style and its relationship with change management. *Verslas: teorija ir praktika*, *19*(1), 17-24.

Al-Taweel, I. R. (2021). Impact of high-performance work practices in human resource management of health dispensaries in Qassim Region, Kingdom of Saudi Arabia, towards organizational resilience and productivity. *Business Process Management Journal*, *27*(7), 2088–2109. doi:10.1108/BPMJ-11-2020-0498

Alter, K. (2013). Social entrepreneurship and sustainability: Why the social element is important for environmental and economic sustainability. *Journal of Business Ethics*, *115*(3), 481–494. doi:10.100710551-013-1808-6

Altieri, M., & Nicholls, C. (2018). *Biodiversity and pest management in agroecosystems*. CRC press. doi:10.1201/9781482277937

Altrichter, H. (2020). The concept of quality in action research: Giving practitioners a voice in educational research. In *Qualitative voices in educational research* (pp. 40-55). Routledge.

Compilation of References

Alvarez, B. (2021). *What to know about invisible disabilities*. National Education Association. https://www.nea.org/advocating-for-change/new-from-nea/what-know-about-invisible-disabilities

Alvoid, L., & Black, W. L. (2014). The changing role of the principal. Center for American Progress, 1–33.

Alysse, B. (2022). Fact Check: What percentage of Black people go to therapy? *REVOLT.* https://www.revolt.tv/article/2022-05-06/167497/black-people-in-therapy-fact-check/#:~:text=Statistics%20tell%20us%20that%20roughly%2025%20percent%20of,the%20Harvard%20Medical%20School%E2%80%99s%20affiliate%20McLean%E2%80%99s%20latest%20essay

Amabile, T. M., Conti, R., Coon, H., Lazenby, J., & Herron, M. (1996). Assessing the work environment for creativity. *Academy of Management Journal*, *39*(5), 1154–1184. doi:10.2307/256995

Amanchukwu, R. N., Stanley, J. G., & Ololube, P. N. (2015). A review of Leadership Theories, Principles and Styles and Their Relevance to Educational Management. *Management*, *5*(1), 6–14.

American Medical Association. (2021). *Medical students, residents and fellows making an impact.* Author.

American Psychiatric Association. (2017). *Mental health disparities: African Americans.* APA. https://www.psychiatry.org/File%20Library/Psychiatrists/Cultural-Competency/Mental-Health-Disparities/Mental-Health-Facts-for-African-Americans.pdf

American Psychological Association (A.P.A.). (2019). *Racial and ethnic disparities in mental health care*. APA. https://www.apa.org/pi/oema/resources/ethnicity-health/mental-health

American Psychological Association. (2017). *Clinical practice guideline for treatment of post traumatic stress disorder (PTSD).* Retrieved from https://www.apa.org/ptsd-guideline/ptsd.pdf

Aminah A., Sylvia N., Syed J., & Nelson L. (2020). The Effect of Transformational Leadership on Employees' Performance in Malaysia's Public Sector. *International Journal of Academic Research in Business and Social Sciences*, *10*(11).

Amjad, A., & Rehman, M. (2018). Resistance to change in public organization: Reasons and how to overcome it. *European Journal of Business Science and Technology*, *4*(1), 56–68. doi:10.11118/ejobsat.v4i1.129

Amor, A. M., Vázquez, J. P. A., & Faíña, J. A. (2020). Transformational leadership and work engagement: Exploring the mediating role of structural empowerment. *European Management Journal*, *38*(1), 169–178. doi:10.1016/j.emj.2019.06.007

Anca-Ioana, M. (2013). New approaches of the concepts of human resources, human resource management and strategic human resource management. *Annals of the University of Oradea. Economic Science Series*, *22*(1), 1520–1525.

Andersén, J. (2012). Protective capacity and absorptive capacity: Managing the balance between retention and creation of knowledge-based resources. *The Learning Organization*, *19*(5), 440–452. doi:10.1108/09696471211239730

Anderson, D., & Anderson, L. A. (2002). *Beyond change management: Advanced strategies for today's transformational leaders.* John Wiley & Sons.

Anderson, J. (2015). Barking up the wrong tree. On the fallacies of the transformational leadership theory. *Leadership and Organization Development Journal*, *36*(6), 765–777. doi:10.1108/LODJ-12-2013-0168

Anderson, M. (n.d.). *Gain the clarity and confidence you need to lead well.* Anderson Leadership Resources. https://andersonlr.com/

Andersson, L. (2015). Resistance to change: A literature review. *International Journal of Management Reviews*, *17*(1), 1–13.

Andoh, E. (2021). Psychology's urgent need to dismantle racism. American Psychological Association, 25(3), 38.

Angelini, E., Wolf, A., Wijk, H., Brisby, H., & Baranto, A. (2021). The impact of implementing a person-centered pain management intervention on resistance to change and organizational culture. *BMC Health Services Research*, *21*(1), 1–11. doi:10.118612913-021-06819-0 PMID:34895215

Anita, M., Kawaii, S., Yosia, K., & Rizky, D. (2021). *The impact of transformational leadership on employee performance with psychological ownership and organizational commitment Jurnal Manajemen* (Vol. 1). Edisi Elektronik.

Ansari, T., & Usmani, A. (2018). Students' perception towards feedback in clinical sciences in an outcome-based integrated curriculum. *Pakistan Journal of Medical Sciences*, *34*(3), 702.

Anshari, M., Hamdan, M., Ahmad, N., Ali, E., & Haidi, H. (2022). COVID-19, artificial intelligence, ethical challenges and policy implications. *AI & Society*, •••, 1–14. doi:10.100700146-022-01471-6 PMID:35607368

Antonopoulou, H., Halkiopoulos, C., Barlou, O., & Beligiannis, G. N. (2021). Transformational leadership and digital skills in higher education institutes: during the COVID-19 pandemic. *Emerging science journal*, *5*(1), 1-15.

Antonopoulou, H., Halkiopoulos, C., Barlou, O., & Beligiannis, G. N. (2021). Transformational leadership and digital skills in higher education institutes: during the COVID-19 pandemic. *Emerging science journal*, *5*(1), 1-15. doi:10.28991/esj-2021-01252

Anyolo, E. O. (2012). *Investigating the incorporation of education about, in/through and for the environment in the Geography Junior Phase curriculum: a case study of three Namibian schools*. Academic Press.

APM Research Lab. (2022). *Color of Coronavirus: COVID-19 Deaths by race and ethnicity in the U.S.* APM Research Lab. https://www.apmresearchlab.org/covid/deaths-by-race

Appelbaum, S. H., St-Pierre, N., & Glavas, W. (1998). Strategic organizational change: The role of leadership, learning, motivation and productivity. *Management Decision*, *36*(5), 289–301. doi:10.1108/00251749810220496

Arafat, A., Maged, M., Abdulrahman, M., & Ramez, A. (2021). The Impact of Transformational Leadership on Employees Performance Among Employees in IWPPS, Saudi Arabia. *International Journal of Contemporary Management and Information Technology*, *2*(1).

Aras, G., Tezcan, N., & Furtuna, Ö. K. (2018). Çok boyutlu kurumsal sürdürülebilirlik yaklaşımı ile Türk bankacılık sektörünün değerlemesi: Kamu-Özel banka farklılaşması. *Ege Academic Review*, *18*(1), 47–61. doi:10.21121/eab.2018131895

Ärlestig, H., Day, C., & Johansson, O. (2016). *A decade of research on school principals: Cases from 24 Countries*. Springer. doi:10.1007/978-3-319-23027-6

Armanious, M., & Padgett, J. D. (2021). Agile learning strategies to compete in an uncertain business environment. *Journal of Workplace Learning*, *33*(8), 635–647. doi:10.1108/JWL-11-2020-0181

Arredondo, P. (2017). *Culturally inclusive leadership – The lived experience*. Arredondo Advisory Group. https://www.arredondoadvisorygroup.com/2017/07/18/culturally-inclusive-leadership-the-lived-experience/

Arrizabalaga, P., Abellana, R., Vinas, O., Merino, A., & Ascaso, C. (2014). Gender inequalities in the medical profession: Are there still barriers to women physicians in the 21st century? *Gaceta Sanitaria*, *28*(5), 363–368. doi:10.1016/j.gaceta.2014.03.014 PMID:24889702

Asbari, Hidayat, & Purwanto. (2021). Managing Employee Performance: From Leadership to Readiness for Change. *International Journal of Social and Management Studies*, *2*(1).

Asbari, M. (2020). Is transformational leadership suitable for future organizational needs? *International Journal of Social. Policy and Law*, *1*(1), 51–55.

Compilation of References

Ashforth, B. (1994). Petty tyranny in organizations. *Human Relations*, *47*(7), 755–778. doi:10.1177/001872679404700701

Astuty, I., & Udin, U. (2020). The Effect of Perceived Organizational Support and Transformational Leadership on Affective Commitment and Employee Performance. *Journal of Asian Finance, Economics, and Business, 7*(10).

Atmojo, M. (2015). The influence of transformational leadership on job satisfaction, organizational commitment, and employee performance. *International Research Journal of Business Studies*, *5*(2), 113–128. doi:10.21632/irjbs.5.2.113-128

Austin, J. E., Stevenson, H., & Wei-Skillern, J. (2006). Social and commercial entrepreneurship: Same, different, or both? *Entrepreneurship Theory and Practice*, *30*(1), 1–22. doi:10.1111/j.1540-6520.2006.00107.x

Avolio, B., & Bass, B. (2004). Multifactor Leadership Questionnaire Manual (3rd ed.). Mind Garden, Inc.

Avolio, B. J., Sosik, J. J., Kahai, S. S., & Baker, B. (2014). E-leadership: Re-examining transformations in leadership source and transmission. *The Leadership Quarterly*, *25*(1), 105–131. doi:10.1016/j.leaqua.2013.11.003

Avolio, B. J., Walumbwa, F. O., & Weber, T. J. (2009). Leadership: Current theories, research, and future directions. *Annual Review of Psychology*, *60*(1), 421–449. doi:10.1146/annurev.psych.60.110707.163621 PMID:18651820

Avolio, B. J., & Yammarino, F. J. (Eds.). (2013). *Transformational and charismatic leadership: The road ahead*. Emerald Group Publishing. doi:10.1108/S1479-357120135

Ayers, R. S. (2013). Building goal alignment in federal agencies' performance appraisal programs. *Public Personnel Management*, *42*(4), 495–520. doi:10.1177/0091026013496077

Ayoko, O. B. (2021). Resiliency and leadership in organizations. *Journal of Management & Organization*, *27*(3), 417–421. doi:10.1017/jmo.2021.44

Azmi, F. T. (2010). Devolution of HRM and organizational performance: Evidence from India. *International Journal of Commerce and Management*, *20*(3), 217–231. doi:10.1108/10569211011076910

Baba, M. M., Makhdoomi, U. M., & Siddiqi, M. A. (2021). Emotional intelligence and transformational leadership among academic leaders in institutions of higher learning. *Global Business Review*, *22*(4), 1070–1096. doi:10.1177/0972150918822421

Badal, A. (2015). Human intellectual value: An organizational spectrum. *Asian Journal of Research in Business Economics and Management*, *5*(6), 44–48. doi:10.5958/2249-7307.2015.00125.5

Badsha, N. (2000) South African Higher Education: Diversity Overview. In Beckham, E. F. (eds) Diversity, Democracy, and Higher Education: A View from Three Nations-India, South Africa, the United States. Association of American Colleges and Universities.

Badsha, N., & Wickham, S. (2013). *Review of initiatives in equity and transformation in three universities in South Africa*. Cape Higher Education Consortium.

Bagga, S. K., Gera, S., & Haque, S. N. (2023). The mediating role of organizational culture: Transformational leadership and change management in virtual teams. *Asia Pacific Management Review, 28*(2), 120–131. https://doi-org.captechu.idm.oclc.org/10.1016/j.apmrv.2022.07.003

Bailey, J., & Axelrod, R. H. (2001). Leadership lessons from Mount Rushmore: An interview with James MacGregor Burns. *The Leadership Quarterly*, *12*(1), 113–121. doi:10.1016/S1048-9843(01)00066-2

Bak, H., Jin, M. H., & McDonald, B. D. III. (2022). Unpacking the transformational leadership-innovative work behavior relationship: The mediating role of psychological capital. *Public Performance & Management Review*, *45*(1), 80–105. doi:10.1080/15309576.2021.1939737

Bakker, A. B., Hetland, J., Olsen, O. K., & Espevik, R. (2022). Daily transformational leadership: A source of inspiration for follower performance? *European Management Journal*. Advance online publication. doi:10.1016/j.emj.2022.04.004

Balasuriya, B. L. L. A., & Perera, G. D. N. (2021). The Impact of Transformational Leadership on Employee Performance: The Mediating Role of Employee Engagement in Selected Porcelain Manufacturing Companies in Sri Lanka, Vidyodaya. *Journal of Management*, 7(2).

Bandura, A. (1986). Social foundations of thought and action. Academic Press.

Bandura, A. (1997). *Self-efficacy: The exercise of control*. W.H. Freeman and Company.

Bandura, A. (2000). Exercise of human agency through collective efficacy. *Current Directions in Psychological Science*, 9(3), 75–78. doi:10.1111/1467-8721.00064

Banholzer, M., Birshan, M., Doherty, R., & LaBerge, L. (2023). *Innovation: Your solution for weathering uncertainty*. McKinsey Consulting. https://www.mckinsey.com/~/media/mckinsey/business%20functions/strategy%20and%20corporate%20finance/our%20insights/innovation%20your%20solution%20for%20weathering%20uncertainty/innovation-your-solution-for-weathering-uncertainty_vf.pdf

Banks, G. C., Dionne, S. D., Mast, M. S., & Sayama, H. (2022). Leadership in the digital era: A review of who, what, when, where, and why. *The Leadership Quarterly*, 33(5), 101634. doi:10.1016/j.leaqua.2022.101634

Bansal, S., Garg, I., & Sharma, G. D. (2019). Social entrepreneurship as a path for social change and driver of sustainable development: A systematic review and research agenda. *Sustainability (Basel)*, 11(4), 1091. doi:10.3390u11041091

Barasade, S. G. (2002). The ripple effect: Emotional contagion and influence on group behavior. *Administrative Science Quarterly*, 47(4), 644–675. doi:10.2307/3094912

Bareil, C. (2013). Understanding resistance to change. *Human Resource Management International Digest*, 21(2), 40–43.

Barling, J., Slater, F., & Kelloway, E. K. (2000). Transformational leadership and emotional intelligence: An exploratory study. *Leadership and Organization Development Journal*, 21(3), 157–161. doi:10.1108/01437730010325040

Barnes, L. L., & Spangenburg, J. M. (2018). When leadership fail: A view from the lens of four employees. *American Journal of Business Education*, 11(3), 49–54. doi:10.19030/ajbe.v11i3.10188

Barnett, M. L., & Huskamp, H. A. (2020). Telemedicine for Mental Health in the United States: Making Progress, Still a Long Way to Go. *Psychiatric Services (Washington, D.C.)*, 71(2), 197–198. doi:10.1176/appi.ps.201900555 PMID:31847735

Barney, J. (2001). Is the resource-based view a useful perspective for strategic management research? Yes. *Academy of Management Review*, 26(1), 41–56.

Baron, J. S., Specht, A., Garnier, E., Bishop, P., Campbell, C. A., Davis, F. W., ... Guru, S. M. (2017). Synthesis centers as critical research infrastructure. *Bioscience*, 67(8), 750–759. doi:10.1093/biosci/bix053

Bar-On, R. (1996). *The Emotional Quotient Inventory (EQ-i): A Test of Emotional Intelligence*. Multi-Health Systems.

Barron, B., & Darling-Hammond, L. (2008). *Teaching for Meaningful Learning: A Review of Research on Inquiry-Based and Cooperative Learning. Book Excerpt*. George Lucas Educational Foundation.

Barsade, S., & O'Neill, O. A. (2016). Manage your emotional culture. *Harvard Business Review*, 58–66.

Compilation of References

Bartels, J., Douwes, R., Jong, M., & Pruyn, A. (2006). Organizational Identification During a Merger: Determinants of Employees' Expected Identification with the New Organization. *British Journal of Management, 17*(S1), 49–67. doi:10.1111/j.1467-8551.2006.00478.x

Basoro, T. S., & Tefera, B. (2021). Ethical leadership practices and factors affecting it in South Addis Ababa district commercial bank of Ethiopia. *European Journal of Business and Management, 13*(1), 1–11.

Bass, B. M. (1985), Leadership and Performance. *N.Y. Free Press.* https://www.langston.edu/sites/default/files/basic-content-files/TransformationalLeadership.pdf

Bass, B. M., & Bass Bernard, M. (1985). *Leadership and performance beyond expectations.* Academic Press.

Bass, B. M., & Riggio, R. E. (2010). The transformational model of leadership. *Leading organizations: Perspectives for a new era, 2*, 76-86.

Bass, B. M. (1985). *Leadership and performance beyond expectations.* Free Press.

Bass, B. M. (1985). *Leadership and Performance beyond Expectations.* Free Press.

Bass, B. M. (1985). *Leadership and Performance Beyond Expectations.* Free Press.

Bass, B. M. (1990). *Bass & Stogdill's Handbook of Leadership: Theory, research & managerial applications* (3rd ed.). Free Press.

Bass, B. M. (1997). Does the transactional–transformational leadership paradigm transcend organizational and national boundaries? *The American Psychologist, 52*(2), 130–139. doi:10.1037/0003-066X.52.2.130

Bass, B. M. (2012). *The Bass handbook of leadership: Theory, research, and managerial applications* (4th ed.). Free Press.

Bass, B. M., & Avolio, B. J. (1990). Developing transformational leadership: 1992 and beyond. *Journal of European Industrial Training, 14*(5). Advance online publication. doi:10.1108/03090599010135122

Bass, B. M., & Avolio, B. J. (1996). Multifactor leadership questionnaire. *Western Journal of Nursing Research.*

Bass, B. M., & Avolio, B. J. (2004). *Multifactor Leadership Questionnaire: MLQ; manual and sampler set.* Mind Garden.

Bass, B. M., & Riggio, R. E. (2006). *Transformational leadership.* Lawrence Erlbaum Publishers. doi:10.4324/9781410617095

Bassett, N. (2021). *Sustainable Fashion Through Circular Business Innovations: New Business Models Reduce Waste. In Sustainable Textile and Fashion Value Chains: Drivers.* Concepts, Theories and Solutions.

Basu, P. S. (2022). Organisational Csr Practices: A Strategic Lever Towards Harnessing Higher Employee Engagement. *Journal of Organisation & Human Behaviour, 11*(1), 40–49.

Bates, R., & Khasawneh, S. (2005). *Organizational learning culture, learning transfer climate and perceived innovation in Jordanian organizations.* doi:10.1111/j.1468-2419.2005.00224.x

Bayiz Ahmad, A., Liu, B., & Saleem Butt, A. (2020). Predictors and outcomes of change recipient proactivity in public organizations of the Kurdistan region of Iraq. *International Public Management Journal, 23*(6), 823–851. doi:10.1080/10967494.2019.1588812

Baykal, E. (2020). A Model on Authentic Leadership in The Light Of Hope Theory. *Sosyal Bilimler Arastirmalari Dergisi, 10*(3).

Beauty, M., & Aigbogun, O. (2022). Effects of Leadership Styles on Employee Performance: A Case Study of Turnall Holdings LTD, Harare. *International Journal of Academic Research in Business & Social Sciences*, *12*(1). doi:10.6007/IJARBSS/v12-i1/12037

Becerra-Fernandez, I., & Sabherwal, R. (2015). *Knowledge management: systems and processes* (2nd ed.). Routledge.

Becker, L., Coussement, K., Büttgen, M., & Weber, E. (2022). Leadership in innovation communities: The impact of transformational leadership language on member participation. *Journal of Product Innovation Management*, *39*(3), 371–393. doi:10.1111/jpim.12588

Bedoya, E. (June 2018). *Contributions of transformational leadership style to change management*. Ferenc Farkas 1st International Conference, Pécs, Hungary. https://www.researchgate.net/publication/345344646_Contributions_of_transformational_leadership_style_to_change_management

Bedwell, W. L., & Ramos, A. J. (2022). Remote leadership: A review and future directions. *Journal of Organizational Behavior*, *43*(1), 33–51.

Begum, S., Ashfaq, M., Xia, E., & Awan, U. (2022). Does green transformational leadership lead to green innovation? The role of green thinking and creative process engagement. *Business Strategy and the Environment*, *31*(1), 580–597. doi:10.1002/bse.2911

Behery, M. H. (2008, June). Retracted: Leadership behaviors that count in an organization's performance in the middle east: The case of Dubai. *Journal of Leadership Studies*, *2*(2), 6–21. doi:10.1002/jls.20058

Behfar, K. J., Peterson, R. S., Mannix, E. A., & Trochim, W. M. K. (2008). The critical role of conflict resolution in teams: A close look at the links between conflict type, conflict management strategies, and team outcomes. *The Journal of Applied Psychology*, *93*(1), 170–188. doi:10.1037/0021-9010.93.1.170 PMID:18211143

Belschak, F., Jacobs, G., Giessner, S., Hortin, K., & Bayerl, P. S. (2020). When the going gets tough: Employee reactions to large-scale organizational change and the tole of employee Machiavellianism. *Journal of Organizational Behavior*, *41*(9), 830–850. doi:10.1002/job.2478

Benassi, M., & Landoni, M. (2019). State-owned enterprises as knowledge-explorer agents. *Industry and Innovation*, *26*(2), 218–241. doi:10.1080/13662716.2018.1529554

Benmira, S., & Agboola, M. (2021). Evolution of leadership theory. *BMJ Leader*.

Bergh, D., & Ngah-Kiing Lim, E. (n.d.). *Learning how to restructure: Absorptive capacity and improvisational views of restructuring actions and performance*. Academic Press.

Berinato, S. (2014). A framework for understanding VUCA. *Harvard Business Review*, *59*(9).

Berkovich, I. (2016). School leaders and transformational leadership theory: Time to part ways? *Journal of Educational Administration*, *54*(5), 609–622. doi:10.1108/JEA-11-2015-0100

Berkowitz, E. (2017). George Bush and the Americans with Disabilities Act. *Social Welfare History Project*. https://socialwelfare.library.vcu.edu/recollections/george-bush-and-the-americanswith-disabilities-act/

Bernstein, B., & Solomon, J. (1999). 'Pedagogy, identity and the construction of a theory of symbolic control': Basil Bernstein questioned by Joseph Solomon. *British Journal of Sociology of Education*, *20*(2), 265–279. doi:10.1080/01425699995443

Bertocci, D. I. (2009). *Leadership in organizations: There is a difference between leaders and managers*. University Press of America.

Compilation of References

Bethune, S. (2021). *One year on: Unhealthy weight gains, increased drinking reported by Americans coping with pandemic stress.* American Psychological Association (APA.). https://www.apa.org/news/press/releases/2021/03/one-year-pandemic-stress

Bhagavad Gita & Artificial Intelligence. (2023). *Bhagavad Gita & Artificial Intelligence.* https://www.linkedin.com/pulse/bhagavad-gita-artificial-intelligence-dr-ing-srinivas-jagarlapoodi

Bhardwaj, B. R. (2021). Adoption, diffusion and consumer behavior in technopreneurship. *International Journal of Emerging Markets, 16*(2), 179–220. doi:10.1108/IJOEM-11-2018-0577

Bhasin, H. (2019, October 18). *What Causes Change in an Organization? 10 Factors Explored.* https://www.marketing91.com/change-in-an-organization/#:~:text=What%20Causes%20Change%20in%20an%20Organization%3F%2010%20Factors,8%208%29%20Merger%20and%20acquisition%20...%20More%20items

Bhatnagar, K., & Srivastava, K. (2012, January). Job satisfaction in healthcare organizations. *Industrial Psychiatry Journal.* https://www.ncbi.nlm.nih.gov/pmc/articles/PMC3678186/

Bhattathiri, M. P. (2004). Bhagavad Gita and Management. *Eubios Journal of Asian and International Bioethics; EJAIB, 14*, 138–142.

Bıçakçı, A. B. (2012). Sürdürülebilirlik yönetiminde halkla iliskilerin rolü. *Sosyal ve Beseri Bilimler Dergisi, 4*(1), 47–56.

Biddle, C., & Brown, L. M. (2020). Banishing "Siberia" and student seclusion: Leading trauma-informed systems change in a rural school. *Journal of Cases in Educational Leadership, 23*(2), 85–97. doi:10.1177/1555458920910771

Bingham, D., & Bubb, S. (2017). Leadership for wellbeing. In P. Earley & T. Greany (Eds.), *School Leadership and Education System Reform* (pp. 173–181). Bloomsbury.

Birasnav, M., Albufalasa, M., & Bader, Y. 2013. The role of transformational leadership and knowledge management processes on predicting product and process innovation: an empirical study developed in Kingdom of Bahrain. *TÉKHNE - Review of Applied Management Studies, 11*, 64-75. http://dx.doi.org/ doi:10.1016/j.tekhne.2013.08.001

Birasnav, M., Rangnekar, S., & Dalpati, A. (2011). Transformational leadership and human capital benefits: The role of knowledge management. *Leadership and Organization Development Journal, 32*(2), 106–126. doi:10.1108/01437731111112962

Bisht, I. S., Rana, J. C., & Pal Ahlawat, S. (2020). The future of smallholder farming in India: Some sustainability considerations. *Sustainability (Basel), 12*(9), 3751. doi:10.3390u12093751

Bittner, E. A. C., & Leimeister, J. M. (2014). Creating shared understanding in heterogeneous work groups: Why it matters and how to achieve it. *Journal of Management Information Systems, 31*(1), 111–144. doi:10.2753/MIS0742-1222310106

Blanchard, B. (2015). Leading at a higher level (Revised & Expanded ed.). Pearson.

Blanchard, B. (2010). *Leading at a higher level.* BMC Press.

Blanco-Canqui, H., Shaver, T. M., Lindquist, J. L., Shapiro, C. A., Elmore, R. W., Francis, C. A., & Hergert, G. W. (2015). Cover Crops and Ecosystem Services: Insights from Studies in Temperate Soils. *Agronomy Journal, 107*(6), 2449–2474. doi:10.2134/agronj15.0086

Blasi, S., & Sedita, S. R. (2022). Mapping the emergence of a new organisational form: An exploration of the intellectual structure of the B Corp research. *Corporate Social Responsibility and Environmental Management, 29*(1), 107–123. doi:10.1002/csr.2187

Blau, P. (1964). *Exchange and power in social life.* Wiley.

Bloome, D. (2017). Childhood Family Structure and Intergenerational Income Mobility in the United States. *Demography*, *54*(2), 541–569. doi:10.100713524-017-0564-4 PMID:28315158

Bloomfield, J., Ackland, T. R., & Elliot, B. C. (1994). *Applied anatomy and biomechanics in sport*. Blackwell Scientific.

Bloom, I., & Smith, J. (2010). Scaling Social Impact. *Stanford Social Innovation Review*, *8*(3), 46–51.

Böckel, A., Hörisch, J., & Tenner, I. (2021). A systematic literature review of crowdfunding and sustainability: highlighting what really matters. *Management Review Quarterly, 71*, 433-453. https://link.springer.com/article/10.1007/s11301-020-00189-3

Bolkan, S., & Goodboy, A. K. (2009). Transformational leadership in the classroom: Fostering student learning, student participation, and teacher credibility. *Journal of Instructional Psychology*, *36*(4).

Bonaccio, S., Connelly, C. E., Gellatly, I. R., Jetha, A., & Martin Ginis, K. A. (2020). The participation of people with disabilities in the workplace across the employment cycle: Employer concerns and research evidence. *Journal of Business and Psychology*, *35*(2), 135–158. doi:10.100710869-018-9602-5 PMID:32269418

Bonchek, M. (2013). Purpose is good. Shared purpose is better. *Harvard Business Review*. https://hbr.org/2013/03/purpose-is-good-shared-purpose

Bono, J. E., & Judge, T. A. (2004). Personality and transformational and transactional leadership: A meta-analysis. *The Journal of Applied Psychology*, *89*(5), 901–910. doi:10.1037/0021-9010.89.5.901 PMID:15506869

Bonuses, N. (n.d.). *How to Land a Big Payout*. Retrieved July 19, 2020, from https://www.nursingschool.org/nursing-careers/salaries/bonuses/#context/api/listings/prefilter

Bordia, P., Restubog, S., Jimieson, N., & Imer, B. (2011). Haunted by the Past: Effects of Poor Management History on Employee Attitudes and Turnover. *Group & Organization Management*, *32*(2), 191–222. doi:10.1177/1059601110392990

Borgès Da Silva, R., Brault, I., Pineault, R., Chouinard, M. C., Prud'homme, A., & D'Amour, D. (2018). Nursing Practice in Primary Care and Patients' Experience of Care. *Journal of Primary Care & Community Health*, *9*, 2150131917747186. doi:10.1177/2150131917747186 PMID:29357748

Bormann, K. C., & Diebig, M. (2021). Following an Uneven Lead: Trickle-Down Effects of Differentiated Transformational Leadership. *Journal of Management*, *47*(8), 2105–2134. doi:10.1177/0149206320931584

Boubakary, A. (2016). Change management: The need for successful integration of corporate social responsibility in organizations. *The International Journal of Organizational Analysis*, *24*(2), 231–250.

Boudrias, J.-S., Morin, A. J., & Lajoie, D. (2014). Directionality of the associations between psychological empowerment and behavioral involvement: A longitudinal autoregressive cross-lagged analysis. *Journal of Occupational and Organizational Psychology*, *87*(3), 437–463. doi:10.1111/joop.12056

Boulton, J., & Preiser, R. (2021). Action Research. In Reinette Biggs, Alto De Vos, Rika Preiser, Hayley Clements, Kristine Maciejewski, Maja Schlüter (Eds.) *The Routledge Handbook of Research Methods for Social-Ecological,* (pp. 2017-229). Routledge. Systemshttps://www.taylorfrancis.com/chapters/oa-edit/10.4324/9781003021339-18/action-research-jean-boulton-rika-preiser

Boulware, L. E., Corbie, G., Aguilar-Gaxiola, S., Wilkins, C. H., Ruiz, R., Vitale, A., & Egede, L. E. (2022). Combating Structural Inequities — Diversity, Equity, and Inclusion in Clinical and Translational Research. *The New England Journal of Medicine*, *386*(3), 201–203. doi:10.1056/NEJMp2112233 PMID:35029847

Compilation of References

Bourke, J., & Espedido, A. (2020). The key to inclusive leadership. *Harvard Business Review*, 2–5. https://hbr.org/2020/03/the-key-to-inclusive-leadership

Bourne, P. A. (2018). Ultimate leadership winning execution strategies for your situation. *Academy of Educational Leadership Journal*, *22*(1), 1–6.

Bowers, D. G., & Seashore, S. E. (1966). Predicting organizational effectiveness with a four-factor theory of leadership. *Administrative Science Quarterly*, *11*(2), 238–263. doi:10.2307/2391247

Boyatzis, R. E., Goleman, D., & Rhee, K. (2000). In R. Bar-On & J. D. A. Parker (Eds.), *"Clustering competence in emotional intelligence: insights from the emotional competence inventory (ECI),"* in *Handbook of Emotional Intelligence* (pp. 343–362). Jossey-Bass.

Boyce, M. E. (2003). Organizational learning is essential to achieving and sustaining change in higher education. *Innovative Higher Education*, *28*(2), 119–136. doi:10.1023/B:IHIE.0000006287.69207.00

Bozeman, B. (2007). *Public values and public interest: Counterbalancing economic individualism*. Georgetown University Press.

Bozhikin, I., Macke, J., & da Costa, L. F. (2019). The role of government and key non-state actors in social entrepreneurship: A systematic literature review. Journal of Cleaner Production, 226, 730–747. https://doi.org/10.1016/j.jclepro.2019.04.076

Bozlağan, R. (2005). Sürdürülebilir gelişme düşüncesinin tarihsel arka planı. *Journal of Social Policy Conferences*, *0*(50), 1011–1028.

Bradach, J. (2003). *Scale and Scope: The Dynamics of Industrial Capitalism*. Harvard University Press.

Bradford, T. Jr, Hock, G., Greenhaw, L., & Kingery, W. L. (2019). Comparing Experiential Learning Techniques and Direct Instruction on Student Knowledge of Agriculture in Private School Students. *Journal of Agricultural Education*, *60*(3), 80–96.

Braun, V., & Clarke, V. (2006). Using thematic analysis in psychology. *Qualitative Research in Psychology*, *3*(2), 77–101. doi:10.1191/1478088706qp063oa

Brave Heart, M. Y. H., & Brave Heart Debruyn, L. M. (1998). The American Indian holocaust: Healing historical unresolved grief. *American Indian and Alaska Native Mental Health Research*, *8*(2), 56–78. PMID:9842066

Brazill, S., & Ruff, W. (2022). Using Transformational Leadership to Create Brave Space in Teaching Multicultural Education. *International Journal of Multicultural Education*, *24*(2), 114–131. doi:10.18251/ijme.v24i2.2847

Breevaart, K., Bakker, A., Hetland, J., Demerouti, E., Olsen, O. K., & Espevik, R. (2014). Daily transactional and transformational leadership and daily employee engagement. *Journal of Occupational and Organizational Psychology*, *87*(1), 138–157. doi:10.1111/joop.12041

Bridges, W. (1980). *Transitions: Making Sense of Life's Changes*. Addison-Wesley.

Briggs, A. R. J., Coleman, M., & Morrison, M. (2012). *Research methods in educational leadership & management* (3rd ed.). Sage. doi:10.4135/9781473957695

Bromley, H. R., & Kirschner-Bromley, V. A. (2007). Are you a transformational leader? *Physician Executive*, *33*(6). PMID:18092620

Brostow, D. P., Gunzburger, E., Abbate, L. M., Brenner, L. A., & Thomas, K. S. (2019). Mental illness, not obesity status, is associated with food insecurity among the elderly in the health and retirement study. *Journal of Nutrition in Gerontology and Geriatrics*, *38*(2), 149–172.

Brown, R. L. (2013). Common good and common ground: The inevitability of fundamental disagreement. *The University of Chicago Law Review*. https://lawreview.uchicago.edu/sites/default/files/15_Brown_BKR.pdf

Brown, J. L., & Moffett, C. A. (1999). *The hero's journey: How educators can transform schools and improve learning*. Association for Supervision and Curriculum Development.

Brown-Jackson, K. (2017). *Disrupting and Retooling: A Model for an Effective Community-Based Telehealth Program (Order No. 28144638)*. ProQuest Central. https://www.proquest.com/dissertations-theses/disrupting-retooling-model-effective-community/docview/2440009177/se-2

Brown, N. R., & Kelsey, K. D. (2013). Sidewalks and City Streets: A Model for Vibrant Agricultural Education in Urban American Communities. *Journal of Agricultural Education*, *54*(2), 57–69.

Brown, P., & Keep, E. (2018). Rethinking the race between education and technology. *Issues in Science and Technology*, 31–39.

Bruce, K., & Nyland, C. (2011). Elton Mayo and the deification of human relations. *Organization Studies*, *32*(3), 383–405. doi:10.1177/0170840610397478

Bucknor, A., Kamali, P., Phillips, N., Mathijssen, I., Rakhorst, H., Lin, S., & Furnas, H. (2018). Gender inequality for women in plastic surgery: A systematic scoping review. *Plastic and Reconstructive Surgery*, *141*(6), 1561–1577. doi:10.1097/PRS.0000000000004375 PMID:29794715

Buil, I., Martínez, E., & Matute, J. (2019). Transformational leadership and employee performance: The role of identification, engagement and proactive personality. *International Journal of Hospitality Management*, *77*, 64–75. doi:10.1016/j.ijhm.2018.06.014

Bureau of Labor Statistics. (2013). Persons with a disability: labor force characteristics - 2022. *BLS.*. https://www.bls.gov/news.release/pdf/disabl.pdf

Bureau, J. S., Gagné, M., Morin, A. J. S., & Mageau, G. A. (2021). Transformational Leadership and Incivility: A Multilevel and Longitudinal Test. *Journal of Interpersonal Violence*, *36*(1-2), NP448–NP473. doi:10.1177/0886260517734219 PMID:29294943

Burke, W. W., Roloff, K. S., & Mitchinson, A. (2016). *Learning agility: A new model and measure (Working Paper)*. Teachers College, Columbia University.

Burnes, B. (2004). *Managing change: a strategic approach to organizational dynamics* (4th ed.). Financial Times Prentice Hall.

Burnes, B. (2009). Reflections: Ethics and organizational change–Time for a return to Lewinian values. *Journal of Change Management*, *9*(4), 359–381. doi:10.1080/14697010903360558

Burnes, B., & Jackson, P. (2011). Success and failure in organizational change: An exploration of the role of values. *Journal of Change Management*, *11*(2), 133–162. doi:10.1080/14697017.2010.524655

Burns, J.M. (1978). *Transforming Leadership: A New Pursuit of Happiness*. Grove Press.

Burns, J. M. (2003). *Leadership*. Harper & Row.

Burris, E. R., Detert, J. R., & Chiaburu, D. S. (2008). Quitting before leaving: The mediating effects of psychological attachment and detachment on voice. *The Journal of Applied Psychology*, *93*(4), 912–9222. doi:10.1037/0021-9010.93.4.912 PMID:18642993

Compilation of References

Burton, S. L. (2014). *Best Practices for Faculty Development Through Andragogy in Online Distance Education* (Order No. 10758601). ProQuest Central. https://www.proquest.com/dissertations-theses/best-practices-faculty-development-through/docview/1989663912/se-2

Burton, S. L. (2022). Cybersecurity Leadership from a Telemedicine/Telehealth Knowledge and Organizational Development Examination (Order No. 29066056). ProQuest Central. https://www.proquest.com/dissertations-theses/cybersecurity-leadership-telemedicine-telehealth/docview/2662752457/se-2

Busch, G., Bayer, E., Spiller, A., & Kühl, S. (2022). 'Factory farming'? Public perceptions of farm sizes and sustainability in animal farming. *PLOS Sustainability and Transformation, 1*(10), e0000032. doi:10.1371/journal.pstr.0000032

Bushe, G. R., & Marshak, R. J. (2016). The dialogic mindset: Leading emergent change in a complex world. *Organization Development Journal, 34*(1), 37–65.

Butler, J. (2020). Learning to lead: A discussion of development programs for academic leadership capability in Australian Universities. *Journal of Higher Education Policy and Management, 42*(4), 424–437. doi:10.1080/1360080X.2019.1701855

Buys, D. R., & Rennekamp, R. (2020). Cooperative extension as a force for healthy, rural communities: Historical perspectives and future directions. *American Journal of Public Health, 110*(9), 1300–1303. doi:10.2105/AJPH.2020.305767 PMID:32673106

Buys, N., Wagner, S., Randall, C., Harder, H., Geisen, T., Yu, I., Hassler, B., Howe, C., & Fraess-Phillips, A. (2017). Disability management and organizational culture in Australia and Canada. *Work (Reading, Mass.), 57*(3), 409–419. doi:10.3233/WOR-172568 PMID:28800348

Buzby, J. C., Farah-Wells, H., & Hyman, J. (2014). The estimated amount, value, and calories of postharvest food losses at the retail and consumer levels in the United States. *USDA-ERS Economic Information Bulletin*, (121).

Byrd, M. Y. (2022). Inclusive Leadership: Critical Practice Perspectives From the Field. *Advances in Developing Human Resources, 24*(4), 223–224. doi:10.1177/15234223221120180

Byrne, D. (2022). A worked example of Braun and Clarke's approach to reflexive thematic analysis. *Quality & Quantity, 56*(3), 1391–1412. doi:10.100711135-021-01182-y

Byrne-Haber, S. (2019, June 13). The importance of Disability Employee Resource Groups. *Medium*. https://sheribyrnehaber.medium.com/the-importance-of-disability-employee-resource-groups-21ea6552ea2e

Cagle, M. (2022). Why you need to identify your ideal clients. *[BLOG] Mark Cagle LPC Supervisor*. https://lpcsupervisiontexas.com/identify-your-ideal-clients/#:~:text=An%20ideal%20client%20is%20someone,feel%20comfortable%20working%20with%20you

Cahyono, Y., Novitasari, D., Sihotang, M., Aman, M., Fahlevi, M., Nadeak, M., ... Purwanto, A. (2020). The effect of transformational leadership dimensions on job satisfaction and organizational commitment: Case studies in private university Lecturers. *Solid State Technology, 63*(1s), 158–184.

Caillier, J. G. (2014). Toward a better understanding of the relationship between transformational leadership, public service motivation, mission valence, and employee performance: A preliminary study. *Public Personnel Management, 43*(2), 218–239. doi:10.1177/0091026014528478

Cambridge Dictionary. (2023). *Too many cooks spoil the broth*. Cambridge Dictionary. https://dictionary.cambridge.org/us/dictionary/english/too-many-cooks-spoil-the-broth

Camilleri, E. (2006). Towards developing an organisational commitment – public service motivation model for the Maltese public service employees. *Public Policy and Administration, 21*(1), 63-83. . doi:10.1177/095207670602100105

Campbell, H. (2014). *Managing Organizational Change: A practical toolbook for leaders.* Kogan Page, Limited. https://ebookcentral.proquest.com/lib/bayloru/detail.action?docID=1679159

Campbell, R. D. (2018, October 10). Stigma of depression hurts African American populations more than others. *University of Georgia (UGA) Today.* https://news.uga.edu/stigma-depression-hurts-african-american-populations/

Campos, A. (2020, November). *Transformational Leadership Theory.* Academic Press.

Campos, J. A. D. B., Campos, L. A., Martins, B. G., Valadão Dias, F., Ruano, R., & Maroco, J. (2022). The Psychological Impact of COVID-19 on Individuals with and without mental health disorders. *Psychological Reports, 125*(5), 2435–2455.

Canaslan, A., & Güçlü, N. (2020). Öğretmenlerin öğrenme çevikliği: Ölçek geliştirme çalışması. *Kastamonu Education Journal, 28*(5), 2071–2083.

Candy, P. (1991). *Self-direction for lifelong learning: A comprehensive guide to theory and practice.* Jossey-Bass.

Canrinus, E. T., Helms-Lorenz, M., Beijaard, D., Buitink, J., & Hofman, A. (2012). Self- efficacy, job satisfaction, motivation, and commitment: Exploring the relationships between indicators of teachers' professional identity. *European Journal of Psychology of Education, 27*(1), 115–132. doi:10.100710212-011-0069-2

Canrinus, E. T., Lorenz-Helms, M., Beijaard, D., Buitink, J., & Hofman, A. (2011). Profiling teachers' sense of professional identity. *Educational Studies, 37*(5), 593–608. doi:10.1080/03055698.2010.539857

Canterino, F., Cirella, S., Piccoli, B., & Shani, A. (2020). Leadership and change mobilization: The mediating role of distributed leadership. *Journal of Business Research, 108,* 42–51. doi:10.1016/j.jbusres.2019.09.052

Carolissen, R., & Bozalek, V. (2017). Addressing dualisms in student perceptions of a historically white and black university in South Africa. *Race, Ethnicity and Education, 20*(3), 344–357. doi:10.1080/13613324.2016.1260229

Carson, J. B., & Farh, J. L. (2023). The role of transformational leadership in overcoming resistance to change: A theoretical perspective. *Journal of Change Management, 23*(1), 1–15.

Carson, J., Tesluk, P., & Marrone, J. (2007). Shared leadership in teams: An investigation of antecedent conditions and performance. *Academy of Management Journal, 50*(5), 1217–1234.

Cartwright, S., & Holmes, N. (2006). The meaning of work: The challenge of regaining employee engagement and reducing cynicism. *Human Resource Management Review, 16*(2), 199–208. doi:10.1016/j.hrmr.2006.03.012

Casciano, R., & Massey, D. S. (2008). Neighborhoods, employment, and welfare use: Assessing the influence of neighborhood socioeconomic composition. *Social Science Research, 37*(2), 544–558. doi:10.1016/j.ssresearch.2007.08.008 PMID:19069058

Cavalcante, S., Kesting, P., & Ulhoi, J. (2011). Business model dynamics and innovation: (Re)establishing the missing linkages. *Management Decision, 49*(8), 1327–1342. doi:10.1108/00251741111163142

CEB. (2014). *The rise of the network leader: Reframing leadership in the new work environment.* CEB. https://www.multivu.com/assets/59760/documents/59760-CEB-Annual-EG-2014-original.pdf

CEE. (1998). *Education for Sustainable Development in the Schools Sector: A Report to DfEE/QCA from the Panel for Education for Sustainable Development.* Council for Environmental Education.

Cemil, T., Bryar, M., Sharif, A., Akar, H., & Mahmood, F. (2020). Transformational leadership Impact on employee performance in the Kurdistan region of Iraq. *Eurasian Journal of Management & Social Sciences.*

Compilation of References

Centers for Disease Control and Prevention (CDC). (2018). Prevalence of self-reported invisible disability among U.S. adults aged ³18 years, 2015–2017. *MMWR. Surveillance Summaries, 67*(18), 1–8.

Cervero, R. M., & Wilson, A. L. (2006). *Working the planning table: Negotiating democratically for adult, continuing and workplace education*. Jossey-Bass.

Chater, N. (2020). *We might dream of a world where there are no rules, but how practical would it be?* BBC. https://www.bbc.com/future/article/20200220-could-we-live-in-a-world-without-rules

Chatterjee, D. (2014). *Timeless Leadership: 18 Leadership Sutras from the Bhagavad Gita,Wiley Publications*. Sage Publications.

Chattopadhyay, S., Prasad, I., Henley, A. Z., Sarma, A., & Barik, T. (2020, April). What's wrong with computational notebooks? Pain points, needs, and design opportunities. In *Proceedings of the 2020 CHI conference on human factors in computing systems* (pp. 1-12). 10.1145/3313831.3376729

Chenarides, L., Grebitus, C., Lusk, J. L., & Printezis, I. (2021). Who practices urban agriculture? An empirical analysis of participation before and during the COVID-19 pandemic. *Agribusiness, 37*(1), 142–159. doi:10.1002/agr.21675 PMID:33362336

Chen, W., & Zhang, J. H. (2023). Does shared leadership always work? A state-of-the-art review and future prospects. *Journal of Work-Applied Management, 15*(1), 51–66. doi:10.1108/JWAM-09-2022-0063

Cherkowski, S., & Walker, K. (2016). Flourishing leadership: Engaging purpose, passion, and play in the work of leading schools. *Journal of Educational Administration, 54*(4), 378–392. doi:10.1108/JEA-10-2014-0124

Chilisa, B. (2021). Indigenous research methodologies. *Sage (Atlanta, Ga.)*.

Chin, J. H., & Wang, H. (Eds.), *Handbook of partial least squares*. Springer., doi:10.1007/978-3-540-32827-8_29

Chin, W. W. (1998). The partial least squares approach to structural equation modeling. In G. A. Marcoulides (Ed.), *Modern methods for business research* (pp. 295–336). Erlbaum.

Chirichello, M. (2004). Collective leadership: Reinventing the principalship. *Kappa Delta Pi Record, 40*(3), 119–123. doi:10.1080/00228958.2004.10516420

Chopra, R. (2017). Strategic human resource management and its impact on organisational performance. *Global Journal of Enterprise Information System, 9*(3), 89–93. doi:10.18311/gjeis/2017/16057

Choudhury, P., & Heras, M. (2023). The impact of war on global leadership. *Journal of Global Leadership, 5*(2), 115–130.

Chouinard, J. A., & Cousins, J. B. (2013). Participatory evaluation for development: Examining research-based knowledge from within the African context. *African Evaluation Journal, 1*(1), 9. doi:10.4102/aej.v1i1.43

Chumbley, S. B. (2016). The impact of a career and technology education program. *SAGE Open, 6*(4), 2158244016678036.

Clark, H. H., & Brennan, S. (1991). Grounding in communication. *Perspectives on socially shared cognition*.

Clark, H. H. (1996). *Using language*. Cambridge University Press. doi:10.1017/CBO9780511620539

Clemons, C., Lindner, J. R., Murray, B., Cook, M. P., Sams, B., & Williams, G. (2018). Spanning the Gap: The Confluence of Agricultural Literacy and Being Agriculturally Literate. *Journal of Agricultural Education, 59*(4), 238–252. doi:10.5032/jae.2018.04238

Cletzer, D. A., Mott, R. L., Simonsen, J. C., Tummons, J. D., Peckman, J. Y., & Preston, K. (2022). Agricultural leadership: A national portrait of undergraduate courses. *Journal of Agricultural Education, 63*(1), 165–181.

Clò, S., Di Giulio, M., Galanti, M. T., & Sorrentino, M. (2016). Italian State-Owned Enterprises after Decades of Reforms." Still public? *Economia Pubblica*, *3*, 11–49.

Coblentz, J. B. (2002). *Organizational Sustainability: The three aspects that matter*. Academy for Educational Development.

Cohen, L., Manion, L., & Morrison, K. (2011). *Research methods in education* (7th ed.). Routledge.

Cohen, W. M., & Levinthal, D. A. (1990). Absorptive capacity: A new perspective on learning and innovation. *Administrative Science Quarterly*, *35*(1), 128–152. doi:10.2307/2393553

Coleman, A. M. (201). *A dictionary of Psychology*. (4th ed.). Oxford University Press.

Coleman-Jensen, A., Rabbitt, M. P., Gregory, C. A., & Singh, A. (2022). Household food security in the United States. *Economic Research Report*, *155*.

Coleman, R. A., & Donoher, W. J. (2022). Looking Beyond the Dyad: How Transformational Leadership Affects Leader–Member Exchange Quality and Outcomes. *Journal of Leadership Studies*, *15*(4), 6–17. doi:10.1002/jls.21792

Collins, C., & Kehoe, R. (2017). Examining strategic fit and misfit in the management of knowledge workers. *Industrial & Labor Relations Review*, *70*(2), 308–335. doi:10.1177/0019793916654481

Conger, J. A. (1999). Charismatic and transformational leadership in organizations: An insider's perspective on these developing streams of research. *The Leadership Quarterly*, *10*(2), 145–179. doi:10.1016/S1048-9843(99)00012-0

Conger, J. A., & Kanungo, R. N. (1988). The empowerment process: Integrating theory and practice. *Academy of Management Review*, *13*(3), 471–482. doi:10.2307/258093

Conger, J. A., & Kanungo, R. N. (1998). *Charismatic Leadership in Organizations*. Sage Publications. doi:10.4135/9781452204932

Connective Leadership Institute. (2022). *Connective leadership*. Connective Leadership Institute. https://connective-leadership.com/

Connors, C. (2020). *Emotional Intelligence for the Modern Leader*. Rockridge Press.

Constantinou, C. S., Andreou, P., Nikitara, M., & Papageorgiou, A. (2022). *Cultural competence in healthcare and healthcare education*. Academic Press.

Cook, B. G. (2011). Invisible disabilities in the workplace: Challenges and strategies. *Journal of Vocational Rehabilitation*, *35*(3), 199–207. doi:10.3233/JVR-2011-0528

Cook, D. A., & Artino, A. R. Jr. (2016). Motivation to learn: An overview of contemporary theories. *Medical Education*, *50*(10), 997–1014. doi:10.1111/medu.13074 PMID:27628718

Cooks-Campbell, A. (2022, February 28). *Understanding invisible disabilities in the workplace*. Understanding Invisible Disabilities in the Workplace. https://www.betterup.com/blog/invisible-disabilities#:~:text=A%20simple%20way%20to%20provide,for%20people%20with%20chronic%20conditions

Corporate Leadership Council. (2005). Realizing the Full Potential of Rising Talent: Vol. I. *A Quantitative Analysis of the Identification and Development of High-potential Employees*. Corporate Executive Board.

Cortellazzo, L., Bruni, E., & Zampieri, R. (2019). The role of leadership in a digitalized world: A review. *Frontiers in Psychology*, *10*, 1938. doi:10.3389/fpsyg.2019.01938 PMID:31507494

Cosby, A., Manning, J., Power, D., & Harreveld, B. (2022). New decade, same concerns: A systematic review of agricultural literacy of school students. *Education Sciences*, *12*(4), 235. doi:10.3390/educsci12040235

Compilation of References

Costa-Font, M., & Gil, J. M., & Traill, W. B. (2008). Consumer acceptance, valuation of Dalgaard, T., Hutchings, N. J., & Porter, J. R. (2003). Agroecology, scaling and interdisciplinarity. *Agriculture, Ecosystems & Environment*, *100*(1), 39–51.

Cote, R. (2017). Vision of effective leadership. *Journal of Leadership, Accountability and Ethics*, *14*(4), 52–63.

Coton, F. (2019). *What are invisible disabilities?* University of Glasgow. https://www.gla.ac.uk/media/Media_702849_smxx.pdf

Coulter, K., & Punj, G. (2013). The effects of cognitive resource requirements, availability, and argument quality on brand attitudes: A melding of elaboration likelihood and cognitive resource matching theories. *Journal of Advertising*, *33*(4), 53–64. doi:10.1080/00913367.2004.10639177

Cousins, J. B. (2011). Intervention action research: A methodology for developing, enacting, and evaluating interventions. *New Directions for Evaluation*, *2011*(130), 7–20.

Covarrubias, V. B., Thill, K., & Domnanovich, J. (2017). The importance of strategic competence in HRM. Evidence from Austria, Czech Republic, Hungary and Slovakia. *Journal of Eastern European & Central Asian Research*, *4*(2), 1–11. doi:10.15549/jeecar.v4i2.145

Covey, S. R. (1988). *7 basic habits of highly effective people*. Free Press.

Cox, T. H., & Blake, S. (1991). Managing cultural diversity: Implications for organizational competitiveness. *The Academy of Management Perspectives*, *5*(3), 45–56. doi:10.5465/ame.1991.4274465

Cox, W. T. L. (2023). Developing scientifically validated bias and diversity trainings that work: Empowering agents of change to reduce bias, create inclusion, and promote equity. *Management Decision*, *61*(4), 1038–1061. doi:10.1108/MD-06-2021-0839 PMID:37090785

Crane, A., & Matten, D. (2016). *Business ethics: Managing corporate citizenship and sustainability in the age of globalization* (4th ed.). Oxford University Press.

Crase, D., & Rosato, F. D. (1992). Single versus multiple authorship in professional journals. *Journal of Physical Education, Recreation & Dance*, *63*(7), 28–32. doi:10.1080/07303084.1992.10609913

Creasey, T. (2020). The cost and risks of poorly managed change. *Prosci: People, Change, Results*. https://blog.prosci.com/the-costs-risks-of-poorly-managed-change

Creswell, J. (2005). *Educational research: Planning, conducting, and evaluating quantitative and qualitative research*. Pearson.

Creswell, J. W., & Creswell, J. D. (2018). *Research design: qualitative, quantitative & mixed methods approaches* (5th ed.). Sage.

Creswell, J. W., & Plano Clark, V. L. (2018). *Designing and conducting mixed methods research* (3rd ed.). Sage.

Crittenden, J. (1992). *Beyond individualism: Reconstituting the liberal self*. Oxford University Press.

Crosby, B. (2008). Theoretical foundations of integrative leadership. *Integral Leadership Review*. http://integralleadershipreview.com/5000-feature-article-theoretical-foundations-of-integrative-leadership/

Crosby, B. C., & Bryson, J. M. (2005). *Leadership for the common good: Tackling public problems in a shared-power world* (Vol. 264). John Wiley & Sons.

Crosby, B. C., & Bryson, J. M. (2010). Integrative leadership and the creation and maintenance of cross-sector collaborations. *The Leadership Quarterly*, *21*(2), 211–230. doi:10.1016/j.leaqua.2010.01.003

Cross, M. (2004). Institutionalising campus diversity in South African higher education: Review of diversity scholarship and diversity education. *Higher Education*, *47*(4), 387–410. doi:10.1023/B:HIGH.0000020854.04852.80

Croucher, G., & Woelert, P. (2021). Administrative transformation and managerial growth: A longitudinal analysis of changes in the non-academic workforce at Australian universities. *Higher Education*, 1–17. doi:10.100710734-021-00759-8

Crowther, F. (1997). Teachers as Leaders—An Exploratory Framework. *International Journal of Educational Management*, *11*(1), 6–13. doi:10.1108/09513549710155410

Crucke, S., Servaes, M., Kluijtmans, T., Mertens, S., & Schollaert, E. (2022). Linking environmentally-specific transformational leadership and employees' green advocacy: The influence of leadership integrity. *Corporate Social Responsibility and Environmental Management*, *29*(2), 406–420. doi:10.1002/csr.2208

Cultural Relativism. (2000). In A. G. Johnson (Ed.), *The Blackwell dictionary of sociology* (2nd ed.). Blackwell Publishers. https://search-credoreference-com.portal.lib.fit.edu/content/entry/bksoc/cultural_relativism/0?institutionId=5457

Cummings, T. G., & Worley, C. G. (2008). *Organization Development & Change*. South-Western/Cengage Learning.

Cummings, T., & Worley, C. (2009). *Organization Development and Change* (9th ed.). South-Western Cengage Learning.

Cunliffe, A. L., & Eriksen, M. (2011). Relational leadership. *Human Relations*, *64*(11), 1425–1449. doi:10.1177/0018726711418388

Curran-Everett, D. (2015). Best Practices: A series of theory, evidence, and implementation. *Advances in Physiology Education*, *39*(4), 253. doi:10.1152/advan.00099.2015 PMID:26628644

Cutcher, L. (2009). Resisting change from within and without the organization. *Journal of Organizational Change Management*, *22*(3), 275–289. doi:10.1108/09534810910951069

Dabke, D. (2020). Impact of leader's perfectionism on team performance: An empirical study. *Journal of Organizational Behavior*, *41*(7), 620–634.

Dachler, H. P. (1992). Management and leadership as relational phenomena. In M.V. Cranach, W. Doise, & G. Mugny (Eds.), Social representations and social bases of knowledge (p. 169–178). Hogrefe and Huber.

Daniel, G. R. (2020). Safe spaces for enabling the creative process in Danso, A., Adomako, S., Amankwah-Amoah, J., Owusu-Agyei, S., & Konadu, R. (2019). Environmental sustainability orientation, competitive strategy and financial performance. *Business Strategy and the Environment*, *28*(5), 885–895.

Darling-Hammond, L. (2008). *Introduction: Teaching and learning for understanding. Powerful Learning: What We Know About Teaching for Understanding*. Jossey-Bass.

Dave, D. (2019). An Analytical Study of the Role of ICT in Higher Education. *Journal of Global Economics*, *15*(1), 56–61.

Davenport, T., & Prusak, L. (1998). *Working knowledge*. Harvard Business School Press.

Davies, S., Fong, C. Y., & Yau, O. H. M. (2020). Destructive leadership in the workplace: A cross-cultural study. *International Journal of Business and Management*, *15*(4), 272–285.

Day, D. V., & Dragoni, L. (2015). Leadership development: An outcome-oriented review based on time and levels of analyses. *Annual Review of Organizational Psychology and Organizational Behavior*, *2*(1), 133–156. doi:10.1146/annurev-orgpsych-032414-111328

Day, D. V., & O'Connor, P. M. (2003). Leadership development: Understanding the process. In S. E. Murphy & R. E. Riggio (Eds.), *The Future of Leadership Development*. Lawrence Erlbaum Associates.

Day, J., Chin, N., Sydnor, S., Widhalm, M., Shah, K. U., & Dorworth, L. (2021). Implications of climate change for tourism and outdoor recreation: An Indiana, USA, case study. *Climatic Change*, *169*(3-4), 1–21. doi:10.100710584-021-03284-w PMID:34924649

de Costa, J., Chen-Xu, J., Bentounsi, Z., & Vervoort, D. (2018). Women in surgery: Challenges and opportunities. *International Journal of Surgery: Global Health*, *1*(2), 1–3.

de Fatima Nery, V., Sanches Franco, K., & Rabelo Neiva, E. (2019). Attributes of the organizational change and its influence on attitudes toward organizational change and well-being at work: A longitudal study. *The Journal of Applied Behavioral Science*, *56*(2), 216–236. doi:10.1177/0021886319865277

De MeuseK. P. (2015). Using science to identify future leaders: Part III-The TALENTx7 assessment of learning agility. (Technical Report). Doi doi:10.13140/RG.2.1.4905.7769

De Meuse, K. P. (2017). Learning agility: Its evolution as a psychological construct and empirical relationship to leader success. *Consulting Psychology Journal*, *69*(4), 267–295. doi:10.1037/cpb0000100

De Meuse, K. P., Dai, G., Eichinger, R. W., Page, R. C., Clark, L. P., & Zewdie, S. (2011). The development and validation of a self-assessment of learning agility. In *Society for Industrial and Organizational Psychology Conference*. IEEE.

De Paula Vieira, A., & Anthony, R. (2020). Recalibrating veterinary medicine through animal welfare science and ethics for the 2020s. *Animals (Basel)*, *10*(4), 654. doi:10.3390/ani10040654 PMID:32283812

De Smet, A., Gast, A., Lavoie, J., & Lurie, M. (2023). *New leadership for a new era of thriving organizations*. McKinsey. https://www.mckinsey.com/capabilities/people-and-organizational-performance/our-insights/new-leadership-for-a-new-era-of-thriving-organizations

de Wit, H., & Altbach, P. G. (2021). Internationalization in higher education: Global trends and recommendations for its future. *Policy Reviews in Higher Education*, *5*(1), 28–46. doi:10.1080/23322969.2020.1820898

Deberry-Spence, B. E. N. E. T., & Torres, L. T. (2019). Multinational Corporation Approaches to Corporate Social Responsibility and Entrepreneurship in Africa. The Oxford Handbook of Corporate Social Responsibility: Psychological and Organizational Perspectives, 391.

Debevoise, N. D. (2021, January 26). The third critical step in problem-solving that Einstein missed. *Forbes Magazine*. https://www.forbes.com/sites/nelldebevoise/2021/01/26/the-third-critical-step-in-problem-solving-that-einstein-missed/?sh=acfa24f38079

Deci, E. L., & Ryan, R. M. (2002). *Handbook of self-determination research*. University of Rochester Press.

Dees, J. G. (2001). The meaning of social entrepreneurship. *Stanford Social Innovation Review*, *1*(1), 1–8. https://ssir.org/articles/entry/the_meaning_of_social_entrepreneurship

Dees, J. G. (2008). Scaling Social Impact: What Every Social Entrepreneur Should Know. *Stanford Social Innovation Review*, *6*(3), 35–41.

Delia, N. (2018). The Concept of Leadership. *"Ovidius" University Annals, Economic Sciences Series 8*(2). https://stec.univ-ovidius.ro/html/anale/RO/wp-content/uploads/2019/02/24.pdf

DeMarsh, N. (2022). Redefining the role of young farmers: Participatory action youth-led urban agriculture. *The International Journal of Sociology and Social Policy*, *42*(7/8), 727–742.

Demir, A., & Budur, T. (2019). Roles of leadership styles in corporate social responsibility to non-governmental organizations (NGOs). *International Journal of Social Sciences & Educational Studies*, *5*(4).

Deng, R., He, X., Liu, Y., Fu, Y., & Hu, X. (2020, January). Analysis on the Application Strategy of "4V" Marketing Mix Theory: Based on the Perspective of the Perceived Value of Agricultural Products Consumer. In *5th International Conference on Economics, Management, Law and Education (EMLE 2019)* (pp. 501-504). Atlantis Press.

DeNisi, A. S., & Freeman, A. B. (2017). Performance appraisal and performance management: 100 years of progress. Journal of Applied. *The Journal of Applied Psychology*, *102*(3), 421–433. doi:10.1037/apl0000085 PMID:28125265

Denis, J. L., Langley, A., & Sergi, V. (2012). Leadership in the plural. *The Academy of Management Annals*, *6*(1), 211–283. doi:10.5465/19416520.2012.667612

Densen, P. (2011). Challenges and Opportunities facing medical education. *Transactions of the American Clinical and Climatological Association*, *122*, 48–58. PMID:21686208

DeRue, D. S., & Ashford, S. J. (2010). Who will lead and who will follow? A social process of leadership identity construction in organizations. *Academy of Management Review*, *35*(4), 627–647. https://www.jstor.org/stable/29765008

Derue, D. S., Nahrgang, J. D., Wellman, N. E. D., & Humphrey, S. E. (2011). Trait and behavioral theories of leadership: An integration and meta-analytic test of their relative validity. *Personnel Psychology*, *64*(1), 7–52. doi:10.1111/j.1744-6570.2010.01201.x

Dharma, J., Mahendra, F., Putu, M., Ida, N., & Bachruddin, S. (2021). The Effect of Transformational Leadership Style on Employee Performance with Job Stress as Intervening Variables in PT. *Pos Indonesia, Proceedings of the 11th Annual International Conference on Industrial Engineering and Operations Management Singapore*.

Di Domenico, M., Daniel, E., & Nunan, D. (2014). Mental mobility in the digital age: Entrepreneurs and the online home-based business. *New Technology, Work and Employment*, *29*(3), 266–281. doi:10.1111/ntwe.12034

Dimitri, C., & Effland, A. (2020). From farming to food systems: The evolution of US agricultural production and policy into the 21st century. *Renewable Agriculture and Food Systems*, *35*(4), 391–406. doi:10.1017/S1742170518000522

Dimitrov, A. (2018). The digital age leadership: A transhumanistic perspective. *Journal of Leadership Studies*, *12*(3), 79–81. doi:10.1002/jls.21603

Dinc, M. S., & Aydemir, M. (2014). Ethical leadership and employee behaviours: an empirical study of mediating factors. *International Journal of Business Governance and Ethics*, *9*(3).

Dinh, J. E., & Lord, R. G. (2023). Role of context in the moral compass of leadership. *Journal of Business Ethics*, *167*(2), 201–217.

Dirani, K. M., Abadi, M., Alizadeh, A., Barhate, B., Garza, R. C., Gunasekara, N., Ibrahim, G., & Majzun, Z. (2020). Leadership competencies and the essential role of human resource development in times of crisis: A response to Covid-19 pandemic. *Human Resource Development International*, *23*(4), 380–394. doi:10.1080/13678868.2020.1780078

Ditlevsen, K., Denver, S., Christensen, T., & Lassen, J. (2020). A taste for locally produced food-Values, opinions and sociodemographic differences among 'organic' and 'conventional' consumers. *Appetite*, *147*, 104544. doi:10.1016/j.appet.2019.104544 PMID:31786190

Diwanji, V. S., Chen, Y., & Erba, J. (2023). Automated Linguistic and Visual Content Analysis of Diversity, Equity, and Inclusion Perspectives in Advertising and Public Relations Program Websites. *Journal of Public Relations Research*, 1-25.

Djourova, N. P., Rodríguez Molina, I., Tordera Santamatilde, N., & Abate, G. (2020). Self-efficacy and resilience: Mediating mechanisms in the relationship between the transformational leadership dimensions and well-being. *Journal of Leadership & Organizational Studies*, *27*(3), 256–270. doi:10.1177/1548051819849002

Compilation of References

Doane, D., & MacGillivray, A. (2001). Economic sustainability: The business of staying in business. *New Economics Foundation*, *1*, 52.

Dobbins, C. E., Edgar, D. W., Cox, C. K., Edgar, L. D., Graham, D. L., & Perez, A. G. P. (2021). Perceptions of Arkansas agriculture county extension agents toward urban agriculture. *Journal of Agricultural Education*, *62*(1), 77–94.

Dobre, O.-I. (2013). Employee motivation and organizational performance. *Review of Applied Socio-Economic Research*, *5*(1), 53–60.

Dóci, E., & Hofmans, J. (2015). Task complexity and transformational leadership: The mediating role of leaders' state core self-evaluations. *The Leadership Quarterly*, *26*(3), 436–447. doi:10.1016/j.leaqua.2015.02.008

Doeze Jager, S. B., Ph. Born, M., & van der Molen, H. T. (2022). The relationship between organizational trust, resistance to change and adaptive and proactive employees' agility in an unplanned and planned change context. *Applied Psychology*, *71*(2), 436–460. doi:10.1111/apps.12327

Dogru, C. (Ed.). (2023). *Role of human resources for inclusive leadership, workplace diversity, and equity in organizations*. IGI Global. doi:10.4018/978-1-6684-6602-5

Dolas, R. S. (2023). *Analytic-driven decision support in cybersecurity: towards effective IP risk management decision-making process*. University of Twente.

Donate, M. J., & de Pablo, J. D. S. (2015). The role of knowledge-oriented leadership in knowledge management practices and innovation. *Journal of Business Research*, *68*(2), 360–370. doi:10.1016/j.jbusres.2014.06.022

Donkor, F., Dongmei, Z., & Sekyere, I. (2021). The Mediating Effects of Organizational Commitment on Leadership Styles and Employee Performance in SOEs in Ghana: A Structural Equation Modeling Analysis. *SAGE Open*, *11*(2). doi:10.1177/21582440211008894

Dou, D., Devos, G., & Valcke, M. (2016). The effects of autonomy gap in personnel policy, principal leadership and teachers' self-efficacy on their organizational commitment. *Asia Pacific Education Review*, *17*(2), 339–353. doi:10.100712564-016-9428-7

Downey, L. (2012). *Calmer classrooms: A guide to working with traumatised children*. AUS, Child Safety Commissioner.

Downton, J. V. (1973). *Rebel Leadership: Commitment and Charisma in a Revolutionary Process*. Free Press.

Doyle, T. (2008). *Helping Students Learn in a Learner-Centered Environment: A Guide to Facilitating Learning in Higher Education*. Sterling. Stylus Publishing.

Drath, W. (2001). *The deep blue sea: Rethinking the source of leadership*. Jossey-Bass and Center for Creative Leadership.

Drouin, N., Müller, R., Sankaran, S., & Vaagaasar, A. L. (2021). Balancing leadership in projects: Role of the socio-cognitive space. *Project Leadership and Society*, *2*, 100031. doi:10.1016/j.plas.2021.100031

Duan, J., Wang, X. H., Janssen, O., & Farh, J. L. (2022). Transformational Leadership and Voice: When Does Felt Obligation to the Leader Matter? *Journal of Business and Psychology*, *37*(3), 543–555. doi:10.100710869-021-09758-z

Dubinsky, A. J., Yammarino, F. J., Jolson, M. A., & Spangler, W. D. (1995). Transformational leadership: An initial investigation in sales management. *Journal of Personal Selling & Sales Management*, *15*(2), 17–31.

Dumitru, A., Motoi, A. G., & Budica, A. B. (2015). What kind of leader is a manager? *Annals of the University of Craiova for Journalism. Communications Management*, *1*, 50–60.

Dunstan Rajkumar, A., Nilavathy, K., & Ida Merlin, J. (2021). A Review - Emotional Intelligence An Important Predictor Of Leadership Potential. *Turkish Online Journal of Qualitative Inquiry*, *12*(7), 3966–3975.

Duplechain, R., Reigner, R., & Packard, A. (2008). Striking differences: The impact of moderate and high trauma on reading achievement. *Reading Psychology*, *29*(2), 117–136. doi:10.1080/02702710801963845

Durowoju, S., Sakiru, G., & Kolapo, O. (2013). Influence of leadership styles on job satisfaction of employees in small and medium enterprises. *European Journal of Business and Management*, *5*(21), 40–49.

Durst, S., & Zieba, M. (2018). Mapping knowledge risks: Towards a better understanding of knowledge management. *Knowledge Management Research and Practice*, *17*(1), 1–13. doi:10.1080/14778238.2018.1538603

Durst, S., & Zieba, M. (2020). Knowledge risks inherent in business sustainability. *Journal of Cleaner Production*, *251*, 1–10. doi:10.1016/j.jclepro.2019.119670

Dwivedi, Y. K., Kshetri, N., Hughes, L., Slade, E. L., Jeyaraj, A., Kar, A. K., ... Ahuja, M. (2023). "So what if ChatGPT wrote it?" Multidisciplinary perspectives on opportunities, challenges and implications of generative conversational AI for research, practice and policy. *International Journal of Information Management*, *71*, 102642. doi:10.1016/j.ijinfomgt.2023.102642

Dyllick, T., & Hockerts, K. (2002). Beyond the Case for Corporate Sustainability. *Business Strategy and the Environment*, *11*(2), 130–141. doi:10.1002/bse.323

Earley, P. (2020). Surviving, thriving, and reviving in leadership: The personal and professional development needs of educational leaders. *Management in Education*, *34*(3), 1–5. doi:10.1177/0892020620919763

Earley, P. C., & Mosakowski, E. (2004). Cultural intelligence. *Harvard Business Review*, *82*(10), 139–146. PMID:15559582

Earley, P., & Weindling, D. (2007). Do school leaders have a shelf life? Career stages and headteacher performance. *Educational Management Administration & Leadership*, *35*(1), 73–88. doi:10.1177/1741143207071386

Eastwood, C., Klerkx, L., Ayre, M., & Dela Rue, B. (2019). Managing socio-ethical challenges in the development of smart farming: From a fragmented to a comprehensive approach for responsible research and innovation. *Journal of Agricultural & Environmental Ethics*, *32*(5-6), 741–768. doi:10.100710806-017-9704-5

Ebbesen, D. K., & Olsen, J. (2022). Exploring Non-locality in Psychology. *Human Arenas*, *5*(4), 770–782. doi:10.100742087-021-00189-z

Eberle, F. (2019). The 5 Levers of Reciprocal Leadership. *Linkedin*. https://www.linkedin.com/pulse/5-levers-reciprocal-leadership-francis-eberle/

Ehiorobo, O. A. (2020). Strategic agility and ai-enabled resources capabilities for business survival in post-COVID-19 global economy. *International Journal of Information, Business and Management*, *12*(4), 201–213.

Eisenbeiss, S. A., Knippenberg, D. v., & Boerner, S. (2008). *Transformational Leadership and Team*. Academic Press.

Eisenbeiss, S., van Knippenberg, D., & Boerner, S. (2008). Transformational leadership and team innovation: Integrating team climate principles. *The Journal of Applied Psychology*, *93*(6), 1438–1446. doi:10.1037/a0012716 PMID:19025260

Eisenmenger, A. (2020, September 14). *Five things you didn't know about invisible disabilities*. Access Living. https://www.accessliving.org/newsroom/blog/five-things-you-didnt-know-about-invisible-disabilities/

Ekowati, D., Abbas, A., Anwar, A., Suhariadi, F., & Fahlevi, M. (2023). Engagement and flexibility: An empirical discussion about consultative leadership intent for productivity from Pakistan. *Cogent Business & Management*, *10*(1), 2196041. doi:10.1080/23311975.2023.2196041

Compilation of References

Ekpenyong, J. (2020). The Impact of Leadership Style on Employees Performance in a Business Organization: A Case Study of Guarantee Trust Bank Plc. Academic Press.

Eli, H., & Stiem, B. (2017). *The Effect of Transformational Leadership on Employee Job Satisfaction and Performance*. Academic Press.

Eliasson, K., Wiréhn, L., Neset, T. S., & Linnér, B. O. (2022). Transformations towards sustainable food systems: Contrasting Swedish practitioner perspectives with the European Commission's Farm to Fork Strategy. *Sustainability Science*, *17*(6), 2411–2425. doi:10.100711625-022-01174-3

Eliyana, A., Ma'arif, S., & Muzakki. (2019). Job satisfaction and organisational commitment effect in the transformational leadership towards employee performance. *European Research on Management and Business Economics*, *25*(3), 144–150. doi:10.1016/j.iedeen.2019.05.001

Elizabeth, R., Margaretha, G. I. E., Ivan, G. S., & Tukiran, M. (2023). The Influence Of Transformational Leadership: Accelerating Farmer Group Empowerment To Realize Export-Oriented Agribusiness. *Asian Journal of Management. Entrepreneurship and Social Science*, *3*(01), 413–427.

Elkington, R. (2018). Leadership Decision-Making Leveraging Big Data in VUCA Contexts. *Journal of Leadership Studies*, *12*(3), 66–70. doi:10.1002/jls.21599

Ellinger, A. D., & Keller, S. (2019). Destructive leadership: A review and research agenda. *The Leadership Quarterly*, *30*(2), 291–310. doi:10.1016/j.leaqua.2018.11.003

Ellingsen, T., & Östling, R. (2010). When Does Communication Improve Coordination? *The American Economic Review*, *100*(4), 1695–1724. doi:10.1257/aer.100.4.1695

Elliott, E. S., & Dweck, C. S. (1988). Goals: An approach to motivation and achievement. *Journal of Personality and Social Psychology*, *54*(1), 5–12. doi:10.1037/0022-3514.54.1.5 PMID:3346808

Elrehail, H., Emeagwali, O. L., Alsaad, A., & Alzghoul, A. (2018). The impact of transformational and authentic leadership on innovation in higher education: The contingent role of knowledge sharing. *Telematics and Informatics*, *35*(1), 55–67. doi:10.1016/j.tele.2017.09.018

Elshout, R., Scherp, E., & van der Feltz-Cornelis, C. (2013). Understanding the link between leadership style, employee satisfaction, and absenteeism: A mixed methods design study in a mental health care institution. *Neuropsychiatric Disease and Treatment*, *9*, 823–837. doi:10.2147/NCT.S43755 PMID:23818784

Empson, L. (2017). *Leading professionals: Power, politics, and prima donnas*. Oxford University Press. doi:10.1093/oso/9780198744788.001.0001

Endrejat, P. C., Klonek, F. E., Müller-Frommeryer, L. C., & Kaufeld, S. (2021). Turning change resistance into readiness: How change agents' communication shapes recipient reactions. *European Management Journal*, *39*(5), 595–604. doi:10.1016/j.emj.2020.11.004

Erdel, D., & Takkaç, M. (2020). Instructor Leadership In Efl Classrooms And The Outcomes: The Effects Of Transformational And Transactional Leadership Styles. *Teflin Journal*, *31*(1), 70–87. Https://Doi.Org/10.15639/Teflinjournal.V31i1/70-87

Eren, N. S., & Ravitch, S. M. (2021). Trauma-informed leadership: Balancing love and accountability. In *Critical leadership praxis: Leading educational and social change* (Vol. E). Teachers College Press.

Erickson, J., Lyytinen, K., & Siau, K. (2005). Agile modeling, agile software development, and extreme programming: The state of research [JDM]. *Journal of Database Management*, *16*(4), 88–100. doi:10.4018/jdm.2005100105

Erina. (2023). The Effect of Transformational Leadership and Organizational Commitments on Employee Performance in Cv Artha Mega Mandiri Medan. *Journal of Industrial Engineering & Management Research, 2*(3).

Ernst, J., & Jensen Schleiter, A. (2019). Organizational identity struggles and reconstruction during organizational change: Narratives as symbolic, emotional and practical guides. *Organization Studies, 42*(6), 891–910. doi:10.1177/0170840619854484

Errida, A., & Lotfi, B. (2021). *The determinants of organizational change management success: Literature review and case study*. https://journals.sagepub.com/doi/full/10.1177/18479790211016273

Erro-Garcés, A., & Alfaro-Tanco, J. A. (2020). Action research as a meta-methodology in the management field. *International Journal of Qualitative Methods, 19*. doi:10.1177/1609406920917489

Erwin, D., & Garman, A. (2010). Resistance to organizational change: Linking research and practice. *Leadership and Organization Development Journal, 31*(1), 39–56. doi:10.1108/01437731011010371

Esobi, I. C., Lasode, M. K., Anyanwu, C. I., Barriguete, M. F., Okorie, M. A., & Lasode, D. O. (2021). Food insecurity, social vulnerability, and the impact of COVID-19 on population dependent on public assistance/SNAP: A case study of South Carolina, USA. *Journal of Food Security, 9*(1), 8–18.

Esters, L. T., & Bowen, B. E. (2004). Factors influencing enrollment in an urban agricultural education program. *Journal of Career and Technical Education, 21*(1), 25-37.

Etzioni, A. (1965). Dual leadership in complex organizations. *American Sociological Review, 30*(5), 688–698. doi:10.2307/2091137 PMID:5824934

Evans-Lacko, S., Aguilar-Gaxiola, S., Al-Hamzawi, A., Alonso, J., Benjet, C., Bruffaerts, R., Chiu, W. T., Florescu, S., de Girolamo, G., Gureje, O., Haro, J. M., He, Y., Hu, C., Karam, E. G., Kawakami, N., Lee, S., Lund, C., Kovess-Masfety, V., Levinson, D., & Thornicroft, G. (2018). Socio-economic variations in the mental health treatment gap for people with anxiety, mood, and substance use disorders: Results from the WHO World Mental Health (W.M.H.) surveys. *Psychological Medicine, 48*(9), 1560–1571. doi:10.1017/S0033291717003336 PMID:29173244

Ewenstein, B., Smith, W., & Sologar, A. (2015, July 1). Changing change management. *Featured Insights*. https://www.mckinsey.com/featured-insights/leadership/changing-change-management

Exworthy, G. M., Jones, J. R. I., & Smith, G. (2019). Professional autonomy and surveillance: The case of public reporting in cardiac surgery. *Sociology of Health & Illness, 41*(6), 1–16. doi:10.1111/1467-9566.12883 PMID:30874329

Fachri & Onsard. (2020). The Effect of Transformational Leadership Style and Work Spirit on Employee Performance at Raffles City Hotel Bengkulu. Academic Press.

Fagbadebo, O. M. (2022). State-owned enterprises and public service delivery in Africa. In F. G. Netswera, O. M. Fagbadebo, & N. Dorasamy (Eds.), *State-owned enterprises in Africa and the economics of public service delivery* (pp. 11–25). AOSIS Publishing. doi:10.4102/aosis.2022.BK270.01

Fagbemi, F., Oke, D. F., & Fajingbesi, A. (2023). Climate-resilient development: An approach to sustainable food production in sub-Saharan Africa. *Future Foods, 7*, 100216. doi:10.1016/j.fufo.2023.100216

Fapohunda, T. (2014). Increasing organizational effectiveness through better talent management. *Research Journal of Human Resource, 2*(4), 1–14.

Farinha, L., Sebastião, J. R., Sampaio, C., & Lopes, J. (2020). Social innovation and social entrepreneurship: Discovering origins, exploring current and future trends. *International Review on Public and Nonprofit Marketing, 17*(1), 77–96. https://link.springer.com/article/10.1007/s12208-020-00243-6 doi:10.100712208-020-00243-6

Compilation of References

Farmers, U. S., & Alliance, R. (2011). *Nationwide surveys reveal disconnect between Americans and their food*. PR Newswire.

Farny, S., & Binder, J. (2021). Sustainable entrepreneurship. In *World Encyclopedia of Entrepreneurship* (pp. 605–611). Edward Elgar Publishing. doi:10.4337/9781839104145.00076

Faupel, S., & Süß, S. (2019). The effect of transformational leadership on employees during organizational change–an empirical analysis. *Journal of Change Management*, *19*(3), 145–166. doi:10.1080/14697017.2018.1447006

Fawzy, R., & Saad, M. (2023). The relationship between agility drivers, agility capabilities, and organizational sustainability. *The Journal of Business*, *11*(2), 101–114. doi:10.1016/j.orp.2020.100171

Feder, J. (n.d.). *Considerations for supporting and accommodating invisible disabilities*. Accessibility.com. https://www.accessibility.com/blog/considerations-for-supporting-and-accommodating-invisible-disabilities

Feiler, J. (2023). The Artificially Intelligent Trolley Problem: Understanding Our Criminal Law Gaps in a Robot Driven World. *Hastings Science and Technology Law Journal*, *14*(1), 1–34.

Feinberg, B. J., Ostroff, C., & Burke, W. W. (2005). The role of within-group agreement in understanding transformational leadership. *Journal of Occupational and Organizational Psychology*, *78*(3), 471–488. doi:10.1348/096317905X26156

Fenitra, R. M., Abbas, A., Ekowati, D., & Suhairidi, F. (2022). Strategic Intent and Strategic Leadership: A Review Perspective for Post-covid Tourism and Hospitality Industry Recovery. In P. Mohanty, A. Sharma, J. Kennell, & A. Hassan (Eds.), *The Emerald Handbook of Destination Recovery in Tourism and Hospitality* (pp. 23–44). Emerald Group Publishing. doi:10.1108/978-1-80262-073-320221003

Fenitra, R. M., Premananto, G. C., Sedera, R. M. H., Abbas, A., & Laila, N. (2022). Environmentally responsible behavior and Knowledge-Belief-Norm in the tourism context: The moderating role of types of destinations. *International Journal of Geoheritage and Parks*, *10*(2), 273–288. doi:10.1016/j.ijgeop.2022.05.001

Ferrari Braun, A. (2022). The Elon Musk experience: Celebrity management in financialised capitalism. *Celebrity Studies*, 1–18. doi:10.1080/19392397.2022.2154685

Fiedler, F. E., & Garcia, J. E. (1987). *New approaches to leadership: Cognitive resources and organizational performance*. Wiley.

Fischer, T., & Sitkin, S. B. (2023). Leadership styles: A comprehensive assessment and way forward. *The Academy of Management Annals*, *17*(1), 331–372. doi:10.5465/annals.2020.0340

Fisk, L. (2021, February 10). Council post: Breaking down workplace barriers for those with invisible disabilities. *Forbes*. https://www.forbes.com/sites/forbesbusinesscouncil/2021/02/11/breaking-down-workplace-barriers-for-those-with-invisible-disabilities/

Fitzsimons, D. (2016). How Shared Leadership Changes Our Relationships at Work. *Harvard Business Review*. https://hbr.org/2016/05/how-shared-leadership-changes-our-relationships-at-work

Fletcher, C., & Carr, A. (2011). Destructive leadership: The impact of negative leadership behaviours and the moderating influence of organizational culture. *The Leadership Quarterly*, *22*(3), 467–481.

Flocco, N., Canterino, F., & Cagliano, R. (2021). Leading innovation through employees' participation: Plural leadership in employee-driven innovation practices. *Leadership*, *17*(5), 499–518. doi:10.1177/1742715020987928

Flynn, J., Välikoski, T., & Grau, J. (2008). Listening in the Business Context: Reviewing the State of Research. *International Journal of Listening*, *22*(2), 141–151. doi:10.1080/10904010802174800

Foley, J. A., Ramankutty, N., Brauman, K. A., Cassidy, E. S., Gerber, J. S., Johnston, M., Mueller, N. D., O'Connell, C., Ray, D. K., West, P. C., Balzer, C., & Zaks, D. P. (2011). Solutions for a cultivated planet. *Nature*, *478*(7369), 337–342. doi:10.1038/nature10452 PMID:21993620

Føllesdal, H., & Hagtvet, K. (2013). Does emotional intelligence as ability predict transformational leadership? A multilevel approach. *The Leadership Quarterly*, *24*(5), 747–762. doi:10.1016/j.leaqua.2013.07.004

Follett, M. P. (1926). The Giving Orders. Scientific Foundations of Business Administration, 29-37.

Forbes. (2020). *The Seven Characteristics of great leaders*. Retrieved from https://www.forbes.com/sites/forbescoachescouncil/2020/10/21/the-seven-characteristics-of-great-leaders/?sh=5e8eb515f7f4

Ford, T. G., Lavigne, A. L., Fiegener, A. M., & Si, S. (2020). Understanding district support for leader development and success in the accountability era: A review of the literature using social-cognitive theories of motivation. *Review of Educational Research*, *90*(2), 264–307. doi:10.3102/0034654319899723

Foster, W., Sweet, L., & McNeill, L. (2020). Linking Out Loud (LOL): Developing critical thinking. *MedEdPublish*, *9*(42), 42.

Frankema, E. H. (2012). The origins of formal education in sub-Saharan Africa: Was British rule more benign? *European Review of Economic History*, *16*(4), 335–355. doi:10.1093/ereh/hes009

Franken, E., Edwards, D., & Lambert, S. (2009). Strategy execution: Making it happen. *Strategy and Leadership*, *37*(4), 12–17.

Freedhoff, Y., & Stevenson, R. (2008). Frying up hospital cafeteria food. *CMAJ: Canadian Medical Association journal = journal de l'Association medicale canadienne*, *179*(3), 213–214. https://doi.org/ doi:10.1503/cmaj.080975

Fries, A., Kammerlander, N., & Leitterstorf, M. (2021). Leadership styles and leadership behaviors in family firms: A systematic literature review. *Journal of Family Business Strategy*, *12*(1), 100374. doi:10.1016/j.jfbs.2020.100374

Friesen, S., & Scott, D. (2013). *Inquiry-based learning: A review of the research literature*. Alberta Ministry of Education.

Friesner, J., Colón-Carmona, A., Schnoes, A. M., Stepanova, A., Mason, G. A., Macintosh, G. C., Ullah, H., Baxter, I., Callis, J., Sierra-Cajas, K., Elliott, K., Haswell, E. S., Zavala, M. E., Wildermuth, M., Williams, M., Ayalew, M., Henkhaus, N., Prunet, N., Lemaux, P. G., ... Dinneny, J. R. (2021). Broadening the impact of plant science through innovative, integrative, and inclusive outreach. *Plant Direct*, *5*(4), e00316. doi:10.1002/pld3.316 PMID:33870032

Fuchs, G. E., Ness, L., Booker, J. M., & Fusch, P. I. (2020). *People and Process: Successful Change Management Initiatives*. https://scholarworks.waldenu.edu/cgi/viewcontent.cgi?article=1264&context=jsc

Fuentelsaz, L., González, C., & Mickiewicz, T. (2023). Entrepreneurial growth aspirations at re-entry after failure. *International Journal of Entrepreneurial Behaviour & Research*, *29*(2), 297–327. doi:10.1108/IJEBR-05-2022-0433

Fuglie, K., Heisey, P., King, J. L., Day-Rubenstein, K., Schimmelpfennig, D., Wang, S. L., Pray, C.E., & Karmarkar-Deshmukh, R., (2011). Research investments and market structure in the food processing, agricultural input, and biofuel industries worldwide. *USDA-ERS Economic Research Report*, (130).

Fullan, M. (2008). *The Six Secrets of Change: What the Best Leaders Do to Help Their Organizations Survive and Thrive*. John Wiley & Sons, Inc.

Gabriel, A., & Gandorfer, M. (2021). Have City Dwellers Lost Touch with Modern Agriculture? In Quest of Differences between Urban and Rural Population. *Engineering Proceedings*, *9*(1), 25.

Galileo Educational Network Association. (2008). Retrieved from: http://www.galileo.org/research/publications/rubric.pdf

Compilation of References

Galindo-Martín, M. A., Castaño-Martínez, M. S., & Méndez-Picazo, M. T. (2020). The relationship between green innovation, social entrepreneurship, and sustainable development. *Sustainability (Basel)*, *12*(11), 4467. doi:10.3390u12114467

Gallagher, D. J. (2009). Disability studies and the ethics of research on disability. In P. L. Baker (Chair), *Interdisciplinary research symposium*. University of Northern Iowa.

Galletta, M., Portoghese, I., & Battistelli, A. (2011). Intrinsic motivation, job autonomy and turnover intention in the Italian healthcare: The mediating role of affective commitment. *Journal of Management Research*, *3*(1), 1–19. doi:10.5296/jmr.v3i2.619

Galli, B. J. (2018). Change management models: A comparative analysis and concerns. *IEEE Engineering Management Review*, *46*(3), 124–132. doi:10.1109/EMR.2018.2866860

Gamble, J. E., Peteraf, M. A., & Thompson, A. A. Jr. (2019). *Essentials of Strategic Management: The Quest for Competitive Advantage, 6e*. McGraw Hill Education.

Gamero-Burón, C., & Lassibille, C. (2018). Work engagement among school directors and its impact on teachers' behaviour at work. *Journal of Developing Areas*, *52*(2), 27–39. doi:10.1353/jda.2018.0020

Gandolfi, F., & Stone, S. (2018). Leadership, leadership styles, and servant leadership. *Journal of Management Research*, *18*(4), 261–269.

Ganguly, A., Nilchiani, R. & Farr, J. (2009). Evaluating agility in corporate enterprises. *Int. Journal of Production Economics*, *118*, 410–423, https://doi.org/ doi:10.1016/j.ijpe.2008.12.009

García, S., & O'Driscoll, T. (n.d.). Networks not Hierarchy: Expanding Leadership Capacity and Impact in a Complex World. *Institute For Contemporary Leadership*. https://contemporaryleadership.com/wp-content/uploads/2021/10/Network-Leadership.pdf

García-Morales, V. J., Lloréns-Montes, F. J., & Verdú-Jover, A. J. (2008). The effects of transformational leadership on organizational performance through knowledge and innovation. *British Journal of Management*, *19*(4), 299–319. doi:10.1111/j.1467-8551.2007.00547.x

Gardner, H., & Laskin, E. (1995). *Leading minds: An anatomy of leadership*. Harper Collins Publishers.

Gardner, W. L. (2010). Destructive leadership: A review and synthesis of the empirical literature and implications for future research. *The Leadership Quarterly*, *21*(2), 212–218.

Gardner, W. L., Avolio, B. J., Luthans, F., May, D. R., & Walumbwa, F. (2005). "Can you see the real me?" A self-based model of authentic leader and follower development. *The Leadership Quarterly*, *16*(3), 343–372. doi:10.1016/j.leaqua.2005.03.003

Garton, B. L. (2019). Trends and Challenges Facing Higher Education: Implications for Agricultural Education. *Journal of Agricultural Education*, *60*(1), 1–13. doi:10.5032/jae.2019.01001

Garza, E. Jr, Drysdale, L., Gurr, D., Jacobson, S., & Merchant, B. (2014). Leadership for school success: Lessons from effective principals. *International Journal of Educational Management*, *28*(7), 798–811. doi:10.1108/IJEM-08-2013-0125

Geisler, E., & Beauvais, A. (2013). Organizational diagnosis: A review of the literature. *International Journal of Management Reviews*, *15*(3), 339–360. doi:10.1111/ijmr.12004

Gencel, İ. E., & Erdoğan, M. (2022). Kolb'un Yenilenen Öğrenme Stili Sınıflamasına İlişkin Bir İnceleme. *Yaşadıkça Eğitim*, *36*(3), 813–833. doi:10.33308/26674874.2022363492

Georgalis, J., Samaratunge, R., Kimberley, N., & Lu, Y. (2015). Change process characteristics and resistance to organizational change: The role of employee perceptions of justice. *Australian Journal of Management*, *40*(1), 89–113. doi:10.1177/0312896214526212

Gerber, P. J., Henderson, B., & Makkar, H. P. (2013). Mitigation of greenhouse gas emissions in livestock production: a review of technical options for non-CO2 emissions (No. 177). Food and Agriculture Organization of the United Nations (FAO).

Getachew, D. S., & Zhou, E. (2018). The influences of transformational leadership on collective efficacy: The moderating role of perceived organizational support. *International Journal of Organizational Innovation*, *10*(4), 7–15.

Ghasabeth, M. S., & Provitera, M. J. (2018). Transformational leadership and knowledge management: Analysing the knowledge management models. *The Journal of Values Based Leadership*, *11*(1), 1–14. doi:10.22543/0733.111.1206

Ghavifekr, S., & Fung, H. Y. (2021). Change management in digital environment amid the Covid-19 pandemic: a scenario from Malaysian higher education institutions. *Pandemic, Lockdown, and Digital Transformation: Challenges and Opportunities for Public Administration, NGOs, and Businesses*, 129-158.

Ghosh, K. (2015). Teaching and developing leadership in business schools: A multilevel evaluative approach in the Indian context. *International Journal of Indian Culture and Business Management*, *10*(2), 178–192. doi:10.1504/IJICBM.2015.068169

Gibeau, É., Reid, W., & Langley, A. (2016). Co-leadership: Contexts, Configurations and Conditions. In The Routledge Companion to Leadership (pp. 247-262). Routledge.

Gierszewska, G., & Seretny, M. (2019). Sustainable behaviors—The need of change in consumer and business attitudes and behavior. *Foundations of Management*, *11*.

Gigliotti, R. A. (2019). Crisis leadership in higher education. In *Crisis Leadership in Higher Education*. Rutgers University Press.

Gignac, M. A., Bowring, J., Jetha, A., Beaton, D. E., Breslin, F. C., Franche, R.-L., Irvin, E., Macdermid, J. C., Shaw, W. S., Smith, P. M., Thompson, A., Tompa, E., Van Eerd, D., & Saunders, R. (2020). Disclosure, privacy, and workplace accommodation of episodic disabilities: Organizational perspectives on disability communication-support processes to sustain employment. *Journal of Occupational Rehabilitation*, *31*(1), 153–165. doi:10.100710926-020-09901-2 PMID:32410153

Gingras, A. (2020, October 21). *24 companies with innovative and award-winning Accessibility Practices*. RippleMatch. https://ripplematch.com/insights/companies-with-innovative-and-award-winning-accessibility-practices-972ec8a4/

Gisma Business School. (2020). *The evolution of leadership in the past decade*. Gisma Business School. https://www.gisma.com/blog/the-evolution-of-leadership-in-the-past-decade

Givens, D. (2020, August 25). The Extra Stigma of Mental Illness for African-Americans. *The New York Times*. https://www.nytimes.com/2020/08/25/well/mind/black-mental-health.html

Glad, B., & Blanton, R. (1997). F. W. de Klerk and Nelson Mandela: A Study in Cooperative Transformational Leadership. *Presidential Studies Quarterly*, *27*(3), 565–590.

Global Impact Investing Network. (2019). *What is impact investing?* Retrieved from https://thegiin.org/impact-investing/need-to-know/#what-is-impact-investing

Goering, S. (2015). Rethinking disability: The Social Model of disability and chronic disease. *Current Reviews in Musculoskeletal Medicine*, *8*(2), 134–138. doi:10.100712178-015-9273-z PMID:25862485

Compilation of References

Goethals, G. R., & Allison, S. T. (2016). Transforming motives and mentors: The heroic leadership of James MacGregor Burns. In Politics, Ethics and Change (pp. 59-73). Edward Elgar Publishing.

Goksoy, S. (2016). Analysis of the relationship between shared leadership and distributed leadership. *Eurasian Journal of Educational Research*, *16*(65), 295–312. doi:10.14689/ejer.2016.65.17

Goldman, S. L., Nagel, R. N., & Preiss, K. (1995). *Agile Competitors and Virtual Organizations –Strategies for Enriching the Customer*. Van Nostrand Reinhold.

Goldsmith, M. (2014, July 28). *The many facets of leadership*. Financial Times Prentice Hall. https://www.scribd.com/document/235260851/Marshall-Goldsmith-the-Many-Facets-of-Leadership

Goldsmith, M. (2020). Sharing Leadership to Maximize Talent. *Harvard Business Review*. Retrieved from https://hbr.org/2010/05/sharing-leadership-to-maximize

Goleman, D. (1995). *Emotional Intelligence*. Bantam Books.

Goleman, D. (1998). *Emotional intelligence: Why it can matter more than IQ*. Bantam Books.

Goleman, D. (1998). *Working with emotional intelligence*. Bantam Books.

Goleman, D. (2005). *Emotional Intelligence: Why it can matter more than IQ*. Bantam Books.

Gomes-Casseres, B., & Bamford, J. (2001). The Corporation is Dead. Long Live the Constellation. In *The Alliance Enterprise* (p. 31). Global Strategies for Corporate Collaboration. doi:10.1142/9781848161405_0004

Gomez, M. (2010). *Exchanging our country marks: The transformation of African identities in the colonial and antislavery world*. University of North Carolina Press.

Gomiero, T., Pimentel, D., & Paoletti, M. G. (2011). Environmental impact of different agricultural management practices: Conventional vs. organic agriculture. *Critical Reviews in Plant Sciences*, *30*(1-2), 95–124. doi:10.1080/07352689.2011.554355

Gonzalez-Morales, M. G., McNeese-Smith, D., & Ilies, R. (2015). Destructive leadership, workplace deviance, and employee stress. *Journal of Managerial Psychology*, *30*(2), 133–149.

Gonzalez-Perez, M. A., & Leonard, L. (Eds.). (2015). *The UN Global Compact*. Emerald Group Publishing.

Goodman, J. (2005). Accommodating the Invisible Disability: Mental Illness in the Workplace. *Employee Responsibilities and Rights Journal*, *17*(3), 211–222.

Good, T. L., & Brophy, J. E. (1990). *Educational psychology: A realistic approach* (4th ed.). Longman.

Gopalkrishnan N. (2018). Cultural Diversity and Mental Health: Considerations for Policy and Practice. *Frontiers in Public Health*, *6*, 179. doi:10.3389/fpubh.2018.00179

Gotz, O., Liehr-Gobbers, K., & Krafft, M. (2010). Evaluation of structural equation models using the Partial Least Squares (PLS) approach. In V. E. Vinzi, W. W. Chin, J. Henseler, & H. Wang (Eds.), *Handbook of partial least squares*. Springer. doi:10.1007/978-3-540-32827-8_30

Graamans, E., Aij, K., Vonk, A., & Have, W. (2020). Case study: Examining failure in change management. *Journal of Organizational Change Management*, *33*(2), 319–330. doi:10.1108/JOCM-06-2019-0204

Grant, R.M. (1996). Towards a knowledge-based theory of the firm. *Strategic Management Journal*, *17*(Winter special issue), 109-122.

Grant, A. (2021). *Think Again: The Power of Knowing What You Don't Know*. Viking.

Grayson, C., & Baldwin, D. (2011). *Leadership networking: Connect, collaborate, create* (Vol. 125). John Wiley & Sons.

Grebitus, C., Chenarides, L., Muenich, R., & Mahalov, A. (2020). Consumers' perception of urban farming—An exploratory study. *Frontiers in Sustainable Food Systems*, *4*, 79. doi:10.3389/fsufs.2020.00079

Grebitus, C., Printezis, I., & Printezis, A. (2017). Relationship between consumer behavior and success of urban agriculture. *Ecological Economics*, *136*, 189–200. doi:10.1016/j.ecolecon.2017.02.010

Greer, C. R., Lusch, R. F., & Hitt, M. A. (2017). A service perspective for human capital resources: A critical base for strategy implementation. *The Academy of Management Perspectives*, *31*(2), 137–158. doi:10.5465/amp.2016.0004

Greer, C. R., & Stevens, C. D. (2015). HR in collaborative innovation with customers: Role, alignment, and challenges. *International Journal of Human Resource Management*, *26*(20), 2569–2593. doi:10.1080/09585192.2014.1003086

Griebel, T. (2018). Corporate social responsibility: An overview and introduction. *Journal of Corporate Citizenship*, (72), 5–24.

Grieg, J., Bailey, B., Abbot, L., & Brunzell, T. (2021). Trauma-informed integral leadership: Leading school communities with a systems-aware approach. *International Journal of Whole Schooling*, *17*(1), 62–97.

Gubanova, A., Mineva, O., & Gadzhieva, E. (2021). Transformation of the Scientific Paradigm of Leadership Under the Influence of Digital Reality. In *SHS Web of Conferences* (Vol. 110, p. 04008). EDP Sciences.

Gudykunst, W. B., & Ting-Toomey, S. (1988). Culture and affective communication. *The American Behavioral Scientist*, *31*(3), 384–400. doi:10.1177/000276488031003009

Guillen, L., & Florent-Treacy, E. (2011). *Emotional intelligence and leadership effectiveness: The mediating influence of collaborative behaviors*. Social Science Research Network.

Gultekin, H., & Acar, E. (2014). The intrinsic and extrinsic factors of teacher motivation. *revista de cercetare si interventie sociala*, *47*, 291-306.

Gumede, W. (2018). Positioning Africa's SOEs to deliver on the developmental mandate, viewed. *Democracy works*. https://democracyworks.org.za/policy-brief-30-positioning-africas-soes-to-deliver-on-the-developmental-mandate/

Gumusluoglu, L., & Ilsev, A. (2009). Transformational leadership, creativity, and organizational innovation. *Journal of Business Research*, *62*(4), 461–473. doi:10.1016/j.jbusres.2007.07.032

Gupta, P., Chauhan, S., Paul, J., & Jaiswal, M. P. (2020). Social entrepreneurship research: A review and future research agenda. Journal of Business Research, 113, 209–229.

Gupta, V., & Jones, G. (2023). Leadership in the face of intersecting crises: Navigating pandemics, war, and AI. *Journal of Business and Psychology*, *38*(2), 189–204.

Gupta, V., & Krishnan, V. R. (2019). Impact of transformational leadership on followers' self-efficacy: Moderating role of followers' demographics. *Leadership and Organization Development Journal*, *40*(7), 821–837.

Gurin, P., Nagda, B., & Lopez, G. (2004). The benefits of diversity in education for democratic citizenship. *The Journal of Social Issues*, *60*(1), 17–34. doi:10.1111/j.0022-4537.2004.00097.x

Gürlek, M. (2020). *Tech development through hrm*. Emerald Publishing Limited. doi:10.1108/9781800433120

Compilation of References

Gürlek, M., & Çemberci, M. (2020). Understanding the relationships among knowledge- oriented leadership, knowledge management capacity, innovation performance and organizational performance. *Kybernetes*, *49*(11), 2819–2846. doi:10.1108/K-09-2019-0632

Gürlek, M., & Tuna, M. (2018). Reinforcing competitive advantage through green organisational culture and green innovation. *Service Industries Journal*, *38*(7/8), 467–491. doi:10.1080/02642069.2017.1402889

Gururani, K., Sood, S., Kumar, A., Joshi, D. C., Pandey, D., & Sharma, A. R. (2021). Mainstreaming Barahnaja cultivation for food and nutritional security in the Himalayan region. *Biodiversity and Conservation*, *30*(3), 551–574. doi:10.100710531-021-02123-9 PMID:33526962

Guthman, J. (2008). Neoliberalism and the making of food politics in California. *Geoforum*, *39*(3), 1171–1183. doi:10.1016/j.geoforum.2006.09.002

Guttman, H. (2004). The leader's role in conflict management. *Leader to Leader*, *31*(31), 48–53. doi:10.1002/ltl.63

Gutu, I., Agheorghiesei, D. T., & Alecu, I. C. (2022). The Online Adapted Transformational Leadership and Workforce Innovation within the Software Development Industry. *Sustainability (Basel)*, *14*(12), 7408. doi:10.3390u14127408

Haas, M., & Vanhala, M. (2022). AI and leadership: The shift towards algorithmic management and what it means for leaders. *Organizational Dynamics*, *51*(1), 100787.

Haddad, L. M., Annamaraju, P., & Toney-Butler, T. J. (2020). *Nursing Shortage*. StatPearls Publishing. Available from: https://www.ncbi.nlm.nih.gov/books/NBK493175/

Hadziahmetovic, N., & Dinc, M. S. (2020). Linking reward types to organizational performance in Central and Eastern European universities: The mediating role of affective commitment. *Journal for East European Management Studies*, *25*(2), 325–359. doi:10.5771/0949-6181-2020-2-325

Haesevoets, T., De Cremer, D., Hirst, G., De Schutter, L., Stouten, J., van Dijke, M., & Van Hiel, A. (2021). The effect of decisional leader procrastination on employee innovation: Investigating the moderating role employees' resistance to change. *Journal of Leadership & Organizational Studies*, *29*(1), 131–146. doi:10.1177/15480518211044166

Hair, J. F., Black, W. C., Babin, B. J. B., & Anderson, R. E. (2014). *Multivariate data analysis* (7th ed.). Pearson Education Limited.

Hair, J. F. Jr, Ringle, C. M., & Sarstedt, M. (2013). Partial least squares structural equation modeling: Rigorous applications, better results and higher acceptance. *Long Range Planning*, *46*(1-2), 1–12. doi:10.1016/j.lrp.2013.01.001

Hair, J. F., Ringle, C. M., & Sarstedt, M. (2011). PLS-SEM: Indeed a silver bullet. *Journal of Marketing Theory and Practice*, *19*(2), 139–151. doi:10.2753/MTP1069-6679190202

Hair, J. F., Sarstedt, M., Ringle, C. M., & Mena, J. A. (2012). An assessment of the use of partial least squares structural equation modeling in marketing research. *Journal of the Academy of Marketing Science*, *40*(3), 414–433. doi:10.100711747-011-0261-6

Haldar, S. (2019). Towards a conceptual understanding of sustainability-driven entrepreneurship. *Corporate Social Responsibility and Environmental Management*, *26*(6), 1157–1170. doi:10.1002/csr.1763

Haleem, A., Javaid, M., Singh, R. P., & Suman, R. (2021). Telemedicine for healthcare: Capabilities, features, barriers, and applications. *Sensors International*, *2*, 100117. doi:10.1016/j.sintl.2021.100117 PMID:34806053

Hallegatte, S., Bangalore, M., Bonzanigo, L., Fay, M., Narloch, U., Rozenberg, J., & Vogt-Schilb, A. (2014). Climate change and poverty--an analytical framework. *World Bank Policy Research Working Paper*, (7126), 2-47.

Hallenbeck, G., & Santana, L. (2019). *Great leaders are great learners: How to develop learning-agile high potentials.* Creative Center for Leadership. (https://files.eric.ed.gov/fulltext/ED596166.pdf) (23.03.2023).

Han, J. H., Sullivan, N., Leas, B. F., Pegues, D. A., Kaczmarek, J. L., & Umscheid, C. A. (2015). Cleaning Hospital Room Surfaces to Prevent Health Care-Associated Infections: A Technical Brief. *Annals of Internal Medicine, 163*(8), 598–607. doi:10.7326/M15-1192 PMID:26258903

Hanson, S. (2020). *What Is Social Entrepreneurship?* Retrieved April 13, 2021, from https://www.entrepreneur.com/article/352759

Hanson, C. (2013). Crossing borders: Developing collaborations with Indigenous communities. *Proceedings of the National Conference of Canadian Association for the Study of Adult Education,* 211–217.

Hao, J., & Yazdanifard, R. (2015). Change management: Strategies and practices in different contexts. *International Journal of Business Research and Management, 3*(2), 157–167.

Hapeta, J., Palmer, F., & Kuroda, Y. (2019). Cultural identity, leadership and well-being: How indigenous storytelling contributed to well-being in a New Zealand provincial rugby team. *Public Health, 176,* 68–76. doi:10.1016/j.puhe.2018.12.010 PMID:30739731

Haris, N. B. M., Yunus, N. A., & Shah, J. A. (2022). *Community Readiness of Urban Farming Practices in Malaysia.* Academic Press.

Harris, A., & Muijs, D. (2003). *Teacher Leadership: A Review of Research.* General Teaching Council.

Harris, K. J., Kacmar, K. M., & Zivnuska, S. (2007). An investigation of abusive supervision as a predictor of performance and the meaning of work as a moderator of the relationship. *The Leadership Quarterly, 18*(3), 252–263. doi:10.1016/j.leaqua.2007.03.007

Harris, N. (2018). *The deepest well: Healing the long-term effects of childhood adversity.* Houghton Mifflin Harcourt.

Harrison, K. (2013). Building resilient communities. *M/C Journal, 16*(5), 1-8.

Hartmann, K., & Martin, M. J. (2021). A critical pedagogy of agriculture. *Journal of Agricultural Education, 62*(3), 51–71. doi:10.5032/jae.2021.03051

Hartmann, N., & Lussier, B. (2020). Managing the sales force through the unexpected exogenous COVID-19 crisis. *Industrial Marketing Management, 88,* 1–30. doi:10.1016/j.indmarman.2020.05.005

Hart, T., & Fassett, D. (2021). Slow your role: Troubling (our) assumptions about higher education. *Communication Teacher, 35*(3), 214–221. doi:10.1080/17404622.2021.1923770

Harvard Business Review. (1998). *On leadership.* Harvard Business School Press.

Harvard Business School. (2013). *Understanding the Impact of Corporate Social Responsibility on Companies.* Retrieved from https://www.hbs.edu/socialenterprise/research/Pages/understanding-the-impact-of-corporate-social-responsibility-on-companies.aspx

Harvey, S. (2014). Creative synthesis: Exploring the process of extraordinary group creativity. *Academy of Management Review, 39*(3), 324–343. doi:10.5465/amr.2012.0224

Haryanto, B., Suprapti, A. R., Taufik, A., & Fenitra, R. M. (2022). *Moderating role of transformational leadership in the relationship between work conflict and employee performance* (Vol. 9). Cogent Business & Management.

Compilation of References

Haslam, S. A., Steffens, N. K., Reicher, S. D., & Bentley, S. V. (2021). Identity leadership in a crisis: A 5R framework for learning from responses to COVID-19. *Social Issues and Policy Review*, *15*(1), 35–83. doi:10.1111ipr.12075 PMID:33821168

Hassan, A., Evelyn, D., & Titus, K. (2018). Effect of Leadership Styles on Employee Performance in the Somali National Civil Service Commission. *International Journal of Novel Research in Humanity and Social Sciences*, *5*(3).

Hater, J. J., & Bass, B. M. (1988). Superiors' evaluations and subordinates' perceptions of transformational and transactional leadership. *The Journal of Applied Psychology*, *73*(4), 695–702. doi:10.1037/0021-9010.73.4.695

Hatfield, J. L., & Prueger, J. H. (2015). Temperature extremes: Effect on plant growth and development. *Weather and Climate Extremes*, *10*, 4–10. doi:10.1016/j.wace.2015.08.001

Hay, I. (2006). Transformational leadership: Characteristics and criticisms. *E-journal of Organizational Learning and Leadership*, *5*(2).

Hay, A., & Hodgkinson, M. (2006). Rethinking leadership: A way forward for teaching leadership? *Leadership and Organization Development Journal*, *27*(2), 144–158. doi:10.1108/01437730610646642

Haymanot, A. (2020). *The Effect of Leadership Styles on Employee Performance a case study in Army Foundation*. Academic Press.

Head, G. (2003). Effective collaboration: Deep collaboration as an essential element of the learning process. *Journal of Educational Enquiry*, *4*(2), 47–62.

Healthcare Value Hub. (2017, November). Telemedicine: Decreasing barriers and increasing access to healthcare. *Altarum*. https://www.healthcarevaluehub.org/advocate-resources/publications/telemedicine-decreasing-barriers-and-increasing-access-healthcare

He, C., Liu, Z., Wu, J., Pan, X., Fang, Z., Li, J., & Bryan, B. A. (2021). Future global urban water scarcity and potential solutions. *Nature Communications*, *12*(1), 4667. doi:10.103841467-021-25026-3 PMID:34344898

Hechanova, R. M., & Cementina-Olpoc, R. (2013). Transformational leadership, change management, and commitment to change: A comparison of academic and business organizations. *The Asia-Pacific Education Researcher*, *22*(1), 11–19. doi:10.100740299-012-0019-z

Heckman, J. J., & Kautz, T. (2014). Fostering and measuring skills: Interventions that improve character and cognition. In J. J. Heckman, J. E. Humphries, & T. Kautz (Eds.), *The myth of achievement tests: The GED and the role of character education in American life* (pp. 341–430). The University of Chicago Press.

Heiser, S. (2019, December 9). *The Majority of U.S. Medical Students Are Women, New Data Show*. American Associate of Medical College. https://www.aamc.org/

Heizmann, H., & Liu, H. (2018). Becoming green, becoming leaders: Identity narratives in sustainability leadership development. *Management Learning*, *49*(1), 40–58. doi:10.1177/1350507617725189

Hejkrlik, J., Chaloupkova, P., & Sokolska, T. (2023). The role of transformational leadership and leaders' skills for new agricultural cooperatives in post-soviet countries. *Annals of Public and Cooperative Economics*, *94*(1), 109–129.

Helgesen, S. (1996). *Leading from the grass roots: The leader of the future*. Jossey-Bass Publishers.

Hellman, T., Molin, F., & Svartengren, M. (2020). A mixed method study of providing and implementing a support model focusing on systematic work environment management. *Journal of Occupational and Environmental Medicine*, *62*(4), 62. doi:10.1097/JOM.0000000000001829 PMID:32032185

Henley, D. (2023). The Surprising Benefits Of Co-Leadership. *Forbes magazine.* https://www.forbes.com/sites/dedehenley/2023/01/22/the-surprising-benefits-of-co-leadership/?sh=15853f943e92

Henwood, B. F., Derejko, K. S., Couture, J., & Padgett, D. K. (2015). Maslow and mental health recovery: A comparative study of homeless programs for adults with serious mental illness. *Administration and Policy in Mental Health, 42*(2), 220–228. doi:10.100710488-014-0542-8 PMID:24518968

Herman, J. (1992). *Trauma and recovery: The aftermath of violence—from domestic abuse to political terror.* Basic Books.

Hermann, R. R., & Bossle, M. B. (2020). Bringing an entrepreneurial focus to sustainability education: A teaching framework based on content analysis. *Journal of Cleaner Production, 246.* https://doi.org/10.1016/j.jclepro.2019.119038

Herr, K., & Anderson, G. (2005). *The action research dissertation: A guide for students and faculty.* Sage.

Hershcovis, M. S. (2007). Implications of destructive leadership behavior: Review, synthesis, and research agenda. *Group & Organization Management, 32*(3), 409–439.

Hess, A. J., & Trexler, C. J. (2011). A Qualitative Study of Agricultural Literacy in Urban Youth: Understanding for Democratic Participation in Renewing the Agri-Food System. *Journal of Agricultural Education, 52*(2), 151–162.

Hewlett, S. A., Marshall, M., & Sherbin, L. (2013). How diversity can drive innovation. *Harvard Business Review, 91*(12), 30.

Hezlett, S., & Kuncel, N. (2012). Prioritizing the learning agility research agenda. *Industrial and Organizational Psychology: Perspectives on Science and Practice, 5*(3), 296–301. doi:10.1111/j.1754-9434.2012.01449.x

Hiatt, J. M. (2006). *ADKAR: A model for change in business, government and our community.* Prosci Learning Center.

Hickman, G. R., & Sorenson, G. J. (2013). *The power of invisible leadership: How a compelling common purpose inspires exceptional leadership.* Sage Publications.

Hiller, N. J., Day, D. V., & Vance, R. J. (2006). *Collective enactment of leadership roles and team.*

Hiller, N. J., Day, D. V., & Vance, R. J. (2006, August). effectiveness: A field study. *The Leadership Quarterly, 17*(4), 387–397. doi:10.1016/j.leaqua.2006.04.004

Hite, K. (1996). The formation and transformation of political identity: Leaders of the Chilean left, 1968–1990. *Journal of Latin American Studies, 28*(2), 299–328. doi:10.1017/S0022216X0001302X

Hoch, J. E., Bommer, W. H., Dulebohn, J. H., & Wu, D. (2018). Do ethical, authentic, and servant leadership explain variance above and beyond transformational leadership? A meta-analysis. *Journal of Management, 44*(2), 501–529. doi:10.1177/0149206316665461

Hodson, R., & Brouer, R. L. (2016). Workplace stress: Causes, consequences, and interventions. In R. Hodson & R. L. Brouer (Eds.), *Workplace stress: A comprehensive guide for assessment, prevention, and management* (pp. 1–35). ABC-CLIO.

Hoffman, K., Alford, D., Bialik, A., Blanchard, M., Calogero, R., Carter, R., & Wampold, B. (2020). The psychological impact of the COVID-19 pandemic on the public: Mental health considerations. *The American Psychologist, 75*(7), 778–788.

Hogan, R., & Hogan, J. (2017). Personality and destructive leadership. *The Leadership Quarterly, 28*(1), 16–30. doi:10.1016/j.leaqua.2016.09.005

Hollard, M. (2007). Pourquoi une action collective peut-elle exister? In M. Bensaïd, N. El Aoufi, & M. Hollard (Eds.), *Economie des organisations. Tendances actuelles* (pp. 125–153).

Hollaus, A., Schunko, C., Weisshaidinger, R., Bala, P., & Vogl, C. R. (2022). Indigenous farmers' perceptions of problems in the rice field agroecosystems in the upper Baram, Malaysia. *Journal of Ethnobiology and Ethnomedicine*, *18*(1), 26. doi:10.118613002-022-00511-1 PMID:35351170

Holmes, G., & Abington-Cooper, M. (2000). Pedagogy vs. andragogy: A false dichotomy? *The Journal of Technology Studies*, *26*(2), 1–6. https://scholar.lib.vt.edu/ejournals/JOTS/Summer-Fall-2000/holmes.html. doi:10.21061/jots.v26i2.a.8

Homans, G. C. (1958). Social Behavior as Exchange. *American Journal of Sociology*, *63*(6), 597–606. https://www.jstor.org/stable/2772990. doi:10.1086/222355

Hong, Y. H., Liao, H., Hu, J., & Jiang, K. (2013). Missing link in the service profit chain: A meta-analytic review of the antecedents, consequences, and moderator of service climate. *The Journal of Applied Psychology*, *98*(2), 237–267. doi:10.1037/a0031666 PMID:23458337

Hooker, C., & Csikszentmihalyi, M. (2003). Flow, creativity, and shared leadership. In C. L. Pearce & J. A. Conger (Eds.), *Shared Leadership* (pp. 217–234). Sage.

HossniM. (2019). *Human relations theory of management*. doi:10.13140/RG.2.2.12893.56804

House, T. W. (2022, March 1). *FACT SHEET: President Biden to Announce Strategy to Address Our National Mental Health Crisis, As Part of Unity Agenda in his First State of the Union*. The White House. https://www.whitehouse.gov/briefing-room/statements-releases/2022/03/01/fact-sheet-president-biden-to-announce-strategy-to-address-our-national-mental-health-crisis-as-part-of-unity-agenda-in-his-first-state-of-the-union/

Huang, S. Y., Li, M. W., & Lee, Y. S. (2021). Why do medium-sized technology farms adopt environmental innovation? The mediating role of pro-environmental behaviors. *Horticulturae*, *7*(9), 318. doi:10.3390/horticulturae7090318

Hughes, M. (2007). The tools and techniques of change management. *Journal of Change Management*, *7*(1), 37–49. doi:10.1080/14697010701309435

Hulland, J. (1999). Use of partial least squares (PLS) in strategic management research: A review of four recent studies. *Strategic Management Journal*, *20*(2), 195–204. doi:10.1002/(SICI)1097-0266(199902)20:2<195::AID-SMJ13>3.0.CO;2-7

Hunter, S. T., Cushenbery, L. D., & Jayne, B. (2017). Why dual leaders will drive innovation: Resolving the exploration and exploitation dilemma with a conservation of resources solution. *Journal of Organizational Behavior*, *38*(8), 1183–1195. doi:10.1002/job.2195

Hussinki, H., Kianto, A., Vanhala, M., & Ritala, P. (2017). Assessing the universality of knowledge management practices. *Journal of Knowledge Management*, *21*(6), 1596–1621. doi:10.1108/JKM-09-2016-0394

Ibarra, H., & Hunter, M. (2007). How leaders create and use networks. *Growth*, *35*(1), 101–103. PMID:17286073

Iezzoni, L. I. (2003). Invisible disabilities: Challenges to diagnosis and treatment. *Quality in Primary Care*, *11*(5), 373–380.

Imad, M. (2022). Teaching to empower: Leveraging the neuroscience of how to help students become self-regulated learners. *Journal of Undergraduate Neuroscience Education*, *20*(2), 252–260.

Imran, R., Kamaal, A., & Mahmoud, A. B. (2017). Teacher's turnover intentions. The International. *Journal of Education Management*, *31*(6), 828–842. https://do.org/10.1108/IJEM-05-2016-0131

Ince, F. (2023). Transformational Leadership in a Diverse and Inclusive Organizational Culture. Handbook of Research on Promoting an Inclusive Organizational Culture for Entrepreneurial Sustainability, 188-201.

Indian Management Thought. (2013). *Gravity, The Great Lakes Magazine, 17*.

Innovates, Diversity & Cultural Competency: Workshops. (n.d.). Retrieved from https://www.inclusioninnovates.com/cultural-diversity-training

Innovation: Integrating Team Climate Principles. *Journal of Applied Psychology*, 6(93), 1438-1446.

International Institute for Management Development (IMD). (2010). *Corporate Social Responsibility: A role for senior management*. Retrieved from https://www.imd.org/publications/corporate-social-responsibility-role-senior-management/

Invisible Disabilities Association. (2023). *What is an invisible disability?* IDA. https://invisibledisabilities.org/

Islami, X., & Mulolli, E. (2020). A conceptual framework of transformational leadership as an influential tool in the team performance. *European Journal of Management Issues*, 28(1-2), 13–24. doi:10.15421/192002

Islam, J., & Hu, H. (2012). A review of literature on contingency theory in managerial accounting. *African Journal of Business Management*, 6(15), 5159–5164.

Islam, M. Z., Jasimuddin, S. M., & Hasan, I. (2015). Organizational culture, structure, technology infrastructure and knowledge sharing: Empirical evidence from MNCs based in Malaysia. *Vine*, 45(1), 67–88. doi:10.1108/VINE-05-2014-0037

Ismail, K. (2009). Corporate social responsibility: An Islamic perspective. *International Journal of Social Economics*, 36(8), 704–717.

Ivandic, I., Kamenov, K., Rojas, D., Cerón, G., Nowak, D., & Sabariego, C. (2017). Determinants of Work Performance in Workers with Depression and Anxiety: A Cross-Sectional Study. *International Journal of Environmental Research and Public Health*, 14(5), 466. doi:10.3390/ijerph14050466 PMID:28445433

Iwelunmor, J., Blackstone, S., Nwaozuru, U., Obiezu-Umeh, C., Uzoaru, F., Mason, S., ... Airhihenbuwa, C. (2022). Social Enterprises for Child and Adolescent Health in Sub-Saharan Africa: A Realist Evaluation. *Child Behavioral Health in Sub-Saharan Africa: Towards Evidence Generation and Policy Development*, 317-332.

Jackson, S. E., Hitt, M. A., & DeNisi, A. S. (2003). Managing human resources for knowledge-based competition: new research directions. In, S.E. Jackson, M.A. Hitt., & A.S. DeNisi (Eds), Managing knowledge for sustained competitive advantage: designing strategies for effective human resource management (pp.399-428). Jossey-Bass.

Jacobs, E. A., Shepard, D. S., Suaya, J. A., & Stone, E. L. (2004). Overcoming language barriers in health care: Costs and benefits of interpreter services. *American Journal of Public Health*, 94(5), 866–869. doi:10.2105/AJPH.94.5.866 PMID:15117713

Jain, P., Asrani, C., & Jain, T. (2018). Resistance to Change in an Organization. *Journal of Business and Management*, 20(5), 37–43.

Jaiswal, N. K., & Dhar, R. L. (2016). Fostering employee creativity through transformational leadership: Moderating role of creative self-efficacy. *Creativity Research Journal*, 28(3), 367–371. doi:10.1080/10400419.2016.1195631

Jankelová, N., Joniaková, Z., Némethová, I., & Blštáková, J. (2020). How to support the effect of transformational leadership on performance in agricultural enterprises. *Sustainability*, 12(18), 7510.

Jansen, M., Guariguata, M. R., Raneri, J. E., Ickowitz, A., Chiriboga-Arroyo, F., Quaedvlieg, J., & Kettle, C. J. (2020). Food for thought: The underutilized potential of tropical tree-sourced foods for 21st century sustainable food systems. *People and Nature*, 2(4), 1006–1020. doi:10.1002/pan3.10159

Jaramillo, P. L., Alpizar, A. B., Forno, C. M., & Landaverde, R. Q. (2021). Agricultural education and migration: A comparison of rural youth in El Salvador and Honduras. *Advancements in Agricultural Development*, 2(1), 70–82.

Compilation of References

Jashari, A., & Kutllovci, E. (2020). The Impact of Human Resource Management Practices on Organizational Performance Case Study: Manufacturing Enterprises in Kosovo. *Business: Theory and Practice, 21*(1), 222–229. doi:10.3846/btp.2020.12001

Jay, A. (2023). *Planting the Seed: Reframing Agriculture Education and Leadership to Cultivate Diversity, Agriculture Literacy, and Sustainable Food Security* [Doctoral dissertation, St. Thomas University]. Proquest Dissertations and Theses Global.

Jaycox, L., Cohen, J. A., Mannarino, A. P., Walker, D. W., Langley, A. K., Gegenheimer, K. L., Scott, M., & Schonlau, M. (2010). Children's mental health care following Hurricane Katrina: A field trial of trauma-focused psychotherapies. *Journal of Traumatic Stress, 23*, 223–231. doi:10.1002/jts.20518 PMID:20419730

Jermsittiparsert, K., Chankoson, T., Malik, I., & Thaicharoen, W. (2021). Linking Islamic Work Ethics With Employee Performance: Perceived Organizational Support And Psychological Ownership As A Potential Mediators In Financial Institutions. Journal of Legal. *Ethical and Regulatory Issues, 24*, 1–11.

Jetten, J., O'Brien, A., & Trindall, N. (2002). Changing identity: Predicting adjustment to organizational restructure as a function of subgroup and superordinate identification. *British Journal of Social Psychology, 41*(2), 281–297. doi:10.1348/014466602760060147 PMID:12133229

Jeve, Y. B., Oppenheimer, C., & Konje, J. (2015). Employee engagement within the NHS: A cross-sectional study. *International Journal of Health Policy and Management, 4*(2), 85–90. doi:10.15171/ijhpm.2015.12 PMID:25674571

Ji, H. (2018). *Uncovering the dark side of shared leadership: a perspective of hierarchical functionalism.* [Doctoral dissertation, Zhejiang University, Hangzhou].

Johns, M. L. (2013). Breaking the glass ceiling: Structural, cultural, and organizational barriers preventing women from achieving senior and executive positions. *Perspectives in Health Information Management, 10*(Winter). PMID:23346029

Johnson, S. (2020). *The advantages of equity in the workplace.* Hearst Newspapers, LLC. https://work.chron.com/advantages-equity-workplace-2635.html

Johnson, D. G., & Wetmore, J. M. (2021). *Technology and society: Building our sociotechnical future.* MIT Press.

Joiner, B. (2019). Leadership agility for organizational agility. *Journal of Creating Value, 5*(2), 139–149. doi:10.1177/2394964319868321

Jones, A., & Matthews, R. (2021). The role of emotional intelligence in leadership decision-making. *Journal of Business and Psychology, 19*(3), 345–358.

Jones, G. R., George, J. M., & Hill, C. W. L. (2000). *Contemporary management* (2nd ed.). Irwin McGraw-Hill.

Jones, S. L., & Van de Ven, A. H. (2016). The changing nature of change resistance: An examination of the moderating impact of time. *The Journal of Applied Behavioral Science, 52*(4), 482–506. doi:10.1177/0021886316671409

Jongen, C., McCalman, J., & Bainbridge, R. (2018). Health workforce cultural competency interventions: A systematic scoping review. *BMC Health Services Research, 18*(1), 232. doi:10.118612913-018-3001-5 PMID:29609614

Jordan, P. J., & Troth, A. C. (2020). Common method bias in applied settings: The dilemma of researching in organizations. *Australian Journal of Management, 45*(1), 3–14. doi:10.1177/0312896219871976

Joseph, P. (2012). Mahatma Gandhi" s concept of educational leadership. *International Journal of Economics Business and Management Studies, 1*(2), 60–64.

Judge, T. A., & Piccolo, R. F. (2004). Transformational and transactional leadership: A meta-analytic test of their relative Validity. *The Journal of Applied Psychology*, *89*(5), 755–768. doi:10.1037/0021-9010.89.5.755 PMID:15506858

Judge, T., Ilies, R., & Colbert, A. (2004). Intelligence and leadership: A quantitative review and test theoretical propositions. *The Journal of Applied Psychology*, *89*(3), 542–552. doi:10.1037/0021-9010.89.3.542 PMID:15161411

Justice, C., Rice, J., Roy, D., Hudspith, B., & Jenkins, H. (2009). Inquiry-based learning in higher education: Administrators' perspectives on integrating inquiry pedagogy into the curriculum. *Higher Education*, *58*(6), 841–855. doi:10.100710734-009-9228-7

Kaiser Family Foundation. (2022). *Mental Health Care Health Professional Shortage Areas (H.P.S.A.s)*. K.F.F. https://www.kff.org/other/state-indicator/mental-health-care-health-professional-shortage-areas-hpsas/

Kaiyatsa, S., Ricker-Gilbert, J., & Jumbe, C. (2019). What does Malawi's fertiliser programme do to private sector fertiliser sales? A quasi-experimental field study. *Journal of Agricultural Economics*, *70*(2), 332–352. doi:10.1111/1477-9552.12286

Kale, G., & Shimpi, S. (2020). Testing Role of Hrm Practices and Organizational Commitment on Organizational Performance with Reference to Seasonality in Tourism Employment. *Journal of Hospitality Application & Research*, *15*(2), 23–46.

Kamel, S., Khalifa, E., & Noermijatib. (2014). The Influences of Transformational Leadership on Employees Performance (A Study of the Economics and Business Faculty Employee at University of Muhammadiyah Malang). *Asia-Pacific Management and Business Application*, *3*(1).

Kaminski, J. (2022). Theory applied to informatics–The Prosci ADKAR Model. *Canadian Journal of Nursing Informatics*, *17*(2). https://cjni.net/journal/?p=10076

Kane, G. C., Phillips, A. N., Copulsky, J., & Andrus, G. (2019). How digital leadership is (n't) different. *MIT Sloan Management Review*, *60*(3), 34–39.

Kanekar, A., & Sharma, M. (2020, September). COVID-19 and mental well-being: guidance on the application of behavioral and positive well-being strategies. In Healthcare (Vol. 8, No. 3, p. 336). MDPI.

Kang, S. K., & Kaplan, S. (2019). Working toward gender diversity and inclusion in medicine: Myths and solutions. *Lancet*, *393*(10171), 579–586. doi:10.1016/S0140-6736(18)33138-6 PMID:30739693

Kanitz, R., & Gonzalez, K. (2021). Are we stuck in the predigital age? Embracing technology-mediated change management in organizational change research. *The Journal of Applied Behavioral Science*, *57*(44), 447–458. doi:10.1177/00218863211042896

Kaplan, R. E., Drath, W. H., & Kofodimos, J. R. (1991). *Beyond ambition: How driven managers can lead better and live better*. Jossey-Bass.

Karami, A., Sahebalzamani, S., & Sarabi, B. (2015). The influence of HR practices on business strategy and firm performance: The case of banking industry in Iran. *IUP Journal of Management Research*, *14*(1), 30–53.

Karanth, S., Benefo, E. O., Patra, D., & Pradhan, A. K. (2022). Importance of artificial intelligence in evaluating climate change and food safety risk. *Journal of Agriculture and Food Research*, 100485.

Karliner, L. S., Jacobs, E. A., Chen, A. H., & Mutha, S. (2007). Do professional interpreters improve clinical care for patients with limited English proficiency? A systematic review of the literature. *Health Services Research*, *42*(2), 727–754. doi:10.1111/j.1475-6773.2006.00629.x PMID:17362215

Compilation of References

Kashima, Y., Klein, O., & Clark, A. E. (2007). Grounding: Sharing Information in Social Interaction. In K. Fiedler (Ed.), *Social communication* (pp. 27–77). Psychology Press.

Katz, D. (2019). Plastic bank: launching social plastic® revolution. *Field Actions Science Reports. The Journal of Field Actions*, (19), 96–99.

Kaufman, E. K. (2010). *Leadership program planning: Assessing the needs and interests of the agricultural community.* Academic Press.

Kaul, E., & Weber, P. (2021). *Overcoming barriers to collaborative learning: Pioneering a virtual student-led longitudinal interprofessional education program.* American Medical Association.

Kazim, F. A. (2019). Digital transformation and leadership style: A multiple case study. *The ISM Journal of International Business*, *3*(1), 24–33.

Kazimoto, P. (2013). Analysis of conflict management and leadership for organizational change. *International Journal of Research in Social Sciences*, *3*(1), 16–25.

Kconvery. (2022, September 30). *Invisible disabilities in the Workplace.* Harvard Pilgrim Health Care - HaPi Guide. https://www.harvardpilgrim.org/hapiguide/seen-supported-destigmatizing-invisible-disabilities-at-work/

Kellerman, B. (2012). *The End of Leadership.* Harper Collins.

Keller, R. T. (1992). Transformational leadership and the performance of research and development project groups. *Journal of Management*, *18*(3), 489–501. doi:10.1177/014920639201800304

Kelly-Turner, K., & Radomsky, A. (2020). The fear of losing control in social anxiety: An experimental approach. *Cognitive Therapy and Research*, *44*(4), 834–845. doi:10.100710608-020-10104-5

Kemerer, D., & Ćwiekala-Lewis, K. (2016). *Emotional Intelligence for Leaders in Nursing. Polish Nursing / Pielegniarstwo Polskie*, *62*(4), 562–565. https://doi.org.dyc.idm.oclc.org/10.20883/pielpol.2016.60

Kemp, J. (2006). Foundations for systemic change: Social evolution and the need for systemic change in education. *TechTrends*, *50*(2), 20–26. doi:10.100711528-006-7582-1

Kepa, M., Pittman, B., Williams, M., & Bruce-Iri, P. (2021). *Whakaora ngā Whenua Whāma: Utilising mātauranga Māori and Western science to protect and restore the soil on rural farms in Te Tai Tokerau.* Academic Press.

Kernis, M. H. (2003). Toward a conceptualization of optimal self-esteem. *Psychological Inquiry*, *14*(1), 1–26. doi:10.1207/S15327965PLI1401_01

Kets de Vries, M. (2021). Two CEOs, No Drama: Ground Rules for Co-Leadership. *INSEAD.* https://knowledge.insead.edu/leadership-organisations/two-ceos-no-drama-ground-rules-co-leadership

Kets de Vries, M. F. R., & Korotov, K. (2010). Developing Leaders and leadership development. SSRN *Electronic Journal.* doi:10.2139/ssrn.1684001

Kezar, A., & Eckel, P. (2002). Examining the institutional transformation process: The importance of sense making, interrelated strategies, and balance. *Research in Higher Education*, *43*(3), 295–328. doi:10.1023/A:1014889001242

Kezar, A., Holcombe, E., Harper, J., & Ueda, N. (2023). Culture Change Requires Personal and Organizational Changes: Lessons from the Shared Equity Leadership Model. *Change*, *55*(1), 39–46. doi:10.1080/00091383.2023.2151806

Khan, Z., A., Irfanullah, A., N. & Khan, D., I. (2016). Leadership Theories and Styles: A Literature Review. *Journal of Resources Development and Management, 16.*

Khan, A. N., & Khan, N. A. (2022). The nexuses between transformational leadership and employee green organisational citizenship behaviour: Role of environmental attitude and green dedication. *Business Strategy and the Environment*, *31*(3), 921–933. doi:10.1002/bse.2926

Khan, H., Rehmat, M., Hassan Butt, T., Farooqui, S., & Asmin, J. (2020). Impact of transformational leadership on work performance, burnout and social loafing: A mediation model. *Future Business Journal*, *6*(1), 1–13. doi:10.118643093-020-00043-8

Khan, M. A. S., Jianguo, D., Ali, M., Saleem, S., & Usman, M. (2019). Interrelations between ethical leadership, green psychological climate, and organizational environmental citizenship behavior: A moderated mediation model. *Frontiers in Psychology*, *10*, 1977. doi:10.3389/fpsyg.2019.01977 PMID:31555173

Khan, N. (2017). Adaptive or Transactional Leadership in Current Higher Education: A Brief Comparison. *International Review of Research in Open and Distance Learning*, *18*(3), 178–183. doi:10.19173/irrodl.v18i3.3294

Kho, J., Gillespie, N., & Khan, M. (2020). *A systematic scoping review of change management practices used for telemedicine service implementations.* https://bmchealthservres.biomedcentral.com/articles/10.1186/s12913-020-05657-w

Kianto, A., Sáenz, J., & Aramburu, N. (2017). Knowledge-based human resource management practices, intellectual capital and innovation. *Journal of Business Research*, *81*, 11–20. doi:10.1016/j.jbusres.2017.07.018

Kidido, J. K., Bugri, J. T., & Kasanga, R. K. (2017). Youth agricultural land access dimensions and emerging challenges under the customary tenure system in Ghana: Evidence from Techiman Area. *Journal of Land and Rural Studies*, *5*(2), 140–163.

Kirkbride, P. (2006). Developing transformational leaders: The full range leadership model in action. *Industrial and Commercial Training*, *38*(1), 23–32. doi:10.1108/00197850610646016

Kish-Gephart, J. J., Detert, J. R., Treviño, L. K., & Edmondson, A. C. (2010). Bad apples, bad cases, and bad barrels: Meta-analytic evidence about sources of unethical decisions at work. *The Journal of Applied Psychology*, *95*(1), 1–31. doi:10.1037/a0017103 PMID:20085404

Kitch, S., McGregor, J., Mejía, G. M., El-Sayed, S., Spackman, C., & Vitullo, J. (2021). Gendered and Racial Injustices in American Food Systems and Cultures. *Humanities (Washington)*, *10*(2), 66.

Klaus, G., Ernst, A., & Oswald, L. (2020). Psychological factors influencing laypersons' acceptance of climate engineering, climate change mitigation and business as usual scenarios. *Technology in Society*, *60*, 101222. doi:10.1016/j.techsoc.2019.101222

Kline, R. (2022). Emotional intelligence and transformational leadership: An exploratory study. *Journal of Leadership & Organizational Studies*, *29*(1), 45–59.

Klingborg, D. J., Moore, D., & Varea-Hammond, S. (2006). What is leadership? *Journal of Veterinary Medical Education*, *33*(2), 280–283. doi:10.3138/jvme.33.2.280 PMID:16849311

Klinger, M. G. M. (2002). Organizational culture and people with disabilities. *Disability Studies Quarterly*, *22*(1). doi:10.18061/dsq.v22i1.332

Klopotan, I., Mjeda, T., & Kurečić, P. (2018). Exploring the motivation of employees in a firm: A Case-Study. *Business Systems Research*, *9*(1), 151–160. doi:10.2478/bsrj-2018-0012

Knapp, S. (2016). *Importance of Bhagavad Gita in this Day and Age.* http://www.stephenknapp.com/importance_of_bhagavadgita_in_this_day_and_age.htm

Compilation of References

Knight, J. (2018). Decolonizing and transforming the Geography undergraduate curriculum in South Africa. *The South African Geographical Journal, 100*(3), 271–290. https://hdl.handle.net/10520/EJC-10c31734cd. doi:10.1080/03736245.2018.1449009

Knight, L., & Pemberton, C. (2022). Perfectionism in leadership and team dynamics. *Leadership and Organization Development Journal, 43*(2), 183–198.

Knowles, M. S. (1980). *The modern practice of adult education: From pedagogy to andragogy* (2nd ed.). Cambridge Books.

Knowles, M. S., & ... (1984). *Andragogy in action: Applying modern principles of adult learning.* Jossey-Bass.

Kocolowski, M. D. (2010). Shared Leadership: Is it Time for a Change? *Emerging Leadership Journeys, 3*(1).

Koester, L. (2015). Destructive leadership and its impact on employees: A review of the literature. *Human Resource Management Review, 25*(3), 254–267.

Kohl, K. (2016). *Becoming a sustainable organization.* Auerbach Publications. doi:10.1201/b20789

Kohn, M. (2008). *Trust: Self-interest and the common good.* OUP Oxford.

Kohtamäki, V. (2019). Academic leadership and university reform-guided management changes in Finland. *Journal of Higher Education Policy and Management, 41*(1), 70–85. doi:10.1080/1360080X.2018.1553499

Kolb, D. (1984). *Experiential learning: Experience as the source of learning and development.* Prentice Hall.

Kolb, D. A. (2014). *Experiential Learning Experience as the Source of Learning and Development* (2nd ed.). Pearson Education.

Kollenscher, E., Poper, M., & Ronen, B. (2018). Value-creating organizational leadership. *Journal of Management & Organization, 24*(1), 19–39. doi:10.1017/jmo.2016.33

Kolzow, D. R. (2014). *Leading from within: Building organizational leadership capacity.* IEDC. https://www.iedconline.org/clientuploads/Downloads/edrp/Leading_from_Within.pdf

Konrad, A. M. (2018). Toxic leadership: A review of the literature. *Leadership and Organization Development Journal, 39*(1), 1–17.

Konu, A., & Viitanen, E. (2008). Shared leadership in Finnish social and health care. *Leadership in Health Services (Bradford, England), 21*(1), 28–40. doi:10.1108/17511870810845888

Kopelovich, S. L., Monroe-DeVita, M., Buck, B. E., Brenner, C., Moser, L., Jarskog, L. F., Harker, S., & Chwastiak, L. A. (2021). Community Mental Health Care Delivery During the COVID-19 Pandemic: Practical Strategies for Improving Care for People with Serious Mental Illness. *Community Mental Health Journal, 57*(3), 405–415. doi:10.100710597-020-00662-z PMID:32562033

Korejan, M. M., & Shahbazi, H. (2016). An analysis of the transformational leadership theory. *Revue des Sciences Fondamentales et Appliquées, 8*(3), 452–461. doi:10.4314/jfas.v8i3s.192

Köşker, Z., & Gürer, A. (2020). Sürdürülebilirlik Çerçevesinde Yeşil Örgüt Kültürü. *Ekonomi İşletme Siyaset ve Uluslararası İlişkiler Dergisi, 6*(1), 88–109.

Kotter, J. P. (1996). *LeadingChange.* Harvard Business School Press.

Kotter, J. P., & Cohen, D. S. (2002). *The heart of change: Real-life stories of how people change their organizations.* Harvard Business Press.

Kotter, J., & Rathgeber, H. (2005). *Our Iceberg is Melting: Changing and Succeeding Under Any Conditions* (10th ed.). Penguin Random House LLC.

Kotterman, J. (2006). Leadership versus management: what's the difference?. *The Journal for Quality and Participation, 29*(2), 13. *leadership, 31*, 43.

Kountios, G., Konstantinidis, C., & Antoniadis, I. (2023). Can the Adoption of ICT and Advisory Services Be Considered as a Tool of Competitive Advantage in Agricultural Holdings? A Literature Review. *Agronomy (Basel), 13*(2), 530. doi:10.3390/agronomy13020530

Kouzes, J. M., & Posner, B. Z. (2017). *The Leadership Challenge* (6th ed.). John Wiley & Sons.

Kovar, K. A., & Ball, A. L. (2013). Two decades of agricultural literacy research: A synthesis of the literature. *Journal of Agricultural Education, 54*(1), 167–178.

Krill, T. L. (1993). *An exploration of the leadership practice" enabling others to act": a case study*. Iowa State University.

Kuban, C., & Steele, W. (2011). Restoring safety and hope: From victim to survivor. *Reclaiming Children and Youth, 20*(1), 41–44.

Kubler-Ross, D., & Kessler, E. (2014). On grief and grieving. Simon & Schuster.

Kuckertz, A., Brändle, L., Gaudig, A., Hinderer, S., Reyes, C. A. M., Prochotta, A., Steinbrink, K. M., & Berger, E. S. C. (2020). Startups in times of crisis—A rapid response to the COVID-19 pandemic. *Journal of Business Venturing Insights, 13*, 1–13. doi:10.1016/j.jbvi.2020.e00169

Kugelmass, H. (2016). Sorry, I'm not accepting new patients. *Journal of Health and Social Behavior, 57*(2), 168–183. doi:10.1177/0022146516647098 PMID:27251890

Kumah, P. (2022). Impact of SHRM on Employee Commitment in Tertiary Educational Institutions in Ghana. [IJAMSE]. *International Journal of Applied Management Sciences and Engineering, 9*(1), 1–22. doi:10.4018/IJAMSE.312849

Kumari, K., Abbas, J., Hwang, J., & Cioca, L. I. (2022). Does Servant Leadership Promote Emotional Intelligence and Organizational Citizenship Behavior among Employees? A Structural Analysis. *Sustainability (Basel), 14*(9), 5231. doi:10.3390u14095231

Kumar, K. L. S., & Reddy, M. L. (2019). Strategic Human Resource Management: The Calibrated Catalysts for Indian IT-SMEs Performance Optimization. *SDMIMD Journal of Management, 10*(1), 31–42. doi:10.18311dmimd/2019/21493

Kumar, S. (2020). Knowledge risk management for state-owned enterprises-Indian scenario. In S. Durst & T. Henschel (Eds.), *Knowledge risk management: from theory to praxis* (pp. 89–106). Springer. doi:10.1007/978-3-030-35121-2_6

Kunze, F., Boehm, S., & Bruch, H. (2013). Age, resistance to change, and job performance. *Journal of Managerial Psychology, 28*(7/8), 741–760. doi:10.1108/JMP-06-2013-0194

Kutsyuruba, B., & Walker, K. D. (2016). The Destructive Effects of Distrust: Leaders as Brokers of Trust in Organizations. The Dark Side of Leadership: Identifying and Overcoming Unethical Practice in Organizations (Advances in Educational Administration, Vol. 26), Emerald Group Publishing Limited, Bingley, pp. 133-154. doi:10.1108/S1479-366020160000026008

Kyngäs, H., Kääriäinen, M., & Elo, S. (2020). The trustworthiness of content analysis. In *The Application of Content Analysis in Nursing Science Research, H. Kyngäs, M. Kääriäinen, and S. Elo* (pp. 41–48). Springer. doi:10.1007/978-3-030-30199-6_5

Lai, F.-Y., Tang, H.-C., & Lu, S.-C. (2020). Transformational Leadership and Job Performance: The Mediating Role of Work Engagement. *Organizational Research Methods*, *10*(1).

Laig, R. B. D., & Abocejo, F. T. (2021). Change management process in a mining company: Kotter's 8-Step change model. *Journal of Management, Economics, and Industrial Organization*, *5*(3), 31–50. doi:10.31039/jomeino.2021.5.3.3

Lajoie, D., Boudrias, J., Rousseau, V., & Brunelle, E. (2017). Value congruence and tenure as moderators of transformational leadership effects. *Leadership and Organization Development Journal*, *38*(2), 254–269. doi:10.1108/LODJ-04-2015-0091

Laker, B. (2022, November 9). Culture is a company's single most powerful advantage. Here's why. *Forbes*. https://www.forbes.com/sites/benjaminlaker/2021/04/23/culture-is-a-companys-single-most-powerful-advantage-heres-why/?sh=51c110d679e8

Lamba, S., Omary, M. B., & Strom, B. L. (2022). Diversity, equity, and inclusion: Organizational strategies during and beyond the COVID-19 pandemic. *Journal of Health Organization and Management*, *36*(2), 256–264. doi:10.1108/JHOM-05-2021-0197

Lambe, A., Anthoney, F., & Shaw, J. (2018). One door closes, another opens: Surviving and thriving through organizational restructure by ensuring knowledge continuity. *Business Information Review*, *35*(4), 145–153. doi:10.1177/0266382118802651

Lameck, W. U. (2022). The influence of ethical leadership in the delivery of agricultural advisory services in Tanzania local government authorities. *Public Administration and Policy*, *25*(1), 78–88. doi:10.1108/PAP-05-2021-0031

Lamm, K. W., Holder, M., Randall, N. L., Edgar, D. W., & Lamm, A. J. (2021). Agricultural leadership development program participant personality and demographic characteristics: An empirical analysis. *SAGE Open*, *11*(4), 21582440211061577. doi:10.1177/21582440211061577

Langley, A., Santiago, C. D., Rodríguez, A., & Zelaya, J. (2013). Improving implementation of mental health services for trauma in multicultural elementary schools: Stakeholder perspectives on parent and educator engagement. *The Journal of Behavioral Health Services & Research*, *40*(3), 247–262. doi:10.100711414-013-9330-6 PMID:23576136

Lang, R., & Fink, M. (2019). Rural social entrepreneurship: The role of social capital within and across institutional levels. *Journal of Rural Studies*, *70*, 155–168. doi:10.1016/j.jrurstud.2018.03.012

Lardjane, S., Laveuve, F., & Nutinen, M. (2017). The need for fundamental change in education. *E-Journal of Environmental Education*, 1–7.

Latif, S. A., & Ahmad, M. A. S. (2020). Learning agility among educational leaders: A Luca-ready leadership competency? *Jurnal Pengurusan Dan Kepimpinan Pendidikan*, *33*(1), 105–116.

Laub, J. (2018). *Leveraging the power of servant leadership: Building high performing organization*. Palgrave Macmillan. doi:10.1007/978-3-319-77143-4

Laurie, R., Nonoyama-Tarumi, Y., Mckeown, R., & Hopkins, C. (2016). Contributions of Education for Sustainable Development (ESD) to Quality Education: A Synthesis of Research. *Journal of Education for Sustainable Development*, *10*(2), 226–242. doi:10.1177/0973408216661442

Le Glaz, A., Haralambous, Y., Kim-Dufor, D. H., Lenca, P., Billot, R., Ryan, T. C., Marsh, J., DeVylder, J., Walter, M., Berrouiguet, S., & Lemey, C. (2021). Machine learning and natural language processing in mental health: Systematic review. *Journal of Medical Internet Research*, *23*(5), e15708. doi:10.2196/15708 PMID:33944788

Lee, C., Liu, J., Rousseau, D. M., Hui, C., & Chen, Z. X. (2011). Inducements, contributions, and fulfillment in new employee psychological contracts. *Human Resource Management*, *50*(2), 201–226. doi:10.1002/hrm.20415

Lee, J., & Song, J. H. (2022). Developing a Conceptual Integrated Model for the Employee's Learning Agility. *Performance Improvement Quarterly, 34*(4), 367–394. doi:10.1002/piq.21352

Le, H., Palmer Johnson, C., & Fujimoto, Y. (2021). Organizational justice and climate for inclusion. *Personnel Review, 50*(1), 1–20. doi:10.1108/PR-10-2019-0546

Leibowitz, B., Bozalek, V., Van Schalkwyk, S., & Winberg, C. (2015). Institutional context matters: The professional development of academics as teachers in South African higher education. *Higher Education, 69*(2), 315–330. doi:10.100710734-014-9777-2

Leithwood, K. (1992). *Transformational Leadership and School Restructuring.*

Leithwood, K., & Jantzi, D. (2005). Transformational leadership. *The essentials of school leadership, 31*, 43.Perrin, C. (2010). Leader vs. Manager: What's the Distinction? *Catalyst, 21519390*(39), 2.

Leithwood, K. (1994). Leadership for school restructuring. *Educational Administration Quarterly, 30*(4), 498–518. doi:10.1177/0013161X94030004006

Leithwood, K., Harris, A., & Hopkins, D. (2020). Seven strong claims about successful school leadership revisited. *School Leadership & Management, 40*(1), 5–22. doi:10.1080/13632434.2019.1596077

Leithwood, K., & Jantzi, D. (1990). Transformational leadership: How principals can help reform school cultures. *School Effectiveness and School Improvement, 1*(4), 249–280. doi:10.1080/0924345900010402

Lelli, C. (2014). Ten strategies to help the traumatized child in school. *Kappa Delta Pi Record, 50*(3), 114–118. doi:10.1080/00228958.2014.931145

Lencioni, P. (2016). *The ideal team player: How to recognize and cultivate the three essential virtues.* Jossey-Bass.

Lensges, M., Hollensbe, E., & Masterson, S. (2016). The human side of restructures: The role of shifting identification. *Journal of Management Inquiry, 25*(4), 382–396. doi:10.1177/1056492616630140

Leon, R. D. (2013). From sustainable organization to sustainable knowledge-based organization. *Economic Insights - Trends and Challenges, 65*(2), 63–73.

Le, P. B., & Le, H. (2019). Determinants of innovation capability: The roles of transformational leadership, knowledge sharing and perceived organisational support. *Journal of Knowledge Management, 23*(3), 527–547. doi:10.1108/JKM-09-2018-0568

Lerner, M., & Shimazu, A. (2021). Adaptive and maladaptive perfectionism in leadership: A case study. *Journal of Business and Psychology, 36*(4), 499–513.

Lewin, K. (1951). *Field Theory in Social Science: Selected Theoretical Papers* (D. Cartwright, Ed.). Harper & Row.

Lewin, K., Lippitt, R., & White, R. K. (1939). Patterns of aggressive behavior in experimentally created "social climates.". *The Journal of Social Psychology, 10*(2), 269–299. doi:10.1080/00224545.1939.9713366

Lewis, T. (2018). The Black Church and African-American Communities: A Historical Perspective. *Journal of African American History, 103*(2), 181–190.

Liang, Q., Ma, K., & Liu, W. (2023). The role of farmer cooperatives in promoting environmentally sustainable agricultural development in China: A review. *Annals of Public and Cooperative Economics.*

Compilation of References

Liaw, Y.-J., Chi, N.-W., & Chuang, A. (2010). Examining the Mechanisms Linking Transformational Leadership, Employee Customer Orientation, and Service Performance: The Mediating Roles of Perceived Supervisor and Coworker Support. *Journal of Business and Psychology*, *25*(3), 477–492. doi:10.100710869-009-9145-x

Li, L., & Liu, Y. (2022). An integrated model of principal transformational leadership and teacher leadership that is related to teacher self-efficacy and student academic performance. *Asia Pacific Journal of Education*, *42*(4), 661–678.

Lin, L., Stamm, K., & Christidis, P. (2018). How diverse is the psychology workforce: News from APA's Center for Workforce Studies. *American Psychological Association (APA)*. https://www.apa.org/monitor/2018/02/datapoint

Lin, S.-Y., Hirst, G., Wu, C.-H., Lee, C., Wu, W., & Chang, C.-C. (2023). When anything less than perfect isn't good enough: How parental and supervisor perfectionistic expectations determine fear of failure and employee creativity. *Journal of Business Research*, *154*, 113341. doi:10.1016/j.jbusres.2022.113341

Linklater, R. (2014). *Decolonizing trauma work*. Fernwood Publishing.

Linuesa-Langreo, J., Ruiz-Palomino, P., & Elche-Hortelano, D. (2017). New Strategies in the New Millennium: Servant Leadership as Enhancer of Service Climate and Customer Service Performance. *Frontiers in Psychology*, *8*, 786. doi:10.3389/fpsyg.2017.00786 PMID:28559873

Linzenich, A., Arning, K., & Ziefle, M. (2021). Acceptance of energy technologies in context: Comparing laypeople's risk perceptions across eight infrastructure technologies in Germany. *Energy Policy*, *152*, 112071. doi:10.1016/j.enpol.2020.112071

Lipman-Blumen, J. (1988). *Individual and organizational achieving styles: A technical manual for researchers and human resource professionals*. Achieving Styles Institute.

Lipman-Blumen, J. (1996). *The connective edge: Leading in an interdependent world*. Jossey-Bass.

Lipman-Blumen, J. (2017). Connective leadership in an interdependent and diverse world. *Roeper Review*, *39*(3), 170–173. doi:10.1080/02783193.2017.1318994

Li, Q., Huang, J., Luo, R., & Liu, C. (2013). China's labor transition and the future of China's rural wages and employment. *China & World Economy*, *21*(3), 4–24. doi:10.1111/j.1749-124X.2013.12019.x

Litz, D., & Blaik-Hourani, R. (2020). Transforamtional Leadership and Change in Education. *Oxford Research Encyclopedia of Education*. Retrieved 1 Aug. 2023 from https://oxfordre.com/education/view/10.1093/acrefore/978019026493.001.001/acrefore9780190264093-e-631

Liu, Y., Fu, W., Zou, L., Wen, L., Zhang, P., Zhang, L., Bai, X., Wang, J., & Mao, J. (2022). Posttraumatic stress disorder and depression of Chinese medical staff after 2 years of COVID-19: A multicenter study. *Brain and Behavior*, *12*(11), 1–9. https://doi-org.captechu.idm.oclc.org/10.1002/brb3.2785. doi:10.1002/brb3.2785 PMID:36259949

Li, X., & He, Z. (2022). Function of psychological analysis of painting based on image information in cultivating college students' entrepreneurship. *Journal of Sensors*, *2022*, 1–12. doi:10.1155/2022/3564884

Logofătu, M. (2019). Integrating Organizational Culture in Strategic Human Resource Management of the Educational Institutions. Ovidius University Annals. *Series Economic Sciences*, *19*(1), 443–449.

Lombardo, M. M., & Eichinger, R. W. (2000). High potentials as high learners. *Human Resource Management*, *39*(4), 321–329. doi:10.1002/1099-050X(200024)39:4<321::AID-HRM4>3.0.CO;2-1

Lopez, J. (2020). How the COVID-19 pandemic is affecting children's mental health. *Medical News Today*. https://www.medicalnewstoday.com/articles/how-the-covid-19-pandemic-is-affecting-childrens-mental-health

Lorenz, F. G. (2014). A study of wellness and academic leadership. *Journal of Applied Research in Higher Education*, *6*(1), 30–43. doi:10.1108/JARHE-11-2012-0029

Loveless, A. (2002). Literature review in creativity, new technologies and learning. NESTA Futurelab Research Publisher.

Lo, W.-Y., Lin, Y.-K., Lee, H.-M., & Liu, T.-Y. (2023). The lens of Yin-Yang philosophy: The influence of paradoxical leadership and emotional intelligence on nurses' organizational identification and turnover intention. *Leadership in Health Services*, *36*(3), 434–457. doi:10.1108/LHS-09-2022-0095 PMID:36853757

Luca, N. R. (2021). Overview of stakeholder involvement in social marketing. In *The Palgrave Encyclopedia of Social Marketing*. Palgrave Macmillan., doi:10.1007/978-3-030-14449-4_99-1

Lucatello, S., & Sánchez, R. (2022). Climate Change in North America: Risks, Impacts, and Adaptation. A Reflection Based on the IPCC Report AR6–2022. *Revista Mexicana de Economía y Finanzas Nueva Época REMEF*, *17*(4), 794.

Luc, É. (2016). Le leadership partagé: Du mythe des grands leaders à l'intelligence collective. *Gestion*, *41*(3), 32–39. doi:10.3917/riges.413.0032

Ludwikowska, K. (2021). The Mediating Role of Employee—Oriented Human Resource Policy in the Relationship between Strategic Human Resource Management and Organisational Performance. *Forum Scientiae Oeconomia*, *9*(2), 131–150.

Lueneburger, C., & Goleman, D. (2010). The change leadership sustainability demands. *MIT Sloan Management Review*, *51*(4), 49–55.

Luthans, F. (2006). *Organizational Behavior*. McGraw-Hill.

Luthans, K. W., Luthans, B. C., & Palmer, N. F. (2016). A positive approach to management education: The relationship between academic PsyCap and student engagement. *Journal of Management Development*, *35*(9), 1098–1118. doi:10.1108/JMD-06-2015-0091

Lwi, B. (2019). The influence of elementary school leadership in promoting a learning-centered Classroom. *Philippine Social Science Journal*, *2*(1), 69–82. doi:10.52006/main.v2i1.56

MacGregor, B. J. (1978). *Leadership*. Torchbooks.

MacKenzie, S. B., Podsakoff, P. M., & Rich, G. A. (2001). Transformational and transactional leadership and salesperson performance. *Journal of the Academy of Marketing Science, 29*(2).

Madalina, O. (2016). Conflict management: A new challenge. *Procedia Economics and Finance*, *39*, 807–814. doi:10.1016/S2212-5671(16)30255-6

Mahadevan, B. (2012, July). Leadership lessons from Bhagavad Gita. *Impact*, 13–16.

Mahmood, Z., & Humphrey, D. (2013). The impact of corporate social responsibility on organizational performance in Malaysian manufacturing firms. *International Journal of Business and Social Science*, *4*(2), 145–154.

Mahmudi. (2010). *Manajemen Kinerja Sektor Publik, Edisi Kedua*. Yogyakarta: Sekolah Tinggi Ilmu Manajemen YKPN.

Mair, J., & Marti, I. (2006). Social entrepreneurship research: A source of explanation, prediction, and delight. *Journal of World Business*, *41*(1), 36–44. doi:10.1016/j.jwb.2005.09.002

Malhotra, N., Zietsma, C., Morris, T., & Smets, M. (2020). Handling resistance to change when societal and workplace logics conflict. *Administrative Science Quarterly*, *66*(2), 475–520. doi:10.1177/0001839220962760

Compilation of References

Mamorobela, S. P. (2022). Understanding a social media-enabled knowledge management adoption model for small and medium enterprises in South Africa. In P. Ngulube (Ed.), *Handbook of research on mixed methods research in information science* (pp. 324–339). IGI Global. doi:10.4018/978-1-7998-8844-4.ch016

Man, X., Zhu, X., & Sun, C. (2020, May 11). The positive effect of workplace accommodation on creative performance of employees with and without disabilities. *Frontiers*. https://www.frontiersin.org/articles/10.3389/fpsyg.2020.01217/full

Mancini, M. C., Arfini, F., Antonioli, F., & Guareschi, M. (2021). Alternative agri-food systems under a market agencements approach: The case of multifunctional farming activity in a peri-urban area. *Environments (Basel, Switzerland)*, *8*(7), 61. doi:10.3390/environments8070061

Mangkunegara, A. P., & Huddin, M. (2016). The effect of transformational leadership and job satisfaction on employee performance. *Universal Journal of Management*, *4*(4), 189–195. doi:10.13189/ujm.2016.040404

Mann, P. (1991). Permanence and evolution of the repertoire of collective action of French farmers since 1970. *Economie Rurale*.

Manuaba, I. B. A. P., No, Y., & Wu, C. C. (2022). The effectiveness of problem based learning in improving critical thinking, problem-solving and self-directed learning in first-year medical students: A meta-analysis. *PLoS One*, *17*(11), e0277339.

Manz, C., Shipper, F., & Stewart, G. (2009). Everyone a Team Leader: Shared Influence at W. L. Gore & Associates. *Organizational Dynamics*, *38*(3), 239–244. doi:10.1016/j.orgdyn.2009.04.006

Maphoto, A. R., & Matlala, M. E. (2022). Prospects for, and challenges of, knowledge sharing in the South African public sector: a literature review. *Social Sciences International Research Conference*, 19-21 Oct, pp. 1109-1125.

Martic, K. (2022, November 14). Transparency in the workplace: 7 benefits and 6 best practices. *Haiilo*. https://haiilo.com/blog/transparency-in-the-workplace/

Martin, S. L., Liao, H., & Campbell, E. M. (2013). Directive versus empowering leadership: A field experiment comparing impacts on task proficiency and proactivity. *Academy of Management Journal*, *56*(5), 1372–1395. doi:10.5465/amj.2011.0113

Martins, E. C., & Meyer, H. W. J. (2012). Organisational and behavioural factors that influence knowledge retention. *Journal of Knowledge Management*, *16*(1), 77–96. doi:10.1108/13673271211198954

Maslach, C., & Leiter, M. P. (2018). *The truth about burnout: How organizations cause personal stress and what to do about it* (3rd ed.). Jossey-Bass.

Massoudi, A. H., & Hamdi, S. S. (2019). Reciprocal leadership influence on organizational change. *Cihan University-Erbil Journal of Humanities and Social Sciences*, *3*(1), 20–26. doi:10.24086/cuejhss.v3n1y2019.pp20-26

Mathis, R. L., & Jackson, J.H. (2006). Human Resource Management: Manajemen Sumber Daya Manusia. Terjemahan Dian Angelia. Jakarta: Salemba Empat.

Mathis, R. L., & Jackson, J. H. (2000). *Human resource management* (9th ed.). South-Western College Publishing.

Matošková, J., & Směšná, P. (2017). Human resources management practices stimulating knowledge sharing. *Management & Marketing. Challenges for Knowledge Society*, *12*(4), 614–632.

Mattson, D. (2017, August 29). *6 Principles of change management for leaders*. Sandler Blog. https://www.sandler.com/blog/principles-change-management/

Maurer, R. (2022, October 25). Employers can do more for workers with disabilities. *SHRM*. https://www.shrm.org/hr-today/news/hr-news/pages/ndeam-employers-can-do-more-for-workers-with-disabilities.aspx

Maxwell, D. O., Lambeth, D. T., & Cox, J. T. (2015). Effects of using inquiry-based learning on science achievement for fifth-grade students. Asia-Pacific Forum on Science Learning & Teaching, 16(1).

Maxwell, J. (2015). *The leadership handbook*. Harper Collins Leadership.

Mbugua K. (2012). Respect for cultural diversity and the empirical turn in bioethics: a plea for caution. *Journal of Medical Ethics and History of Medicine, 5*, 1.

McCall, T., Bolton, C. S., III, Carlson, R., & Khairat, S. (2021). A systematic review of telehealth interventions for managing anxiety and depression in African American adults. MHealth, 7, 31–31. doi:10.21037/mhealth-20-114

McCall, M. W. (2004). *Leadership development through experience*. Academy of Management Executive. doi:10.5465/ame.2004.14776183

McCall, M.W., & Lombardo, M.M., Lombardo. (1983). What Makes a Top Executive? *Psychology Today, 17*(2), 26–31.

McCall, T., Schwartz, T. A., & Khairat, S. (2020). The Acceptability of Text Messaging to Help African American Women Manage Anxiety and Depression: Cross-Sectional Survey Study. *JMIR Mental Health, 7*(2), e15801. doi:10.2196/15801 PMID:31909720

McClellan, J. L. (2022). Post pandemic leadership in Latin America: Responding to wicked problems using adaptive leadership in organizational contexts. *Estudios de Administración, 29*(1), 52–65. https://doi-org.captechu.idm.oclc.org/10.5354/0719-0816.2022.65372

McDonald, P., & Gandz, J. (1992). Getting value from shared values. *Organizational Dynamics, 20*(3), 64–77. doi:10.1016/0090-2616(92)90025-I

McFarland, R., Rode, J., & Shervani, T. (2016). A contingency model of emotional intelligence in professional selling. *Journal of the Academy of Marketing Science, 44*(1), 108–118. doi:10.100711747-015-0435-8

McHugh, M. D., Kutney-Lee, A., Cimiotti, J. P., Sloane, D. M., & Aiken, L. H. (2011). Nurses' widespread job dissatisfaction, burnout, and frustration with health benefits signal problems for patient care. *Health Affairs (Project Hope), 30*(2), 202–210. doi:10.1377/hlthaff.2010.0100 PMID:21289340

McKimm, J., Lomax, P., & White, P. (2012). Using action research for school improvement. *Sage (Atlanta, Ga.)*.

McKinzie, S. (2000). Twenty-five years of collegial management: The Dickinson College model of revolving leadership and holistic librarianship. *Library Philosophy and Practice, 2*(2), 1–8.

McLearney, A. S. (2006). Leadership development in healthcare: A qualitative study. *Journal of Organizational Behavior, 27*(7), 967–982. doi:10.1002/job.417

McShane, S. L., Tas, K., & Steen, S. L. (2015). *Canadian organizational behaviour* (11th ed.). McGraw Hill.

Meachem, L. (2021). *Mental health in the church & community*. Lulu Publications.

Medical facilities in Aruba - Hospitals, Pharmacies & Clinics. (n.d.). Retrieved from https://www.aruba.com/us/organization/medical-facilities

Meiryani, N., Yorick, K., Gatot, S., Mohammed, A., & Fakhrul, H. (2022). *The Effect of transformative leadership and Remote working on Employee performance During the COVID-19 Pandemic*. Academic Press.

Compilation of References

Men, L. R., Qin, Y. S., Mitson, R., & Thelen, P. (2023). Engaging Employees Via an Inclusive Climate: The Role of Organizational Diversity Communication and Cultural Intelligence. *Journal of Public Relations Research*, 1-22.

Mendel, S. C. (2017). Workarounds in nonprofit management: Counter theory for best practices innovation. *Journal of Ideology, 38*(2), 1–31.

Mendy, V. L., Vargas, R., Cannon-Smith, G., Payton, M., Enkhmaa, B., & Zhang, L. (2018). Food insecurity and cardiovascular disease risk factors among Mississippi adults. *International Journal of Environmental Research and Public Health, 15*(9), 2016.

Mental Health America. (2019). Mental health in the workplace: How employers can support employees. *Mental Health America.*. https://www.mentalhealthamerica.net/issues/mental-health-workplace-how-employers-can-support-employees

Mercer, J. R. (1965). Social System Perspective and Clinical Perspective: Frames of Reference for Understanding Career Patterns of Persons Labelled as Mentally Retarded. *Social Problems, 13*(1), 18–34. doi:10.2307/799303

Merkens, B. J., & Spencer, J. S. (1998). A successful and necessary evolution to shared leadership: A hospital's story. *International Journal of Health Care Quality Assurance, 11*(1), 1–4. PMID:10177364

Merriam, S. B., & Bierema, L. L. (2014). Adult learning: Linking theory and practice. John Wiley & Sons, Inc.

Merriam, S. (2009). *Qualitative research: A guide to design and implementation* (3rd ed.). Jossey-Bass.

Mertens, M. M. (2014). *Implications of Local and Regional Food Systems: Toward a New Food Economy in Portland, Oregon* [Doctoral dissertation]. Portland State University.

Mertens, D. M. (2015). Mixed methods and wicked problems. *Journal of Mixed Methods Research, 9*(1), 3–6. doi:10.1177/1558689814562944

Meuer, J., Koelbel, J., & Hoffmann, V. H. (2020). On the nature of corporate sustainability. *Organization & Environment, 33*(3), 319–341. doi:10.1177/1086026619850180

Meuter, R. F., Gallois, C., Segalowitz, N. S., Ryder, A. G., & Hocking, J. (2015). Overcoming language barriers in healthcare: A protocol for investigating safe and effective communication when patients or clinicians use a second language. *BMC Health Services Research, 15*(1), 371. doi:10.118612913-015-1024-8 PMID:26357948

Meyer, J. (2002). Strategic communication enhances organizational performance. *Human Resource Planning, 25*(2), 7–10.

Mezirow, J. (1978). *Education for perspective transformation: Women's re-entry programs in community colleges.* Teachers College.

Mezirow, J. (1991). *Transformative dimensions of adult learning.* Jossey-Bass.

Mhazo, T., & Thebe, V. (2021). 'Hustling Out of Unemployment': Livelihood Responses of Unemployed Young Graduates in the City of Bulawayo, Zimbabwe. *Journal of Asian and African Studies, 56*(3), 628–642.

Miao, Q., Newman, A., Yu, J., & Xu, L. (2012). The relationship between ethical leadership and organizational performance: The mediating role of knowledge-sharing culture. *Journal of Business Ethics, 159*(3), 828–839.

Michael, E. (2023, February 27). *Understanding the economic consequences of the covid-19 pandemic.* Economist Impact. https://impact.economist.com/perspectives/economic-development/understanding-economic-consequences-covid-19-pandemic

Michigan State University. (2022, November 22). *What Is Change Management?* https://www.michiganstateuniversity-online.com/resources/leadership/what-is-change-management/

Micić, R. (2015). Leadership role in certain phases of knowledge management processes. *Ekonomika (Nis)*, *61*(4), 47–55. doi:10.5937/ekonomika1504047M

Migeon, D. (2018). Bienveillance, éthique et empathie en entreprise. *Petod digest de philo á l'usage du monde professionnel Paris: Maxima*.

Miles, M. B., & Huberman, A. M. (1994). *Qualitative data analysis: An expanded sourcebook* (2nd ed.). Sage.

Miller, K. (2020, March 19). *5 critical steps in the change management process*. Harvard Business School Insights.

Miller, B. A. (2011). Marketing and branding the agronomy major at Iowa State University. *Journal of Natural Resources and Life Sciences Education*, *40*(1), 1–9.

Miller, H., McNeal, K., & Herbert, B. (2010). Inquiry in the physical geology classroom: Supporting students' conceptual model development. *Journal of Geography in Higher Education*, *34*(4), 595–615. doi:10.1080/03098265.2010.499562

Minnesota Department of Mental Health. (2023). *differences in rates of drug overdose deaths by race*. MDMH. https://www.health.state.mn.us/communities/opioids/data/racedisparity.html

Mitchinson, A., & Morris, R. (2014). *Learning about learning agility*. Center for Creative Leadership. doi:10.35613/ccl.2014.1012

Mitra, P., Kickul, J., Gundry, L., & Orr, J. (2019). The Rise of Hybrids: A Note for Social Entrepreneurship Educators. *International Review of Entrepreneurship*, *17*(2).

Mizrak, K. C. (2021). A Research on Effect of Performance Evaluation and Efficiency on Work Life. In Management Strategies to Survive in a Competitive Environment: How to Improve Company Performance (pp. 387-400). Springer International Publishing.

Mohammedshum, A. A., Mannaerts, C. M., Maathuis, B. H. P., & Teka, D. (2023). Integrating Socioeconomic Biophysical and Institutional Factors for Evaluating Small-Scale Irrigation Schemes in Northern Ethiopia. *Sustainability (Basel)*, *15*(2), 1704. doi:10.3390u15021704

Moin, M. F., Omar, M. K., Wei, F., Rasheed, M. I., & Hameed, Z. (2021). Green HRM and safety: How transformational leadership drives follower's job satisfaction. *Current Issues in Tourism*, *24*(16), 2269–2277. doi:10.1080/13683500.2020.1829569

Mongelli, F., Georgakopoulos, P., & Pato, M. T. (2020). Challenges and Opportunities to Meet the Mental Health Needs of Underserved and Disenfranchised Populations in the United States. *Focus - American Psychiatric Publishing*, *18*(1), 16–24. doi:10.1176/appi.focus.20190028 PMID:32047393

Moore, J., & Continelli, T. (2016). Racial/Ethnic Pay Disparities among Registered Nurses (R.N.s) in U.S. Hospitals: An Econometric Regression Decomposition. *Health Services Research*, *51*(2), 511–529. doi:10.1111/1475-6773.12337 PMID:26932449

Moore, M. H. (1995). *Creating public value: Strategic management in government*. Harvard University Press.

Moore, S. D. M., Jayme, B. D. O., & Black, J. (2021). Disaster capitalism, rampant edtech opportunism, and the advancement of online learning in the era of COVID19. *Critical Education*, *12*(2), 2–23. doi:10.14288/ce.v12i2.186587

Morantz, A. (2022). In praise of multi-headed leadership. *Smith*. https://smith.queensu.ca/insight/content/In-Praise-of-Multi-Headed-Leadership.php

Morgan, A. C., King, D. L., Rudd, R. D., & Kaufman, E. K. (2013). *Elements of an undergraduate agricultural leadership program: A Delphi study*. Academic Press.

Morgan, P. (2020, October 27). A rise in invisible disabilities calls for a corporate culture change. *Forbes.* https://www.forbes.com/sites/paulamorgan/2020/10/27/a-rise-in-invisible-disabilities-calls-for-a-corporate-culture-change/?sh=58bdd4ca60f6

Morris, G., Ehlers, S., Tormohlen, R., Field, B., & Rudolph, M. (2022). A Review on Agricultural Academic Safety and Biosecurity Curriculum Standards. In *2022 ASABE Annual International Meeting* (p. 1). American Society of Agricultural and Biological Engineers. 10.13031/aim.202200852

Muhaimin, A. W., Retnoningsih, D., & Pariasa, I. I. (2023, May). The role of women in sustainable agriculture practices: evidence from east java Indonesia. In *IOP Conference Series: Earth and Environmental Science* (Vol. 1153, No. 1, p. 012005). IOP Publishing.

Muhl, C. J. (2002). What is an employee? The answer depends on the Federal law; in a legal context, the classification of a worker as either an employee or an independent contractor can have significant consequences. *Monthly Labor Review*, *125*(1).

Mukherjee, S. (2017). Bhagavad Gita: The key source of modern management. *Asian J. Management, 8*(1).

Muluneh, G. (n.d.). *Leading change through adaptive design/Change management practice in one of the universities in a developing nation.* Academic Press.

Muniapan, B. A. L. (2007). Transformational leadership style demonstrated by Sri Rama in Valmiki Ramayana. *International Journal of Indian Culture and Business Management*, *1*(1-2), 104–115. doi:10.1504/IJICBM.2007.014473

Muniappan, B. (2013) *The Bhagavad-Gita on Leadership Development for Sustainability.* http://www.siv-g.org/index.php/columnists/16-balakrishnan-muniappan/121thebhagavadgitaonleadershipdevelopmentforsustainability?tmpl=component&print=1&page

Musa, S. F. P. D., & Basir, K. H. (2021). Smart farming: Towards a sustainable agri-food system. *British Food Journal*, *123*(9), 3085–3099. doi:10.1108/BFJ-03-2021-0325

NAB. (2018). *Number of accredited tertiary institutions in Ghana per category as at January, 2018.* NAB. http://www.nab.gov.gh/news1/414-accredited-published-tertiary-institutions-as-at-august-2016-summary

Nabi, M. N., Liu, Z., & Hasan, N. (2022). Examining the nexus between transformational leadership and follower's radical creativity: the role of creative process engagement and leader creativity expectation. *International Journal of Emerging Markets*. doi:10.1108/IJOEM-05-2021-0659

Nadim, A., & Singh, P. (2019). Leading change for success: Embracing resistance. *European Business Review*, *31*(4), 512–523. doi:10.1108/EBR-06-2018-0119

Nagata, J. M., Seligman, H. K., & Weiser, S. D. (2021). Perspective: The convergence of coronavirus disease 2019 (COVID-19) and food insecurity in the United States. *Advances in Nutrition*, *12*(2), 287–290. doi:10.1093/advances/nmaa126 PMID:32970098

Nair, A., & Rao, N. (2016). Spiritual competencies for an exemplary organizational work culture outlined in Bhagavad-Gita. *Journal of Organisation and Human Behaviour*, *5*(3).

Nair, L., & Adetayo, O. A. (2019). Cultural Competence and Ethnic Diversity in Healthcare. *Plastic and Reconstructive Surgery. Global Open*, *7*(5), e2219. doi:10.1097/GOX.0000000000002219 PMID:31333951

Nalini, D. V. (1997). *Vedanta and Management.* Deep and Deep Publications.

Naqshbandi, M. M., & Jasimuddin, S. M. (2018). Knowledge-oriented leadership and open innovation: The role of knowledge management capability in France-based multinationals. *International Business Review*, *27*(3), 701–713. doi:10.1016/j.ibusrev.2017.12.001

Nasir, J., Ibrahim, R. M., Sarwar, M. A., Sarwar, B., Al-Rahmi, W. M., Alturise, F., Samed Al-Adwan, A., & Uddin, M. (2022). The effects of transformational leadership, organizational innovation, work stressors, and creativity on employee performance in SMEs. *Frontiers in Psychology*, *13*, 1379. doi:10.3389/fpsyg.2022.772104 PMID:35529553

National Council for Tertiary Education. (2017). *Summary of basic statistics on tertiary educational institutions 2016/2017*. NCTE. ncte.gov.gh

National Council on Labor-Management Relations. (2012). *Council receives GEAR report*. Labor Management Council. http://www.lmrcouncil.gov/index.aspx

National Institute of Mental Health (NIMH). (2018). *Mental Health Disparities*. NIMH. https://www.nimh.nih.gov/health/statistics/mental-health-disparities.shtml

National Institute of Mental Health. (2018). *Any disorder among adults*. NIH. https://www.nimh.nih.gov/health/statistics/any-disorder-among-adults.shtml

Nayak, A. K. (2018). Effective leadership traits from Bhagavad Gita. *International Journal of Indian Culture and Business Management*, *16*(1), 1–18. doi:10.1504/IJICBM.2018.088593

Naylor, R. L. (2019). Long-Run Uncertainties for U.S. Agriculture. *Economic Review-Federal Reserve Bank of Kansas City*, 51-84.

Nazuri, N. S., & Ahmad, N. (2019). Social Capital Among Urban Agriculture Program Participants in Klang Perdana Selangor, Malaysia. *International Journal (Toronto, Ont.)*, *2*(10), 47–56.

Netswera, F. G. (2022). Counting the cost of state-owned enterprises failure in South Africa: Post-apartheid betrayals or mere inefficiency? In F. G. Netswera, O. M. Fagbadebo, & N. Dorasamy (Eds.), *State-owned enterprises in Africa and the economics of public service delivery* (pp. 109–118). AOSIS Publishing. doi:10.4102/aosis.2022.BK270.06

Neuendorf, K. A. (2019). Content analysis and thematic analysis: Introducing content analysis and thematic analysis. In P. Brough (Ed.), *Advanced Research Methods for Applied Psychology* (pp. 211–223). Routledge.

Ngulube, P. (2019, January-March). Mapping methodological issues in knowledge management research, 2009- 2014. *International Journal of Knowledge Management*, *15*(1), 85–100. Advance online publication. doi:10.4018/IJKM.2019010106

Ngulube, P. (2020). Mixed methods research in knowledge management studies (2009-2014): A content analysis of journal articles. *Journal of Information & Knowledge Management*, *19*(3), 1–23. doi:10.1142/S0219649220500161

Nguyen, A. W. (2018). African American Elders, Mental Health, and the Role of the Church. *Generations (San Francisco, Calif.)*, *42*(2), 61–67.

Nguyen, V. Q., Turner, N., Barling, J., Axtell, C. M., & Davies, S. (2023). Reconciling general transformational leadership and safety-specific transformational leadership: A paradox perspective. *Journal of Safety Research*, *84*, 435–447. doi:10.1016/j.jsr.2022.12.006 PMID:36868673

Nicholas, L., & West-Burnham, J. (2016). *Understanding leadership: Challenges and reflections*. Crown House.

Nicholls, A. (2007). *Social Entrepreneurship: New Models of Sustainable Social Change*. Oxford University Press.

Nichols, R. G., & Stevens, L. A. (1978). Listening to people. *Reporter*, *4*, 8. https://heinonline.org/HOL/LandingPage?handle=hein.journals/report4&div=6&id=&page=

Compilation of References

Niken, W., Habibullah, J., & RR, E. (2022). The Effect of Transformational Leadership on Employee Performance Mediated by Work Motivation in Car Rental Services Companies in Lampung Province. *SSRG International Journal of Economics and Management Studies, 9*(3).

Nonaka, I., & Takeuchi, H. (1995). *The knowledge-creating company*. Oxford University Press.

Noopila, M. Y., & Pichon, H. W. (2022). Leadership education at Hispanic serving institutions in the southwest united states: What does it look like? *Journal of Leadership Education, 21*(2). Advance online publication. doi:10.12806/V21/I2/R6

Noori, A. Q., Orfan, S. N., & Noori, N. (2023). Principals' Transformational Leadership and Teachers' Emotional Intelligence: A Cross-Sectional Study of Takhar High Schools, Afghanistan. *Leadership and Policy in Schools*, 1–16. Advance online publication. doi:10.1080/15700763.2023.2176780

Norlin, D. (2020). Emotional intelligence: An integral part of positive leadership. *Journal of Organizational Behavior, 41*(3), 260–279.

Northouse, P. G. (2013). Leadership: Theory and practice (6th ed.). Thousand Oaks.

Northouse, P.G. (2012). *Leadership: Theory and practice*. Sage.

Northouse, P. G. (2010). *Leadership: Theory and practice* (5th ed.). Sage.

Northouse, P. G. (2019). *Interactive: Leadership: Theory and Practice*. SAGE Publications.

Northouse, P. G. (2019). *Leadership Theory and Practice* (8th ed.). SAGE Publications.

Northouse, P. G. (2021). Leadership: Theory and practice. *Sage (Atlanta, Ga.)*.

Nowak, Z., Pavelock, D., Ullrich, D. R., & Wolfskill, L. A. (2019). Leadership Styles of Successful FFA Advisors and FFA Programs. *Journal of Leadership Education, 18*(1).

Nunes, B., Gholami, R., & Higón, D. A. (2021). Sustainable farming practices, awareness, and behavior in small farms in Brazil. *Journal of Global Information Management, 29*(6), 1–23.

Nunes, L. J., Meireles, C. I., Gomes, C. J. P., & Ribeiro, N. M. A. (2021). The impact of climate change on forest development: A sustainable approach to management models applied to Mediterranean-type climate regions. *Plants, 11*(1), 69. doi:10.3390/plants11010069 PMID:35009073

Nunez, M. D., Gudema, M., & Gallegos-Carrillo, K. (2017). Disability inclusion in the workplace: A review of best practices. *Journal of Management, 43*(7), 2056–2089.

Nunnally, J. C. (1976). *Psychometric theory*. McGraw-Hill.

Nyarko, D. A., & Kozári, J. (2021). Information and communication technologies (ICTs) usage among agricultural extension officers and its impact on extension delivery in Ghana. *Journal of the Saudi Society of Agricultural Sciences, 20*(3), 164–172. doi:10.1016/j.jssas.2021.01.002

Nyberg, A., Holmberg, I., Bernin, P., & Alderling, M. (2011). Destructive managerial leadership and psychological well-being among Swedish, Polish, and Italian hotel employees. *Work (Reading, Mass.), 39*(3), 267–281. doi:10.3233/WOR-2011-1175 PMID:21709363

O'Keefe, D. F., Peach, J. M., & Messervey, D. L. (2019). The combined effect of ethical leadership, moral identity, and organizational identification on workplace behavior. *Journal of Leadership Studies, 13*(1), 20–35. doi:10.1002/jls.21638

O'Leonard, K. (2010). *The Corporate Learning Facebook: Statistics, Benchmarks, and Analysis of the US Corporate Training Market*. Bersin & Associates.

O'Malley, L. (2021). Addressing the lack of black mental health professionals. *Insight Into Diversity*. https://www.insightintodiversity.com/addressing-the-lack-of-black-mental-health-professionals/

O'Shannassy, T. (2021). The challenges of strategic leadership in organizations. *Journal of Management & Organization*, 27(2), 235–238. doi:10.1017/jmo.2021.36

O'Shea, E., O'Connor, M., Deeds, R., & Thompson, A. (2013). The effectiveness of employee assistance programs. *Human Resource Management Review*, 23(2), 149–158. doi:10.1016/j.hrmr.2012.08.003

Ody, M., & Shattuck, A. (2023). 'Our struggle is for humanity': A conversation with Morgan Ody, general coordinator of La Via Campesina International, on land, politics, peasant life and a vision for hope in our changing world. *The Journal of Peasant Studies*, 50(2), 539–558. doi:10.1080/03066150.2023.2174857

Oehlberg, B. (2008). Why schools need to be trauma informed. *Trauma and Loss: Research and Intervention*, 8(2). Retrieved from http://www.tlcinstitute.org

Ogaga, I. A., Ezenwakwelu, C. A., Isichei, E. E., & Olabosinde, T. S. (2023). Ethical leadership and sustainability of agro-allied firms: Moderating role of environmental dynamism. *International Journal of Ethics and Systems*, 39(1), 36–53. doi:10.1108/IJOES-12-2021-0226

Ogden, T. H. (2004). The analytic third: Implications for psychoanalytic theory and technique. *The Psychoanalytic Quarterly*, 73(1), 167–195. doi:10.1002/j.2167-4086.2004.tb00156.x PMID:14750469

Oh, H., & Kilduff, M. (2008). The ripple effect of personality on social structure: Self-monitoring origins of network brokerage. *The Journal of Applied Psychology*, 93(5), 1155–1164. doi:10.1037/0021-9010.93.5.1155 PMID:18808233

Ojo, O. O., Shah, S., & Coutroubis, A. (2020). Impacts of Industry 4.0 in sustainable food manufacturing and supply chain. *International Journal of Integrated Supply Management*, 13(2-3), 140–158. doi:10.1504/IJISM.2020.107851

Oldham, G. R., & Cummings, A. (1996). Employee creativity: Personal and contextual factors at work. *Academy of Management Journal*, 39(3), 607–634. doi:10.2307/256657

Olley, R. (2021). A focussed literature review of power and influence leadership theories. *Asia Pacific Journal of Health Management*, 16(2), 7–17. doi:10.24083/apjhm.v16i2.807

Olson, M. (1978). *Logique de l'action collective*. Puf.

Omodan, B. I., Tsotetsi, C. T., & Dube, B. (2020). Analysis of human relations theory of management: A quest to re-enact people's management towards peace in university system. *SA Journal of Human Resource Management*, 18. doi:10.4102ajhrm.v18i0.1184

Omolawal, S. A. (2015). Delegation of responsibilities: A leadership tool for subordinates' competence development in selected organizations in Ibadan metropolis. The Nigerian. *Journal of Sociology and Anthropology*, 13(1), 68–83. doi:10.36108/NJSA/5102/13(0140)

Onorato, M. (2013). Transformational leadership style in educational sector: An empirical study of corporate managers and educational leaders. *Academy of Educational Leadership Journal*, 17(1), 33–47.

Opoku, F. K., & Arthur, D. D. (2015). Human resource management practices and its influence on organizational performance: An analysis of the situation in the Ghana Postal Services Company Limited. *International Journal of Scientific and Research Publications*, 5(6), 2250–3153.

Oreg, S. (2003). Resistance to change: Developing an individual differences measure. *The Journal of Applied Psychology*, 88(4), 680–693. doi:10.1037/0021-9010.88.4.680 PMID:12940408

Compilation of References

Ormrod, J. E. (2020). Human learning (8th ed.). Pearson Education, Inc.

Orr, D. (1992). *Ecological Literacy: Education and the Transition to a Postmodern World*. State University of New York Press.

Ovans, A. (2015). How emotional intelligence became a key leadership skill. *Harvard Business Review*. https://hbr.org/2015/04/how-emotional-intelligence-became-a-key-leadership-skill

Owa, O. (2022). Mainstreaming Diversity, Equity, and Inclusion as Future Workplace Ethics: Effect of Diversity, Equity, and Inclusion on Organizational Performance. In Mainstreaming Diversity, Equity, and Inclusion as Future Workplace Ethics: Effect of Diversity, Equity, and Inclusion on Organizational Performance (pp. 28-48). doi:10.4018/978-1-6684-3657-8.ch002

Owens, R., & Valesky, T. (2009). *Organizational behavior in education: Leadership and school reform*. Pearson.

Owings, W. A., & Kaplan, L. S. (2010). *Leadership and organizational behaviour in education: Theory into Practice*. Pearson.

Owusu-Agyeman, Y. (2021). Transformational leadership and innovation in higher education: A participative process approach. *International Journal of Leadership in Education*, 24(5), 694–716. doi:10.1080/13603124.2019.1623919

Öztürk Çiftci, D. (2021). *21. Yüzyılda Değişen Örgütlerin Oluşturduğu Yeni Liderlik Yaklaşımları: Kavramsal Bir Değerlendirme, 20*. Uluslararası İşletmecilik Kongresi, Giresun.

Palmer, B. (Ed.). (2023). *Practical social justice: Diversity, equity, and inclusion strategies based on the legacy of Dr. Joseph L. White*. ProQuest.

Palmer, R. E. (2008). *Ultimate leadership: Winning execution strategies for your situation*. Pearson Education Inc.

Papin, S. (2021). Le leadership de demain. La confiance dans le bien commun. *Hermés la Revue*, 88(2), 226–229.

Pappas, S. (2021). Effective Theory for Black Women. *Monitor on Psychology*. https://www.apa.org/education-career/ce/effective-therapy-black-women.pdf

Pardo del Val, M., & Martinez Fuentes, C. (2003). Resistance to change: A literature review and empirical study. *Management Decision*, 41(2), 148–155. doi:10.1108/00251740310457597

Pargament, K. I. (2013). Spirituality as an irreducible Human Motivation and Process. *The International Journal for the Psychology of Religion*, 23(4), 271–281. doi:10.1080/10508619.2013.795815

Parr, J. F., Papendick, R. I., Youngberg, I. G., & Meyer, R. E. (2020) Sustainable agriculture in the United States. In *Sustainable agricultural systems* (pp. 50–67). CRC Press. doi:10.1201/9781003070474-5

Parsons, T., Bales, R. F., & Shils, E. A. (1953). *Working Papers in The Theory of Action*. Cambridge, UK: The Free Press.

Pasmore, W. A., Woodman, R. W., & Shani, A. B. (2010). Research in Organizational Change and Development (Vol. 18). Emerald Publishing Limited.

Patterson, D. (2022). *In-depth look: Tuckman's Model – Five Stages of Team Development*. In *Strategic Project Management Theory and Practice for Human Resource Professionals*. Press Books. https://ecampusontario.pressbooks.pub/hrstrategicprojectmanagementtheory/chapter/4-6-in-depth-look-tuckmans-model-five-stages-of-team-development/

Paulsen, N., Callan, V. J., Ayoko, O., & Saunders, D. (2013). Transformational leadership and innovation in an R&D organization experiencing major change. *Journal of Organizational Change Management*, 26(3), 595–610. doi:10.1108/09534811311328597

Pawlak, S. (2017). The impact of diversity and inclusion on employee satisfaction and morale. *Journal of Business and Psychology*, *32*(5), 615–631.

Peano, C., Massaglia, S., Ghisalberti, C., & Sottile, F. (2020). Pathways for the amplification of agroecology in African sustainable urban agriculture. *Sustainability (Basel)*, *12*(7), 2718. doi:10.3390u12072718

Pearce, C. L. (2012). Shared Leadership. Encyclopedia of Leadership. Thousand Oaks.

Pearce, C. L., & Conger, J. A. (2002). *Shared leadership: Reframing the hows and whys of leadership*. Sage Publications.

Pellicer, L. (2008). Caring enough to lead: How reflective practice leads to moral leadership (3rd ed.). Corwin Press.

Pendell, R. (2022, December 2). Avoid virtue signaling; embrace culture-changing dei initiatives. *Gallup.com*. https://www.gallup.com/workplace/396593/avoid-virtue-signaling-embrace-culture-changing-dei-initiatives.aspx

Peng, J., Li, M., Wang, Z., & Lin, Y. (2021). Transformational leadership and employees' reactions to organizational change: Evidence from a meta-analysis. *The Journal of Applied Behavioral Science*, *57*(3), 369–397. doi:10.1177/0021886320920366

Pennington, C. (n.d.). *We are hardwired to resist change*. Change Management.

Penny, M., Jeffries, R., Grant, J., & Davies, S. (2014). Women and academic medicine: A review of the evidence on female representation. *Journal of the Royal Society of Medicine*, *107*(7), 259–263. doi:10.1177/0141076814528893 PMID:24739380

Perry, J. L. (2010). *The Jossey-Bass reader on nonproftit and public leadership*. John Wiley & Son.

Peters, T. (2014). *Leading: People first*. WP Content. https://tompeters.com/wp-content/uploads/2014/02/Leadership_052914.pdf

Peterson, K. (2016). Understanding and responding to the effects of toxic leadership. *Journal of Leadership & Organizational Studies*, *23*(4), 439–453.

Petrou, P., Demerouti, E., & Schaufeli, W. B. (2018). Crafting the change: The role of employee job crafting behaviours for successful organizational change. *Journal of Management*, *44*(5), 1766–1792. doi:10.1177/0149206315624961

Pew Research. (2022). *Religious Landscape Study. Pew Research Center's Religion & Public Life Project*. Pew Research. https://www.pewresearch.org/religion/religious-landscape-study/

Phaladi, M. P. (2011). *Knowledge transfer and retention: The case of a public water utility in South Africa* [Master's Thesis, University of Stellenbosch, Stellenbosch, South Africa].

Phaladi, M. P. (2021). *Framework for integrating knowledge management and human resource management for the reduction of organisational knowledge loss in selected South African state-owned enterprises* [PhD Thesis, University of South Africa, Pretoria, South Africa].

Phaladi, M. P. (2022a). Studying knowledge management and human resource management practices in the state-owned entities using mixed methods research design. In P. Ngulube (Ed.), *Handbook of research on mixed methods research in information science* (pp. 340–361). IGI Global. doi:10.4018/978-1-7998-8844-4.ch017

Phaladi, M. P. (2022b). Human resource management as a facilitator of a knowledge-driven organisational culture and structure for the reduction of tacit knowledge loss in South African state-owned enterprises. *South African Journal of Information Management*, *24*(1), 1–10. doi:10.4102ajim.v24i1.1547

Phaladi, M., & Ngulube, P. (2022). Mitigating risks of tacit knowledge loss in state-owned enterprises in South Africa through knowledge management practices. *South African Journal of Information Management, 24*(1), 1–9. doi:10.4102ajim.v24i1.1462

Phillips & Klein. (2022, September 9). *Change management: From theory to practice*. Retrieved from, https://link.springer.com/article/10.1007/s11528-022-00775-0

Phillips, J. M., & Malone, B. (2014). Increasing racial/ethnic diversity in nursing to reduce health disparities and achieve health equity. *Public Health Reports, 2*(Suppl 2), 45–50. doi:10.1177/00333549141291S209

Phillips, W., Alexander, E. A., & Lee, H. (2019). Going it alone won't work! The relational imperative for social innovation in social enterprises. *Journal of Business Ethics, 156*(2), 315–331. doi:10.100710551-017-3608-1

Pierce, W. (1998). Reciprocal leadership, a practical approach to leadership. *University of Richmond UR Scholarship Repository*. https://scholarship.richmond.edu/cgi/viewcontent.cgi?article=2205&context=honors-theses

Pimentel, D., & Burgess, M. (2013). Soil erosion threatens food production. *Agriculture, 3*(3), 443–463. doi:10.3390/agriculture3030443

Piper, R. F. (1954). In Support of Altruism in Hinduism. *Journal of the American Academy of Religion, 22*(3), 178–183. doi:10.1093/jaarel/XXII.3.178

Plan-do-study-act (PDSA) directions and examples. (n.d.). AHRQ. https://www.ahrq.gov/health-literacy/improve/precautions/tool2b.html

Pollock, S. (2022, January 14). *The importance of employee feedback*. ClearCompany. https://blog.clearcompany.com/importance-employee-feedback#:~:text=Asking%20for%20employee%20feedback%20is,environment%20for%20well%2Drounded%20insights

Pondicherry, N., & Peabody, C. (2021). *E-drive: Analyzing a health system to expand access to clinical guidelines*. American Medical Association.

Pope, L. (2019). Racial disparities in mental health and criminal justice. *National Alliance on Mental Health (NAMI)*. https://www.nami.org/Blogs/NAMI-Blog/July-2019/Racial-Disparities-in-Mental-Health-and-Criminal-Justice

Popescu, C. R. G., & González, A. L. (2023). Digital Transformation Impact on Organizations' Culture and Employees' Motivation: Shaping the "New Normal" and Addressing Sustainable Development Goals. In C. R. G. Popescu (Ed.), *Positive and Constructive Contributions for Sustainable Development Goals* (pp. 114–130). IGI Global.

Popoola, O. O., Monde, N., & Yusuf, S. F. G. (2019). Climate change: Perception and adaptation responses of poultry smallholder farmers in Amathole District Municipality, Eastern Cape Province of South Africa. *South African Journal of Agricultural Extension, 47*(3), 108–119. doi:10.17159/2413-3221/2019/v47n3a519

Poturak, M., Mekić, E., Hadžiahmetović, N., & Budur, T. (2020). Effectiveness of transformational leadership among different cultures. *International Journal of Social Sciences & Educational Studies, 7*(3), 119–129.

Poudel, P. B., Poudel, M. R., Gautam, A., Phuyal, S., Tiwari, C. K., Bashyal, N., & Bashyal, S. (2020). COVID-19 and its global impact on food and agriculture. *Journal of Biology and Today's World, 9*(5), 221–225.

Prabhavananda, S., & Isherwood, C. (1954). *The Song of God: Bhagavad Gita*. The New American Library.

Prabhu, J. U. (2015). *Social entrepreneurship: A global perspective*. Palgrave Macmillan.

Prager, J. (2016). Disrupting the intergenerational transmission of trauma: Recovering humanity, repairing generations. In P. Gobodo-Madikizela (Ed.), *Breaking intergenerational cycles of repetition: A global dialogue on historical trauma and memory* (pp. 12–26). Verlag Barbara Budrich. doi:10.2307/j.ctvdf03jc.7

Prashanth, G. P. (2022). COVID-19 pandemic impact on mental health in children: a call for longitudinal datasets on prevalence of post-traumatic stress disorder. *Middle East Current Psychiatry, 29*(1), 1–3. https://doi-org.captechu.idm.oclc.org/10.1186/s43045-022-00266-1

Pratt, B. (2023). Equitable Urban Planning for Climate Change. *Journal of Planning Literature, 38*(1), 59–69. doi:10.1177/08854122221138125

Pretty, J. (2008). Agricultural sustainability: Concepts, principles and evidence. *Philosophical Transactions of the Royal Society of London. Series B, Biological Sciences, 363*(1491), 447–465. doi:10.1098/rstb.2007.2163 PMID:17652074

Price, J., & Murnan, J. (2004). Research limitations and the necessity of reporting them. *American Journal of Health Education, 35*(2), 66–67. doi:10.1080/19325037.2004.10603611

Proctor-Thomson, S. B. (2008). Constellations or Stars? What Is Being Developed in Leadership Development. Lancashire, England: Lancaster University Management School, Centre for Excellence in Leadership (CEL).

Pulrang, A. (2019, November 4). How to make workplaces more welcoming for employees with disabilities. *Forbes*. https://www.forbes.com/sites/andrewpulrang/2019/11/04/how-to-make-workplaces-more-welcoming-for-employees-with-disabilities/?sh=2304782353d8

Puni, A., Hilton, S. K., Mohammed, I., & Korankye, E. S. (2022). The mediating role of innovative climate on the relationship between transformational leadership and firm performance in developing countries: The case of Ghana. *Leadership and Organization Development Journal, 43*(3), 404–421. doi:10.1108/LODJ-10-2020-0443

Purcell, W., & Chahine, T. (2019). Leadership and governance frameworks driving transformational change in an entrepreneurial UK university. *Leadership and Organization Development Journal, 40*(5), 612–623. doi:10.1108/LODJ-07-2018-0280

Purdy, M., & Dupey, P. (2005). Holistic flow model of spiritual wellness. *Counseling and Values, 49*(2), 95–106. doi:10.1002/j.2161-007X.2005.tb00256.x

Purg, P., Cacciatore, S., & Gerbec, J. Č. (2023). Establishing ecosystems for disruptive innovation by cross-fertilizing entrepreneurship and the arts. *Creative Industries Journal, 16*(2), 115–145. https://doi-org.captechu.idm.oclc.org/10.1080/17510694.2021.1969804. doi:10.1080/17510694.2021.1969804

Purwanto, A., Bernarto, I., Asbari, M., Wijayanti, L. M., & Hyun, C. C. (2020). Effect of transformational and transactional leadership style on public health centre performance. *Journal of Research in Business, Economics, and Education, 2*(1).

Purwanto, A., Purba, J. T., Bernarto, I., & Sijabat, R. (2021). Effect of transformational leadership, job satisfaction, and organizational commitments on organizational citizenship behavior. *Inovbiz: Jurnal Inovasi Bisnis, 9*(1), 61–69. doi:10.35314/inovbiz.v9i1.1801

Qayyum, A., & Khan, B. S. (2017). Practice of self-help group in Pakistan: A traditional saving instrument. *WALIA Journal, 33*(1), 74–80.

Qiu, J., Zhao, H., Bravo, L., & Ryals, J. (2023). Urban Agriculture and its Sustainability Implications on the Food-Water-Energy Nexus: FOR391/FR463, 3/2023. *EDIS, 2023*(1).

Rabarison, K., Ingram, R. C., & Holsinger, J. W., Jr (2013). Application of situational leadership to the national voluntary public health accreditation process. *Frontiers in Public Health, 1*, 26. doi:10.3389/fpubh.2013.00026

Rada, D. R. (1999). Transformational leadership and urban renewal. *The Journal of Leadership Studies*, *6*(3-4), 18–33.

Raelin, J. A. (2003). *Creating leaderful organizations: How to bring out leadership in everyone*. Berrett-Koehler Publishers.

Rafferty, A. E., & Griffin, M. A. (2004). Dimensions of transformational leadership: Conceptual and empirical extensions. *The Leadership Quarterly*, *15*(3), 329–354. doi:10.1016/j.leaqua.2004.02.009

Raghid Al, H., & Vongas, J. G. (2022). Leadership and contempt in organizations: A conceptual model and research agenda. *Journal of Business and Behavioral Sciences*, *34*(1), 20–34.

Rahmadani, V. G., & Schaufeli, W. B. (2022). Engaging leadership and work engagement as moderated by "diuwongke": An Indonesian study. *International Journal of Human Resource Management*, *33*(7), 1267–1295.

Raineri, A. (2009). Change management practices: Impact on perceived change results. *Journal of Business Research*, *64*(3), 266–272. doi:10.1016/j.jbusres.2009.11.011

Rajaram, K. (2021). Transformation in Higher Education: Twenty-First-Century Teaching and Learning Competencies. In *Evidence-Based Teaching for the 21st Century Classroom and Beyond*. Springer. doi:10.1007/978-981-33-6804-0_1

Ramey, D. M. (2015). The social structure of criminalized and medicalized school discipline. *Sociology of Education*, *88*(3), 181–201. doi:10.1177/0038040715587114

Ramos, D. (2022, November 9). *8 Elements of an Effective Change Management Process*. https://www.smartsheet.com/8-elements-effective-change-management-process

Ramthun, A. J., & Matkin, G. S. (2014). Leading Dangerously: A Case Study of Military Teams and Shared Leadership in Dangerous Environments. *Faculty Publications: Agricultural Leadership, Education & Communication Department*, 97. https://digitalcommons.unl.edu/aglecfacpub/97

Rao, K. R. (2018). Mahatma Gandhi's pragmatic spirituality: Its relevance to psychology East and West. *Psychological Studies*, *63*(2), 109–116. doi:10.100712646-017-0394-x

Rasheed, M. A., Shahzad, K., & Nadeem, S. (2021). Transformational leadership and employee voice for product and process innovation in SMEs. *Innovation & Management Review*, *18*(1), 69–89. doi:10.1108/INMR-01-2020-0007

Rashid, M., Clarke, P. M., & O'Connor, R. V. (2020). A mechanism to explore proactive knowledge retention in open source software communities. *Journal of Software (Malden, MA)*, *32*(3), 1–10. doi:10.1002mr.2198

Rashid, R. (2021, April 03). Updating the PhD: Making the case for interdisciplinarity in twenty-first-century doctoral education. *Teaching in Higher Education*, *26*(3), 508–517. doi:10.1080/13562517.2021.1892624

Rasmussen, C. M., Pardello, R. M., Vreyens, J. R., Chazdon, S., Teng, S., & Liepold, M. (2017). Building social capital and leadership skills for sustainable farmer associations in Morocco. *Journal of International Agricultural and Extension Education*, *24*(2), 35–49.

Rayner, C., & Holden, R. (2016). Destructive leadership: A review and agenda for future research. *The Leadership Quarterly*, *27*(1), 4–20. doi:10.1016/j.leaqua.2015.11.003

Razael, F., Khalilzadeh, M., & Soleimani, P. (2021). Factors affecting knowledge management and its effect on organisational performance: Mediating the role of human capital. *Advances in Human-Computer Interaction*, *2021*, 1–16. doi:10.1155/2021/8857572

Reason, P., & Bradbury, H. (2008). *The SAGE Handbook of Action Research: Participative Inquiry and Practice* (2nd ed.). SAGE. doi:10.4135/9781848607934

Record, J. (2016). *How Mutual Leadership Helps High-Performing Teams Avoid Meetings And Increase Productivity. Leaderonomics.* https://www.leaderonomics.com/articles/business/mutual-leadership-in-teams

Reece, B., & Reece, M. (2017). *Effective human relations: Interpersonal and organizational applications* (13th ed.). CENGAGE Learning.

Reed, G. E., & Bullis, R. C. (2009). The impact of destructive leadership on senior military officers and civilian employees. *Armed Forces and Society, 36*(1), 5–18. doi:10.1177/0095327X09334994

Reger, R. K., Mullane, J. V., Gustafson, L. T., & DeMarie, S. M. (1994). Creating earthquakes to change organizational mindsets. *The Academy of Management Perspectives, 8*(4), 31–43. doi:10.5465/ame.1994.9412071701

Rehman. (2021). *The Psychology of Resistance to Change: The Antidotal Effect of Organizational Justice, Support and Leader-Member Exchange.* https://www.frontiersin.org/articles/10.3389/fpsyg.2021.678952/full

Ren, S., & Jackson, S. E. (2020). HRM institutional entrepreneurship for sustainable business organizations. *Human Resource Management Review, 30*(3), 100691. doi:10.1016/j.hrmr.2019.100691

Report and Declaration of the Presidents Conference at the Tufts University European Center. (1990). *The role of universities and university presidents in environmental management and sustainable development.* Medford, MA: Tufts University.

Resick, C. J., Whitman, D. S., Weingarden, S. M., & Hiller, N. J. (2009). The bright-side and the dark-side of CEO personality: Examining core self-evaluations, narcissism, transformational leadership, and strategic influence. *The Journal of Applied Psychology, 94*(6), 1365–1381. doi:10.1037/a0016238 PMID:19916649

Retno, R., Achmad, S., & Sunaryo. (2020). The Effect of Transformational Leadership on Employee Performance Mediated by Job Satisfaction and Employee Engagement on the Civil Servants of Public Housing and Settlement Areas of Central Java Province. *International Journal of Business, Economics, and Law, 21*(5).

Revoltella, D., Brutscher, P.-B., Tsiotras, A., & Weiss, C. (2016). Linking local business with global growth opportunities: The role of infrastructure. *Oxford Review of Economic Policy, 32*(3), 410–430. doi:10.1093/oxrep/grw019

Reyes, Y. D. (2018). Teachers' and school administrators' perception on the strategic leadership practices of school administrators. *Educational Review, 2*(8), 432–446. doi:10.26855/er.2018.08.004

Riaz, A., & Mahmood, H. Z. (2017). Cross-level relationship of implemented high performance work system and employee service outcomes: The mediating role of affective commitment. *Pakistan Journal of Commerce & Social Sciences, 11*(1), 351–373.

Richter, D., Riedel-Heller, S., & Zürcher, S. J. (2021). Mental health problems in the general population during and after the first lockdown phase due to the SARS-Cov-2 pandemic: Rapid review of multi-wave studies. *Epidemiology and Psychiatric Sciences, 30*, e27. doi:10.1017/S2045796021000160 PMID:33685551

Rickard, J. W., Boerngen, M. A., Lorenz, S. M., & Baker, E. (2017). Assessing student demographics in a non-land-grant university department of agriculture. *Natural Sciences Education, 46*(1), 1–5.

Rickley, M., & Stackhouse, M. (2022). Global leadership effectiveness: A multilevel review and exploration of the construct domain. In J. S. Osland, B. S. Reiche, B. Szkudlarek, & M. E. Mendenhall (Eds.), *Advances in global leadership* (Vol. 14, pp. 87–123). Emerald Publishing Limited. doi:10.1108/S1535-120320220000014004

Rider, E. (2002). Twelve strategies for effective communication and collaboration in medical teams. *BMJ (Clinical Research Ed.), 325*(7359), 45. doi:10.1136/bmj.325.7359.S45

Rinaldi, A., Yunia, W., & Susi, E. (2018). *The effect of Transformational leadership on employee performance in Faculty of Economics, State University of Padang* (Vol. 64). Advances in Economics, Business and Management Research.

Ritter, G. D., Acuff, G. R., Bergeron, G., Bourassa, M. W., Chapman, B. J., Dickson, J. S., Opengart, K., Salois, M. J., Singer, R. S., & Storrs, C. (2019). Antimicrobial-resistant bacterial infections from foods of animal origin: Understanding and effectively communicating to consumers. *Annals of the New York Academy of Sciences, 1441*(1), 40–49. doi:10.1111/nyas.14091 PMID:30924543

Rivai. (2005). *Peformance Appraisal: Sistem yang tepat untuk Menilai Kinerja Karyawan dan Meningkatkan Daya Saing Perusahan*. Jakarta: PT. RajaGrafindo Peral-sada

Rizki, W., Eloh, B., & Sri, N. (2022). *The effect of transformational leadership style, work environment, and work motivation on employee performance* (Vol. 1). MSR Journal.

Robbins, J. (2020). *The mental health impact of the coronavirus pandemic*. Harvard Health Publishing. https://www.health.harvard.edu/mind-and-mood/the-mental-health-impact-of-the-coronavirus-pandemic

Robbins, S. P., & Judge, T. A. (2011). *Organizational behavior* (14th ed.).

Roberts, N. C. (1985). Transforming leadership: A process of collective actio. *Human Relations, 38*(11), 1023–1046. doi:10.1177/001872678503801103

Robinson, G. S., & Wick, C. W. (1992). *Organizational development that makes a business difference*. Human Resource Planning.

Rodríguez-Pose, A., & von Berlepsch, V. (2019). Does population diversity matter for economic development in the very long term? Historic migration, diversity and county wealth in the US. *European Journal of Population, 35*(5), 873–911. doi:10.100710680-018-9507-z PMID:31832029

Rodriguez, R. (2015). Corporate social responsibility: An analysis of corporate social responsibility practices in the Indian Companies Act, 2013. *International Journal of Management and Applied Science, 1*(7), 15–21.

Roka, P. (2011). *Bhagavad Gita on Effective Leadership: Timeless Wisdom for Leaders*. Jaico Publishing House.

Romero-Cabrera, J., Yubero-Serrano, E., Diaz-Caceres, A., Serran-Jimenez, A., Arenas-Montes, J., & Alcala-Diaz, J. (2022). Educational strategy to improve cardiovascular health and mitigate food insecurity: Rationale for the E-DUCASS program. *Span J Med, 2*, 1–8.

Roome, E. (2012). *Hiring by knowledge-intensive firms in China*. [PhD thesis: Manchester Business School].

Rosdiana, N., & Aslami, N. (2022). The Main Models of Change Management in Kurt Lewin's Thinking. *Jurnal Akuntansi, Manajemen dan Bisnis Digital, 1*(2), 251-256.

Rose, J., & Johnson, C. W. (2020). Contextualizing reliability and validity in qualitative research: Toward more rigorous and trustworthy qualitative social science in leisure research. *Journal of Leisure Research, 51*(4), 432–451. doi:10.1080/00222216.2020.1722042

Rosen, P. (2022, November, 1). Invisible disabilities in the workplace. *Understood*. https://www.understood.org/en/articles/understanding-invisible-disabilities-in-the-workplace

Ross, S. M., & Offermann, L. R. (1997). Transformational leaders: Measurement of personality attributes and work group performance. Personality and Social Psychology Bulletin, 23 (10), 1078-1086.Runkle, G. (1976). Is violence always wrong? *The Journal of Politics, 38*(2), 367–389.

Rotemberg, J. J. (1994). Human Relations in the Workplace. *Journal of Political Economy*, *102*(4), 684–717. https://www.jstor.org/stable/2138761. doi:10.1086/261951

Rothwell, W. J. (2005). *Effective succession planning: Ensuring leadership continuity and building talent from within* (3rd ed.). American Management Association.

Rothwell, W. J., & Sullivan, R. L. (Eds.). (2005). *Practicing organization development: A guide for consultants* (Vol. 27). John Wiley & Sons.

Rubens, A., Schoenfeld, G. A., Schaffer, B. S., & Leah, J. S. (2018). Self-awareness and leadership: Developing an individual strategic professional development plan in an MBA leadership course. *International Journal of Management Education*, *16*(1), 1–13. doi:10.1016/j.ijme.2017.11.001

Rubenstein, E. D., Thoron, A. C., & Estepp, C. M. (2014). Perceived Self-Efficacy of Preservice Agriculture Teachers toward Specific SAE Competencies. *Journal of Agricultural Education*, *55*(4), 72–84. doi:10.5032/jae.2014.04072

Rubin, H. (2009). *Collaborative leadership: Developing effective partnerships for communities and schools*. Corwin Press.

Ruggieri, S. (2009). Leadership in virtual teams: A comparison of transformational and transactional leaders. *Social Behavior and Personality*, *37*(8), 1017–1021. doi:10.2224bp.2009.37.8.1017

Russo, M. V. (2010). *Companies on a mission: entrepreneurial strategies for growing sustainably, responsibly, and profitably*. Stanford University Press.

Ryan, R. M., & Deci, E. L. (2017). *Self-determination theory: Basic psychological needs in motivation, development and wellness*. The Guilford Press. doi:10.1521/978.14625/28806

Ryback, D. (1998). *Putting Emotional Intelligence to Work: Successful Leadership is More Than IQ*. Butterworth-Heinemann.

Ryu, J. Y., Kim, M. J., & Yun, S. Y. (2021). The effects of agricultural experience program on agricultural literacy and hand function improvement of adolescents living in self-reliance residence hall. *Journal of People, Plants, and Environment*, *24*(3), 277–283.

Saad Alessa, G. (2021). The dimensions of transformational leadership and its organizational effects in public universities in Saudi Arabia: A systematic review. *Frontiers in Psychology*, *12*, 682092. doi:10.3389/fpsyg.2021.682092 PMID:34867578

Saaty, T. L. (1990). An exposition of the AHP in reply to the paper "remarks on the analytic hierarchy process". *Management Science*, *36*(3), 259–268. doi:10.1287/mnsc.36.3.259

Saaty, T. L., & Hu, G. (1998). Ranking by eigenvector versus other methods in the analytic hierarchy process. *Applied Mathematics Letters*, *11*(4), 121–125. doi:10.1016/S0893-9659(98)00068-8

Sabir, A. (2017). A leader: One, who knows the way, goes the way, and shows the way. *European Business and Management*, *3*(5), 82–85. doi:10.11648/j.ebm.20170305.12

Saboe, K. N., Taing, M. U., Way, J. D., & Johnson, R. E. (2015). Examining the unique mediators that underlie the effects of different dimensions of transformational leadership. *Journal of Leadership & Organizational Studies*, *22*(2), 175–186. doi:10.1177/1548051814561028

Sadeghi, A., & Pihie, Z. A. L. (2012). Transformational leadership and its predictive effects on leadership effectiveness. *International Journal of Business and Social Science*, *3*(7).

Sadeghi, A., & Rad, F. M. (2018). The role of knowledge-oriented leadership in knowledge management and innovation. *Management Science Letters*, *8*, 151–160. doi:10.5267/j.msl.2018.1.003

Compilation of References

Sadia, A., Mohd Salleh, B., Abdul Kadir, Z., & Sanif, S. (2016). The relationship between organizational communication and employees' productivity with new dimensions of effective communication flow. *Journal of Business and Social Review in Emerging Economies*, 2(2), 93–100. doi:10.26710/jbsee.v2i2.35

Sadiq, M., Nonthapot, S., Mohamad, S., Chee Keong, O., Ehsanullah, S., & Iqbal, N. (2022). Does green finance matter for sustainable entrepreneurship and environmental corporate social responsibility during COVID-19? *China Finance Review International*, 12(2), 317–333. doi:10.1108/CFRI-02-2021-0038

Sadler, R. R. (2021, November 3). How to support employees with Invisible Disabilities. *She+ Geeks Out*. https://www.shegeeksout.com/blog/how-to-support-employees-with-invisible-disabilities/

Sağbaş, M., & Erdoğan, F. A. (2022). Digital Leadership: A Systematic Conceptual Literature Review. *İstanbul Kent Üniversitesi İnsan ve Toplum Bilimleri Dergisi*, 3(1), 17-35.

Sale, Bass, & Stogdills. (1991). Handbook Of Leadership-Theory, Research, And Managerial Applications. Personnel Psychology Inc.

Saleh, C., & Riyadi, B. S. (2023). The Relationship of Community Empowerment and Social Capital towards Production Capacity of Agricultural Product in Indonesia. *International Journal of Membrane Science and Technology*, 10(3), 435–448.

Salovey, P., & Mayer, J. D. (1990). Emotional intelligence. *Imagination, Cognition and Personality*, 9(3), 185–211. doi:10.2190/DUGG-P24E-52WK-6CDG

Samimi, M., Cortes, A. F., Anderson, M. H., & Herrmann, P. (2022). What is strategic leadership? Developing a framework for future research. *The Leadership Quarterly*, 33(3), 101353. doi:10.1016/j.leaqua.2019.101353

Sandelin, S. K., Hukka, J. J., & Katko, T. S. (2019). Importance of knowledge management at water utilities. *Public Works Management & Policy*, 00(0), 1–17. doi:10.1177/1087724X19870813

Sanders, C., Cox, C., Edgar, L., Graham, D., & Perez, A. P. (2021). Exploring the needs of urban producers in a rural state: A qualitative needs assessment. *Journal of Agriculture, Food Systems, and Community Development*, 11(1), 99–113.

Sandler, T. (1992). *Collective Action: Theory and Applications*. University of Michigan Press.

Santamaría, L. J. (2014). Critical change for the greater good: Multicultural perceptions in educational leadership toward social justice and equity. *Educational Administration Quarterly*, 50(3), 347–391. doi:10.1177/0013161X13505287

Santa, R., Moros, A., Morante, D., Rodríguez, D., Scavarda, A., & Al-Adwan, A. S. (2023). The impact of emotional intelligence on operational effectiveness: The mediating role of organizational citizenship behavior and leadership. *PLoS One*, 18(8), e0284752–e0284752. doi:10.1371/journal.pone.0284752 PMID:37531386

Santoso, H., Elidjen, E., Abdinagoro, S., & Arief, M. (2019). The role of creative self-efficacy, transformational leadership, and digital literacy in supporting performance through innovative work behavior: Evidence from telecommunications industry. *Management Science Letters*, 9(13), 2305–2314. doi:10.5267/j.msl.2019.7.024

Santuzzi, A. M., Waltz, P. R., Finkelstein, L. M., & Rupp, D. E. (2014). Invisible disabilities: Unique challenges for employees and Organizations. *Industrial and Organizational Psychology: Perspectives on Science and Practice*, 7(2), 204–219. doi:10.1111/iops.12134

Sanzo, K. L., Myran, S., & Clayton, J. K. (2011). Building bridges between knowledge and practice: A university-school district leadership preparation program partnership. *Journal of Educational Administration*, 49(3), 292–312.

Saputra, N., Chumaidah, E., & Aryanto, R. (2021). Multi-layer agility: A proposed concept of business agility in organizational behavior perspective. *Diponegoro International Journal of Business*, 4(1), 30–41. doi:10.14710/dijb.4.1.2021.30-41

Sarker, A. H., Bornman, J. F., & Marinova, D. (2019). A framework for integrating agriculture in urban sustainability in Australia. *Urban Science*, *3*(2), 50.

Satiani, A., Niedermier, J., Satiani, B., & Svendsen, D. P. (2018). Projected Workforce of Psychiatrists in the United States: A Population Analysis. *Psychiatric Services (Washington, D.C.)*, *69*(6), 710–713. doi:10.1176/appi.ps.201700344 PMID:29540118

SavageM.SavageC.BrommelsM.MazzocatoP. (2019). Physicians in the management and leadership of health care: A systematic review of the conditions conducive to organizational performance. medRxiv, 19011379. doi:10.1101/19011379

Savitz, A. W., & Weber, K. (2013). *Talent, transformation, and the triple bottom line: how companies can leverage human resources to achieve sustainable growth*. John Wiley & Sons, Inc.

Sawney, P., & Niven-Jenkins, N. (2007). Medical education- the need for change. *Occupational Medicine*, *57*(6), 395–396. doi:10.1093/occmed/kqm062 PMID:17728310

Sawyer, K. (2006). *The Cambridge handbook of the learning sciences*. Cambridge University Press.

Scharmer, C. O. (2012). *Théorie U: diriger à partir du futur émergent*. Pearson.

Schein, E. H. (1992). *Organizational culture and leadership*. Jossey-Bass.

Schuessler, R. (2020). Why deontologists should reject agent-relative value and embrace agent-relative accountability. *Zeitschrift für Ethik und Moralphilosophie*, *3*(2), 315–335. doi:10.100742048-020-00084-2

Schulz, W., Hammett, R., & Low, G. (2022). Using an Emotional Intelligence Learning System for Person-Centered Curriculum Development and Teaching. In Advancing DEI and Creating Inclusive Environments in the Online Space (pp. 40-61). Academic Press.

Schut, M., Leeuwis, C., & Thiele, G. (2020). Science of Scaling: Understanding and guiding the scaling of innovation for societal outcomes. *Agricultural Systems*, *184*, 102908. doi:10.1016/j.agsy.2020.102908

Schutte, N. S., Malouff, J. M., Hall, L. E., Haggerty, D. J., Cooper, J. T., Golden, C. J., & Dornheim, L. (1998). Development and validation of a measure of emotional intelligence. *Personality and Individual Differences*, *25*(2), 167–177. doi:10.1016/S0191-8869(98)00001-4

Schwab, G. *Haunting legacies: Violent histories and transgenerational trauma*. Columbia University Press.

Schwarz, G., Bouckenooghe, D., & Vakola, M. (2021). Organizational change failure: Framing the process of failing. *Human Relations*, *74*(2), 159–179. doi:10.1177/0018726720942297

Schwind, U., & Fassina, W. (2013). *Canadian human resource management: A strategic approach* (13th ed.). McGraw Hill.

Schyns, J. F., Hogeboom, R. J., & Krol, M. S. (2022). Water Footprint Assessment: towards water-wise food systems. In Food Systems Modelling (pp. 63-88). Academic Press. doi:10.1016/B978-0-12-822112-9.00006-0

Schyns, B., & Schilling, J. (2013). How bad are the effects of bad leaders? A meta-analysis of destructive leadership and its outcomes. *The Leadership Quarterly*, *24*(1), 138–158. doi:10.1016/j.leaqua.2012.09.001

Scott, S. G., & Bruce, R. A. (1994). Determinants of innovative behavior: A path model of individual innovation in the workplace. *Academy of Management Journal*, *37*(3), 580–607. doi:10.2307/256701

Scuotto, V., Nespoli, C., Tran, P. T., & Cappiello, G. (2022). An alternative way to predict knowledge hiding: The lens of transformational leadership. *Journal of Business Research*, *140*, 76–84. doi:10.1016/j.jbusres.2021.11.045

Compilation of References

Searle, J. R. (1990). Collective intentions and actions. In P. Cohen, J. Morgan, & M. E. Pollack (Eds.), *Intentions in communication* (pp. 401–415). Bradford Books.

Sebastian, J., Huang, H., & Allensworth, E. (2017). Examining integrated leadership systems in high schools: Connecting principal and teacher leadership to organizational processes and student outcomes. *School Effectiveness and School Improvement*, *28*(3), 463–488. doi:10.1080/09243453.2017.1319392

Selamata, N., Nordin, N., & Adnan, A. A. (2013). Rekindle teacher's organizational commitment: The effect of transformational leadership behavior. *Procedia: Social and Behavioral Sciences*, *90*, 566–574. doi:10.1016/j.sbspro.2013.07.127

Sergiovanni, T. J. (1992). Reflections on administrative theory and practice in schools. *Educational Administration Quarterly*, *28*(3), 304–313. doi:10.1177/0013161X92028003004

Serrat, O. (2017). Understanding and Developing Emotional Intelligence. In *Knowledge Solutions*. Springer. doi:10.1007/978-981-10-0983-9_37

Sessa, V. I., Kabacoff, R. I., Deal, J., & Brown, H. (2007). Generational differences in leader values and leadership behaviors. *The Psychologist Manager Journal*, *10*(1), 47–74. doi:10.1080/10887150709336612

Sethumadhavan, T.N. (2010). *Managerial Effectiveness-A Holistic View from the Bhagavad Gita*. Academic Press.

Sevilla, M. (2022). *How respectful dialogue can reduce mental health stigma*. American Hospital Association. https://www.aha.org/news/blog/2022-07-13-how-respectful-dialogue-can-reduce-mental-health-stigma

Seyawash, F., & Yongjin, C. (2021). *Transformational Leadership and Its Impact on Employee Performance: Focus on Public Employees in Afghanistan*. Academic Press.

Shah, D., & Sharer, R. (2021). *Role of telemedicine in health care delivery to vulnerable populations during COVID-19. In Clinical Informatics and Health Technology*. American Medical Association.

Shah, F., & Wu, W. (2019). Soil and crop management strategies to ensure higher crop productivity within sustainable environments. *Sustainability (Basel)*, *11*(5), 1485. doi:10.3390u11051485

Shamblin, S., Graham, D., & Bianco, J. A. (2016). Creating trauma-informed schools for rural Appalachia: The partnerships program for enhancing resiliency, confidence, and workforce development in early childhood education. *School Mental Health*, *8*(1), 189–200. doi:10.100712310-016-9181-4

Shamim, S., Cang, S., & Yu, H. (2019). Impact of knowledge-oriented leadership on knowledge management behaviour through employee work attitudes. *International Journal of Human Resource Management*, *30*(16), 2387–2417. doi:10.1080/09585192.2017.1323772

Shariq, S. Mukhtar, U., & Anwar, S. (2019). Mediating and moderating impact of goal orientation and emotional intelligence on the relationship of knowledge-oriented leadership and knowledge sharing. *Journal of Knowledge Management*, *23*(2), 332-350). doi:10.1108/JKM-01-2018-0033

Sharma, R. (2010). *The leader who had no title*. Simon & Schuster.

Shekhawat, D. (2022). A Comparative Analysis Of Organizations Supporting Social Entrepreneurship. *Social Innovations Journal*, *15*.

Sheppard, J. M., & Young, W. B. (2006). Agility literature review: Classifications, training, and testing. *Journal of Sports Sciences*, *24*(9), 919–932. doi:10.1080/02640410500457109 PMID:16882626

Shigekawa, E., Fix, M., Corbett, G., Roby, D. H., & Coffman, J. (2018). The Current State of Telehealth Evidence: A Rapid Review. *Health Affairs*, *37*(12), 1975–1982. doi:10.1377/hlthaff.2018.05132 PMID:30633674

Shiiba, N., Singh, P., Charan, D., Raj, K., Stuart, J., Pratap, A., & Maekawa, M. (2023). Climate change and coastal resiliency of Suva, Fiji: A holistic approach for measuring climate risk using the climate and ocean risk vulnerability index (CORVI). *Mitigation and Adaptation Strategies for Global Change*, *28*(2), 9. doi:10.100711027-022-10043-4 PMID:36685809

Shin, S. J., & Zhou, J. (2003). Transformational leadership, conservation, and creativity: Evidence from Korea. *Academy of Management Journal*, *46*(6), 703–714. doi:10.2307/30040662

Shonk, K. (2022). What Is Collective Leadership? *Program On Negotiation*. Harvard Business School. Retrieved from https://www.pon.harvard.edu/daily/leadership-skills-daily/what-is-collective-leadership/

Shood, S. (2021, March 18). *Impact of COVID-19 on Food Services and Drinking Places, First Quarter of 2021*. StatCan COVID-19. https://www150.statcan.gc.ca/n1/pub/45-28-0001/2021001/article/00010-eng.htm

Showers, B. (1987). Synthesis of research on staff development: A framework for future study and a state-of-the-art analysis. *Educational Leadership*, *45*(3), 77–87.

SHRM. (2019). *Diversity and inclusion*. SHRM. https://www.shrm.org/hr-topics/talent-acquisition/diversity-and-inclusion

Siangchokyoo, N., Klinger, R. L., & Campion, E. D. (2020). Follower transformation as the linchpin of transformational leadership theory: A systematic review and future research agenda. *The Leadership Quarterly*, *31*(1), 101341. doi:10.1016/j.leaqua.2019.101341

Silva, I. D. D. L., Nascimento, J. A. D. A., de Moraes Filho, L. E. P. T., Caetano, V. F., de Andrade, M. F., de Almeida, Y. M. B., Hallwass, F., Brito, A. M. S. S., & Vinhas, G. M. (2022). Production of potential antioxidant and antimicrobial active films of poly (vinyl alcohol) incorporated with cashew tree extract. *Journal of Food Processing and Preservation*, *46*(10), e16831. doi:10.1111/jfpp.16831

Simões-Coelho, M., Figueira, A. R., & Russo, E. (2023). Motivations for a sustainable ethos: Evidence from the globally present Brazilian multinational Natura &Co. *Environment Systems & Decisions*, *43*(3), 1–16. doi:10.100710669-022-09890-y PMID:36628130

Simon, D. M. (2011). *Assumptions, limitations, and delimitations*.

Simon, S. K. (2002). Participative Decision Making and Employee Performance in Different Cultures: The Moderating Effects of Allocentrism/Idiocentrism and Efficacy. *Academy of Management Journal*, *45*(5), 905–914. doi:10.2307/3069321

Simonson, J., & Rahman, K. S. (2020). The Institutional Design of Community Control. *California Law Review*, 108.

Sinek, S. (2014). *Leaders eat last*. Penguin Group LLC. https://d-pdf.com/book/595/read

Singh, J., Sharma, G., Hill, J., & Schnackenberg, A. (2013). Organizational agility: What it is, what it is not, and why it matters. In Academy of Management proceedings. Briarcliff Manor: Academy of Management.

Singh, M.K., & Gupta, V. (2020). Critical types of knowledge loss in military organisations. *VINE Journal of Information and Knowledge Management* Systems, (pre-print), 1-18. doi:10.1108/VJIKMS-09-2019-0152

Singh, M. (2021). Organic farming for sustainable agriculture. *Indian Journal of Organic Farming*, *1*(1), 1–8.

Singh, Wood, G., Darwish, T. K., Fleming, J., & Mohamed, A. F. (2019). Human resource management in multinational and domestic enterprises: A comparative institutional analysis in Southeast Asia. *Thunderbird International Business Review*, *61*(2), 229–241. doi:10.1002/tie.21997

Compilation of References

Skala, K., Chuang, R. J., Evans, A., Hedberg, A. M., Dave, J., & Sharma, S. (2012). Ethnic differences in the home food environment and parental food practices among families of low-income Hispanic and African-American preschoolers. *Journal of Immigrant and Minority Health*, *14*(6), 1014–1022. doi:10.100710903-012-9575-9 PMID:22262411

Skogstad, A., Aasland, M. S., Nielsen, M. B., Hetland, J., Matthiesen, S. B., & Einarsen, S. (2015). The Relative Effects of Constructive, Laissez-Faire, and Tyrannical Leadership on Subordinate Job Satisfaction. *Zeitschrift für Psychologie mit Zeitschrift für Angewandte Psychologie*.

Smith, J. (2022, May 19). Half of people aren't comfortable talking about disability in the Workplace. *Workplace Insight*. https://workplaceinsight.net/half-of-people-arent-comfortable-talking-about-disability-in-the-workplace/

Smith, W. (2019). Mental Health Stigma in African-American Communities. *The Huffington Post*. https://www.huffpost.com/entry/mental-health-stigma-in-african-american-communities_b_5d32d726e4b0faa7bacd5362

Smith, B. C. (2015). *How does learning agile business leadership differ? Exploring a revised model of the construct of learning agility about organizational performance*. Columbia University.

Smith, J., & Hunsaker, P. (2023). Emotional intelligence in leadership: Why it matters. *Business Horizons*, *66*(1), 54–60.

Snyder, H. (2019). Literature review as a research methodology: An overview and guidelines. *Journal of Business Research*, *104*, 333–339. doi:10.1016/j.jbusres.2019.07.039

Sobieralski, J. B. (2020). COVID-19 and airline employment: Insights from historical uncertainty shocks to the industry. *Transportation Research Interdisciplinary Perspectives*, *5*, 1–9. doi:10.1016/j.trip.2020.100123 PMID:34173453

Sohail, R., Saleem, S., Ansar, S., & Azeem, M. A. (2014). Effect of work motivation and organizational commitment on job satisfaction: A case of education industry in Pakistan. *Global Journal of Management and Business Research*, *14*(6), 1–7.

Soklaridis, S., Lin, E., Black, G., Paton, M., LeBlanc, C., Besa, R., MacLeod, A., Silver, I., Whitehead, C. R., & Kuper, A. (2022). Moving beyond 'think leadership, think white male': The contents and contexts of equity, diversity, and inclusion in physician leadership programmes. *BMJ Leader*, *6*(2), 146–157. doi:10.1136/leader-2021-000542 PMID:36170540

Solution, O. C. M. (2021, February 2). *Importance of Change Management in an Organization | All You Need to Know – OCM Solution*. https://www.ocmsolution.com/importance-of-change-management/

Somers, M. (2022). Why distributed leadership is the future of management. *MIT*. https://mitsloan.mit.edu/ideas-made-to-matter/why-distributed-leadership-future-management

Sorensen, L. B., Germundsson, L. B., Hansen, S. R., Rojas, C., & Kristensen, N. H. (2021). *What skills do agricultural professionals need in the transition towards a sustainable agriculture? A qualitative literature review*. Academic Press.

Soubbotina, T. P. (2004). *Beyond economic growth: An introduction to sustainable development*. The World Bank. doi:10.1596/0-8213-5933-9

Southwick, D. A., Tsay, C.-J., & Duckworth, A. L. (2021). Grit at work. Elsevier, 39, 1–17.

Specht, K., Zoll, F., Schümann, H., Bela, J., Kachel, J., & Robischon, M. (2019). How will we eat and produce in the cities of the future? From edible insects to vertical farming—A study on the perception and acceptability of new approaches. *Sustainability (Basel)*, *11*(16), 4315. doi:10.3390u11164315

Spender, J.C. (1996). Making knowledge the basis of a dynamic theory of the firm. *Strategic Management Journal*, *17*(Winter Special Issue), 45-62.

Spreitzer, G., Porath, C. L., & Gibson, C. (2012). Toward human sustainability: How organizations can enable more thriving at work. *Organizational Dynamics*, *41*(2), 155–162. doi:10.1016/j.orgdyn.2012.01.009

Spurk, D., & Straub, C. (2020). Flexible employment relationships and careers in times of the COVID19 pandemic. *Journal of Vocational Behavior*, *119*, 1–14. doi:10.1016/j.jvb.2020.103435 PMID:32382161

Srirangarajan, G. S., & Bhaskar, R. K. (2011). Key dimensions of spirit at work—An Indian perspective. *Journal of Human Values*, *17*(2), 93–120. doi:10.1177/097168581101700201

Stagich, T. (2006). *Collaborative Leadership and Global Transformation: Developing Collaborative Leaders and High Synergy Organizations*. Global Leadership Resources.

Stanford-Blair, N., & Gesner, D. (2019). Transformational Leadership: A Call for Action. *School Leadership & Management*, *39*(5), 476–497.

Stanford-Blair, N., & Gesner, J. M. (2019). Leading from the middle: A case study of people-centered leadership. In R. Papa (Ed.), *Handbook of Research on Ethical Challenges in Higher Education Leadership* (pp. 152–177). IGI Global.

Stanley, D., Bennett, C. L., & James, A. H. (2022). *Clinical leadership in nursing and healthcare*. Available Online. doi:10.1002/9781119869375

Statistics Canada. (2020). Food services and drinking places, April 2020. *The Daily*. https://www150.statcan.gc.ca/n1/daily-quotidien/200624/dq200624c-eng.htm

Steed, J. (2003). *A question of leadership*. O'Reilly. https://learning.oreilly.com/library/view/a-question-of/01520110027SI/chapter-02.html

Stefan, T. A. L. U., & Nazarov, A. D. (2020, November). Challenges and competencies of leadership in Covid-19 pandemic. In Research technologies of pandemic coronavirus impact (RTCOV 2020) (pp. 518-524). Atlantis Press.

Stewart, J., & Hocking, C. (2020). Adaptive sustainability for business in times of uncertainty and hyper disruption. *Journal of Applied Business and Economics*, *22*(12), 24–43.

Stoeber, J., & Otto, K. (2006). Positive conceptions of perfectionism: Approaches, evidence, challenges. *Personality and Social Psychology Review*, *10*(4), 295–319. doi:10.120715327957pspr1004_2 PMID:17201590

Stokes, H., & Brunzell, T. (2019). Professional learning in trauma informed positive education: Moving school communities from trauma affected to trauma aware. *School Leadership Review*, *14*(2).

Stone, A. G., & Patterson, K. (2023). The history of leadership focus. *Springer Books*, 689-715.

Stone, B. (2022). *Amazon unbound: Jeff Bezos and the invention of a global empire*. Simon and Schuster.

Storey, J. (Ed.). (2004). *Leadership in organizations: Current issues and key trends*. Psychology Press.

Storrs, C. (2016, June 1). Therapists often discriminate against black and poor patients, study finds. *CNN*. https://www.cnn.com/2016/06/01/health/mental-health-therapists-race-class-

Stoute, B. J. (2020). Racism: A Challenge for the Therapeutic Dyad. *American Journal of Psychotherapy*, *73*(3), 69–71. doi:10.1176/appi.psychotherapy.20200043 PMID:32927960

Struik, P. C., & Kuyper, T. W. (2017). Sustainable intensification in agriculture: The richer shade of green. A review. *Agronomy for Sustainable Development*, *37*(5), 1–15. doi:10.100713593-017-0445-7

Substance Abuse and Mental Health Administration. (2014). *SAMHSA's concept of trauma and guidance for a trauma-informed approach*. Author.

Substance Abuse and Mental Health Services Administration. (2023). *Living well with serious mental illness: What are serious mental illnesses?* SAMHSA. https://www.samhsa.gov/serious-mental-illness

Suhandiah, S., Suhariadi, F., Yulianti, P., & Abbas, A. (2023). Autonomy and Feedback on Innovative Work Behavior: The Role of Resilience as a Mediating Factor In Indonesian Islamic Banks. *Cogent Business and Management*, *10*(1), 2178364. doi:10.1080/23311975.2023.2178364

Suhariadi, F., Sugiartib, R., Hardaningtyasc, D., Mulyatid, R., Kurniasarie, E., Saadahf, N., ... Abbas, A. (2023). Work from home: A behavioral model of Indonesian education workers' productivity during Covid-19. *Heliyon*, *9*(3), e14082. Advance online publication. doi:10.1016/j.heliyon.2023.e14082 PMID:36855679

Sumbal, M. S. U. K., Irfan, I., Durst, S., Sahibzada, U. F., Waseem, M. A., & Tsui, E. (2023). Knowledge retention in oil and gas industry – the case of contract workforce. *Kybernetes*, *52*(4), 1552–1571. doi:10.1108/K-06-2021-0458

Sumbal, M. S., Tsui, E., Durst, S., Shujahat, M., Irfan, I., & Ali, S. M. (2020). A framework to retain the knowledge of departing knowledge workers in the manufacturing industry. *VINE Journal of Information and Knowledge Management Systems*, *50*(4), 631–651. doi:10.1108/VJIKMS-06-2019-0086

Sundi, K. (2013). Effect of Transformational Leadership and Transactional Leadership on Employee Performance of Konawe Education Department at Southeast Sulawesi Province. *International Journal of Business and Management Invention*, *2*(12).

Sun, H., Pofoura, A. K., Mensah, I. A., Li, L., & Mohsin, M. (2020). The role of environmental entrepreneurship for sustainable development: Evidence from 35 countries in Sub-Saharan Africa. *The Science of the Total Environment*, *741*, 140132. doi:10.1016/j.scitotenv.2020.140132 PMID:32886991

Supermane, S. (2019). Transformational leadership and innovation in teaching and learning activities: The mediation effect of knowledge management. *Information Discovery and Delivery*, *47*(4), 242–250. doi:10.1108/IDD-05-2019-0040

Sur, S. (2022, October 27). Why is it important to set realistic goals? 8 strong reasons. *Wealthful Mind*. https://wealthfulmind.com/why-is-it-important-to-set-realistic-goals/

Suransky, C., & Van der Merwe, J. C. (2016). Transcending apartheid in higher education: Transforming an institutional culture. *Race, Ethnicity and Education*, *19*(3), 577–597. doi:10.1080/13613324.2014.946487

Susanty, L., Hartati, Z., Sholihin, R., Syahid, A., & Liriwati, F. Y. (2021). Why English teaching truth on digital trends as an effort for effective learning and evaluation: opportunities and challenges: analysis of teaching English. *Linguistics and Culture Review*, *5*(S1), 303–316. doi:10.21744/lingcure.v5nS1.1401

Swartz, T. H., Palermo, A.-G. S., Masur, S. K., & Aberg, J. A. (2019). The science and value of diversity. Closing the gaps in our understanding of inclusion and diversity. *The Journal of Infectious Diseases*, *220*(Supplement_2), S33–S41. doi:10.1093/infdis/jiz174 PMID:31430380

Swisher, V. (2013). Learning agility: The "X" factor in identifying and developing future leaders. *Industrial and Commercial Training*, *45*(3), 139–142. doi:10.1108/00197851311320540

Szamosi, L., & Duxbury, L. (2002). Development of a measure to assess organizational change. *Journal of Organizational Change Management*, *15*(2), 184–201. doi:10.1108/09534810210423107

Tajeddini, K. (2015). *Using the integration of disparate antecedents to drive world-class innovation performance: An empirical investigation of Swiss watch*. Academic Press.

Takeshita, J., Wang, S., Loren, A. W., Mitra, N., Shults, J., Shin, D. B., & Sawinski, D. L. (2020). Association of racial/ethnic and gender concordance between patients and physicians with patient experience ratings. *Journal of the American Medical Association (JAMA). JAMA Network Open, 3*(11), e2024583. doi:10.1001/jamanetworkopen.2020.24583 PMID:33165609

Tallon, P. P., & Pinsonneault, A. (2011). Competing perspectives on the link between strategic information technology alignment and organizational agility: Insights from a mediation model. *Management Information Systems Quarterly, 35*(2), 463–486. doi:10.2307/23044052

Talukder, B., Blay-Palmer, A., Hipel, K. W., & VanLoon, G. W. (2017). Elimination method of multi-criteria decision analysis (mcda): A simple methodological approach for assessing agricultural sustainability. *Sustainability, 9*(2), 287.

Tangdigling, D. E., Nursyamsi, I., & Yusuf, R. M. (2019). The Effect of Situational Leadership and Work Ethics on Employee Performance through Organizational Climate as Intervening Variables at Gowa Agricultural Development Polytechnic. *Hasanuddin Journal of Business Strategy, 1*(4), 43–50. doi:10.26487/hjbs.v1i4.285

Tanneau, C., & McLoughlin, L. (2021, June 22). Effective global leaders need to be culturally competent. *Harvard Business Review*.

Taplin, I. (2006). Strategic change and organizational restructuring: How managers negotiate change initiatives. *Journal of International Management, 12*(3), 284–301. doi:10.1016/j.intman.2006.06.002

Taylor, M. J., McNicholas, C., Nicolay, C., Darzi, A., Bell, D., & Reed, J. E. (2014, April 1). A systematic review of the application of the plan–do–study–ACT method to improve quality in healthcare. *BMJ Quality & Safety*. https://qualitysafety.bmj.com/content/23/4/290

Team, W. (2019, August 4). *These are the 5 Best Theories of Change Management*. The Change Management Blog. https://change.walkme.com/theories-of-change-management/

Teboul, J., & Damier, P. (2022). *Le Mirage du leadership à l'épreuve des neurosciences*. Odile Jacob.

Tecosky, K., & Hollister, R. (2021, August 10). Why every executive should be focusing on culture and change now? MIT Sloan Management Review. https://sloanreview.mit.edu/article/why-every-executive-should-be-focusing-on-culture-change-now/

Tepper, B. J., Duffy, M. K., Hoobler, J., & Ensley, M. D. (2004). Moderators of the relationships between coworkers' organizational citizenship behavior and fellow employees' attitudes. *Journal of Applied Psychology, 89*, 455–465.

Tepper, B. J. (2000). Consequences of abusive supervision. *Academy of Management Journal, 43*(2), 178–190. doi:10.2307/1556375

Tessier, C., Chaudron, L., & Muller, H.-J. (Eds.). (2002). *Conflicting agents: Conflict management in multi-agent systems*. Kluwer Academic. doi:10.1007/b116057

Test, L. (2022, April 5). How to start an employee resource group at your company. *Culture Amp*. https://www.culture-amp.com/blog/start-employee-resource-group

Tetty, D., Emmy, A., & Fahmi, A. (2019). *The Influence of Transformational Leadership on Employee Performance at PT VVF Indonesia* (Vol. 4). International Research Journal of Advanced Engineering and Science.

Thamrin, H. M. (2012). The Influence of Transformational Leadership and Organizational Commitment on Job Satisfaction and Employee Performance. *International Journal of Innovation, Management and Technology, 3*(5).

Compilation of References

Thapa, A., & Parimoo, D. (2022). Transactional Leadership Style and Organizational Performance: The moderating role of emotional intelligence. *Parikalpana: KIIT Journal of Management*, *18*(1), 53–70. doi:10.23862/kiit-parikalpana/2022/v18/i1/212345

The ADA: Your employment rights as an individual with a disability. (n.d.). US EEOC. https://www.eeoc.gov/publications/ada-your-employment-rights-individual-disability#:~:text=Under%20the%20ADA%20%2C%20you%20have,even%20if%20you%20don't

The relationship between an individual's margin in life and readiness for change. (2003). In *Positivistic Research* (pp. 759–766). Academic Press.

The Strategy Institute. (2020, April 9). *Personal goals and organizational strategy: The virtue of perfect alignment*. The Strategy Institute.

Thévenot, L. (2006). *L'action au pluriel: sociologie des régimes d'engagement*. Éd. La Découverte. doi:10.3917/dec.theve.2006.02

Thomas International Limited. (2022, May 3). *How to develop leadership skills in employees*. Thomas. https://www.thomas.co/resources/type/hr-blog/how-develop-leadership-skills-employees

Thomas, D. A. (2001). Cultural diversity at work: The effects of diversity perspectives on work group processes and outcomes. *Administrative Science Quarterly*, *46*(2), 229–273. doi:10.2307/2667087

Thomas, E. E., Haydon, H. M., Mehrotra, A., Caffery, L. J., Snoswell, C. L., Banbury, A., & Smith, A. C. (2022). Building on the momentum: Sustaining telehealth beyond COVID-19. *Journal of Telemedicine and Telecare*, *28*(4), 301–308. https://journals.sagepub.com/doi/pdf/10.1177/1357633X20960638. doi:10.1177/1357633X20960638 PMID:32985380

Thomas, R. J., & Cheese, P. (2005). Leadership: Experience is the best teacher. *Strategy and Leadership*, *33*(3), 24–29. doi:10.1108/10878570510594424

Thompkins, S. (2022). *Leading With Emotional Intelligence*. Center for Creative Leadership. https://www.ccl.org/articles/leading-effectively-articles/emotional-intelligence-and-leadership-effectiveness/

Thompson, J. P., & Cavaleri, S. (2010). Dynamic knowledge, organizational growth, and sustainability: The case of Prestwick memory devices. *International Studies of Management & Organization*, *40*(3), 50–60. doi:10.2753/IMO0020-8825400303

Thoms, C. L. V., & Burton, S. L. (2015). Understanding the impact of inclusion in disabilities studies education. In C. Hughes (Ed.), *Impact of diversity on organization and career development* (pp. 186–213). IGI-Global Publishing. doi:10.4018/978-1-4666-7324-3.ch008

Thoms, C. L. V., & Burton, S. L. (2018). Transculturalized diversity and inclusion model: A new framework for disabilities. [Sage Journal]. *Advances in Developing Human Resources*, *20*(30), 359–369. doi:10.1177/1523422318778015

Thorsborne, M., & Blood, P. (2013). *Implementing restorative practices in schools: A practical guide to transforming school communities*. Jessica Kingsley Publishers.

Thude, B. R., Thomsen, S. E., Stenager, E., & Hollnagel, E. (2017). Dual leadership in a hospital practice. *Leadership in Health Services*, *30*(1), 101–112. doi:10.1108/LHS-09-2015-0030 PMID:28128047

Tien, N. H., Anh, D. B. H., Ngoc, N. M., & Do Thi, Y. N. (2019). Sustainable social entrepreneurship in Vietnam. *International Journal of Entrepreneurship*, *23*(3), 1–12.

Tillotson, J., Laker, B., Pereira, V., & Bhatnagar, K. (2023). How to make workplaces more inclusive for people with invisible disabilities. *Harvard Business Review*. https://hbr.org/2023/04/how-to-make-workplaces-more-inclusive-for-people-with-

Tilman, D., Balzer, C., Hill, J., & Befort, B. L. (2011). Global food demand and the sustainable intensification of agriculture. *Proceedings of the National Academy of Sciences of the United States of America*, *108*(50), 20260–20264. doi:10.1073/pnas.1116437108 PMID:22106295

Tinker, J. E., & Latta, G. F. (2020). Decoding leaders experiences of innovation, adaptation and change through the lens of dispositional attitudes toward risk in a global fortune 500 organization. *Journal of Strategic Innovation & Sustainability*, *15*(8), 70–87. https://doi-org.captechu.idm.oclc.org/10.33423/jsis.v15i8.3922

Todnem, R. (2005). Change management: A review of current thinking. Leadership &amp. *Organization Development Journal*, *26*(3), 195–204.

Toker, A. (2022). Importance of leadership in the higher education. *International Journal of Social Sciences & Educational Studies*, *9*(2), 1- 8. https/www.doi: . v9i2p230 doi:10.23918/ijsses

Toolkits. (2022, April 26). SHRM. https://www.shrm.org/ResourcesAndTools/tools-and-samples/toolkits/Pages/default.aspx

Torraco, R. J. (2005). Writing integrative literature reviews: Guidelines and examples. *Human Resource Development Review*, *4*(3), 356–367. doi:10.1177/1534484305278283

Torraco, R. J. (2016). Writing integrative reviews of the literature: Methods and purposes. *International Journal of Adult Vocational Education and Technology*, *7*(3), 62–70. doi:10.4018/IJAVET.2016070106

Traver-Marti, J. A., Ballesteros-Velazquez, B., Beldarrain, N. O., & Maiquez, M. D. C. C. (2023). Leading the curriculum towards social change: Distributed leadership and the inclusive school. *Educational Management Administration & Leadership*, *51*(3), 554–574. doi:10.1177/1741143221991849

Treslan, D. L. (2010). Transformational Leadership in the Classroom: Any Evidence? *Education Canada*, *46*, 58–61.

Treviño, L. K., Hartman, L. P., & Brown, M. (2000). Moral person and moral manager: How executives develop a reputation for ethical leadership. *California Management Review*, *42*(4), 128–142. doi:10.2307/41166057

Tripathi, A., Srivastava, R., & Sankaran, R. (2020). The role of learning agility and learning culture on turnover intention is an empirical study. *Industrial and Commercial Training*, *52*(2), 105–120. doi:10.1108/ICT-11-2019-0099

Trivedy, K. (2019). The Perfectionistic Leader: The Bright and Dark Side. *Leadership and Organization Development Journal*, *40*(7), 816–831.

Truth and Reconciliation Commission of Canada. (2015). *Canada's residential schools: The final report of the Truth and Reconciliation Commission of Canada*. McGill-Queen's University Press.

Turgut, S., & Neuhaus, A. E. (2020). The relationship between dispositional resistance to change and individual career management: A matter of occupational self-efficacy and organizational identification. *Journal of Change Management*, *20*(2), 171–188. doi:10.1080/14697017.2020.1720774

Turk, A., Cevher, M. F., & Mizrak, K. C. (2021). The effect of informal relations and executive support on organizational commitment in the aviation cector. International Journal of Innovative Science and Research Technology, 6(2), pp. 243-253.

Türk, A., & Mızrak, K. C. (2021). Bibliometric analysis of research in the field of organizational communication in the web of science database. Business & Management Studies: An International Journal, 9(3), pp. 1173-1185.

Tüyen, Z. (2020). İşletmelerde Sürdürülebilirlik Kavramı Ve Sürdürülebilirliği Etkileyen Etmenler. *İstanbul Ticaret Üniversitesi Sosyal Bilimler Dergisi, 19*(37), 91-117.

Tykkyläinen, S., & Ritala, P. (2021). Business model innovation in social enterprises: An activity system perspective. *Journal of Business Research, 125*, 684–697. https://doi.org/10.1016/j.jbusres.2020.01.045 doi:10.1016/j.jbusres.2020.01.045

Tyssen, A. K., Wald, A., & Spieth, P. (2013). Leadership in temporary organizations: A review of leadership theories and a research agenda. *Project Management Journal, 44*(6), 52–67. doi:10.1002/pmj.21380

U. S. Equal Opportunity Commission. (2023). *The ADA: Your employment rights as an individual with a disability*. EEOC. https://www.eeoc.gov/publications/ada-your-employment-rights-individual-disability#:~:text=Reasonable%20accommodation%20is%20any%20change,equal%20to%20those%20enjoyed%20by

U.S. Census Bureau. (2016). *Disability status*. US Census. https://www.census.gov/data/tables/2016/demo/disability/disability-status.html

U.S. Centers for Disease Control and Prevention (C.D.C.). (2022, October 27). *Training from Organizations Other than C.D.C. U.S. Centers for Disease Control and Prevention*. CDC. https://www.cdc.gov/healthliteracy/non-cdc-training.html

U.S. Centers for Disease Control and Prevention. (2020). Mental health, substance use, and suicidal ideation during the COVID-19 pandemic—United States, June 24–30, 2020. *Morbidity and Mortality Weekly Report, 69*(32), 1049–1056. doi:10.15585/mmwr.mm6932a1 PMID:32790653

U.S. Department of Labor. (2019). *Disability inclusion in the workplace*. DoL. https://www.dol.gov/agencies/odep/topics/disability-inclusion-workplace

U.S. Equal Employment Opportunity Commission. (1991). *Americans with Disabilities Act: Questions and Answers*. EEOC. https://www.eeoc.gov/laws/guidance/ada-questions-and-answers

Uhl-Bien, M. (2006). *Relational Leadership Theory: Exploring the social processes of leadership and organizing*. Leadership Institute Faculty Publications. https://digitalcommons.unl.edu/leadershipfacpub/19

Uhl-Bien, M. (2021). Complexity leadership and followership: Changed leadership in a changed world. *Journal of Change Management, 21*(2), 144–162. https://doi-org.captechu.idm.oclc.org/10.1080/14697017.2021.1917490 doi:10.1080/14697017.2021.1917490

Ulrich, D., & Yeung, A. (2019). Agility: The new response to dynamic change. *Strategic HR Review, 18*(4), 161–167. doi:10.1108/SHR-04-2019-0032

Unger, D., Goh, S. K., Whelan, J., & Burns, P. (2019). Toxic leadership: A meta-analytic review of negative outcomes for individuals and teams. *Journal of Occupational and Organizational Psychology, 92*(3), 577–599.

UNICEF. (2020). *What will a return to school during COVID-19 look like?* https://www.unicef.org/coronavirus/what-will-return-school-during-covid-19-pandemic-look

United Nations. (2020). *Policy Brief: Education during COVID-19 and beyond*. https://www.un.org/development/desa/dspd/wp-content/uploads/sites/22/2020/08/sg_policy_brief_covid-19_and_education_august_2020.pdf

USDA. ARS. (2021). *Food Security in the United States: Key Statistics & Graphics*. Retrieved from https://www.ers.usda.gov/topics/food-nutrition-assistance/food-security-in-the-us/key-statistics-graphics.aspx

USDA. ERS - Ag and Food Sectors and the Economy. (2021). https://www.ers.usda.gov/data-products/ag-and-food-statistics-charting-the-essentials/ag-and-food-sectors-and-the-economy/

Valaei, N., Nikhashemi, S. R., & Javan, N. (2017). Organisational factors and process capabilities in a KM strategy: Toward a unified theory. *Journal of Management Development*, *36*(4), 560–580. doi:10.1108/JMD-04-2016-0057

Valamis. (2023). *Shared leadership*. Valamis. https://www.valamis.com/hub/shared-leadership

Valeriu, D. (2017). The significance of emotional intelligence in transformational leadership for public universities. *Euromentor Journal*, *8*(1), 35.

Vallera, F. L., & Bodzin, A. M. (2020). Integrating STEM with AgLIT (agricultural literacy through innovative technology): The efficacy of a project-based curriculum for upper-primary students. *International Journal of Science and Mathematics Education*, *18*(3), 419–439. doi:10.100710763-019-09979-y

van de Ven, A. H., & Poole, M. S. (1995). Explaining development and change in organizations. *Academy of Management Review*, *20*(3), 510–540. doi:10.2307/258786

Van Dick, R., Cordes, B. L., Lemoine, J. E., Steffens, N. K., Haslam, S. A., Akfirat, S. A., ... Avanzi, L. (2021). Identity leadership, employee burnout and the mediating role of team identification: Evidence from the global identity leadership development project. *International Journal of Environmental Research and Public Health*, *18*(22), 12081. doi:10.3390/ijerph182212081 PMID:34831833

Van Dijk, D., Kark, R., Matta, F., & Johnson, R. E. (2021). Collective aspirations: Collective regulatory focus as a mediator between transformational and transactional leadership and team creativity. *Journal of Business and Psychology*, *36*(4), 633–658. doi:10.100710869-020-09692-6

van Manen, M. (1997). *Researching lived experience: Human science for an action sensitive pedagogy* (2nd ed.). The Althouse Press.

Van Velsor, E., & McCauley, C. D. (2004). Our view of leadership development. In C. D. McCauley & E. Van Velsor (Eds.), *The center for creative leadership handbook of leadership development* (2nd ed., pp. 1–22). Jossey-Bass.

Van Zyl, E. (2014). The role of self-leadership in becoming an ethical leader in the South African work context. *African Journal of Business Ethics*, *8*(2). Advance online publication. doi:10.15249/8-2-82

Vance, T. A. (2019). *Addressing mental health in the Black community*. Columbia University Department of Psychology. https://www.columbiapsychiatry.org/news/addressing-mental-health-black-community

Vargas-Hernández, J. G. (2021). Strategic Organizational Sustainability. *Circular Economy and Sustainability*, *1*(2), 457–476. Advance online publication. doi:10.100743615-020-00003-y

Vedenik, J., & Leber, P. (2015). Change management: The view through the prism of three different models. Management &amp. *Marketing Challenges for the Knowledge Society*, *10*(1), 5–17.

Vekved, M., McNeil, D. A., Dolan, S. M., Siever, J. E., Horn, S., & Tough, S. C. (2017). Invested in success: A qualitative study of the experience of CenteringPregnancy group prenatal care for perinatal educators. *Journal of Perinatal Education*, *26*(3), 125–135.

Velez, J. J., Moore, L. L., Bruce, J. A., & Stephens, C. A. (2014). Agricultural leadership education: Past history, present reality, and future directions. *The Journal of Leadership Studies*, *7*(4), 65–70.

Venkatesan, M. (2022). Marketing Sustainability: A Critical Consideration of Environmental Marketing Strategies. In Products for Conscious Consumers (pp. 151-166). Emerald Publishing Limited. doi:10.1108/978-1-80262-837-120221009

Vera, E. M. (2022). Social emotional learning and cultural relevancy: Real world challenges. *Preventing School Failure*, 1-12.

Compilation of References

Vermeulen, M., Kreijns, K., & Evers, A. T. (2022). Transformational leadership, leader–member exchange and school learning climate: Impact on teachers' innovative behaviour in the Netherlands. *Educational Management Administration & Leadership*, *50*(3), 491–510. doi:10.1177/1741143220932582

Vickery, S. K., Droge, C., Setia, P., & Sambamurthy, V. (2010). Supply chain information technologies and organisational initiatives: Complementary versus independent effects on agility and firm performance. *International Journal of Production Research*, *48*(3), 7025–7042. doi:10.1080/00207540903348353

Viegnes, M. (2014). Risquer la confiance. In: Colloques interdisciplinaires sur les valeurs - Troisième série Codirigé avec Simone de Reyff et Michel Viegnes. Neuchâtel: Alphil - Presses universitaires suisses, 11-18.

Vineeta, K. (2022). Cultural evolution – Theory of Cultural Change. *Anthromania*. https://www.anthromania.com/2022/03/04/cultural-evolution-theory-of-cultural-change/

Violanti, M. T. (2021). Addressing Workplace Bullying Behaviors Through Responsible Leadership Theory: Essential Skills for Strategic Communicators. In Public Relations for Social Responsibility (pp. 71-82). Academic Press.

Vogels, E. a. (n.d.). The digital divide persists even as lower-income Americans benefit from tech adoption. *Pew Research Center*. https://www.pewresearch.org/fact-tank/2021/06/22/digital-divide-persists-even-as-americans-with-lower-incomes-make-gains-in-tech-adoption/

Volkwein, J. F. (1999). The four faces of institutional research. *New Directions for Institutional Research*, *104*(104), 9–19. doi:10.1002/ir.10401

Von Culin, K., Tsukayama, E., & Duckworth, A. (2014). Unpacking grit: Motivational correlates of perseverance and passion for long-term goals. *The Journal of Positive Psychology*, *9*(4), 306–312. doi:10.1080/17439760.2014.898320 PMID:31404261

Vu, T., Vu, M., & Hoang, V. (2020). The impact of transformational leadership on promoting academic research in higher educational system in Vietnam. *Management Science Letters*, *10*(3), 585–592.

Wadumestrige Dona, C. G., Mohan, G., & Fukushi, K. (2021). Promoting urban agriculture and its opportunities and challenges—A global review. *Sustainability*, *13*(17), 9609.

Wales, T. (2013). Organizational sustainability: What is it, and why does it matter? *Review of Enterprise and Management Studies*, *1*(1), 38–49.

Walker, K. D., & Kutsyuruba, B. (2019). The role of school administrators in providing early career teachers' support: A Pan-Canadian perspective. *International Journal of Educational Policy and Leadership*, *14*(3), 1-19. https://doi.org/doi:10.22230/ijepl.2019v14n3a862

Walker, K. (2017). 884 *critical policy making in education; Early readings* (2nd ed.). Turning Point Global Publishing.

Wang, C., Ghadimi, P., Lim, M. K., & Tseng, M. L. (2019). A literature review of sustainable consumption and production: A comparative analysis in developed and developing economies. *Journal of Cleaner Production*, *206*, 741–754. doi:10.1016/j.jclepro.2018.09.172

Wang, F., Pollock, K., & Hauseman, C. (2018). School principals job satisfaction: The effects of work intensification. *Canadian Journal of Educational Administration and Policy*, *85*, 73.

Wang, Y., & You, J. (2022). The Operation Mode of Agricultural Supply Chain Finance Using Blockchain. *Computational Intelligence and Neuroscience*, *2022*, 2022. doi:10.1155/2022/3338030 PMID:36188687

Warrior, P. (2022). You need a leadership community. *Lifelong Learning*. Linkedin. https://www.linkedin.com/pulse/you-need-leadership-community-heres-how-build-one-padmasree-warrior/

Washington, M., & Hacker, M. (2005). Why change fails: Knowledge counts. *Leadership and Organization Development Journal*, *26*(5), 400–411. doi:10.1108/01437730510607880

Wathes, C. (2010). Guarding the welfare of farm animals. *The Veterinary Record*, *167*(15), 583–584. doi:10.1136/vr.c4785 PMID:21257423

Waxman, B. (2021). Future of workforce TALENT PROCUREMENT: Changes ahead in talent search and remote logistics from startup to big tech. *HR Future*, *2021*(11), 20–21.

Webster, N. (2021). *Webster's Dictionary* (11th ed.). https://www.merriam-webster.com/

Webster, J., & Watson, R. T. (2002). Analyzing the past to prepare for the future: Writing a literature review. *Management Information Systems Quarterly*, *26*(2), xiii–xxiii.

Wee, B., Shepardson, D., Fast, J., & Harbor, J. (2007). Teaching and learning about inquiry: Insights and challenges in professional development. *Journal of Science Teacher Education*, *18*(1), 63–89. doi:10.100710972-006-9031-6

Weiner, S. (2022, August 9). *A growing psychiatrist shortage and an enormous demand for mental health services*. A.A.M.C. https://www.aamc.org/news-insights/growing-psychiatrist-shortage-enormous-demand-mental-health-services

Weissenberg, C. (2018). Inclusive leadership. *Inclusive Leadership*. https://inclusiveleadership.eu/blog/ildocs/christine-weissenberg/

Welbourne, T. M., & McLaughlin, L. L. (2013). Making the business case for employee resource groups. *Employment Relations Today*, *40*(2), 35–44. doi:10.1002/ert.21409

Wells, J. C., & Stock, J. T. (2020). Life history transitions at the origins of agriculture: A model for understanding how niche construction impacts human growth, demography and health. *Frontiers in Endocrinology*, *11*, 325. doi:10.3389/fendo.2020.00325 PMID:32508752

Wexley & Yuki. (1984). *Organizational behavior People and Process in management*. Academic Press.

White, B. (2020). IFAD Research Series 48: Rural Youth, Today and Tomorrow. *Today and Tomorrow*.

White, R. R., & Hall, M. B. (2017). Nutritional and greenhouse gas impacts of removing animals from US agriculture. *Proceedings of the National Academy of Sciences of the United States of America*, *114*(48), E10301–E10308. doi:10.1073/pnas.1707322114 PMID:29133422

Whittinghill, L., & Sarr, S. (2021). Practices and Barriers to Sustainable Urban Agriculture: A Case Study of Louisville, Kentucky. *Urban Science (Basel, Switzerland)*, *5*(4), 92. doi:10.3390/urbansci5040092

Widiana, M. E. (2017). Tranformational Leadership Effect On The Marketing Performance Through Market Orientation. *Advances in Social Sciences Research Journal*, *4*(9), 118–132. doi:10.14738/assrj.49.3150

Wilkinson, R., & Pickett, K. (2010). *Why Greater Equality Makes Societies Stronger: The Spirit Level*. Bloomsbury Press.

Williams, B., & Davis, D. (2021). Public administration in a diverse society: The impact of transformational leadership and DEI. *Public Administration Review*, *81*(4), 562–574.

Williamson, P. C. (2011). *Social Impact: A Definition*. Retrieved from http://www.socialimpactcenter.com/social-impact/

Willink, J., & Babin, L. (2017). *Extreme Ownership: How US Navy SEALs Lead and Win*. St. Martin's Press.

Wilmore, E., & Thomas, C. (2001). The new century: Is it too late for transformational leadership? *Educational Horizons*, *79*(3), 115–123.

Wilson, E., & Breault, J. (2018). The core of demand planning and data science. *Journal of Business Forecasting*, *37*(1), 28–31.

Wilson, S. (2008). *Research is ceremony: Indigenous research methods*. Fernwood Publishing.

Winfrey Avant, D. (2011) Unwrapping tradition: shifting from traditional leadership to transformative action. Counterpoints, 409, 114-127.

Winnie, N., Josphat, N., Martin, D., Maxwell, C., Elias, K., & Andrew, J. (2021). Achieving High Employee Performance through Transformational Leadership in the Banking Sector. *International Journal of Research and Innovation in Social Science*.

Wittmayer, J. M., Backhaus, J., Avelino, F., Pel, B., Strasser, T., Kunze, I., & Zuijderwijk, L. (2019). Narratives of change: How social innovation initiatives construct societal transformation. *Futures*, *112*, 102433. doi:10.1016/j.futures.2019.06.005

Wöcke, A., & Barnard, H. (2021). Turnover in South Africa: the effect of history. In D. G. Allen & J. M. Vardaman (Eds.), *Global talent retention: Understanding employee turnover around the world* (pp. 239–259). Emerald Publishing. doi:10.1108/978-1-83909-293-020211012

Wolfensberger, M., & Hogenstijn, M. (2016). Slow shift- developing provisions for talented students in Scandinavian higher education. *Education Sciences*, *6*(31), 1–15. doi:10.3390/educsci6030031

Wong, E., & Swanson, A. (2023). How Russia's War on Ukraine Is Worsening Global Starvation. *New York Times*.

Wong, C. S., & Law, K. S. (2002). Wong and law emotional intelligence scale. *The Leadership Quarterly*.

World Bank. (2011). Promoting Gender Equality through Human Development. World Bank. www.worldbank.org

World Business Council for Sustainable Development. (2010). *Sustainability: A Global Survey of Corporate Practices*. Retrieved from https://www.wbcsd.org/web/publications/WBCSD_Survey_2010.pdf

World Health Organization (WHO). (2020). *COVID-19 disrupting mental health services in most countries*. WHO. https://www.who.int/news/item/05-10-2020-covid-19-disrupting-mental-health-services-in-most-countries-who-survey

World Health Organization. (2015). Retrieved from https://www.who.int/

World Health Organization. (2020). *Mental health*. WHO. https://www.who.int/mental_health/en/

Wright, P. M., & McMahan, G. C. (2011). Exploring human capital: Putting 'human' back into strategic human resource management. *Human Resource Management Journal*, *21*(2), 93–104. doi:10.1111/j.1748-8583.2010.00165.x

Wu, Q., & Cormican, K. (2021). *Shared Leadership and Team Effectiveness: An Investigation of Whether and When in Engineering Design Teams*. Frontiers Psychology., doi:10.3389/fpsyg.2020.569198

Yammarino, F. J., & Bass, B. M. (1990). Transformational leadership and multiple levels of analysis. *Human Relations*, *43*(10), 975–995. doi:10.1177/001872679004301003

Yammarino, F. J., Dubinsky, A. J., Comer, L. B., & Jolson, M. A. (1997). Women and transformational and contingent reward leadership: A multiple-levels-of-analysis perspective. *Academy of Management Journal*, *40*(1), 205–222. doi:10.2307/257027

Yankee, D. K. (2017). A measure of attributes and benefits of the co-leadership model: Is co-leadership the right fit for a complex world? [Doctoral dissertation, Pepperdine University].

Yauch, C. A. (2011). Measuring agility as a performance outcome. *Journal of Manufacturing Technology Management*, *22*(3), 384–404. doi:10.1108/17410381111112738

Yigitbasioglu, O., Furneaux, C., & Rossi, S. (2023). Case management systems and new routines in community organisations. *Financial Accountability & Management*, *39*(1), 216–236. doi:10.1111/faam.12297

Yin, Z., Liu, Z., & Tong, P. (2022). Core entrepreneurial competences of Chinese college students: Expert conceptualisation versus real-life cases. *The Asia-Pacific Education Researcher*, *31*(6), 781–801. doi:10.100740299-022-00656-3

Yu, H., Lin, Z., Lin, M. S., Neal, J. A., & Sirsat, S. A. (2022). Consumers' Knowledge and Handling Practices Associated with Fresh-Cut Produce in the United States. *Foods*, *11*(14), 2167. doi:10.3390/foods11142167 PMID:35885411

Yukl, G. (2013). *Leadership in Organizations*. Pearson.

Yukl, G. A. (2006). *Leadership in organizations* (6th ed.). Pearson-Prentice Hall.

Yusuf, M., Sani, D., Fadele, A., Rajab, R., Abulwafa, M., Ludfi, D., & Tutut, H. (2018). *An Impact of Transformational Leadership on Employees' Performance: A Case Study in Nigeria*. Academic Press.

Zada, I. (2022, July 2). *Organizational Change Management: Leadership Roles in Adapting New Norms*. https://www.ejbmr.org/index.php/ejbmr/article/view/1477

Zahmatkeshan, M., Zakerabasali, S., Farjam, M., Gholampour, Y., Seraji, M., & Yazdani, A. (2021). The use of mobile health interventions for gestational diabetes mellitus: A descriptive literature review. *Journal of Medicine and Life*, *14*(2), 131–141. doi:10.25122/jml-2020-0163 PMID:34104235

Zakerabasali, S., Ayyoubzadeh, S. M., Baniasadi, T., Yazdani, A., & Abhari, S. (2021). Mobile health technology and healthcare providers: Systemic barriers to adoption. *Healthcare Informatics Research*, *27*(4), 267–278. doi:10.4258/hir.2021.27.4.267 PMID:34788907

Zakszeski, B. N., Ventresco, N. E., & Jaffe, A. R. (2017). Promoting resilience through traumafocused practices: A critical review of school-based implementation. *School Mental Health*, *9*(4), 310–321. doi:10.100712310-017-9228-1

Zamani, R., Lari Dashtbayaz, M., & Hesarzadeh, R. (2023). Transformational leadership of audit managers and supervisors on the quality of team interactions of independent auditors. *Majallah-i Danish-i Isabdari*.

Zeiger, S. (2021). *The cost benefit evaluation and cost effectiveness evaluation methods*. Hearst Newspapers, LLC. https://smallbusiness.chron.com/cost-management-strategies-business-decisions-78054.html

Zhai, X., Zhu, C. J., & Zhang, M. M. (2022). Mapping promoting factors and mechanisms of resilience for performance improvement: The role of strategic human resource management systems and psychological empowerment. *Applied Psychology*, 1.

Zhang, B., Krajcik, J. S., Sutherland, L. M., Wang, L., Wu, J., & Qian, Y. (2005). Opportunities and challenges of China's inquiry-based education reform in middle and high schools: Perspectives of science teachers and teacher educators. *International Journal of Science and Mathematics Education*, *1*(4), 477–503. doi:10.100710763-005-1517-8

Zhang, L., & Guo, H. (2019). Enabling knowledge diversity to benefit cross-functional project teams: Joint roles of knowledge leadership and transactive memory system. *Information & Management*, *56*(8), 1–13. doi:10.1016/j.im.2019.03.001

Zhang, Y., Mandell, B., & Wang, L. (2022). Emotional intelligence in cross-cultural leadership: A qualitative study. *Journal of Global Leadership*, *8*(1), 27–39.

Zhang, Y., Zhou, F., & Mao, J. (2018). Ethical leadership and follower moral actions: Investigating an emotional linkage. *Frontiers in Psychology*, *9*, 1881. doi:10.3389/fpsyg.2018.01881 PMID:30337900

Compilation of References

Zhao, H., & Zhou, Q. (2020). Socially responsible human resource management and hotel employee organizational citizenship behavior for environment: A social cognitive perspective. *International Journal of Hospitality, 95*, 1–9.

Zhao, L., Yang, M. M., Wang, Z., & Michelson, G. (2023). Trends in the dynamic evolution of corporate social responsibility and leadership: A literature review and bibliometric analysis. *Journal of Business Ethics, 182*(1), 135–157. doi:10.100710551-022-05035-y

Zhao, Y., & Watterston, J. (2021). The changes we need: Education post COVID-19. *Journal of Educational Change, 33*(1), 3–12. doi:10.100710833-021-09417-3

Zheng, W., Yang, B., & McLean, G. (2010). Linking organizational culture, structure, strategy, and organizational effectiveness: Mediating role of knowledge management. *Journal of Business Research, 63*(7), 763–771. doi:10.1016/j.jbusres.2009.06.005

Zhu, J. L., Liao, Z. Y., Yam, K. C., & Johnson, R. E. (2018). Shared leadership: A state-of-the-art review and future research agenda. *Journal of Organizational Behavior, 39*(7), 834–852. doi:10.1002/job.2296

Zia, M. Q., Decius, J., Naveed, M., & Anwar, A. (2022). Transformational leadership promoting employees' informal learning and job involvement: The moderating role of self-efficacy. *Leadership and Organization Development Journal, 43*(3), 333–349. doi:10.1108/LODJ-06-2021-0286

Zia, N. U. (2020). Knowledge-oriented leadership, knowledge management behaviour and innovation performance in project-based SMEs. The moderating role of goal orientations. *Journal of Knowledge Management, 24*(8), 1819–1839. doi:10.1108/JKM-02-2020-0127

Zieba, M., & Schivinski, B. (2015). Knowledge management driven leadership, culture and innovation success – an integrative model. *Proceedings of IFKAD 2015: 10th International Forum on Knowledge Asset Dynamics: Culture, Innovation and Entrepreneurship: Connecting the Knowledge Dots.* BBK. https://eprints.bbk.ac.za/id/eprint/19951/

Zieba, M. (2020). Knowledge risk management in companies offering knowledge-intensive business services. In S. Durst & T. Henschel (Eds.), *Knowledge risk management: from theory to praxis* (pp. 13–31). Springer. doi:10.1007/978-3-030-35121-2_2

Zohar, D. (2021). What Is a Quantum Society? In *Zero Distance: Management in the Quantum Age* (pp. 221–228). Springer.

Zohar, D. (2022). *Zero distance: Management in the quantum age*. Springer Nature. doi:10.1007/978-981-16-7849-3

Zohar, D., & Zohar, D. (2022). Thinking Principles for the Quantum Leader. In *Zero Distance: Management in the Quantum Age* (pp. 147–154). Springer. doi:10.1007/978-981-16-7849-3_14

Zulaikha, Y., Martono, E., & Himam, F. (2021). Perceptions of students of the faculty of agriculture on the social status and career prospects in agricultural sector *Agrisocionomics: Jurnal Sosial Ekonomi Pertanian, 5*(1), 11–18.

About the Contributors

Darcia Roache worked for private and public sector organizations in Jamaica in the capacity of accountant, director of administration, and acted as chief executive officer. Her work experiences also included research assistant, programme leader, and faculty for organizations and universities in Canada, America, and Jamaica. Her passion for education led to her completion of a master and doctoral degrees in Business Administration. Dr. Roache is a member of the Finance and Operations' Committee at British Educational Research Association (BERA), London, as well as the Canadian Society for the Study of Education (CSSE) and the Canadian Associate for the Study of Educational Administration (CASEA). Dr. Roache's career is driven by her passion for administrative work, education, and learning. She works as research supervisor, second examiner, and faculty for the University Canada West, Capilano University, University of the People and University of the Commonwealth Caribbean, and The Management Institute for National Development (Jamaica). Dr. Roache obtained her second PhD in Educational Administration from the University of Saskatchewan. She has published several peer reviewed articles, book chapters, and book reviews on educational leadership, transformational leadership, positive leadership practices, social inequities, manifestation of microaggression, mid-career leadership, and promoting wellbeing in higher education. Dr. Roache is a firm believer in the Lord Jesus, who guides and directs her pathway. Her career ambition is to become a professor at any university in the world.

* * *

Ansar Abbas received an Airlangga Development Scholarship to complete his doctoral degree at the University of Airlangga in Surabaya, Indonesia. During his studies, he wrote several journal articles, qualitative and quantitative, and book chapters. Some papers are already published in prestigious journals while others are still under the peer-review process. Some of the key areas of research he developed are leadership theories, leadership psychology, modern slavery, human capital value creation, positive and negative elements of psychology, spirituality, spiritual intelligence, research modeling and framework design, well-being, and positive psychology research. In addition, he is broadening his expertise to contribute to various worthwhile academic activities for research advancement, such as serving as a reviewer, editorial assistant, and editor for several national and international journals. He has 15 years of diverse experience in various fields, including management, administration, academia, and research.

Endalsasa Belay Abitew has born on February 1988 in Gondar, Ethiopia. He got his first degree (in Public Administration and Development Management) and second degree (with Public Management and Policy specialization in Development Management) for Addis Ababa University, Ethiopia. He has

About the Contributors

worked for five years at Wollega University, Ethiopia, and currently, he is an Assistant Professor working at the Department of Governance and Development Studies, Bahir Dar University, Ethiopia. He served as head of the Department of Governance and Development Studies for the last three years.

Anna Amsler is an independent consultant and researcher affiliated to the Observatory of Competitiveness and New Ways of Working. She holds a Bachelor's Degree in International Relations and a Master's in Political Communication and Marketing, having worked in private and public institutions in areas related to public policy, strategic planning, and project evaluation.

Gretchen Blow, MSL, is a recent doctoral graduate in the department of Curriculum & Instruction at Baylor University. Gretchen earned her B.S. and her M.A. in Business and Leadership from Stephens College. As a top student, Gretchen was elected into Baylor Beta Xi Chapter of Kappa Delta Pi, Gretchen professionally focuses on medical education. Gretchen has been in medical education for over 10 years and primarily spent time working with administrative teams to streamline processes and training. Her past leadership positions include serving as neurosurgery's coordinator for medical student curriculum, and establishing junior-resident training bootcamps as they enter their specialty. Her research interests and publications include topics on leadership's influence over employees, how leadership's influence impacts employees morale and motivation, and gender inequality in medical education.

Darrell Norman Burrell is visiting scholar at the Samuel DeWitt Proctor Institute for Leadership, Equity, and Justice at Rutgers University. Dr. Burrell has two doctorate degrees and five graduate degrees. Dr. Burrell received his first doctoral degree in Health Education from A.T. Still University in 2010. In 2021, Dr. Burrell completed his 2nd doctorate, a Doctor of Philosophy (Ph.D.) in Cybersecurity Leadership and Organizational Behavior at Capitol Technology University, Laurel, MD. Dr. Burrell completed a Master of Arts in Interfaith Action at Claremont Lincoln University as a Global Peacemaker Fellow in 2016. He has an EdS (Education Specialist Post Master's Terminal Degree) in Higher Education Administration from The George Washington. He has two graduate degrees, one in Human Resources Management/Development and another in Organizational Management from National Louis University. Dr. Burrell has a graduate degree in Sales and Marketing Management from Prescott College. He has over 20 years of management, teaching, and training experience in academia, government, and private industry.

Sharon Burton delivers more than 25 years of experience. She earned a Ph. D. in Cybersecurity Leadership and a DBA in Quality Management: Business Process Improvement. She is recognized for exhibiting an aptitude for leading organizational change, as well as developing and managing process improvement, documenting high-impact business requirements, writing/authoring, and driving continuous improvement. Publications include more than 90 peer-reviewed and academic texts: journal articles, textbook chapters, business books, and conference proceedings. Publications - Artificial Intelligence, Cyber Security, Leadership, Andragogy, Business Process Improvement, Diversity and Inclusion, Entrepreneurship, Quality Customer Service, Engaged Scholarship and Civic Responsibility, and Mentoring & Coaching. Certifications: Master Lean Six Sigma Black Belt, Change Management, Advanced Telemedicine and Telehealth, Kaizen Leadership, Strategic Workforce Planning, and Kirkpatrick Four Levels Evaluation. Certificates: Diversity, Equity, & Inclusion, and Artificial Intelligence/Robotic Processing. Diplomas: Artificial Intelligence Computer Vision 2.0, Robotic Starter Training, and Business Analyst

Training. One badge is earned in Artificial Intelligence (AI) Computer Vision. Dr. Burton serves as a dissertation chair for Capitol Technology University and an adjunct faculty member for Post University and Capitol Technology University.

Margie Crowe is a retired United States Air Force lieutenant colonel, leadership & DEI consultant, published writer, higher education director and professor with broad experience in government and civilian programs, strategic planning, as well as published works focused on leadership practices affecting policies and programs in social justice, anti-racism, and DEI. She has consulted for the military, law enforcement, and private sector, as well as presented at academic and professional conferences on topics related to leadership, DEI, and digital equity and literacy. Margie holds a BA in political science, MS in international relations/national security, MA in special education, a postgraduate degree and a doctorate degree in educational leadership, and a training certificate in racial equity literacy facilitation.

Murat Culduz, after studying at Çukurova University Tourism and Hotel Management department for two years, transferred to Ege University English Language and Literature department and graduated from here in 1997. He worked in special-purpose classrooms at Ankara University for 2 years. He came to Istanbul in 1999 as a Staff Ensign. After completing his military service, he taught English in the Prep Class of a private college for 9 years. He started working at Istanbul Aydın University in 2009. After working here for a year, he became the founder of Istanbul Medipol University Preparatory Department in 2010.Murat Culduz, having completed his master's degree in English Language and Literature at Namık Kemal University in 2014, successfully earned his Ph.D .from Bahçeşehir University, and became a scholar in the field of Educational Technologies. Additionally, he joined the Fulbright program in the USA to further enrich his academic expertise and cross-cultural understanding.

Henry Dimingu holds a bachelor's degree in accounting from Davenport University, Michigan, USA, and a master's degree in accounting from Brock University, St Catherine's, Canada. Additionally, he holds Chartered Professional Accountants of Canada certification (CPA Canada). Henry is currently finishing his doctoral work in Business Administration at California Southern University, California, USA. Henry is an experienced educator who has worked at a number of Canadian universities and colleges. He presently teaches business at Aurora College in Canada. Henry's research interest includes leadership, corporate governance, equity, diversity, and inclusion (EDI).

Dian Ekowati is currently assigned as the Head of Planning and Development Board, Universitas Airlangga. She is responsible for strategic analysis for the purpose of planning and development at the university. Previously, she was the Director of Airlangga Global Engagement, where she was responsible to manage and coordinate internationalization initiatives and activities in Universitas Airlangga. She is also skilled in qualitative research and analysis, organizational theories and behavior, management of change, and internationalization. She is an education professional with a Doctor of Philosophy (Ph.D.) focused in Management of Change and Strategies, Interorganizational Network, Organization Politics/Power and Organizational Territoriality from the University of York, United Kingdom.

Rakotoarisoa Fenitra graduated from the Faculty of Economics and Business, Department of Business Administration, Universitas Airlangga, Surabaya Indonesia. His area of interest falls in Entrepreneur-

About the Contributors

ship, human behavior, tourism, and marketing in particular, while general interests are related to human development approaches and empirical research.

Suzzette Harriott is an accomplished Conflictologist and Life Strategist with a solid history of success in leadership consulting, transformative research, diversity, equity, and inclusion strategy, corporate HR management, personal development, education, and speaking. She has been speaking at multiple conferences for over a decade, sharing her expertise and passion for conflict resolution, emotional intelligence, personal development, diversity, equity, and inclusion with a wide range of audiences. Dr. Harriott's extensive educational background includes a Doctor of Philosophy in Conflict Analysis and Resolution/Peace Studies with a concentration in Organizational, Healthcare, and School Conflict from Nova Southeastern University, Fort Lauderdale, FL. She also holds a Master of Science in Human Resource Management and a Bachelor of Science in Psychology from the same institution. Her core research topics of imposter syndrome, self-compassion, hate, and empathy have been the focus of her study for over two decades. As a consultant, Dr. Harriott has served in various senior leadership positions, providing guidance, feedback, and quality data to inform decision-making. Her focus on conflict resolution, diversity, equity, and inclusion has helped organizations to create more productive and harmonious workplaces, driving employee engagement and overall business success. In addition to her consulting work and speaking engagements, Dr. Harriott is also an accomplished author, blogger, and educator. Her research on imposter syndrome, self-compassion, hate, empathy, and her extensive experience in conflict resolution, emotional intelligence, personal development, diversity, equity, and inclusion make her a respected and sought-after expert in these areas. Dr. Harriott has authored several books, including Echoes, Synergy, BLUSH, Hate, and Revolution, as well as a children's book series, The Adventures of Busy Issey & DEBI. Her active blog also gives people and organizations valuable insights and advice on a wide range of topics, which helps them improve their communication, relationships, and overall effectiveness. As an educator, Dr. Harriott has served as an adjunct professor at Florida International University, teaching various subjects within the Department of Teaching and Learning. Her expertise in conflict resolution, emotional intelligence, personal development, diversity, equity, and inclusion, as well as her research on imposter syndrome, self-compassion, hate, and empathy, has made her a sought-after instructor and mentor for students pursuing careers in education.

Marsha Hilton, MS, is a passionate Career Coach and Diversity, Equity, and Inclusion Strategist who empowers individuals to achieve their dreams by building agility and confidence to explore different paths. Marsha's specialties include career planning, reframing negative inner dialogue, and uncovering purpose to help clients thrive. She teaches professionals the importance of language and transferable skills like Adaptability Quotient and Emotional Intelligence. Marsha's methodology focuses on understanding the individual behind the role and curating their lives to identify the next steps by helping clients find their "why," Marsha increases their chances of achieving the life and career they envision.

Allison Huff, as an assistant professor in UArizona's Department of Family & Community Medicine, focuses on technology to address complex disorders, particularly focusing on how technology impacts SDOH. Previously, she was a behavioral health clinician working with individuals with serious mental illnesses and substance use disorders. Dr. Huff is PI and Co-I on several NSF, HRSA, and industry sponsored grants and leads clinical trials and research programs. She also is a mentor for several underserved pre-professional health and pre-med students each summer and through the academic year. Dr.

Huff's Doctor of Health Education is from A.T. Still University, her Master of Education in Instructional Technology is from University of Oklahoma, and her Bachelor's in Psychology is from University of West Florida.

Ashli Jay is an Agribusiness Educator and Academy Leader at William H. Turner Technical Arts High School's Academy of Veterinary Science & Agriculture Technology (VSAT). Armed with a Ph.D. in Ethical Leadership from St. Thomas University, she leverages her academic prowess to promote urban agriculture and sustainable living. Ashli's research spans transformational leadership, urban sustainable living through urban farming, and community engagement concerning the environment. With a keen interest in these domains, she remains at the forefront of initiatives championing sustainable urban development. She integrates these thematic areas into her teaching, molding the minds of her students with updated knowledge of the contemporary challenges affecting our environment. As an educator, she plays a crucial role in fostering a culture of sustainability among her students, engaging them in experiential learning about urban farming and organic food systems. Her teaching method ensures students learn theoretically and get hands-on experience in agriculture. A passionate advocate for community education in urban farm settings, Ashli, believes in the transformative power of education to create healthier and more resilient neighborhoods. Her commitment to sustainability goes beyond the classroom; she works tirelessly to translate her teachings into actionable steps for sustainable practices. Her approach emphasizes community participation and underscores the transformative power of education in building healthier, more sustainable communities at both local and global levels. Dr. Ashli Jay embodies the spirit of transformational leadership, bringing her vision of sustainable urban living to life through her work in education and community engagement.

Laura Jones is regarded as a strategist and practitioner in the risk management sector. She has spoken internationally on the topics of risk management and quality assurance. Dr. Jones has also served as an Associate Dean as well as a guest lecturer for various institutions. She currently serves as a Doctoral Chair at Capitol Technology University and an Adjunct Instructor at Carnegie Mellon University. Jones has published several multidisciplinary, indexed chapter books.

Peace Kumah holds a doctorate degree in Business Administration. She has an MBA (Human Resource Management) degree from Wisconsin International University College, Accra, Ghana. She has several years of teaching experience and occupies leadership positions in various educational institutions. She is a member of international editorial review board for International Journal of Human Capital and Information Technology Professionals. Her research interest includes strategic human resource management, organizational leadership and motivation, change management, and employment relations.

Dewaine Larmond is an accomplished and dynamic urban planner, project manager, and food & beverage specialist with a distinguished 15-year track record in local government, policy, and community development. Leveraging expertise cultivated through the successful execution of over 80 community development initiatives, Dewaine Larmond has consistently delivered positive impacts across multiple Jamaican communities. Renowned as an expert in the Local Government field, he has held key roles in Jamaica, including: Director of Urban Planning and Projects, Manchester Municipal Corporation - Jamaica Urban Planner, Manchester Municipal Corporation - Jamaica Local Economic Development Specialist, Caribbean Local Economic Development Project (CARILED), Government of Canada Geographic

About the Contributors

Information System Specialist, National Environment and Planning Agency - Jamaica Former CEO, Freight Express and Backyard Farms and Supplies At Maple Leafs Sport and Entertainment (MLSE), Dewaine spearheads the management and facilitation of over 120 food and beverage outlets, showcasing his prowess in the industry. Additionally, his versatility extends to professional photography, specializing in corporate events, portraits, weddings, and product imagery. Currently pursuing an aviation pilot career at Canadian Flyers International, Dewaine is dedicated to continuous growth. Qualifications: Master of Business Administration, University of the People, Pasadena, California Post Graduate Diploma in Marketing Management, Centennial College, Scarborough, ON Post Graduate Diploma in Project Management, Centennial College, Scarborough, ON Certificate in Fundamentals of Community Economic Development, University of Waterloo, ON Bachelor of Science in Urban and Regional Planning, University of Technology, St. Andrew, Jamaica Diploma in Urban and Regional Planning, University of Technology, St. Andrew, Jamaica Dewaine Larmond exemplifies a remarkable blend of strategic leadership, expertise, and ambition, continuously advancing both personally and professionally.

Yvonne Lomas-Montaudon is a Business Engineer, holding a Doctorate in Administration and a Master's in Logistics and Supply Chain Management. Passionate about pioneering solutions to drive positive business impact through process simulation, statistical analysis, and efficiency enhancement across various industries. Committed to advancing knowledge that fuels progress for organizations and society. A dedicated explorer of strategies like supply chain management and socially responsible business practices. Skilled in data analysis and proficient in specialized software. A firm advocate for teamwork and novel concepts. Co-founded Honey Bunny, a fusion of jewelry and technology. Currently, the coordinator of Universidad Iberoamericana Puebla's Business Engineering Program. Actively engaged in interdisciplinary research spanning Business Engineering, Logistics Engineering, Industrial Engineering, and Advanced Manufacturing Engineering programs.

Ngoako Marutha is a full Professor in the Department of Information Science at the University of South Africa (UNISA). The Limpopo born Professor in Sekgopo also serves as a representative of the Unisa Department of Information Science on the International Council on Archives (ICA) and he is an ICA Regular Member of Section on University and Research Institution Archives (ICA/SUV), where he also serves as an executive member for bureau. He is also a regular member for ICA section for Archival education (SAE) and section for the National Assembly. He has recently been appointed ICA New Professionals mentor for year 2022/2023. He is also a member of the South African Society of Archivists and serves on the National Executive Committee. He is an editor-in-chief of the Journal of the South African Society of Archivists since 2022. He is also a review editor for the journal Frontiers in Research Metrics and Analytics. He teaches archival principles and practice as well as honours research in archives and records management. He has published several books, chapters and articles in different national and international publications and presented conference papers. His research interest includes knowledge, archives, and records management, especially on patients and hospital records, electronic records, cloud computing, Blockchain technology, enterprise content management, big data management and police case records security. The other field of his interest includes library management and marketing as well as Open Distance electronic learning (ODeL). His professional industry background includes working as an information and records manager as well as librarian in several public and private institutions over 13 years. He has been in the academic industry over five years so far. He holds Bachelor of Information studies and Bachelor of Information Studies honour from University of the North (UNIN)-now known as University of Limpopo (UL), Master of Information Science and Doctor of literature and philosophy (PhD) from University of South Africa (UNISA). He serves as external examiner for masters and doctoral research studies for over seven universities.

Shannon McCrory-Churchill is Acting Dean and Associate Professor at the Patricia H. Garman School of Nursing at D'Youville University. Her research interests include leadership, global health and cultural competence.

Quatavia McLester is a PhD candidate in the Business and Industrial/Organizational Psychology program at The Chicago School of Professional Psychology – Washington, D.C. She holds a Master of Science in Industrial/Organizational Psychology from Austin Peay State University. She holds a Bachelor of Science in Psychology and a minor in Applied Statistics and Data Analysis from Kennesaw State University. She is currently serving as a Board Certified Behavior Analyst for a private mental healthcare agency. Her research interests include processes and outcomes of organizational development and change at the individual, group, and systems levels and the effects of destructive leadership within organizations.

Filiz Mizrak is an Assistant Professor holding a Doctorate degree in Management and Strategy from Istanbul Medipol University. She was born on May 12, 1986. She completed her undergraduate studies in American Culture and Literature at Istanbul University in 2009. Later, she pursued her Master's degree in Executive MBA at Bahçeşehir University in 2015. Filiz MIZRAK's passion for research and academia led her to obtain her doctoral degree in Management and Strategy from Istanbul Medipol University in 2021. Currently, she is working as an Assistant Professor at Istanbul Medipol University. Her research interests include strategic management, organizational behavior, and business strategy.

Idowu Mogaji is a seasoned educator and a national board-certified teacher from the Teacher Registration Council of Nigeria (TRCN) and the Ontario College of Teachers, Canada (OCT). She is a member of the International Society of Female Professionals, USA. Idowu is also a certified K-12 administrator, a program and curriculum specialist, an instructional coach and facilitator, a workshop facilitator, as well as a leadership coach. She is currently the Manager of Curriculum Development at Aurora College, Canada. Idowu holds a Ph.D. in Educational Administration from the University of Saskatchewan, Canada, a Masters' degree in Educational Leadership and School Improvement from the University of Manchester, UK, and a Bachelor's degree in Educational Management from the University of Ibadan, Nigeria.

Cynthia Montaudon is the Dean of UPAEP Business School and a business consultant. In September 2018, she became head of the Observatory on Competitiveness and New Ways of Working, which deals with numerous issues related to social problems and creates awareness about current and future social needs. She has obtained a Post Doctorate Certificate In Organizational Leadership from Regent University in Virginia, USA; a Ph.D. in Strategic Planning and Technology Management from UPAEP, in Puebla, Mexico; a Ph.D. in Business from the University of Lincoln in Lincolnshire, UK, and three masters degrees: one in Quality Engineering from the Universidad Iberoamericana in Puebla, Mexico, another in Communication and media from the Jean Moulin, Lyon II University in Lyon, France, and the last one in Business Administration from the Tec de Monterrey in Mexico.

About the Contributors

Ivonne Montaudon-Tomas is a researcher, author, and Coordinator of Strategic Projects for the General Directorate of Higher Secondary Education at UPAEP. Master's Degree in Latin American Literature from Universidad Iberoamericana Puebla, and Doctorate in Literature from CIDHEM. Her line of research includes Education, socio-critic, gastronomy, and Latin American studies.

Yaw Owusu-Agyeman is a Senior Lecturer at the Department of Adult Education and Human Resource Studies, University of Ghana. Before joining University of Ghana, Yaw served as a Postdoctoral Research Fellow at the Directorate for Institutional Research and Academic Planning, University of the Free State from December 2018 to November 2021.

Didem Öztürk Çiftci is an Associate Professor in the Fatsa Vocational School at Ordu University, where she has been a faculty member since 2009. She has been the Head of the Accounting and Tax Department since 2013. Didem Öztürk Çiftci completed her doctorate at Bolu Abant İzzet Baysal University, her graduate education at Karadeniz Technical University and her undergraduate education at Gazi University. Her research interests are organizational behavior and leadership. Dr. Öztürk Çiftci is married and has a son.

Malefetjane Phineas Phaladi (PhD) is Director of the Durban University of Technology (DUT) Library Services, external examiner, reviewer, postgraduate students' supervisor and researcher affiliated to the Department of Information Systems. Dr. Phaladi is strategist, an emerging exceptional leader and researcher with more than 20 years library and information service industry experience mainly in the academic and corporate sectors. He is a member of Library and Information Association of South Africa (LIASA) and serves as a trustee at South African Library and Information (SALI) Trust, Board of Trustees and represent DUT on the Committee of Higher Education Libraries of South Africa (CHELSA). Dr Phaladi is a holder of five degrees including four postgraduate qualifications in different information science-related disciplines, namely a PhD in Information Science from UNISA, MPhil degree in Information and Knowledge Management from Stellenbosch University, BCom Honours in IT Management from University of Johannesburg), Bachelor of Information Studies Honours (BInfHons) & Bachelor of Information Studies in Education (BInf.Ed) from University of Limpopo. He serves as a reviewer for South African Journal of Libraries and Information Science (SAJLIS), South African Journal of Information Management (SAJIM), South African Journal of Human Resource Management (SAJHRM) and has also reviewed 5 book chapters for book publications published or accepted for publication by US-based IGI Global. His recent peer reviews include the book chapter in Ngulube, P (Editor), Handbook of Research Connecting Research Methods for Information Science Research published by IGI Global in 2020, book chapter published in Ngulube P (Editor) in 2022, Handbook of Research on Mixed Methods Research in Information Science by the same publisher. Dr Phaladi has presented papers at local and international conferences and published scholarly works in the field of knowledge management, knowledge risk management and mixed methods research. His research interests include mixed methods research, organisational tacit knowledge loss, knowledge management, knowledge risk management, human resource management, open access and open science, library management, information technology management and governance, and state-owned enterprises. He served on the editorial committees for SCANUL-ELS Conference (Standing Conference of African and University Librarians – Eastern, Central & Southern) and LIASA-SCECSAL Conference (hosted by Library and Information

Association of South Africa and Standing Conference of Eastern, Central and Southern African Library and Information Associations).

Kevin Richardson currently serves as an Associate Professor of Business & Technology at Edward Waters University. He is a Certified Diversity Professional and a Certified Trainer. Dr. Richardson has two doctoral degrees and three graduate degrees. In 2016, he received his first doctorate degree in Operations and Quality Management Systems from The National Graduate School (Washington, DC). In 2021, Dr. Richardson received a Philosophy of Doctorate (Ph.D.) in Technology Management of Information Systems from Capitol Technology University (Laurel, MD). He completed a Master of Science in Natural Resources Economics and Corporate Sustainability at Virginia Tech University (Blacksburg, VA). Dr. Richardson has a graduate degree in Information Systems Engineering Management from Harrisburg Science & Technology University (Harrisburg, PA), and his third master's degree in Counseling Psychology from Springfield College (Charleston, SC). Dr. Richardson has over 25 years of management, teaching, and training trainer experience in academia, government, and private industries. His university teaching experience included teaching at Edward Waters University, Bethune Cookman University, Allen University, The National Graduate School of Quality Management, and Morris College.

Ingrid Robinson (BA, BEd, MEd, PhD) is an Associate Professor in the Faculty of Education at St. Francis Xavier University. She teaches a variety of undergraduate and graduate level courses in the areas of educational leadership and administration, research methods, foundations of education, and Social Studies education. Her research interests include Indigenous educational leadership, women and educational leadership, culturally relevant pedagogy, action research, and Social Studies education.

Tarek Salem (DBA, MBA, PPM, B.Sc. Civil Eng.) is an assistant professor of innovation and entrepreneurship at MacEwan University, Edmonton, Alberta. He holds a Doctorate degree in Business Administration-DBA. and a Master of Business Administration MBA from F. W. Olin Graduate School of Business, Babson College, MA, USA (Magna Cum Laude) He honed a long track record and diversified experience in supporting innovation, entrepreneurial activities, and education in North America, Europe, China, and the Middle East. He has been involved in startups, consultation, and project management roles with multi-disciplinary entrepreneurs and startups. His experience expands to cover a spectrum of industries including, Utilities, Construction, Real estate, manufacturing, government agencies, education, and others. Recently he served as a senior strategy adviser for a national massive healthcare transformation program in the Middle East.

Pooja Sharma is presently working as an assistant professor in the School of Commerce and Business Management, Geeta University. She is having more than six years of teaching and research experience. Her area of interest includes HRM, strategic leadership styles and banking. She is a teacher by profession and always ready to learn and explore new areas of research.

Amy Sloan, Ed.D., is a lecturer in the department of Curriculum & Instruction. Dr. Sloan earned her B.A. as a University Scholar from Baylor University, her M.A. in English from the University of Tennessee in Knoxville, and her Ed.D. in Postsecondary and Higher Education from Argosy University. She was named the top junior of her class at Baylor and was elected into Phi Beta Kappa. Dr. Sloan has been in higher education for almost two decades, with the majority of that time spent in postsecondary

About the Contributors

education primarily working within online education programs. Her past leadership positions include serving as the University Dean of the College of General Education and Psychology, a Director of Academic Operations, a Program Chair, and as an associate professor. With few exceptions, her postsecondary teaching and leadership positions have been within programs designed for non-traditional adult learners. Prior to transitioning into postsecondary education, Amy served several years as the Director of Grant Management for a charter secondary school district focusing on at-risk high school youth. Her research interests and publications include topics on effective student engagement and community within postsecondary education programs aimed at nontraditional learners, preparing students for leadership in a rapidly evolving educational system, first-year student success, mentoring in higher education, and the role of instruction in online education platforms. She also serves as the Co-Director of the IMPACT Mentoring Program.

Tamica Small is the Workforce Development Training Consultant at Tourism Saskatchewan where she specializes in awareness and training for tourism operators as well as evaluates existing training programs for alignment with the requisite needs of the tourism industry. Before joining Tourism Saskatchewan, Tamica was the Equity and Inclusion Coordinator at Saskatchewan Intercultural Association where she developed and facilitated diversity and equity presentations as well as coordinated cultural programs and activities to promote inclusion and opportunities to learn about diverse cultures which exist in Saskatoon. Tamica does have a passion for education and understands the importance of quality education to any nation, its people to think critically, solve problems, and make informed decisions. Hence, she has invested many years inculcating these skills in children at the elementary level. Tamica earned a Master of Education in Educational Foundations from the University of Saskatchewan, a Master of Education in Educational Measurement from the University of the West Indies- Mona, Jamaica. She also has a Diploma in Teacher Education. Tamica is a lifelong learning and savors every opportunity to learn and impart what she has learnt.

Fendy Suhariadi holds the position of professor and serves as the dean of the Doctoral Program at the postgraduate school of Airlangga University in Surabaya, Indonesia. Profeross is a highly esteemed social scientist and industrial psychologist known for their expertise in the region of East Java, Indonesia.

S. Bruce Thomson is with the School of Business at MacEwan University, Alberta. His PhD is from Monash University in Melbourne, Australia. His research interests include diversity management, job turnover, human resource management, strategic human resource management, and qualitative research methods. Current research projects are diversity management, intellectual capital and human resource management in Chinese firms, and human resource management effectiveness in government agencies in developing countries. He has published in leading academic journals such as Human Resource Management, International Journal of Human Resource Management, Thunderbird International Business Review and Journal of Contemporary Asia. His previous work on religion in the workplace was published as a book by Palgrave/McMillian in 2015 – Religion and Organizational Stigma at Work and published a co-edited volume of work on stigmas in the workplace in 2017.

Denise Toney (BA, BEd, MEd) is an Elementary School Principal at Eskasoni Elementary and Middle School in Mi'kmaw Kina'matnewey (MK). She is also serves as a part-time Instructor in both Indigenous Studies and Teacher Education at Cape Breton University. She has also taught curriculum and instruction courses including Diverse Cultures and Elementary Social Studies in the Faculty of Education at St. Francis Xavier University. Her research interests include post-colonial theory, school improvement in Indigenous education, educational leadership, Indigenous teacher education, Indigenous language revitalization and acquisition.

Jia Tyson is a Human Resource Strategist and consultant with over 22 years of cross-industry experience in both private industry and education. She holds a Bachelor's degree in Education and a Master's degree in Education with a specialization in persons with disabilities. Jia has a particular specialty within DEIB in relation to individuals with disabilities. She is a sought-after speaker, trainer, and thought leader on disability inclusion and accommodation, and has worked with a range of organizations and schools to design and implement effective DEIB strategies. Her in-depth knowledge within the education sector, particularly where individuals with disabilities are concerned, has allowed her to develop expertise in creating inclusive and equitable learning environments for all students. Jia's work is grounded in her own experiences as a person with a disability, and her deep commitment to creating more inclusive and equitable workplaces and learning environments for people with disabilities. She has worked with organizations to create more accessible physical and virtual environments, develop disability-specific policies and procedures, and provide disability sensitivity training to employees. In addition to her expertise in disability inclusion, Jia has also been at the forefront of the paradigm shift that has occurred post-pandemic. As organizations and schools have had to rapidly adapt to remote and hybrid work and learning environments, Jia has provided critical guidance on how to ensure that these environments are accessible and inclusive for individuals with disabilities. She has also helped organizations and schools to think more broadly about how they can leverage technology and flexible work arrangements to create more inclusive and equitable workplaces and learning environments for all employees and students.

Kiana Zanganeh has significant research interests in women's health, health disparities, healthcare management, public health, and medicine. She is a first year medical student at Lake Erie College of Osteopathic Medicine - Bradenton. She completed a Master of Science in Healthcare Management from the Florida Institute of Technology. She completed her undergraduate degree in May 2020 from the Florida Institute of Technology where she was a student athlete.

Index

A

Accountability 2, 6, 16, 35, 120, 153, 156, 162-163, 167, 169, 173-174, 236, 273, 277, 279-280, 286, 308, 317, 321, 329, 343, 354, 426, 430, 447

Accuracy 118

Africa 20-24, 30, 32-35, 128-131, 135-136, 138, 141-143, 145-148, 363, 365-366, 441, 446

Agency 15, 251, 308, 315, 329

AI 258, 264, 307-311, 314, 317-318, 324-328, 332-339

AI Algorithms 311

AI Technology 264

Artificial Intelligence (AI) 258, 311, 324-325, 327-328, 332, 334

Assessment 7, 43-44, 53, 62, 75, 95, 153, 157, 201, 203-204, 212, 244, 266, 276, 301, 313, 345, 380, 409, 419, 436, 447

B

Best Practices 12, 14, 53-54, 71, 190, 192, 198, 203-204, 219, 240-241, 245, 278, 381, 410, 427

bias 45, 205, 207, 210, 217, 310, 339, 383, 411

Blended Learning 27

C

challenges 2, 6 8, 11, 13, 15, 18, 21 23, 26-28, 30-31, 53, 60-61, 65, 68, 71, 75, 79, 83-85, 87, 90, 93, 96, 102, 121-122, 126, 129-130, 134-135, 143, 146, 169, 175, 185, 187, 189, 191-194, 196-197, 199, 201, 203, 207-208, 217, 221, 224, 230-232, 234-235, 240-242, 244, 247, 249-251, 253, 258, 269, 273, 276, 288, 305, 308-309, 311, 315-318, 322, 324-328, 331-336, 339-340, 342-343, 349, 351-354, 357-362, 366, 368, 380, 393-394, 397-399, 402, 405, 413-416, 418-421, 423-426, 428-430, 435-437, 440-441, 443, 448-449

ChatGPT 318

Classroom 36, 68, 232, 234, 275, 341-349, 382, 417, 430-431

Collaborative Learning 290

Consequentialism 428

COVID-19 Pandemic 33, 74-75, 78, 201, 204, 208, 220-223, 239-243, 248-255, 270, 273, 324, 326-328, 372, 375, 394, 412, 423, 439-440, 448

Curriculum 35, 71, 207, 266, 343, 347-348, 405, 413, 417, 422, 424, 428, 432-433, 437, 444, 449

D

Deontological Ethics 431

E

Education 1, 3, 5-6, 8-10, 12-13, 15-21, 23, 29, 31-36, 38, 42, 52-53, 55, 57, 66-67, 71, 73-75, 91, 94-97, 111, 125, 143, 145, 181, 189-190, 194, 196, 199, 203, 206, 208-209, 211, 214, 217-219, 222, 225-226, 234, 236-237, 243, 247, 252, 258, 270-271, 273-275, 279-283, 285, 287-293, 306, 309, 316-318, 320-321, 339, 341-345, 347-349, 352, 356, 358-361, 364, 370, 375, 385, 393, 395, 405, 411, 414, 416-417, 420-422, 424-425, 427-428, 430-433, 435-447, 449

Education Sector 21

Emotional Intelligence 2, 23, 30-31, 33, 35, 54, 74, 101, 105, 109, 112, 118-119, 123, 125-126, 148, 156, 266, 294-295, 297, 299, 301-303, 317, 324-328, 330-332, 335-340, 393-396, 398-410, 412-413

Engagement 2, 8, 17, 23, 28, 34, 52, 65-66, 74, 107, 111-112, 118, 121-122, 124, 150, 166, 182, 190, 211, 213, 237, 242, 245, 253, 266, 283-285, 290, 299, 308, 318, 325, 342, 345-346, 353, 362, 370-371, 373, 375, 377, 379, 381, 385, 389, 397-398, 406-407, 409-411, 416-420, 424, 429-430, 433-434, 446

Ethics 16, 24, 54, 75, 175, 197, 254, 263, 265, 298,

317, 322, 338-339, 362-363, 365, 373, 389, 407, 409, 412, 414, 417-418, 428, 431-432, 439-440, 445, 448-449

Experiences 4, 7, 11, 14, 21, 24-25, 27, 30, 71, 82-85, 89, 91-92, 98, 123, 154, 156, 194, 205, 209-210, 223-225, 228, 231, 241, 251, 262, 273, 277, 298-299, 306, 308-309, 311-312, 316, 342-343, 391, 393-395, 397, 430

F

Fairness 165, 215, 328, 331, 333, 335, 421, 431
Feedback 7, 24-28, 30-31, 79, 83-85, 89-90, 92, 116, 156, 168, 189-190, 195, 198, 244-245, 301, 321, 344-345, 409, 422, 425, 437

G

game 264
Guidelines 31, 244, 250-251, 292, 320-321, 405, 435

H

Higher Education 1, 3, 8-10, 18-21, 23, 31-36, 38, 52, 74-75, 274-275, 283, 289, 292-293, 316-318, 339, 348-349, 405, 433, 441

I

implications 50, 149, 151, 155, 157, 189, 265, 284-285, 317-318, 320, 324-325, 331, 335, 337-338, 354, 387, 393, 396, 399-400, 402, 404-406, 410, 424-426, 429, 439, 441, 444, 446
Inclusivity 193, 301, 392-395, 397-399, 401, 404, 407, 409, 417, 428
Instructor 348
Intrinsic Motivation 13, 17, 104, 108, 110, 169

L

learners 2-3, 6, 11, 66, 72, 96, 236, 273, 275, 277, 280-281, 298, 341, 345-346, 430, 436
Learning 3-4, 6-8, 10, 12-13, 15, 21, 27, 31-36, 38-39, 58, 63, 66, 71-72, 75, 77-80, 82-86, 88-98, 101, 120, 122-123, 125-126, 129, 131-132, 135, 140, 144, 182, 185-186, 189, 192, 195, 203, 228-230, 232-235, 237-238, 240, 254, 260-262, 264, 266-267, 277-279, 286-287, 290-291, 295, 298, 308, 310-311, 319-320, 322, 327, 332, 341-349, 351, 361, 363, 383, 395, 407, 409-411, 413, 415, 417, 429-431, 433, 438, 444, 448

Literacy 207, 209, 225, 320, 349, 415-417, 422-423, 433-435, 437, 439, 442-443, 447, 449

M

Machine learning 308, 327, 444

N

Nigeria 370, 372, 376

P

Pandemic 33, 56-57, 73-75, 78, 201-204, 208, 217-218, 220-223, 240-243, 248-255, 270, 273, 275, 279, 295, 324, 326-328, 332-333, 335, 372, 375, 394, 398, 412, 423, 439-440, 448
Pedagogy 19, 34, 220, 275, 290, 343-344, 346, 348, 442
Privacy 192, 194, 197, 263, 309, 311, 327, 391
Professional Development 12, 16, 31-33, 36, 63, 66, 68, 71, 97, 121-122, 227, 231-233, 349
Prospects 122, 146, 176, 450

R

Reliability 36, 43-47, 63

S

Safeguards 270, 418
Social Interactions 114, 130
Student engagement 111, 342

T

teaching 9, 13, 21, 25, 27, 30-31, 36, 38-39, 68, 71, 75, 77, 111, 225, 236, 238, 267, 292, 341, 344, 346-349, 364, 413, 417, 425, 428, 431-434, 436, 448
Technology 39, 55, 57, 63, 66, 75, 77, 90, 92, 95, 98, 128, 133-134, 145, 149, 184, 189, 201, 211-212, 214, 220, 223, 243-245, 248-249, 252-253, 258, 264, 270, 272-273, 275, 286-287, 292, 301, 304, 306-319, 321-323, 325, 350, 372, 376-377, 393-394, 398, 415, 417, 420, 424, 432, 439, 442, 447, 449
Transparency 116, 118, 162, 164, 169, 174, 189-190, 198, 252-253, 276, 302, 331, 357, 407, 426
Trust 10, 12, 14-15, 60-61, 63-64, 72, 92, 100, 104, 114-120, 122, 152-153, 156, 160-161, 165-166, 168-169, 171, 173-174, 179, 183, 190, 217, 227, 230, 252, 262-263, 274, 280, 285-286, 288, 299-300, 305, 307, 310, 314, 328-329, 331, 333, 335,

Index

345, 368, 372, 374, 382, 384, 392, 396, 406-408,
414-416, 429, 434, 437

V

Validity 17, 35-36, 43-44, 46-47, 80, 93, 339, 342, 374
Virtual Reality 394
Virtue Ethics 414, 417, 431-432

Recommended Reference Books

IGI Global's reference books are available in three unique pricing formats:
Print Only, E-Book Only, or Print + E-Book.

Order direct through IGI Global's Online Bookstore at
www.igi-global.com or through your preferred provider.

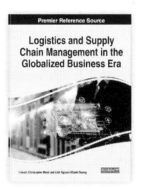

Logistics and Supply Chain Management in the Globalized Business Era

ISBN: 9781799887096
EISBN: 9781799887119
© 2022; 413 pp.
List Price: US$ **250**

Food Safety Practices in the Restaurant Industry

ISBN: 9781799874157
EISBN: 9781799874164
© 2022; 334 pp.
List Price: US$ **240**

Implementing Diversity, Equity, Inclusion, and Belonging Management in Organizational Change Initiatives

ISBN: 9781668440230
EISBN: 9781668440254
© 2022; 320 pp.
List Price: US$ **215**

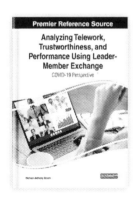

Analyzing Telework, Trustworthiness, and Performance Using Leader-Member Exchange: COVID-19 Perspective

ISBN: 9781799889502
EISBN: 9781799889526
© 2022; 263 pp.
List Price: US$ **240**

Digital Communications, Internet of Things, and the Future of Cultural Tourism

ISBN: 9781799885283
EISBN: 9781799885306
© 2022; 587 pp.
List Price: US$ **360**

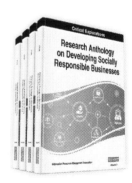

Research Anthology on Developing Socially Responsible Businesses

ISBN: 9781668455906
EISBN: 9781668455913
© 2022; 2,235 pp.
List Price: US$ **1,865**

Do you want to stay current on the latest research trends, product announcements, news, and special offers?
Join IGI Global's mailing list to receive customized recommendations, exclusive discounts, and more.
Sign up at: **www.igi-global.com/newsletters**.

Publisher of Timely, Peer-Reviewed Inclusive Research Since 1988

www.igi-global.com | Sign up at www.igi-global.com/newsletters | facebook.com/igiglobal | twitter.com/igiglobal | linkedin.com/igiglobal

Ensure Quality Research is Introduced to the Academic Community

Become an Evaluator for IGI Global Authored Book Projects

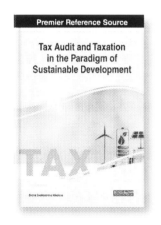  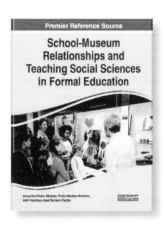 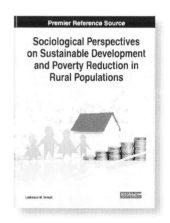

The overall success of an authored book project is dependent on quality and timely manuscript evaluations.

Applications and Inquiries may be sent to:
development@igi-global.com

Applicants must have a doctorate (or equivalent degree) as well as publishing, research, and reviewing experience. Authored Book Evaluators are appointed for one-year terms and are expected to complete at least three evaluations per term. Upon successful completion of this term, evaluators can be considered for an additional term.

If you have a colleague that may be interested in this opportunity, we encourage you to share this information with them.

Easily Identify, Acquire, and Utilize Published Peer-Reviewed Findings in Support of Your Current Research

IGI Global OnDemand

Purchase Individual IGI Global OnDemand Book Chapters and Journal Articles

For More Information:
www.igi-global.com/e-resources/ondemand/

Browse through 150,000+ Articles and Chapters!

Find specific research related to your current studies and projects that have been contributed by international researchers from prestigious institutions, including:

- Accurate and Advanced Search
- Affordably Acquire Research
- Instantly Access Your Content
- Benefit from the InfoSci Platform Features

> It really provides *an excellent entry into the research literature of the field.* It presents a manageable number of *highly relevant sources* on topics of interest to a wide range of researchers. The sources are *scholarly, but also accessible* to 'practitioners'.

- Ms. Lisa Stimatz, MLS, University of North Carolina at Chapel Hill, USA

Interested in Additional Savings?

Subscribe to

IGI Global OnDemand Plus

Learn More

Acquire content from over 128,000+ research-focused book chapters and 33,000+ scholarly journal articles for as low as US$ 5 per article/chapter (original retail price for an article/chapter: US$ 37.50).

7,300+ E-BOOKS. ADVANCED RESEARCH. INCLUSIVE & AFFORDABLE.

IGI Global e-Book Collection

- Flexible Purchasing Options (Perpetual, Subscription, EBA, etc.)
- Multi-Year Agreements with No Price Increases Guaranteed
- No Additional Charge for Multi-User Licensing
- No Maintenance, Hosting, or Archiving Fees
- Continually Enhanced & Innovated Accessibility Compliance Features (WCAG)

Handbook of Research on Digital Transformation, Industry Use Cases, and the Impact of Disruptive Technologies
ISBN: 9781799877127
EISBN: 9781799877141

Handbook of Research on New Investigations in Artificial Life, AI, and Machine Learning
ISBN: 9781799886860
EISBN: 9781799886877

Handbook of Research on Future of Work and Education
ISBN: 9781799882756
EISBN: 9781799882770

Research Anthology on Physical and Intellectual Disabilities in an Inclusive Society (4 Vols.)
ISBN: 9781668435427
EISBN: 9781668435434

Innovative Economic, Social, and Environmental Practices for Progressing Future Sustainability
ISBN: 9781799895909
EISBN: 9781799895923

Applied Guide for Event Study Research in Supply Chain Management
ISBN: 9781799889694
EISBN: 9781799889717

Mental Health and Wellness in Healthcare Workers
ISBN: 9781799888130
EISBN: 9781799888147

Clean Technologies and Sustainable Development in Civil Engineering
ISBN: 9781799898108
EISBN: 9781799898122

Request More Information, or Recommend the IGI Global e-Book Collection to Your Institution's Librarian

For More Information or to Request a Free Trial, Contact IGI Global's e-Collections Team: eresources@igi-global.com | 1-866-342-6657 ext. 100 | 717-533-8845 ext. 100

Are You Ready to Publish Your Research

IGI Global offers book authorship and editorship opportunities across 11 subject areas, including business, computer science, education, science and engineering, social sciences, and more!

Benefits of Publishing with IGI Global:

- Free one-on-one editorial and promotional support.
- Expedited publishing timelines that can take your book from start to finish in less than one (1) year.
- Choose from a variety of formats, including Edited and Authored References, Handbooks of Research, Encyclopedias, and Research Insights.
- Utilize IGI Global's eEditorial Discovery® submission system in support of conducting the submission and double-blind peer review process.
- IGI Global maintains a strict adherence to ethical practices due in part to our full membership with the Committee on Publication Ethics (COPE).
- Indexing potential in prestigious indices such as Scopus®, Web of Science™, PsycINFO®, and ERIC – Education Resources Information Center.
- Ability to connect your ORCID iD to your IGI Global publications.
- Earn honorariums and royalties on your full book publications as well as complimentary content and exclusive discounts.

Join Your Colleagues from Prestigious Institutions, Including: Australian National University, Massachusetts Institute of Technology, Johns Hopkins University, Harvard University, Tsinghua University, Columbia University in the City of New York

Learn More at: www.igi-global.com/publish
or Contact IGI Global's Aquisitions Team at: acquisition@igi-global.com

Individual Article & Chapter Downloads
US$ 29.50/each

Easily Identify, Acquire, and Utilize Published Peer-Reviewed Findings in Support of Your Current Research

- Browse Over **170,000+ Articles & Chapters**
- **Accurate & Advanced** Search
- Affordably Acquire **International Research**
- **Instantly Access** Your Content
- Benefit from the **InfoSci® Platform Features**

THE UNIVERSITY of NORTH CAROLINA at CHAPEL HILL

" *It really provides an excellent entry into the research literature of the field. It presents a manageable number of highly relevant sources on topics of interest to a wide range of researchers. The sources are scholarly, but also accessible to 'practitioners'.* "

- Ms. Lisa Stimatz, MLS, University of North Carolina at Chapel Hill, USA

Interested in Additional Savings?

Subscribe to
IGI Global OnDemand Plus

Learn More

Acquire content from over 137,000+ research-focused book chapters and 33,000+ scholarly journal articles for as low as US$ 5 per article/chapter (original retail price for an article/chapter: US$ 29.50).